APR 25			
OCT 09			
NOV 21			
DEC 2			
			PRINTED IN U.S.A.

GAYLORD

The Police and the Community

Jewels Among Swine
(Front cover, *Harper's Weekly,* June 13, 1874)
from

The Art and Politics of Thomas Nast
by Morton Keller

New York, Oxford University Press, 1968
Plate 70

The Police and the Community

Louis A. Radelet

Director, National Center on Police
and Community Relations
Michigan State University

with research and complementary materials prepared by

Hoyt Coe Reed
Coordinator, Research Library
National Center for Police and Community Relations

GLENCOE PRESS
A division of Benziger Bruce & Glencoe, Inc.
Beverly Hills

GLENCOE PRESS
A division of Benziger Bruce & Glencoe, Inc.
8701 Wilshire Boulevard
Beverly Hills, California 90211
Collier-Macmillan Canada, Ltd., Toronto, Ontario

Library of Congress Catalog Card Number: 72-93310

Third printing, 1974

Contents

Foreword

Some persons in America today advocate the concept that the greatest threat to civil liberties is the police; and, by so doing, place the police and the public in separate camps. Actually, in a democracy, the police and the people in the community are inseparable. The police are the agents of the people they serve. The importance of public support of the police cannot be overemphasized, for the police constitute only a small fraction of the community, and can never discharge their obligations unless they are reinforced by the good will and cooperation of the citizenry.

The widespread riots, civil disorder protest demonstrations, street crime, and other symptoms of a troubled society occurring during the past decade and a half have made necessary an agonizing reappraisal by the police not only of their community relations efforts, but also of their basic concepts of the police role and police function in society.

In the broadest terms, the police have two paramount functions: law enforcement and crime suppression; and social service and maintenance of order. Since the two roles are clearly interrelated, we are not faced with a question of choice, but one of emphasis. Until very recently, and to a large extent even today, the emphasis has been on law enforcement and crime suppression. This role concept by the police is reflected in the nature of the education and training they receive on

vii

and off the job. All studies conducted to date, however, have shown that by far the greatest part of a policeman's time is spent performing his social service and order maintenance functions. Although such conflicting views of social institutional roles are inevitable in a free society, the problem is especially critical in police-community relations, since the police have society's maximum power—the power to take from citizens their liberty and even their lives.

Police do their work under conflicting pressures to protect the inherently conflicting values of public order and individual freedom. They are seeking a balance between freedom and order, and the quest is not easy. In recent years, the growing complexity of laws and their interpretation has sharpened the conflict between the protection of personal rights and the freedom which police feel they need to perform their duties. As James Q. Wilson says, "Some people want crime suppressed even at some cost in civil liberties; others want civil liberties protected even at some cost in crime." This conflict is demonstrated all the way from activists attempting to gain civil rights, to citizens griping about motor vehicle regulations. In these and other areas, public annoyance and anger are easily transferred to the police, who are responsible for enforcing society's rules and who are the visible symbols of the Establishment.

Another paramount issue affecting police-community relations is the discretionary use of police power. Law enforcement is not an end in itself but, rather, only a means to an end: the maintenance of an orderly society that places great import on justice and individual liberty. Although the police are expected to enforce all laws, this is not possible or even desirable. Everyone knows this, especially the police, but they and their agencies continue to ignore it officially. Clearly, the police cannot, because of manpower limitations, enforce all laws. And the community will not tolerate strict enforcement of all laws all the time. Also, laws must be interpreted before they are applied.

A policeman spends most of his time in social service functions, the least controlled aspect of his work. He has the decision-making responsibility of a professional, but is, unfortunately, too often poorly prepared to handle that responsibility. Also, in relying so much on personal judgment in dealing with people-related situations, a policeman is subject to his personal prejudices. It is not surprising that the question often arises of which of his decisions are properly discretionary and which are unjust and discriminatory. The community, therefore, calls for tighter control of his conduct by civilian review boards, neighborhood control, or other devices that tend to further alienate the police and make community relations more difficult.

So far I have used the term *police-community relations* as if everyone agrees on its meaning. This is not so. To some persons it means public relations; to others, public information; some hold it synonymous with race relations; and still others consider it community service, or perhaps community participation in crime prevention and law enforcement. A sound conception favors a combination of all these.

No one is better qualified to present this vital subject of police-community relations than is Louis A. Radelet, Professor, School of Criminal Justice, and Coordinator of the National Center on Police and Community Relations at Michigan State University.

After serving for some years on the faculty of the University of Notre Dame, Professor Radelet was the director of national program development for community services of the National Conference of Christians and Jews from 1959 to 1963, when he was appointed to the faculty of Michigan State University. He has served as director of the Annual National Institutes on Police and Community Relations at Michigan State University since 1955, and as coordinator of the National Center on Police and Community Relations at that university since 1965. He has also served as director or staff member for numerous college and university workshops in human relations and is the author of articles, monographs, reports, and books in the fields of intergroup relations and police-community relations. An earlier (1968) work published by The Glencoe Press, *Police and Community Relations: A Source Book,* has been done in collaboration with A. F. Brandstatter.

Written as a companion volume to *The Police and the Community* but designed to enhance the study of any other textbook on the subject, is a second volume, *The Police and the Community: Studies.* The *Studies* volume has a co-author, Hoyt Coe Reed. Dr. Reed is Emeritus Professor of Social Science at Michigan State University and has served as coordinator of the research library of the National Center on Police and Community Relations. He holds an Ed.D. from Columbia University, and he has been Secretary of the National Institutes at Michigan State and editor of their annual Proceedings.

Although a careful reading of either *The Police and the Community* or *Studies* will result in an excellent understanding of their subject, a greater depth of understanding will certainly result from the simultaneous use of both volumes. They are the fabric of extensive experience and the highest quality of scholarship, research, and writing. They are thorough, complete, relevant, and current. I enthusiastically endorse them and recommend their reading and study not only by policemen and police students, but by sociologists and by practitioners and students in probation, parole, corrections, and the courts.

G. Douglas Gourley
Chairman, Department of
Criminal Justice
California State University
at Los Angeles

GLENCOE PRESS CRIMINAL JUSTICE SERIES

General Editor:

G. DOUGLAS GOURLEY

Inspector (Ret.), LA Police Department
Chairman, Department of Criminal Justice
California State University at Los Angeles
Los Angeles, California

Preface

This text is dedicated to students, for it was inspired by a student's question, "Why all the fuss about police-community relations?" It was one of those small queries that can generate a stadium, a hundred-story building, a concerto, or a national park by way of a response. Lest this seem pretentious, I should add that a good teacher is usually able to come up with a simple answer to a simple question. This text may well be the defense of a teacher with much to learn.

What has happened to the relationship between the police and the policed in recent years to make it eligible for the special attention it continues to hold? This is what the student was asking, and it is what this book is all about. My colleague and I found so much we thought important to say on the subject that the publisher decided on two volumes, one for a text volume and one for a study volume. The studies are assembled under the title *The Police and the Community: Studies,* and dovetail with the text as I have put it together in the first volume.

This college text is based largely on a course syllabus that I first prepared in 1963, and have emended many times since. As a text, it is probably better suited to a semester than to a trimester or a ten-week term. The two volumes, together with some supplementary reading and some modest field studies, might easily constitute a basis for a year of study in a sequence of courses adapted to the calendar and curriculum of the particular institution. Our intention was to provide as comprehensive, while yet as flexible, an educational tool as possible.

This work has reunited a trio whose experience with police and community relations problems and programs goes back to the first National Institute on Police and Community Relations at Michigan State University in 1955. Dr. Reed and I are two of these; Mr. Robert H. Scott, co-author of Chapter Seventeen of the text, is the other. Nostalgia alone has made the present effort a joy.

It is customary in such prologues for authors to acknowledge that they could not have done the job without helpers. By the time all the helpers have been listed and their respective contributions gratefully identified, the reader wonders what remained for the author to do. Alas, authors are just like most people—they do what they do, in considerable measure, because of what other people do for them. Come to think of it, there is a message in that for police-community relations too.

In any case, let it be known that our wives endured many inconveniences during the two years that this task required. Our numerous children and the grandchildren were politely interested in the enterprise, and my son, Joseph, was of special assistance in several tedious editorial chores. Some of our professional colleagues lent us a hand or a head on specific topics. My students, and participants in police and community programs, have permitted me to bounce ideas back and forth with them through the years, and their contribution to the result has been substantial. To all of these helpers, and others we should mention, we extend our hearty thanks.

Some themes recur throughout the work that may as well be set down here. If this were a musical piece, the refrain would be that—

> In the functional sense that is the essence of its meaning, *community* is salvageable in many facets of our society, despite all the obstacles.

> What the police do, no matter how it may be defined, requires the utmost in community participation, involvement, cooperation. The police-community relationship can be, ideally, participative democracy at its best.

> The goal in police and community relations is not good relations as an end in itself. The goal is good relations resulting from teamwork in problem-solving endeavors dedicated to the common good.

> Problems in police and community relations lie in a matrix of broader and deeper social problems, progress in solving which will be to a considerable degree interrelated.

> Good community relations are possible for the police to the extent that they see themselves as community leaders and "change agents," as befits fledgling professionals. To the extent that their behavior fails to measure up to this description, professionalism in police work is idle chatter and "community relations" is meaningless.

Not surprisingly, this text reflects the author's conception of what a text should be: a synthesis, a convenient format, pulling together whatever of significance has been written by advanced students of a subject. The beginning student is usually not sure just how interested in the subject he or she may be. A text ought to help him or her to decide. Yet it ought not to pretend to settle every quesion. Indeed, it should be a device to help formulate questions more sensibly, and more systematically, to place side by side the agreeing and disagreeing opinions as one would many dishes and courses of a banquet. A text should be a feast of thought and ideas; an ally of education, not propaganda.

If I were asked to set this work in its appropriate academic discipline, I would say that social psychology is as close as I can come to it. The "sociology of the police" may be a better way to put it. Further, it has the flavor of social pathology, if I may be forgiven for using a term little used today. We are still guessing about many social problems, as we were when I first heard such terms more than three decades ago. Sweeping changes in social and institutional structures have made the problems more complex, but in many cases the cures are worse than the diseases.

In one respect, at least, there may be an inkling of real progress. The 1960s helped immeasurably to bring home the importance of conflict theory in the study of societal problems. In the study of programs on police and community relations, this may have been *the* major revelation of the past decade. To put it briefly, we are learning that social order and social disorder must be studied interrelatedly, much the same as we study heredity and environment. Lewis A. Coser says it neatly: "Man's best hope is not the eradication of conflicts, for that is impossible, but rather their channelling and regulation, their domestication if you wish, so that their destructive impact can be successfully minimized."

The problems of living together will not go away. In fact, they seem to become increasingly interconnected, therefore more impossible to understand. Bewilderment and frustration thrive until community action to solve problems becomes more personal psychotherapy than a rational, systematic approach to the external matter. Mix politics with this therapy, and it is small wonder that sometimes rationality seems to have so little chance. Responses to social problems involve countless nonscientific factors. But this can hardly be taken as an excuse for resigning from "the human condition."

I have said that this text is dedicated to students because I am optimistic, even confident, that they hold the hope for a better world; not, mind you, a problemless world—for that would be a perfect bore—but a world with more people believing that our problems can be solved, and willing to do their part to that end.

Louis A. Radelet

Part One

Scope
of the
Problem

Chapter One

Police and the Community

The more or less familiar, modern municipal police department dates back only to 1829, when Sir Robert Peel managed to secure approval by an apprehensive English Parliament of his Bill For a Metropolitan Police (Lee, *A History of Police*). There was considerable opposition to the idea, as some members were apprehensive that such a force might become a mechanism of political tyranny. A Parliamentary committee had reported on an earlier Peel proposal ". . . that forfeiture or curtailment of individual liberty which the creation of an effective police system would bring with it would be too great a sacrifice on behalf of improvements in police or facilities in detection of crime" (Reith, *British Police*). However, Sir Robert's bill finally became law, and the "Peelers," or "Bobbies," set the stage for our city police of today.

Peel's principles of law enforcement are interesting to review in today's circumstances, particularly because of a notable prevailing emphasis on the important part to be played by the ordinary citizen in police services (see Table 1–1). This idea contrasts with the modern misconception that the police are paid to do what civilians would prefer not to do—one expression of popular nonsense at the root of current police-community separatism.

3

Why have the police been viewed as pigs from historical times? (See frontispiece.) Clearly, the reference is neither complimentary nor indicative of an always wholesome relationship between the police and the public. While we know that most people have a favorable view of the police most of the time, many people frankly prefer to avoid contact with the police if at all possible, and the outright hostility of some groups toward the police is a well-established reality. There would seem to be something peculiar to the police relationship with the community that makes it the object of special study by scholars interested in such social processes as human and intergroup relations, governmental operations, bureaucratic organizations, and the administration and management of public service agencies.

Police-community relations is a subject that has come prominently to the forefront of social concern in the United States during the past two or three decades, especially in recent years. It has been one of the important concentrations of the civil rights movement, in the theme of equal protection of the law for all citizens, and in the sense that the uniformed police officer is viewed by minorities as the most visible representative of the dominant elements of society.

We hear it said that successful police work depends on the cooperation of the public with the police. In fact, in a democracy every citizen has a serious *obligation to do police work,* and the existence of a paid police force does not alter this duty. Some historical background will be useful for putting the subject in perspective.

TABLE 1–1
Peel's Principles of Law Enforcement

1. The basic mission for which the police exist is to prevent crime and disorder as an alternative to the repression of crime and disorder by military force and severity of legal punishment.

2. The ability of the police to perform their duties is dependent upon public approval of police existence, actions, behavior, and the ability of the police to secure and maintain public respect.

3. The police must secure the willing cooperation of the public in voluntary observance of the law to be able to secure and maintain public respect.

4. The degree of cooperation of the public that can be secured diminishes, proportionately, the necessity for the use of physical force and compulsion in achieving police objectives.

5. The police seek and preserve public favor, not by catering to public opinion, but by constantly demonstrating absolutely impartial service to the law, in complete independence of policy, and without regard to the justice or injustice of the substance of individual laws; by ready

Table 1–1 continued

offering of individual service and friendship to all members of the society without regard to their race or social standing; by ready exercise of courtesy and friendly good humor; and by ready offering of individual sacrifice in protecting and preserving life.

6. The police should use physical force to the extent necessary to secure observance of the law or to restore order only when the exercise of persuasion, advice, and warning is found to be insufficient to achieve police objectives; and police should use only the minimum degree of physical force which is necessary on any particular occasion for achieving a police objective.

7. The police at all times should maintain a relationship with the public that gives reality to the historic tradition that the police are the public and that the public are the police; the police are the only members of the public who are paid to give full-time attention to duties which are incumbent on every citizen in the interest of community welfare.

8. The police should always direct their actions toward their functions and never appear to usurp the powers of the judiciary by avenging individuals or the state, or authoritatively judging guilt or punishing the guilty.

9. The test of police efficiency is the absence of crime and disorder, not the visible evidence of police action in dealing with them.

Medieval Police Service

In the Anglo-Saxon England of a thousand years ago, every able-bodied freeman was a policeman. As Peel later asserted, ". . . the police are the public and the public are the police." Every male from fifteen to sixty maintained such arms as he could afford. When the hue and cry was raised, every man within earshot dropped whatever he was doing and joined in the pursuit of the transgressor. Not to do so was a serious offense.

Later, the constable became the chief peace officer; but the job was still unpaid and was rotated among many. Then came the justice of the peace, who was both judge and police officer, discharging certain police duties even in modern times, especially in the suppression of riots (Lee, Ch. 1–3). This was the beginning of judicial surveillance over the police. As towns developed, watchmen were employed for full-time work. But ordinary citizens retained the solemn duty to perform police functions.

By the seventeenth century, many abuses had appeared in this medieval police system. Unpaid constables sought to avoid duty. Some persons maneuvered their police responsibilities to serve their private interests. As towns grew into cities, this watch-and-ward system was severely

strained. Thugs of varying description became the terror of the community. Finally, in the early eighteenth century, Sir John Fielding
organized the "Bow Street Runners," a small corps of paid police
officers who rapidly acquired a reputation for their success in apprehending hoodlums and undoubtedly helped to persuade Parliament of
the wisdom of Peel's proposals. Anxiety regarding the possible abuse of
treasured English civil liberties by overzealous, paid policemen gradually
dissolved in the face of accumulating evidence to the contrary.

So it is that the English declare, to this day, that a policeman is
someone who is paid to do what it is a citizen's duty to do without pay.
Consider, for example, the law of arrest. In a seventeenth century
treatise, *The Country Justice,* by Michael Dalton, there appears this
sentence: "The Sherife, Bailifes, Constables and other of the King's
Officers may arrest and imprison offenders in all cases where a private
person may . . ." This order of topics, the emphasis upon arrest by
every man and the selection of the private person as the standard by
which the right of officers to arrest is measured, is significant when
compared with modern treatises.[1]

It was not, in fact, until 1827 that the rule differentiating the
legal powers of lay persons from those of peace officers was established
in England. It is also interesting that numerous private police agencies
existed in England and Europe as far back as the eleventh century—for
example, associations of merchants such as the Hanseatic League, and
of property owners as self-appointed "thief catchers," anxious to protect
their special interests.

The American Experience

In the United States, Peel's plan of police organization was copied
in New York by 1844, and during the ensuing ten years similar organizational patterns appeared in Chicago, Philadelphia, and Boston. By
1870, the main features of the London Metropolitan Police were firmly
established in this country (Fosdick, *American Police Systems*). The
idea of laymen participating in police work was certainly evident in the
early history of the western states. Public tribunals, councils, and vigilante activities were common, just as many private protective and security organizations exist today in business and industry.[2]

Every society quickly recognizes that the police function is essential to its survival. The question is simply one of means necessary to
maintain the function. In the free society, it is understood that order is
not an end in itself, that it is a means to the end of justice and the sanctity
of individual liberty. Three additional points are implied:

1. Since in the democratic society the police are the public and the
   public are the police, the police accurately mirror the general

culture of the society they represent.[3] We will examine this point more thoroughly in a later chapter.

2. In a democratic society, unlike totalitarian systems, the police function depends on a considerable amount of self-policing by every citizen. The system is rooted in personal responsibility. Law observance is the most vital part of law enforcement. Paid police officers, even under conditions of intensive specialization and extensive training, cannot possibly perform their duties effectively without abundant self-policing by the citizen. This custom is not merely a matter of cooperation or good relations between police and community. Ideally, it is a matter of *organic union,* with the police *as part of,* and *not apart from* the community they serve.

3. The police in the democratic society are a living expression, an embodiment, an implementing arm of democratic law. If such a principle as due process, for example, is to have practical meaning, the nature of police behavior is important. What the police officer does and how he does it is one weighty measure of the value of the entire legal system for each person with whom he comes in contact. For many people, it is the only contact that they may ever have with the legal system. If democratic law is to be credible and ethical to ordinary citizens, with standards of fairness, reasonableness, and human decency, it will be so to the extent that police behavior reflects such qualities.

The importance of the police officer in our system of democratic legal process and institutions could hardly be stressed more emphatically than in this line of reasoning. Similarly, the overall importance of police-community relations is evident. To view the police as "pigs" or as "dirty workers" carries with it an implied indictment of the system far more fundamental and far more serious than the momentary titillation of "bugging the fuzz." This does not mean that the system should be spared from criticism. But criticism should be grounded in an understanding of the meaning of police service in democratic society. Only through genuine police-community partnership can a police force be created that will discharge its duties in a manner that strengthens the democratic way of life and maintains the stability of the community.

The test case is the quality of police service in relation to so-called minorities, sometimes called "the powerless" in society. Certainly antisocial conduct must be controlled. Vital as this task is, however, there must be more to the police-community partnership. Order must be maintained in ways that preserve and extend the values of democratic society: in short, by police methods conducive to human dignity, not by uncontrolled force. Associate Supreme Court Justice Louis Brandeis[4] once said:

Those who won our independence . . . recognized the risks to which all human institutions are subject. But they knew that order cannot be secured merely through fear of punishment for its infraction; that it is hazardous to discourage thought, hope, imagination; that fear breeds repression; that repression breeds hate; that hate menaces stable government; that the path of safety lies in the opportunity to discuss freely supposed grievances and proposed remedies; and that the fitting remedy for evil counsels is good ones. Believing in the power of reason as applied through public discussion, they eschewed silence coerced by law—the argument of force in its worst form.

Police and Social Change

Seemingly, the police today are more in the public eye than ever. Why so? The general reason lies in the shift from a predominantly agricultural society to a predominantly urban one. It includes the effect of social change upon social control. It is related to the concentration of the population in big cities, and to the unprecedented physical mobility of people. Twenty percent of our population is estimated to have changed residence annually since 1956, with approximately half of them moving across state and regional lines. Some 70 percent of the population occupy only 5 percent of the land area (Mundy, "Police and Community Relations," in Brandstatter and Radelet, eds.).

These are social conditions in which the police are likely to be prominently in public view. Order is more apt to be disrupted, crime more likely to be committed, a variety of social services more needed, civil rights and civil liberties more often championed and contested. Instantaneous news coverage of social conflict situations guarantees plentiful publicity for the police. The essential tension between collective security and individual liberty, the ancient teeter-totter of government, is severely tested. The entire apparatus of government has lately come under closer public scrutiny, the police included. As taxes spiral upward, disgruntled taxpayers hold public servants increasingly accountable. As the number of automobiles on public roads increases, more demanding rules of driving increase the odds that more citizens will experience contact with the police. Many of these contacts will not be joyful for the citizen, nor will they leave either citizen or police officer ecstatic over their partnership. In the same vein, many people will blame the police for the rising crime rate, for riots and disorders, and for general social bankruptcy. As a result, some policemen may occasionally feel sorry for themselves.

Police Response to Social Change

How have the police responded to this focus upon them? To some extent negatively, as would be expected, by feeling self-pity, by evincing defensiveness, by attempting to shift public attention elsewhere, by occasionally—and unavoidably—apologizing; more generally by retreating into their own subculture and isolating themselves, sometimes rather bitterly, from the community. Alas, as Gilbert and Sullivan observed, the policeman's lot is not a happy one. Typical expressions of negative reaction include such remarks as—

"Being a cop is a no-win deal."

"They expect us to solve all the problems in town."

"I don't go for these freaks spitting on me."

"We spend so much time these days doing social work that we haven't got time to do real police work."

"People just don't care anymore."

However, there has also been a positive police response. During the past twenty to thirty years, this response has been made through professional development. Without pausing here to define professional development (to be dealt with in a later chapter), we can say that it includes such things as the elevation of recruitment standards, a police service somewhat less likely to submit to the demands of politicians, and the development of a great variety of training and educational facilities and resources for the police. In addition, there are more sophisticated activities of professional organizations in the law enforcement field; at least a beginning in crystallizing a systematic theory of criminal justice administration; and the gradual emergence of police leadership in community relations. Since the latter is of special interest here, it merits further chronicling.

Early Programs for Police Training

Programs usually grow out of problem identification, when enough people are affected by a problem to care about trying to solve it. So far as can be determined, the first systematic programs in the field that is today captioned *Police-Community Relations* trace back about thirty years. These were special training courses for the police.

In 1931, the National Commission on Law Observance and Law Enforcement—popularly known, after its chairman, as the Wickersham Commission—presented its voluminous report to President Herbert Hoover. It recommended many reforms in dealing with crime and order problems, e.g., putting the police in civil service and giving them better training. The slogan "Take the police out of politics" was bandied about widely, and suddenly the idea of training the police was considered a means to that end. Training was also viewed, however narrowly, as a way of making the police more proficient in restraining crime. The fact that the police alone, no matter how well trained, cannot possibly prevent or control crime was largely ignored.

Much earlier, some American law enforcement leaders, such as August Vollmer, had been talking about the necessity of police training. But now training became respectable; some police officers began to take seriously the idea of going to school. Ten years later, as this country became involved in World War II, a sociological "happening" was of decisive influence in shaping a new type of specialized police training.

The first large migratory wave of American Negroes, generally from South to North, had occurred during World War I. It had helped substantially in breaking the manpower bottleneck in war production industries. As European immigration diminished, Negroes constituted a ready, unskilled labor supply, especially since the cotton industry, as the cornerstone of economy in the South, was declining. This internal Negro mobility was greatly accelerated with World War II, when the nonwhite population of many metropolitan areas doubled within a few years.

The social frictions, potential and actual, from these shifts in population became a matter of increasing concern to the police in many cities. Consequently, during the war years, police training courses in human relations, under such titles as "The Police and Minority Groups," were initiated. One such course, in the Chicago Park District Police Training School, was developed by Joseph D. Lohman, a lecturer in sociology at the University of Chicago, who began teaching it in 1942. The course became something of a model for other such courses. The text, mimeographed at first for Lohman's own classes, but later printed for general classroom use, stated the case for this type of police training as follows:

> All of us have our jobs to do and unless we can do them with a minimum of friction and conflict, the very fabric of society will be so rent and torn as to be beyond repair. Indeed, it is questionable whether a democracy can even continue to exist unless it develops a means for peacefully mediating these differences. . . . Not only individuals but also nationality and racial groups are in competition with one another as they strive . . . to improve their economic and social status. It is almost inevitable that such competition for jobs, a place to live, access to higher social position, and the struggle for a generally higher plane of living will bring about some measure of conflict; and each in our separate ways will seek to retain whatever superior advantages we may already possess. . . . There are two essentials in the encouragement of the (police) professional attitude as it affects race and minority group problems: First, there must be brought into clearer relief the nature of the race and minority group tensions with which a police officer may be confronted . . . Second, the individual police officer must possess the most accurate and authenticated information on the nature of racial, nationality and religious differences. He must understand the reasons for discrimination and bigotry. In addition, he must possess the best knowledge available regarding

ways in which the police officer can function when incidents occur and in situations of great tension. [*The Police and Minority Groups*]

Lohman's course included sessions on these topics:

- Worldwide and Neighborhood Aspects of Human Relations
- Background of Racial, Nationality and Religious Tensions
- The Facts About Race
- The Social Situations in Which Tensions Arise
- The Role of the Police Officer in Dealing with Tensions
- The Law and Administrative Controls as They Affect Human Relations

The course devoted considerable attention (for example, by the use of spot maps) to ecological factors in social disorganization, consistent with the approach of Robert Park and his colleagues in sociology on the Midway campus in the 1920s and 1930s.

Harvard Professor Gordon W. Allport took more of a socio-psychological route in a similar course he developed for the Boston Police Academy in 1942. In 1944, the International City Managers' Association (now the International City Management Association) reported that more than twenty metropolitan police departments had initiated human relations training (Weckler and Hall, *Police and Minority Groups*) during the war years.

These early police training programs in human relations had certain general characteristics:

1. They focused exclusively on racial, religious, and ethnic conflict.

2. They introduced police officers to the nature and causes of these sociological problems, and their relationship to crime.

3. They stimulated the police to think about crime and social disorders in *preventive* terms.

4. They often used especially trained police officers as instructors.

5. They mostly disregarded concerns of broad community relations, and did not involve community leaders and citizens.

Program Development: 1946–1955

Following World War II, interest in programs of this type waned for a time. A few publications with relevant content appeared,[5] along with many general books dealing with race relations, prejudice, and the like. Milwaukee Chief of Police Joseph T. Kluchesky made news when he addressed the 1945 annual meeting of the International Association of Chiefs of Police on the topic, "Police Action on Minority Problems."[6] It was a speech that would be as appropriate today as it was then. President Truman's Committee on Civil Rights (1947), in its report *To Secure These Rights,* devoted some space to law enforcement and judicial processes, calling attention to the difficulties encountered by some Americans in these as well as in other institutional facets of the society.

Summer workshops in human relations for teachers and other community leaders were pioneered by the National Conference of Christians and Jews and other organizations dedicated to reducing tensions between elements of the community. A few police officers enrolled in these workshops as early as 1947, seeking help in understanding human relations problems, and sometimes with a specific departmental charge, for instance, to fashion a unit of instruction for a training program in the subject.[7]

The Southern Police Institute, established at the University of Louisville in 1950, scheduled twenty-six hours of instruction in human behavior and human relations in its thirteen-week curriculum. This instruction followed immediately upon the initiation of a Lohman-designed training program, *Principles of Police Work,* in the Louisville Division of Police. In 1952, the Los Angeles County Conference on Community Relations (Senn, *Programs in Minority Relations*) reported on police departments in more than thirty major cities that had some sort of specialized training in human relations, race relations, the police and minority groups, and similar problems. In the summer of 1952, at the University of Chicago, Lohman conducted the first national seminar on the subject, "The Police and Racial Tensions." Of three weeks duration, it was attended by twenty-nine police officers from approximately twenty municipalities.

Philadelphia was the site, in February 1954, of a two-day conference jointly sponsored by the International Association of Chiefs of Police and the National Association of Intergroup Relations Officials, and attended by top police executives and intergroup relations professionals from approximately thirty cities. The agenda anticipated the decision of the Supreme Court in the school desegregation cases, which came a few months later, in that the conference participants asked themselves how they might effect cooperation at the local level to secure the coveted goal of orderly and just communities.

Community Programs: 1955–1967

The Philadelphia conference set in motion a process of thought and a series of steps by the National Conference of Christians and Jews (NCCJ) that led to the establishment, in 1955, of the National Institute on Police and Community Relations at Michigan State University, as a cooperative venture of NCCJ and the MSU School of Police Administration and Public Safety. Only a few highlights from a more detailed source need be noted here.[8]

The Institute was a five-day conference, the recognized usefulness of which caused it to be repeated each May up to 1970. It brought together teams of police officers and other community leaders, recruited largely through the more than sixty NCCJ regional offices across the country, to discuss a wide range of problems of common interest and to develop leadership for similar programs at the local or state levels. In certain years, well over 400 participants came from as many as 165 communities in 30 states and several foreign countries, and only 7 states were never represented. As a result of the Institute, such programs proliferated rapidly across the nation. Programs of this type are considered in a later chapter.

The stated purposes of the many programs initiated during this period tended to follow those of the National Institute, expressed as follows:

1. To encourage police-citizen partnership in the cause of crime prevention.

2. To foster and improve communication and mutual understanding between the police and the total community.

3. To promote interprofessional approaches to the solution of community problems, and stress the principle that the administration of justice is a total community responsibility.

4. To enhance cooperation among the police, prosecution, the courts, and corrections.

5. To assist police and other community leaders to achieve an understanding of the nature and causes of complex problems in people-to-people relations, and especially to improve police-minority group relationships.

6. To strengthen implementation of equal protection under the law for all persons.

In addition, certain basic assumptions supported these programs:

That the law enforcement officer occupies a crucially important position in the maintenance of order in the community. Yet it is vital that the police recognize that order in itself is not the ultimate end of government in the free society.

That, therefore, the principle of equal protection of the law for ALL citizens, and respect for their rights *as persons,* are absolutely fundamental under our system of government.

That police interested in police-community relations are committed to their own professional development. At a minimum this means fair and impartial law enforcement regardless of personal opinions or prejudices.

That today's community which the police officer is endeavoring to serve is vastly different in community relations from the community of yesteryear. This implies a need for new concepts in police education and police training, especially as to social and behavioral science.

That police-community relations programs should involve a genuine educational process, the cultivation of dialogue across lines of diversity, and real effort to make communication more effective and mutual understanding a practical objective.

That each of us has something to learn from others regarding complex community problems, in their definition, diagnosis and remedies. The police officer has something to learn from people who are not policemen, and the converse.

That police education in community relations does not add *new* burdens for law enforcement officers. That because police are in a unique position for dealing with social problems, they need help so that they may do so more effectively, particularly since conflict management has become the *central* task of the police in today's society.

That current problems in race relations and civil rights represent extremely important subject matter in any police-community relations Institute. Yet basic issues affect the police-community relationship that have little or nothing to do with race.

That there is also much more to the field of police-community relations than the traditional (and important!) matter of public relations.

That the improvement of the police-community relationship should not be an end in itself. The relationship is improved as the dialogue matures, in the process of working together in interprofessional approaches to the solution of community problems. Thus, a good police-community relations program may very well be, chiefly, a program in crime prevention . . . or a series of discussions focusing on the attitudes of youth toward law and authority . . . or an action project in traffic safety. Any of the great issues in the administration of justice today may conceivably be the focus or pivot for police-community relations programs or projects.

The National Conference of Christians and Jews, the mainspring of so many programs in this field since 1955, was founded in 1928, against the background of the religious bigotry which characterized the presidential election campaign of that year. It was conceived as a civic organization of religiously motivated individuals seeking, through education, to promote cooperation and mutual understanding among men of goodwill of diverse religious belief, and racial and ethnic origin, without compromise of any particular creed or faith. Through the years, this organization has fostered a great variety of programs by means of its regional offices across the country. These programs have been directed mainly toward leaders in the social institutional "trunklines" of society, which strongly influence the formation of attitudes: religious, educational, familial, political; community organizations, the mass media of public information, and labor and management groups. Since 1934, the NCCJ has sponsored the annual observance of Brotherhood Week. Religious News Service is another of its creations. The organization became interested in police-community relations because of its commitment to orderly and just interaction among all citizens.

Generally, the programs that emerged during the 1955–1967 period—

1. developed what has come to be called a *concept* of police-community relations—with which Chapter Two will deal. Scholarly interest in the "sociology of the police" was stimulated.

2. widely encouraged a teamwork or interprofessional approach to problems of police-community relations, by using a kind of laboratory method that brought together citizens of widely diversified community interests and the police and other criminal justice people for discussing problems of common interest. The essential question was, how can we work together to build a better community for all citizens?

3. promoted the idea of police-community relations program development on a national scale.

In 1961, on a grant of funds from the Field Foundation, the School of Police Administration and Public Safety, Michigan State University, conducted a national survey of 168 law enforcement agencies. The results of this survey strongly documented a case for the establishment of a National Center on Police and Community Relations. This Center, with year-round services available, was activated August 1, 1965 at Michigan State, with the further help of a substantial enabling grant from the Field Foundation. To the present, the Center's functions include—

1. undertaking action-related research projects;

2. preparing, publishing, and circulating literature in the field of its interest;

3. developing, and sometimes conducting, educational and training programs;

4. providing direct consultative service to interested police and community organizations;

5. training young professionals for work in the field of police and community relations;

The Center has been the recipient of several Federal grants, including one with which it conducted a national survey of police-community relations (*Field Surveys V*) for the President's 1966 Commission on Law Enforcement and Administration of Justice (also referred to as the President's Crime Commission), completed in January 1967.

Another study (*Police-Community Relations Policies and Practices: A National Survey*), jointly undertaken in 1954 by the International Association of Chiefs of Police and the U.S. Conference of Mayors, surveyed police-community relations in cities with a population of 30,000-plus, with the following conclusions:

1. Less than a third of the police departments studied had continuing, formalized community relations programs.

2. Two-thirds of the departments studied had, or were developing, plans to cope with racial demonstrations and disturbances.

3. In cities with more than a 5 percent nonwhite population, 70 percent of the departments reported that they were experiencing difficulties in recruiting nonwhite officers.

4. While more than 60 percent of the reporting departments indicated that they offered some training in police-minority group relations, there was wide diversity in the type and quality of training involved.

5. In only two regions did the responding departments report that they restricted the power of arrest of nonwhite officers—10 percent of those in the South Atlantic and 14 percent of those in the West South Central. Assignment of officers either on a nonracial basis or to racially mixed teams was becoming increasingly general.

6. More than half of the departments studied were being charged by racial groups with police brutality or differential treatment, or both. Nearly two out of ten departments reported that such complaints were increasing; about the same number reported them to be decreasing.

Several Federal government agencies substantially encouraged programs in police-community relations in the 1960s. One was the United States Commission on Civil Rights, whose 1961 report devoted one of five volumes to the subject of *Justice*. It was the most thorough job yet done in laying bare the problems of our criminal justice system, by exposing deficiencies in fulfilling the principle of equal justice under law for all.

The Community Relations Service, initially in the Department of Commerce, and later shifted to the Department of Justice, still provides consultant and programmatic services for many police departments and community organizations concerned about problems of police-community relations. Numerous state and local public agencies for intergroup relations also help in this cause, as do several of the better known private organizations, in addition to the NCCJ; e.g., The Anti-Defamation

League of B'nai B'rith, the National Association for the Advancement of Colored People, the Urban League, the American Jewish Committee, the Southern Regional Council, and Jewish Community Relations Councils in many cities. Many private educational consultant agencies have also become interested in police-community relations projects during the past few years.

A perennial obstacle in efforts to build programs is the cost. Beginning in 1965, the Office of Law Enforcement Assistance of the U.S. Department of Justice (now known as the Law Enforcement Assistance Administration) took a special interest in police-community relations programs at the local level and has since funded many diversified projects. One of its most significant contributions was the work of President Lyndon Johnson's Commission on Law Enforcement and Administration of Justice (1966–1967), whose studies were financed entirely by the Office of Law Enforcement Assistance. Many of these studies had dimensions of police-community relations. Consider this passage from *Task Force Report: The Police* of the Commission report, for example:

> The need for strengthening police relationships with the communities they serve is critical today in the Nation's large cities and in many small cities and towns as well. The Negro, Puerto Rican, Mexican-American, and other minority groups are taking action to acquire rights and services which have been historically denied them. As the most visible representative of the society from which these groups are demanding fair treatment and equal opportunity, law enforcement agencies are faced with unprecedented situations on the street which require that they develop policies and practices governing their actions when dealing with minority groups and other citizens.

> Even if fairer treatment of minority groups were the sole consideration, police departments would have an obligation to attempt to achieve and maintain good police-community relations. In fact, however, much more is at stake. Police-community relationships have a direct bearing on the character of life in our cities, and on the community's ability to maintain stability and to solve its problems. At the same time, the police department's capacity to deal with crime depends to a large extent upon its relationship with the citizenry. Indeed, no lasting improvement in law enforcement is likely in this country unless police-community relations are substantially improved. [Ch. 6, p. 144]

Since 1967

The riots and disorders that occurred in various cities during the summer of 1967, and thereafter, marked a turning point in programs on police-community relations, as well as in other features of intergroup activities. Suddenly, the nation was jolted into a realization of how intense and profound were the divisions among our people, both racial and social. The assumptions of goodwill and commitment to the brotherhood of man that had more or less motivated programs in police-community relations during the 1955–1967 period were abruptly called into question. Reliance on the possibilities of developing dialogue to build communication bridges across the chasms of intergroup differences was brought into instant doubt. Programs cast in traditional patterns of community organization (block committees, precinct councils, etc.) were evidently not doing the job; many police officers and others began to express skepticism about whether it was "worth the effort" and to ask "what have we done wrong?" There was widespread bewilderment. Some simply withdrew from further efforts; many adopted a get tough philosophy. Another presidential commission, The National Advisory Commission on Civil Disorders (popularly known as the Kerner Commission, after its chairman), proclaimed in its report that "Our Nation is moving toward two societies, one black, one white—separate and unequal," (p. 1) and as for police-community relations,

> The police are not merely a "spark" factor. To some Negroes police have come to symbolize white power, white racism, and white repression. And the fact is that many police do reflect and express these white attitudes. The atmosphere of hostility and cynicism is reinforced by a widespread belief among Negroes in the existence of police brutality and in a "double standard" of justice and protection—one for Negroes and one for whites. [P. 5]

For those across the country who had been active in police-community relations programs of one kind or another during the 1955–67 period, there may have been some tendency to overreact to the catastrophes of 1967 in our cities. Perhaps it should not have been so great a shock to discover that police-community relations programs were not, indeed, doing the job; and that there were quite legitimate questions to be raised about the quality of these programs, without suggesting that the programs had no merit at all. Actually, there had been little effort to evaluate programs carefully and scientifically. In fact, there was even some resistance to such research by eager program developers who preferred not to be reminded that the attitudes of many people were not being changed, and that many people were not being reached. The truth was that there had been little or no progress in solving basic societal problems that vitally affect police-community relations.

What has happened since 1967? Seemingly, more programs than ever in police-community relations have been initiated, many of them grandiosely viewed as preventive treatment for civil disorders. Many of these programs have been heavily oriented toward improving public relations for the police. A few programs, almost entirely funded by the Law Enforcement Assistance Administration, have been designed with truly innovative features. Almost none are adequately evaluated. Although there is widespread malaise, there is also a yearning for fresh thinking and new ideas in the field, and a latent, haunting realization that the goal of better police-community relations is closely allied with other goals in social justice and criminal justice that remain in the category of things we can't change overnight.

The Urban Coalition, a private action-research organization headquartered in Washington, D.C., issued a report in 1969, indicating that the nation had made little progress in coping with the problems identified a year earlier by the Kerner Commission. Another presidential commission was activated in the wake of the assassinations of Dr. Martin Luther King and Senator Robert F. Kennedy—the National Commission on the Causes and Prevention of Violence, headed by Dr. Milton Eisenhower. This commission has since presented sweeping recommendations relative to violent crime, e.g., that cities should undertake "increased police-community relations activity in slum ghetto areas in order to secure greater understanding of ghetto residents by police, and of police by ghetto residents." This commission has also made recommendations pertaining to group violence, firearms, television programs, and campus disorders. Various "Safer City" organizations have pleaded that these recommendations should be carefully studied.

The National Institute on Police and Community Relations at Michigan State University was discontinued at the end of 1969. Its demise was a commentary on the evolution of issues and social forces pertinent to the field. The purposes, assumptions, and Institute design of past years may have been relevant in their time. But it became imperative now to think about police-community relations programs in different terms, with more precise purposes that could be better measured as to results, and with somewhat less universalistic assumptions. In Michigan, a newly designed state-wide Institute on Community Relations in the Administration of Justice was initiated, to test some new ideas in program techniques with built-in evaluation aspects.

Realistic hopes of improving police relations with the community depend considerably upon fundamental work that remains to be done (for example, in urgently needed reforms in the criminal justice system, as well as in the broader social milieu). For there is an inescapable connection between police-community relations and powerlessness, despair, hopelessness, and authority arbitrarily imposed, just as there is with racism, slum living, poverty, substandard housing, unemployment and unemployability, discrimination in education, and other such social malignancies. This does not mean, of course, that all efforts to improve police-community relations should be abandoned until these correlative problems are solved. But correlative problems demand correlative approaches. It is not our intention at this point to describe existing programs or to present recommendations for future program development. (This will be done later in the book.)

The outlook is not altogether melancholy. The late Elmo Roper struck a positive chord in *Saturday Review*:

> There are literally dozens of areas where responsible and intelligent whites and responsible and intelligent Negroes can be seen working together because of some mutuality of interest. The next step is to make these contacts more frequent and more personal.
>
> That the racial heat is on is no excuse for faltering in the long-range, step-by-step effort to bring the races together; it is reason to redouble these efforts. There must be a model of racial friendliness and good-will to counter the image of racial contempt and antagonism so visible today. I have no illusions that small, individual efforts to bridge the gulf between the races present a magical solution to the problems of racial disharmony. But it seems clear to me that if educated, high-minded people who believe in the concept of racial brotherhood cannot make a reality of closeness between the races, no one can. ["Beyond the Riots," pp. 24, 25]

Notes to Chapter One

1. This discussion relies heavily on a series of three papers, "Police and Law in a Democratic Society," by Professor Jerome Hall of the Indiana University Law School.

2. For a further discussion of lay participation in law enforcement, see Jerome Hall, *Theft, Law and Society*.

3. For an elaboration of this point, see Geoffrey Gorer, "Modification of National Character: The Role of the Police in England."

4. In a concurring opinion in *Whitney* v. *California,* 274 U.S. 357, 375 (1927).

5. For example, Alfred McClung Lee and Norman D. Humphrey, *Race Riot* (a study of the 1943 Detroit riot). See also *Guide to Race Relations for Peace Officers* by Davis McEntire and Robert B. Powers, for the Attorney General, State of California, 1946 (republished in 1952). Again republished by the same source in 1958 as *Guide to Community Relations for Peace Officers* (Edmund G. Brown, Attorney General; Emmet Daly, Assistant Attorney General).

6. New York: Freedom House, 1946.

7. As an example, see the training syllabus by Detroit Officer Irvin Lawler in Study 1, Part I, *The Police and the Community: Studies,* Louis A. Radelet and Hoyt Coe Reed.

8. See "Introduction," *Police and Community Relations: A Sourcebook,* A. F. Brandstatter and Louis A. Radelet, eds.

Chapter Two

The Concept of Police-Community Relations

A basic difficulty in police-community relations is to define the concept. There appear to be as many answers to the question of what it means as there are those disposed to respond to the question. Individual police officers have different conceptions of it, not to mention various factions of the community. To some, police-community relations simply means public relations, that is, activities directed at creating and maintaining favorable impressions of a product, a firm, or an institution; in Madison Avenue terms, *imagery*. The emphasis is on *looking good*, not necessarily on *being* good, although public relations people themselves insist that the best public relations is a quality product. For a police department, this would mean good service to the community.[1]

Differing Views of Police-Community Relations

But what a police department views as good for the department may not be good for the community. Or it may be good for only that part of the community to whom the police are particularly responsive, not for other parts. Frequently, some parts of the community are not adequately consulted in matters in which someone decides what is good for "everybody." Public relations sometimes have a tendency to be a one-way communications process.

X Good public relations are important for any police agency. This area has been neglected in the past, apparently on the grounds that it is something of a luxury for a tax-supported service. It may have been also that some police agencies preferred privacy! Some apparently still do. In any event, public relations and community relations, though often used interchangeably, are not identical. The President's 1966 Crime Commission, in *The Challenge of Crime in a Free Society*, made the distinction:

> A community relations program is not a public relations program "to sell the police image" to the people. It is not a set of expedients whose purpose is to tranquilize for a time an angry neighborhood by, for example, suddenly promoting a few Negro officers in the wake of a racial disturbance. It is a long-range, full-scale effort to acquaint the police and the community with each other's problems and to stimulate action aimed at solving those problems. [P. 100]

This statement suggests police-community teamwork as a methodological and community action concept, a way to approach complex problem solving. More about this shortly.

Another View of the Relationship

As we noted earlier, another popular way of defining police-community relations is to see it as concerned primarily with racial and ethnic relationships, civil rights, the police and minority groups, with parrying charges of "police brutality," and with clamor for establishing civilian review boards. Closely akin to this is the notion that police-community relations means the control of riots, demonstrations, civil disturbances, and such. This latter view gained momentum following the 1967 disorders, proposed especially by those believing that forceful suppression of political dissent and social deviance is the ideal program for police-community relations. Thus, more and better equipment ("hardware") for police tactics in civil disorder situations is seen as the answer. "Law and order must prevail; support your local police!"

There is little doubt that the rather spectacular development of police-community relations programs in recent years may be explained largely in terms of the tumult in race relations and civil rights in this country. But again, police-Negro relations or police-Puerto Rican relations, important though they surely are, do not constitute the whole story of police-community relations. As with public relations, while one is an aspect of the other, the substance of one is not wholly the substance of the other. There are problematic aspects of the police relationship with the community that have little or nothing to do with racial or ethnic considerations.

The Difficulty of Definitions

Perhaps the first question in trying to define police-community relations is agreeing on a concept of "community." By and large, inter-group relationship problems are most acute in metropolitan areas. It is there that what Maurice Stein called "the eclipse of community" (in his book of the same title) has occurred most dramatically. In fact, it may be argued that it is precisely because "community" in the functional sense has ceased to exist—or, more accurately, because the community is less *functional* than it once was—that relationship problems germinate. A definition of the functional community has interpersonal and inter-group relations at its heart. Closely knit social relations is its very metabolism. When a community becomes dysfunctional, the chief aim of remedial programs is the restoration of social cohesiveness—to build unity where there is fragmentation. The author has discussed this in "The Idea of a Community."

In the same line of reasoning, when we say, "police-community," we are associating entities that are quite dissimilar, sociologically, and at the same time suggesting a false dichotomy. If the police are part of the community, why the hyphen? Moreover, "police" suggests a fairly unitary, compassable, intellectually manageable occupational grouping. The "community" on the other hand is an amorphous, elusive, quick-silverish concept, especially when it is applied to the modern metropolis. To speak of the police relationship with "the community" is therefore misleading. Which community? It might be preferable to use the socio-logical concept of a "public," and speak of the police interaction with this or that public, were it not that this induces confusion of another sort, as earlier noted. (Why not, then, call it "public relations"?)

To complicate the matter further, we will be saying, for instance, that the police function is a part of several social systems—the criminal justice system, for one. On the one hand, community relations, for the *police* must be seen more comprehensively than in most discussions. On the other hand, *society's* attitude toward the police is in some meas-ure society's attitude toward the entire criminal justice system, and toward government as a whole. As previously indicated, correlative problems require correlative approaches.

General Definition

Having suggested some of the pitfalls in the formidable task of defining terms, we may proceed. A general definition of police-commu-nity relations might specify simply that it refers to the reciprocal attitudes of police and civilians. We are interested in the sum total of activities by which it may be emphasized that police are an important part of, not apart from, the communities they serve. We are also interested in the factors that contravene this positive principle. Properly understood, the principle is one for total *orientation* of a police organization. It is an attitude and an emphasis for all phases of police work, not merely for a specialized unit in the department. It is a way for a police officer to view his work in dealing with citizens. For citizens, it is a way of viewing the police officer: what he does and how he does it. Ideally, it is a matter of striving to achieve mutual understanding and trust, as with any human relationship. Every problem in police work today is in some way a problem of police-community relations. Its solution depends in some sense upon police and community cooperation, indeed *partnership*.

As the President's Crime Commission put it in *Challenge of Crime:*

> Improving community relations involves not only instituting programs and changing procedures and practices, but re-examining fundamental attitudes. The police will have to learn to listen patiently and under-standingly to people who are openly critical of them or hostile to them, since those people are precisely the ones with whom relations need to be improved. ... police-citizen relationships on the street [must] become person-to-person encounters rather than the black-versus-white, oppressed-versus-oppressor confrontations they too often are. [P. 100]

So conceived, the police-and-community relation has a *preventive* character. Its thrust is in working together in the community to anticipate and to *prevent* problems, to do something constructive about problems *before crisis occurs*. It entails planning to avert crises. Police-community relations programs should operate on the premise that the best way to control a riot is to prevent it; the best way to control a crime is to prevent it. When the police are in the streets armed with shotguns, volleying tear gas, and crouched behind protective shields, it is too late for police-community relations.

Three Aspects of Community Relations

Community relations may be more specifically defined. It may be viewed as a kind of tripod,[2] based on three equal components: public relations, community service, and community participation. One leg of the tripod, *public relations,* has already been defined. For a police de-partment, an example of *community service* would be a youth program comprising a variety of activities for children—recreation, sports, skill games, camping, music, etc. Community service is good public relations, but with the plus factor of providing some beneficial service to the community.

The third leg of the tripod, *community participation,* is the aspect that has been emphasized in police and community relations programs in recent years. It stresses interprofessional or teamwork approaches to solving community problems. It is the widely used social-work concept

Look on p.22

of community organization, with particular attention to the participation of the police and other criminal justice agencies.

The idea of community participation may be clarified by an illustration. Take the crime problem. Clearly, the police are concerned about it. So are the courts and other criminal justice institutions. So are the schools, religious bodies, social work agencies, various community organizations, labor unions and business management; the mass media, etc. The crime problem is extremely complicated. No single community force, not even the police, have the total answer. Policemen have a certain experience with the problem. It is not the same experience that, say, school principals have. Thus, the police have something to contribute, out of their experience, to the definition, diagnosis, and solution of the crime problem. So do school people. And so on, with other community entities.

The art of devising programs, therefore, is that of bringing together all these forces in some sort of cooperative, coordinated venture, to cope with problems too complex for any single force to solve alone. It is in this sense that the police-community relations activity takes on a problem-solving function. The program might be, primarily, one of comprehensive crime prevention. Or it might focus on some other problem—any problem concerning which there is a sense of common social consequence and shared responsibility.

The Relationships of Teamwork

But what is the point of such an indirect approach to improving police and community relations? To reply to this in a somewhat roundabout way, we refer to research (known as the Robbers' Cave Experiment) by Muzafer and Carolyn Sherif and their colleagues at the University of Oklahoma more than two decades ago (*An Outline of Psychology,* pp. 301–331). They demonstrated that within a period of a few weeks they could produce two contrasting patterns of behavior in a group of normal children. First, they could bring the group to a state of intense hostility, and then they could completely reverse the process by inducing a spirit of friendship and cooperation.

The Sherifs showed that mere interaction—pleasant social contact between antagonists—would not reduce hostility. The critical element for achieving harmony in human relations, according to the Sherifs, is joint activity in behalf of a *superordinate goal.* Hostility gives way when groups pull together to achieve overriding goals that are real and compelling for all concerned. The Sherif team accomplished this by certain stratagems, such as interrupting the water supply to the camp where two groups of youngsters had been turned against each other bitterly by a series of conflict-inducing incidents. The boys volunteered to search the water line for trouble; they located it and worked together harmoniously to correct the difficulty.

To translate the principle into police-community relations terms, another illustration may be helpful. Bruce J. Terris, a member of the staff of the President's Crime Commission, describes the idea in the following way, with crime control and community stability as the superordinate goals:

> The problem of violent crime must be met in our ghettos where it principally occurs. Yet the state of police-community relations in these areas now makes it almost impossible for the police to deal with crime there. At the same time, both the prevalence of violent crime and the threat of disorders compound the already serious problems in our cities. Consequently, relations between the police and minority groups must be drastically and immediately improved if our cities are to reduce crime and to have the reasonable degree of stability necessary to solve their other problems. ["The Role of the Police," *The Annals*]

Yet a precautionary note should perhaps be recorded. Maintaining good relationships with all elements of the population of a community should be regarded by police officials as a goal of the greatest importance, on its own merits. But good relationship also has great pragmatic value in dealing with social problems, such as crime, that are of grave concern to police and community. Herman Goldstein, of the University of Wisconsin Law School, puts it in perspective:

> Any improvement in citizen contact obviously serves in a very direct manner to improve the cooperation which the police can expect from the public in combatting crime. This is a consideration of the utmost importance when one reflects upon the degree to which the police depend upon the public for assistance in reporting crimes and suspicious circumstances and in serving as witnesses and complainants in the prosecution of criminal cases. But if lasting improvements are to be made in that aspect of police functioning that is unrelated to crime, they must be justified on their merits rather than be rationalized on the basis of the relationship such improvements will have to those police efforts that more directly relate to crime. ["Police Response to Urban Crises"][3]

To make our point clear, the prevention and control of crime is a superordinate goal, in which all elements of the community have an important stake. The problem can be coped with only with input from all sources: police and community teamwork. In this process, police and community relations are likely to be improved.

Distinguishing Activities

It is not always easy, nor probably is it in practical terms too important, to distinguish among public relations, community service, and community participation. Perhaps Table 2–1 will help to clarify it.

Each activity is listed in its *primary* purpose, acknowledging that some may span more than one category.

Table 2-1
Police Activities Fostering Favorable Public Response

Public Relations	Personal cleanliness and good grooming (wearing uniform smartly, having shoes polished, etc.)
	General politeness, courtesy, and good manners
	Telephone etiquette
	Car cleanliness (keeping cars washed, etc.)
	Modifications in the military-type uniform (redesigned blazers, jackets, etc.; inconspicuous carrying of weapons)
	Speaker's bureau activities, skill demonstrations, equipment exhibits, etc.
	Open houses at police stations
	Dog shows, water safety shows, etc.
	Displays on bumper stickers, car cards, billboards
	Awards and citations for outstanding policemen and citizens
	Liaison for press personnel and facilities
	Cooperation between the chief and media executives
	Tidiness and good order in administrative facilities
	American flag insignia worn
Community Service	Informational or interpretive newspaper or magazine features, newsletters and door knob hangers, radio and television presentations (e.g., education on drugs, auto safety, auto theft, house burglaries)
	Safety instruction for operating autos, bicycles, and other vehicles
	Youth programs (e.g., Police Athletic League, summer camping, etc.)
	Store-front centers in neighborhoods
	Annual or periodic reports, *if* designed for public understanding
	Complaint procedure
	Public fund-raising solicitation for tuition to help improve the education of police officers (by a citizens' organization)
	Ride-in-a-patrol-car programs
	Sponsorship of scouting units (e.g., Explorers)
	Police junior band or drum-and-bugle corps
	Law enforcement career clinics in high schools
	Policeman Bill and *Officer Friendly* types of programs in elementary schools
	Police aid and advice for parades, demonstrations, etc.

Table 2–1 continued

Community **Service** continued	Emergency facilities for demonstrations Police assignments to job opportunity centers Assistance to crisis intervention agencies Crime prevention literature Helping Hand programs Distribution of information to new residents Tire changing assistance Checks on vacationers' residences Ambulance service Lost-and-found auctions (e.g., bicycles) School counselling assistance Social service referrals
Community **Participation**	Councils of Social Agencies, United Fund, Community Chest, etc. Family and Neighborhood Stabilization Councils Coordinating Council on Community Relations XYZ Council on Police-Community Relations Precinct or District Police-Citizens Committees or Work- shops ABC Council on Crime and Delinquency 77th Street Interdenominational Clergy-Police Council Police-Community Relations seminars (potentially) Edison Park—Hamilton Community (neighborhood) Council Citizens United for a Safer City (not vigilante groups)

Some Implications of Relationships

The approach to police and community relations stressing problem solving through community participation has some implications that should be noted. It suggests, for instance, that it is not the goal of programs to persuade everyone to fall in love with the police. If, as a by-product of programs, some people learn to appreciate policemen more —even to the point of seeing them as "human," as neighbors and fellow-citizens, and possibly even as friendly and personable "good guys"—this may be credited as a nice dividend. But the *primary* purposes in the community participation approach should be to solve hard problems, to improve the quality of police services, and to elevate the level of public respect for the police officer and for the system of government by law which he represents. Respect is, of course, something that is earned, and the attitude and behavior of the police officer himself is the most important factor in this process. But citizens, also, should recognize their responsibilities in what a police officer may expect from them.

Full police participation in community problem-solving efforts assumes that police will be encouraged and motivated to rise to the highest level of their professional potential. In effect, this means the emergence of the police as authentic *community leaders.* The English social anthropologist Michael Banton refers in *The Police Chief* (April 1963) to the policeman as "a professional citizen," no doubt mindful of the Anglo-Saxon background referred to in the preceding chapter. However, the idea of the police officer as a community leader comes on even stronger in other statements, for example, this by University of Illinois sociologist David Bordua in "Comments on Police-Community Relations":

> We are, in short, asking the police to lead the community in race relations. For them merely to reflect the community would be a disaster ... It is ... no help to have the police closely linked into the local community if that community's main concern is the suppression of Negroes ... The modern police cannot function simply as representatives of community culture—assuming it is coherent enough to be represented. They must stand aside from the culture to a large degree and function as community managers.

Real and Imaginary Problems

In defining police-community relations and the problems associated with it, a question frequently arises whether a distinction should be drawn between what really *is* a problem and what people *think* is a problem. The positions taken by various segments of the population are clearly based upon differing perceptions. Individuals believe something because they see it as being so. Both police malpractice and community misunderstanding bear upon the relationship between police and community. While police officers sometimes behave in discriminatory ways, it is just as accurate to say that much of the friction between police and community results from misunderstanding and misinterpretation. As in any other area of human relations, some attitudes are based on fact and some on assumption and some assumptions are incorrect. Eleanor Harlow of the National Council on Crime and Delinquency makes the point:

> Where there is anonymity of individual officers, there is generalization and stereotyping by citizens; where there is racial hatred and distrust, there is misinterpretation of police actions; and where there is lack of communication with and confidence in the police, there is also a tendency on the part of citizens to believe the worst. Thus, the actions of those police who do behave unprofessionally reflect not only upon the entire department but on police in general, and whenever questionable tactics are employed against minority groups anywhere,

hostility to police everywhere is increased. [*Problems in Police-Community Relations*, p. 4]

Her analysis continues:

One important fact to consider is that whether or not police brutality exists, if significant numbers of people believe that it does, it then becomes a serious and very real problem. For example, a widespread belief that police are unjust or brutal results in loss of respect for and cooperation with any police officer. When people do not accept police authority at every point of contact, the police feel the need to assert personal authority by force in order "to handle the situation" in the absence of respect for the badge and uniform. Thus the belief that police are brutal often becomes a self-fulfilling expectation.

Harvard political scientist James Q. Wilson adds a telling point in "Police Morale, Reform and Citizen Respect":

The fact that the police can no longer take for granted that non-criminal citizens are also non-hostile citizens may be the most important problem which even the technically proficient department must face. [P. 158]

The evaluation of police-community relations at a given place and time is an offshoot of the perceptions which the police have of the community and which the community has of the police. These perceptions are commonly divergent. Public perceptions of the police represent a complex side of the matter; police perceptions of various "publics" also affect the relationship, and are equally complex. Reciprocal attitudes are rooted in these reciprocal perceptions. The police, for instance, often resent not being able to take action before violence occurs, and sometimes claim that minority groups receive preferential treatment by the courts (Watson, *Police-Community Relations*). On the other hand, community groups are extremely sensitive to any police behavior that conjures up the image of a "police state."

The main thought that we are suggesting is that police-community relations problems are defined at a given time and place by diverse, often conflicting and ambiguous perceptions and attitudes of police officers on the one side and of individual citizens and community groups on the other. This is hardly a startling revelation; the author has dealt with it more extensively in "Attitudes Involved in Relating Community and Police"; and later chapters in this book will analyze it further.

The matter of defining the police-community relations concept may be summarized with this statement by the author, writing in *The Christian Science Monitor*, in 1968:

Police-community relations is not merely a number of schemes and machines, or greater technical efficiency, or more socio-psychological training for police officers, or recruiting more Negro policemen, or a store-front operation in a ghetto, or a truly open system for handling citizen complaints, or the activities of a specialized unit in the department. Good police-citizen relations is, ideally, a TOTAL ORIENTATION in the attitudes and behavior of a police department, bearing upon everything it does, every facet and level of the organization. If it is less than this, then police-community relations may be simply gamesmanship, a kind of insult and mockery, and a particularly ignominious species of self-serving social placation. If it is this, it makes absurd the hope for police professionalization.

Police and community relations refers to the many aspects of the relationship between the police and the public. The term *police-community relations* must be broadly interpreted, emphasizing preventive activity in containing crime and in maintaining order and community stability. Community relations combines public relations, community service, and community participation. The relationship between police and community is determined, not only by what actually happens in police-citizen contacts but also by how people perceive what happens.

Notes to Chapter Two

1. A broad overview of the field of police-community relations is provided in a chapter by the author entitled, "Public Information and Community Relations," in the 1969 edition of *Municipal Police Administration* (International City Management Association).

2. This three-way analysis of community relations relies on *Community Organization: Theory and Principle*, by Murray G. Ross, pp. 23–26.

3. Professor Goldstein adds this note: "Otherwise, continuing opposition is likely because of suspicion as to the true motives of the police. Thus, a recent proposal by the Washington, D.C., Police Department to establish a wide range of services in a 'model precinct' was opposed by militant civil rights groups who viewed it as an effort by the police to develop a network of informants."

Chapter Three

The Role of the Police in Today's Society

Let us consider one of the central, most perplexing, most fundamental questions affecting police-community relations: the role of the police in today's society. In 1968, the National Advisory Commission on Civil Disorders (Kerner Commission) clearly touched on this question in the opening of its chapter on police and the community:

> The policeman in the ghetto is a symbol of increasingly bitter social debate over law enforcement. One side, disturbed and perplexed by sharp rises in crime and urban violence, exerts extreme pressure on police for tougher law enforcement. Another group, inflamed against police as agents of repression, tends toward defiance of what it regards as order maintained at the expense of justice.

> . . . police responsibilities in the ghetto are even greater than elsewhere in the community since the other institutions of social control have so little authority: the schools, because so many are segregated, old and inferior; religion, which has become irrelevant to those who have lost faith as they lost hope; career aspirations, which for many young Negroes are totally lacking; the family, because its bonds are often snapped. It is the policeman who must deal with the consequences of this institutional vacuum and is then resented for the presence and the measures this effort demands. [P. 157]

Our discussion in the preceding chapter of the concept of police-community relations had implications for the role of the police. For example, if the idea of the police as community leaders—or *managers,* to use Bordua's term—is to be taken seriously, it has certain implications for role concept and role expectations. Part of the shock in considering this seemingly rash idea is in its role implications, so vastly different from a popular image which is a holdover from a past era of American police work. If on the other hand one claims that police-community relations is simply another term for public relations, and the police are seen not as community leaders but as followers, the role implications are quite different.

Conflicting Expectations of Police Role

Police and community relations has to do with what the police expect from the community and with what the community expects from the police. *What* the police do, then, and *how* they do it, are vitally important considerations in the status of the relationship. As suggested earlier, divergent perceptions and attitudes are involved in this relationship, to a point where some scholars describe the problems of police-community relations as essentially a matter of conflicting role perceptions and conflicting role expectations, which cause what Lohman called "dissonance" between the community and the police.

Perhaps it should be stated immediately that conflicting role perceptions are not unique to police and community relations. Problems of school and community relations are created by conflicting perceptions of what teachers should do and how they should do it. School teachers themselves do not agree on this, any more than do various factions of the community. Nor does everyone agree on what clergymen or mayors or welfare workers or college presidents should do and how they should do it.

In a free society, such conflicting views of social institutional roles and functions are inevitable and, to a considerable extent, socially beneficial. But they make relationship problems inevitable, too, and pose the challenge of achieving the minimal working consensus necessary to the survival of the free society and its institutions. In police and community relations, moreover, a special consideration makes the role question particularly vexing, as well as particularly important: the police hold society's greatest power, that of discretion in the use of force and the authority, under certain conditions, to initiate legal process against citizens. A social role with such repressive or punitive dimensions is bound to be the object of unusual public (and scholarly) interest, and sometimes apprehension.

Historical Review of Police Role

It is instructive to study the police role question in historical perspective. Recall, for instance, that Peel referred to "the basic mission

for which the police exist—to prevent crime and disorder as an alternative to the repression of crime and disorder by military force and
severity of legal punishment." This is a description of the police role
that has tended to dominate British policing since Peel's time and looms
large in a comparative study of American and British police-community
relations. Banton, for example, refers to the difference between *law
officers* and *peace officers*: the public contacts of law officers tend to be
of a punitive or inquisitory character; whereas the public contacts of the
peace officers are more in the nature of assisting citizens. In *The Policeman in the Community* (pp. 6, 7), Banton distinguishes between a
police *force* and a police *service*.

The Anglo-American system of civilian policing has brought together a variety of explicit and implicit functions. In the United King-
dom, since 1829, the primary functions have been the preservation of
the Queen's peace and the prevention of crime—as suggested by Peel's
first principle. Other functions have been regarded as ancillary. While
it is generally assumed that civilian policing in the United States has
followed the British model, the relationship has actually been more
theoretical than real. For in this country, the functions of peace keeping
and crime prevention have not had the priority in police attention that
has marked the British system.

In analyzing the difference, the distinguished American social
historian Oscar Handlin, in *Community Organization,* has cited "the
exceptional diffusion of violence in our society." He points out that ours
has been, from the beginning, a much more violent society than that of
most European countries. Carrying arms and rounding up a posse were
aspects of American history still glamorized in today's movies and television fare. Handlin also says that early American police forces had
"undifferentiated functions." They were public servants with duties pertaining to public health, clean streets, and all sorts of other odds and
ends. Thus, it was easy to make scapegoats of the police for every
problem. Until after 1900, the most important aspects of police work,
as we now see it, were not performed by the police. Various private
agencies took care of apprehending crooks, while the police busied
themselves with menial chores, thereby cultivating the public impression
that a policeman was a rather backward character "with a strong back
and a weak mind."

The literature dealing with police administration in England and
in the United States indicates the British stress on the prevention of
crime and the maintenance of peace as the two most important functions
of the civilian police; on the other hand, American writers tend to stress
the protection of security and the enforcement of law as the two primary functions. This difference is much more than a semantic inci-
dental. It has a direct, practical application in the manner in which
police agencies have been organized, the standards regarded as germane

in recruiting, the nature of training that a police officer receives, and in beliefs and values considered important in the craft. Every police recruit inherits these ambiguities of "the system" about his functions—what he is expected to do and to what he is expected to give priority.[1]

That there is widespread confusion and lack of consistency or consensus among police officers on the question of their role has been pointed out by many observers. One difficulty is the number of persons and groups professing some right to speak about what policemen do and how they do it. Police administrators and supervisors, police officers themselves (through their professional and fraternal organizations, and recently their unions), legislative bodies, the courts, governmental executives, assorted bureaucrats, and of course "the people"—many different factions of the population, with different perceptions of and expectations from the police—all these forces and some others not mentioned rightfully demand some voice and vote in the question of what the police should do and how they should do it. Thus, the officer is in the position of attempting to do what is obviously impossible for him to do—to discover some consensus among many discordant and disparate views and adopt this as his modus operandi. That he gets into hot water so frequently is not surprising.

Toward Further Clarification

Perhaps a few concrete examples will help to illustrate the complexity of the problem. With respect to certain decisions by the United States Supreme Court in recent years, many police officers have asked why they are criticized for performing their duty of enforcing the law. Why are they denied vital tools of law enforcement when the crime rate is increasing as it is? How can they be expected to cope with the increased demands made by the courts on undermanned and underfinanced departments? These are frustrating questions for many policemen today (Michigan State University, *Field Surveys V,* 1967, p. 23).

Another case in point pertains to the overcoming of resistance to arrest. Law generally defines in broad terms the degree of force that a police officer may use in carrying out his duties. However, departmental regulations and policies, procedures and traditions may define the *specific* types of force that may be used in typical situations. Sometimes departmental prescriptions and local *mores* are not well harmonized with existing, applicable statutes, and the result—in what a particular policeman does under particular circumstances—can be disastrous. As Lohman and his associates said in *Field Surveys IV* (University of California):

> The obedient policeman performs, to the best of his own ability, up to the expectations which are set for him. If the department has not taken measures to restrict the officer's use of force, it, rather than the officer, may be to blame. [Vol. 1, p. 28]

We have noted that in the nineteenth century law enforcement in the United States was not a duty of the "watchmen" police. As Roger Lane describes it in *Policing the City,* the Boston Police Department was organized mainly as a night watch, to keep peace in the streets. Even after detectives began to appear on police forces, they served private interests. They recovered loot, for a percentage; the best detectives knew the haunts and methods of thieves (James Q. Wilson, *The Atlantic,* March, 1969).

It was the increasing incidence of civil disorder, not mounting crime rates, that brought the municipal police force to fruition. The Boston police were not fully armed at public expense until 1884. And the growth of formally organized police departments did not lead initially to changes in function. Wilson points out that the maintenance of order was still the principal objective:

> What did lead to a change was twofold: the bureaucratization of the detectives (putting them on salary and ending the fee system), and the use of the police to enforce unpopular laws governing the sale and use of liquor. The former change led to the beginning of the popular confusion as to what the police do. The detective became the hero of the dime novel and the cynosure of the public's romantic imagination; he, and not his patrolman colleague, was the "real" police officer doing "real" police work. [P. 132]

Because the public was sharply divided in opinion regarding liquor laws and such questions as Sunday closing of saloons—situations in which the police could initiate prosecutions on their own authority, rather than on citizen complaint—disastrous police-community relations problems were averted when the police simply chose to do no more than was absolutely necessary. Their motto was: better to do too little than too much. Wilson explains that the police began to provide various services to citizens who seemed likely to become instigators of public disorder. Thus, in the 1850s, the police in Boston, Philadelphia, and New York were heavily engaged in overnight lodging service, in addition to supplying coal for poor families, soup kitchens for the hungry, and jobs as domestics for girls they thought might be lured away from prostitution. Such social services by the police helped to soften their public image whereas liquor law enforcement hardened it. Eventually, however, the organized charities opposed the aspect of social services, apparently because they thought it inappropriate for the police to render such services, but more likely because it reflected unfavorably on them.

At the turn of the century, the maintenance of order was still the paramount function of the American police. But two early twentieth century influences shifted emphasis away from maintaining order to that of enforcing law. One was Prohibition, which put police in the position "of choosing between corruption and making a nuisance of themselves," as Wilson phrases it; and the other was the Great Depression of the 1930s, which focused public attention "on the escapades of bank robbers and other desperadoes." Wilson observes:

> Police venality and rising crime rates coincided in the public mind, though in fact they had somewhat different causes. The watchman function of the police was lost sight of; their law enforcement function, and their apparent failure to exercise it, were emphasized. [P. 133]

It was at this time that President Hoover appointed the Wickersham Commission. The Commission considered both police and politicians as principally blameworthy, and reform became the slogan. The argument was that since the police *can* prevent crime, intolerable crime rates mean that the police are not doing their job because of political influence. Wilson analyzed the consequences:

> If the job of the police is to catch crooks, then the police have a technical, ministerial responsibility in which discretion plays little part. Since no one is likely to disagree on the value of the objective, then there is little reason to expose the police to the decision-making processes of city government. *Ergo,* take the police "out of politics." [P. 133]

All "superfluous" police services were questioned. These were not "real police work." The police were portrayed mainly as "crook catchers"; both the police view of themselves and the public's view of them were adjusted accordingly, over a period of several ensuing decades.

Yet as Wilson says, it was a view of police work that really did not correspond with reality. The patrolman knew that he was still handling family fights and troublesome teen-agers. The police also knew that they alone could not prevent crime. So they turned to manipulating crime records, to make things look better from the standpoint of public expectations. The "good pinch" and the "G Man" became symbols of "real police work." Rewards and incentives in the department—for example, promotion to detective—were geared to the crook-catching function. And the *means* of apprehending criminals were not always open to public scrutiny. Indeed, one summarization of the Wickersham Commission Report was published under the title, *Our Lawless Police* (Hopkins).

Jerome Skolnick discusses an implication of this point in *Justice Without Trial*:

> ... it is not surprising that the solution to "the police problem" in America has been frequently conceived as changing the quality of people, rather than the philosophies of policing. ... Police reform means finding a new source of police, and police control is a matter of having the "right" sort of people in control. "Reform" of police means increasing the efficiency of police personnel. It is rarely recognized that the conduct of police may be related in a fundamental way

to the character and goals of the institution itself—the duties police are called upon to perform, associated with the assumptions of the system of legal justice—and that it may not be men who are good or bad, so much as the premises and design of the system in which they find themselves. [Pp. 4, 5]

The Role Question Today

Today, the question of police role is being examined by many analysts. The President's Crime Commission (1967), the Kerner Commission (1968), and the National Commission on the Causes and Prevention of Violence (1969–70) have all pointed out that the vast majority of the situations in which the police intervene are not crime situations calling for arrests. Another Presidential Commission, headed by former Pennsylvania Governor William Scranton, studied student unrest and college campus disorders in the aftermath of the Kent State University and Jackson State College tragedies of the spring of 1970. This Commission also underscored the police responsibilities of maintaining order.

Today, the emphasis appears to have shifted back to maintaining order and keeping the peace. However, as Wilson states, the picture is hazy because of the public interest in crime in the streets, which is leading many still to emphasize crime deterrence as the principal function of the police. Wilson's summary of the situation in the March 1969 *Atlantic* is classic:

> The simultaneous emergence of a popular concern for both crime and order does put in focus the choices that will have to be made in the next generation of police reforms. In effect, municipal police departments are two organizations in one, serving two related but not identical functions. The strategy appropriate for strengthening their ability to serve one role tends to weaken their ability to serve the other. Crime deterrence and law enforcement require, or are facilitated by, specialization, strong hierarchical authority, improved mobility and communications, clarity in legal codes and arrest procedures, close surveillance of the community, high standards of integrity, and the avoidance of entangling alliances with politicians. The maintenance of order, on the other hand, is aided by departmental procedures that include decentralization, neighborhood involvement, foot patrol, wide discretion, the provision of services, an absence of arrest quotas, and some tolerance for minor forms of favoritism and even corruption.
>
> There is no magic formula [Wilson concludes]—no prepackaged "reform"—that can tell a community or a police chief how to organize a force to serve, with appropriate balance, these competing objectives. Just as slogans demanding "taking the police out of politics" or "putting the police in cars" have proved inadequate guides to action in the past, so also slogans demanding "foot patrolmen" or "community

control" are likely to prove inadequate in the future. One would like to think that since both points of view now have ardent advocates, the debate has at last been joined. But I suspect that the two sides are talking at, or past, each other, and not *to* each other, and thus the issue, far from being joined, is still lost in rhetoric. [P. 135]

It is crucial, of course, in discussing the role question, to recognize that the debate is not over whether the police should be relieved of either of their principal functions. The argument is not one of law enforcement versus order maintenance. It is recognized that the police must work in both functions. The debate has to do, rather, with *emphasis*. If, for example, the police spend most of their time in keeping peace (often called *conflict management*), why should a police agency be organized as if this were not so? And why should police officers be trained as if most of their time were spent catching crooks, when most of their time is not spent catching crooks? What then is the desirable relationship between the major functions of the police, granting that these functions are not mutually exclusive? Sometimes making an arrest helps to preserve civic peace; sometimes it can set off a riot. Is crime to be suppressed at any price? Such questions highlight the gist of the issue.

More of the Wilson Analysis

In his fascinating study of the management of law and order in eight communities, *Varieties of Police Behavior,* Wilson describes three styles of policing—the watchman, the legalistic, and the service—and relates each to local politics. He explains why the question of the role of the police is of special interest: a big-city police department is a special kind of complex, bureaucratic organization, with perplexing pressures for the patrolman "to do the right thing." As a public agency, such a police department affects the lives of many people. Wilson also points out that "the ability of the police to do their job well may determine our ability to manage social conflict, especially that which involves Negroes and other minority groups, and our prospects for maintaining a proper balance between liberty and order" (p. 3).

Some students of police role speak of four functional categories: order maintenance (conflict management or peace keeping); law enforcement (or "crook catching"); crime prevention; and social services. Wilson reduces these to two: order maintenance and law enforcement. He dismisses social services from consideration, on the ground that such services "are intended to please the client and no one else. There is no reason in principle why these services could not be priced and sold on the market. It is only a matter of historical accident and community convenience that they are provided by the police." Wilson's special concern is with police activities "the quality of which the client cannot be allowed to judge for himself: in short, with police efforts to enforce laws and maintain order" (pp. 4–6).

In *Dilemmas of Police Administration,* Wilson describes *order maintenance* as the handling of disputes or behavior which threatens to produce disputes, among persons who disagree over what ought to be right or seemly conduct, or over the assignment of blame for what is agreed to be wrong or unseemly conduct (p. 407). Examples of this would be a family quarrel, a noisy drunk, a tavern brawl, a street disturbance by teen-agers, and idle young men congregating on a street corner. Although a law may be broken in these examples of conduct, the police do not see their responsibility as simply the comparing of particular behavior to a clear legal standard and making an arrest if the standard has been violated. In many order maintenance situations, the legal rule is ambiguous. Blame may be more important to the participants than guilt.

To illustrate the ambiguity, by what standard is "peace" defined in peace-keeping activities? Skolnick notes that there are communities which appear disorderly to some observers (for example, a bohemian neighborhood), but which nevertheless maintain a substantial degree of legality. The converse may also occur: order is well maintained, but legality may be questionable. More often than not in peace-keeping situations, the officer will not make an arrest, since most such infractions are misdemeanors; and in most states an arrest cannot be made unless the illegal act is committed in the officer's presence or unless the victim is willing to sign a complaint.

Law enforcement, on the other hand, is defined by Wilson as the application of legal sanctions, usually by means of an arrest, to persons who injure or deprive innocent victims; for example, burglary, purse snatching, mugging, robbery, or auto theft. Once guilt is established, there is no question of blame. The officer is expected either to make an arrest or to act to prevent the violation from occurring in the first place. His task is to apprehend or to deter the criminal. But in most instances involving crime, he lacks the resources to do this. Therefore, few cases are "cleared by arrest." Moreover, the President's Crime Commission said that a high proportion of crimes go unreported. Nobody knows how many crimes the police prevent, but the number is not thought to be large. And certain police tactics in so-called high-crime areas that might have the effect of preventing certain types of crime may also place the police in conflict with some elements of the community (p. 408).

Order and Justice

Role conflict is further complicated by varying expectations (and tolerances) in the community as to the means that the police should use, either in maintaining order or in enforcing the law. Wilson states that some people believe that crime should be suppressed even at some cost in civil liberties; others believe that civil liberties must be protected even at some cost in crime. Again, this is the ancient riddle of freedom and order. In the culturally homogeneous community of yesteryear, there was general agreement on the norms of behavior for both policeman and citizen, and the meaning of order and justice. Today's community has no common normative guide, which suggests why there is some question whether it really is a community.

Skolnick believes that the police frequently are criticized for behavior that is, to a considerable extent, integral to "the system," or "the way things work," etc. Reform movements often concentrate on what should be done to improve police officers, rather than on what fundamental changes should be contemplated in the system itself. Wilson joins Skolnick in making the same point. He observes that police departments are often charged with such things as hiring unqualified personnel, manipulating crime statistics, condoning improper procedures on the street, and using patrol tactics that irritate people and heighten tensions. Community groups volunteer solutions for these matters. Since their diagnosis is often that the problems are caused by incompetent, stupid, rude, brutal, and prejudiced policemen, the suggested remedies usually include elevated recruitment standards, more and better education for police officers, tougher internal discipline, exterior review of police behavior, and other measures focusing on police officers.

But suppose, Wilson argues, that "better men" should somehow suddenly become available, i.e., more college-educated policemen, more black officers, more police officer participants in the best "sensitivity training," and even more neighborhood control of the police. Under such conditions, deemed ideal by many critics of the police, the crime rate might well go up rather than down, at least temporarily. It would not necessarily resolve the conflict in the community between those who want less police surveillance and those who want more. Formal education might make police officers more civil, yet more impersonal in their dealings with people. A college degree for a police officer is not a guarantee that he would be any more sensitive to the feelings and needs of poor, young blacks in a ghetto. The college degree might even be a handicap in such situations, in terms of communication and rapport. In short, the ingredients that are often identified by community groups as important in creating better police-community relations must be carefully delineated and qualified.

This is not an argument against "better men" in police work, but a suggestion that getting better men is not in itself a magic formula that will settle all police-community relations problems. What counts is the extent to which better men in police and criminal justice work seek basic changes in the system itself, and then carry them out.

Other Views of the Role Question

Having relied so much on the views of James Q. Wilson on the role question, it is useful to cite others who have studied the matter. Albert Morris, professor emeritus of sociology at Boston University, has this to say (*Correctional Research,* November 1969):

> The responsibilities that have accrued to police departments, then, are broad and encompass more than a concern with criminal behavior. The police are, indeed, expected to assume direct and major responsibility for maintaining order under the law and in so-doing protect the property and persons of citizens from the consequences of unlawful criminal acts by deterring, detecting, and apprehending the small proportion of offenders they are equipped to deal with. They may conduct prosecutions in court for minor offenses and may be witnesses in trial proceedings. They have responsibility for traffic regulation and control. They may be required to carry out other specific duties such as taking an annual census, locating jurors, and reporting public dangers. But traditionally they are also expected to help people in time of emergencies and this is the aspect of their work whose value and importance seem largely underestimated when laymen think of the work of the police. [P. 7]

Gordon Misner has noted that it has become "increasingly fashionable" for the police in various parts of the country to refer to themselves as "law enforcement officers." He thought that this implies an intention to convey to the public that law enforcement is the primary and highest goal of the police profession in America, probably because many policemen feel angry, frustrated, and anxious about what they think is expected of them under current conditions.

"Law and order" is really a matter of law *or* order, Misner says (*The Nation,* April 21, 1969), and "the dilemma arises from the conflicting set of instructions which society has historically given to policemen." He continues, echoing both Wilson and Skolnick:

> The policeman really has two role models from which to choose: he can conceive of himself as a "rule enforcer," or as a "guardian of the peace." He is helped in the choice by the role preferred by his chief and immediate superiors. In many departments, being a rule enforcer is viewed as a necessary stage of development in the growth of a mature policeman. . . . The older policeman hopes that the young prospect will realize eventually that strict enforcement of the laws is a gigantic inconvenience, not only to the public but also to the policeman himself. It is part of police folklore that an experienced policeman knows how to "stay out of trouble," and has necessarily learned that law enforcement is simply a means and not an end in itself. [P. 488]

Misner also indicates that if law enforcement is stressed as the primary role of the police in this country, it affects the manner in which police agencies should be organized, the priorities ascribed to particular tasks, and the nature of training policemen are to receive, and it defines the departmental system of rewards. Misner is one of many, including the President's Crime Commission, who emphasize that uniformed police officers in large urban areas typically spend less than 30 percent of their working time dealing with crime or other enforcement duties. He adds another point we have made:

> There are situations when non-enforcement of certain laws or regulations may actually contribute to the peace and tranquility of the community. Enforcement, therefore, is a two-edged sword that must be used with a delicate sense of balance and timing. To suggest that "total enforcement" is a magic formula for reinstituting order in a troubled community simply lulls the public into a false sense of security. It also diverts public attention from seeking more basic, long-term solutions to social problems. [P. 489]

Herman Goldstein, former administrative assistant to Chicago Police Superintendent O. W. Wilson, and now professor of law at the University of Wisconsin, is another widely respected analyst who is concerned with police perspective regarding the importance of their crime control function as against their social service function. His position is substantially the same as that of Misner and Wilson. Writing in *Public Administration Review* (1968), he argues that the police must become more, not less, involved in noncriminal activities, if they are to be effective in dealing with civil disorder and civil disobedience:

> The police function in two worlds. They play an integral part, along with the prosecutor, the courts, and correctional agencies, in the operation of the criminal justice system. As the first agency in the system, their primary responsibility is to initiate a criminal action against those who violate the law. This is a highly structured role, defined by statutes and court decisions and subjected to strict controls.

> The second world is less easily defined. It comprises all aspects of police functioning that are unrelated to the processing of an accused person through the criminal system. Within this world, a police department seeks to prevent crimes, abates nuisances, resolves disputes, controls traffic and crowds, furnishes information, and provides a wide range of other miscellaneous services to the citizenry. In carrying out these functions, officers frequently make use of the authority which is theirs by virtue of their role in the criminal process. . . . Police spend most of their time functioning in the second of these two worlds. . . . Despite this distribution of activity, police agencies are geared primarily to deal with crime. [P. 417]

Goldstein teamed up with his colleague at the University of Wisconsin, Frank J. Remington, in shaping a chapter of the *Police Task Force Report* of the President's 1966 Crime Commission—the chapter dealing with the role of the police. The following is indicative of their central emphasis.

There are two alternative ways in which police can respond to the difficult problems currently confronting them:

1. The first is to continue, as has been true in the past, with police making important decisions, but doing so by a process which can fairly be described as "unarticulated improvisation." This is a comfortable approach, requiring neither the police nor the community to face squarely the difficult social issues which are involved, at least until a crisis—like the current "social revolution"—necessitates drastic change.

2. The second alternative is to recognize the importance of the administrative policy-making function of police and to take appropriate steps to make this a process which is systematic, intelligent, articulate, and responsive to external controls appropriate in a democratic society; a process which anticipates social problems and adapts to meet them before a crisis situation arises.

Of the two, the latter is not only preferable; it is essential if major progress in policing is to be made, particularly in the large, congested urban areas. [*Task Force Report: The Police,* p. 18]

The view of Jerome Skolnick on the role question has already been suggested. The distinction between law and order has been particularly emphasized in his writings—more specifically, the conflict between two goals that might guide police behavior. One is adherence to the rule of law: police attitudes and actions that give high priority to the rights of citizens and to legal restraints upon government officials. The other is managerial efficiency: the goal of maintaining order with an efficient, technically sophisticated police organization. Skolnick feels that police in the United States tend to emphasize order as their goal, at the expense of legality. For Skolnick, maintaining order means controlling criminal behavior. His use of these terms differs from Wilson's. In *Professional Police in a Free Society,* Skolnick states his position this way:

... the common juxtaposition of "law and order" is an oversimplification. Law is not merely an instrument of order, but may frequently be its adversary. ... The phrase "law and order" is misleading because it draws attention away from the substantial incompatibilities existing between the two ideas. Order under law is not concerned merely with achieving regularized social activity, but with the means used to come by peaceable behavior—certainly with procedure but also with the law itself. ... In short, "law" and "order" are frequently found to be in opposition precisely because law implies rational restraint upon the rules and procedures utilized to achieve order. Order under law, therefore, subordinates the ideal of conformity to the ideal of legality. [Pp. 10, 11]

The Skolnick thesis has some implications for police professionalism, which will be explored further in the next chapter.

Still Other Views of the Police Role

Skolnick's concern for the rule of law and the importance he attaches to the police officer's role in it is shared by other observers, for instance, Jerome Hall, in the *Indiana Law Journal* (Winter 1953):

> In sum, the policeman who conforms to law is the living embodiment of the law, he is its microcosm on the level of its most specific incidence. He is literally law in action, for in action law must be specific. He is the concrete distillation of the entire mighty, historic *corpus juris*, representing all of it, including the constitution itself.

On a subject as complex as police role, it is interesting to look at European developments. George Berkley has written a pertinent book, *The Democratic Policeman*, in which he describes significant changes that have occurred in recent years in the approach of various European police forces to their work. He outlines developments in police education, social service activities, and in the use of civilians in police work, which appear to be reducing the traditional isolation of the police from the community.

The British Royal Commission on the Police (1962) also had some relevant things to say in its *Final Report*:

> ... efficiency is not the sole end of a good and wise administration of the police, and that the apparently confused police system which this country has inherited reflects not merely the British habit of adapting old institutions to meet new needs, but the interplay of conflicting principles of great constitutional importance which human minds have always found, and still find, the utmost difficulty in reconciling.

The English social anthropologist Michael Banton has written an authoritative comparative analysis of the British and the American police in questions of community relations. His distinction between a *law* officer and a *peace* officer merits attention:

> A division is becoming apparent between specialist departments within police forces (detectives, traffic officers, vice and fraud squads, etc.) and the ordinary patrolman. The former are "law officers" whose contacts with the public tend to be of a punitive or inquisitory character, whereas the patrolmen ... are principally "peace officers" operating within the moral consensus of the community. Whereas the former have occasion to speak chiefly to offenders or to persons who can supply information about an offense, the patrolmen interact with all sorts of people and more of their contacts center upon assisting citizens than upon offenses. [*The Policeman in the Community,* p. 7]

Banton maintains, first, that the enforcement of social regulations is central to the nature of the British police; second, that to reduce "real crime," close attention must be paid to social regulations; and third, that if the rising level of crime in England is to be held in check, "we should not divert inquisitions to administrative tribunals but should make maximum use of the public aspects of our criminal procedures in order to educate people in what is entailed." Banton's position controverts that of Lord Devlin, who insists that the police should concentrate on criminal matters—that enforcing social regulations is foreign to the nature of the police (he sees drunken driving, for example, as a breach of social regulations rather than real crime)—and that such matters should be dealt with by administrative tribunals, not the police. Banton accepts Skolnick's argument that social control must deal not only with the maintenance of order (in Skolnick's terms, deterring crime), but with the *quality* of the order that a given system is capable of sustaining and the procedures appropriate to the achievement of such order. In short, law enforcement policy should not be to maintain the status quo, but to improve the quality of life in the community.

Another writer, California criminal justice Professor A. C. Germann, stresses that what the police do and how they do it, in today's urban "noncommunity," is best understood in terms of political power. In effect, police administrators count votes; their definition of police role, their interpretation of relative emphasis upon crook-catching and peace-keeping, is finely attuned to the wishes of the community's dominant political elements. If the dominant demand is for expanding the coercive role of the police, as it has seemed to be nationally since the summer of 1967, the police will act accordingly. Germann recognizes this as "political policing" in a certain sense. As he puts it, "our police continually become more efficient in doing the same old ineffective operations." To quote him further, and to clarify what he means:

If the majority community is more interested in order than liberty, more interested in property than human beings, more interested in community security than personal freedom, more interested in entertainment than in injustices, that community surely is inviting the police state. Its police may form an accurate barometer of community values; its police may precisely mirror the attitudes of the majority. And any police agency that accepts the task of "community bully," even if tacitly agreed to by community silence, and regularly bugs the living hell out of its minority groups, peace groups, hippie groups, youth groups—unpopular groups—will sooner or later have "a lot of chickens coming home to roost," and be forced to increase repression and coercion. Anyone who would seek to blame the American police service for current orientation and attitudes would be well advised to study the majority community in terms of orientations and attitudes.[2]

Bruce Terris' view of the role question, in "The Role of the Police," is consistent with that of others quoted:

> ... improved police-minority relations require a radical change in the conception, of both the police and the community, of what police work is all about. ... The situations in which police officers most frequently find themselves do not require the expert aim of a marksman, the cunningness of a private eye, or the toughness of a stereotyped Irish policeman. Instead, they demand knowledge of human beings and the personal, as opposed to official, authority to influence people without the use or even the threat of force. These characteristics are not commonly found in police officers because police departments do not consider these values as paramount. As a result, persons with these abilities are not attracted to police work nor rewarded by promotion or other incentive if they happen to enter a department.

A Conflicting View of the Police Role

A conflicting view of the police role question is one for which there is considerable support. It is the position of Lord Devlin in England, which has also been well articulated in this country by Dean Richard Myren of the School of Criminal Justice, State University of New York at Albany, in a paper, *The Role of the Police,* written for the President's 1966 Crime Commission.

Myren sees police functions in three categories: the performance of miscellaneous social services; the enforcement of nuisance (or convenience) norms—what Devlin and Banton call "social regulations"; and the enforcement of the criminal code. He considers the alleged advantages and disadvantages of police performance of each of these types of function, and concludes that only the enforcement of the criminal code is an appropriate police role. He argues that police performance of the other two types of function indefinitely postpones the transfer of these tasks to other, more appropriate agencies—either existing or needing to be created for a particular purpose. Furthermore, Myren thinks that police performance of what he deems inappropriate duties is a serious handicap to genuine professional development of the police. And he believes that regulating traffic, handling drunks, and performing other "nuisance norm" enforcement by the police invite corruption, actual or fancied.

Myren contends that police-community relations, based upon a desirable mutual respect, cannot be improved unless and until the role of the police is narrowed to no more than the enforcement of the criminal code. He concedes that the police have an important role to play in civil defense in case of invasion, but that they do not have authority or responsibility for maintaining tank, paratroop, and similar military units as do the paramilitary police organizations of other countries. He adds:

Police in the United States are also not lawfully assigned the role of controlling and suppressing political opposition to the party in power, although there have been instances, at particular times and places, when they have seemingly assumed or been assigned this role illicitly.

Relationship of the Police Role to Values and Beliefs

An interesting ramification of the police role question is its relationship to occupational and professional value and belief systems. While this is a topic to be discussed more thoroughly in later chapters, some attention to it here is in order.

John Pfiffner, professor emeritus of public administration at the University of Southern California, has devoted considerable study to the matter. Pfiffner reminisces that in American society at the close of the last century, people knew their neighbors, though they may not always have liked what they saw. He refers to Jane Jacobs' commentary on the police function in such a society, "folk policing through constant surveillance by one's neighbors" (*The Death and Life of Great American Cities*). This folk society had ample room for people with lower skills and potentiality. Today, many such people are regarded as a social problem.

About one fourth of our families in the United States today have inadequate incomes. Many of them live in large cities. Among them are a large number of people with mental, educational, or vocational handicaps. As Pfiffner[3] puts it, "substandard human beings are multiplying into succeeding generations of public charges." People who are economically, mentally, vocationally, educationally, socially, and genetically handicapped represent a large proportion of "police problems." There has long been controversy as to "how these people got that way." Is it nature or nurture?

Depending upon where one stands in this debate, Pfiffner observes, one takes his position as to how the police should deal with antisocial behavior. Those who say that individuals should be held morally and legally responsible for what they do tend to take a punishment approach to the treatment of antisocial behavior. Those who feel that environment should be blamed tend to take a rehabilitative approach. Pfiffner makes the two schools of thought distinct, in what he admits are "free-wheeling generalizations":

> People engaged vocationally in dealing with violators of the law fall into two opposing belief systems: in the first category are the police and the custody-minded prison personnel; in the second, those engaged in rehabilitation such as probation and parole, social workers, and therapy-oriented workers in general. For convenience I have labelled the latter as "rehabs."

Pfiffner allows for individuals in any vocation who entertain beliefs that vary from the mode, but asserts that law enforcement officials generally subscribe to the classical theory of criminology. They tend to see the violator as a wrong-doer, morally responsible for his conduct, and therefore liable for the consequences. This school of thought maintains that the fear of punishment is a powerful deterrent to law transgression. Those who commit crime should be treated as enemies of society; "soft" treatment is regarded as a waste.

On the other hand, the "rehab" stereotype, Pfiffner states, is fairly common to people with "humanistic predilections, a value system tolerant of man's foibles." Pfiffner phrases the eternal optimism of this school of thought that man can be directed away from criminal behavior:

> The applied social scientists dealing with the criminal elements in our courts, prisons, institutions and social agencies are committed to the efficacy of a therapeutic approach based on counseling, supervision and guidance. They readily admit that their techniques have not been developed to a state of high maturity, and that they are not too sure how effective they are. But they are convinced that great effort should be made to rehabilitate criminals and that, in the absence of more mature know-how, what they are doing seems to be the most efficacious procedure available.

We will reserve for later discussion the implications of Pfiffner's theory for relationships among the various components of the criminal justice system. For the moment, it is the implications of his ideas for the question of police role that are intriguing. He contends that there is fundamental conflict between the two schools of thought he identifies. One is oriented to force and intimidation, the other to kindness and "loving sensitivity." Of course this is an oversimplification, as Pfiffner concedes, but he says it is nonetheless a handy theoretical construction. The question he poses is whether it may not be timely to redefine these roles. He asks: does the welfare-therapeutic-bureaucratic society require a new concept of the police function? If so, will it be one in which the police participate more widely in the whole process of dealing with the problems of handicapped humanity? Will more of a team approach be demanded for these problems, in which the police role will be but one phase of society's cooperative effort to deal with the problems of personal and social disorganization?

These questions bring us back to our description of police-community relations as "an interprofessional approach to community problem solving," with the police (and other criminal justice agencies) as vital members of the community team, so to speak. Pfiffner's conclusion is provocative:

...society will soon redefine the police role to include ideas, perceptions and insights which will bring the police into the area of dealing
with social pathology on a scale larger than the present holding and
containing operation. That role has not yet been spelled out, and is
not even dimly perceived by many police administrators; indeed, perhaps most would feelingly deny it to be within the police purview.

For Pfiffner, then, the role choice is this: should the police deal
with criminals only as deserving of punishment, or should the police be
called upon to take part in some aspects of criminal rehabilitation?

Applicable Role Theory

Sociologists devoted to role theory are not satisfied with the
generalizations in which we have so far indulged. A few have found the
police role question of special research interest. They have their own
terminology for dealing with the question, e.g., *role, role reciprocal,
role set, role concept, role expectations, role performance, reference
group, role model, generalized other, role conflict, isomorphism,* etc.
An example of the possibilities in the application of sociological role
theory to the police is Martin Miller's *Systemic Model of Police Morale.*[4]
James Sterling[5] of the staff of the International Association of Chiefs of
Police has conducted an interesting study in this vein, about which we
shall have more to say shortly.

A systematic empirical study of the police, applying sociological
role theory, is that done by Jack Preiss and Howard Ehrlich (*Examination of Role Theory*). Their study of a state police organization testifies
to the complexity of the question. They found that there is indeed a
great deal of confusion and ambiguity in role perceptions by police
officers themselves. Trial-and-error learning (occupational socialization)
and "playing it by ear" are intrinsic elements of police role behavior.
Preiss and Ehrlich agree that certain dilemmas faced by policemen are
part of the structure of police organization itself. They found little
consensus in role perception among police officers at the same or at
different levels of the organization. In turn, there was little consensus in
how police officers perceived what others ("audience expectations,"
"significant others," etc.) required of them in role performance. Often
this left the police officer (the actor) choosing from among behavioral
roles without adequate guidelines.

An example of what occurs under such circumstances would be
a particular police department that lacks clearly defined organizational
goals, objectives, and strategies. The result is a paucity of well-
delineated departmental policy and procedures, and a correlative lack
of effective supervision. As a result, the patrolman is handicapped in
attempting to determine his responsibilities. Unsure of requirements or
of subsequent reactions, such policemen tend to be guided by informal
communication among peers and are inclined to apply personal values

and interests, as well as "situational opportunism," as criteria for decision making. If a police officer is unsure of the standards being used to evaluate his performance, he is left to decide for himself whether it is better to be technically proficient or to be personable and decently sensitive to people. This kind of decision bears on the nebulous nature of personnel evaluation processes that are frequently observable in police as well as in other kinds of organizations.

Preiss and Ehrlich make a telling point:[6]

> Since many of the policeman's audiences were not in agreement about their perceptions and expectations of him, they also varied in their evaluative criteria and their judgments of his performance. This variability could have lessened the impact that a precise and uniform evaluation procedure would have had on the role performance of a policeman by providing him with options and alternatives rather than one highly constraining set of role prescriptions. Perhaps . . . the existence of an acceptable range of permissible behaviors in a group provides the very flexibility which makes group survival possible. [P. 92]

In role expectations from a police officer, consider the difference between saying to him, "All persons checked by radar as driving more than 10 mph over the posted speed limit are to be ticketed"; or "Use your judgment in arresting those exceeding the posted speed limit"; or "Cars transporting suspicious-looking persons should be stopped and investigated."

It would appear that Myren is correct in at least one respect, although the example of a traffic situation would probably be unacceptable to him: police-community relations would probably be less jeopardized if the police were expected only to enforce the criminal code, and to do so with a policy of strict enforcement. But is it actually so simple? The test appears to be in perceptions and expectations that underlie *specific* judgments, i.e., decisions to do a certain thing in a certain way under certain circumstances. If, in making an arrest or in quelling a teen-age disturbance, the police officer makes a decision that deviates seriously from "audience expectations," a relationship problem may result. In police work, it is inevitable that this will happen. Good police-community relations, as previously noted, is not a matter of police popularity. Yet the essential problem is the reconciliation of expectations—the try for working consensus—and, to be functional, the consensus need not be popular in every respect. It is a question of authority combined with responsibility.

Variations in Police Role Expectations

Clearly, there are variations in the expectations of various audiences on what the police do and how they do it. There is much inconsistency and ambivalence in these expectations. Age, educational level, region of the country, type of police agency, race, sex, religion, ethnic and cultural values, and socio-economic status appear to be among the significant variables affecting expectations from the police. Add to these departmental policies, supervisory practices, specific police assignments, departmental morale, legislative actions, and executive and judicial decisions to see the many influences on expectations from any public service.

We are beginning to see the kind of research that deals with such matters, clearly so important in police and community relations. The Preiss and Ehrlich study is an example. The Field Surveys of the President's 1966 Crime Commission are especially helpful; for instance, Field Surveys I and II pertain to the victims of crime. What attitudes exist, among those victimized by crime, toward the police and other parts of the criminal justice system? If the victim is black and poor, will these attitudes more likely be different than if the victim is white and wealthy?

Field Survey III (two volumes) is a comprehensive study, with quantities of data on public perceptions of crime, law enforcement and criminal justice. Field Survey IV, referred to earlier in this chapter, also contains much relevant information.

Can the Police Role Dilemma Be Resolved?

Can the dilemma of police role be resolved? Various scholars we have quoted have recommended measures of coping with the problem. None of them is overly optimistic. If, for example, social class looms as large in the problem diagnosis as Wilson thinks it does, what can be done in the short run? First, he believes that the police should recognize clearly that maintaining order is their central function. He does not prescribe how a "consensus of audience expectations" is to be secured in this regard. But Wilson would hold that the police themselves have some responsibility to lead the community toward a minimal consensus. Skolnick, Misner, and Goldstein would agree.

Police leadership means "getting good men to serve," not simply as automatons in a set system but as critics and *agents of change* in that system. The recently established *Police Foundation,* subsidized by the Ford Foundation, has promising possibilities along this line. The Law Enforcement Assistance Administration has the potential of contributing substantially to constructive research and program expansion. News events underline the difficulties of the police role question and of the idea of the police as community leaders, but should not discourage continuing efforts to elevate the status of police work. Following are examples of some such reports:

1. The commissioner of a major metropolitan police department announced that after September 1, 1973, police officers taking promotional examinations must have one year of college credit;

then two years by 1976, etc. The police officers' association protested on the ground that the requirement was an "unfair labor practice."

2. The faculty of one of the nation's leading university-based schools of criminal justice approved a resolution recommending that the president of that university appoint an appropriate committee to study thoroughly the matter of whether police officers stationed on, or entering, that campus should be armed. Several nearby police agencies immediately threatened to withdraw officers who were enrolled there.

3. The mayor of a certain large city appointed a citizen's committee to investigate allegations of widespread corruption in the police department. The police officers' association promptly threatened court action and sought an injunction to block the investigation.

Summing Up

We have said that there is a relationship between one's position on the police role question and how one organizes a police department—how it is administered and supervised, what kind of training its personnel receive, and other such matters. Many police agencies are organized to emphasize the law enforcement function; a few seem now to be shifting to conflict management. Wilson indicates that various combinations of the three styles of policing he describes exist among police agencies across the country.

We should repeat that police officers themselves reflect a wide range of views on the role question. A good way to start an argument in any group of policemen is to quiz them about priorities in police work. Which specific tasks are most important? Which tasks are inappropriate for the police and ought to be handled by some other agency? Is it proper for a police department to operate, say, a rehabilitative facility for "drying out" chronic alcoholics? Should policemen be assigned to the staff of job opportunity centers? Should they function as guidance counselors in high schools?

Questions of this type will not be settled here, but by analyzing what lies behind such questions we advance communication. With this in mind, several additional considerations, directly related to the role question, merit attention. One is the relationship between police role and police professionalism. This, in turn, suggests the several social systems in which the police function. These matters (along with the discretionary use of police power) that depend so much on how the police role is defined will be our concern in the next two chapters.

Notes to Chapter Three

1. For a more detailed discussion of this point, see *Field Surveys IV: The Police and the Community*, vol. 1, pp. 25–28, University of California, School of Criminology. Report of a research study submitted to the President's 1966 Commission on Law Enforcement and Administration of Justice.

2. A. C. Germann, "The Police: A Mission and Role." For an analysis of how societies condition social control, see Allan Silver, "The Demand for Order in Civil Society: A Review of Some Themes in the History of Urban Crime, Police and Riot."

3. John M. Pfiffner, *The Function of the Police in a Democratic Society*. Research dealing with value and belief systems of different occupations and professions, including the police, is being done currently by Professor Milton Rokeach of the Department of Psychology, Michigan State University. Pfiffner's earlier work is reflected in his *The Supervision of Personnel*.

4. See Martin Miller, "Systemic Model of Police Morale," Study 2, Part II, in *The Police and the Community: Studies*, Radelet and Reed.

5. James W. Sterling, *Changes in Role Concepts of Police Officers During Recruit Training*. Report (June 1969) of an IACP research project with a grant from the National Institutes of Health, U.S. Department of Health, Education and Welfare. Sterling describes this as a study of "occupational socialization—the process by which an individual acquires the necessary attitudes, knowledge and skills to perform his occupational role." Much more than training (in the sense of academy instruction) is inherent in this process. The research was conducted in the police departments of Baltimore, Cincinnati, Columbus, Ohio, and Indianapolis. A modest sampling of data from this noteworthy study may be found in Part I of *Studies* (Radelet and Reed).

6. This point has also been suggested by S. A. Stouffer in "An Analysis of Conflicting Social Norms."

7. Several studies in Parts I and II of the Radelet and Reed *Studies* have been developed on the basis of these data.

Chapter Four

Police Professionalism and Its Implications for Police and Community Relations

Logically, our idea of what it means to be a professional police-man is governed by our notion of the policeman's role in society. If we emphasize the law enforcement function, professionalism means attri-butes deemed to be conducive to this function, e.g., courage, respect for superiors, reliability, and obedience. If, instead, we emphasize the con-flict management function in policing, then professionalism means such attributes as intelligence, common sense, friendliness, courtesy, and patience.

There also appear to be both law enforcement and peace-keeping orientations for our view of police-citizen interaction. A law enforcement *of police* orientation tends to stress what the community should do to assist the *relatns* police in such measures as containing crime, catching crooks, and pro-viding information about "suspicious persons." A peace-keeping orien-tation for police and community relations is more likely to stress what the police and community can do together, helping each other in part-nership. *Preventing* crime as well as disorder is seen as an important objective of this partnership. Information becomes more a matter of mutual exchange than of one-way, police intelligence. For the police, a law enforcement orientation for police-citizen interaction tends to emphasize public relations; while a peace-keeping orientation empha-sizes community participation. The essence of the peace-keeping orientation is mutual trust; helping the police is regarded by citizens as, in effect, helping themselves—to create a better community for all.

The Policeman's Role

Perhaps these distinctions are useful only as generalized abstractions. In practice, a given police agency may be difficult to characterize in such terms because the elements of both orientations may be present in its activities, just as the views will be mixed on the role question. Likewise, a discussion of police professionalism reveals the same mixed views. One of the marks of a profession is that its constituency has arrived at some consensus regarding the "product" of the profession. Thus, it may be said that policing will come to be recognized as truly professional when some consensus is reached on the role question. But this is not likely to occur overnight.

Since professional recognition depends upon public attitudes toward the police, consensus on role or product must then involve both police and community. To influence public attitude favorably will require unprecedented police leadership, another mark of true professionalism. Medicine is a favorite example in discussions of professionalism. Generally speaking, public education in matters of health is carried on under the leadership of medical professionals. Instructive campaigns *influence* and *shape* public attitudes, at the same time helping to convince the public that the promoters are truly professional. Medical professionals do not follow in the wake of community opinions in health matters. They secure factual data through research from which the public is informed and educated as to what its attitudes and expectations should be. There is no great problem of consensus about role or product in the medical profession.

As with any analogy, the comparison of medicine or public health with policing has some limitations. But it is adequate to suggest a simple point: true professionals *lead* the community in their area of competence. While they are careful listeners to community opinions by way of learning about needs, they do not wait for the community to tell them what should be done.

The Definition of Professionalism

We begin to see that our definition of professionalism, or of a professional, will depend considerably upon what we regard as important in a particular field—what we feel ought to be emphasized as priorities by workers in that field.

Webster defines a profession as "a calling requiring specialized knowledge and often long and intensive academic preparation, used by way either of instructing, guiding or advising others, or of serving them in some art." Special knowledge and proficiency are among the earmarks of a profession. Service to others with a clearly defined purpose is another; so is a technical terminology. Still another is the assumption that financial return is not the primary object in rendering a service. A profession has a certain ethic, guiding moral principles, for which a self-policing provision is maintained within the profession. Members are associated in organizations for the purpose of regulating and improving the service they render. It is in this connection that professional organizations are concerned with such matters as licensing, accreditation of schools, establishment of training standards, separation of the qualified from the unqualified, etc.[1]

Sometimes reference is made to what is called *attitude*: for example, in such aphorisms as "attitude makes the professional." Attitude, although elusive and difficult to define in a concrete way, becomes somewhat more manageable when it is applied to the relationship between a professional and a client. The late Alexander Woolcott had attitude in mind when he defined a professional as "someone who does his best job when he feels worst."

Some Useful Distinctions About Professionalism

Views expressed on professionalim are frequently corrupted by the careless intermixture of terms that complicate communications. For instance, what is the difference between a professional and a technician, between a professional and a specialist, between a professional and an artist or a craftsman? What is the relationship between professionalism and bureaucracy?

Specialist and technician are closely related concepts. A specialist is someone with proficiency or unique knowledge in a particular branch of study. A professional may be a specialist, for instance, in a particular aspect of medicine or law. A technician is a specialist in the technical details of a subject or occupation. To be a technician necessitates *practical* aptitude, as distinct from theoretical, especially in a mechanical or scientific subject. A hospital is a place where professionals, technicians, students, and others work, some of whom are specialists. Can this be said of a police station?

A professional is sometimes an artist, i.e., one who professes and practices an art in which "conception and execution are governed by imagination and taste" (Webster). A craftsman is one engaged in an occupation or trade requiring manual dexterity or artistic skill.

Professionalism and bureaucracy have become increasingly correlated in our society. Bureaucracy is a system of administration characterized by specialization of functions, by adherence to fixed rules (frequently referred to as Standard Operating Procedure, or simply

S.O.P.), and by a hierarchy of authority. The question of whether bureaucracy and professionalism are compatible has been widely argued. The professional and bureaucratic models clearly clash at certain points.

In an excellent article written several years ago, *The Professionalization of Everyone,* sociologist Harold Wilensky claimed that the distinctive standards of a profession are its *technical* basis (systematic knowledge or doctrine acquired only through long prescribed training), and its adherence to *professional norms* (ethic, attitude, client relations, etc.). He emphasized *autonomous expertise* and the service ideal. Bureaucracy enfeebles the service ideal more than it threatens autonomy, Wilensky asserted, and he concluded that very few occupations will achieve the authority of the established professions. If we call everything a profession, he said, we obscure its meaning and make it less a prize to be earned only by meeting demanding requirements. Quoting Wilensky—

> ... the role orientations of many professionals reflect a resolution of the clash between the requirements of profession, organization and social movement ... End products of broad movements of social reform, these men combine professional standards of work with programmatic sense and constitute an important link between professional culture and civil culture, the man of knowledge and the man of power. As we assess the mixed organizational forms and mixed role orientations of the future, we must attend not only to the barriers to the professionalization of newer occupations, but to the emergence from existing professions of such policy-minded staff experts. [Pp. 137–158]

Effects of Social Change on Professionalism

Underlying Wilensky's analysis is the emergence of many new occupations in an increasingly technocratic society, and a surge for professional identification. It raises interesting questions about the differences between doctors and plumbers, between clergymen and computer technicians, between lawyers and trade union members. A more complex society requires more specialty services. As the society relies more and more upon specialists, experts, professionals, to make more and more decisions in its behalf—decisions requiring technical know-how in matters of public affairs and public responsibility—the gap widens between the individual and the decision making that affects his destiny. This is another commentary on the question of "community."

Social change has radically altered the traditional professional categories. By and large, the qualifications for being accepted in the new professional groupings that have surfaced in recent years are more demanding than in the relatively few professions of the past. The professional requirements of medicine and law are more rigorous today than years ago, if for no other reason than that these fields require more knowledge. In police work, which is an occupation or craft, as James Q. Wilson tabs it, that has become more demanding as social control in society has become more intricate, the tests of modern professionalim are challenging indeed. Judged by the recognized marks of a profession, any claims that policing has achieved such status amount simply to wishful thinking. Remember, however, that professionalism has a relativistic character. Police work is relatively more professionalized today than it was years ago. Police Department *A* may be relatively more professionalized than Police Department *B*. Police Officer Smith may be relatively more professionalized than Police Officer Jones. Police *departments* tend to be relatively more professionalized than police *officers*. Of course, all such judgments involve criteria about which there is sharp disagreement.

How important is professional recognition in police work? The preponderance of opinion strongly favors such recognition. Still, professionalization may not be an unmixed blessing—depending again on how it is defined. Perhaps some insight along this line can be gained by considering some specific aspects of police professional development.

Sundry Views of Police Professionalism

In 1959, James Slavin—then Chief of the Kalamazoo (Michigan) Police Department, later the Chief in Denver and director of the Traffic Institute at Northwestern University—told the Fifth National Institute on Police and Community Relations at Michigan State University of a number of obstacles to the professional development of American police. One was the hesitancy to carry out vigilant internal monitoring of police practices. Another was his impression that some so-called professional police organizations and associations were indistinguishable from labor and craft unions. Slavin hastened to add, on this point, that he was not critical of labor and craft unions; he was merely calling attention to the difference that is generally believed to exist between a union and a professional association.

Continuing his provocative commentary, Slavin pointed to "almost imperceptible progress in establishing documented standards for selection of police personnel from our citizenry." He said that little information was available describing what kind of person and what qualifications were necessary to predict a probably successful police career. Another shortcoming, according to Slavin, was the inadequacy of training for supervisory responsibility in police agencies. He advocated wider uses of supervisory training, similar to that of business and industry.

Slavin concluded his remarks with one more drawback to arriving at professionalism:

> Another disturbing and impeding factor in the goal of professional police service is our manner of talking about professionalizing. There

is need to recognize that attaining professional status is the result of acquiring . . . certain characteristics which entitle our activity to be called a professional endeavor. The thing we fail to emphasize in our writings and discussions is that it is the characteristics that mark a profession that are worthwhile, rather than talking frequently as though what we want most of all is to be identified as a professional occupation. ["How Can Policing Become a Profession?"]

Slavin's is a disquieting approach to the subject of police professionalism, one to which some policemen responded rather caustically. A more popular commentary among police officers is exemplified by Quinn Tamm, executive director of the International Association of Chiefs of Police, in which he also revealed a point of view in *The Police Chief,* regarding police role:

I know of no period in recent history when the police have been the subject of so many unjustified charges of brutality, harassment and ineptness. It almost seems that the better we do our job enforcing the law, the more we are attacked. The more professional we become, the more effective we become and the more effective we are, the more we impinge upon the misbehavior of society.

But for this we should offer no apology. A police force is established, among other things, for the purpose of enforcing existing laws. In this respect, we are dutybound. Those who damn our actions in this regard must be made to understand that the police do not make the laws, that laws are the direct product of public desires, and if the public does not like those laws or believe them to be fair, then the public should change the laws rather than criticize the police . . . We can no longer afford to answer unjust criticism with thinly veiled innuendoes and pusillanimous generalities. If we are right, let's say so. ["Police Professionalism and Management"]

Writing in *Police Organization and Management,* V. A Leonard, a well-known authority on police administration, strikes a related but discordant note:

A system of legal justice based upon the thesis of punishment has exerted a tremendously negative effect on the professionalization of police service. As a corollary, the low quality of personnel required to exercise the police power under these conditions was not conducive to good public relations, with the result that a negative public opinion had been created. The withdrawal of public interest and support, together with public apathy and indifference, has further served to retard the advance toward professionalization. No less important has been the fact that a substandard personnel became easy prey for corrupt political figures and others in the community who profit when the risks associated with vice operations are reduced.

Another policeman-analyst, Bernard Brannon—former Kansas City Police Chief and professor at the University of Missouri—has stressed the importance of *attitude* in his discussion of professionalism in police work. He believes that being a professional policeman begins with seeing oneself as a professional and acquiring the feeling of a professional. He alludes to the effort and sacrifice necessary to becoming a professional, emphasizing that there are responsibilities of such status accompanying the privileges. He speaks of self-discipline, dedication to the public service ideal, the importance of individual words and deeds, constant emphasis upon study and learning, and the importance of participation in community affairs. He favors the establishment of an accrediting agency for police professional education, and the enforcement of uniform standards and examinations in each state.[2]

The attitude of the true professional is difficult to pin down. Using the medical analogy again, we might quote Norman Cousins, former editor of *The Saturday Review* (August 22, 1970):

> Finally, the good doctor is not only a scientist but a philosopher. He knows that the facts of medicine will continue to change and that, therefore, his professional training can never be an absolute guide to good practice. It is his philosophy of medicine that has to serve as the solid base of his practice. The doctor's respect for life, his special qualities of compassion and tenderness—even under the most devilish of circumstances—these are the vital ingredients of his art. To such a doctor, the most exotic diagnostic machines are not more important than the simple act of sitting at the bedside of a patient. In this sense, the ultimate art of the good doctor is to make good patients. He does this by making the patient a full partner in his recovery. Such a doctor is worth all the recognition and reward a society is capable of offering. [P. 32]

Professionalism and Police-Community Relations

An abundance of literature deals with police professionalism in general terms. It is a required subject in every standard text in police administration, with each author advancing his particular pitch on what constitutes professionalism. Most of these positions on the subject have merit from one standpoint or another. A central problem of police professionalism—closely related as it is to the question of police role—is the problem of consensus. This means simply that police professionalization is essentially a police-community transaction. Community attitudes toward the police are crucial, for professionalism implies public certification of professional competence, with commensurate status, privileges, and responsibilities.

There is, therefore, special significance to the professionalizing of police service from a police-community standpoint. This author once wrote an article on this topic for *Police* (1966), a few sentences of which may make a point here:

> Now I would maintain that a profession serves *needs,* not *wants.* I don't particularly care about being a pal with my doctor, but I do want to respect him for his competence, his skill and his attitude as a professional. I don't think he should go out of his way to be a pal to me either. When I need his help, I want something more from him than soothing assertions that he'll never let me down.... May I suggest [then] what I regard as the first implication of the professional concept [in law enforcement] for police-community relations: to woo the client's respect, not his favor—in short, to reassert authority as a necessary corollary to responsibility.

As we examine more closely the matter of police professionalism, which is an extension of the nature of police role, we observe that the police *are* indeed professionalizing—in terms of education and training, improved "tools" and "hardware," better communication systems, etc. Yet at the same time, as Quinn Tamm suggests, the more professionalism the police achieve, the more the public seems to criticize, even to ridicule and caricature. This, of course, underscores the fundamental role dilemma and what we have referred to as the consensus problem.

If professionalism is defined conventionally, from the benchmarks previously noted, the police have some distance to go before they arrive. Agreement seems general on this point, even among policemen. Yet in certain respects they want very much to be viewed as professionals, for example, in the matter of civilian review. However, as Eleanor Harlow points out in *Problems in Police-Community Relations,* "those who argue that civilian review of police is wrong because as a 'professional' organization, the police department should be subject only to its own surveillance are basing their conclusion on a faulty comparison. If civilian review is inappropriate, as it well may be, it is for other reasons" (p. 13).

Professionalism, as applied to the police, tends to be rather loosely and elastically defined. Efficiency in suppressing crime is widely equated with professionalization. It would be easier to evaluate these twin goals if they were kept distinct. As Skolnick explains (*The Police and the Urban Ghetto,* 1968):

> The problem of police in a democratic society is not merely a matter of obtaining new police cars or more sophisticated equipment, or communication systems, or of recruiting men who have to their credit more years of education. What is necessary is a significant alteration in the philosophy of police, so that police "professionalization" rests upon the values of a democratic legal polity, rather than merely on the notion of technical proficiency to serve the public order of the state. [P. 11]

Skolnick's view is supported in the Michigan State University study for the President's 1966 Crime Commission (Field Surveys V):

> The peace and security of the community do not rest alone upon the efficient and technological performance of law enforcement. More important is *law observance* or the consent of the governed, which involves meaningful participation in the formulation as well as the implementation of law as a means of social control ... A fundamental error is made when too heavy a reliance is placed upon law enforcement and too little reliance is placed upon other means of social control. [P. 360]

In sum, when Tamm says "the more the police professionalize ... ," he is talking about management and criminal investigation efficiency, about hardware, about training and educational expansion. Why, then, he asks, are some elements of the public still so critical of the police? The answer must be that these citizens believe that there is more to professionalism than efficiency and hardware—or perhaps it is that police professionalism *without a human dimension* is not a very significant goal after all.

The Human Dimension in Police Work

Police work in a democratic society cannot escape from its human dimension. Its public service aspects need re-emphasis, and a military-technological orientation tends to obscure its fundamental concern for relating to people and for what Jerome Hall stressed in his discussion of the democratic ethic. The Michigan State study recommends—

> ... that the police place greater emphasis upon the concept of public service as a legitimate goal of their organizations. For the police, professionalism has been viewed in too narrow a focus. True professionalism is rooted in broad-based public service which commands popular respect for the police officer and the system of government by law which he represents. Increased efficiency in police work is laudable, but as a means to an end, not as an end in itself. When efficiency is coupled with a goal of crime suppression at any cost, the community is often faced with a police agency which is not responsive to community needs. Certain elements in the community do not see it as their police department. [Field Survey V, pp. 377, 78]

Eleanor Harlow makes a further useful distinction:

> The term professionalization is used by those who wish to free the police from community "interference" to support their contention that a professional organization is responsible for regulating and supervising its own members, free from the control of outsiders, who lack the knowledge and experience to make appropriate judgments. It is used—simultaneously but with different meaning—by those who

believe that the community should "police the police" to insist that only the establishment of specific standards and procedures (presumably based on dictates from the community power structure) will insure "professional" police operations. [*Problems in Police-Community Relations*, p. 14]

There are difficulties with either of these interpretations of police professionalization. In our society, with the police ultimately accountable to the people and consequently subject to political process,[3] it is evident that police work cannot be professionalized by conceding autonomy to the point of complete isolation from the community. On the contrary, we maintain that the police are integral to the community—*part of*, not *apart from*. Both community relations and justice are jeopardized, however, if the police allow themselves to become the marionettes of this or that politically dominant group in the community.

There is also some difficulty with the second interpretation of professionalization, suggested by Harlow (*Problems in Police-Community Relations*):

Those who use the term professionalization to mean the establishment of standards for police operation advocate the provision to police of specific instructions for handling those situations not clearly defined by law. This is an admirable goal and one which would probably please everybody; certainly the police would be relieved to know what, precisely, is expected of them. However, such procedural standards often cannot be made specific enough to apply to any given situation. Ultimately, the individual officer must be sufficiently trained and educated to use his discretion when the standard procedure is inapplicable. [P. 15]

We will deal with the implications of this point in the next chapter.

Professionalism and the Line Officer

Sociologist Albert Reiss makes the observation in "Professionalization of the Police" that our larger American police departments have become major bureaucratic organizations. Many of their problems are therefore peculiar to bureaucracy. Reiss contends that most attempts to professionalize police work have led to a professionalization of the police department, to a lesser extent the professionalization of those in staff positions, and only to a relatively minor extent to professionalization of the rank and file officer in the line. He states that the nature of changes within police departments has tended to work against the professionalization of the line officer. The department has been professionalized, says Reiss, through bureaucratization, and the line officer accordingly becomes no more than a technician, taking orders. Reiss also maintains that broader societal changes work against professionalization of the line officer, primarily through redefinition of the police role. He argues that the nature of police work "coerces discretionary decision-making in social situations, and both the end and the means valued by our society require that in the long run at least part of the line must be 'professional' " (Ibid., p. 216).

Reiss is particularly interested in the relationship of the professional with clients. He characterizes this relationship as technical, in the sense of specialized knowledge to be applied in practice. The client relationship, moreover, is moral and ethical. But its central feature, Reiss asserts, is a decision about the client in which the professional decides something relating to the future of the client. This feature of the professional-client relationship is especially critical when the client has little choice whether to abide by the decision of the professional.

To support his view that the professionalization of police departments through bureaucratization has worked against the professionalization of the line officer, Reiss points to three factors:

1. The increasing centralization of decision-making in departments. A bureaucratic system where decision-making is decentralized to the line would be more consistent with professionalization of the line.

2. The tendency of specialization in police organizations to be more technical than professional. It has been more "professionalization of the organizational system" than it has been professional role specialization. Writing tickets in traffic enforcement, for example, is a work assignment, a technical job specialty. It does not involve professional decision-making by the line officer.

3. The making of decisions at the staff rather than the operating level of police departments, and the bringing in of professional specialists at the staff rather than the operating level. As an illustration, "human relations" in many departments is largely a staff function. It is handled through central orders, leaving little room for "professional treatment of clients" by the line officer.

His summarizing statement is helpful in our discussion at this point[4]:

Despite dissatisfaction with the "new" role emerging for the police officer, it seems clear that the changes underway involve a reinterpretation of client role and behavior in terms of a more "professional" ideology and practice. The dilemma for the police is to somehow balance traditional moral and quasi-legal concerns with enforcing the law and catching criminals who are to be "punished," with the emerging concerns for civil rights and legal requirements on police methods. "Professionalization" of police work appears to be one "legitimate" way to deal with the dilemma. [Ibid., p. 227]

The Service Ideal

Analysts of professionalism, in any field, emphasize the service ideal and the client relationship. These considerations are closely akin to what we mean by *attitude*. Wilensky discusses the idea (*Am. J. Soc.,* Sept. 1964):

> The criterion of "technical" is not enough however. The craftsman typically goes to a trade school, has an apprenticeship, forms an occupational association to regulate entry to the trade, and gets legal sanction for his practice. But the success of the claim to professional status is governed also by the degree to which the practitioners conform to a set of moral norms that characterize the established professions. These norms dictate not only that the practitioner do technically competent, high-quality work, but that he adhere to a service ideal—devotion to the client's interests more than personal or commercial profit should guide decisions when the two are in conflict. [P. 140]

Wilensky goes on to state that the professional norm of selflessness is more than mere lip service: ". . . the service ideal is the pivot around which the moral claim to professional status revolves." It would be difficult to express more eloquently a major implication of police professionalism for police and community relations.

The Police as Community Managers

An earlier quotation (*Comments on Police-Community Relations*) reflected David Bordua's view of the police as "community managers" and "monitors of social change." Bordua suggested that after a transitional period of professionalizing police *departments,* it will be necessary really to professionalize police *officers.* If the police are to be community managers, they will have to participate more in the goal-setting functions of government, as recommended in Chapter 2 of the *Police Task Force Report* of the President's Crime Commission. The participation will involve the police in some aspects of politics, but this is nothing new.

It means simply a legitimate political role for the police, which is not quite the same as "political policing" in the past. Reforms in police work cannot occur without intelligent political role-playing by police administrators. This does not imply a police state. As Bordua says, ". . . if they [the police] are to avoid being politically maneuvered into being hired oppressors by reactionary whites or manipulated targets by extremist Negro leaders, they will have to present themselves as detached and principled specialists in community order."

Some may think this notion a lofty ideal, or sheer fantasy. But the police response to current social challenges in many places already reflects this ideal in some measure. In a number of jurisdictions, the police

have responded to service needs by new programs, both of direct assistance and of referral to other agencies. Several examples come to mind:
special police training programs have been devised in family crisis intervention; police are being assigned to job centers to assist young men
with records find jobs; some departments are experimenting with hiring
certain individuals with felony records; lateral placement is not quite the
anathema in police organizations that it has been in the past; officers
are being assigned to antipoverty centers; some police departments have
established community service units, are operating store-front stations
in numerous cities, and are beginning promising ventures in team policing. A few departments are even taking the initiative in pointing out
deficiencies that need correcting in other governmental and private
services. These are evidences of fresh thinking about what police professionalism means in the way of client services and community
leadership.

As Herman Goldstein observes in *Police Response to Urban Crises*:

> Efforts to communicate with the public more effectively are in sharp
> contrast with the commitment to secrecy, isolation, and aloofness
> that has marked the "professional" approach in the past. The will-
> ingness to accept criticism and the acknowledgement of existing
> inadequacies represent a substantial modification of the customary
> police commitment to maintaining an all-powerful image of invulner-
> ability. Involvement in social services reflects a recognition of these
> tasks as appropriate police responsibilities. [P. 422]

Yet, as various writers have told us, some of the more progressive
police administrators in our large cities are confronted by a difficult
dilemma. At a time when the need for new and enlightened approaches
to policing is so vital, they are forced by weight of public opinion and
by political "gamesmanship" to retain traditional methods. Some of the
pressure to maintain the status quo comes from within departments and
is wielded by police officers and their associations who feel threatened
by change. This results in a kind of tug-of-war for administrative control
of the department. Visionary and able administrators do not always win
this kind of battle!

Professionalism and Law vs. Order

Skolnick has written extensively on the subject of police professionalism, rooted in the distinction he draws between law and order.
To add to what we have already said about this earlier in this chapter,
the following, again from *The Police and the Urban Ghetto* (1968), is
indicative of his position:

> ... if the police are ever to develop a conception of legal as opposed
> to managerial professionalism, two conditions must be met: First,

the police must accustom themselves to the seemingly paradoxical yet fundamental idea of the rule of law, namely, that the observance of legal restraints may indeed make their task more difficult. That's how it is in a free society. Second, the civic community must support compliance with the rule of law by rewarding police for observing constitutional guarantees, instead of looking to the police as merely an institution responsible for controlling criminality. In practice, regrettably, the reverse has been true. The police function in a milieu tending to support, normatively and substantively, the idea of administrative efficiency as an index of police professionalism. Steps must be taken to reverse this trend. The observance of the principles of legality will indeed be the hallmark of professional police in a free society. [P. 12]

Skolnick sees two other important aspects of the problem of police professionalization calling for reform. One is *overcriminalization* or *legal moralism:* making the policeman the guardian and enforcer of conventional morality. The other is the traditional military model of police organization. These matters will be considered in later chapters.

Various observers, Skolnick among them, have noted that the police system in democratic society is the inevitable result of the give-and-take of free discussion and political bargaining. The *Final Report* of the British Royal Commission on the Police made the point well:

The police systems in England, Scotland and Wales are the products of a series of compromises between conflicting principles or ideas. Consequently, in contrast to other public services such as health and education, the rationale of the police service does not rest upon any single and definite concept of the public good. Thus, it is to the public good that the police should be strong and effective in preserving law and order and preventing crime; but it is equally to the public good that police power should be controlled and confined so as not to interfere arbitrarily with personal freedom. The result is compromise. The police should be powerful but not oppressive; they should be efficient but not officious; they should form an impartial force in the body politic, and yet be subject to a degree of control by persons who are not required to be impartial and who are themselves liable to police supervision. [P. 9]

One clear implication is that police professionals should have autonomy, but not too much. Writing in *The Saturday Review* (August 22, 1970), Dr. John H. Knowles, director of Massachusetts General Hospital, makes this point:

The major issue besetting the AMA over the past 50 years has been the struggle for the absolute power of self-determination. That is, the autonomy to decide what is best for the profession and what is best for the public, without "outside" interference. Looked at narrowly, the battle pits conservatives against liberals; self-reliant individualists against paternalistic socialists; creative artists against power hungry bureaucrats. Looked at more broadly, it represents the fears of a proud profession steadily losing power and territory to "others" in the health field. Narrowly, this has been characterized as a battle for money and economic security; more broadly, as a loss of freedom and a reaction to the interposition of outside forces between a doctor and his patient, much as a father resents the interposition of anyone or anything between him and his sons.

Police Authority and Police Power

Banton makes much of the point (*Social Integration*) that the police officer functions most effectively (professionally?) when what he does is supported by the moral consensus of the community. The officer possesses both authority and power. Authority is rightful power; it has a moral element. Banton declares that public resentment against police is usually directed against their power, not their authority, because the latter is conferred upon policemen by the community. Therefore, the officer who wields moral authority acts in a predictable fashion, that is, in a manner that is socially approved. The policeman whose responses are uncertain, Banton suggests, is the man who relies on his individual powers, unconcerned with whether the subject feels he is exercising them rightfully. This is the type of officer in whom the public will lack confidence, because he is unpredictable.

Banton's point is again one with implications for both police role and police professionalism. In the preceding chapter, we spoke of the hypothetical police department which lacks clearly defined goals, with corresponding inadequacies in administrative policy and supervision that leave individual policemen unsure of departmental requirements. We said that police officers in such situations tend to be guided by informal communication among peers, by their personal values and interests, and by their own interpretations of what the community expects of them. These are the conditions that produce the unpredictable behavior to which Banton refers.

On the other hand, there is the concept of a professional police department suggested by the description "a tight ship." It is one that attempts to have a policy or rule applicable to every conceivable situation in which a policeman might find himself. It is a department so oriented toward efficiency that it strives for guidelines in every police activity. Its operation is sometimes called a "by the book" operation. The policeman on the street is stringently limited in his exercise of discretion; as Reiss describes it, decisions are made for him "up the line" or "down town." Idle conversation with residents of the community is discouraged as a waste of time. Instead, policemen should engage in "aggressive patrol" and be on the lookout for suspicious persons, especially in high crime areas. Citizens should be treated civilly, but policemen should never show sympathy or other emotion toward a "mere civilian."

Bruce Terris declares that a police department can be so "professional" that it destroys community relations. He observes that "there is no inherent reason why professional police departments must . . . adopt procedures which interfere with improved police-minority relations" (*The Annals,* 1967). He believes that true police professionalism can be a functional combination of management efficiency and good community relations. In fact, he says that efficiency is meaningless if it is secured at the cost of further isolating the police from the community, especially in high crime areas where police-community relations tend to be poor. It will be recalled that policing in democratic society rests on the assumption that a cooperative public is to a large extent a self-policing public.

The Isolation Syndrome and Professionalism

Yet it is countered that lofty principles have a way of being tested in the crucible of reality—a reality in which practical political considerations play a decisive part. Misner suggests this in terms similar to others quoted in Chapter Three of *The Nation.*

> Now, at the very time when we find ourselves confronted with the most compelling need to redefine our whole set of public services, the political climate is such that a genuine redefinition may be impossible. In the nation's urban centers, social upheavals make a reexamination of police resources and their utilization imperative; but the general public seems to find the environment so threatening that its fears may forestall any meaningful attempts at police reform. [*The Nation,* April 21, 1969, p. 489]

What this means in practical terms for many big city police officers has been well described also in *The Nation* (April 21, 1969) by William Brown, a retired New York City Police Inspector, now professor of criminal justice at the State University of New York in Albany. He feels that the new isolation of the police is a recoil from pressures exerted by human relations specialists, by some college professors in the police field, by other "activist academics," and by the courts. Many police officers feel, Brown believes, that these pressure groups generally propose that more restrictions be placed on the police, rather than provide support for the police by devising workable solutions to difficult problems.

So it is, Brown continues, that the police have turned "to their own councils." Leadership has developed from police fraternal organizations, which are "for the policeman." As Brown puts it, "they are his unquestioning champions and today's policeman needs a champion."

Thus it is that the police respond to current pressures "by withdrawing from the professional arena to the blue-collar world." With this goes apathy, "the classic reaction of a group to what it sees as a hopeless situation." In Brown's terms:

> Obviously, the leitmotiv of professional police apathy holds no future for our society, but what is it that we want the police to do? . . . The need is for the police to remain calm, to be fair, to bring in the black policemen as co-professionals, to serve rather than to control the black communities, to meet a standard of performance under difficulties which we could not even have visualized a few years ago. Above all, they must develop a faith that if they do perform at this level, they will eventually win the support that can make their future job possible.

Pfiffner develops basically the same thought in *Function of the Police*. He refers to the "isolation syndrome" of the police, and his diagnosis of the pressures which explain it is similar to Brown's. As a result, Pfiffner says, the police turn to what he calls "guild protectionism," born out of self-pity and the failure to make personal adjustment to extreme vocational tensions.

Police Responses to the Isolation Syndrome

James Q. Wilson, writing in *Police and their Problems,* has analyzed the phenomenon of police misconduct and corruption in big city departments in the same terms, but more intensively. He considers two general responses of police forces to the isolation syndrome. Each response provides a different definition of "a good cop." Wilson calls one response (or code of police behavior), the system; he calls the other, professionalism. By the system, he means "the institutionalized rules and norms which express the policeman's position as a member of a group which feels keenly its *pariah* status." By professionalism, he means "an institutionalization of rules and norms expressing, not feelings of group separateness, but an external body of 'expert' knowledge about 'correct' police work."

The code of the system is internal and, in sociological terms, is *particularistic:* its value standards are derived from the significance to a particular person of his relations with particular others. The code of the professional is external, is *universalistic,* its values derived from general, impersonal, and presumably valid rules binding upon all persons possessing certain qualifications. Wilson[5] makes this pertinent point:

> Professionalism is a term that must be understood in a special sense when applying it to policemen. Generally speaking, a profession provides a service (such as medical aid or legal advice) the quality of which the client is not in a position to judge for himself; therefore, a

professional body and a professional code must be established to protect both the client from his ignorance and the profession from the client who supposes that he is not ignorant. The policeman differs from the doctor or lawyer, however, in important respects: first, his role is not to cure or advise but to restrain; and second, whereas health and counsel are welcomed by the recipients, restraint is not. If this is true, then professionalism among policemen will differ from professionalism in other occupations in that the primary function of the professional code will be to protect the practitioner from the client rather than the client from the practitioner. [Ibid.]

Wilson proceeds to consider the difference between the codes of the system and of professionalism in certain specific issues in police work: recruitment, law enforcement, informers, graft, authority, secrecy, violence, and public relations. His conclusions are interesting:

1. The prospects for a high level of professionalism in the police forces of many, if not most, large American cities seem dim.

2. The elimination of wholesale corruption of police forces by gamblers and syndicate hoodlums may be a necessary condition for the growth of police professionalism, but it is not a sufficient one.

3. Police professionalism is part of a "package"; it is possible that the benefits of police professionalism may be outweighed by the costs of other, necessarily related institutions. It is even possible that a professionalized police force is not always superior to its alternative.

The Desirability of Professionalism

Is professionalism of the police an unmixed blessing? In "Dilemmas of Police Administration," Wilson states flatly that the patrolman is neither a bureaucrat nor a professional, but a member of a *craft*. (Wilson also takes this position in *Varieties of Police Behavior*, p. 278) As with other crafts, there is in the police field no generalized, written body of special knowledge. Learning is imparted by apprenticeship, largely on the job; the primary reference group is composed of colleagues on the job; and the members think of themselves as set apart from society because they have a special task to perform. Unlike other crafts, however, police work produces no product that can be easily judged, and it is carried on often in an apprehensive or hostile atmosphere. Consider this passage in which Wilson speculates that efforts to change policing into a profession will be largely ignored, simply because it is irrelevant:

Such gains as can be made in the way the police handle citizens are not likely to come primarily from either proliferating rules (i.e., bureaucratizing the police) or sending officers to colleges, special training programs, or human relations institutes (i.e., "professionalizing" the police). Instead, the most significant changes will be in organization and leadership in order to increase the officer's familiarity with and sensitivity to the neighborhood he patrols and rewarding him for doing what is judged (necessarily after the fact) to be the right thing rather than simply the "efficient" thing. ["Dilemmas," p. 414]

Wilson is speaking here of the order maintenance function of the police, which he regards as paramount. He admits that the law enforcement function requires a different approach, though he acknowledges that it is sometimes difficult to separate the two functions.

We may conclude, then, that professionalism in police work is a desirable goal provided that—

1. it is recognized that not everyone who works in the police station need be a professional.

2. it is recognized that police officer professionalism pivots in the *human* dimensions of police work—in such things as attitude, ethic, service and sensitivity to people of all kinds (client relations), and manifold activities directed toward earning public trust and respect.

The Outlook for Professionalism

We have tried to show that the quandary of police professionalism is intimately related to the quandary of police role. Discussion of police professionalism is apt to be frustrating, because of the problem of definition, complicated as it is by the role question; and also because some doubt can be raised about whether police professionalism, in some understandings of the term, is an altogether desirable or feasible thing in the first place. These difficulties seem great when analysis turns to the implications of professionalism for police and community relations. As Wilson points out, there is no clear evidence, for example, that middle-class, college-educated people make better police officers. Moreover, he adds that it is highly unlikely that many such persons will find a police career in a large city very attractive.

Several questions are closely related. What factors of personality, attitude, background, education, values, and beliefs are most important in the effective policeman for good community relations? How should a police organization cultivate these qualities? Do certain personality types gravitate to policing as a career? If so, how can the decisive traits be described?

Researchers[6] are only beginning to deal with such questions. For example, the Industrial Relations Center at the University of Chicago, on a grant from the Office of Law Enforcement Assistance, conducted research in the Chicago police department dealing with the psychological assessment of the patrolman's qualifications as related to field performance. David Bayley and Harold Mendelsohn of the

University of Denver were co-researchers in a study of the Denver police department, which produced information bearing upon such questions. Sociologist James Walsh of Oberlin College, having interviewed police officers in four police departments in small and medium-sized cities in the Midwest, concluded that police officers who see policing as a profession have attitudes toward the work sharply contrasting with police officers who see policing simply as a job. Arthur Niederhoffer and Seymour Martin Lipset are among those with related research interests. John McNamara has studied the occupational socialization of recruits in the New York City police department, focusing on the uncertainties of the police role and the processes which determine the fitness of recruits to do police work.

The outlook for police professionalism in the police departments of big American cities is rather glum, in the opinion of such observers as Wilson, Goldstein, Misner, and Skolnick. Wilson, for one, does not regard this as necessarily disastrous. As a political scientist, he is inclined to emphasize the pragmatic. He says, for instance, that police and city administrators will have to work with the human material they now have, or something close to it (*Varieties of Police Behavior,* p. 281). Under such circumstances, they will tend to rely heavily on organizational and legal "prodding," to persuade the policeman "to do his duty": in short, bureaucracy. This has frequently meant "the tight ship," doing things "by the book"—what Wilson labels the *legalistic* style of policing. In effect, this approach reduces the amount of discretion the officer can exercise. It makes him a technician, sometimes a specialist, but *not* a professional. It gives the appearance of efficiency, oriented to the law enforcement function rather than to peace keeping. The similarities of the Wilson and Reiss positions are discernible, but there are also some differences. Reiss seems more hopeful than Wilson for eventual professionalization of the line officer. Wilson simply says that it may be irrelevant.

Another school of thought (loosely combining Wilson's *service* and *watchman* styles) wants policemen to be professionals stressing their community service functions. In this view, the emphasis should be on good community relations. The police officer should be trained to take a broad view of his role, with maximum initiative and discretion. Perhaps, Wilson speculates, the answer is that "the police should be bureaucratized for some purposes, professionalized for others, and left alone for still others" (ibid., p. 283). In this vein, the issue is not so simple as a choice of emphasis between law enforcement and order maintenance. Where there is agreement that the order maintenance role is central and primary, there is sometimes disagreement on how best to maintain order. Wilson concludes:

> In sum, the police can cope with their problems but they cannot solve them. If they were expected to do less, they might not be so frus-

trated by their inability to do much of anything. . . . The "problems of the police" are long standing and inherent in the nature of their function, but our definition of those problems has changed and, by changing, has misled or unsettled us. [P.·299]

The Police and Their Social Systems

A point made by Wilson is that police professionalism is part of a "package." This may be interpreted several ways. One way is to observe that the police operate in the context of several social systems, each of which has an influence upon police role interpretation and all its ramifications, including the possibilities of professionalism; indeed, even how professionalism is defined in a given department. In short, "systemic analysis" is essential to understanding police problems. What does this mean?

A *social system* may be defined as an ordered arrangement of interrelated roles. While there is some question that our legal or criminal justice system is truly a social system, it may be said that to the extent that it is a system, the police are part of it—one of its important components. It is ordinarily the police who initiate the process of the system, with the prosecutor's role, the judicial role, and the corrections role as other important components. It is a more or less ordered arrangement of interrelated roles, at least theoretically. Actually, there are many problems in the system pertaining to its interrelationships, which we shall examine in a later chapter.

In any case, this so-called criminal justice system is one of the packages that significantly affect what the police do and how they do it. By the same token, it may be said that the professionalization of the police, whatever this may mean, will inevitably proceed more or less apace of the professionalization of the other components in this system. It is "a package deal." The problems of police and community relations tend to be systemic problems. To be sure, there *are* unique and specific problems of police and community relations. But, beyond this are broader, systemic problems of community relations in the administration of justice.

But the situation of the police, as a component of a social system is more complicated. The police are, in fact, part of several social systems, and these systems overlap and conflict at certain points. Police are part of a political and governmental social system, and operate in interrelated roles with legislative, executive, and judicial branches of government. Within this system, as earlier suggested, the police are influenced in what they do and how they do it by Federal, state, and local law-making bodies, by city managers and mayors, and corporation counsels and city planners and, surely again, in this system, by what the courts do. As an illustration of conflicts between interrelated social systems: what a state legislature may decide about some aspect of the treatment of offenders may not coincide with the judgment of professional corrections personnel.

Another, broad social system comprises the social institutions of society—the familial, educational, political, religious, and economic institutions and the mass media. Clearly, what the police do and how they do it is influenced by this network of social institutions. Social disorganization occurs when social institutions break down, or when interrelationships and coordination among social institutions cease. Crime, for example, is such a problem. These are matters discussed at length in introductory sociology texts, and we will not explore them here, but, again, this is another social system of significance for the police.

In the identification of the various social systems that influence police behavior, one must also consider the kind of social environment or background of the individual policeman. This background is also a type of social system, although only in the loosest sense, since the arrangement of interrelated roles is more disordered than ordered and it is difficult to distinguish it from social institutional influences. In any event, the individual policeman is the product of a particular "world," a particular set of experiences, of family, socioeconomic class, nationality, and ethnic factors, race, religion, education, and political views. He has a personality with certain attitudes, beliefs, and values. What he does as a police officer and how he does it will probably be influenced to some extent by these "background variables," as John McNamara's study indicated. One important aspect of his maturing (socialization) as an effective and professional police officer in today's society will be the extent to which he comes to recognize that the world of which he is a product, and therefore the world as he perceives it, is not the only world there is. As the work of Trager and Yarrow has put it, "they learn what they live."

Summing Up

We have suggested the several social system references of the police that bear directly on the questions of police role and police professionalism. We have also reviewed the complex question of police professionalism, integral as it is to the equally complex role question. If this discussion seems to have reflected confusion, ambiguity, and lack of consensus, it still accurately mirrors the state of the art. The next chapter, which revolves around the questions of role and professionalism, may help in getting the main issues appropriately identified.

Notes to Chapter Four

1. For a further discussion of these benchmarks of a profession, see Bernard C. Brannon, "Professional Development of Law Enforcement Personnel."

2. Ibid. Brannon made this presentation in 1960; some progress has been made since that time, in numerous states, in setting minimum professional standards for policemen.

3. President's Crime Commission report, *Field Surveys IV*, vol. 2, p. 298, University of California.

4. Some of the data supporting Reiss's views are given in Study 5 (Part 1) *The Police and the Community: Studies* (Radelet and Reed).

5. Wilson relies here on a differentiation developed by Everett C. Hughes in *Men and Their Work*.

6. The Industrial Relations Center, University of Chicago (Baehr, Furcon, and Froemel), *Psychological Assessment of Patrolman's Qualifications;* Bayley and Mendelsohn, *Minorities and the Police;* James Leo Walsh, "The Professional Cop" (a paper for the 64th annual meeting of the American Sociological Society, September, 1968); Niederhoffer, *Behind the Shield;* Lipset, "Why Cops Hate Liberals"; McNamara, "Uncertainties in Police Work."

Chapter Five

Discretionary Use of Police Power

It is said that ours is a government by law, not a government by men. This means, of course, that those empowered by the people, from whom their authority is derived, are not free to exercise that power by whim or caprice. They are held accountable to the people to discharge their responsibilities within the limits of established law. A police officer, for example, might describe his job (however naïvely) by saying that it is his duty to enforce the law, no more and no less, equally for all.

Would that it were so simple! If it were, there would probably be much less concern for police and community relations. But the fact is that the law is not really so impersonal; not so detached from what men do with it, from how men interpret it, indeed from how policemen enforce it. Moreover, the law does not cover every situation in which a police officer may find himself. Where there seems to be applicable law, the policeman may be well advised to conduct himself as though ignorant of the law; for to attempt to enforce it might invite Armageddon.

The Human Side of the Law

The law is not an end in itself. Properly understood, it is a means to higher ends in human affairs, such as good order, justice, and individual liberty. Law is an indispensable instrument of social control.

It comes to life through what men make of it and what men do with it. In the totalitarian social system, law is a mechanism of tyranny, dedicated to order as an end in itself, coldly efficient because it is little concerned with the means used to maintain peaceable, conformist behavior. In the democratic society, however, there is (or should be) as much attention to procedural law as there is to substantive law. As Skolnick puts it, "the procedures of the criminal law . . . stress the protection of individual liberties *within* a system of social order" (*Professional Police in a Free Society*). Thus, we are reminded again of Jerome Hall's depiction of the police officer as "the living embodiment of democratic law. (*Indiana Law Journal,* 1953).

We said earlier that police work and police-community relations are of extraordinary importance in our society because the policeman is authorized by the community he serves to exercise extraordinary power under certain circumstances. Both Reiss and Wilson refer, in their analyses of the policeman-client relationship, to decisions by the policeman that seriously affect the client's future, concerning which the client has little or no choice. The policeman's disposition of a case is, then, a *professional* judgment, a *discretionary* decision. As such, it presumes some latitude in choosing from among alternative possible actions, and there is responsibility for whatever determination is made. (Reiss, "Professionalization of the Police," p. 216).

An implication in this again brings to mind Banton's distinction between police authority and police power (*The Police Chief,* April, 1963). For in some decisions that the police officer must make, he cannot be sure that he has the moral support of the community. In such situations, when he acts with power but not necessarily with authority, the validity of his judgment in decision making is especially tested. An example would be the enforcing of gambling laws when the weight of opinion in the community prefers that such laws be ignored. In Wilson's terms, "the system" would suggest "discretion"; "professionalism" would suggest making arrests, including perhaps even one or two "city fathers." Either way, the effects on police-community relations are interesting to contemplate.

Pulling Things Together

We are suggesting that the exercise of personal discretion in decision making by the police officer, in both his law enforcement and order maintenance functions, represents an exceedingly sensitive issue of police-community relations. One reason for this is simply the police power to restrain. Another reason is the lack of consensus on the question of police role; ambiguity in this basic consideration means that the police officer will be a loser no matter what his decisions, because he is asked to do the impossible.

Because ours is a government by law, vast effort has been made to minimize the opportunities for the system to be manipulated to the advantage of the tyrant. *Officially,* therefore, police officers are allowed little room for discretion, or, one might say, little professional autonomy. It is ticklish indeed for police officials to speak publicly of discretionary use of police power—often called *selective enforcement.* One reason for this is that the frank admission that police departments function constantly with discretionary use of police power as a basic assumption might be interpreted by the public as undermining government by law in a fundamental way and tantamount to a police state.

By law and in theory, the police are expected to enforce all laws, to arrest everyone they see committing an offense. Clearly, this is absurd. Everybody knows it is absurd, policemen perhaps most of all, but this seems to be some kind of secret. A police officer cannot function without considerable latitude in the exercise of personal discretion, but the several systems in which he finds himself often act as if it were not so. Departmental policies and regulations almost always ignore it. (After all, it is a secret!) In what they sometimes impose upon police departments, city councils and city executives act to *appear* to deny that police discretion is a fact. Prosecutors and the courts sometimes reprimand police officers for exercising discretion, even as they wink at their own more extensive use of the same prerogative.

In short, police discretion is inevitable partly because the police cannot do everything, partly because many laws require interpretation before they can be applied, and partly because the community will not tolerate full enforcement of all laws all the time. Wilson adds a striking thought:

> In almost every public organization, discretion is exercised—indeed, from the client's viewpoint, the problem arises out of how and whether it is exercised—but the police department has the special property (shared with a few other organizations) that within it discretion increases as one moves *down* the hierarchy. In many, if not most, large organizations, the lowest ranking members perform the most routinized tasks and discretion over how those tasks are to be performed increases with rank. . . . [But in police organizations] the lowest ranking police officer—the patrolman—has the greatest discretion, and thus his behavior is of greatest concern to the police administrator. [*Varieties of Police Behavior,* pp. 7–8]

Discretion and Police Role

This presents the central issue in a manner inviting further analysis. We have noted that autonomy in decision making is one of the marks of the professional. Wilson indicates that the line policeman has the greatest autonomy, at least theoretically. Reiss focuses on police officer autonomy in client relations and coerced decisions relating to the future of clients. The key question from the client's viewpoint is correctly identified by Wilson as that of *how* and *whether* autonomy (discretion) is exercised. This is the central problem in the relationship between police and community.

Herman Goldstein points out that the law enforcement function of the police officer is relatively structured, i.e., defined by statutes and court decisions. Therefore, it is somewhat controlled. Policy and supervision in the department may tighten these controls further. Even so, the patrolman is left with considerable discretion in his law enforcement function. The use of discretion is simply a sine qua non of the job, however much it may be denied officially. When one considers the policeman's order maintenance function, one sees even more room for the exercise of discretion. We earlier noted Goldstein's point that in carrying out his non-law enforcement duties, the policeman frequently uses the authority he has by virtue of his role in the criminal process. Goldstein adds:

> Thus, the ability of a police officer to resolve a dispute and to elim- inate a nuisance stems, in large measure, from widespread recognition of the fact that he has the authority to initiate criminal prosecutions. Indeed, in some situations, a police officer may actually exercise his authority—for example, by arresting an intoxicated person for safe keeping—even though he has no intention to initiate a criminal prose- cution. ["Police Response to Urban Crises," p. 418][1]

Now the issue begins to get more complicated. If, as more and more observers insist, the order maintenance and public service func- tions of the police are or ought to be paramount, it develops that the city patrolman spends most of his time in the least defined, least con- trolled aspects of his work. Here, the nature of responses is left almost entirely to the discretion of the individual. He has, in effect, the decision- making responsibility of a highly trained professional, but too often is ill-prepared to handle that responsibility professionally. Hence, the community calls for a tighter rein on his conduct, by one means or another, including civilian review boards and neighborhood control.

It may be, as some have speculated, that police departments insist on making their case for professionalism by stressing efficiency in law enforcement (a lesser part of their activity) partly because they sense a credibility gap were they to base their case on their performance in the order maintenance work that takes most of their time. Yet it is clearly in this part of their work that their cherished professionalism is continually tested. Law enforcement can be handled by technicians and specialists; it probably does not require professionals on the line, depending on how professionalism is defined. But order maintenance and peace keeping today call for officers possessing the autonomy of true professionals.

Some community groups clamor for tighter control of patrolmen, by both external and internal means, basically because patrolmen are not sufficiently professional to handle effectively what they spend most of their time doing. The question eventually becomes whether a sufficient number of professionalized patrolmen can become available to permit some relaxation of controls—and to that extent, encourage and gain public support for truly professional, autonomous police behavior in the principal function of maintaining peaceable, stable communities through conflict management.

Emphasis on Patrolmen

Our emphasis in this discussion is on the patrolman who, as Wilson observes, "is almost solely in charge of enforcing those laws that are the least precise, or most ambiguous (those dealing with disorderly conduct, for example); or whose application is most sensitive to the availability of scarce resources and the policies of the administrator (those governing traffic offenses, for example)" (*Varieties of Police Behavior,* p. 8). Wilson goes on to mention that detectives, on the other hand, are mainly concerned with more precisely defined and more serious crimes, after the crime has been committed. The patrolman is more apt (except for vice squad detectives) to deal with offenses about which there are sharp differences in public opinion. Detectives are not much concerned with peace keeping, nor (except in juvenile work) with crime prevention.

It is seldom possible to specify in advance adequate guidelines for the patrolman's intervention, or how he should handle a given situation, especially when maintaining order. He may be told what *not* to do, but it is much more difficult to specify what he *should* do. At roll call, sergeants or lieutenants may exhort "going by the book," but experienced patrolmen know that "you can't always go by what the book says," and that there are many situations about which "the book" has nothing to say (ibid., p. 66).

It is therefore apparent that even in cities where police departments are enthusiastic about going by the book, much of the police work on the street is performed at the discretion of the line officer. And this is the basis for considerable police-community relations tension and conflict. What is considered disorderly conduct or disturbing the peace, for example, varies widely by community and by neighborhood. In the absence of a complaint by a citizen, the police officer determines what is disturbing or disorderly.

There are two ancillary considerations. One is that many people believe in the myth that the police are the impartial enforcers of all the laws for all persons. It is when a police officer is thought to have substituted too much of his own discretion for the letter of the law that a demand arises for more controls. "In reality," Eleanor Harlow says,

> while no doubt clear-cut violation of the law by police does occur, in many cases personal discretion is unavoidable and the problem becomes not one of eliminating discretion (an impossible goal) but of improving the ability of those men exercising it to do so in accord with community norms and values. [*Problems in Police-Community Relations*]

The other consideration is that the police officer believes that he has been endowed with special authority to guard the community against immorality, impropriety, and sundry affronts (as he sees them) to public decency. Here we may recall our initial point: problems pertaining to discretionary use of police power revert in some measure to the ambiguity of the police role. Any attempt to change the way in which patrolmen exercise personal discretion must consider the extent to which they may be persuaded to act in accordance with rules set down in advance. And this, in turn, depends upon how the policeman's job is defined (Wilson, p. 11).

Discretion vs. Discrimination

Another extremely sensitive aspect of the discretionary use of police power comes to mind. If a patrolman relies so much upon personal judgment in dealing with people-related situations, it follows that his decisions are subject to his own personal prejudices, hang-ups, and predilections. In specific instances, it is a question of which of his decisions are legitimately discretionary or understandably "differential," and which of his decisions are patently unjust and discriminatory.

To be more concrete, Wilson states that "the patrolman believes, with considerable justification, that teenagers, Negroes, and lower income persons commit a disproportionate share of all reported crimes." Simply to be in one of these population categories makes one, statistically, more suspect than another. If, in addition, a person identified with one of these categories behaves unconventionally, the tab of *suspicious person* is promptly applied. The police would regard it as dereliction of their duty if they did not treat such persons with suspicion (to be suspicious is an important quality of the police subculture, as we shall see later), routinely question them on the street (stop and frisk!), and detain them for further interrogation if a crime has occurred in the area (Wilson, p. 40).

George Edwards, now a judge of the United States Court of Appeals, a former Detroit Police Commissioner and justice of the

Michigan Supreme Court,[2] has pointed to the situation of the previous
paragraph in what is commonly referred to as "curbstone justice" and
"alley court":

> . . . a few police officers are sincerely convinced that they are unable
> to maintain peace and order unless they are allowed to bolster their
> authority in the streets by use of a fist or billy when they feel it nec-
> essary. . . . "Alley court" is ordinarily used against minority groups.
> . . . It produces cries of "police brutality," and it deprives the police
> department of its most important weapon against crime—the support
> of the law-abiding populace residing in the core areas of our big cities.
> There are relatively few police officers who believe in "alley court";
> they cannot be allowed to perpetuate an utterly indefensible institu-
> tion. [*Police and the Community*]

Again, Beware of Oversimplification

Once more in this matter of discretion versus discrimination, however, it is easy to blame the police officer and to overlook the factors
that make his behavior more understandable, if not more acceptable.
For example, the class composition of the particular community influences police behavior. Wilson points out in "Dilemmas of Police Administration" that because relatively little public disorder occurs in a
middle-class suburban community, it is rarely necessary for the police
to intervene in situations of intense conflict:

> When the chief law enforcement problem involves crimes of stealth
> (burglary and larceny) rather than street crimes (assaults, robberies,
> muggings), the police need not practice aggressive preventive patrol
> or otherwise keep persons on the streets under close surveillance;
> accordingly, it is rare for a suburban resident walking the streets at
> night to feel he is being "harassed." . . . A socially homogeneous
> middle-class area provides the police with relatively unambiguous
> cues as to who should be regarded as a "suspicious person" and thus
> who should be made the object of police attention. [P. 411]

Wilson holds that harsh and unjust police treatment of blacks is
as much a problem of social class as it is a problem of prejudiced police
officers. He does not question that many police officers are racially
prejudiced. But according to Wilson, even if all police officers were free
of prejudice, blacks would still regard their treatment by the police as
unjust. The reason for this is that a high proportion of violent crime is
basically a lower class phenomenon.[3] Blacks (and some other minority
groups) are disproportionately lower class; therefore, a greater probability exists that blackness (or other visible signs of minority group
status) will trigger the suspicion of police officers. The same thing often
occurs with lower class whites. This is stereotypic reaction, but it is no
less real in understanding police behavior. Writing in *Justice Without*

Trial, Skolnick says that the "disposition to stereotype is an integral part of the policeman's world." It is typical bureaucratic behavior.

Actually the behavior we are discussing involves something more complex than police stereotypes. There are also *counterstereotypes,* held by members of minority groups toward police officers. We shall deal with this in a later chapter. A further point from Skolnick is illuminating:

> The policeman ... claims freedom from racial prejudice. He is, according to his own standards, not "biased," but merely truthful. Thus, the policeman would object ... to the term racial bias as a portrayal of his attitude on two grounds: it is not descriptive, but accusatory; and it singles out the policeman when in fact he represents a wider body of opinion. His most important objection, however, would be to the ambiguity of the term when applied to the issue of how he does his job. Whatever his personal preferences, and indeed their influence upon his work, the policeman sees himself as a man who extends justice evenhandedly, a factor which in itself exerts some control over his behavior. [Ibid.]

Discretion and the Pertinent Variables

We have suggested that the exercise of police discretion depends upon a number of variables, one of which is the character and disposition of the community. Another, of course, is administrative policy and the pattern of supervision in the particular department. Still another is the officer's personal assessment of gain or loss that he can anticipate from his intervention—for the suspect, the community, and the officer himself.[4]

It is a somewhat startling thought, but as the President's Crime Commission, in *Challenge of Crime,* stated, law enforcement policy is actually made by the patrolman on the street. The Commission referred to the criminal code, in practice, not as a set of specific instructions for police officers, but as "a more or less rough map of the territory in which policemen work. How an individual policeman moves around that territory depends largely on his personal discretion." The Commission said that a policeman is "an arbiter of social values." Our point regarding the officer's assessment of probable gains and losses as he determines manner of intervention in a particular situation is stated by the Commission in practical terms: the legal strength of the available evidence, the willingness of victims to press charges and of witnesses to testify, the temper of the community, and the time and information at the policeman's disposal.

The repeated reference to the temper of the community needs a brief comment. In a quite basic sense, no matter what the criminal code, the particular community or neighborhood governs largely the level and pattern of policing that will be tolerated. Banton implies this in his distinction between police authority and police power:

> ... the policeman obtains public cooperation, and enjoys public esteem because he enforces standards accepted by the community. This gives his role considerable moral authority ... It will be agreed that nothing is more important to police-public relations or to police efficiency generally than that the individual police officer should have good judgment in handling people. [*The Police Chief*, 1963]

Banton goes on to say that policemen are assisted by the courts in developing "good judgment" (". . . a good expression of the consensus of responsible opinion . . ."), and by the influence of his own private life wherein he becomes aware of what other citizens think of him.

Communities and neighborhoods vary considerably in what they expect of the police. In effect, modern social conditions prescribe significant differences in both law enforcement and order maintenance, depending upon where one looks. In practical police terms, this means that a single metropolitan police department may work at its job quite differently in different precincts or divisions. Some observers regard this practice as administratively unsound, but such opinions are rapidly being reassessed. There are implications in this for neighborhood control of the police (as of schools), with which we will deal in Chapter Fifteen.

The Question of Policy

The President's Crime Commission thought it "curious" that police administrators have seldom attempted to develop and articulate policies aimed at guiding the way policemen exercise their discretion on the street. There are policies and rules which deal extensively with many things, but, the Commission said in *Challenge of Crime*, many choices are not covered:

> What such manuals almost never discuss are the hard choices policemen must make every day: whether or not to break up a sidewalk gathering, whether or not to intervene in a domestic dispute, whether or not to silence a street-corner speaker, whether or not to stop and frisk, whether or not to arrest. Yet these decisions are the heart of police work. How they are made determines to a large degree the safety of the community, the attitude of the public toward the police and the substance of court rulings on police procedures. [P. 103]

The Commission recognized the difficulty of designing such policies. But it insisted that the job can and should be done, departmentally. The alternative is that the line officer will make policy—an administrative decision—by what he does or fails to do on the street. Adequate policy guidelines will still leave ample and inevitable latitude for "professional autonomy." A surgeon in a hospital is not seriously inhibited in his professional autonomy by the procedural regulations of the hospital for its staff. The policeman, as well as the public, is entitled to know in advance what police policy is. In tune with Banton's point, it helps to make police conduct more "predictable." Formulating and executing policy can also help to make the police more conscious of neighborhood problems, more "culturally sensitive," as the Crime Commission phrased it.

The Commission recommended more guidance[5]:

> Police departments should develop and enunciate policies that give police personnel specific guidance for the common situations requiring exercise of police discretion. Policies should cover such matters, among others, as the issuance of orders to citizens regarding their movements or activities, the handling of minor disputes, the safeguarding of the rights of free speech and assembly, the selection and use of investigative methods, and the decision whether or not to arrest in specific situations involving specific crimes. [Ibid., p. 104]

Police Accountability

Again, the theme of the Commission's recommendation is the need to *control* police discretion through legitimate authority, not to pretend to eliminate it. The courts control, to be sure, and—rather reluctantly—legislative bodies occasionally do it too. But there seems to be substantial support for the principle that it is best done mainly by police departments themselves. If controls are not satisfactorily handled internally by the departments, then they will be handled in one form or another by civil review. Reiss succinctly summarizes the issue:

> The issue of professionalization of the police is one of whether civic accountability will take the form of an inquiry into an individual's work within an organization, whether it will take the form of accountability of an occupational organization of police, or whether accountability rests with a local police organizational system headed by a chief as the "accountable officer." ["Professionalization," p. 222]

Reiss suggests that the central question is whether decision making by patrolmen is of a kind that is "open to professionalization." He asserts, as have others, that the tendency has been to professionalize police organization rather than police practice: the department rather than the individual. Thus the key question for Reiss: whether the patrolman's work requires truly professional competence. If it does, then the patrolman should have considerable professional autonomy in decision making.

Reiss concludes that the evidence is mixed. In the long run, he thinks that at least some aspects of police patrol work will require professionals, while other aspects of the work can be handled by technical, clerical, and maintenance personnel. He insists that such differentiation in occupational specialties is necessary if we are to cope realistically with the problem of police professionalism.

The Matter of Traffic Law Enforcement

The logic of such differentiation is illustrated by policemen specializing in traffic law enforcement. A study by John Gardiner concludes that traffic ticket writing is a bureaucratic, technical specialization.[6] It is a specialization in *work assignment,* not one of professionalism. Such decision making is technical, and subject to strict bureaucratic rules and review. Traffic enforcement officers themselves do not feel that they have autonomy; they see themselves simply as specialists. It is a job, not a profession.

Traffic law enforcement is, of course, only one branch of police work. Other branches constitute a better case for professionalism, with correspondingly greater latitude assumed in decision making. Yet traffic law enforcement is a fascinating area for the study of discretion. Preiss and Ehrlich devote a chapter in *Examination of Police Theory,* for example, to analyzing the similarities and differences in the way traffic enforcement officers in a state police agency on the one side, and the public on the other side, view such activities as enforcing the speed limit, and using unmarked cars, semi-marked cars, and radar. They found that both the officers and the public agreed on the goal: discreet enforcement. The problem was disagreement on the interpretation of *discreet.* Thus, the police-public relationship here was predicated on conflict:

> With high consensus on their goals, they clash not so much on the means to be employed but on how and by whom control is to be maintained over these means. The respective interests of both were mirrored openly not only in the claims they made for discretionary law enforcement but also in the *policeman's* concern for an uncontestable arrest and the *public's* appeal for consideration of intent. [P. 153]

Policemen dislike writing traffic tickets. They do not enjoy the public resentment and hostility that traffic law enforcement engenders. This is one reason why the so-called quota system was invented. Traffic patrol duty may be analyzed as adding to the social isolation of the policeman from the community. So may the automated processing of traffic tickets, which allows for no discretion (Skolnick, *Justice Without Trial,* pp. 55–56, 73–80).

Authorized and Unauthorized Discretion

The police-community interest in police discretion is broader, however, than simply with traffic law enforcement. Skolnick believes that the issue of police discretion is the epitome of the problem of order and legality. The basic issue is whether there should be, in his language, "a loosening or a tightening of restraints on the decisional latitude of the police" (p. 71). An important distinction should be made, he argues, between *delegated* and *unauthorized* discretion; most of the problems revolve around lack of clarity on what discretion is authorized —how much, under what circumstances, etc. Again, this confusion suggests the importance of control by policy guidelines and other means.

Even when the useful distinction between authorized and unauthorized discretion is applied, however, some difficulties remain. Complexities in decision making are still present even when discretion is clearly authorized; and they are compounded when discretion is unauthorized. Unauthorized discretion appears especially to be the issue in tense encounters where the police officer exercises discretion and his authority to do so is contested by citizens. This exemplifies Banton's distinction between authority and power. The latter is popularly expressed in the term *arbitrary police behavior*. For the street policeman, however, his uniform constitutes authority and, as Skolnick says, he is "usually willing to back up a challenge with all the force he can command," particularly if he perceives himself to be in danger. This is when the book is no help.

The element of perceived danger is generally believed to be an important conditioner of police behavior and the degree to which it may be viewed as arbitrary by some viewers. Banton discusses this point at some length; and Skolnick states that when the street policeman feels that he is in control of the situation, his behavior is apt to be more tempered. When he encounters hostility, he is tempted to make strong claims of authority, sometimes with frail, if any, legal justification (p. 90). Another influence upon his behavior is the history of possible prior relations with a particular type of suspect: the perceptual shorthand that Skolnick tabs the *symbolic assailant,* i.e., the person who uses gesture, language, and attire that the policeman has come to associate with violence and danger. The summarizing point is this: street police officers are influenced in their discretionary determinations, subtly but firmly, by perceived threats to their survival. Whether or not they are delegated authority, hence legal grounds, for a particular judgment seems to be of lesser importance.

Some of the problem has to do with the training of policemen. Prevailing training methods and content do not contribute much toward inculcating qualities of good judgment, prudence, and common sense in police recruits. What *is* taught along this line is often culture-bound; these are matters mainly of training techniques and methods. To illustrate the point simply, case analysis and various projective instructional techniques such as role playing, with the opportunity for considerable small group discussion, surpass straight lecture and tidy notebook keeping—if the educational objective is that of developing good judgment. Training method (or content) is not, of course, a panacea for the patrolman's problems in the street, where instant decisions are routinely required. But some approaches to training are surely more relevant to the real world than others.

Legal Grounds

The law, under our system, unquestionably allows and indeed encourages discretionary evaluation and judgment throughout the criminal justice process, by the policeman, the prosecutor, the courts, and the correctional factions. A cardinal principle is that of dealing with each offender as an individual. The misuse or usurpation of delegated power in the system is not uniquely a police problem; judges and prosecutors have been known to stretch their discretion to unconscionable extremes of either leniency or severity.

Judges and prosecutors enjoy the luxury of time in their deliberations. The street policeman frequently has no such advantage. For this chief reason, legal scholars have become increasingly concerned about what Skolnick terms "introducing arrangements to heighten the visibility of police discretion to permit its control by higher authority" (ibid., p. 71). Wayne LaFave is one of these legal analysts, author of *Arrest* one work in a series[7] dealing with the range of the criminal justice system, with a primary premise stated as follows:

> From the point of view of either the individual suspect or the community as a whole, the issue is not so much whether police are efficient, or whether the corrections process is effective, but whether the system of criminal justice administration in its entirety is sensible, fair, and consistent with the concepts of a democratic society. [In *Foreword*]

LaFave joins those who contend that there has been a traditional failure to recognize the existence and importance of police discretion. His discussion on the reasons for this attitude includes such matters as overly strict interpretation of substantive criminal law, the assumption that only legislative and judicial bodies should decide what conduct is criminal, concern and uncertainty whether the rule of law is adequately safeguarded by police exercise of discretion, and the assumption that prosecutors are more competent to exercise discretion than are the police.

LaFave observes that the question of police discretion has not received careful legislative attention. Evidence is considerable that legislative bodies either specifically deny police discretion, or consciously ignore it. Generally, appellate courts have not recognized the propriety of police discretion either. LaFave writes that where discretion is recognized as proper, courts have not indicated what standards ought to control the exercise of such discretion:

The exercise of discretion by the police, which seems inevitable in current criminal justice administration, continues unrecognized. In practice, policies to guide the individual officer in deciding whether to make an arrest are not formally developed within the police agency, and no sustained effort is made to subject existing practices to re-evaluation. [Pp. 81–82]

LaFave then analyzes the measures existing, and others that might be established, to acknowledge the need for police discretion while yet coping effectively with the hazards involved. These measures include wider public understanding of the issue (with correspondingly greater likelihood that the public will support the principle of necessary, though regulated, police discretion); the elevation of the level of police professional competence; improved intradepartmental review and control of discretion through administrative policy, supervision, and discipline; more use of criminal action against officers who abuse their discretionary power; and more use by defendants of their constitutional right to equal protection—which would provoke challenges of the criteria used by the police in invoking criminal process.

As we have noted, the issue of discretion exercised by an individual police officer on the street in dealing with an individual citizen incorporates the question of dealing differently with groups of citizens —for example, because of racial or cultural considerations, or social class differentials—and of dealing differently with various neighborhoods or areas in a city. The policy questions involved are extremely complex, no doubt one reason why they are seldom discussed. As LaFave says:

Notwithstanding the great importance and significance of these and other instances of discretionary enforcement, the police have failed to evaluate carefully such enforcement policies or even to acknowledge that such practices exist. Rather, most departments attempt to maintain the existing stereotype of the police as ministerial officers who enforce all of the laws, while they actually engage in a broad range of discretionary enforcement. [P. 494]

"It is understandable," LaFave continues:

that a police administrator may be willing to have the myth of full enforcement continue. Full enforcement is consistent with impartiality, while acknowledged discretionary enforcement may be challenged as unfair, inconsistent, or arbitrary. The image of full enforcement raises less of a public relations problem than does the image of the police agency as a formulator of enforcement policy. Finally, police training is an easier task in a department committed to the facade of full enforcement than in one in which it is assumed that police officers must share some responsibility for making decisions with important social implications. [Pp. 494, 495]

Jerome Hall is among the legal scholars (Joseph Goldstein of the Yale Law School is another) taking a more conservative stance on the subject of police discretion. Hall subscribes to the thesis that there must be a sharp demarcation between police and judicial functions, and that therefore the police should be strictly confined to so-called ministerial duties. It is not the police officer's job, he insists, to decide whether a person under arrest is guilty of a crime; the police arrest only "on reasonable ground." Nor is it the police job, he continues, to define or declare any general rules of law. And finally, he says, "whatever the police in our system may think the rules of law mean, their interpretations are not authoritative" (*Police and Law*).

However, most of those who have studied the issue of police discretion would probably agree with LaFave:

> There are ways of recognizing police discretion and of controlling its exercise. Legislatures can give explicit attention to police discretion and prescribe criteria to guide the exercise of that discretion. This is the trend at the sentencing and correctional stages of the criminal process, and there is no reason to believe that this sort of legislation would be less appropriate at the arrest stage. Courts can subject police discretion to the kind of review which sometimes occurs in regard to economic regulatory agencies.
>
> The development [LaFave continues] of an "administrative law" in the enforcement field is as important as it is in the field of economic regulation, but while the one has been given sustained attention, the other has been completely neglected. Greater legislative and judicial recognition of the importance of police discretion might in turn encourage police administrators to acknowledge its importance and attempt to devise methods of meaningful evaluation of existing policies.
>
> The obvious complexity of the task of dealing adequately with police discretion at the arrest stage makes it all the more important that a start be made immediately. [Pp. 494, 495]

The Gravity of the Issue

There is growing evidence of the gravity of the issue of police conduct in general, and of police discretion in particular. Stephen Wildstrom, former managing editor (1968–69) of *The Michigan Daily* at the University of Michigan, expressed an indicative view in an article in *The Nation* (April 21, 1969):

> American society will never be peaceful so long as significant portions of that society are systematically terrorized by the police. There will be no peace because, as blacks have learned and students are learning, the cops are above the law, and the only satisfying way to respond to their violence is with violence of one's own. And no matter what kind of pronouncements come down from the police brass, the terror

will continue as long as individual cops are immune from attempts by citizens to make them responsible for their acts. Despite the assertions of commissioners, chiefs and mayors, police departments have proved themselves to be at best unable, and at worst unwilling, to discipline their own. ["Mugged by the Sheriffs: An Anecdote"]

W. H. Ferry, a consultant to foundations and nonprofit institutions, is even stronger in stating his position. He contends that a police state already exists in our large cities, comparable to Hitler's Germany:

> The police are the effective rulers of blacktown today. Theirs is the paraphernalia of any police state: the procedures, the weapons, the psychological instruments of intimidation and repression. Theirs is the most important possession of all, the knowledge that they have the backing of white America. I invoke here the memory of the good Germans.[8]

Such views of police activities reveal the nature and degree of police-community separation, particularly when one considers the typical police officer's view side by side with that conveyed in the quotations just given. This brings us back to Skolnick's question considered earlier: what are the conditions under which police, as authorities, may be threatened? William Westley was one of the first to raise this question about the police, when he studied the conditions under which the police tend to become violent ("Violence and the Police").[9] We have already discussed the symbolic assailant, how the policeman responds to what he construes as disrespect for and attacks on his authority, "handling the situation," saving face, "not taking any crap," etc.

We are suggesting values that are important in the working class backgrounds of many police officers. As Westley said, when physical force *is* used, it is often justified by officers as a way of dealing with disrespect for the police. As police officers perceive more and more challenge to their authority, there is an increasing tendency for the police to close ranks, to shore up their own internal solidarity, and to defend themselves against outside influences—what Pfiffner calls guild protectionism.

Both Westley and William Kephart found in their research that a negative attitude toward blacks was a common norm among white police officers. Kephart observed that the higher the actual rate of black arrests in a district, the higher was the degree of overestimation of that rate by white policemen in that district (*Racial Factors and Urban Law Enforcement*).

The point here is one Skolnick makes:

> The Negro population is no longer so cowed as it once was, unfortunately for the patrol police. . . . When a policeman pushes a man who knows his rights, he receives an understandably hostile response.

In an earlier period (as Westley found), the police used outright violence to maintain respect. It is now more difficult for them ... to maintain control through these techniques. ... But it is not color that is necessarily the determining factor. ... When a citizen (read: *any* citizen) makes a policeman sweat to take him into custody, he has created the situation most apt to lead to police indignation and anger. [*Justice Without Trial*]

Arthur Niederhofer, a retired New York City police officer, vividly portrays the policeman's approach to a situation in terms of the vital importance of "handling his beat" (*Behind the Shield*). We referred earlier to policemen pleading that "you can't always go by the book." Showing "who is boss" appears to be very high on the list of values that street policemen hold most sacred. As such, it is a consideration of great weight in understanding what the police officer calls the *practicalities* of his job, with particular relevance in understanding his exercise of discretion.

Summing Up

Our discussion has moved into the intriguing matter of the self-image of the police officer, inevitably, because it is closely related to questions of police role, police professionalism (it is said that a professional police officer is first of all an officer who *sees himself* as a professional), and into the difficult question of discretionary use of police power. The self-image of the police officer will be our focus as we begin Part Two.

How to conclude on the matter of discretion? We may say that the street patrolman necessarily exercises discretion, both in keeping order and in suppressing crime. Herman Goldstein has neatly summarized the reasons why discretion must be exercised, the reasons why the exercise of discretion is not openly and freely acknowledged, and the advantages inherent in a policy of publicly acknowledging the exercise of discretion (*Public Administration Review,* September 1963).

In managing conflict, the patrolman's task is to maintain civic peace amidst circumstances in which various parties often disagree on what constitutes a fair settlement. In these circumstances, the officer is frequently aware of hostility toward him, of challenges to his authority as represented by disrespect, and of the ever-present danger of violence in which his own survival may be at stake. He is all out to control the situation by whatever means he deems necessary, often without too much attention to its by-the-book legality.

In suppressing crime, the officer is likely to base judgments about persons on their appearance, their attitude, the possible history of past relations, and stereotypic images of "symbolic assailants" and "suspicious persons." Often such judgments are based upon questionable authority (for instance, authority to question or to search suspects), and thus create an ambiguous and oftentimes controversial basis for his actions, in point of departmental policy (often lacking), or of law (often nondirective).

As James Q. Wilson concludes:

> In any particular case, the patrolman may act improperly by abusing or exceeding his authority, making arrests or street stops on the basis of personal prejudice or ill-temper, or handling a situation differently from the way the administrator or the mayor might handle it. But to say that in a given case the observer or the community could have prescribed a better course of action is not to say that a better course of action, applicable to all or most situations, could be prescribed generally and in advance. Put another way, the possibility of deciding in a particular instance that the police behaved wrongly does not mean that one can formulate a meaningful policy for how the police should behave in all cases. [*Varieties of Police Behavior,* p. 278]

Herman Goldstein provides an appropriate sequel:

> The police have sought professional status. But professional status does not normally accrue to individuals performing ministerial functions. One of the marks of a true profession is the inherent need for making value judgments and for exercising discretion based upon professional competence. To deny that discretion is exercised gives support to those citizens who maintain that the job of a police officer is a simple one, that it is not worthy of professional status. By acknowledging the discretionary role the police do fulfill, the drive toward a higher degree of respect and recognition for law enforcement personnel is given impetus. ["Full Enforcement vs. Police Discretion," p. 391]

Notes to Chapter Five

1. A penetrating analysis of police discretion and the role of the police and the law in the decision to arrest, including the use of arrest for purposes other than prosecution, is provided by Wayne R. LaFave in *Arrest: The Decision to Take a Suspect Into Custody.*

2. George C. Edwards, "Police and the Community—A Judicial View." See also by the same author, *Police on the Urban Frontier.*

3. For documentation of this point see, for example, Marvin E. Wolfgang, *Crimes of Violence,* a report to the President's Crime Commission.

4. James Q. Wilson has devised a helpful chart with these and other important variables, which appears in Study 8, Part I, *The Police and the Community: Studies,* by Radelet and Reed.

5. For an interesting case study of the adaptation of a metropolitan police department to community *mores* and temper, see "Deviance and Democracy in San Francisco," *Transaction,* April 1970. See also Egon Bittner, "The Police on Skid-Row."

6. The principle enunciated in this recommendation by the President's Commission is more thoroughly analyzed in Chap. 2 of its *Task Force Report: The Police.*

7. John A. Gardiner, "Police Discretion: The Case of Traffic Law Enforcement." Unpublished Ph.D. dissertation, Harvard University, 1966.

8. Wayne R. LaFave, *Arrest.* See also Sanford H. Kadish, "Legal Norm and Discretion in the Police and Sentencing Processes"; Joseph Goldstein, "Police Discretion Not to Invoke the Criminal Process"; Edward J. Barrett, "Police Practices and the Law."

9. W. H. Ferry, "The Police State, American Mode," Starr King Commencement Speech, Unitarian Church of Berkeley, California, October 10, 1969.

10. Also Westley's unpublished Ph.D. dissertation, "The Police: A Sociological Study of Law, Custom, and Morality," University of Chicago, Department of Sociology, 1951.

Summary of Part One

Our main objective in Part One has been to lay a foundation for the study of police-community relations. We began by reviewing the historical background. We next discussed its scope through various concepts. Then we analyzed three interrelated, fundamental issues that must be considered in order to gain an understanding of current problems of police-community relations:

1. The question of police role.
2. The question of police professionalism.
3. The question of discretionary use of police power.

The Anglo-Saxon background of English and American policing was based on the principle of self-policing, with every citizen expected to do police work. The people were the police, and the police were the people. When the idea of an organized metropolitan police force appeared in the early nineteenth century, British parliament was forthrightly opposed to it on the ground that it threatened liberty. But the so-called Peelers came into being, and their influence soon became evident even in the United States. Gradually, however, the important principle of self-policing—of widespread participation by private citizens in police work—faded. Today, the isolation of the police from the community has reached a serious stage in the United States.

In democratic society, the conduct of the policeman is ideally the living expression of the rule of law, with all its values and potentialities. Democratic law is *ethical* law, and this must be stressed in the training of all policemen. If the policeman's behavior conforms with the values of this system, he becomes the most important official in its hierarchy.

The policeman of today seems to be more in the public eye than in the past. Social change, particularly its effect on people-to-people relations, broadly explains this phenomenon to which the police have responded both negatively and positively. Among evidences of positive response has been the development during the past thirty years of police leadership in community relations.

Specialized police training in community relations dates back to the 1940s. Institutes on police and community relations were initiated in the 1950s, and many varied projects and programs were undertaken throughout the country in the ensuing years. Dramatization of the deficiencies of these programs in the later 1960s produced greater concern for the effects of such programs on the attitudes and behavior of both police and nonpolice participants.

The idea of police-community relations has been defined many different ways. A sound conception views it as a combination of public relations, community service, and community participation. The community participation aspect uses interprofessional or teamwork approaches to solving community problems: for example, crime prevention through some form of combined efforts of police and community. The appropriate emphasis in police-community relations programs is *preventive,* with both crime and civic disorder. The concept is also increasingly systemic in its scope, recognizing that the community relations problems of the police are in large part problems of the entire criminal justice and governmental systems. Thus, it follows that police problems must be studied in systemic perspective.

Assuming that there is, theoretically at least, a certain ideal relationship between police and community, it would clearly depend upon mutual expectations: what should the community expect from the police? what should the police expect from the community? The question of the role of the police in today's society is, therefore, a central consideration in effecting an ideal relationship of police and community.

In broad terms, the police have two primary and complementary functions: (a) law enforcement, and (b) order maintenance and social service. In the early years of organized American policing, the emphasis was placed upon the second function, coinciding with the British model. Twentieth century American policing, however, has moved toward emphasizing law enforcement and crime suppression. With the two main roles clearly interrelated, and every police department expected to work at both, the present predicament regarding the role of the police is basically a question of *emphasis:* which function is or ought to be paramount? The two roles place demands upon the police that are conflicting and literally impossible for them to fulfill, because the demands (expectations) require conflicting responses. In the terms of sociological role theory, it is a classic case of role conflict and role ambiguity.

The essence of the role hang-up lies in the absence of general agreement between police and socially heterogeneous communities on what should be stressed in police work, and how it should be carried out. Techniques that may conceivably result in suppressing crime are at times techniques that may conceivably cause civic tension and turmoil. Some people want crime suppressed even at some cost in civil liberties; others want civil liberties protected even at some cost in crime.

Where one stands on this teeter-totter—for instance, as a police administrator—will strongly influence such matters as departmental organization, operational strategies and tactics, recruitment standards for policemen, training methods for police recruits, and every other significant facet of the manner in which a given police agency handles its responsibilities. Both traditionalist and progressive positions appear on the role question, in and out of police departments, and the dispute is currently lost in rhetoric. Hence, we see one more example of contemporary political and social groups drawing away from each other instead of seeking to reconcile their views through reasoned communication. There is, in effect, a combative encounter of opposing political and occupational value systems.

Questions hinging directly on the role perplexity concern the meaning of police professionalism, how desirable a goal professionalism is, and how it may be achieved. If, for example, the primary duty of the police is to suppress crime through organization for law enforcement, the model of a professional police agency will stress managerial and operational efficiency. If, on the other hand, the primary police responsibility is seen as peace keeping and conflict management, the model of a professional police agency will underline the importance of humanistic values. The problem of police professionalism will not be resolved until that of the police role is resolved and, in turn, so also will the enigma of police-community relations remain unresolved. This is so because the key to police professionalism lies in client relationships with the police, and in public attitudes (expectations) toward the police.

This point is well illustrated in the matter of discretionary use of police power. The desirable relationship of order and freedom, of authority and liberty, is routinely tested in the decisions of the street patrolman. Again, there is a dilemma in this, a crucially important extension into the realm of practical police work of the role and professionalism puzzles. So intense is this philosophical conflict that the police refrain from publicly acknowledging that they exercise discretion—

indeed that it is impossible to conceive of their work without it—for fear that they would not be supported in the discretionary principle, fearful, in fact, they might even be accused of undermining the system.

The issue is complex, but comes down to this: modern police work makes discretion in the exercise of police power inevitable and, in fact, desirable. This idea harmonizes with the assertion that street patrol duty in our cities requires genuine professional competence, and professionals must have a certain amount of professional autonomy, albeit not without some departmental guidelines and controls. But the difficulty is that because most patrolmen today lack this professional competence, their appropriate authority is too often misused.

In the recent move to shift police work to a professional level, more attention has been devoted to professionalizing police organizations than to professionalizing police practices. Discretion and discrimination are frequently confused. Police power is commonly imposed arbitrarily, especially where the police officer feels that his authority is challenged or that his life is endangered by "suspicious persons" or "symbolic assailants."

Some guidelines are essential, therefore, in controlling police behavior, even when the patrolman is assumed to be a full-fledged professional. Legislatures and courts have some responsibility in providing such controls, but most of it should be provided by departmental policies, supervision, and discipline. The growing concern that it is already very late for this action has been reflected in agitation for establishment of various forms of external control. One way or another, the police must be held accountable to the community for what they do and how they do it. This means to *all* the community, for the police must be the police of all the people.

Part Two

Psychological Considerations

Chapter Six

The Self-Image
of the
Police Officer

Much of what is being said and written today about the police reflects public concern. The police are being called upon to cope simultaneously with antiwar demonstrations, with the youth revolution, with "The Movement" in race relations and civil rights, and with what is widely regarded as unprecedented crime. The police are blamed for what is wrong in each of these stressful areas, by reason of either overacting or underacting. In view of popular generalizations, usually vituperative, regarding their activities, police officers must have developed a certain hardiness, else we would have few policemen remaining in our big cities. There are serious recruiting problems, and not many officers choose to remain in police service beyond retirement age when circumstances allow them a choice.

The Morale Problem

The situation commonly referred to as the "morale problem" of the police is as variously defined as is police professionalism, with a tendency to settle for rather superficial explanations; for example, that the police morale problem is largely a matter of money. Accordingly, improved police salaries and pension benefits are seen as the answer. There is certainly no opposition here to improvement of the financial security of policemen. But, would that the problem were so simple!

To explore the morale problem requires some analysis of the psychological dynamics of police work, with special focus on the individual police officer. Morale pertains to mental and emotional attitudes of an individual about the functions or tasks expected of him by his group—the group to which he is expected to be loyal. It is a state of well-being that stems from a sense of purpose and confidence in the future. It is esprit de corps, rooted in role conception, role performance, and role satisfaction. Morale is intimately related to self-respect which, in turn, contributes to a positive self-image.

Simply to define in these terms what morale means is to provide a clue to the particular problem of the police officer. If morale is related to role, and if police work is a classic example of role conflict and role ambiguity, it follows that policemen must have some kind of self-image problem. Our purpose in this chapter is to discuss this hypothesis.

The Question of Personal Identity

How does a person learn who he is? Psychologists tell us that each of us discovers a large part of the answer to this question in the feedback he gets from the way others behave toward him. To illustrate this point, we may say that people harbor certain attitudes regarding what a man does—his job or calling. This is basically what is meant by *ascribed status*. Some jobs have high status, others low status, depending upon such attitudes. The status of our job or occupation is an important factor in the satisfaction we get from it, but it is, of course, not the only factor.

What a person does for a living is one basis of feedback for his self-image, for learning who he is and how he rates, so to speak, in the status hierarchy of a given society—sometimes called the pecking order. The feedback process was referred to years ago as "the looking glass self" by University of Michigan sociologist Charles H. Cooley. It means simply that each of us governs his actions according to the estimate he believes others are making of him—what we think others think of us. This may be tabbed the *social self*. One discovers who he is by seeing himself reflected in the actions of others toward him.

We have said that our occupation is one source of personal identity. Our possessions, where we live, what we do for recreation, what we wear, are others. It is basically the attitudes and behavior of people toward us that provide the feedback. "Mirror, mirror on the wall," said the witch in the fairy tale, "who's the fairest of them all?" She expected to be told that she was beautiful, which made her very much like the rest of us. We expect the mirror to give us the answer we want (Mildred Peters, "A Look at Ourselves," pp. 53ff). Furthermore, we tend to screen or filter the information that comes to us in the feedback process, to be selective in what we perceive and accept about ourselves. We tend to see and accept what is pleasant about ourselves and provides a "good" image, to reject what is "bad," and often to project on others what we cannot accept in ourselves. Some psychologists say that the closer our self-image is to the image that most people hold of us, the nearer we are to good mental health. The process is ideally one of becoming increasingly mature.

The Socialization Process in Childhood

What we are describing is the essence of socialization, which begins in infancy. The helpless infant identifies with the adults around him for elementary need satisfaction. In time, the child begins to see himself through the eyes of these adults. Through their behavior toward him he develops self-confidence and self-respect—or the opposite. His actions are strongly affected by the picture he has of himself. As Oberlin College sociologist J. Milton Yinger[1] puts it:

> Environments that fill a child with self-doubt and even self-hatred lay the basis for later attacks on one's self, in the form of alcoholism, mental illness, or irresponsibility—or attacks on the community, in the form of crime and disregard of the interests of others.

Davis and Havighurst, in *Father of the Man,* express the idea as follows:

> If a child is to develop an effective conscience, two conditions should be met. First, the child should receive complete *love* from his parents, or from his parent-substitutes; second, he should receive socially appropriate *prohibitions* from them. The love-relationship seems to be necessary as a basis for the best type of identification. The prohibitions are necessary in order that the child may take into himself a warning and punishing voice. Thus, parents who never punish their children (either by corporal punishment or by withdrawing affection from them) would not be able to instill a warning, punishing conscience in them. On the other hand, parents who never show affection to their children would not instill a conscience in them either, *no matter how much they punished them,* because their children would not love them enough to want to be good.

Wayne State University educational psychologist Mildred Peters adds this point:

> It is a well known fact that children and adults who find it hard to relate to others, or who are unwilling to show respect for the rights of others, are people who have either been denied love returns for giving up instinctual demands, or they are people who have never been helped to bear frustration. [P. 55]

Conscience and self-respect, then, are basic requirements in sound personality development. Needless to say, many children grow up without either. Clear, consistent standards of behavior are not provided by parents or by "significant others"; neither is supportive affection. If a child is to be a successful adult, he needs models of successful adults with whom to identify. This is expressed, for example, in the collecting of baseball cards. Boys need adult male models to teach them what it is to be a man. When such models are not available, crude and inadequate definitions of mankind are created, which may result in painful answers to the question, who am I? And as Yinger points out, there is a self-perpetuating quality to this kind of pattern; children who have had such a problem of identity become the parents of another generation for whom they cannot supply the proper balance of affection and discipline.

The most difficult task in growing up is in coming to terms with one's self, of learning who one is, what one can do, and how one stands in relation to others. For those in seriously disadvantaged environments, this task is especially difficult. Deeply insecure, self-hating and frustrated, they often invent a cultural world of their own, a world in which they can be dominant and set the standards. Rohrer and Edmonson refer to this as the world of the gang, which is not necessarily a criminal group, but one in which youngsters try to salvage some sense of dignity and control. They search for the feeling that they are "somebody," at least to each other. The behavior is described in this way:

> . . . The gang demands aggressive independence, a touchy and exaggerated virility, and a deep, protective secrecy. Acceptance by the gang provides almost the only source of security for its members, but such acceptance is conditional upon continual proof that it is merited, and this proof can only be furnished through physical aggressiveness, a restless demonstration of sexual prowess, and a symbolic execution of those illegal deeds that a "sissy" would not perform. These activities victimize women, but it would seem that they are not specifically directed toward women. Rather the enemy of the gang is the world of people (especially men) too unmanly for survival in what has often been described as a social jungle. [Rohrer and Edmonson, *Eighth Generation,* p. 160]

The "us kids" groups of little boys may become the gangs of older boys, a seemingly tough and masculine answer to the question, what is a man and the related question, who am I? The exaggerated assertions of manliness are often a camouflage for doubts.

Multiple Roles, Multiple Selves

All of us belong to many groups, and each group judges us by different standards. The average adult plays a number of social roles in the course of a day, each involving a pattern of conduct that a person occupying a specific position in society is expected to follow. Being a parent, for example, is a social role. A person may be a male, a husband, a father, a police officer, a student or teacher, a PTA officer, and a scoutmaster, and be active in sundry religious or civic organizations.

Each involves a social role. Each implies a certain pattern of socially prescribed behavior. As we have seen, role behavior may involve conflict or ambiguity when standards are not clear or consistent. Our primary example was in the matter of discretionary use of police power.

Multiple social roles mean, in effect, multiple selves. Thus, from adolescence onward, a person faces the problem of integrating the several different selves required by different and sometimes conflicting roles. Our perceptions of self depend on the context, varying somewhat with what has gone before and who we have been thinking of or dealing with, as well as the immediate problem or situation. Another point worth noting is that we encounter and relate to different people in the various social roles we play. Some people see us exclusively in a certain role, others in another role. Therefore, it is possible that the feedback will vary, so that a person may receive more positive feedback in one role than he does in another. In short, he may be viewed as a more successful husband or father than he is a police officer or a teacher, or vice versa.

In the complex of the many selves of the individual, each one may be far from simple. A rapid shift in roles requires quick changes in habits (roles standardize behavior) and often in attitudes and values as well. Since roles tend to become self, adjustments to the requirements of changed roles are often difficult. Role changes frequently involve frustrations, nowadays called hang-ups, as experienced by civilians becoming soldiers or by soldiers becoming civilians. Our behavior patterns in dealing with frustrations are identified in the language of psychologists by such terms as compensation, rationalization, projection, displacement, repression, sublimation, and regression. We shall have more to say about some of these. The point of emphasis here is that all these patterns are relevant in a consideration of learning to live with one's self, that is, in *personality integration*. The matters we have touched on relate to our initial question about the morale problem of the police.

Yinger makes an additional point:

> A successful adult is often required to postpone many satisfactions. He has learned that denying an immediate desire may contribute to greater satisfactions later.... Now this ability to postpone is not born in a child; it is learned by the way he is treated. If to miss the opportunity for an immediate pleasure carried no promise of later rewards, only a foolish child would skip the immediate pleasure. The kind of discipline that becomes an important part of a person's character is learned in childhood when his small capacities to postpone pleasure ... are rewarded by praise and by a recognition that he is growing up. If children are simply disregarded in this matter, they will take the immediate pleasure. We should scarcely be surprised when, as adults, they are irresponsible with regard to their jobs, their families, their communities.

The Policeman's Self-Image

With the above as a cursory review of some relevant general considerations pertaining to the self-image, our focus now becomes the self-image of the police officer.

In a recent national survey conducted by the International Association of Chiefs of Police, police officers from various departments, ranging in rank from patrolman to inspector, were asked a series of questions as to how they saw themselves and their job (Watson and Sterling, *Police and Their Opinions*). Following are some of the questions and responses:

	Percent answering "yes"
Do you feel tense and "under pressure" during duty hours?	47%
Do you find your home life made difficult by annoyances, irritations, and aggravations which are a "hangover" from your job?	41%
Is your physical condition suffering or deteriorating from duty requirements?	32%
Is the police "image" favorable in your community as far as you can determine?	40%
Do you feel that officers in your department are just "cogs in a big machine"?	60%

It may be added that 90 percent of the same officers answered yes to the question, "Do you plan to make law enforcement your life career?"; 66 percent said that the dangerous aspects of police work seldom worried them. Two out of three believe that punishment is effective in crime control. Four out of five think that punishment for crime ought to be more severe. Seven out of ten think that the police today do not have enough authority. Only 55 percent think that the police should be concerned with social problems such as education, jobs, and housing discrimination. But 90 percent believe that the police should be involved in recreation programs for youth. They are accustomed to the latter concept.

In their written comments on the same questionnaires, about one out of three officers complained about one aspect or another of their work, some with marked bitterness and defensiveness. Yet only a few admitted occasional shame at being a police officer. Many revealed characteristics of a persecuted minority: hypersensitivity, the feeling that everyone is against them, cynical despair, displaced aggression, etc. When asked why they continue as police officers, the main reasons given were:

- The position offers good fringe benefits other than salary.
- It is an interesting job.

- It's steady work; I don't have to worry about layoffs, strikes, plant shut downs, etc.

- I'm trapped. I'd quit if I didn't have so much time invested; I have to go on now until I retire.

On the whole, these officers seem to value their job for its security, but many do not think that it rates very highly in affording them social status.

Reasons for Becoming a Policeman

Why does one become a policeman in the first place? The IACP survey shows that 46 percent of white policemen, 52 percent of black policemen, and 54 percent of policewomen came into police work almost by accident; they had tried several jobs and finally settled on police work. A substantial majority stated that the job turned out to be different from what they anticipated. An even larger proportion (approximately 80 percent) had given little or no thought to leaving police service; however, the higher the educational level of the respondents, the larger was the percentage who had thought about leaving.

The same survey revealed that police officers consider "too much paper work" and "not enough chance for advancement" as their two main job-related problems, followed by such things as "ineffective supervision," "many officers don't know what they are doing," and "not enough freedom of judgment." As to personal problems, 57 percent said "not enough pay"; 16 percent said "little respect shown by others for my profession"; and 11 percent cited "inability to relax at home; can't leave the job behind." Other responses showed 47 percent of the officers citing the manpower shortage as the most pressing problem facing their department. Only 14 percent thought the most pressing problem was lack of understanding and support by citizens. These are not mutually exclusive categories.

For an article that appeared in *The Atlantic Monthly,* Patricia Lynden asked a number of New York City policemen why they joined the force. Their responses are illuminating, as given in the following selections:

... a year ago, I was a cop-hater. I decided to try to find out. I was a beatnik when I came on. It's a noble profession. I'd rather have it in my hands than someone else's.

... I always wanted to become a cop. It was a matter of getting up some Saturday morning and taking the test. ... I came to the police force because I felt I could better myself here monetarily and social-wise.

... I really don't know why I came on. I used to work for Chase-Manhattan, and I was about to become head teller. The money was better here. I never was a cop-hater.

...I have no desire to be other than what I am. ...I was a pro baseball player. Then I went into the Marine Corps. I was out in California. I never had any bad or superstitious attitudes toward the police. They weren't the bogeyman to me. [The police in California] have an *esprit de corps*. On being discharged [from the Marines], we got a recruitment lecture from the Los Angeles Police Department. I was impressed.

...Why did I become a cop? I don't actually know. I used to take all the city tests as a hobby. I was a butcher by trade. In 1957 I had taken the test for policeman, and I got called in November, 1958. I didn't really want to become a policeman, but I was working all hours as a butcher. I thought that every city job was a form of retirement. When I went on, I had every intention of taking it easy. I found out my first day at the academy that it wasn't an easy job, but I like it. ...I think it's the greatest work a person could go into. ...I get a lot of personal satisfaction from it. ["Why I'm a Cop: Interviews"]

It is not known whether these views are representative of police officers in general. But they do provide some insight into the range of motivation for entering police service, from "I always wanted to be a police officer," to "I really don't know why I came on."

Actually, the reasons why some policemen join the force are somewhat more complicated. James Q. Wilson surveyed (1960–61) all the sergeants of one large American police department to secure data illustrating the continuing importance of police careers to second-generation Irish.[2] He found several reasons for this. One was the possibility that the Irish patrolman was the beneficiary of a promotional system that had been biased in his favor. At least the non-Irish respondents saw it that way—an interesting correlation between perceived unfairness and ethnicity. However, there was no evidence that such a bias actually existed in the promotional system.

Another factor disclosed in the study was that the second-generation Irish sergeant was more likely than the non-Irish sergeant to come from a police family, to associate mainly with other police officers, and to have a police officer as his closest friend. In short, the son of the Irish immigrant was more likely than the son of the European immigrant or native American to have a family background and a set of attitudes predisposing him toward a police career. Incidentally, over 75 percent of all the sergeants felt that financial security was the principal incentive *for other officers* to have joined the force; when asked what the chief incentive was *for themselves*, the proportion mentioning security was much lower.

In his study of the black policeman, *Black in Blue*, Nicholas Alex considers the questions of why blacks enter police work, and why they stay in it once they join. His findings indicate that most black policemen in New York City applied for police work only as one possibility among other, similar civil service jobs. As Alex puts it, "their goal was not police work as such but the benefits of a civil service job." He continues:

> For those Negroes whose aims are to enter the mainstream of American society and to move up from predominantly lower-class positions, civil service is a crucially important path. . . . to gain economic mobility, they selected a relatively low prestige job that had little intrinsic meaning for them. . . . Police work was actually considered an occupational area to avoid because it was thought of as a routine job, menial and onerous, limited in scope for the individual with talent and imagination, and the "butt of everybody's problems." [Pp. 34, 35]

We should note that both white and black police officers, in several studies, responded to the question of why they joined the police force in ways that suggested that their choice contributed to self-hatred, for selecting an unsatisfying job because there was no available alternative. This implicit incongruency of goals between officer and department, and the resultant inevitable frustrations, has an obvious bearing on the question of morale. In the case of the black officer, this problem may be especially complicated. Where the "Movement" in racial justice makes a claim on his conscience as a black man who happens to be a policeman, there is additional stress between his occupational role and the pressures put on him to join in the "rebellion against The Man." As Alex observes, the problem is one of double marginality, in classic sociological terms.

While most of the black police interviewed in Alex's study signed up for the reasons given, it should be noted that approximately 30 percent chose the police occupation specifically, and not merely for economic reasons. They *wanted* to be police officers, because they thought police work promised more prestige than other jobs they had had, and because it "offered the potential of satisfying their personal interests in youth, community work, and law." They felt that police work had brought them status and mobility, and they identified strongly with its high ideals. For the *civil-service-oriented* black policeman, staying in police work is largely a matter of finding no alternative paying as well. For the *police-oriented* black policeman, on the other hand, staying in is a kind of calling, with a sense of mission (*Black in Blue,* p. 52).

Securing Good Men for Police Work

One school of thought maintains that there is no gain in securing "good men" (whatever that may mean) for police work, because after a few years of experience in the field, "they become like all the rest of them." That is to say, the role shapes the self, as opposed to the position that a relatively immutable self shapes the role. Those taking the latter position would argue that high quality personnel (in terms of initial selection) will substantially help to improve police service.

James Sterling has given some attention to this conflict of views in his study *Changes in Role Concepts of Police Officers During Recruit Training.* His research suggests that experienced policemen expect that police experience will bring about some change in police recruits as persons. As Sterling observes, "where the expectation for change is widely perceived, conditions are favorable for change." His hypothesis is that "subjects who did not feel that others held the expectation that police experience will change them will themselves show less change over time . . ." This is significant for those interested in occupational socialization, since one of its goals—for the police recruit—is an awareness of and sensitivity to the expectations of role-related reference groups. In Sterling's terms:

> Socialization for the police recruit includes both the adoption of normative modes of police behavior and the extinction of certain other behaviors which were appropriate for his previous civilian roles. In learning the new role, the police recruit undertakes a complex process of learning which includes more than just knowledge and skills. He will also learn a system of attitudes, beliefs, perceptions and values. The most important learning related to perception concerns the identification of role relevant reference groups and a sensitivity to their expectations and evaluations.

John McNamara was interested in similar questions in his study of the backgrounds and training of New York City police department recruits ("Uncertainties in Police Work."). He describes the orientation of many police training programs and the strong influence these programs may have on individuals, whether or not they are "good men" when recruited. Following are some of his summarizing conclusions:

> In attempting to develop an *esprit de corps,* the academy seems not to have been successful in immunizing patrolmen against experiencing a strong feeling that their work is one that rates quite low in prestige in the eyes of the public. At the same time, the emphasis on police professionalization in recruit training probably increases the patrolman's perception of the discrepancy between the socioeconomic status that officers should have and the status they actually have. . . . Although it is difficult to conceive of a training program that would prepare recruits effectively for immersion in the belief system about supervision and use of punitive tactics by supervisors and the administration, the academy experiences of the recruits were likely to create a receptivity to the belief that supervisors often took punitive actions. [P. 250]

In the same vein (and pertinent to certain of our considerations in preceding chapters), McNamara continues:

Perhaps our most significant inference . . . is that a training program for police recruits faces two major dilemmas in preparing recruits for their later duties in the field. The first involves the question of whether to emphasize training strategies aimed at the development of self-directed and autonomous personnel, or to emphasize strategies aimed at developing personnel over whom the organization can easily exercise control. It appears that the second strategy is the one most often emphasized.

The second dilemma is that involving the inconsistencies between what the academy considers ideal practices in police work and what the majority of men in the field consider to be the customary and perhaps more practical procedures in the field. The training program appears to emphasize the former approach. [P. 251]

Bruce Olson found, in his study "The City Policeman: Inner- or Other-Directed?" conducted in one midwestern police department, that respondents in each of five police ranks rated "other directed" traits as more important than "inner directed" traits (using David Reisman's categories) in job success for patrolmen. This would be surprising to those expecting emphasis on such "inner directed" qualities as forceful-ness, imagination, independence, self-confidence, and decisiveness, as compared with "other directed" qualities of cooperation, adaptability, caution, agreeableness, and tact. But the results of Olson's research were not easy to reconcile. For example, the higher ranking officers rated imag-ination nearly twice as high as the lower ranking officers, but the same higher ranking respondents rated independence very low.

Seeing Oneself as a Professional

We have observed that getting "good men" to enter the police field is not the whole story in achieving professionalism. It was sug-gested that good men must be committed to basic structural, functional, and systemic change, if they are to make a real difference. The same thought may now be repeated regarding morale problems in police work. In fact, the goal is essentially the same: professionalism in police work and a better self-image (more self-respect, improved morale, etc.) are parallel concepts. While more than attitude is involved in the making of a professional, believing deeply that one is a professional and striving to behave in a manner consistent with a professional model are surely important in making an earnest effort toward that objective.

Also important are elements bearing upon the job survival of young careerists entering the system with a commitment to change. Conditions *ought* to be such as to retain them in the system long enough so their influence can begin to be felt. But the fact is that *any* system (banking, teaching, preaching) tends to be set in such a way as, in effect, to protect itself against change. The result is that young career-ists, with some inspiration and competence to be agents of change, are discouraged from entering the system initially, or become frustrated and drop out at some later point, or survive only to the extent that they compromise their commitment to change. Thus the system remains self-insulated and self-perpetuating, a haven only for those conforming to its standpat values.

A glimmer of hope for the change-minded is the possibility that the community served by the system will demand change and insist upon the creation of conditions conducive to it. Where police work is concerned, this has happened far too rarely in the past. Sophisticated police-community partnership could bring it about more widely in the future. However, genuine commitment as a change agent is a tender and precious thing, while at the same time necessarily hardy and not easily thwarted. To be committed to change is to anticipate no easy path, whatever the field. Relatively few have what it takes, precisely because it involves the heart of "a lonely hunter that hunts on a lonely hill."

The Walsh research referred to earlier had something significant to say about attitude.[3] His study of police officers in four midwestern departments led him to conclude that officers who see policing as a profession have attitudes toward their work considerably different from those who see what they do as just a job. This contrast extends to attitudes toward minorities and to the use of force, as well as to other matters. Walsh found, for example, that the "professionals" were much more concerned about public approbation, respect, and support than were the "jobbers." The latter were more apt than the professionals to say that riots and the poor constitute the number one police problem today. Nearly half of the jobbers felt that the use of force in police work actually helped their standing in the community, while 60 percent of the professionals said that the use of force, although sometimes necessary, was detrimental to their efforts to achieve professional status.

The professionals were inclined to attach much more importance than the jobbers to public service in police work today. The jobbers tended to stress, much more than the professionals, physical size and strength as desirable qualifications for police work. Walsh also discovered some political differences; the jobbers were more likely than the professionals to have voted for far-right candidates in the 1968 election. Thus, occupational self-conception appears to affect voting behavior. Incidentally, the Walsh study also suggests that generalizations regarding the values and beliefs of policemen as a group are, as with other groups, hazardous indeed.

Bayley and Mendelsohn, in their study *Minorities and the Police*, conducted in Denver, observed (p. 148) that "very little credence is given by policemen to charges that policemen treat minority people unfairly or improperly."[4] This has also been indicated by Skolnick, as earlier noted. Walsh found that the jobbers were much more likely than

the professionals to claim that unequal treatment was the fault of minorities themselves. Some 62 percent of the jobbers felt that the poor and
minority groups actually get better treatment than do the middle class
and the rest of us. Another 23 percent of the jobbers felt that the poor
and minority groups have problems because they are "too lazy" to improve their lot in life. Only a small percentage of the professionals
subscribed to these notions.

Walsh described a central hypothesis of his study as follows:

> To be proud of one's occupation and to view it as a profession enjoy-
> ing positive standing in the community should lead to attitudes toward
> the work done by members of the profession different from those one
> would expect from other practitioners whose view of the occupation
> is that it is simply a job—something one does because he can't find
> anything else, or because it is the most secure position available, or
> something that anyone could handle with little or no training. ["The
> Professional Cop"]

Cynicism the Result of Conflicting Roles

We are still left with the question, why is it that many police officers are not proud of their occupation, especially in our big cities? Why
are so many of them so cynical about their professional prospects? Why
the continuing evidences of corruption and other signs of low morale?

James Q. Wilson examined this phenomenon some years ago and
produced a provocative analysis in "The Police and Their Problems:
A Theory." He recognizes that there is no single explanation for the
problem of police morale. Many forces bear on it. The crucial concern
of the individual police officer is in finding some consistent, satisfying
basis for his self-conception: to be able to live with himself in reasonable tranquility. The gravity of this concern, of course, varies with individual officers and departments. Wilson contends that the problem of
morale or self-interest results from two aspects of the policeman's role.
First, he often deals with his client as an adversary. Secondly, the policeman is frequently under pressure to serve incompatible ends. We have
already noted this latter point in relation to the functions of law enforcement and order maintenance. The public cannot make up its mind
what it wants from the police.

To alleviate the police morale problem, therefore, some consensus
must be reached as to what is expected of the police, community by
community. It is basically the role question again. The police must be
taken off the hook in the quandary they face constantly as to the ends
a particular community may want served only symbolically; for example, gambling, prostitution, homosexuality, etc. Police and community
must move together toward clearer directional signals than presently
exist as to the police exercise of discretion, as previously discussed. This

can happen only in communities motivated to function in an integrated manner, not *despite* differences but *because* of them. On the police side, the reality of the heterogeneity of the community must be recognized and dignified—another way of saying that the police must become the police of *all* the people.

Wilson's description of the policeman's difficulty is best conveyed in his language:

> The awareness that he is viewed with hostility and judged in terms of inconsistent standards can, unless other factors intervene, lead a policeman to believe that he has chosen an occupation which sets him apart from others. Even during off-duty hours, he is rarely allowed to forget that he is a policeman—even if by nothing more than the joking remarks of his friends. To live with himself and with others, he must develop some acceptable and consistent standards by which to evaluate himself. In the extreme case of which we are here speaking, such standards cannot be found in the expectations of others. In adapting to this situation, the policeman comes to be governed by norms different from, and sometimes in conflict with, those which govern the persons with whom he comes in contact. [Ibid.]

Wilson continues, and his point regarding the disparity between role (viewed as of the highest importance) and status (pretty well down on the totem pole) should be underscored:

> To the extent that the policeman feels the need to develop a police "sub-culture" or "code" different from that of civilians, he can be said to be "alienated".... The two major causes of the morale problem for policemen seem analogous to two of the many meanings of alienation. First, the "pariah feeling" implies not only that the individual (or his occupation) is given low esteem, but more particularly that the esteem accorded is much lower than the ostensible importance of the goals he is to serve. The individual (in this case, the policeman) is obliged to perform a social function of the highest importance but is told that he will not be given an appropriately high status even if he is successful. Second, the problem of serving incompatible ends implies that society has so defined the policeman's situation that he can never act in accord with that definition. Stated another way, the inconsistent expectations of society imply that the policeman will be called upon either to use socially unapproved behavior to attain socially approved goals, or vice versa. [Ibid.]

Wilson states that his usages are close to what Melvin Seeman ("On the Meaning of Alienation") calls "isolation" and "normlessness" as types of alienation. Wilson expands his analysis of police morale in "Police Morale, Reform and Citizen Respect: The Chicago Case."

It bears repeating that the morale problem of the police, where it exists, is invariably the result of a complex of factors. Wilson's diagnosis suggests the subtlety of what may be involved in an indeterminant number of situations. It goes considerably deeper than the superficialities often blamed by the public, and sometimes by the police themselves, for the police morale problem. But Wilson's explanation is frequently complicated further, in departmental realities, by such things as incredibly poor administrative leadership and supervision, by bureaucratic inertia and the failure of a department to use effectively the competencies of personnel, and by the feelings of police officers that they are ill-prepared, in training and education, for what is expected of them. These and other considerations of this type have an important bearing upon morale also. In short, any single-dimensional answer to this problem is patently inadequate.

The Subculture of the Police

For our purpose, *subculture* may be defined as the meanings, values, and behavior patterns that are unique to a particular group in society. Toward the end of Chapter Four, we alluded to the various social systems that affect what the police do and how they do it: the criminal justice system, the governmental-political system, and the social institutional system. We referred also to the system of which the police officer is a product: his social class, racial, ethnic, value, and belief background, all of which have pertinence in understanding the nuances of the police subculture.

Most communities seem to be unaware that they expect their police to perform impossible tasks. The police, quite naturally, are defensive in their reactions to community expectations that they cannot fulfill. They are too often reminded of their failures by people who do not understand the basic problem of the police. Because policemen are, by occupational prescription, inclined to be suspicious, they tend to isolate themselves from an unsympathetic, critical, untrustworthy, and uncomprehending community, and to form their own in-group alliances with fellow officers. This supplies needed emotional and ideological support—what Wilson calls a "code"—with elements of secrecy and sometimes of ritual, even a special language and other subgroup trappings.

In "When Subcultures Meet," Victor Strecher, professor of criminal justice at Michigan State University, bases his conception of police subculture on a theoretical paradigm of occupational subculture presented in a study of medical students by Becker et al.[5] Beyond childhood and adolescent socialization, the police officer, Strecher asserts, undergoes a process of occupational socialization (as we have observed) through which he becomes identified as a policeman and begins to share all the perspectives relevant to the police role. There is substantial coherence and consistency among these perspectives. Moreover, because all police officers occupy the same social institutional position, they tend to face the same kind of problems, arising out of the character of the position. Therefore, the demands and inhibitions of the *police role,* as we have suggested, are decisive in shaping the kaleidoscopic perspectives of the police officer.

Strecher holds that policemen do not simply apply the perspectives they carry over from previous experience or backgrounds. He believes that background may have some indirect influence in many ways, and goes on to say:

> ... The problems of the police officer are so pressing and the policeman's initial perspectives so similar that the perspectives developed are much more apt to reflect the pressures of the immediate *law enforcement* situation than of ideas associated with prior roles and experiences. ["When Subcultures Meet"]

To Strecher, therefore, police subculture is a shorthand term for "the organized sum of *police perspectives* relevant to the *police role.*" He presents an interesting comparison of police subculture with that of medical students (adapting medical perspectives of Becker et al.[6]):

Medical	*Police*
... the concept of medical responsibility pictures a world in which patients may be in danger of losing their lives and identifies the true work of the physician as saving these endangered lives. Further, where the physician's work does not afford (at least in some symbolic sense) the possibility of saving a life or restoring health through skillful practice ... the physician himself lacks some of the essence of physicianhood.	... the concept of police responsibility pictures a world in which the acts and intended acts of criminals threaten the lives or well-being of victims, and the security of their property. The true work of the police officer is the protection of life and property by intervention in, and solution of criminal acts. Further, where the policeman's work does not afford (at least in some symbolic sense) the possibility of protecting life or property by intervening in criminal acts, the police officer himself lacks some of the essence of police identity.
... Those patients who can be cured are better than those who cannot.	... Those cases which can be solved are better than those which cannot.
... "Crocks" ... are not physically ill and ... are not regarded as worthwhile patients because nothing can be done for them. (*Note:* To a medic, a "crock" is a hypochondriac.)	... Chronic neighborhood complainants are not worth taking seriously because there is no substance to their complaints, and nothing can be done for them.

... Students worry about the dangers to their own health involved in seeing a steady stream of unscreened patients, some of whom may have communicable diseases.

... Policemen worry about dangers to their own safety involved in approaching a steady stream of unknown persons, some of whom may have serious behavioral problems and intentions of causing them injury or even death, because of circumstances unknown to the policemen.

... Perhaps the most difficult scenes come about when patients have no respect for the doctor's authority. Physicians resent this immensely.

... When a citizen makes a policeman sweat to take him into custody, he has created the situation most apt to lead to police indignation and anger. (Skolnick)

[Strecher, "When Subcultures Meet"]

Strecher does not attach much direct importance to the background perspectives of persons entering police work. Other researchers would argue with him on this point. "Background" is an all-encompassing term that covers a great deal of territory. Skolnick is interested in the sociology of occupations and devotes considerable attention to what he calls "the working personality" of the policeman—an analysis of the effects of the occupation on the personality of the officer—some features of which we noted earlier. The literature dealing with the effects of one's work on world outlook is extensive.[7] Skolnick suggests that

... the police, as a result of combined features of their social situation, tend to develop ways of looking at the world distinctive to themselves, cognitive lenses through which to see situations and events. The strength of the lenses may be weaker or stronger depending on certain conditions, but they are ground on a similar axis. [*Justice Without Trial*, p. 42]

In another study, "The Police and the Urban Ghetto," Skolnick observes that the policeman's attitude toward his work is much like that of the combat soldier. For the working policeman, life is "combat." People are either good or bad, the situation is safe or unsafe—the "we-versus-they attitude." Like the soldier, the policeman is irritated by minor organizational rules, what he calls "legal technicalities," and long-winded, "sociological" explanations. Quoting Skolnick again:

Additionally, as one observes police, one notices their employment of two predominant models of discourse. One of these models, which might be termed "office language" or "working language," is frequently profane, loud, and good-humored. Transported into the cold light of print, the words might have a shocking effect upon delicate sensibilities. But such discourse would ring familiar to a steelworker or longshoreman, a ball-player or a soldier. . . .

. . . .
Off the street, police frequently resort to an alternative model—"offi-cialese"—out of fear that "working language" might spill out and offend officialdom. An outstanding example of police officialese is the substitution of the word "altercation" for "fight" . . . So the policeman is often not a graceful or moderate speaker or writer, and his inability or perhaps unwillingness to conceal true feelings gets him into trouble. [Ibid., pp. 5, 6]

To relate these insights of Strecher and Skolnick to our initial point, we may note the variables: the influence of childhood develop-ment, of the experiences one has had before taking a certain job, and the influence of the job itself upon personality. Each of these factors comes into play for an individual's developing self-image; the degree to which one factor or another may predominate depends on the indi-vidual and his situation. It appears to Strecher and Skolnick that in a police situation the occupational influence upon attitudes and the self-image is especially strong. But as we shall see in a moment, this view is qualified by other analysts.

Personality Traits of Policemen

As we have indicated in general terms, the questions of why a person would want to be a police officer and what type of personality tends to gravitate to police work are of interest to researchers. We are beginning to see helpful studies of these and related questions, which dig beneath surface generalizations. Ruth Levy, for example, believes that certain personality traits established early in life are clues as to whether a person will be able to stand the pressures of a police career. She says:

. . . we find that the appointees most likely to remain in law enforce-ment are probably those who are more unresponsive to the environ-mental stresses introduced when they become officers of the law than are their fellow-appointees. These stresses include becoming a member of a "minority" (occupationally speaking) group, need to adhere to semi-military regimen, community expectation of incongruous roles and the assumption of a position of authority complete with the trap-pings of uniform, badge, holster and gun, and all these imply. The officers who remain in law enforcement may well be the sons of fathers who imposed a rigid code of behavior to which their children learned to adhere, and who do not feel a strong need to defy or rebel against authority. ["Predicting Police Failures"]

Levy's work suggests some further implications for those committed to systemic change and reminds us of Pfiffner's analysis of vocational belief systems and stereotyped patterns of thought in *The Function of the Police in a Democratic Society.* He says that the police subculture possesses a set of values, standards, and job goals "more appropriate to the days of public hangings than to a society which is making some progress toward ameliorating the lot of those who for one reason or another have not adjusted to the demands of society."

Pfiffner raises some provocative questions regarding the police subculture:

> How strong is the right-wing orientation of those engaged in the police vocation? ("One senses that it may be more prevalent than in the general population.")

> Do the police tend to think didactically? (". . . the police may regard themselves as the custodians of a public conscience to which society gives only lip service.")

> Are the police anti-social science? (". . . the investigators are in a sense natural enemies because of their opposite values . . . [thus] it is little wonder that the police should adopt a certain skepticism or aloofness toward social science research.")

> How prevalent is the anti-social work bias among law enforcement people? (". . . this implication [that police work is social work] is distasteful to some policemen who regard the rehabilitation apparatus as foreign territory . . .")

> Is "authoritarian" leadership a product of the police sub-culture, or does police work attract men with natural tendencies in that direction? ("If this is authentically an ingredient of the police sub-culture, certain other questions present themselves.")

> To what extent does the police operation resist administrative coordination? (". . . there may have been at one time and among certain officers a feeling that because police receive their powers from the state [sic.], they are therefore immune from general administrative supervision.")

> Is there an equitation complex among the police, using that term as symbolic of the survival of outmoded procedures? (". . . equitation thinking is resistence to change. . . . Are they [the police] now hung in their Maginot Line of technical effectiveness in meeting traditional police problems?") [Ibid.]

We have already referred to what Pfiffner calls the "guild protectionism" of the police, growing out of what he labels as their "isolation syndrome." His delineation of the isolation syndrome is pertinent here:

> Some police administrators prefer to deny, or at any rate overlook, the statement that the police feel isolated from the opinion-making elements in the community, but one cannot probe their intimate thoughts without becoming aware of the existence of an isolation syndrome. There is quite definitely this feeling of being at cross-purposes with the social scientists and social workers . . . In a very generalized

sort of way, it may also be said that the intellectual community has an anti-authority complex which in a vague manner is transferred to the police. The police also harbor a feeling that they have been deserted by that portion of the legal profession which sits on the judicial bench, and the civil libertarians. [Ibid.]

Psychologist Hans Toch has referred to the oft-heard description of the police as a "minority group":

> The police inhabit a ghetto of their own, and they are doomed to segregation. They have little hope of man-to-man conversation with civilians, who—even if favorably disposed to law enforcement—tend to be nervous and self-conscious in encounters with officers. The average person finds it difficult to feel open and at ease with a man who sports a conspicuous firearm, who is entitled to question, search and arrest him. ["Cops and Blacks: Warring Minorities"]

Toch contends that police officers sense these attitudes by civilians, and their defensive reaction is typical of minority groups: they become self-righteous. They seek the exclusive company of one another, and "regale one another with their own virtues, sometimes enhancing these to super-man proportions. Self-regard and pride slide into chauvinism, especially . . . built on a foundation of persistent self-doubt." Toch continues:

> In the code of minorities, it is important to present a united front. There must be no break in the ranks, no visible division to be exploited by the hostile majority. . . . Among police, "brother officers" are supported, even when they have proved trigger-happy or brutal. Review boards are anathema to police, because they expose fellow officers to public view. . . . The police . . . feel themselves discriminated against and unpopular. They feel themselves stigmatized by indices of status. They feel their ambitions thwarted and their objectives misunderstood. They feel impotent and without recourse. They feel hated and persecuted. And they sense that the situation is steadily degenerating into a future of complete hopelessness and utter helplessness. [Ibid.]

This is Toch's explanation of the underlying psychological dynamics of police militancy—generally known as "Blue Power." Incidentally, Toch points out the limitations in referring to the police as a "minority group," if an analogy to blacks is implied.

The Pariah Feeling

Some writers have used a stronger term than "isolation syndrome"; Westley, for example, in "Violence and the Police" referred to the pariah feeling of the policeman—an outcast, a person despised by society. James Q. Wilson and Michael Banton use the same term; Banton says for example:

Couple this experience of the public with the policeman's feelings that in his social life he is a pariah, scorned by citizens who are more respectable but no more honest, and it need surprise no one that the patrolman's loyalties to his department and his colleagues are often stronger than those to the wider society. [*The Policeman in the Community*, p. 170]

There are other, similar characterizations in the literature, although only a few are supported by adequate research.

The American Civil Liberties Union has acquired, by the nature of its purpose, the reputation of being antipolice. The following is a typical ACLU statement:

... studies of persons who elect police work as a career, mostly before new professional methods began to be employed in recruitment and screening, suggested a heavy percentage with an authoritarian approach to individual relationships. Another study advanced the theory that police self-esteem is probably not high and that the officer himself accepts some of the stereotypes about that "flat-foot" who is not overly supplied with integrity. This low self-image possibly leads to a higher incidence of wrongful police actions than is encountered in other levels of the law enforcement hierarchy.[8]

As we have noted, many writers also have dealt with the reactions of the police to their perceived low social status and with their alleged cynical, bitter, and defensive posture.[9] Sterling questions the validity of the emphasis placed on police clannishness, in comparison with certain other occupations. He thinks the point is a weak one; what is not considered is the fact that clannishness is a characteristic of all occupations where shift work is practiced.[10]

Research of the type conducted by Sterling is exemplary in testing the factual basis for allegations as to the hardness or cynicism of police officers, or their tendency to conform to authority, or their conservatism. The Sterling hypothesis is that hardness and cynicism increases with the experience of the policeman, and rigid conformity to authority decreases. Again, however, unsubstantiated generalizations are perilous, as Sterling repeatedly warns.

Patterns for Success in Police Work

The University of Chicago research by Baehr, Furcon, and Froemel is an expansion of Ruth Levy's work. A battery of psychological tests was developed that the researchers claim accurately predicts future performance of patrolmen, determines specific patterns of good and poor performance, and identifies subgroups exhibiting these patterns among the patrolmen tested. The patterns may be used for purposes of selection, placement, duty assignment, and promotion.

The tests show that, apart from an average level of intelligence, the most important personal attributes of successful patrolmen are all related to *stability*—stability stemming from personal self-confidence and the control of emotional impulses, stability in the maintenance of cooperative rather than hostile or competitive attitudes, and stability deriving from a resistance to stress and a realistic rather than a subjective and feeling-oriented approach to life. Underlying this stability (deriving from the background of "better" patrolmen) was early assumption of family responsibilities and involvement in family activities. All the desirable attributes were measured by the tests, and patrolmen who scored high in these attributes were, in general, those who were independently given high ratings for performance by their supervisors. The study focused on Chicago patrolmen in the Patrol Division, who had at least one year of service and who were currently assigned to uniformed street patrol.

Both the Chicago research and that by Levy point to the importance of stability, or what may be called "stress resistance" in successful police careers. Levy observed that young policemen do not find conformity to the system stressful. Conformism is a psychological trait related to security. The conformist, as stated by Watson and Sterling (*Police and Their Opinions,* p. 4) receives approbation from the wielders of power and at the same time rids himself of the uncertainty of decision making so far as matters covered by the rules are concerned. Wenninger and Clark make the point in "A Theoretical Orientation for Police Studies" that the police have both a value maintenance and a goal attainment function (Talcott Parsons' categories).

When one shares the values of the larger society, as Banton says policemen do, his behavior tends to harmonize with society's expectations as dictated by shared values. Accordingly, many policemen as well as many others who hold strongly to established values are inclined to react strongly against those who wish to change these values. Student rebels and black or white extremists are regarded as threats to stability. The larger society actually encourages the police to exercise their discretion in handling such threats in ways that would probably not be tolerated with more "respectable" adversaries. For their part, the police are committed by their oath to maintaining the status quo. Moreover, if Levy and others are correct, they are also so committed by psychological disposition, hence "do not find it distasteful"—as Watson and Sterling put it—"to function in this manner." Again, this point carries implications for agents of change within police organizations.

Reiss and Bordua comment on a variation of this point, focusing on "curbstone justice":

> Police dissatisfaction with the administration of justice by the courts results in their doing justice, a tendency to settle things outside the courts to be sure that "justice is done." Nowhere is this more apparent

than when police are expected to continue law enforcement involving violators that the court sends back to the community. The police then may take the law in their own hands and dispense justice, even if it means using violence. ["Environment and Organization: A Perspective on the Police"]

Fletcher Knebel adds that many policemen are ambivalent toward their work ("Police in Crisis"). They like much of what they do, but there are many things about it that they do not like. It will be recalled that McNamara's observations on the uncertainties in police work cast light on some of the sources of the policeman's ambivalence.[11]

Policing "by the book" helps to relieve anxieties rooted in ambivalence and uncertainty. Hillard Trubitt in an article in *The Nation* puts it this way:

> Rules formulated for the conduct of police business, originally enacted to restrain unfettered police action, have become ends in themselves. Many police procedures and actions are followed simply because they are "in the book." All the petty tyrannies of officialdom which form the basis of complaints against the police establishment today are reflections of this unthinking adherence to "rules," to form, without regard for social effect. The charge of being "irregular" frightens the police at least as much as the charge of being ineffective. ["Going By the Book"]

Conservatism in Police Work

Harvard political scientist Seymour Martin Lipset has pointed to the increasing body of evidence "which suggests an affinity between police work and support for radical-right politics, particularly when linked to racial unrest" (*The Atlantic*, "Why Police Hate Liberals—and Vice Versa"). Lipset contends that this is because police are recruited largely from the undereducated, typically conservative working class, and because their job inevitably stresses toughness, authority, and "a skeptical view of human behavior." Skolnick alludes to conservatism as the dominant political and emotional persuasion of the police. The late Los Angeles Chief of Police William H. Parker asserted that the majority of the nation's peace officers were "conservative, ultraconservative, and very right wing." Various observers have suggested that the John Birch Society has been popular in police circles.

Research of the type done by Levy and by the University of Chicago group provides some information as to the generally conservative orientation of the "police establishment." Lipset believes that this is the result of a combination of social background and occupational role factors. For example, he cites Niederhoffer's observation[12] that in the past fifteen years, during relative economic prosperity, the bulk of New York City police candidates has been upper lower class with a

sprinkling of lower middle class, 95 percent having had no college training. Lipset quotes McNamara's findings to substantiate other aspects of
his thesis, of which this is an expression:

> In general, the policeman's job requires him to be suspicious of people,
> to prefer conventional behavior, to value toughness. A policeman must
> be suspicious and cynical about human behavior. As Neiderhoffer
> points out, "he needs the intuitive ability to sense plots and conspira-
> cies on the basis of embryonic evidence." The political counterpart of
> such an outlook is a monistic theory which simplifies political conflict
> into a black-and-white fight, and which is ready to accept a con-
> spiratorial view of the sources of evil, terms which basically describe
> the outlook of extremist groups, whether of the left or right. [Lipset,
> p. 78]

Lipset goes on to say:

> The police have faced overt hostility and even contempt from spokes-
> men for liberal and leftist groups, racial minorities, and intellectuals
> generally. The only ones who appreciate their contribution to society
> and the risks they take are the conservatives, and particularly the
> extreme right. The radical left has almost invariably been hostile, the
> radical right friendly. It is not surprising therefore that police are
> more likely to be found in the ranks of the right. . . . The liberal world
> . . . is perceived as an enemy, an enemy which may attack directly in
> demonstrations or riots—or indirectly through its pressure on the
> courts. [P. 80]

It will be recalled that James Q. Wilson (*Varieties of Police
Behavior,* pp. 33, 34) referred to the working class backgrounds of
police officers in many communities and their preoccupation with working class values: maintaining self-respect, proving one's masculinity,
"not taking any crap," and not being "taken in."[13] The literature is rich
with similar references. Westley early alluded to the working class
origins of most policemen. Gunnar Myrdal described the American
policeman as economically and socially insecure and always on the defensive, creating the impression with the public that he is crude and
hard-boiled (*An American Dilemma,* p. 540). In the same vein, Sam
Blum writes in *Redbook*:

> The police therefore have been forced to write off the better-educated
> as a source of recruits. In addition, no one can say precisely what type
> of person (if there is any one specific type) can function most suc-
> cessfully as a policeman. In large cities it is a virtual certainty, how-
> ever, that police recruits will be drawn from the less-well-educated
> and the lower income groups. According to Milton Rector, "There is
> a high correlation between violence and the lower cultural-economic
> levels. If you recruit from these levels, you run the risk of obtaining
> people who have built-in violent reactions when they run into prob-

lems, as the police do. Before you recruit from these levels, you have to assess carefully their attitudes and stability." ["The Police"]

A. L. Cornelius said essentially the same thing forty years ago:

> Policemen as a class are usually not well educated, skilled mechanically or industrially. They are men above average in physical strength and appearance who have lacked sufficient persistence to acquire an education or learn a trade. [*Cross Examination*]

Watson and Sterling provide a contradicting analysis of various ramifications of social class factors and the police, based on their national opinion sampling (*Police and Their Opinions*, pp. 105–119). They raise questions regarding the assumptions prevailing in the views quoted above:

> This data shows that today's police officers have come from the families of craftsmen and foremen, and service workers (including police) in larger proportion than is true for the general adult work force. Conversely, the data shows that proportionately fewer police officers than other adults are the children of professional, technical and managerial workers; clerical and sales workers; operatives; farmers; and laborers. By and large, ... the data cast doubt on the accuracy of the view that "most policemen are products of lower-middle-class environments. [P. 119]

Watson and Sterling concluded that differences in *educational attainment* among policemen were more significant than any other variable in the contrasting opinions expressed by officers they sampled regarding many issues affecting police work. One might argue that educational attainment is class-oriented, and therefore that social class is actually the most important variable. Implicit in the entire discussion is, of course, the assumption that persons from class levels other than lower-middle or working class would make better police officers, by some definition of "better." Banton may have the key point:

> To do his job properly, the policeman, like the minister of religion, has to be to some extent a "classless" figure. He has to deal with subjects of different class and his relationships with them must be determined by his office, not by his class position. [*The Policeman in the Community*, p. 181]

To which Watson and Sterling (p. 124) append: "... we would hasten to add that the policeman should be an *educated* classless figure."

Value Gap Between Police and Policed

Rokeach, Miller, and Snyder of Michigan State University have probed the question of whether there are noteworthy contrasts in the value patterns of police, compared with representative samples of other black and white Americans ("The Value Gap Between Police and Policed"). They discovered a somewhat larger value gap, on the whole, between police and blacks than between police and whites, but the gap was considerable in both cases. The police officers tested ranked high such values as *a sense of accomplishment, capable, intellectual,* and *logical.* They devalued such modes of behavior as being *broadminded, forgiving, helpful,* and *cheerful.* They ranked *equality* significantly lower than a national sampling of whites and far lower than a national sampling of blacks. This ranking of equality is interpreted as a telling indicator of conservatism.

The Michigan State University researchers regard this discrepancy in value for equality as the most significant component of the value gap between police and policed. Their findings support Lipset's contention that police derive their conservatism from their working class backgrounds, with the added consideration that police work appeals primarily to those of working class background "whose personalities have been shaped in such a way that they value subservience to authority and an 'escape from freedom' [Eric Fromm's term]." In effect this suggests what Bayley and Mendelsohn concluded, that the background and "pre-police personality" of police recruits are more important in shaping their value patterns than is the occupational socialization process after they enter police work. There appears to be some dissent on this point from Sterling, from Strecher, and from Walsh.

The Uniform as Symbol

Lipset cites the various analysts (Westley, James Q. Wilson, Skolnick, and others) who have underlined the importance that police officers attach to respect for law and authority, and more specifically to respect for the individual policeman. Several studies reflect that policemen feel that lack of respect for the police is America's primary law enforcement problem. We mentioned this in our discussion of discretionary use of police power. We noted the symbolic importance ascribed by the officer to his uniform, especially in situations where he perceives that his authority is being challenged. He expects deference to be shown; as Skolnick points out, for a citizen to make a policeman sweat to take him into custody—as for instance in "going limp"—is to create a situation calculated to elicit the officer's anger and indignation.

Walsh looked into the question of the meaning of the uniform to the policeman,[14] as did Bayley and Mendelsohn (*Minorities and the Police,* pp. 50, 51). Walsh asked the question of the officers he interviewed: "Some have suggested that police work could improve its image if it were to encourage officers to wear suits, not uniforms, while on duty. Do you agree?" Almost 90 percent of the respondents disagreed. Among these, the importance of the uniform as a "symbol of our identity or mark of distinction" went up as professional striving went up;

U.S.C. 242* or interviewed such witnesses in a perfunctory and hostile manner.

b. More aggressive efforts to implement 18 U.S.C. 242 by the Department of Justice are needed.

Underrepresentation of Mexican-Americans on juries

There is serious and widespread underrepresentation of Mexican-mericans on grand and petit State Juries in the Southwest:

a. Neither lack of knowledge of the English language nor low-incomes of Mexican-Americans can explain the wide disparities between the Mexican-American percentage of the population and their representation on juries.

b. Judges or jury commissioners frequently do not make affirmative efforts to obtain a representative cross section of the community for jury service.

c. The peremptory challenge is used frequently both by prosecutors and defendants' lawyers to remove Mexican-Americans from petit jury venires.

The underrepresentation of Mexican-Americans on grand and petit juries results in distrust by Mexican-Americans of the impartiality of verdicts.

7. Bail

Local officials in the Southwest abuse their discretion:

a. In setting excessive bail to punish Mexican-Americans rather than to guarantee their appearance for trial.

b. In failing to give Mexican-American defendants an opportunity to be released until long after they were taken into custody.

c. By applying unduly rigid standards for release of Mexican-Americans on their own recognizance where such release is authorized.

In many parts of the Southwest, Mexican-American defendants are hindered in their attempts to gain release from custody before trial

---

*The principal Federal criminal sanction against violence or other unlawful action by state and local officials is Title 18, Section 242 of the U.S. Code. It provides:

Whoever, under color of any law, statute, ordinance, regulation, or custom, willfully subjects any inhabitant of any State, Territory, or District to the deprivation of any rights, privileges, or immunities secured or protected by the Constitution or laws of the United States, or to different punishments, pains, or penalties, on account of such inhabitant being an alien, or by reason of his color or race, than are prescribed for the punishment of citizens, shall be fined not more than $1,000 or imprisoned not more than one year, or both, and if death results shall be subject to imprisonment for any term of years or for life.

because they cannot afford the cost of bail under the traditional ba
system.

8. *Counsel*

There are serious gaps in legal representation for Mexica
Americans in the Southwest:

a. The lack of appointed counsel in misdemeanor cases results i
serious injustices to indigent Mexican-American defendants.

b. Even in felony cases, where counsel must be provided for indige
defendants, there were many complaints that appointed counse
often was inadequate.

c. Where public defender's offices are available to indigent crimina
defendants, they frequently did not have enough lawyers or othe
staff members to adequately represent all their clients, many o
whom are Mexican-Americans.

d. In parts of the Southwest, there are not enough attorneys to pro
vide legal assistance to indigent Mexican-Americans involved i
civil matters.

e. Many lawyers in the Southwest will not handle cases for Mexican
American plaintiffs or defendants because they are "controversial"
or not sufficiently rewarding financially.

f. Despite the enormous need for lawyers fluent in Spanish and
willing to handle cases for Mexican-American clients, there are
very few Mexican-American lawyers in the Southwest.

9. *Attitudes toward the courts*

Mexican-Americans in the Southwest distrust the courts and think
they are insensitive to their background, culture, and language. The
alienation of Mexican-Americans from the courts and the traditional
Anglo-American legal system is particularly pronounced in northern
New Mexico.

10. *Language disability*

Many Mexican-Americans in the Southwest have a language disability that seriously interferes with their relations with agencies and
individuals responsible for the administration of justice:

a. There are instances where the inability to communicate with police
officers has resulted in the unnecessary aggravation of routine situations and has created serious law enforcement problems.

b. Mexican-Americans are disadvantaged in criminal cases because
they cannot understand the charges against them nor the proceedings in the courtroom.

c. In many cases Mexican-American plaintiffs or defendants have difficulty communicating with their lawyers, which hampers preparation of their cases.

d. Language disability also adversely affects the relations of some Mexican-Americans with probation and parole officers.

11. *Interpreters*

Interpreters are not readily available in many Southwestern courtrooms:

a. In the lower courts, when interpreters were made available, they are often untrained and unqualified.

b. In the higher courts, where qualified interpreters were more readily available, there has been criticism of the standards of their selection and training and skills.

12. *Employment by law enforcement agencies*

Employment of Mexican-Americans by law enforcement agencies throughout the five Southwestern states does not reflect the population patterns of these areas:

a. Neither police departments, sheriffs' offices, nor state law enforcement agencies employ Mexican-Americans in significant numbers.

b. State and local law enforcement agencies in the Southwest do not have programs of affirmative recruitment which would attract more Mexican-American employees.

c. Failure to employ more Mexican-Americans creates problems in law enforcement, including problems in police-community relations.

13. *Courts and prosecutors*

Other agencies in charge of the administration of justice—courts, district attorneys' offices, and the Department of Justice—also have significantly fewer Mexican-American employees than the proportion of Mexican-Americans in the general population.

Conclusion

This report paints a bleak picture of the relationship between Mexican-Americans in the Southwest and the agencies which administer justice in those States. The attitude of Mexican-Americans toward the institutions responsible for the administration of justice—the police, the courts, and related agencies—is distrustful, fearful, and hostile. Police departments, courts, and the law itself are viewed as Anglo institutions in which Mexican-Americans have no stake and from which they do not expect fair treatment.

The U.S. Civil Rights Commission found that the attitudes of Mexican-Americans are based, at least in part, on the actual experience of injustice. Contacts with the police represent the most common encounters with the law for the average citizen. There is evidence of police misconduct against Mexican-Americans. In the Southwest, as throughout the nation, remedies for police misconduct are inadequate. Mexican-Americans have been excluded from full participation in many of the institutions that administer justice; they are underrepresented in employment in police departments, state prosecutors' offices, courts, and other official agencies. Consequently, these agencies tend to reflect a lack of knowledge about and understanding of the cultural background of Mexican-Americans.

The Commission's report shows that Mexican-Americans believe they are subjected to such treatment again and again because of their ethnic background. Moreover, their complaints bear striking similarities to those of other minority groups which have been documented in earlier Commission studies of the administration of justice, namely, that on black Americans (*Justice,* 1961) and Indians (*Law Enforcement,* 1965). Consequently, the Commission's recommendations in this report are designed to be sufficiently broad to be applicable to all minority groups.

The essence of this situation is summed up in the words of a Mexican-American participant in the California State Advisory Committee meeting, who said, "I think that my race has contributed to this country with pride, honor, and dignity, and we deserve to be treated as citizens today, tomorrow, and every day of our lives. I think it is the duty of our Government to guarantee the equality that we have earned."

STUDY 5

The Black Panther Phenomenon

The weeping began quietly: 12 slaves stolen in 1441. Over 400 years, 20 million more were taken, draining Africa. Perhaps one third died marching; another third at sea. They were branded and stuffed on ships so crowded that they couldn't stand, shift or lie down. Africans and Europeans profited from their misery. In 1619, some 20 blacks were sold at Jamestown, Va. About 500,000 made it here. By 1744, 300 ships had sailed out of Liverpool. The Africans fought back. They rebelled in Hispaniola in 1522; in Puerto Rico in 1527; in Panama in 1531. And in America in 1969 they were putting the black fist to our lie.

This quotation (from *Look* magazine, January 7, 1969, p. 28) skips over the American phase of the black struggle. Between 1619 and today, we wrote the institution of slavery into the Constitution when we stipulated that a black was 3/5 of a man—not for his sake, but as a sort of bulk count for purposes of establishing white representation in Congress. Since then, the black contribution to the American economy has been so vast that, after the Emancipation, the South collapsed, as did the world-wide clipper ship trade out of Salem and New Bedford when Yankee owners had to start paying their black crews.

The great lie of America to itself that these were something less than people continues, despite the death of Crispus Attucks (1770) at the Boston Massacre; of white John Brown (1859); the innumerable lynchings of yesterday that have been succeeded by gunnings-down in the streets; despite the careers and dignity of Booker T. Washington, Marcus Garvey, and George Washington Carver. Despite, too, the more recent sit-ins, boycotts, Resurrection City, the riots of 1967–68, and the diverse efforts of Martin Luther King, Jr., Roy Wilkins (NAACP), the late Whitney Young (Urban League), James Forman (SNCC and lately National Black Economic Development Conference); James Farmer (CORE, HEW), and Jesse Jackson (Operation Breadbasket). To name only these few is an embarassment, for the list could be so long. The great lie continues despite the careers of writers, actors, athletes, musicians, and such statesmen as Ralph Bunche, Edward Brooke and Thurgood Marshall. Because we still rationalize such names as Paul Robeson and Marian Anderson as exceptions to the great lie, we are, and will continue to be confronted by the Malcolm X's, Stokely Carmichaels, Rap Browns, Huey Newtons, and Eldridge Cleavers of our time. The problem that has burned in all of these remains: an unequal society that must be set aright.

The 1954 Supreme Court decision on desegregating the schools and new voting rights laws—with their half-hearted enforcement—have done little more than dramatize the need for true solutions. Ghettos and poverty remain. Integration itself is being questioned by many of the concerned, black and white alike. For the Negro, black is still painfully black, although—since Malcolm X—it is becoming beautiful.

Now the "revolution of rising expectations" is really being felt. The totally hopeless and the abject do not despair; they know nothing better. But when, as now in America, the door has been opened a crack so that the repressed can glimpse the vision of the possibilities of the world beyond ("I have been to the mountain . . ."), there is a surge of hope mounting to a panic of desire. The mockery of "all deliberate speed" enflames the frustrated. A whole new generation of young blacks has grown up since 1954. As many blacks see it, the maddeningly slow, tedious democratic processes have become totally irrelevant as means of realizing equality in our time.

The wonder is that the Black Panther phenomenon didn't develop sooner (although there was, of course, Marcus Garvey) and that the vast majority of American blacks have not joined them. Perhaps the national expectation was that, after the riots of 1967–68, laws would be passed and public acceptance would assure, at long last, the sought-for equality. The laws *were* passed. But you can't legislate good will. You can only pass laws that will give legal support to those who are disposed to practice good will. And these were still too few. White unions still control the labor market. The black sections of our cities and towns are still walled off by "gentlemen's" agreements in spite of the laws. Most white churches are still searching their souls about admitting black brothers. In the South and North, those schools which achieved at least token integration are having a rough time: there are still riots and cuttings. Most of this is unorganized, but the deadly struggle continues in a dull, disheartening monotony that shows little sign of positive outcome.

It is no surprise, then, that out of this hopelessness there should emerge a small band of the new black youth determined to take their stand. Picture the three black young giants in black jackets and black berets standing on the white steps of the white courthouse in Oakland, California: legs spread in a stance of strength, holding three huge and beautifully painted banners bearing the new symbol of black determination—the Black Panther, with the professionally painted words "Free Huey."

This was 1966: the birth of the Black Panther Party.

Huey Newton, along with Bobby Seale, later joined by Eldridge Cleaver, had quietly conceived the party over cups of expresso at Oakland's Merritt College. It was to be, and became, a tightly disciplined organization of chapters across the country dedicated to wiping out "the pigs" by violence; to start the revolution that would knock over "the White Establishment" and bring in a socialist regime. Racism, they knew, was here to stay, but they believed it would be easier to handle it under a socialist system where everyone would presumably have an equal voice. At first, it was an all-black movement, but Cleaver was later to persuade the Panthers that blacks couldn't do the job alone—that alliances with white, disaffected groups should be solicited.

Huey was jailed, to await trial for killing a policeman. This bestowed upon him a martyr charisma with more associated power than would have been the case if he had tried to build the party as a free man. As *Newsweek* (February 23, 1970, p. 29) put it:

> Revolutions create their own mythologies and their own folk heroes. The Panthers' main man is Huey P. Newton. In prison he is like a lost saint, and tales of his wonders sustain the Panthers. Huey could talk down any professor and throw hands with any blood on the block. Huey faced down a whole cordon of cops with his M-1 and his law book. Huey has even beaten his jailers because he knows they have only his body and that he lives in the revolution. Huey was a figure in the days when the Panther Revolution was still romantic, when he and Seale and Bobby Hutton and David Hilliard rode the streets bird-dogging the Oakland police. Cleaver first laid eyes on Huey in those days, standing down itchy-fingered policemen, and thought to himself, "Goddam, that nigger is crazy!" And Seale, in his jail cell, sorts over the memories like fading photographs. "Those were the days, man," he said, staring into a cloud of cigarette smoke. "Dangerous days. Patrolling the police—that was beautiful."

In the years since the heyday of the movement, the lustre has faded. Huey had the misfortune to be freed on bail. Bobby Seale, the organizer, was jailed in New Haven, but this martyrdom—arousing Yale students to his support—faded with their preoccupation with pollution or other causes. Eldridge Cleaver, the party's philosopher, was jailed for rape of white women (perhaps a symbolic gesture on his part!), released on bail, and fled to Algeria where he tried to form alliances with disaffected youth groups of Europe and the Palestinians. For awhile, the Panthers operated clinics for Negro children, ostensibly to feed and tend their health needs, actually for purposes of indoctrination. But this required funds that proved hard to come by, despite gifts from upper-class groups on Park Avenue whose interest waned with expressed white dismay and black ingratitude.

The Panthers and what they symbolized sputtered on, as reflected in these brief excerpts from the *Information Please Almanac* for 1971 (Dan Golanpaul, pp. 70–86), covering events for 1970:

February 1: Pre-trial hearings begin for 16 members of the Black Panther Party in New York, charged with plotting to kill policemen and dynamite rail lines and major department stores.

March 9: H. Rap Brown, black militant, goes on trial in Bel Air, Md., on charges of treason and inciting to riot.

March 10: Two Negro men, including an associate of H. Rap Brown, die in an explosion that demolishes their car in Bel Air. Second victim not identified, and Brown's whereabouts unknown. (He had been out on bail). FBI investigation later showed blast was accidental. (Where had the men been going with the bomb?)

April 6: Two gunmen slay four California patrolmen; one captured, the other shot dead.

April 30: U.S. troops flown to New England for Black Panther rally in New Haven (re: Bobby Seale trial) of 20,000.

May 1: Demonstrators rally on New Haven green opposite Yale buildings to support Black Panthers. Federal troops and National Guardsmen stand by, but rally is peaceful.

May 11: Five Negro men killed in racial rioting in Augusta, Ga.

May 15: Jackson State College, Miss., predominantly Negro, closes after two black students are killed, nine wounded, by police gunfire.

June 19: Black volunteer peacemakers restore temporary quiet in Negro area racked by four days of violence in Miami, Fla.

August 5: Black Panther leader Huey Newton released on bail pending retrial of his 1967 manslaughter conviction in the death of a policeman.

August 15: Angela Davis, former UCLA instructor in philosophy, an avowed Communist, is sought on warrant charging murder and kidnap in connection with courtroom raid in which judge and three others were killed.

August 29: Black soldier from Vietnam is buried in all-white cemetery at Fort Pierce, Fla., by court order. Cemetery manager harried with protests and threats as a result.

December 22: Angela Davis, arrested in New York City in October, is extradicted to California to stand trial.

While some of these 1970 events had no apparent direct connection with the Panthers, they testify that the struggle continued, in spite of the 230 arrests that J. Edgar Hoover reported for the 12-month period ending May 1970 and 28 Panther deaths to that date.

What, specifically, do the Panthers want? A few excerpts from Eldridge Cleaver's *Soul on Ice,* written while he was in Folsom prison shortly before the launching of the Black Panther organization, suggest the philosophical base that Cleaver provided for the Panthers:

page 121: We live today in a system that is in the last stages ... of breaking up on a worldwide basis ... Injustice is being challenged at every turn and on every level ... around the world. But at home there is a Trojan Horse, a black Trojan Horse that has become aware of itself ... It, too, demands liberation.

page 123: Black Americans are too easily deceived by a few smiles and friendly gestures, by the passing of a few liberal sounding laws which are left on the books to rot unenforced, and by the speech-making of a President who is a past master at talking out of the thousand sides of his mouth. The black people must be sure beyond all doubt that the reign of terror is ended ... What is being decided right now is the shape of the world tomorrow.

After the Civil War, America went through a period similar to the one we are now in. The Negro problem received a full hearing. Everybody knew that the black man had been denied justice. No one doubted that it was time for changes and that the black man should be made a first class citizen. But Reconstruction ended. Blacks who had been elevated to high positions were brusquely kicked out into the streets and herded with the mass of blacks into the ghettos and the black belts.

page 125: Black Americans number 23 million strong. That is a lot of strength. But it is a lot of weakness if it is disorganized and at odds with itself ... *The need for one organization that will give one voice to the black man's common interest* is felt in every bone and fiber of black America. [*Italics ours.*]

page 130: Every city has its police department ... It would be sheer madness to try operating any American city without the heat, the fuzz, the man. Americans are too far gone, or else they haven't arrived yet ... Take the cops away and Americans would have a coast-to-coast free for all.

page 133: In their rage against police brutality, the blacks lose sight of the fundamental reality: That the police are only an instrument for the implementation of the policies of those who make the decisions. Police brutality is only one facet of the crystal of terror and oppression. Behind police brutality there is social brutality, economic brutality, political brutality ... The real problem is a trigger-happy social order.

These quotations show that Cleaver's rationale for the Panther movement was carefully drawn. But in trying to put the Panther program in operation, frustration and desperation sparked a resort to violence. In 1969, *Time* magazine (December 19, 1969, p. 14) said:

> Their stated aim is to give black Americans full pride and dignity; yet though they claim self-defense, they are committed to organized violence. In a last month issue of *The Black Panther,* Information Minister Eldridge Cleaver wrote: "We call for the violent overthrow of the fascist imperialist United States government."

When the police react, or overreact, to such declarations of intention, as in the raid on the Black Panther Chicago headquarters in which Fred Hampton and Mark Clark were slain (December 1969), other blacks than the Panthers cry "genocide" and claim that the police have a plot to wipe out all Panthers. *Time* continued:

> The Panthers make little secret of stockpiling arms; where it is legal, they brandish them in public. "Off the pigs"—kill the police—is the frequent Panther refrain. (But) what the Panthers view as an extermination plot, says one Federal official, is the human response of a cop confronted by someone who has publicly avowed to kill him. "That's no plot," the official says. "It's a perfectly natural reaction by a policeman facing someone who has boasted that he is prepared to shoot it out." To the Panthers, "violence against the police is not a crime but heroism."

The public was not only alarmed by the Panthers' professed intention of violence, but by their confused ideological verbiage. As the *Time* article put it:

> Much of the Panther rhetoric is couched in Marxist-Maoist terms... "We know we can learn from the struggles of China, Korea and Russia. We use it as a guide to action. An ideology has to be a living thing. But the Black Panther Party is not really Maoist."

Cleaver himself, even with the perspective of his long view from his self-exile in Algiers, became more disposed to violence. Sanche de Gramont interviewed him there for *The New York Times Magazine* (November 1, 1970, pp. 30ff) and quoted him:

> All I do is toward the idea of going back, but not to surrender myself to those pigs... I find it impossible to relate to the judicial system of the United States. I feel like the young brothers who went into the courtroom and offed the judge. That's how black people should treat the courts in Babylon.
>
> ... Reforms are not the solution. Our problems derive from the system itself. We have to completely eliminate the capitalist system and replace it with socialism ... We accepted the principle of revolutionary suicide ... but we feel we must place our lives on the line ... Here

in Algiers we will work on recruiting black G.I.'s who have deserted and are in Europe. During our trip to North Vietnam we learned there were black deserters fighting in the ranks of the Viet Cong ... It would give me great satisfaction if Richard Nixon should be killed. I would consider that an excellent thing ... The answer is not black capitalism, or black athletes, or black actors, or blacks in cigarette ads; that is just a way of incorporating black people in a device. The answer is to do away with the device. It's not a question of black studies; it's white studies that have got to be changed.

Perhaps a more realistic and authentic view of what the Black Panthers want can be gained from examining their objectives as they spelled them out at their September 1970 convention in Philadelphia. The convention was called to write a new Constitution for the United States. According to one estimate, 35 percent of those attending were whites—members of The Young Lords (Puerto Ricans), members of the Women's and Gay liberation movements, and other radical leftists. The conference was orderly and productive, despite some harassment by the Philadelphia police in the preceding three days. The meetings consisted of 15 study groups, each assigned to develop recommendations, plus a plenary reporting session at Temple University, which had leased facilities for the purpose. The recommendations of the final day included (Lansing, Michigan, *State Journal,* September 7, 1970):

1. Guarantee rights to national minorities to integrate, segregate, federate, amalgamate, congregate, secede, or do whatever they wished, provided that no group oppresses any other.

2. Guarantee representation for all ethnic groups in whatever government structure is formed in proportion to their numbers at the local level.

3. Free housing, health care, education, and day care centers for children, all paid for by the government.

4. The right and duty for everyone to bear arms, perhaps in the form of a justice-dispensing "people's militia" that would include women.

5. People to be judged only by their peers.

6. Free abortion, sterilization, and contraceptive devices for men and women.

7. Drastic changes in the present family structure, with more emphasis on communal living and men sharing house work equally with women.

8. Both education and art to serve "the people" and assist in teaching revolutionary ideas.

9. All special privileges would be forbidden; there would be no com-

pulsory servitude or domination of one group by another, and
people would police and defend themselves.

10. Present political boundaries to be abolished and replaced by an
undetermined number of autonomous, continuously evolving, self-
governing communities from which political power would flow
upward.

11. Evolution of a truly stateless society.

12. Exemption from military service.

The convention was due to reconvene in Washington in late November 1970 to formally draw up the Constitution itself. Confusion in
obtaining facilities prevented this, although several thousand delegates
appeared. The foregoing list of recommendations for the new document
reflects the influences of the various white groups present, but these were
approved in the plenary session as part of the Panther program of
cooperation with disaffected white groups. Officially, as of this writing,
these recommendations constitute the position of the Panthers today.
But what do *other* blacks want?

Surveys have revealed that the mass of black people in the United
States reject such extremism. On April 6, 1970, *Time* magazine reported
the results of a *Time*-Louis Harris poll on black attitudes, based on
1,225 nation-wide responses:

WHOM DO BLACKS RESPECT?

	A Great Deal	Some	Hardly at all
N.A.A.C.P.	75%	18%	3%
S.C.L.C.	73	18	3
Cleveland Mayor Carl Stokes	63	20	5
S.C.L.C. President Rev. Ralph Abernathy	62	27	5
Fayette, Miss., Mayor Charles Evers	61	21	5
N.A.A.C.P. Exec. Dir. Roy Wilkins	55	24	6
National Urban League	54	24	5
Justice Thurgood Marshall	54	17	5
The Rev. Jesse Jackson	51	19	7
U.S. Senator Edward Brooke	49	22	7
N.Y. Rep. Shirley Chisholm	48	15	6
Urban League Dir. Whitney Young	44	24	8
N.Y. Rep. Adam Clayton Powell	43	29	17
CORE	43	28	6
Labor Leader A. Philip Randolph	42	17	6
Boxer Muhammad Ali	33	24	27
Panther Eldridge Cleaver	30	19	23
Militant Stokely Carmichael	26	22	33
THE BLACK PANTHERS	23	18	37
Black Muslim Elijah Muhammad	23	23	26

Negroes in general seem to rate the Panthers low as an agency for change. What do they think about the use of violence as a means of achieving reform? The *Time*-Harris poll reported:

IS VIOLENCE NECESSARY?

	Can Win Rights Without Violence	Violence Probably Necessary
1963	63%	22%
1966*	59	21
1970	58	31
South	64	23
Non-South	50	40
Urban	56	34
Rural	64	23
Age Groups:		
14–21	55	40
22–29	58	31
30–49	55	33
50 and over	65	20
Professionals and managers	53	34
Welfare recipients	58	33
Pro-Panthers	44	51

Again, a substantial percentage of blacks reject the use of violence. How *do* they think they can improve their lot?

HOW WILL BLACKS MAKE REAL PROGRESS?

	Yes	No
Getting more blacks better educated	97%	1%
Through black owned businesses	93	3
Electing blacks to public offices	92	4
Cooperating with helpful whites	83	7
Boycotting whites who discriminate	68	20
Taking to streets in protest	42	41
Supporting militant organizations	41	39

rest not sure

There is unmistakable evidence of black socio-economic progress in recent years, although it is chiefly notable in comparison with former years. But this does not mean that the passions are draining from the struggle.** A *Newsweek* survey (June 30, 1969) of black feelings and opinions showed that over half still preferred to be called "Negro" or "colored," but that more than three-quarters were still striving to enter integrated neighborhoods, where their children could attend integrated

---

*Panthers were founded in 1966.
**The third *Newsweek* (June 30, 1969, pp. 19ff) poll of Black America indicates this.

schools, and over half were opposed to the Vietnam war on grounds that they had less freedom to fight for than did whites.

Has the Panther phenomenon caused moderate Negroes to veer to the radical left? One appraisal of the future is presented by Hilary Ng'weno, a former editor of *The Daily Nation* in Nairobi:

> The irony of the Black Panthers and other militant black groups is that though doomed to fail insofar as their own avowed goals are concerned, they will in the end achieve some of the moderate goals for which less militant civil rights groups have unsuccessfully been fighting during the past decade. They will fail in their own program because . . . they are hopelessly out of touch with political realities in America. (They) continue to behave as if in ignorance of the full capacity for violence which the police possess . . .
>
> America may be headed for a revolution. But if Kent State, Jackson, and Vice President Agnew's words have any meaning, it will not come from the Left . . . It is safe to assume that the Panthers have now been reduced to two alternative courses: annihilation by police gunfire, jail and enforced exile; or 'respectable' existence devoid of revolutionary pretensions. The former may be heroic, and the latter repugnant; both spell the same fate as far as the Black Panther Party is concerned.
>
> Nevertheless, the Panthers [have given] the blacks a sense of pride in their own race and heritage . . . that they have not enjoyed for centuries . . . And if it is ironic that the Panthers should perform this services . . . it is tragic that more than a century after Emancipation, America still needs groups such as the Panthers to prod her into granting her black citizens their constitutional rights. ["The Panthers: An African View"]

A less gentle appraisal of the Panthers was provided by Saul Alinsky when he was interviewed by Israel Shenker in connection with the publication of his new book, *Rules for Radicals*:

> When the Panthers began I found myself quite sympathetic. But what's wrong or right about them now is academic. The moment Huey glorified the shooting in Marin County courthouse, they blew it. I think the Panthers are asking for it. They've never been as strong as the press has indicated, and there's a suicidal obsession now.
>
> A guy has to be a political idiot to say all power comes from the barrel of a gun when the other side has the guns. A lot of their rhetoric has become a bore. You start saying 'whitefascistracistpig' and people turn off. Here's Newton saying he can't get justice in an American court, and all the time he's saying that, he's out on a reversal by a superior court. The Panthers will still get a bubble of publicity, but their days are numbered. ["Organizers Clutch Key to the Future"]

These words may sound like a premature obituary. Surely the Panther organization has an obscure future. But it is a symbol of the burgeoning revolution aptly described by *Ebony* magazine (August 16, 1969):

> The revolution of which we speak is not a violent political revolution aimed at overthrowing the established government.... The Black Panthers may seem poles apart from the members of the Urban League or NAACP (but) in their secret heart they share the common blackness which sent them on separate roads toward the same goal ... "Say it loud, I'm black and I'm proud." ... The revolution is black engineers, poets, lawyers, artists, inventors, farmers, builders, nurses, philosophers, space travelers, senators, and secretaries and vice presidents and presidents. It is black men finally free to pursue their personal goals secure in the dignity of their manhood.

Some indication of the immediate future of the Panthers may be gained from this quotation by Don McEvoy, editor, *The Hot Line* (July 1971):

> PANTHER LEADER ANNOUNCES MAJOR POLICY CHANGES:
> Huey Newton, co-founder of the Black Panther Party, recently announced a major change in tactics for the organization—avoiding confrontation with the police, promoting church attendance, and seeking new support within the black community.
>
> Speaking to a conference of San Francisco Bay area theological schools, Newton said the party "was very wrong to think that it could change the police forces the way we tried to do it. All we got was war and a lot of bloodshed."
>
> He also admitted that "we of the Panther Party were arrogant to say 'dump the church.' When we stepped outside the church we defected from the community because the church is the one institution the whole black community is involved in one way or another."
>
> "We lost the favor of the black community and left them behind," he continued. "Now there has been a change in the make-up of the central committee and a change in thinking. We're going to be going to church and get involved in the church and the black community."
>
> Newton's mention of a change in the central committee was an apparent reference to the differences between himself and Eldridge Cleaver which have split the party nationally.
>
> "Our intention to operate within reality does not mean we accept it," Newton declared. "We'll operate within the system so we can change it. It is wrong to say that the system can't give us anything because it is just not true."
>
> A minister's son, Newton said he hadn't attended church for ten years

until recently, but now he is telling party members to go to services and "experience the church."

Uncle Tom was once the symbol of oppression, but because of his "Yassuh", he has been denigrated to a symbol of fawning compliance, his name anathema to The Movement. Today, instead, we have the symbols of the raised black fist of star athletes who, while they wouldn't join the Panthers, burn just as deeply and fight the fight in their own ways—as do the wearers of dashikis and Afro hair styles. All are symbols. Like the Black Panther phenomenon, they may not prove to be lasting. But they or other symbols will remain until the Great Lie is no longer the rationalization for inequalities in America.

Perhaps Frantz Fanon, the black psychiatrist from Martinique whose brief life was spent in the revolutionary movements of North Africa, said it best. A philosopher of The Movement, his *Black Skin, White Masks* (1952) and *The Wretched of the Earth* (1961) raged at the suppression of the black ethos by colonial Europeans. The message is equally pointed for the post-slavery Negro of America. Fanon called for blacks everywhere to rise again to an awareness of their integrity as a people. Horace Sutton commented:

> He preached the necessity of controlled violence to bring about abrupt change whether it be "national liberation or national renaissance or the restoration of nationhood to the people." He said, "humanity is waiting for something from us other than . . . an imitation . . . an obscene caricature . . . We must try to set afoot a new man." ["Fanon: The Revolutionary as a Prophet"]

Ten years after Fanon's death, blacks everywhere were rediscovering him. The Black Panthers may prove to be a transient phenomenon, but the message of Frantz Fanon will continue to be heard until there is indeed a renaissance of both black and white in attitudes that recognize and accept the dignity of all men.

STUDY 6

A Model for Handling Citizen Complaints

From the citizens' point of view, a problem of municipal bureaucracies is that there is seldom a procedure, in the hierarchy of bureaus, departments, and agencies, through which complaints can be channeled to achieve redress for wrongs suffered from the governmental system. In our time of increasing awareness of ethnicity, when all manner of minority groups are conscious of their rights and potential powers, the pressures for instituting a satisfactory complaint system are multiplying. But the question of how power is to be controlled is an ancient problem of government.

Cries of "police brutality" typify the complaints with which government officials are most familiar. But in researching ways to handle such complaints, students of the problem have become increasingly aware of the fact that police are not the only agency from which citizens feel they need protection: that they need protection as well, from wrongs done by other arms of government. As examples, citizens feel the need for relief from the tax assessor, the zoning board, condemnation authorities, criminal and civil courts, welfare agencies, and others which sometimes inadvertently injure where they are supposed to help. But few of these arms of government have provided adequate means of appeal.

For instance, the police, long confronted with demands for redress procedures, have explored the relative usefulness of internal versus external complaint systems—generally defending the former and resisting the latter. The ombudsman plan, so successful in Sweden and elsewhere, has been held suspect by American police as another external agency threatening the competence and right—they feel—of the police to police themselves. Generally their objections have been based on a paucity of information about how the ombudsman system might operate.

Another aspect of the matter has been the sometimes adversarial nature of the citizen versus the police relationship, apparently inevitable when a claimant demands redress for a wrong suffered at the hands of a particular officer. New York City police felt this adversary aspect when there was brief experimentation a few years ago with a citizen-dominated review board. The feeling was that even though the board received the complaints, processed them and reported findings to the Police Commissioner, the ultimate effect was possible disciplinary action upon an individual officer. There was the feeling, too, that the police department —of all the municipal agencies—was being singled out for discriminatory harassment. So the Policeman's Benevolent Association led police opposition to this board in an expensive referendum that presaged liquidation of the board. The New York City Police Department appeared to have an effective disciplinary system. But in the citizens' view—as with the zoning board or the tax assessor—the agency is either too overwhelming to approach, or results of complaints and investigations—if any—are seldom reported back.

To meet these objections, Walter Gellhorn, professor of law at Columbia University, has been prominent among those who have proposed that municipalities create "an official with authority to examine the entire range of administration," with whom citizens can file complaints from which they would not only be assured a response but also relief, where appropriate ("Police Review Boards: Hoax or Hope"). Equally, if not more important, the adversary relationship between accuser and accused would be obviated, and municipal administration would be given guidance in improving governmental services as a whole.

In our model, let us say that the city of Urbanton is in the process of establishing just such a "Citizens' Appeals Office" to meet its urgent needs. The reasons for this decision require a brief background of information.

The population of Urbanton is 250,000, but its SMSA includes 700,000 people. In 1950, its Negro population was 14 percent of the total; in 1970 it had mounted to 30 percent. But the adjustment problems are worse than even these figures suggest because Urban River, which flows through the city, has been used as a device to confine Negroes in one-third of the city's area—an all black ghetto of de facto segregation. Since the black population is growing (high birthrate and continuing in-migration) twice as fast as the white population, which has twice as much room, tensions have mounted accordingly. There have been three serious disorders in the past 17 months. In addition, there is a relatively minor ethnic problem with the Appalachians (SAMs) in the white sector. While their number is only 10 percent of the total population, their cultural characteristics make them only a little easier to assimilate than the Negroes. (See the foregoing Study 2 on SAMs).

The police department consists of 400 officers plus 60 civilians. It is a closed system in which the chief and ranking officers have been promoted from within. Personnel is 96 percent white, and traditionally Negroes have not been encouraged to apply. Feelings of minority groups in the city are hostile in the extreme. In an effort to establish contacts with the community, a Police-Community Relations unit has been created. In its first year, the unit has developed a number of programs:

1. Created a citizens' advisory group to the PCR unit. This group is broadly representative of the community.

2. Assisted in the formation of a youth patrol in the Negro community to help communicate with minority groups in tension and conflict areas. From the original 14 members, the group now numbers nearly 160. Plans are being prepared to form another youth group in the white area. At a later date, plans call for incorporation of the two groups into a city-wide youth patrol.

3. Instituted a program of school visitation in elementary schools. Officers have made contact with 1900 children and plans are to visit each school in the city and make personal contact with children in the first three grades. This includes involving the beat officers.

4. Prepared open-house brochures and other hand-out materials and arranged for distribution of materials through business and industrial outlets.

5. Attended meetings of civil rights groups, particularly hostile or militant groups, to sound out feelings in the community.

6. Made a pilot showing of a film on morals at one of the larger high schools: 900 girls were in attendance, and the success of this showing will lead to showing it in all other high schools in the city.

The mayor and city manager of Urbanton are aware that the newly created PCR unit is having initial success in making contacts with elements of the community with whom communication has not heretofore existed. They know that the police department has a well-organized internal disciplinary structure and trial board. But these officials are also aware that the city lacks a system through which citizens can file complaints against the police and other departments with assurance that the complaints will be accepted, processed, and acted upon. For this reason, the city commission authorized the city manager to issue the following directive:

TO: All Department Directors and Agency Heads

FROM: Frederick Fredericks, City Manager

SUBJECT: Creation of the Position of Citizens' Appeals Officer

1. CITIZENS' APPEALS OFFICER CREATED

The position of Citizens' Appeals Officer is hereby created and established in the Office of the City Manager. Such Citizens' Appeals Officer shall be a deputy of the City Manager within the meaning of Sec. 95,1,D of the Charter, and in the unclassified service.

2. SALARY

The Citizens' Appeals Officer shall be paid a salary of $18,000 per year.

3. DUTIES

The Citizens' Appeals Officer shall have the following duties, subject to the limitations hereinafter contained:

    a. Receive, record, and evaluate all complaints from any person concerning inefficiency, maladministration, arrogance, abuse, or other failure arising out of the operation of any department, board, agency, or office of the city.

    b. Investigate, in the manner hereinafter provided, any of such complaints as he may deem appropriate.

4. ASSISTANCE OF OTHER DEPARTMENTS

All departments, boards, agencies, or offices of the City responsible to the City Manager shall give assistance and provide such data or other information to the Citizens' Appeals Officer as he may request in the performance of his duties as herein provided.

5. INVESTIGATIONS

The authority of the City Manager to conduct investigations, as provided in Sec. 50 of the Charter, is hereby delegated to the Citizens' Appeals Officer for the purpose of investigating such complaints. The Citizens' Appeals Officer may determine who, in his discretion, may attend any hearing held by him. Any information gained as the result of any investigation, including the identities of any complainants or witnesses, shall be kept confidential by the Citizens' Appeals Officer, except when disclosure is necessary to enable him to carry out his duties and to support his recommendations. Any witnesses appearing at any investigation conducted by the Citizens' Appeals Officer shall be entitled to have counsel present while being examined.

6. POWERS AND DUTIES AFTER INVESTIGATIONS

The objective of the Citizens' Appeals Officer in making any investigation shall be to determine whether the act complained of was any of the following, taking into consideration only the facts and circumstances existing at the time the act complained of was taken, and in no way considering any fact or circumstance occurring thereafter:

    a. Contrary to law.

    b. Unreasonable, unjust, oppressive, or discriminatory.

    c. Was taken in accordance with a rule, regulation, or standing operating procedure of the City that is unreasonable, unjust, oppressive or discriminatory.

    d. Based wholly or partially on a mistake of law or fact.

    e. An arbitrary use of discretionary power.

The Citizens' Appeals Officer shall report the findings of his investigations to the City Manager together with his recommendation as to whether the act complained of should be affirmed, reversed, or modified, together with any recommendations he may make as to the manner in which his findings should be implemented.

7. STUDIES, INQUIRIES, SURVEYS, ETC.

The Citizens' Appeals Officer may, with the approval of the City Manager, undertake any studies, inquiries, surveys, or analyses concerning any department, board, agency, or office of the City which he may deem appropriate, and may, with the approval of the City Manager, cooperate with any public or private agencies including educational, civic, or research organizations, colleges, universities, institutions, or foundations in conducting any study, inquiry, survey, or analysis.

8. REPORTS

The Citizens' Appeals Officer shall make a report of all investigations, studies, inquiries, surveys, or analyses to the City Manager. The Citizens' Appeals Officer, shall, with the approval of the City Manager, report any relevant information in his possession, which, in his opinion, relates to the commission of a crime, to the appropriate authority charged with the prosecution thereof, including malicious complaints.

9. LIMITATIONS

The Citizens' Appeals Officer shall *not* have authority to do any of the following:

  a. Impose any penalty upon any individual officer or employee of the City, other than the authority to render findings as hereinbefore provided.
  b. Investigate any complaint until it has been submitted to the director of the department or head of the board, agency, or office involved, except that, in any case where there is reason to believe such referral would result in harassment of the complainant, the Citizens' Appeals Officer may, with the approval of the City Manager, investigate such complaint as hereinbefore provided.
  c. To investigate any practice or policy which has not resulted in a complaint from a citizen.

Frederick Fredericks
City Manager

The above directive was formally approved by the Commission of the city of Urbanton and the program is now operative, financed initially by a grant from the Federal Office of Economic Opportunity.

Discussion

In recent years, there has been widespread consideration of the merits and demerits of various systems for handling citizen complaints at the level of municipal government. The Urbanton model outlined above has both strengths and weaknesses. The intention in presenting it here is to provide a basis for discussion of various alternatives. Questions that might be raised include:

1. The model is essentially an ombudsman plan, so successful in Scandinavia. Are American metropolitan situations such that the plan can(not) be effective here?

2. Does the model provide realistic procedures for achieving satisfaction in complaints concerning the mayor, the members of the city commission, or the city manager himself?

3. Should the Appeals Officer be appointed by, and be responsible to, the city manager? the commission? the governor? or whom?

4. Does the model provide adequately for handling complaints by:
   a. policeman vs. policeman, or vs. his superiors?
   b. policeman vs. the police department?
   c. citizen vs. a specific policeman?
   d. citizen vs. the police department as a whole?

5. Would a board of three Appeals Officers, of heterogeneous background, be more effective? Why, or why not?

6. How (and why) would the procedures described in the model be viewed by:
   a. a patrolman?
   b. a black citizen?
   c. a SAM?
   d. the county prosecutor?
   e. the tax assessor?
   f. the welfare agencies?
   g. the courts?

7. If you were a graduate student in a university and wished to evaluate the Urbanton model for a master's thesis, what would be the main features of your research design?

Part Four

Special Considerations

Four distinct aspects of community relationships that have direct and indirect impact on the police are:

1. Tensions that develop between police, prosecutors, and the courts.

2. Role confusion that arises from community expectations (or lack of them) regarding the corrections system.

3. Tensions between the police and the media.

4. The power struggle between police and political forces in the community.

Studies 1 and 2 here examine the paradoxes in the police role in relation to the juvenile justice system and misdemeanant probation practices. Recent progress has been shown especially in the latter field. Study 3 looks at police and the press. Study 4, on Blue Power, suggests the growing ability of the police to resist political pressures from both government and the community.

Study 5, an assessment of Attica, not only serves to show the current confused thinking of the nation as to remedies, but also brings into focus the interrelatedness of the police, prosecutors, courts, corrections, the media, and the community itself. All of these have an enormous stake in how we are to define "offenders" and how we are to handle them.

Juvenile Justice: System or Nonsystem?

The focus of this text is on relationships: police-community relationships, police–minority-group relationships, and police-youth relationships, and others within the criminal justice system. The relationships between the police and youth will be best understood by studying concrete situations rather than abstract concepts. For example, to underscore the importance of relationships within the system, and between the system and the public, we will consider the handling of juvenile offenders in the reasonably typical state of Michigan.

The study material describes how this system is *supposed* to function at present in Michigan, from the time the policeman comes in contact with the juvenile until, in some cases, the court takes over. The study is organized by the stages of the process:

1. The juvenile problem today.

2. Procedures of the police in apprehension and referral.

3. Procedures of the juvenile courts.

4. Effects of recent court decisions.

The criminal justice system is concerned with two aspects of the welfare of minors: (1) juvenile delinquency, and (2) child abuse and neglect. Although the problems of juveniles are not new, today's problems are increasingly serious. Because you can find extensive descriptions and analyses on this subject in the library,* this study will not duplicate the research efforts of others. Instead, it will show you how the "system," which society has created to handle juveniles, actually works.

The Juvenile Problem Today

"Our youth . . . have bad manners, contempt for authority; they show disrespect for their elders, and love to chatter in place of exercise.

---

*See Edward Eldefonso, *Law Enforcement and the Youthful Offender;* also Donald H. Bouma, *Kids and Cops.*

They no longer rise when their parents enter the room. They contradict their parents, chatter before company, gobble up their food, and tyrannize their teachers" (Ralph T. Hartell, *Reader's Digest Almanac—1971*, p. 634).

A Victorian complaint? No, it was Socrates speaking more than two thousand years ago. A more recent complaint also gives one a sense of *déjà vu* on an old problem: "One of the juvenile gangs was described as 'Eight young rascals' who had terrorized the city's streets and 'stolen and cut off people's purses.' Another group of young troublemakers included five boys, all between the ages of seven and eleven, who could not be controlled without force even inside the walls of the city jail."

This account did not come from the current press. It is part of a study of the urban ills of Nuremburg, Germany, in the late 1700s, made by Dr. Albert G. Hess of the National Council on Crime and Delinquency during his preparation of *The American Juvenile Court—A Handbook*. According to a review of the study, Dr. Hess is "suspicious" of FBI and other statistics that show "an alarming national increase in juvenile crime in recent years." He says that figures on juvenile crime have been collected only in the last decade; that methods of reporting are improving, and that many "offenses" of children, such as smoking, truancy, and loitering in pool halls, would not be considered violations if committed by adults. Youth rebellion has always been a problem. It may be that the publicity arising from the special systems of courts set up to handle the problems of juveniles adds to the impression that the present generation is a particularly delinquent one.

While it is true that the great majority of children become responsible adults without committing more than the normal childish pranks, it is also true that an alarming proportion of children come before the social agencies and the criminal justice system. Whatever one's appraisal of the FBI crime reports may be, official figures for 1969* showed that:

1. Almost 25% of all persons arrested for any major crime were under 15 years old.

2. Of these, 75% were boys; but the rate for girls is rising at the same rate.

3. Delinquencies in the suburbs are rising at an increasing rate.

4. 49% of all persons charged with a major crime in 1968 were juveniles.

5. The number of juveniles arrested for all offenses (except traffic violations) has doubled since 1960, while the number of adults arrested has increased by only 4%.

---

*James E. Clayton, the Washington *Post*, quoted in Lansing, Mich. *State Journal*, September 4, 1969.

A later study by the FBI (Ralph Hartell, p. 881) shows that arrests of juveniles for violent crimes were 148 percent higher in 1969 than in 1960; and that arrests in those under 18 for property crimes went up 85 percent.

Table 4–1 gives a further idea of the incidence of delinquency. These Delinquency Statistics come from the Probate (juvenile) Court of Ingham County, Michigan (population about 140,000).

In Table 4–2, you will see statistics about child abuse and neglect. Even though all 50 states have legislation in this matter, more than 9,000 such cases were reported in 1967 alone, according to the director of the children's division of the American Humane Association (Lansing State Journal, August 22, 1968). And he points out that it will be a long time before our local communities have developed adequate social-police relationships to implement the laws. "We have developed better procedures for protecting animals than for children." The increasing abuse or neglect of children ranges from allowing diaper rash (deliberate neglect) to striking malicious blows with the fist, and homicide, for which sanctions too often remain unimposed for want of adequate agencies, personnel, and courts. The enormous scope of the problem remains beyond the combined efforts of social agencies, volunteers, and the courts to cope with it.

And somewhere between the cases of deliberate juvenile offenders and the cases of neglect and abuse of juveniles are the runaways (Table 4–3). In one recent year a half million youngsters left home. You will see, by looking at Table 4–3, that an issue of Look magazine (July 25, 1967) featured a story on "Jimmy the Cop" who was assigned to some juvenile hangouts in Greenwich Village. He said, "Many are here in unwashed defiance of their parents' demands for good marks and proper conduct. They share food, shelter, mattresses and experiences in drugs with friends whose names they don't even know. They try to prove that it's love, not money, that makes the good life."

Police Procedures in Apprehension and Referral

There is no universal system for police procedures in handling juveniles. In a sense there cannot be, because of the varieties of situations from one jurisdiction to another, and because every child is different, and is different at different times, as are the officers in their reactions to them. Like the old song, "You never can tell about a woman/ That's why they're all so nice:/ You never see two alike at any one time/ And you never see one alike twice." The very essence of juvenile apprehension-adjudication-treatment is, to a certain degree, subjective. In that degree, it cannot be systematic. On the other hand, there must be minimal systemic, basic procedures to protect the rights of the child be he offender or offended. Concern for these rights is currently, as we shall see, the primary interest reflected in recent court decisions.

Table 4–1
Delinquency Statistics*
Ingham County, Michigan, Probate/Juvenile Court 1970

	Jan.	Feb.	Mar.	Apr.	May	June	July	Aug.	Sept.	Oct.	Nov.	Dec.	Total	Average
(1) New children petitioned into court, jurisdiction accepted, and processed for further court action	44	29	45	56	34	24	24	29	24	35	31	29	404	33.7
(2) New children petitioned into court, jurisdiction accepted, but matter resolved at intake level	11	9	24	23	17	16	29	15	6	17	31	26	224	18.6
(3) Children petitioned into court, jurisdiction transferred to county of residence	2	7	10	5	13	9	4	0	0	2	7	3	62	5.2
(4) Children petitioned into court, jurisdiction denied	10	0	3	6	2	0	5	3	4	1	3	1	38	3.2
(5) Children petitioned into court, jurisdiction accepted and transferred to S.D.S.S.**	1	2	1	5	3	5	3	1	3	2	4	2	32	2.7
(6) Children under official jurisdiction petitioned for rehearings	18	19	22	45	25	29	20	28	25	25	18	9	283	23.6

*From the *Annual Report*, Ingham County, Michigan, Probate Court, Juvenile Division.

**State Department of Social Services.

Notes to Chapter Seven

1. J. Milton Yinger, "Who Are We?"

2. See also the University of Michigan study, *Field Surveys III,* by Albert J. Reiss, Jr. and associates, for the President's Crime Commission. This comprehensive study includes information regarding the images and evaluations of owners and managers of businesses toward the police, patterns of behavior in police and citizen transactions, and career orientations of police officers.

3. ACLU undated pamphlet, *Police Power and Citizens' Rights,* p. 8.

4. William A. Westley, "The Police: A Sociological Study," p. 163. Unpublished Ph.D. dissertation, University of Chicago, 1951.

5. University of Houston, et al., p. vi.

6. Karl Menninger was a consultant to the President's Crime Commission in 1966 and also a consultant in the development of the Lemberg Center for the Study of Violence at Brandeis University. See his book *The Crime of Punishment.*

7. The attitudes of victims of crime toward police are examined in Study 4 (Part I) of the Radelet and Reed *Studies.* Study 4 draws on the findings of the study by Albert J. Reiss and associates (University of Michigan) for the President's Crime Commission.

8. Arthur L. Stinchcombe, "The Control of Citizen Resentment in Police Work." Unpublished, undated manuscript.

9. Arthur L. Stinchcombe, "Institutions of Privacy in the Determination of Police Administrative Practice."

10. Skolnick devotes considerable attention to various aspects of this complicated matter in *Justice Without Trial.* See also Skolnick and Woodworth, "Bureaucracy, Information, and Social Control."

11. University of Michigan (Reiss and associates), *Field Surveys III,* vol. 1, pt. 2, pp. 113–114.

12. Quoted by Richard Rogin in "Now It's Welfare Lib." *The New York Times Magazine,* September 27, 1970, p. 83.

Chapter Eight

Perception, Attitudes, Beliefs, and Values

Psychology is concerned primarily with three basic behavioral processes: learning, motivation, and perception. All systems of psychology are interested in these processes, although in different order and emphasis. Some psychologists start with learning, while others start with perception or motivation. They may come out with somewhat different perspectives, but all agree that these processes are closely related.

For example, if one starts with learning, one thinks of behavior as resulting from a stimulus that may be inside or outside the body; therefore, in this context, motivation would be discussed largely in terms of stimulus. If one starts with motivation, he might get into a rather elaborate analysis of body changes and conditions that give rise to certain behavior. It is not necessary for our purpose to discuss all the details of these complex psychological phenomena; it is enough simply to be aware of their existence and implications, as reviewed in this chapter.[1]

Three Schools of Thought

The psychologists who start with learning (often called behaviorists) stress an objective, detached, scientific approach to the study of behavior. It is essentially stimulus and response, "input" and "output," that interests them; the school of thought they represent is often associated with conditioned reflexes. It is a cause-and-effect approach to behavior; a given cause produces a given (largely predictable) result. In this theory, emotion is a conditioned response to environmental elements. Man is basically like other animals, with little allowance for spiritual and judgmental faculties.

Psychologists who start with motivation (often called psychoanalysts) tend to look inside the person to identify the needs, impulses, and emotions that cause his behavior, with special attention to subconscious and irrational elements in human performance. G. M. Gilbert describes this theory:

> ... man gets along in society by suppressing his primitive instincts. This is a continuously frustrating experience, the theory goes, and creates a reservoir of pent-up aggression which must inevitably erupt into overt actions of hostility. ... the best we can hope to do is to contain the aggression which is the price of civilization. ["What Makes Us Behave As People?"]

Then there are those psychologists who start with the process of perception (sometimes called phenomenologists) who assume the individual relates and gives meaning to the world around him. How does the individual come to understand and deal with this world? For this school of thought, behavior is a response to the world *as it is perceived*. The assumption is that man is a rational creature. One individual may see the world in zany terms as judged by another individual, but once it is discovered *how* he sees it, his behavior becomes understandable.

Each of the three schools of thought has produced evidence to support its views, and each has been applied to significant problems. All three schools are represented in reputable professional psychotherapy and on university faculties. In consumer psychology in the business realm, there are those who foster motivational research approaches, while others examine product images, and still others concentrate on advertising stimuli and customer responses.

Perception in Behavioral Processes

In the preceding chapters we discussed how the police officer sees himself and how others see the police officer. Some analysis now of perception as a psychological process in human behavior may be beneficial. We begin with the assumption that people—at least from the point of view of the behaver—behave in a rational, purposeful, logical manner, depending upon how the objective world is perceived. Each of us sees the world and responds in accord with the way he perceives it. Fortunately for human welfare and progress, we do not all see the world in the same way. Yet however we see it, each of us will behave rationally *within that framework*. The base of our individual point of view is the nature of the self, as we have seen, and not necessarily what really happens "out there" in the world outside of self. Each of us helps to create what's "out there." And perhaps the ultimate maturity and wisdom, for each of us, is the recognition that *the world as I perceive it is not the only world there is.*

Hadley Cantril, a communications psychologist, has referred to three baseball umpires who were talking with each other about their job experiences. One said, "Some are balls, some are strikes, I call 'em as they are." The second umpire retorted, "Some are balls, some are strikes, I call 'em as I see 'em." And the third one mused, "Some are balls, some are strikes, and *they ain't nothing until I call 'em.*"

This story goes to the heart of the problem of perception. If we were to combine the truth in the different approaches of the umpires, we might conclude (1) that we respond to things in accordance with the physical realities out there in nature; (2) that the physical reality is perceived in accordance with some possible distortions in our subjective processes; and (3) that we enter into a transaction with the energies of nature and abstract components that integrate with our perceptual processes and create the world within which we operate and to which we respond. "They ain't nothing until I call 'em!"

Essentially the same ideas may be arranged in the following sequence:

1. When we talk or write about something, what we describe is something that happens inside of us as much as what happens outside.

2. What each of us can talk or write about is only a very small part of all that is going on "out there."

3. Many of our problems in communication arise because we forget that individual experiences are never identical.

4. Since each of us perceives (experiences) the world in bits and pieces, we tend to communicate about it in bits and pieces. To a certain extent, our individual experience teaches us *what* to see and hear. Remember the third umpire.

5. Communication is a human transaction. It depends upon symbols—words, gestures, etc. But the symbols do not have the same meaning for others with different experiences. Hence, what we call a "communication breakdown."[2]

Basis in the Self

How we perceive the world, then, is based upon the *self:* my own unique experience and what happens inside me. Earlier we observed that each of us actually has many selves, not just one. We noted that these selves are related to our positions in the social scene—our social roles. We also indicated that our perceptions of self depend upon the context at the moment, varying with what has gone before, who or what we have been thinking of, and the immediate problem or situation we face.

Because our roles are social, the word-symbols we use to designate them often denote reciprocal human relationships (i.e. *transactions*). The associations are often implied "pairings"; for example: man (woman); boy (girl); lecturer (audience); father or mother (child); teacher (student); writer (reader); police officer . . . what? How one answers this will probaby reveal his perception of the principal role of the policeman. Police officer and law breaker? Police officer and lost child? Police officer and derelict drunk?

For efficient functioning, flexibility is required of all of us, as we shift from one self (role) to another. Thus, we should strive to be open-minded in our perceptions of others, not only to be sensitive to the role they are playing at the time, but also so we can relate to (empathize with) the reality they represent. We limit perception when we insist on dealing with them in terms of our own fixed ideas as to what they represent.

Each of us tries to maintain a stable world in spite of evidence to the contrary. We tend to shape things according to our conceptions and our purposes. This tendency, of course, varies by individuals. Some people are relatively more rigid or dogmatic than others and take a long time to accept and adapt to reality. Some people are relatively adaptable and rather easily shift and adjust to situations as they really are. It is a question of how much stability a particular individual needs, regarding either his self-image or the outer world. Some individuals resist the forces of exterior change, inappropriately, by forcing a posture of outer stability. We say "inappropriately" because insensitivity to situational shifts may mean corresponding failure to shift the self and therefore to adjust one's perceptions flexibly and adaptively. This repeats what we said earlier about the difficulty some individuals have in adjusting to rapid and drastic changes in social role; for example, civilian to soldier, soldier to civilian, etc.

Consider again the first two umpires. So long as we think there is a real world out there, we may kid ourselves into believing that we adapt to it reasonably well. "I call 'em as they are." However, as we come to recognize that there may be some truth in what the third umpire said, we should recognize that our "reasonable adaptation" may reflect a greater ability to *distort* the real world than to adjust to it. "They ain't nothing until I call 'em."

Rigidity and Flexibility

A certain professor, let us say, has a student in class who the professor *knows* is cheating in examinations. The student has not been caught at it (the student being very clever!), but the professor is nonetheless sure that the student is guilty. The professor knows this because of the way the student sits and looks around the room and at the ceiling during exams. The professor is certain that some day the student will blunder and be caught red-handed.

Could the professor be wrong in his judgment? "Just a hunch," he might say, "based on years of experience." He could be right. And then again, he could be wrong. Lots of people get fixed ideas about other people for which there is no factual evidence. To maintain our images of self and of others is a human thing to do: to seek consistency and stability and the comfort of predictability. To think stereotypically —"group think"—requires much less effort than to think in individualistic terms. "If you've met (or seen) one, you've met (or seen) them all!" Stereotyping is a form of perceptual shorthand.

This human tendency is something each of us must learn to control. We must stretch our perceptions to enable us to see the contrary evidence, the unfamiliar, the unexpected. True, it is difficult to do this. People of different backgrounds—cultural and social class, racial, ethnic, educational, and occupational differences—not only see things differently; they also *fail* to see things, even though presented right before their eyes. An abundance of psychological research and numerous measures and exercises prove this conclusively. For example, an individual's tendency toward a closed mind (dogmatism) can be scientifically measured. Basically it is a blocking of perception.[3]

We see the accustomed and the familiar; the things that are not emotionally threatening; things related to special professional training; things with which we agree.

Perceptual Shift

Studies have shown that when people are asked to evaluate material that carries strong social and personal importance for them, they will displace the material from what should be its true scale placement.[4] The psychological term for this is *displacement;* a popular term is *perceptual shift.* Perhaps an example will best make the point.

John Q. Trustworthy considers himself a completely law-abiding citizen. He will not knowingly violate a law. He thinks that major violators are evil and minor violators are bad. He is annoyed by people who do not obey parking regulations or who ignore no-littering admonitions. John Q. is also a dog-lover, and when he walks his Border Terriers, their requirements are quite important to him. In his entire life, John Q. has received but one summons from a police officer, and that for creating a public nuisance with his dogs.

John Q. does not see how this could possibly be construed as a nuisance. But a policeman saw it that way. As a result, John Q.'s perception of the police shifted slightly; as a matter of fact, it shifted quite a bit in the immediate aftermath of the incident. John Q.'s feelings were more than a little changed. This is displacement, and any experienced police officer would have no trouble in supplying further examples. Law-abiding citizens often tend to be especially in favor of strict observance of the law when it applies to *other people.*

Perception and Role Performance

Having reflected that how we see ourselves, how we see others, and how others see us are subject to the fundamental psychological dynamic of the perceptual process, with its inherent "booby-traps," it may be useful to return momentarily to role theory. A basic question in this reference is that of the relationship between perceived role expectations and actual role performance. We have devoted some attention to this question. But to underline our point, harking back to some prior references to Reiss and Bordua, to Sterling and others, here is a Preiss and Ehrlich formulation of an important aspect of the matter, drawn from the policeman's world:

> In the eyes of the *new* policeman, the whole evaluation system appeared as "a jungle with a few landmarks." The diversity of post practices and the ambiguities of policies on law enforcement made it necessary for him to "play it by ear" and to cultivate a kind of practiced opportunism with regard to matching others' expectations with appropriate behavior. In the final analysis, the payoff of high evaluation was promotion. Strategic informal contacts and skill in identifying and satisfying the expectations of superior officers were considered more important assets than formal civil service ratings and examination scores. "Getting an inside track" and "playing the game" were seen as the major techniques for achieving career success.[5]

"Playing it by ear" seems to be an intrinsic element of the police officer's role behavior. It is a notable thread in the tapestry of the police subculture. It exemplifies role performance governed by perceived audience expectations, although "the actor" does not necessarily conform to the expectations of any given audience. To the extent that he does not, there will probably be tension in that particular facet of police-community relations, defined in terms of opposing or conflicting perceptions of role. Logically, the general direction of a solution to this problem will be in working toward more *consensual* agreement in the role perceptions (hence, expectations) of diverse audiences or "reference groups."

All of this we have earlier suggested. Again the question of consensus emerges, at this point as a question of how different people *see* things, how they are influenced by their differences in experience, culture, values, etc. To repeat: some consensus is a requisite, some set of basic, minimal agreements is necessary for a social system to operate at all. Beyond this, there must be some further range of consensus for the system to operate efficiently.

It is not difficult to translate this into police and community relations terms. My way of seeing a problem or situation is not the only way there is to see it. If I insist that my way of seeing it is "the whole story—as any fool should see!", my rigidity impedes the prospect for consensus in transactions with others who see it differently. If I insist that problem-solving efforts be "on my terms" exclusively, there is no chance for success. For in effect, I am imposing my experience, my "way of life," my perception of a problem upon others.

In doing this, we often cite our credentials: what we consider a particularly germane kind of experience, our "professional know-how," our educational accomplishments, or merely on the basis of "I knew somebody once who . . ." No doubt such credentials may be valuable in what we can contribute to a given problem-solving effort. Yet it is still only a single experience, one person's perception of the situation. Complex problems in today's world, exemplified by the police-community relations field, require more to solve them than single perceptions and experiences. It is the diversity of perceptions and experiences that creates the problems in the first place. This is a pivotal principle in police and community relations programs.

Some Further Illustrations

Additional illustrations of the congruence of perception and role enactment may be helpful. An interesting one is provided in Martin Miller's *Systemic Model of Police Morale*.[6] One of its features is its composite portrayal of the interrelationships of several social systems— which is also suggested in another study in the same place dealing with community structure.

An aspect of Sterling's research (*Changes in Role Concept of Police Officers*) that should be mentioned again pertains to the manner in which perceptions of role attributes change. His assumption is that training and education are among the variables that affect role perceptions. If a police recruit at the start of training conceives of police work as consisting largely of physical tasks carried out in a hostile environment, he will logically see such role attributes as physical strength and courage as essential for the work. After training, if the recruit comes to recognize an important role for the police in performing various public service tasks and sees that people can be "manipulated" more easily through verbal rather than physical skills, he will value more highly such role attributes as verbal skills, courtesy and "people knowledge."

Niederhoffer makes some additional points that are relevant here:

1. The police are *perceived,* by members of minority groups, as a symbol of white oppression. Members of minority groups are *perceived* by the police as "symbolic assailants" and "suspicious persons." On both sides, there are "experiences" to bolster the perceptions. But both perceptions are nonetheless stereotypic, and the stereotypes are mutually reinforcing, especially if there are no

"break-throughs" on either side of significant contrasting experiences.

2. Having more minority group policemen on the force may be one important possible break-through, with vital effect upon perceptions of the police department. On the other hand, the black policeman may be perceived as an "Uncle Tom," as a "fink" and traitor, as demanding from his own group a standard of behavior more stringent than that expected of others.

3. Certain groups in the community simply do not perceive the police as trustworthy; contrarily, the police do not perceive certain groups in the community as trustworthy. The current term for this is *credibility*. Obviously, it is basically a problem of perception. [*Behind the Shield*, p. 182 ff.]

Hans Toch has dealt with this in a brief article in *Police*. He refers to police officers who often cite their "experience" in support of sundry opinions. But, he says, the kind of person one is (including the kind of job he holds) has much to do with what he experiences, as opposed to what anyone else might experience in the same situation. A policeman is supposed to be good at spotting trouble. Yet the ability to spot trouble does not necessarily mean that one understands the reason for it. There are even those who would argue that the police need not understand the causes of crime—that their job is enforcement.

If one takes this position, Toch continues, then on what basis can a police officer lobby for the death penalty, or criticize probation officers, or insist that sex offenders should be kept in prison? Certainly he may express his views *as an interested citizen*. But he should keep in mind that his *police* experience does not bear on these matters, by his own role definition.

My point here [Toch concludes] is that the police officer's "experience" is highly specialized, and no more conducive to an *accurate* picture of people than that of other observers. It is, of course, experience that is relevant to police work . . . but even here in a rather narrow way. If the professional police officer dealt with the public courteously, fairly and effectively, his relevant experiences would be a string of courteous, fair and effective dealings with people. Unfortunately, many "experienced" officers find themselves substituting for this requirement an imposing string of tense encounters, displays of confidence, "conning" talks, transparently patronizing intimacies, bluffs that may or may not have worked, and force that did. This sort of "experience" may give the *illusion* of competence to deal with people, but the people involved have not been consulted in arriving at this illusion. ["A Note on Police 'Experience'"]

Toch summarizes by saying that all of us have an inordinate capacity for arranging the world in such a way that incorrect perceptions are confirmed. We see, selectively, what we want to see, what we expect to see, and weight it with our values: good-bad, true-false, acceptable-unacceptable, etc. Thus, we have the sorting process, separating the "good guys and the bad guys," the "white hats and the black hats," the "ins and the outs." With youngsters, it's "cowboys and Indians," "cops and robbers." Whatever the particular terms, it's *we-and-they*.

The self-fulfilling principle is also operative in our perceptual transactions. Because we tend to see what we expect to see—blocking out the unexpected, the evidence that does not fit our predisposed picture—there is a tendency to see only what substantiates our predisposition. Persons thought of as suspicious persons therefore act "suspiciously"; policemen thought of as brutal act "brutally."[7]

Every stereotypic "bad" trait that we attribute generally to an entire group of "bad guys" stems from some impulse that all of us have trouble taming. We accuse some groups of being belligerent and hostile, others of being dirty, and others of grabbing all they can get. We were taught in childhood that these are undesirable qualities; therefore, "bad" people are so characterized. We forget that the real war is between the "good guys" and the "bad guys" *within each of us:* the good self and the bad self. Both good and bad feelings are in each of us, and the crucial task is to use those that are appropriate to the reality in which we find ourselves. Refinement of our own perceptions in such a manner helps to modify the perceptions others have of us. (Peters, "A Look at Ourselves," pp. 58–61.)

More Illustrations

To illustrate further the point that reality may be quite different from one's perceptions, we may take the example of research in the social and behavioral sciences. Many observers charge that objectivity in such research is patently impossible, that therefore all results must be interpreted by first of all checking the bias of the particular researcher. But competent social science researchers are aware of their predispositions and take them into account in their work. Banton, for example, confesses that he began his study of five police departments in Scotland and the United States with the assumption that American police officers might well experience more social isolation than their British counterparts. But at the conclusion of the study, Banton wrote:

> American police may seem isolated from the community to an American observer because he compares them with other occupational groups in the same society; they may at the same time seem to an outsider much less isolated than policemen in other societies. [*The Policeman in the Community*, p. 215]

An example of another phase of the perceptual process in police work is indicated in this passage, also in an English context, from Victor Meek:

... When a policeman has stopped a hundred people, which number has included perhaps ten proved guilty persons, he has learned the behaviour under these conditions of ninety innocent people and of ten thieves. In the next hundred stopped, he will have twenty thieves, in the next perhaps thirty. Not altogether because thieves are thicker but because his "Police here," or "Excuse me a moment, Sir," are [sic] enough to satisfy him, by the reaction of the person stopped, whether he is dealing with a sheep or a goat, whether chummy is in the clear or loaded. So to the sheep his next remark is, "I am very sorry to bother you but my watch has stopped. Can you please tell me the time?" The answer will naturally be, "If you want to know the time, I thought you had to ask another policeman," and the mutual appreciation of this witticism sends chummy away chuckling and quite unaware that Section 66 has been tried on him. [*Cops and Robbers*, p. 86][8]

Here we see that experience builds biases that may at times be helpful in role performance. But Toch's caveat must also be kept in mind.

Skolnick comments on the "discretion" of the British policeman:

A key distinction between the English and American policeman is that the former tends to be more *discreet* in an interactional sense as well as *discrete* in an administrative one, thereby avoiding the censure that is often the lot of the American policeman. [*Justice Without Trial*, p. 67]

In line with the reference to objectivity of social science research, statistics often reveal the perils of perception. Jokes are common about "the numbers game," particularly as applied to such problems as poverty, welfare, crime, unemployment, etc. Counting the number of windmills in Delaware is relatively simple. A windmill exists "out there" in a way that is directly countable. But suppose the statistics pertain to intelligence tests administered to children. The test itself is one problem; what it actually measures is another. The inferences drawn from the data are still another. Intelligence is a man-made concept, *socially defined*. In such circumstances, shadow is easily confused with substance. One or two measurable dimensions of a multifaceted problem are often interpreted as "the answer." And the unmeasured or unmeasurable aspects of the problem may be far more important than those that can be measured. Furthermore, even "good" data may be obsolete or irrelevant by the time it is published.

Factors in Perceptual Distortion

Since perception is a behavioral process filled with hazards and limitations, it is well to be aware of the sources of perceptual distortion. Some important ones are these, their relative importance varying by individuals and situations:

1. Personality rigidity or dogmatism. Relative ability to adjust to the forces of change.

2. Emotional "loading." Illustrated by perceptual shift (displacement) in the example of the dog lover.

3. Experiential limitations—difficult sometimes to recognize and accept realistically—but part of the human condition.

4. Cultural myopia—sometimes called "tunnel vision." Our perceptions are weighted by the attitudes, beliefs, and values we accept at our station in life: ethnic, racial, social class and other such considerations.

5. Prejudice and predisposition, stereotyping, etc. This is a kind of *attitude,* of course—one closely associated with personality rigidity and emotional loading—but for that very reason, of special importance in understanding perceptual distortion. Actually, prejudice involves a combination of several factors that distort perception.

Perception and Attitudes

This leads us directly to a consideration of the relationship between perception and attitudes, beliefs, and values. The perceptual process begins with sensation: audio, visual, olfactory, etc. Perception is the meaningful interpretation of sensations as representative of external objects—*apparent* knowledge of "what's out there" (Jozef Cohen, *Sensation and Perception,* pp. 5, 6).

Sensations and perceptions are distinct. A color (sensation) differs from a specific colored object (perception). Hence, as Cohen explains:

> Combinations of sensations, by repetition, become associated with a novel external object and the "memory" retained. The perceiver unconsciously compares sensations present to sensations stored (as a modern computer processes data) and involuntarily "bets" that current sensations are evoked by equivalent external objects. [Ibid., p. 6]

Perceptions are the *sole* internal representatives of "what's out there"—the mind's reflection of matter. Aristotle noted, "Nothing is in the mind that does not pass through the senses," and Leonardo da Vinci declared, "All of our knowledge has its origins in perceptions." Only a few contemporary psychologists would challenge this. Most would agree that perception is an interpretation of sensations; a few would say that perceptions are "invariants" of sensations.[9]

In any case, our perceptions are the basis for our opinions, our viewpoints on any given subject. These are ideas we may or may not have thought out in limited degree and are still open to dispute and subject to relatively easy change. But some of our opinions assume a certain constancy. They take deeper root, and we are less willing to change them. They become judgments (convictions) on which we are prepared to act, positively or negatively. These are *attitudes*. The basis of our attitudes is in social experiences, *as perceived*. A *belief*, in turn, is a kind of attitude. So is a *value*. To distinguish, let us say that one takes the position that people with green hair should not be permitted to live in a certain neighborhood. This is an attitude. Or simply to say, "I can't stand people with green hair." If, however, one goes on to add "... because people with green hair cannot be trusted," one thereby cites a *belief* to explain the attitude. This is the plausible *rationalization* for the attitude; an "accommodation of beliefs and attitudes," as Gordon Allport stated it. The *value* is implicit: the quality of not being trustworthy is evil, wrong, undesirable. A value is a norm of behavior, an index of "the good, the true, and the beautiful." Basically, a value is itself an attitude and a belief—all based upon perception. And as we have observed, perception is a precarious process indeed; it cannot always be trusted.

Attitudes develop primarily because they tie an individual to a group that he feels can aid him in attaining goals important to him. Thus, the choices a person makes, such as to affiliate with this organization rather than that, to join this party rather than that, to read this newspaper rather than that, are often decisions based on a certain set of attitudes, beliefs, and values. *We tend to prefer what coincides with what we already believe.* Our perceptions of opposing attitudes, beliefs, and values tend to support what we already believe. Therefore, our attitudes, beliefs, and values tend to be self-insulating and reinforcing, because we shut out of our perceptions any contrary or opposing evidence. The alternative creates internal *value conflict*, which can be very upsetting, because it involves the recognition that a cherished belief may not be truth.

As we shall see in the next chapter, what we have been suggesting is intimately related to prejudice, which is an attitude functioning as both a cause and an effect of perceptual distortion. It should be emphasized that our attitudes frequently have a significant emotional dimension; we *feel* deeply about something or somebody.

A Quick Look at Learning

Let us consider for a moment how our discussion might have progressed if we had focused on learning rather than on perception. Learning is popularly thought of as what amounts to only one of its dimensions, i.e., the *cognitive*. This means facts, "hard" information, data, ideas and concepts—what children are expected to memorize, e.g., the multiplication tables, the alphabet, the capital city of Thailand, the number of windmills in Delaware, the definition of democracy, the ten leading hitters in the National League, and the like.

This is more or less important knowledge. But it is not all that we learn. We also acquire knowledge of feelings, of emotions—the *affective* dimension of learning (sensitivity)—and as Margaret Heaton put it, "feelings are facts."[10] This kind of learning is surely as important as cognitive learning; in fact, with reference to attitudes and prejudices, it may be much more important.

Another, correlative dimension of learning has to do with the development of certain *skills,* such as objective habits of thought and reasoning (logic), and the art of putting into practice, in relationships with others, what one *knows* and *feels.* Yet again, learning begins with sensation and perception. And if learning is *growth,* is it possible without motivation? The close kinship of the three basic psychological processes in human behavior is evident, no matter which is regarded as primary.

The Communication Problem

Problems of human relations are everywhere referred to as "communication" problems. There is substantial validity in this diagnosis, but the complexity of the communication problem is not readily grasped. There is often a tendency to suggest, for example, that "talk sessions" will cure the problem, communication being defined simply as "talk." If the parties can be brought together for "dialogue," all will be well!

One implication of our discussion in this chapter is that the communication problem—for instance, in police and community relations—will not be solved so easily. This is true for several reasons, each emphasizing that mere messages do no usually produce mutual understanding. We may summarize our analysis by indicating a few of the reasons why the communication problem is so formidable:[11]

1. Any message in a communication situation may touch upon at least three levels of meaning. A message can contain seeming *fact—* a report of reality *as the communicator sees it.* A message may also contain *inference.* And it may also contain *judgment.* Thus, a message may report an event "out there"; it may include conclusions drawn about the event; and it may include a personal evaluation of it. Much argument takes place between people and groups at all three of these levels of meaning—the latter two directly and the first implicitly.

2. A second important barrier to clarity in communication may be in the *value of differences* and *difference of values.* This is sometimes referred to as the problem of "value gap." It pertains to differences in the conditions of life—age, education, occupation, experience, sex, social class, ethnicity, culture, race, religion, etc.—which, as we have seen, vitally influence our perceptions and, correspondingly, our attitudes, beliefs, and values. This is, of course, a common

cause of difficulty in intergroup communication. So ingrained and deeply rooted are our values that we seldom have occasion to identify them specifically, even to ourselves. Thus, when confronted with groups of persons who evaluate differently, we are likely to think of them as strange, primitive, stubborn, inferior, or even badly motivated. Pfiffner suggests this difficulty in somewhat different terms in his treatment of occupational value systems, cited earlier.

To teach values in American classrooms today is an awesome assignment. In a society in which there is consensus about what constitutes the good, the true, and the beautiful, the task of teaching values is simple. In a pluralist society, however, the task is infinitely more difficult.[12]

John Kane asks the question: Why so much personal and social disorganization in our society? His reply: (1) rapid social and cultural change; and (2) *value conflict*.[13]

We referred previously to current research probing the value gap between police and policed.[14]

3. Difficulties in intergroup or interpersonal communication are created by our *defenses against reorientation*. One such defense is selective perception: we see what we want to see, what we expect to see. Another is selective retention: we consciously retain only a very small fraction of our perceptive input—usually that in which we have a personal interest. A relevant experience would be that of explaining to someone else something that is important to us, only to have that person later deny any previous knowledge of it. Another relevant experience is also incongruent: to have someone we do not like say something with which we agree. In such circumstances, we tend to remember the statement but to forget who said it. Campaign speeches seldom change votes.

4. Still another communication obstacle is the tendency *to place too much emphasis on the message*. All communication systems comprise a source, a channel, a message, and a receiver. The relationship between the source and the receiver merits much more attention than it ordinarily gets. This is the essence of the so-called credibility question. In a nutshell, *we believe people whom we trust*. The place, then, to begin establishing more effective communication between police and community is not with the message to be communicated, or even the system by which it is to be communicated. The place to begin is with existing *attitudes* between source and receiver: the police and the community "audiences." It is the *quality* of this relationship that will be decisive—the degree of genuine mutual trust that can be enkindled. And since attitudes begin with perceptions, some exercise in assessing perceptions may be called for on all sides.

5. Having mentioned dialogue, we should consider what is characteristic of authentic dialogue. It is apparent that discussion does not always cast light on problems. Sometimes the deaf talk to the deaf,

and separation is aggravated. Why so? One reason is that each side enters the discussion "with guns loaded." Each insists that experience is all on his side. We ask others to wake up and see the truth, to "let the facts speak for themselves." The difficulty is, of course, that the facts do not speak. So we presume to speak for them. That our neighbor might possess some precious particle of the truth hardly occurs to us. We ask him only to accept our terms for a solution and "to sign on the dotted line."

This is a combat approach to problem solving. True dialogue has no chance. The aim is to vanquish others involved in the discussion, to disqualify them, even to embarrass and humiliate them and sometimes to attack their personhood. Anything goes: smug statements, pretended indignation, mockery, shrugging of the shoulders, irony, play on words, intended ambiguity, pomposity, inflammatory gestures, and all such things. We even gloat over reducing to silence someone with whom we started out to have a discussion. Forceful argument becomes more force than argument.

The French scholar Marcel Deschoux put it this way:

> ... it is the spirit of peace that is the condition for authentic dialogue. War, attack, violence ... have no place here. The essential thing is to accept fully the presence of someone else, and to open ourselves to his influence. What makes a dialogue is reciprocal presence and actions based on recognized equality. In both the action and the presence, there is mutual involvement. Dialogue is related to propaganda as love is to rape. For any authentic dialogue, therefore, there is work to be done first within ourselves. For it is, after all, *truth*—as Emerson insisted—that is the third party in dialogue.[15]

Notes to Chapter Eight

1. This part of our discussion is based generally on two presentations made by Eugene L. Hartley to the National Institute on Police and Community Relations at Michigan State University in May 1961 and May 1965. Professor Hartley was at that time a member of the faculty of the Department of Psychology at City College, New York. He is currently Dean of the College of Community Services at the University of Wisconsin, Green Bay.

2. These ideas are attractively presented in "Communications," *Kaiser Aluminum News*, vol. 23, no. 3, 1965. See also Study 4 (Part II), "Points on Perception," in Radelet and Reed, *Studies*.

3. Milton Rokeach has been prominent among psychologists researching this matter. See, for example, his study *The Open and Closed Mind*.

4. See, for example, Hovland and Sherif, "Judgmental Phenomena and Scales of Attitude Measurement."

5. Preiss and Ehrlich, *An Examination of Role Theory,* p. 30. Both Neider-hoffer and McNamara refer to the "rabbi" system in the New York City Police Department. "Rabbi" means a person with influence in the department, who can help officers to "get ahead."

6. See Martin Miller, "Systemic Model of Police Morale," Study 2, in Part II, Radelet and Reed *Studies.*

7. The International Association of Chiefs of Police has produced a valuable series of training guides in human relations for police officers. See Nelson A. Watson, *Attitudes—A Factor in Performance; Human Relations Training for Police—A Syllabus; Improving the Officer-Citizen Contact;* and *Issues in Human Relations—Threats and Challenges.*

8. Section 66 of the British code states: "Any constable may stop, search and detain any vessel, boat, cart or carriage in or upon which there shall be reason to suspect that anything stolen or unlawfully obtained may be found, and also any person who may be reasonably suspected of having or conveying in any manner anything stolen or unlawfully obtained."

9. For example, James J. Gibson contends, in his book *The Senses Considered as Perceptual Systems,* that sensory inputs generate sensations, and also information about the exterior world. *Changeful* information is not perception; only permanent, stable, *invariant* information is perception, according to Gibson.

10. Margaret Heaton, *Feelings Are Facts.* Intergroup Education Pamphlet, undated. The National Conference of Christians and Jews.

11. This summary is, in part, dependent on an article by William R. Carmack, "Practical Communication Tools for Group Involvement in Police-Community Programs."

12. See, for instance, Max Birnbaum, "Whose Values Should Be Taught?"

13. John J. Kane, "Personal and Social Disorganization."

14. Rokeach, Miller, and Snyder, "The Value Gap Between Police and Policed." Chief of Police Fred Ferguson of Covina, California, has said: "Frequently, the imposition of certain arbitrary, so-called middle-class standards has done a great deal to break down police-community relations. The number one problem in police education and training is how to properly teach officers to respect and utilize the cultural differences in people."

15. Marcel Deschoux, *L'Homme et Son Prochain.* Presses Universitaires de France. Originally, a lecture presented at the Eighth Congress of the Sociétés de Philosophie de Langue Français, held in Toulouse, circa 1960.

Chapter Nine

Prejudice
and Rumor

The author of this text once spoke to a group on the subject of prejudice. Following the talk, several listeners gathered around the speaker. One lady said: "That was a delightful speech. But we are fortunate not to have these problems in our town. We have no X, Y, or Z people here, and we probably never will have, because they know they wouldn't be welcome here!"

The lady had made a better speech than the author about the nature of prejudice. Here is a subject about which a library full of books and articles has been written and countless speeches and exhortations have been delivered. The last of these is not in sight. One hesitates to be critical of high-minded evangelism, yet one may venture the observation that so much of the rhetoric about prejudice seems to deal with other people's prejudices rather than with one's own. Sometimes one wonders if there may not be such a thing as prejudice directed against those whom one regards as prejudiced!

Perception and Prejudice

Recall what we have said about the relationship between perception and attitudes. Prejudice is a kind of attitude. The word means "to prejudge." It is an attitude formulated with reference to objects, persons, groups, or values on the basis of narrow, superficial, or limited information, or association or experience. Because prejudice is an attitude, it involves an *action* element (discrimination), an *emotional* element (we feel strongly about the object of the prejudice), and, of course, it is wholly *acquired* behavior. We are not born with our prejudices, although various studies have indicated that prejudicial attitudes are acquired at an early age. One such study (Trager and Yarrow, *They Learn What They Live*), of preschool age children in Philadelphia, revealed that these subjects had already developed some clearcut we-and-they differentiations in their play patterns. As one author has put it, "Every bigot was once a child."[1]

Prejudice is in large part irrational and therefore results in irresponsible judgment. Yet there is often a tendency to point a finger at "them," with accusations of irresponsibility. "Why do I dislike them? Because they're so irresponsible, that's why!" Remember what was said earlier about projecting on others the traits we have had trouble controlling in ourselves?

Why "irrational"? Because prejudice springs from emotional roots in personality; it is charged with feelings. It is in large part learning in its affective, rather than cognitive, dimension. This is one reason why information alone will rarely cure a prejudice. A person may "know better" and still be prejudiced. Feelings of anti-Semitism might be lessened, even markedly, by facts. The thrust of one definition of prejudice is that it is "being down on what one is not up on." However, as an epidemic social disease, prejudice—as exemplified by anti-Semitism—will not usually submit meekly to facts. Too many of what the Overstreets called "the gentle people of prejudice" do not wish to be deprived of their feelings by mere facts. Anthropologists may prove in a hundred ways that there are no essential differences among the races of man. Alas, there are many people who remain at least mildly skeptical, and many more who refuse to be influenced by objective, scientific information. After all, the scientists themselves are probably prejudiced!

Hostility and Threat

Prejudice implies *hostility*—a sense of *threat*—with we-and-they differentiation at its base. "We" are better than "they" (attitude) because we got here first (belief), or because the Bible says so (at least as we interpret it), or because they are "subhuman." If one grants the premise, for example, that "they" are "subhuman," prejudice and discriminatory behavior seem justified. "Let them stay in their place!" So it is that a hierarchy of mankind is arranged to suit one's perceptions, and one "feels very strongly about it." So strongly, indeed, that we will not bend an inch, will give no ground, will not entertain even the possibility of compromise. So strongly that we are insulted by the suggestion that we could be wrong, and so on.

Just as with the self-image, in which the individual has a generalized self as well as multiple specific selves, each of us has both general and specific attitudes. A person has a general attitude or outlook toward life, toward the world in general, and toward other people. Terms such as introvert and extrovert, optimist and pessimist, refer to such generalized attitudes. A person also has specific attitudes regarding specific things. Psychologists agree that a person who is prejudiced toward one group will usually be prejudiced toward other groups. It becomes a generalized pattern of thinking; Allport said that entire lives are profoundly oriented in values that take for granted, without any question, the innate inferiority of certain others.

Our feelings of superiority about "our" group, as opposed to other groups, is called *ethnocentrism*. Oliver Wendell Holmes described it as the conviction that "the axis of the earth runs down the center of the Main Street of our town." Around "our town," we build a high wall, so to speak, by our selective perceptions and "editing" of "what's out there." The pattern tends to be self-perpetuating: perceptual input is governed by determinations based on attitudes, beliefs, and values for which we will admit no challenge.

The hostile feelings that are the basis of prejudice tend to be most marked when directed against people who are seen to be socially nearest those harboring the prejudice. This implies the threat element. In the 150 years or so of the history of immigration to this country, there is ample evidence of this point. Consider the colorful nomenclature: *Micks, Krauts, dumb Swedes, Bohunks, Polacks, Sheenies, Wops, Spics, Dagoes,* and the especially interesting *Lace Curtain Irish* and *Shanty Irish* (what does this differentiation suggest?). As Philip Hauser observes, "the problem of hostility and distrust and prejudice was never the monopoly of any one group in our history. It was democratically available to everybody."

Hauser continues:

As a matter of fact, one way to tell pretty much whether a people has yet made the grade in terms of disappearing into the community has been the attitude that they have toward the *newest* newcomer. Normally in our history, the 150% Americans were those who had not yet quite made the grade themselves—they had to have someone to look down upon. After they had been here long enough, they could relax and . . . become just one hundred percenters.[2]

The Social Aspect of Prejudice

There are those who take the position that what they think and believe is their own private business, and they resent "busybodies who stick their noses into what doesn't concern them." Perhaps a telling response to this is the song-title from *South Pacific,* "No Man Is an

Island." This title is taken from John Donne's 17th century prose, which reads:

> No man is an island, entire of itself; every man is a piece of the continent, a part of the main. If a clod be washed away by the sea, Europe is the less, as well as if a promontory were, as well as if a manor of thy friend's or of thine own were. Any man's death diminishes me, because I am involved in mankind, and therefore never send to know for whom the bell tolls; it tolls for thee. [*Devotions Upon Emergent Occasions* (XVII)]

A similar theme appears in the writings of many poets and authors and in the work of many other artists.

The plain fact is that our attitudes *are* social. They are transmitted from person to person. Prejudice is *taught,* and it is also *caught,* like a cold; it is, as we suggested above, an epidemiological social malignancy. Our attitudes are not privately held possessions devoid of social significance. They are closely related to our *social status striving.* More about this shortly. We have already noted that attitudes grow because they tie an individual to a group with whose values he wishes to affiliate. One accepts the values of the group, since without such acceptance, one cannot become an integrated member of that group.

However, we have also seen that group-determined values tend to restrict one's perception of, understanding of, and communication with other groups holding different values. This is particularly true if the differing group is perceived as a competitor for treasured goals: jobs, salary hikes, promotions, "getting ahead," and such. Largely because of the absence of free, two-way communication—in the sense in which we described it in the preceding chapter—the groups become hostile and develop suspicions and hatreds that are impervious to logical, rational appeals. This is the typical dynamic of intergroup prejudice in its social sense (Berrian and Bash, *Human Relations*).

Why prejudice will generally not capitulate to information alone becomes increasingly clear. Information has a very difficult time getting past "the high wall." To say, therefore, that prejudice is simply ignorance or stupidity is acceptable, provided that it is understood that it is somewhat more complex than these terms commonly connote. We may add: provided also that an individual is prepared to recognize that each of us is a little ignorant and a little stupid. A judgment by one person as to what constitutes prejudice in another person is in itself based on a value and is therefore a delicate and hazardous venture. We show that we realize this by telling a third person about someone's prejudice, rather than making the accusation directly. Each of us would be well advised to look to his own prejudices, because the malady is universal in the human family.

Someone might retort that, if this is so, why worry about it? This is equivalent to claiming that because the common cold is so common, and there is no presently apparent cure for it, why not simply live with it? Yet there are those in science and medicine who persist in their research (should we call them busybodies, too?) for clues to how to neutralize this disease that takes so great a toll in human misery. So be it with prejudice. This problem will never be entirely resolved because it is as much a part of the human condition as its counterpart, ignorance. Should we therefore close our schools because we cannot entirely eradicate ignorance?

Types of Prejudice

There are various ways of classifying or "typing" prejudice. We have already touched on the difference between prejudice and discrimination: the latter is prejudice "acted out" in our behavior. This is the target in antidiscrimination legislation pertaining to employment, education, housing, public accommodations, etc. Those who shout "you can't legislate against prejudice" find this distinction difficult. A convincing case can be made of the contention that antidiscrimination legislation has significant *educational* effects.

Prejudice connotes a tendency to act; discrimination is overt action. The relationship may be described in this manner (Simpson and Yinger, *Racial and Cultural Minorities*):

1. There can be prejudice without discrimination.

2. There can be discrimination without prejudice. (If discrimination is widely practiced—for example, in employment—individuals who may not be prejudiced come to accept the discrimination tacitly and unquestioningly.)

3. Discrimination can be among the causes of prejudice. (Some of the individuals mentioned above may come to believe that there is "something wrong" with those discriminated against.)

4. Prejudice can be among the causes of discrimination.

5. Most frequently, prejudice and discrimination are mutually reinforcing.

Another way to classify prejudices is to distinguish between harmless and harmful. Obviously, one's prejudice (it may be more a matter of preference) for shrimp and against rattlesnake steak is harmless. No one is hurt by this attitude, although it may not follow the principles of logical deduction. But when the object of prejudice is people, someone is usually hurt; therefore it is harmful.

Prejudice may also be classified as favorable or unfavorable. Can one be prejudiced in favor of something or somebody, as distinct from prejudiced against? Again, there may be prejudgment involved in either case. Some say that a favorable prejudice, in this sense, is bias, whereas prejudice is reserved for the unfavorable. But the two terms are generally used interchangeably, without this distinction, and the dictionary does not so distinguish. We use the term prejudice in this chapter in the sense that Webster defines as "an opinion or leaning adverse to anything without just grounds or before sufficient knowledge," which has irrational, hostile, unfair, and harmful connotations.

Gilbert speaks of three types of prejudice, with the categories clearly overlapping.[3] First, there is the common garden variety of prejudice: that based on our desire for social conformity. To win the approval of others whom we consider important, we will do whatever we think will please them and gain their acceptance. We tend to be steered by our perception of what a given group requires as a "membership card." Such social pressures have the effect of manipulating the values of the individual, leading him to adopt the prejudices of the group.

The second type of prejudice, in Gilbert's classification, is an extension of the first: institutionalized discrimination, legitimized by policy or legislation. In effect, it is the cultivation of prejudice by supportive public practice. It is the epitome of a tragic story: if enough people believe it, feel that they gain by it, and succeed in marshalling the votes for it, injustice becomes law, imposed upon those who view it as immoral. Thus, we have had restrictive immigration laws, justified for the wrong reasons; we have had miscegenation laws, similarly justified; we have had blacks counted as three-fifths of white persons; and we have had an assortment of laws and policies to restrict certain people in voting, housing, etc. Beyond this, custom and ways of doing things have been even more restrictive.

Thirdly, there is what Gilbert calls "pathological prejudice." This is exemplified by the fanatics, the chronic haters for whom bigotry is compulsive paranoia. Such people are seriously ill in a psychiatric sense, and they are dangerous because some of them have demagogic influence with a loose constituency. Fanatic race hatred is viewed by psychologists as an extension of intense self-hatred. It is a defensive mechanism, a type of projection or scapegoating, that compensates for one's own sense of inferiority. Adolph Hitler was a classic case. He used a group with whom he had reason to identify (he thought he might have been partly Jewish) as a scapegoat to divorce himself from them.

The Consequences of Self-Hatred

The rejection of self, or of one's group identification, is a fascinating aspect of the study of prejudice. In our discussion of the self-image in Chapter Six, we observed how the motivations for childhood behavior become increasingly social as the child grows. Gradually, most children take into their range of motivations the values of the people around them. They learn from others what they should want to do, what they should want to be, and what is most important in life.

One does not go very far in studying motivation in human behavior before recognizing that anticipated reward figures prominently in it. A child who is motivated to do his best in school, to show some consideration for the interests and feelings of others, to postpone immediate satisfactions for larger and later satisfactions is a child who has experienced some rewards for such behavior. But what happens when a society more or less systematically cuts off parts of its population from the opportunity to know and share in the rewards for careful preparation and responsible work? Obviously, social motives for good behavior do not flourish in such circumstances. It is therefore fruitless to say: prove yourself a responsible, well-motivated individual, and opportunities will then materialize. Responsible motivations develop only in an environment in which these opportunities are present.

This point was dramatically emphasized by Ralph Ellison:

> I can hear you say, "What a horrible, irresponsible bastard." And you're right. I leap to agree with you. I am one of the most irresponsible beings that ever lived. Irresponsibility is part of my invisibility; any way you face it, it is a denial. But to whom can I be responsible, and why should I be, when you refuse to see me? [*The Invisible Man*, pp. 16, 17]

Self-rejection, then, is basically a question of identity, as we saw earlier. It bears on the answer to the query, who am I? If the answer comes back, "I am a nobody—and nobody cares," we may come to accept prejudice against ourselves as a fact of life or prejudice against other groups as a way of dealing with our own sense of inadequacy. While there are many causes of prejudice—political, economic, social, etc.—*deeply prejudiced people have often had a childhood filled with threat* (Hirsh, *The Fears Men Live By*). People who have difficulty in finding a satisfactory answer to the question, who am I?, will sometimes take steps to establish who they are not. "Whoever I am, I'm superior to *them!*" Among adolescents, this often takes the form of clannishness —of over-identification with a clique or a gang. Forthwith, everything the gang does is good. The relationship to delinquency, crime, and other socially deviant behavior is evident, with psychological roots very similar to those of prejudiced behavior. These are ways of lashing out or of striking back at others and at society in general, out of feelings of insecurity, frustration, hostility, bitterness, hopelessness, and ultimate despair.

Yinger summarizes the matter in this way:

> To an important degree, prejudice is a way of trying to deal with a negative picture of one's self. The world seems threatening, because of early experiences filled with unpredictability and unhappiness. Mem-

bers of another racial or nationality group were not the cause of a person's problems, but if he has been taught a prejudice, he may use it to control his own feelings of threat by blaming and attacking them. Prejudiced persons are often characterized by what psychiatrists call a weak ego. They are fearful of their own impulses; their picture of themselves, which has been reflected back to them by the behavior of others toward them, is an uncomplimentary one, and they are afraid of it. They may love their parents, but because their parents have given them a negative picture of themselves, they also hate them, but they cannot admit their hate. They repress it, and transfer it to the minority group against whom they are prejudiced. Because they are insecure, they become rigid-minded in an attempt to get some stability and predictability in life. Any suggestion that the relationship between the dominant group and the minority group might be changed is rigidly rejected.[4]

The Power of Social Conformity

We have stated that common prejudice is cultivated by our desire for social acceptance. How strong is this influence? Various research experiments have been conducted to find out. The answer has been loud and clear: stronger even than self-preservation, under certain conditions.

Milton Rokeach has noted the point we mentioned earlier in this chapter, that society often encourages evil by "legitimizing" it, by condoning it through norms, laws, and folkways that sanction man's inhumanity to man. Rokeach refers to an experiment carried out at Yale University under the direction of Stanley Milgram, which was designed to test the respondents' reactions to authority. The idea was to discover the extent to which the subjects had an individual conscience, as against mechanically responding to commands from authority figures regardless of the morality of the commands.

In the experiment, described in "Police—As Viewed By a Psychologist," simulated electric shocks were administered to a subject who was really an accomplice of the experimenter. The actual subjects were third persons (taken singly) who were to administer shocks to the accomplice. Of course no electricity was actually transmitted; it was merely set up to appear so. The experimenter issued a series of commands to the accomplice. Each time the accomplice failed to comply with a command, the real subject administered ostensible shock to the accomplice; each shock was apparently graduated in intensity, with 30 volts for the first button pushed, 60 for the second, 90 for the third—all the way to 330 volts, which was labelled: "Danger, severe shock." Each time a shock was administered, the accomplice (a gifted student of drama) screamed with increasing apparent pain. The real subject assumed that shock was actually occurring. It was startling to find that 65 percent of the real subjects, both students and adults, pushed all the buttons, obeying orders all the way. The subjects were all of middle-class background.

Evidently, many people will condone evil when it is socially legitimized, a phenomenon that has come to be known as "the Eichmann syndrome." It appears to Rokeach that much of the social protest of today is directed against socially legitimized evil.

None of us likes to be thought of as an odd ball. If social pressures, particularly from people whom we wish to impress favorably, seem to condone a certain type of attitude or behavior, it is extremely difficult to rebel against the prevailing pattern. Indeed, there is often some reward for conforming and penalty for failure to conform. One frequently hears references to "dead heroes" or "unemployed crusaders." The pressures are often subtle, vicious, hard to prove, shrewdly and adroitly fabricated. If one speaks out in protest, he may be accused of being a lunatic or a trouble maker.

The Multiple Faces of Prejudice

Prejudice is commonly thought of in racial, nationality, or religious terms, sometimes in ethnic and cultural terms, but seldom in other dimensions. Part of the so-called generation gap is prejudice based on age. Prejudice based on sex is hardly uncommon, as those in the women's liberation movement are quick to point out. What about the differentiation suggested by "city slicker" and "hick" or "hayseed"? How about "the other side of the tracks," as distinct from "the folks who live on the hill"? Then there are "hillbillies," "Indian givers," and "skinheads." In industrial relations, there are epithets such as "union goons" and "titans." The poet Thomas Gray reflects the smug security of the rich when he speaks of "the simple pleasures of the poor." In police and community relations, it is "the fuzz," "the pigs," "the freaks," "the jocks". . . and worse. And in other types of intergroup relationships, there are distinctive ways by which the parties brand each other as reprehensible, barbarian products of suspicious or questionable parenthood. One speculates sometimes that even the "armchair psychiatrists" may be working off their hostilities on other people whom they persist in amateurishly diagnosing.

The victims of prejudice become quite adept at recognizing behavior intended to mask prejudice. For example, there is the patronizing, condescending manner of those who begin a conversation with "I'm not prejudiced . . . in fact, some of my best friends are . . . but . . ." Or another version: *"You people* really are happier by yourselves, aren't you? You don't really want all this agitation and stirring things up." Or another: "Haven't I always taken good care of *you people* and looked out for you?"

Only a slight variation of this is the use of first names in referring to unfamiliar persons, where sometimes even the inflection of the voice is telltale. In effect, it is dealing with people's names in terms of a group attitude toward them. The name in itself carries a stereotypic connotation, e.g., "Hi 'ya, Ruby"; "What's new, Mac"; "Nice goin', Abie"; "C'mere, Boy."

The many faces of prejudice suggest that race differences are important chiefly because of cultural attitudes that make them important. Race is a symbol of one type of group differentiation, although anthropologists testify that scientifically it is not a very significant differentiation. (A classic reference work in this field is Ruth Benedict's *Patterns of Culture.*) In some cultures, racial differences are simply disregarded. A number of we-and-they differentiations in interpersonal and intergroup relations have little or nothing to do with the most commonly thought of standards of differentiation in our culture.

The Tools of Prejudice

Stereotyping or overcategorization is one of the working tools of prejudice. It is a sweeping generalization regarding an entire group or category: Norwegians are giants, Englishmen lack a sense of humor, police officers are corrupt, etc. Walter Lippmann *(Public Opinion)* referred to the stereotype as "a picture in the head," "a short-cut for thought," as "looking at all members of a group as if they were alike." Gordon Allport (*The Nature of Prejudice,* p. 195) argued that a stereotype is not a category, but "often exists as a fixed mark of a category." "Policemen" is a category; "corrupt" is the stereotype. Allport indicated that stereotypes may or may not be based on a morsel of truth; that they aid people in simplifying categories; that they are used to justify hostility; and that sometimes they serve as "projection screens for our personal conflict." Stereotypes are often socially supported—by the mass media, novels, short stories, newspaper items, movies, stage, radio and television.

Allport might well have added jokes and anecdotes of the type that would fall flat without stereotypic "props." Comedians have made much of this, particularly in lampooning their own group, though it appears to be a fading practice. Richard Wright in *Black Boy* described the black elevator operator who exaggerated his accent and affected traits ascribed stereotypically to his racial group. The anti-Semitic story, or that of the "two colored boys," or of the priest, rabbi, and minister, or of Pat and Mike, or of the "two Polacks," are variations on these themes. This is still a significant mechanism for perpetuating stereotypic caricatures. Some defend it in the name of humor—"laughing at ourselves," "not taking ourselves too seriously," etc. But as Mark Twain wrote: " 'Tis said that a fish-hook doesn't hurt a fish'. . . but it wasn't a fish who said it."

No aspect of prejudice has been more thoroughly researched than that pertaining to stereotypes. Gilbert, for example, worked with what he called the "fading effect" of stereotypes, years ago at Princeton ("Stereotype Persistence"). Hartley asked several groups of college students to mark, on a standard social-distance scale, their attitudes toward a large number of groups (*Problems in Prejudice*). He included the names of three groups that never existed. Those who revealed the most intolerant attitudes toward groups that do exist tended to display similarly intolerant attitudes toward the nonexistent groups. The conclusion was that prejudice does not necessarily require actual contact between groups. It may be based on contact with attitudes about groups.

Another mechanism or tool of prejudice is called *projection*—more generally known as *scapegoating*. It means that we all tend to look for the causes of our failures outside of ourselves; we blame the hammer for a smashed finger. Allport (p. 360) defines it as "the tendency to attribute falsely to other people motives or traits that are our own, or that in some way explain or justify our own."[5] Scapegoating in itself is not an adequate theory to explain prejudice, but it is closely allied with stereotyping (for example, to hold that one did not secure a promotion because of the characteristic cunning of a certain group. This combines scapegoating and stereotyping).

Another tool of prejudice is rationalization: an accommodation of an attitude and an overgeneralized belief. As Allport puts it (p. 14), "the belief system has a way of slithering around to justify the more permanent attitude." Few people know the real reasons for their prejudicial attitudes. The reasons they invent are usually rationalizations—an effort to make the attitude seem plausible. All of us have trouble recognizing the difference between our *verbalized* reasons for behaving as we do toward others and the *real* reasons; the emotions from which the latter frequently spring may not be understood or acknowledged. Most of us are unaware of the psychological function that prejudice serves in our lives. It is a kind of crutch, to prop up our feelings of insecurity and inadequacy, and to serve as an outlet (Allport calls it "drainage" or catharsis) for feelings of frustration, aggression, and/or guilt.

The Causes of Prejudice

Prejudice has many causes. No single theory of causation is adequate, and the causative factors are undoubtedly interactive. One school of thought regarding causation tends to emphasize *personality* factors. The focus is on the prejudiced person himself. Another theory stresses *social structure* as an explanation for prejudice. The focus is on power arrangements in society. Prejudice is seen as an economic and political weapon. A third concept emphasizes the *cultural* causes of prejudice. Folkways nurture prejudice; social conformity motivates it. This is what psychologist S. H. Britt had in mind when he referred to entire lives oriented to "the ready-made acceptance of ways." This theory of causation holds that prejudice is simply accepted, without challenge, as a cultural norm.[6]

Any single prejudiced individual may reflect all the causes of prejudice because of the mutually reinforcing pattern of these factors. A fascinating research question is why some individuals are less prejudiced than others. If the societal and cultural variables are reasonably constant, the explanation must be in personality terms. However, such generalized formulas are always precarious in the scholarly sphere.

Having identified three broad approaches to the causes of prejudice, it may be well to touch on a few specifics—necessarily selective because the literature on the subject is monumental. Proponents of the personality theory of causation include some who stress that prejudice is a product of frustration. They argue that the blocking of goal-directed behavior frequently generates hostile impulses in the individual. This hostility may be directed toward self, or it may be "stored up" (repression), or it may be directed toward an innocent target (projection or displacement). Stereotyping, scapegoating, and rationalization are the tools, as we have noted. Britt identifies another: "traumatic experience," which is actually a form of rationalization. The person explains his attitude by referring to a harrowing emotional "happening." For example, a member of a minority group may be held responsible for the death of a loved one, as someone once told this author: ". . . and that's how it was, when I was six years old, that my dear old granny passed away, frightened to death by that runaway horse driven by that colored boy . . ."

A variation in the personality theory of causation is represented by the projection hypothesis illustrated by the stereotyping of an outgroup that is perceived as depicting the impulses that we have had trouble taming in ourselves; feelings about sex or the use of violence are reflected in "those over-sexed so-and-sos . . .," or "those barbarians aren't human . . ."

The whole gamut of repression, guilt, and projection is exemplified in the hackneyed conversation-stopper: "Would you want your daughter to marry one of them?" Fear is at the base of it—fear that "one of them" will ask one's daughter, that the daughter might accept, or even that it might eventually be discovered that an interracial marriage is no great social catastrophe. Simpson and Yinger devote an entire chapter to a discussion of intermarriage and sexual relations of an interracial, interreligious, and interethnic character. Allport said that the intermarriage issue is not rational. He called it "a specious rationalization for prejudice." Quoting him:

It [the marriage issue] comprises a fierce fusion of sex attraction, sex repression, guilt, status superiority, occupational advantage, and anxiety. It is because intermarriage would symbolize the abolition of prejudice that it is so strenuously fought. [P. 354][7]

The personality theory as to the causes of prejudice was given considerable impetus twenty years ago by *The Authoritarian Personality* studies (Adorno, et. al.). The central hypothesis of this research was that prejudice is often a symptom of a basic personality pattern or "set." The general finding was that prejudice is directly related to rigidity of outlook, to intolerance for ambiguity, to superstition, and to suggestibility and gullibility. Subsequent studies, for example that by Rokeach, mentioned earlier, substantiated this conclusion.[8]

Other Theories of Causes

The research cited suggests that prejudiced persons look for hierarchy in society. They like definite power arrangements, something predictable. They like authority and discipline; they tend to distrust other people and to see the world as a hazardous place (Allport, p. 382). But again, amateur diagnosticians can cause havoc by going about gleefully pointing to these behavior patterns in others and failing to see that their own behavior in so doing may be pathogenic. Not every advocate of "law and order" is necessarily "sick," "up-tight," or "prejudiced."

The effect of prejudice—for the prejudiced, and for the victims of it—is an aspect of this subject that has had the attention of numerous writers.[9] It is difficult to separate the causes of prejudice from its effects. What is a gain and what is a loss are questions tied up with the values of the prejudiced, the values of the victims of prejudice, or the values of those who make a judgment, including those who write on the subject.

The preceding reference to those who prefer hierarchal, predictable, and definite power arrangements in society illustrates the point that theories of causation for prejudice blend together. So-called authoritarianism in personality pattern accommodates most easily to a highly ordered and orderly social structure. This suggests the second of the broad schools of thought regarding the causes of prejudice: the social structure emphasis. Ethnocentrism is the cornerstone of this theory; the superiority feeling is the sine qua non of a struggle for power and wealth. Sherif described the theory well:

The scale or hierarchy of prejudice in settled or stable times flows from the politically, economically, and socially strong and eminent down to lower hierachies of the established order. . . . The most elaborate "race" superiority doctrines are products of already existing organizations of superiority-inferiority relationships and exploitations. The superiority doctrines have been the deliberate or unconscious standardizations of the powerful and prosperous groups at the top and not the ideas of the frustrated and deprived majority at the bottom. [*An Outline of Social Psychology*, p. 343]

In short, prejudice exists, according to this theory of causation, because a person is convinced, deliberately or unconsciously, that he gains by it. The doctrinaire Marxist holds that the "fundamental" cause of prejudice is class conflict. The doctrinaire psychoanalyst disagrees. But there is a great deal of support today for the power theory of prejudice, manifest in "Black Power," "Brown Power," etc. In police and community relations, particularly since 1967, there appears to be an increasing tendency to believe that there can be no significant improvement, where such relationships are at their worst and most incendiary, unless and until there are "gut-level" changes in existing economic and political power arrangements. "Dialogue" and "block clubs" are regarded by those of this belief as the preoccupations of "do-gooders," having little or no effect upon attitudes or behavior or upon aspects of the system that are thought to be unjust. Militancy, even to the point of violence if necessary, lining up votes and getting eligible voters registered, separatism as a strategy for identity and power —these have become identifying characteristics of the power or social structure school of thought regarding prejudice. Its proponents are little affected by pleas to contain violence and to maintain law and order. Their retort is to center attention on how little is said and done to deal constructively with the human misery, *anomie,* and rank injustice that precipitate violent, desperate, flailing behavior.

With reference to the school of thought that holds that prejudice has its roots mainly in the perpetuation of the cultural heritage, Allport (p. 233) lists ten sociocultural conditions that seem to encourage prejudice:

1. Heterogeneity in the population.

2. Ease of vertical mobility, erratically distributed.

3. Rapid social change with attendant *anomie.*

4. Ignorance and barriers to communication.

5. The relative density of minority group population.

6. The existence of realistic rivalries and conflict.

7. Exploitation sustaining important interests in the community.

8. Sanctions given to aggressive scapegoating.

9. Legend and tradition that sustain hostility.

10. Unfavorable attitudes toward both assimilation and cultural pluralism.

The overlapping of theories regarding the etiology of prejudice is apparent in this listing.

Definition of a Minority Group

Implicit in our discussion is the question of how a *minority group* is defined. Intergroup relations consultant Harold Lett approaches this question in a manner parallel to Allport's preceding listing, identifying six characteristics of a minority group (from "A Look at Others"):

1. Ease of identification of members of the group enables picking them out of a crowd on sight or through casual contact.

2. The out-group is defined by the slowness with which it is assimilated into the total population, i.e., how long "difference" persists in the public mind.

3. The minority group's identity is fixed by the degree to which it exists in such numerical strength in a community that it irritates just by constant presence.

4. Their numbers and their demands for recognition place them in position of threatening the dominant group's notions of its own superior status, or prior claim to desirable jobs, or unchallenged control of political affairs.

5. The intensity of dominant group reaction to the minority group can be measured by the history of emotional contact between the groups, flowing from such things as labor strikes, teenage gang outbursts, sensationalized crimes of violence involving members of minority groups, and even carry-over from Old World conflicts.

6. The number and kind of rumors that circulate, emphasizing the criminality, sexual depravity, or diabolical plotting of the minority group.

The question of whether police are a minority group is interesting to consider in the light of these criteria. Lett's characterization of a minority group blends the various schools of thought regarding the causes of prejudice. Most observers approach the determination of a minority group in terms of power. It has little to do with numerical proportions, as in electoral processes where the majority system is operative. The vital question is, where is the source of power? Who makes the decisions that matter? In these terms, the really significant relationship is that between the *powerful* and the *powerless*.

Lett (pp. 125, 126) goes on to consider the typical patterns of minority group reaction to their status:[10]

1. Adjustment, adaptation, accommodation, repression, etc.

2. Submission, with consequent sacrifice of individuality, incentive and ambition.

3. Resistance, in various ways:
   a. To excel (Show them!)
   b. To repel (Do our own thing!)
   c. To rebel (Burn, baby, burn!)

What about the typical behavior patterns *of the prejudiced?* Allport (pp. 14, 15) offers two types of classification, the first of which focuses on how individuals act out prejudice:

1. *Antilocution.* People tend to talk about their prejudices with like-minded others. Many people never go beyond this talk stage.

2. *Avoidance.* When a prejudice is more intense, the individual will go to considerable trouble to avoid contact with the group he dislikes.

3. *Discrimination.* The prejudiced person makes detrimental distinctions of an active sort. Exclusion in employment, education, housing, etc. Segregation is an institutionalized form of discrimination, enforced legally or by common custom. Obviously, it is a form of social stratification.

4. *Physical Attack.* Under conditions of heightened emotion, prejudice may lead to violence, riots, etc.

5. *Extermination.* Lynching, pogroms, massacres and genocide.

Another Allport classification (pp. 316–321) focuses on how conflict is handled:

1. *Repression.* Illustrated by the story with which this chapter began: "We have no problems here." Or by the individual who says: "Now I'm not prejudiced . . . but . . . ."

2. *Defensive rationalization.* To marshal "evidence" seemingly supportive of the prejudice. Aided by selective perception, and by *bifurcation:* "I like Jews, but I hate kikes"; "Negroes are good; niggers are bad."

3. *Compromise solutions.* Illustrated by *alternation:* turning prejudice on or off, depending on the situation. One kind of behavior in church, and another at a stag party.

4. *Integration.* True resolution. Goes beyond repression, rationalization and compromise. Wholeness; to bring into common and equal membership.

The sociological term for integration is *assimilation.* It is a process of *nearly complete* absorption of one culture by another. Years ago, we spoke of America as a "melting pot." However, it is now recognized that this metaphor had an unfortunate connotation. It conveyed the idea of an eventual goal of *complete* assimilation, with the consequent disappearance of unique and distinctive cultural traits of the many peoples who compose our population. Insistent "Americanization" of our minorities, with the implication that their ways are unacceptable, has come to be recognized as an undesirable way to define the goal. The term "cultural pluralism" is preferable, to signify *almost complete* assimilation, but not to the point of detroying distinctiveness: *unity in diversity*—out of the many, one—*E pluribus unum.*

Intragroup Prejudice

We have been discussing *intergroup* prejudice and *intergroup* relations. What about *intragroup* prejudice and *intragroup* relations? Prejudice may be expressed by a minority group toward the dominant group, toward another minority group, or within the same minority group by some of its members toward other members. Only the latter is intragroup.

The prejudice of a minority group toward the dominant group is at least partially a matter of reciprocity and reaction—a *result* of dominant group prejudice and at the same time a reinforcing *cause* of the same. The prejudice of a minority group toward another minority group, as exemplified by Negro anti-Semitism, is in part displaced prejudice— using another minority group as a substitute target for the hostilities felt toward white gentiles—and in part a reciprocal prejudice against whites in general. Some of it may also be the result of the disenchantment of militant blacks with white liberals; in a particular sense, with white Jewish entrepreneurs who are regarded as exploiters of urban ghetto blacks.

The prejudice of a member of a minority group toward other members of the same group (Shanty Irish vs. Lace-Curtain Irish) is usually a matter primarily of social class differentiation, although other factors may contribute to it; for example, religious and political considerations (again, Irish vs. Irish) or more subtle criteria of "acceptability." Among Puerto Ricans, for instance, there is a term, *troigaño,* which is used to refer to another Puerto Rican who is perceived as an acceptable prospective friend or spouse. The term has no relation to differences in skin pigmentation, or religion, or of family wealth. Apparently, it is a general term for a composite of desirable personal characteristics.

Dealing With Prejudice

The treatment for prejudice should be tailored to the particular causes in a particular situation. The literature on treatment is as extensive as that on causes. The many so-called civil rights organizations in this country, though they work in different ways and with different philosophies, share the common purpose of combating prejudice and discrimination. Some are committed to broad educational-type programs, others to political action.

Because prejudice is so often thought of in intergroup relations terms, numerous programs foster rather far-reaching activity in community relations and community organization. National promotions such as Brotherhood Week seek to make the overt expression of prejudice unpopular. Generally speaking, the trend in organizationally promoted programs has been to try to cope with prejudice as a group or societal problem. To emphasize that it basically comes down to the *individual* would seem to be too threatening, as so-called sensitivity training quickly establishes. It is also less threatening, as we noted earlier, to focus on the other fellow's prejudices, rather than on one's own. "Who, me? Prejudiced? You gotta' be kidding! I just gave $100 to the United Negro College Fund."

Rather than attempt to catalog the various types of programs that have been undertaken to cope with prejudice, we will footnote several pertinent references where such information may be found.[11] To view a few aspects of the treatment question, a good place to begin is with Robert Merton's useful classification[12] of four types of persons, for each of whom a different treatment strategy is appropriate:

1. The unprejudiced, non-discriminator, or all-weather liberal. (Merton comments: "Beware of such liberals, 'who talk to themselves' about prejudice—[obviously, other people's]—and produce all sorts of false assumptions, e.g., that things are getting better—or worse, as the case may be. This is the fallacy of privatized solutions.")

2. The unprejudiced discriminator or fair-weather liberal. Despite his own lack of prejudice, he will support discrimination if he sees it as profitable.

3. The prejudiced non-discriminator or fair-weather illiberal. This is the reluctant conformist, e.g., the bigoted businessman who profits from the trade of the minority group. To convert him, discrimination must be made costly and painful.

4. The prejudiced discriminator or all-weather illiberal. He believes that differential treatment is not discriminatory but discriminating. He is consistent in belief and practice. He may be moved toward Type 3 by legal and administrative controls. But such movement will probably be "kicking and dragging."

Intergroup education in schools has been one important facet of anti-prejudice programs for the past three decades in the United States, with organizations such as the National Conference of Christians and Jews and the Anti-Defamation League of B'nai B'rith in the vanguard.[13]

One of the most dynamic principles to emerge from intergroup relations programs during the past half-century holds that prejudice (unless deeply rooted in the personality structure of the individual) may be reduced by equal status contact between majority and minority groups, in pursuit of common goals. The effect is greatly enhanced if this contact is sanctioned by institutional supports (law, custom, administrative policy and practice), and if it is of a sort that leads to the perception of common interests and common humanity between members of the groups.[14] This principle is, in effect, Sherif's concept of *superordinate goals,* referred to in Chapter Two. An assumption in such a theory is that conflict of interest is inevitable in the free, pluralistic society. This point merits further analysis.

Constructive Conflict

A society that is free and pluralistic is one in which differences not only occur, but one in which differences must be dignified. This is endemic to the American creed. In American society, conflict is inevitable, and to some extent, indispensable.

Both violence and demands for law and order go far back in America's past. Richard Sennett, a social scientist at Brandeis University, writing in *The New York Times,* says this about it:

> The image of "order" in our culture is an image of peace and harmony.... These images of order create a culture where people are inexperienced and terribly frightened when conflict does break out. Because people try to exclude disorder from their daily lives, it seems as though the abyss is opening up whenever a difficult conflict arises. Because people do not know much about how to act in a situation of social conflict, they can only fear the worst.

> This naivete about disorder leads in two directions. It leads people to believe that conflicts not easily solved must inevitably escalate to a violent level, and that in order to prevent this, the forces of law and order must use preventive violence first. ["The Cities: Fear and Hope"]

In *Conflict and Its Resolution,* Morton Deutsch of Columbia University, a leading authority on the subject of conflict resolution and the techniques of inducing cooperation among adversaries, assumes that conflict is potentially of personal and social value, and that it is a pervasive and inevitable aspect of life. He also assumes that conflict is not necessarily destructive, and that in fact it has many positive functions. Conflict, he contends, prevents stagnation, stimulates interest and curiosity, and is a medium through which problems can be aired and solutions arrived at; it is the root of personal and social change.

Deutsch observes that various psychological theories are aimed toward a psychological utopia of conflict-free existence. But fortunately, he says, none of us has to face this prospect. The question is not how to eliminate or prevent conflict, but rather how to make it productive, or minimally, how to prevent it from being destructive. Deutsch speaks of *mutual* gain and *mutual* satisfaction for the parties to the conflict, not of conflict that is productive for the winner and destructive for the loser. His interest is in what he calls "impure conflict," that is, a mixture of cooperative and competitive elements.

What, he asks, is the difference between cooperative and competitive processes in conflict resolution? Since his response to this question touches on matters we have discussed earlier, an illustrative sampling is in order. Concerning perception, Deutsch states that a *cooperative* process tends to increase sensitivity to similarities and common interests, while minimizing the salience of differences. *It stimulates a convergence or conformity of beliefs and values.* A *competitive* process, on the other hand, tends to increase sensitivity to differences and threats, while minimizing the awareness of similarities. It stimulates the sense of complete oppositeness: "You are bad, I am good."

Deutsch considers at length the conditions that give rise to either cooperative or competitive processes in conflict resolution: intrapersonal, interpersonal, and intergroup. With regard to the latter, which is of special interest in police and community relations, he suggests some general propositions:

1. Any attempt to introduce change in the existing mode of relationship between two parties is more likely to be accepted if each expects some net gain from the change than if either side expects that the other side will gain at its expense.

2. Conflict is more likely to be resolved by a competitive process when each of the parties in conflict is internally homogeneous but distinctly different from one another in such characteristics as class, race, religion, political affiliation, etc., than when each is internally heterogeneous and they have overlapping characteristics.

3. The more coincidental conflicts there are in other areas between two parties, the less likely a conflict in any given area will be resolved cooperatively; the more cooperative relationships there are in other areas, the less likely it is that they will resolve a conflict in any area by a competitive process. (*Note:* Sherif's Robbers' Cave Experiment is a good illustration.)

4. A competitive process of conflict resolution is less likely as the exchange of memberships between the groups increases.

5. The institutionalization and regulation of conflict increases the likelihood of a cooperative process of conflict resolution.

6. Conflict is more likely to be regulated effectively when the parties in conflict are each internally coherent and stable rather than disorganized or unstable.

7. Conflict is more likely to be regulated effectively when neither of the parties in conflict see the contest between them as a single con-

test in which defeat, if it occurs, would be total and irreversible with regard to a central value.

8. The anticipation of a hopeless outcome of conflict, such that nothing of value is preserved, makes the effective regulation of conflict less likely.

9. Conflict is less likely to be regulated effectively if the rules for engaging in conflict are seen to be biased, and thus themselves the subject of conflict. [*Conflict and Its Resolutions*]

In intergroup conflict situations, what functions are performed by a third-party mediator? These are some that Deutsch identifies: helping to remove blocks and distortions in communication (translate and interpret); helping to reduce tension between the two sides by careful listening, blunting or narrowing the issue in conflict; reducing stereotypes; reducing the sense of threat; helping to establish norms for rational interaction; helping to determine what solutions are possible; helping to get the issue redefined so that different aspirations may be realized; helping to make a working agreement acceptable to the parties —for example, to establish conditions in which retreat is possible without loss of face; and helping to make the solution attractive and prestigeful to interested audiences.

Clearly, there is a kind of science of conflict resolution; more accurately, conflict resolution is an extremely important facet of social psychology, with great relevance for police and community relations. Deutsch's views are indicative. An impressive bibliography of work in the field explores aspects of the subject not covered here.

Rumor and Prejudice

Rumor is invariably a companion of prejudice.[15] Rumors explain, augment, and justify prejudices and hostilities. Allport and Postman have said, no riot ever occurs without the aid of rumor.[16] It enters into the pattern of violence at several stages:

1. Stories of the misdeeds of the hated out-group, accused of conspiring, plotting, storing up guns and ammunition, preying on women and children, etc. Rumor is a kind of barometer of community tension.

2. General and preliminary rumors build up to "marshalling" rumors: "Something is going to happen tonight in the park by the river."

3. A rumor in itself may be the spark that ignites the powder keg: "Some white cop beat hell out of a black kid, cut his head open and all, because the kid wouldn't tell where he lives." In short order, this may become: "Ten white cops raided this hangout where some black kids were shooting craps, and six of the kids are

in the hospital." A bit later, it might be: "A bunch of cops shot up the neighborhood and killed two black kids, looking for some dudes who knocked off a liquor store."

4. During a riot or disorder, rumors sustain the excitement—sometimes to a point of utter hallucination.[17]

In itself, a rumor is a verbal expression of hope, of fear, or of hate. Thus, the story that a promotional list has been posted on the bulletin board at the police station may engender *hope*. The story that "usually reliable sources" are predicting an earthquake may engender *fear*. The story that Black Panthers are raping white women may engender *hate*. The story that "cops" have machine-gunned three Chicano teen-agers may engender both *fear* and *hate*. And so on. The more inflammatory the story, the greater the emotion it is likely to arouse.

The discrediting of rumors is important, therefore, in controlling tension in the community. Recognizing this, numerous communities have established Tension Control Centers, the chief function of which is to provide factual information to the public in circumstances where rumors are rampant. Newspapers, radio and television stations, human relations agencies, and sometimes police departments have provided facilities and auspices for such centers. Allport (*The Nature of Prejudice*, pp. 61–63) asserts that the exposure of rumors, in itself, probably does not change any deep-rooted prejudices. What it does, he says, is to warn those of mild or negligible prejudice that wedge-driving rumors contribute substantially to community disruption by aggravating and sometimes triggering violence.

A Concluding Consideration

A discussion of perception, attitudes, and prejudice sometimes leaves an individual reflecting, "Well, O.K., I must try to be more careful about these things in my various activities." This is, of course, a commendable resolution. But it is easily forgotten when the chips are down, especially with regard to the big issues.

What we have been discussing is as applicable to the affairs of the United Nations as it is to the transactions of two youngsters at play. Human transactions range in complexity and in sophistication. Take, for example, the long-haired, unmanicured types associated (stereotypically) in the public mind with campus unrest. The line goes as follows: "What's the matter with them? What kind of people do things like that? Why do they do such things? Do they really think anything good can come of such antics?"

The eminent Harvard research psychiatrist Robert Coles addressed himself to this kind of situation in a recent article. His is not apt to be a widely popular analysis; it makes enemies because it is so starkly rational. Some of its flavor may be transmitted in the following quotation:

> In the distant past, but also in recent times, dissenters have been banished to prison or sent to their death (or sent to America!) for their noisy, unorthodox, unsettling, and provocative words and acts. Many of us no doubt find such out-and-out repression distasteful, but we are not beyond our own ability to call a person we oppose only thinly disguised names, to insult him and at the same time ignore the thrust of his declared purposes, his stated intentions, his deeds—which surely ought to be open for discussion on their own merits, rather than the merits of one or another person's psychiatric status. We dismiss, belittle, and run down those we disagree with *substantively* by doing them in *personally*. ["A Fashionable Kind of Slander," *The Atlantic*, p. 54]

Coles brings out how easily we fall prey to our prejudices, especially regarding those toward whom we feel opposition, such as the long-haired, unmanicured types, the freaks, the street people. Saying "O.K., I must try to do better" is not enough in eliminating prejudices. A more thorough response is necessary: "I will examine and try to recognize my prejudices. I will try to understand why I have come to be prejudiced. I will work at eliminating my prejudices because they hurt others and myself."

Notes to Chapter Nine

1. Sister Mary de Lourdes, St. Joseph's College, West Hartford, Connecticut, in an article with that title, published by the National Conference of Christians and Jews.

2. Philip M. Hauser, "Implications of Population Trends for Urban Communities." Paper presented at an Institute on metropolitan problems, held at the University of Wisconsin, Milwaukee, February 1, 1958.

3. G. M. Gilbert, "What Makes Us Behave as People?" (pp. 47, 48). See also by the same author, *Nuremberg Diary* and *The Psychology of Dictatorship*. Dr. Gilbert was chief psychologist for the United States Government at the Nuremberg trials and also a witness at the trial of Adolph Eichmann in Israel.

4. J. Milton Yinger, "Who Are We?"

5. See also Allport's *The ABC's of Scapegoating*.

6. The three-way classification of the cause of prejudice alluded to is borrowed from Simpson and Yinger, *Racial and Cultural Minorities*.

7. What might be called sexual factors in American race relations are analyzed by John Dollard in *Caste and Class in a Southern Town*.

8. Milton Rokeach, *The Open and Closed Mind.*

9. Simpson and Yinger devote a chapter to it. See also such other sources as John Dollard, *Caste and Class;* S. A. Fineberg, *Punishment Without Crime;* Group for the Advancement of Psychiatry, *Emotional Aspects of School Desegregation,* 1960.

10. Simpson and Yinger devote a chapter to "The Consequences of Prejudice: Types of Adjustment to Prejudice and Discrimination," in *Racial and Cultural Minorities.*

11. See, for example, Part III of Simpson and Yinger; Part VIII of Gordon W. Allport, *The Nature of Prejudice.* See also Allport's *The Resolution of Intergroup Tensions;* R. M. Williams, Jr., *The Reduction of Intergroup Tensions;* and Dean and Rosen, a *Manual of Intergroup Relations.*

12. Robert K. Merton, in R. M. MacIver, ed., *Discrimination and National Welfare,* p. 104.

13. See, for example, the various publications produced as a result of "Intergroup Education in Cooperating Schools," a project of the American Council on Education, in cooperation with the National Conference of Christians and Jews, Hilda Taba, Project Director.

14. Allport, *The Nature of Prejudice,* p. 267. A similar approach to community problem-solving is called the *Normative Sponsorship Theory,* originated and developed by Christopher Sower, professor of sociology at Michigan State University. See his *Community Involvement.*

15. Study 5 (Part II) in Radelet and Reed, *Studies,* makes some pertinent points on prejudice.

16. Allport and Postman, *The Psychology of Rumor.* See also E. T. Fitzgerald, "The Rumor Process and Its Effect on Civil Disorders."

17. Graphically described by Lee and Humphrey in *Race Riot,* a study of the 1943 Detroit riot; also in various descriptions of more recent riots and disorders.

Summary
of Part Two

Our principal purpose in Part Two has been to provide an overview of some of the more significant psychological considerations in problems of police-community interaction.

Perhaps the pivotal psychological aspect of police and community relations is the question of the self-image of the police officer. Actually, the self-image and the public image are so intertwined as to constitute an essential whole. Because morale is so much a matter of self-respect, study of the self-image of the police officer must explore what "good" morale means for the individual officer. We started with the query: how does a person learn who he is? To deal with this, we reviewed some salient points pertaining to the childhood socialization process; for example, the formation of conscience and self-respect.

We next examined the relationship between our social selves and our social roles, a crucial facet of personality integration. What this means specifically for the policeman then became our focus. Why become a police officer? How important is it to secure "good men" for police work, and for what objectives? Why is cynicism seemingly so common a characteristic of the policeman's attitude toward his job? Here we discussed the basic predicament of the big-city officer: the paradox between the importance that society ascribes to his role and his relatively low social status; and the problem of incompatible ends, which implies that society has so defined the policeman's situation that he can never act in accord with that definition. How to deal with these perplexing aspects of police morale and self-image goes to the heart of the police-community problem.

The subculture of the police was our next consideration. We defined it as the organized sum of police perspectives relevant to the police role. We weighed the comparative influence of background and occupational socialization in the composition of the police subculture. This is closely related to the question: who "makes it" in police work? Some interesting research is emerging on this and associated matters.

Why do the police appear to hate liberals and vice versa? We looked at this question in terms of the so-called value gap between police and some of the policed. As we considered the public image of the police, we saw that it is the expectations of specific segments of the public that are crucial—and certain of these are known to be quite negative in their assessment of police performance. Numerous surveys in recent years have found that the police have a special public-image problem with youth, with the poor, and with powerless minority groups. Hostility begets hostility; we reviewed the relevance of this hypothesis in particular police-community interactions, with some attention to complicating factors.

This brought us to the so-called adversary concept in police-citizen relations: the position that, to some degree, this relationship is inevitably adversarial and conflict-laden. We sampled the thoughts of a few of the many who support this idea and of one analyst who is not convinced. We also gave some attention to the question of how successful police work is measured.

Self-images and public images are affected by attitudes, beliefs, and values. Relationship problems in a democratic, pluralistic society arise out of conflicts in perceptions that form attitude structure in personality. We started with perception and considered its pitfalls and distortions and related it to role performance of the police officer. We noted in several different ways the axiom that the world as perceived by any one person is not the only world there is. We saw how this is related to one's attitudes, beliefs, and values, and translated it into the terms of what is often called a "communication problem"; for example, in police and community relations. We concluded that the communication problem rooted in value gap is much more complex than is usually assumed in glib diagnosis.

A fundamental reason for this complexity is represented by the omnibus problem of prejudice. This is a type of attitude embodying hostility and threat, springing from emotional roots in personality, nourished by stereotyping, scapegoating, and rationalization. We reviewed typologies of prejudice and described the schools of thought regarding its causes. Strategies for coping with prejudice and discrimination were discussed, with special attention to the principle of equal-status association in efforts to achieve superordinate goals in which there is a shared sense of stake. The constructive use of interpersonal and intergroup conflict was particularly stressed. Rumor, often a companion of prejudice, was briefly considered.

Problems in police and community relations are generally referred to in terms of minority groups and "the disaffected" in society. And it is true that the problems are frequently most acute in these dimensions. On the basis of our analysis to this point, however, it is apparent that a general problem exists in police and community relations, even before specific issues are introduced. The specific is a complication of the general; an already difficult relationship becomes more difficult when certain elements of the population are combined.

What are some of the bench-marks of the general problem of police and community relations? Here are ten we have noted:

1. Social change, in the sense of changed people-to-people relationships, which has drastically altered the dynamics of social control in society and involves a restructuring of the relationship between police and policed.

2. The changing attitudes toward authority systems and toward authority figures, including the criminal justice system and the police officer. Authority viewed as arbitrarily imposed is being questioned and challenged in many spheres, world-wide.

3. Depreciation or deterioration in the United States of the Anglo-Saxon principle of self-policing as a citizen's duty, which has widened the gap between police and the people.

4. The fundamental role paradox of the police in today's democratic society and its manifestation in such matters as discretionary use of police power.

5. The adversarial nature of the law enforcement aspect of police work and of the larger context of the criminal justice system.

6. Alienation of police and community resulting from the paradox of role and status for the police officer and the inconsistency and ambivalence of society's expectations from him.

7. Unrealistic recruitment and educational standards for the police, given the demands and requirements of modern policing in big cities where most of our population is concentrated.

8. The effects upon police and community relations of overcriminalization or legal moralism and the military model of police organization.

9. The dynamics of the perceptual process in human behavior, with particular reference to we-and-they differentiations in our attitudes, beliefs, and values.

10. The metabolism of prejudice and bigotry in interpersonal and intergroup relations.

Part Three

Sociological Considerations

Chapter Ten

Social Processes and Population Trends

College programs in police administration, police science, public safety, and criminal justice have multiplied rapidly in recent years. At a few universities, it is now possible to earn the bachelor's, master's, and doctor's degrees in this field, with a considerable diversification and range of courses. This may include an opportunity to specialize to some extent within the major; for example, administration and executive development, criminal law, evidence and procedure, corrections, the administration of traffic safety programs, police and community relations, security in government and industry, criminalistics, organized crime, and so on.

Some of these university programs are established in a College of Social Science or sometimes in a College of Community Services. It strikes some people as odd that a school or department of criminal justice is found side by side, in the same college, with departments of sociology, psychology, political science, anthropology, and social work. Students of police administration, corrections, or criminal justice are required to earn a substantial number of credits in the social and behavioral sciences for reasons that will become clear as our discussion proceeds.

Institutional recognition of the interdisciplinary requirements of criminal justice heralds an awakening to a new era in all phases of the field, with emphasis on two significant points: (1) Human behavior and "people relatedness" should be priority concerns in the criminal justice process, and (2) the criminal justice system does not function effectively as a system.

It follows that this "system" stands in desperate need of over-hauling, basically because people are caught up in it who are being treated as non-people. In sum, a School of Criminal Justice, as part of a university's social science "family", ought to signify commitment to the need for change in all facets of the criminal justice process. While there may be those who would dissent on this point (the issue being the purpose of a university, which will trigger an argument on any campus), we will resist being detained by it here.

Group Relationships

Psychologists are interested in behavior. Sociologists are also interested in behavior, but with a somewhat different focus: man in his social or group behavior. Social psychology constitutes the blending of these disciplines. That distinctions among the behavioral and social sciences are thin may be illustrated by the question, "Is human personality a social product?" To deal with this question adequately, one would delve into sociology, psychology, anthropology, and biology. For our purpose, it is sufficient to say that as our analysis shifts slightly, and perhaps imperceptibly, from psychological to sociological considerations, we shall focus somewhat more on *group relationships*.

Just as there are psychological processes in human behavior—perception, motivation, and learning—there are also social processes in group interaction. These processes follow upon social contact, by language or other means of communication. When two or more people meet, the ensuing interaction, if sustained to any extent, assumes some sort of pattern. This pattern of interaction is often erratic and inconsistent, jumping from one quality to another (first impressions are not necessarily lasting), but over a period of time, it can be plotted and given an identifying label. It may never go beyond "small talk"; on the other hand, it may develop into an exchange of ideas, perhaps chaotic, perhaps more or less systematic and orderly—or more likely, some of both, varying by circumstances. A dynamic interplay of personal and social forces is involved.[1]

Which pattern predominates in social interaction: cooperation or conflict? Complex systems of social theory have been built around this question, most holding that cooperation is the dominant social process, a few holding that competition and conflict are dominant. To what extent is it a "dog-eat-dog" world? If one takes an extreme position on this question, how explain that people do, in fact, live together in harmony, mutual aid, and trust? Civilization survives and thrives precisely because of helping and sharing and trusting.

Social relations are, of course, an extension of individual human nature: a mixture of plus and minus, positive and negative, love and hate, good and bad, cooperation and competition. Historians and anthropologists tell us that there are cultures and societies that have emphasized one more than the other, either way. In early America, for example, there were peaceful as well as warlike Indian tribes. Cultural considerations seem to explain these differences. Our society contains many examples of limited cooperation among competitors, which exemplifies the practical admixture of the processes.

The Social Process

Competition is the struggle for what are seen as desirable but limited goods: wealth, customers or profits, prestige, jobs, promotions, parental affection, etc. The prevailing culture establishes what is regarded as desirable. People reared in a noncompetitive culture find it difficult to adjust to highly competitive conditions. Unregulated competition easily becomes destructive and takes unfair advantage of others. Thus there develops wide recognition of the need for such ethical norms as Fair Trade laws or agreements. There are also associations of realtors, automobile dealers, and the like, which set "rules of the game" and provide "insurance against cut-throats." If the parties to the competitive process are of unequal strength, exploitation and injustice are the likely results. Again, the ancient political equation emerges: how much individual freedom, how much regulation, in order to achieve the common good?

Competition is usually impersonal and unconscious. It may exist without personal contacts. People may not be aware that what they have acquired through competition might have deprived someone else of that particular good. But sometimes the scarcity of the good is only a *felt* scarcity, as with parental love, when theoretically there is no actual scarcity.

When competition becomes conscious and personal, it is *conflict*. Sometimes it is difficult to distinguish one from the other. Conflict may be internal, as in the concerns of the psychologist or psychiatrist. Sometimes internal conflict is caused by external forces; for example, in the case of value conflict, as we observed in Chapter Eight. What sociologists call *contra-cultural conflict* illustrates this point; it may cause personality disorganization, as Kane ("Personal and Social Disorganization") and others have pointed out. Then there is interpersonal conflict; for instance, in marriage or other prolonged, close associations of human beings. (Should like marry like?) Rubbing other people the wrong way is hardly a rare experience. There are also intergroup conflicts, as when groups compete for limited goods. And there are international conflicts, pitting nation against nation. (Is war inevitable? Or is it, in truth, culturally prescribed?)

Cooperation is a social process in which two or more persons or groups work together in mutual helpfulness. It exemplifies "associative" social interaction: the parties are inclined to want to work with one another, to join together, to gravitate toward each other, to pool their resources. The ultimate of this social process is *love*. Interaction may, on the other hand, cause individuals or groups to draw apart, a "dissociative" tendency. The ultimate of this is *hate* (war). Between these poles, there are varying degrees of association or dissociation.

Conflict tends to be an intermittent rather than a continuous social process. During periods of conflict, social equilibrium is often maintained through some form of *accommodation*. This is a process of limited cooperation—cooperation under certain conditions. Coercion, or forcing people to act contrary to their wishes, is the lowest level of accommodation. It is outward conformity in order to escape an alternate penalty viewed as worse. Less demeaning to human dignity is compromise—a form of accommodation in which each of the conflicting parties agrees to give some ground and accept some losses. Conciliation, mediation, and arbitration are formalized types of compromise in conflict situations among large groups.

Toleration is a type of accommodation in which differences cannot be compromised, but are accepted for what they are, and are subordinated to cooperation and mutual participation. A democratic, pluralistic society depends on toleration. Conversion is the settlement of a conflict situation by a shifting of a person's beliefs, loyalties, or emotional attachments. ("If you can't lick 'em, join 'em!")

The difference between conversion, as a form of accommodation, and *assimilation* is slight. The latter is a process through which persons or groups acquire the habits and values of other persons or groups and become parts of a common system—as we said in Chapter Nine, *nearly* complete absorption of one culture by another. Anthropologists use the term *acculturation* to refer to this process. The sociological concept of *marginality* refers to persons who participate partially in two different cultures. They may not be fully accepted in either. An example is the black police officer. The degree of marginality varies by individuals. Another example would be blacks who have "made it," by the standards of white middle-class society, but who entertain strong sentiments of loyalty and concern for other blacks who have not. Such ambivalence, when translated into behavior, can be difficult. The conflicting standards (and role expectations) are not easily reconciled.

Amalgamation is a biologically oriented term for the social process whereby races or cultures are merged through intermarriage. Because amalgamation implies ultimate assimilation, it is the most drastic of all the social processes. In itself, amalgamation creates no problems. The principal barriers to it are culturally prescribed ethnocentrism (racism), caste systems, and the stratification of fixed class groups. *Stratification* is the division of society into horizontal levels, evaluated and arranged hierarchically on the basis of such standards as learning, sex, occupation, age, effectiveness in war, social class, caste, race, religion, etc. The standards for stratification are many, often quite subtle, frequently pernicious and arbitrary, and not uncommonly, are imposed by law, public opinion, custom, tradition, etc.

In white society in the United States, it is said that ours is an "open class" system. This means that change of social class is possible for all. Many poor whites and blacks feel that the system is actually quasi-caste, which means that the chances of change are remote indeed. Stratification in terms of social class is the point of departure for Marxism. Stratification in terms of sex is the point of departure for the women's liberation movement. Stratification in terms of age (the "generation gap") is the point of departure for gerontology and "Senior Citizen" activities. Stratification is frequently an end result of competition, conflict (Social Darwinism), cooperation, and accommodation. Whether it is a positive or negative social process varies according to the criteria and whether or not it is arbitrarily imposed. In any case, however, it has an inherent quality of divisiveness.

Social Control

Viewed as a whole, social interaction is grounded in the assumption that the participants (role assignees or actors) will follow certain lines (role patterns) of predictable action. It is, in this sense, "coordinated." Obviously, the survival of society depends on a considerable amount of mutual trust. The more complicated the society, the more vital the latent reliance of people on each other. Take the automobile as a simple illustration. How many persons are engaged in building it and in maintaining it in good repair? When I drive it, I rely on the work of these others, whom I do not know and probably will never meet. In driving it, I depend on other drivers to respect the rules of the road, as they rely on me—and I do not know, nor shall I ever meet, most of them. The mutual trust is impersonal, but real. It holds things together.

The automobile is but one facet of a complex social arrangement that depends utterly on such depersonalized mutual trust. This is *social integration.* It is achieved through a variety of techniques, means, and pressures by which society brings individual members and groups into some measure of conformity: what is called "good order," or *social control.* There are institutionalized or formal means of social control and noninstitutionalized, informal means. The law is an example of the former; public opinion, art, ceremony, praise, flattery, rewards, gossip, and ridicule are examples of the latter. The basic idea is to influence behavior according to a certain norm. Advertising, propaganda, name-calling, pressure groups, lobbying: these are further examples of common social control mechanisms. A political campaign involves all of these and many more.

Law as a means of social control is, of course, of special interest to us here. Law is the expressed will of the state and consists—in the United States—of the common law, statutory law, and court decisions. The prohibitions of law are an index of the range of behavior that the people of a democratic society will tolerate. Law is a society's ultimate weapon in controlling the conduct of its members. For law carries with it, as does any other mechanism of social control, a sanctionary element: rewards for conformity and penalties for deviance. Both the rewards and the penalties reflect shifting standards of public opinion, as evidenced in the history of penology.

Social Change and Social Control

Relatively few laws are needed in a culturally homogeneous society in which everyone respects the existing, informal norms, especially if there is little spatial and social mobility. But in a complicated, technological, culturally heterogeneous society such as ours has become, many laws are required. The trend toward legal controls increases as basic institutional means of control, such as the family and religious bodies, diminish in influence. In short, social change and social control are intimately related. This is another basic way of indicating what police-community relations is all about. It pertains to the relationship between social change and social control.

We have discussed the importance attached to the principle of self-policing in the historical background of modern British and American police work. The number of people who obey the law voluntarily and who thereby assume some responsibility that might otherwise fall to the police—without ever a thought to the police—is striking evidence of the power of social norms. The social control exemplified by law observance is the best kind of law enforcement.

Banton provides an excellent comparison of the simple and the complex society, from the social control standpoint. Following is a series of quotations that convey his key points:

> The communities with the highest level of social control are small, homogeneous, and stable . . . In such communities, social control is maintained to a very large extent by informal controls of public opinion, and there is little resort to formal controls such as legislation or the full-time appointment of people to law enforcement duties. . . . The small society with a simple technology can afford to have its "village idiot"; the large and complex one cannot, for many people

would not recognize him and he might easily hurt himself or create havoc in the affairs of others.

. . . .

People who live together like this are agreed in what they consider right and wrong, so it can be said that the highly integrated society is characterized by a high level of consensus, or agreement on fundamental values. . . . The policeman obtains public cooperation, and enjoys public esteem, because he enforces standards accepted by the community. . . . This gives his role considerable moral authority . . .

. . . .

No social changes are without their costs, and one of the principal costs of making the social structure more flexible is the decline of social integration. An index of this is the crime rate. . . . As the problem of maintaining order becomes more severe, societies increasingly adopt formal controls, summarized by an anthropologist as "courts, codes, constables and central authority." [*The Policeman in the Community*, pp. 2–11]

Some police officers today imply that they have made a remarkable discovery when they say, "Being a cop today is a lot tougher than it used to be!" Yes, indeed—and the same is true for school teachers, clergymen, medical practitioners, social workers, and storekeepers. The police officer is an agent of society's system of social control. And social change, in many ways, has made the social control function infinitely more challenging than in the society of yesteryear. Among the obvious evidences are the "automobile revolution," and the related unprecedented mobility of people. But some of the marks of social change are less discernible, as for instance in the matter of community relations.

The Community and Social Control

Banton's analysis suggests that social control is a function of the status of social relations in a given situation. Its level is determined by the kinds of social relationships that exist among individuals and groups who make up a society. Banton describes it in terms of relative social integration or disintegration. This is the essence of a functional definition of *community,* which we touched on in Chapter Two. A true community is socially integrated; it encompasses a sharing of common experiences and a sense of belonging together.

In another place, the author has commented on the idea of community:

The community that is our goal is a community of COMMON UNITY. It is a community which dignifies the right to be different. It is a community in which there is no penalty or sanction exacted upon those who protest. It is a community disposed in spirit to the dialogue. It is a decent society in the sense of Jacques Maritain's emphasis, viz., a society which helps people to be *persons,* i.e., "bearers of values" . . . the root of the idea of community is *participation;* not condescension, not patronage, not rescue, but the dignity and worth that men and women on any level of life experience when they are part of what is important to their fellows. ["The Idea of Community"]

The main point here is to understand the relationship between social change and social control and to emphasize that social control and community relations are interdependent. As change occurs in people-to-people relations, in the transition from a simple to a complex society, social controls—as Banton says—are more apt to be imposed by formal, institutionalized mechanisms.

When someone asks, "What has happened to community?" or declares, "We must restore a sense of community," it is well to keep in mind what we are talking about. A community is not simply a place or a location. It is not necessarily a small town or a big town. Eric Fromm has said simply that "a community is love." He may be accused of over-simplifying, but he has captured the gist of the idea. So did Albert Camus when he wrote: "Each and every man, on the foundation of his own sufferings and joy, builds for all men."

Again, the same point, in Banton's terms:

In contrasting village society with the big industrial nation, it is difficult not to convey a false impression. Even in the small-scale stable society, consensus is never perfect; it is only relatively high. An even greater mistake would be to imply that consensus is absent under urban conditions. Certainly in some urban situations, the moral controls are weak and the formal organization has to impose strict penalties, but there are many basic issues—such as ideas of duty to kinsfolk, work-mates, and neighbors—where popular morality remains powerful. In many urban residential neighborhoods, there is a very real sense of community, even if informal social controls are less extensive than in the village. Policemen, being subconsciously aware of their dependence upon these mechanisms of control, prefer to work as peace officers and to see their role in these terms. [*The Policeman in the Community*, p. 7]

There is a suggestion in this of the police officer playing something of the role of the umpire in a ball game, even to the functions of mediation and arbitration. We are forthwith back again to the police role question, this time in terms of the changing nature of social control and the management of social conflict in today's urban circumstances.

Population Trends

We have referred to social change in the sense of spatial and social mobility. Since this is so important with reference to the police officer's "umpire" function in social conflict, it merits further attention.

An interesting analogy in big league baseball is to consider the qualities that are deemed vital in competent umpires. The same may be said for arbitrators in industrial relations. How about the policeman?

The first sociology course taught at Notre Dame University by the author of this text, as a graduate fellow in 1939, was in *Population Problems*. The class used several standard references on the subject at that time. These sources unanimously predicted that the population of this country would reach a maximum of 165 million toward the end of the century, remain stationary for a time, and possibly decline thereafter. What has actually happened, of course, is that we passed the 165 million mark in 1955, and the 1970 census puts the figure in the neighborhood of 205 million. The explanation is largely in the completely unanticipated boom in marriages and births that has generally characterized the post-1945 period.

That early teaching experience, and what subsequently occurred, left a lasting lesson: avoid assured predictions regarding population trends. But on one point, the evidence seems to be quite clear: contracultural conflict, resulting from spatial and social mobility, is indicated for some time to come.

Several demographic trends of special interest to us may be identified. One is the increasing *concentration* of population in big cities— what the Bureau of the Census calls Standard Metropolitan Statistical Areas, defined as a core city having a population of 50,000 and up, with surrounding suburban satellites in one or more counties. In the early 1900s, about one-third of our population lived in such centers. By 1950, this had become 57 percent of the population, living in what were then 168 such complexes. In 1970, virtually 70 percent of the population resided in about 220 metropolitan areas.

The trend toward concentration may be identified in another way. In the first half of this century, our metropolitan areas absorbed 73 percent of the total population increase of the country. This became 81 percent during the decade 1940–50 and 97 percent during the decade 1950–60. In 1960, the Chicago metropolitan area, by way of a specific example, had a population greater than that of any of 43 states. In effect, somewhat more than two-thirds of our population today is concentrated on approximately 5 percent of our total land area. This is what is meant by "metroplexity."

A second trend relates to the *decentralization* of population within the large metropolitan areas. During the first half of the present century, the growth of suburban communities—outside central cities but within metropolitan areas—compared with the growth of central city population in a ratio of 1⅓ to 1. It was 2½ to 1 for the decade 1940–50; it became 7 to 1 in the decade 1950–60 and was about 8–1 in the decade 1960–70.

A third trend has to do with the *qualitative nature of the decentralization trend* in the metropolitan areas. The outreaches of big cities tend to provide more desirable residential housing than the core. The dwelling units are newer, and they are functionally more efficient. Historically, as newcomers have come to the city, they have tended to settle in the inner, less desirable parts thereof, because so many of them must start at the bottom of the socio-economic ladder. As they have worked their way up this ladder, they have moved out to where the more desirable housing is, while newer newcomers have filtered into the center.

This general pattern has gone on to a point where vast sections of our inner cities—intermixing old dwellings that have become dilapidated, multiple-family units with business establishments, and heavy industry in weird conglomerations—have deteriorated seriously. As a result, our vast urban renewal programs have developed, to bull-doze and rebuild whole neighborhoods. This imposes new ways of living on millions of relocated people and creates manifold adjustment problems for them. Our main point is, however, that the outward movement of people, from core city to suburbia, has been a highly selective phenomenon. The qualification has not been entirely socio-economic, such as whether a family can afford an improved residential situation. It has frequently been a question of race, of language and culture, and sometimes of religion.

Industries have tended to follow the decentralization pattern, moving out to suburban industrial parks and such. The clustering of factory workers, predominately white, in low cost suburban housing near their jobs foreshadows a new type of "slum." Segregated living has not been the monopoly of any one people in our history. People of the same culture, language, and institutions have tended to flock together initially in the inner city, then have moved out and dispersed throughout a metropolitan area. In the beginning, each newcomer group has been viewed with suspicion, hostility, and distrust. There was contra-cultural conflict aplenty, beginning with the Indians and the early settlers.

As each group has moved away from the city's inner zone, they have invaded middle-aged, conservative neighborhoods, bringing cultural habits that often are threatening to established ways. This prompts many who have resided in such neighborhoods to move further out or to form "Neighborhood Protective Associations." Detroit Councilman Mel Ravitz poses a question:

> How do those who are middle class and who administer and control the schools, the churches, the government, the social agencies, and all of the other organizations of the urban community learn to relate effectively with those people who have come and who are coming to these cities and who want to remain and be accepted? ["Contra-Cultural Conflict"]

This becomes a continuing challenge to America's belief in cultural pluralism. It also reflects the challenge facing today's big-city policeman in his role as an "umpire" in the management of social conflict.

Blacks in the Metropolis

For a number of historical reasons, it happens that in recent years, in most of our metropolitan areas, the Negro has been the newest of the newcomers. There are some exceptions to this; for example, Puerto Ricans in some cities, other Spanish-speaking Mexicans and Latin Americans, or the white Southern Appalachian migrant in some. By and large, however, it is the blacks who have been the latest to arrive, and in the largest numbers, although it appears that this trend may now be slackening.

Back in the 1790–1820 period, blacks made up about 20 percent of the population of the United States. By 1930, this proportion had dwindled to 10 percent of the total. Today, it is estimated to be approximately 11 percent. Just prior to the Civil War in 1860, 92 percent of all blacks in this country lived in the South. In 1910, 89 percent still lived there. As we noted in an earlier chapter, the first large migratory wave of blacks from the South to the North occurred during World War I. The reasons were basically economic: the abdication of King Cotton in the South, the need for manpower in northern war-production industries, and the virtual end of European immigration as a source of the needed manpower.

World War II brought a similar internal migration of blacks, generally from rural to urban localities, and from the South to the North and West, although many blacks also moved to Southern cities. The changing proportion of nonwhite to white residents of urban communities is evident in these figures: in 1940, 48 percent of the nonwhite population of the country and 57.5 percent of the white population was urban; by 1950, this had become 59 percent for each; by 1960, the white population in urban areas was 70 percent, while the nonwhite population in urban areas was 72 percent (Paul Mundy, "Implications of Population Trends," p. 67).[2]

How well prepared were black migrants for life in a metropolis? Within the span of a generation and a half, a people from a folk culture in the rural, economically depressed South were catapulted into metropolitan living. For immigrants to this country, the adjustment and adaptation process was one of assimilation, acculturation, or just plain "Americanization." But for the American Negro, we have had a rather peculiar situation. He has been an American longer than most white people, but it is only in the past fifty years that he has found himself suddenly transplanted into the urban way of life. This process of adjustment in the twentieth century has not been "Americanization" in the traditional sense, but rather one of urbanization or metropolitanization.

Adapting to the demanding patterns of big-city living has been, for most blacks, a struggle against monumental disadvantages that few whites are able to comprehend.

There are those who ask, "Why can't *they* do what various immigrant groups did—lift themselves up and prove their worth by hard work and iron-willed determination?" Aside from the ethnocentric and chauvinistic implications of such a question—with reference to one's own ancestors—there are two points to keep in mind. One is the blackness of the Negro, as compared with immigrant groups generally. Relatively whiter people tend to view blackness in and of itself as "bad," "evil," "a curse"—even to citing God, the Bible, and voodooism to bolster their superstition. The second point is that no other immigrant group coming to this country found itself shackled for almost 250 years by a highly institutionalized system of abject slavery. To be reminded of these considerations is still regarded in some quarters of our country, North and South, as highly inflammatory. But the question with which this paragraph began is equally inflammatory for black citizens.

In the matter of the urbanization problems of the Negro, it is also pertinent to note that as recently as 1950, his average schooling in the rural South was 4.8 years. This is below the level of functional literacy —the level at which a person can read a daily newspaper easily. Although this condition has been improved during the past twenty years, it should be observed that the parents of many black teen-agers today in the inner cities are products of this level and type of formal education.

Chicago as an Example

Chicago is typical of what has happened as a result of population shift. In the period 1950–60, about 600,000 whites left the central city and moved to suburbia. During that decade, the central city's net white population loss was 400,000, because there was an excess of 200,000 white births over deaths. The black population increased by about 350,-000 in the same period, from slightly more than 500,000 to almost 850,000. The black population of Chicago was 30,000 in 1900; by 1920, it was 120,000. The nonwhite population of Chicago quadrupled between 1900 and 1920, increased by more than 28 times between 1900 and 1960, and by more than 7 times between 1920 and 1960. By 1960, blacks constituted 14 percent of the population in the six counties of northeastern Illinois and 23 percent of the population of the city of Chicago. These percentages are higher today (Mundy, p. 68).

Many rural white migrants (and a sizable number of Indians) have also settled in our big cities during the past fifty years. The economic and political forces underlying the spatial and social mobility of these years can hardly be ignored. We have alluded in Chapter Nine to "Black Power" and "Brown Power." Analysis of today's political scene in numerous big cities throughout the nation reveals a rapidly changing panorama. In terms of potential if not actual political power, the balance is shifting more and more to nonwhites with voting prerogatives. As in Chicago, it becomes increasingly difficult to determine the majority and the minority in racial terms.

Minority Aspirations

Aspirations for equal rights generated by members of minority groups themselves constitute a dynamic trend that is shaping the course of America's social and political history. These aspirations are matched with determination, increasingly effective organization, and somewhat improved economic status. The goals of minority groups with respect to economic opportunities, civil rights, and social status are becoming more clearly defined, though there are sharp splits as to the means of achieving these goals.

It is, of course, impossible to answer the question, "What do minorities want?" There is too much disagreement. But on some basic considerations, there is agreement—for instance, the rights and privileges guaranteed to every citizen by our Constitution. In those terms, it may be said that minorities want neither more nor less than their fellow Americans want. They want personal safety and security, freedom from violence, and freedom from discriminatory treatment by police officers and courts of law. They want the full rights and responsibilities of citizens: the right to vote, the right to serve on an equal footing in the armed forces, and the right to serve on juries. They want freedom in religion, speech, and the press, the right to form organizations and to assemble in an orderly and peaceful way to advance their group interests. They want fair and equal opportunities in employment, in education, in housing, in health and welfare services, in recreation, and in public accommodations (Vickery and Gittler, "Intergroup Relations in the United States, 1960–1980"). And they want as much attention paid to "law and order" in the protection of these rights as is paid rhetorically to "crime in the streets," which, by the way, concerns them much more directly than it does middle class, suburban whites, because they *live* where the problem is gravest, and they are frequently its victims. More than all else, they want to be accepted—to be "as good as anyone else."

Poverty as a Social Force

We have noted that anticipated improvement in economic status is a prime reason for spatial mobility. To move one's place of residence is often to aspire to movement upward, financially and socially. Minority group status frequently has poverty as its handmaiden.

The 1960s were marked by a declaration of war on poverty at the highest executive and legislative levels. It has appeared sometimes that the war was declared without adequate education as to the nature of "the enemy." William McKenzie of Southern Illinois University identified some of the favorite myths about poverty as follows:[3]

The myth that poverty is inevitable.

The myth that poverty is simply a matter of being without money or other resources. This leads to the faulty conclusion that poor people are "just like us," except that they lack resources. Of course there are people who are temporarily "down on their luck." But the *culture of poverty* is much more complex. Moreover, the discount-store phenomenon operates on the assumption that the poor do have some resources. And there may be considerable question that some of the poor really want to be "like us."

The myth that the poor are Negroes, and that Negroes are poor. This entire concept is false. Negroes belong to many classifications. Twenty-five percent of the population of this country are poor, so obviously many are white. However, having said this, one may proceed to assert that there are many groups of Negroes in poverty—also Indians, Southern Appalachian migrants, Chicanoes, Puerto Ricans, and even some white policemen! No one group should be used as a model for the whole.

The myth that the poor are without culture. One thinks of such expressions as "the culturally deprived," "the culturally disadvantaged," etc. This is patent nonsense. The simple fact is that the poor live in a *different* culture. The Navajos of New Mexico are poor, but no one would suggest that they are "culture-poor."

The myth that poverty breeds crime. Laws define crimes, and laws are made by dominant groups and provide maximum protection for those who make them. Even crime statistics are largely culturally derived. Where there is an apparent coincidence of crime and poverty, one must look beyond poverty for the cause of crime.

There are other, minor myths about the poor that may be mentioned: that poverty causes family disruption (matriarchy among the Negro poor, for example, is not a product of poverty, but of Negro history); that the poor are dependent in spirit as well as in sustenance (poor people are often proud people, and they want no "handouts"); that the poor are deficient in their ability to communicate (this assumes that middle class communication is the best and only way to communicate).

What are some of the significant *truths* about poverty? Some have been implied above. McKenzie adds:

Poverty is more of a culture or subculture than it is a social class. Identifying the poor with the lower class is similar to identifying the upper class with the rich. The difficulty is that a central middle class concern, i.e., economic resources, is taken as the measure of two groups for which it is not a central concern.

Poverty is socially invisible. It is overwhelmingly taken for granted as part of the scenery. Poor people tend to be seen as "picturesque natives, living in the only way they know, therefore happy."

Poverty means institutional non-participation. The poor do not make our institutions and they do not manage them, but they are subject to them. They are expected to live by a moral code established by people with quite a different experience. What have our schools offered the Poor as Poor? Or our churches? Only the model of striving "to be like others, who have made it." To be poor is to live in someone else's world.

Poverty means immediacy. To be poor is, as it is said, "to live from hand to mouth." The poor are not much concerned with the long ago, and even less with the distant future. Thus, the values of the poor are often difficult for others to understand. If fortune smiles, the poor man buys his automobile or television—today. Tomorrow will take care of itself; it can't be any worse than yesterday. To be poor is to live continuously in the NOW.

To be poor is to have identity. Poverty has a place for everyone, and everyone is in his place. The feeling of lack of identity, of dislocation, of disassociation, of alienation is not a product simply of being poor. The poor know who they are; as with crime, we must look beyond poverty for the causes of disaffection.

Poverty is mean, it is brutal, it is frustrating, it is painful, and it blights the spirit. There are few things in this world that are worse than being caught in the grip of poverty.

A Concluding Note

In this chapter, we have briefly reviewed some basic considerations in a sociological approach to problem analysis in police-community relations. Our purpose has been to set the stage for the discussion in forthcoming chapters. The central message of the chapter may be summarized as follows: the relationship of people is fundamentally a matter of social interaction, the possible patterns of which are called social processes—cooperation, competition, conflict, accommodation, assimilation, amalgamation, stratification, etc. In order to maintain stability, and indeed in order for a society to survive, social controls are necessary—controls by which a society or group secures conformity to its norms. Law is an important means to this end, but there are many social control mechanisms, formal and informal, with accompanying sanctions.

Social change, especially as it has affected people-to-people relations, has made social control in our society much more complicated than it once was. Population trends (spatial mobility) provide evidence of this, and the resultant greater probability of contra-culture conflict, particularly in our big cities, has underlined the growing importance of the umpire (conflict management) role of the police officer. The urbanization problems of the American Negro and other minority groups during the past half-century are of special interest today to students of police-community relations. So too are problems of what has come to be called "the culture of poverty."

Someone has said that revolution is a continuing part of the American experience. Another way to say this may be more of a cliché, thus somewhat less startling, but it conveys the same thought: change is the only social constant. In recent years in the United States, specifically since 1954, we have been in the midst of what many people have referred to as a revolution in race relations. "The Movement," in the popular term, has been in the forefront of concerns in police and community relations, to the point where many people have seen it as *the* problem. In the next chapter, we shall undertake to analyze it.

Notes to Chapter Ten

1. Any standard introductory textbook in sociology covers these matters in detail. Our aim in this chapter is to elicit principles relevant to relationships of the police and the community, in particular to the concerns of the following chapters. Some of the discussion is based on the works of Raymond W. Murray, C.S.C., former chairman of the Department of Sociology of Notre Dame.

2. See also Study 1 (Part III), "The Negro Population of the United States," in Radelet and Reed, *Studies*. It may be further added that a report published jointly in February 1969 by Urban America, Inc., and the Urban Coalition showed that whites had sharply accelerated their movement from the central cities in the aftermath of 1967 racial disturbances in many large urban centers. At the same time, blacks had even more dramatically slowed migration into them. Inner-city ghettos were seen as having spread in area, and slums had begun to emerge in the suburbs. The study went on to state that in the year following issuance of the report of the National Advisory Commission on Civil Disorders, polarization between blacks and whites had increased, and no "serious start" had been made in changing national priorities. The latter point was re-emphasized by the U. S. Civil Rights Commission in the fall of 1970.

3. William R. McKenzie, "The Face of the Enemy: A Brief Introduction to the Theory and Practice of Poverty." Paper presented at the Midwest Philosophy of Education Society meeting held in Chicago, December 4, 1965. See also Elizabeth Herzog, *About the Poor: Some Facts and Some Fictions*.

Chapter Eleven

The Movement–
In Race Relations
and Civil Rights

It has often been said that a democratic society has its critical test in how it deals with its minorities. So it is in police relations with the community. While there is, as we have stated, more to police-community relations than police interaction with minorities, there is no question that police treatment of such groups is in some sense what determines whether the principles enunciated by spokesmen for "our way of life" have any real meaning. Further, since the term "minority group" in this country has most frequently been applied to the Negro, there is special reason for students of police and community relations to look into the matter of police-Negro relationships and to be alert to relevances to other minorities.

Where one chooses to begin a study of Negro history in terms of police and community relations is largely a matter of how intensive and extensive one wishes to be. One might well begin with 1619—or as Herskovits did, even earlier, with his classic analysis of the pre-American past of the Negro (*The Myth of the Negro Past*). One might begin with Harper's Ferry or with the so-called Reconstruction period. Some might say that the civil rights movement—The Movement, in to-day's terms—began with the Supreme Court's 1896 decision ("separate but equal") in the Plessy-Ferguson case (163 U.S.537). Others would contend that it was Marcus Garvey who started it all in 1918, with his Universal Negro Improvement Association—a populist organization that claimed two million members and aimed at leading American Negroes back to Africa, where they could develop their own nation and culture.

Where We Begin the Story

For our purpose, it seems logical to begin the story with internal migration of American blacks during World War II, because it coincides with the development of the earliest programs in police and community relations. Gunnar Myrdal's monumental study of our race problem (*An American Dilemma*) was first published in 1944. He said that this problem was America's greatest failure, but also her greatest opportunity for the future. He observed that Negroes have always shared in American ideals, but not in their realization.

Since the economic factors of supply and demand caused the Negro migratory movement during the years of World War II, it was historically logical that President Franklin D. Roosevelt appointed a Committee on Fair Employment Practices by executive order in June 1941. It was a response to a threatened march on Washington organized by A. Philip Randolph, president of the Brotherhood of Sleeping Car Porters. President Roosevelt expanded the powers of this Committee in 1943, and although it did not have the authority to compel compliance with its recommendations, its persuasive power was substantial.

As the war ended, however, Congress failed to pass legislation establishing a permanent FEPC. But several states moved ahead with such laws, beginning with New York in 1945. In 1948, President Harry S. Truman revived the matter at the Federal level, by executive order providing policy and machinery for nondiscrimination in government employment. With regard to discrimination in the Armed Forces during World War II, the various services experimented gingerly with 10 percent quota patterns and such, with rather unsatisfactory results. Another executive order by President Truman in 1948 activated a President's Committee on Equality of Treatment and Opportunity in the Armed Services.

In the criminal justice field, Charles Johnson reported in 1943 (*Patterns of Negro Segregation,* p. 30) that the South had no Negro judges, few Negro policemen, and no Negroes serving even in minor clerical positions in official agencies. In rural counties a Negro juryman was unheard of. In 1951 Carl Rowan reported that 77 Southern cities employed approximately 425 Negro police officers, but in most cities these officers were permitted to arrest only Negroes or "offenders on their beats" (*How Far From Slavery?,* Chap. 6). The 1964 study by the International Association of Chiefs of Police and the United States Conference of Mayors, mentioned in Chapter One, found that such restrictions on the powers of black officers were gradually disappearing.

In 1947 the President's Committee on Civil Rights submitted its report (*To Secure These Rights*) to President Truman. The Committee reviewed the dreary status of civil rights in the United States and made strong recommendations to correct the many violations and abuses its investigations had revealed. It is sobering today to reflect on some of these recommendations, dating back barely twenty-five years. To cite a few: the establishment of a permanent Commission on Civil Rights, the enactment of an anti-lynching act, the enactment of a new criminal statute on involuntary servitude, a review of the dismal wartime evacuation and detention experience with Japanese Americans, Congressional action to end poll taxes, the granting of suffrage to Indians in New Mexico and Arizona, the granting of citizenship to the people of Guam and American Samoa, the enactment of meaningful Fair Employment, Educational, and Health Practices laws at the Federal and state levels, and the enactment of state laws prohibiting restrictive covenants in housing.

It was ten years later, in 1957, that the United States Commission on Civil Rights was finally established by Congress—the first Federal legislation of its type since 1875. This Commission's first report to President Eisenhower in 1959 concentrated on voting rights, education, and housing.[1]

The Rights of the Individual

The Commission concerned chiefly with laws and educational programs aimed at solving what Myrdal had called "an American dilemma." The 1947 report, entitled *To Secure These Rights,* phrased the ideal this way:

> The central theme in our American heritage is the importance of the individual person. From the earliest moment of our history we have believed that every human being has an essential dignity and integrity which must be respected and safeguarded. Moreover, we believe that the welfare of the individual is the final goal of group life. Our American heritage further teaches that to be secure in the rights he wishes for himself, each man must be willing to respect the rights of other men. This is the conscious recognition of a basic moral principle: that all men are created equal as well as free ... [P. 4]

Myrdal detected the gap between ideal and practice.

White supremacy versus *racial equality.* This is a stark statement of the contradiction at the base of the civil rights struggle. But the gap between preachment and practice is complicated. Americans believe strongly in the sanctity of private property and the right of an individual to acquire and dispose of it. Americans also believe in the values of competition and in the right to privacy. Beliefs of this type are often fundamental in understanding how and why racial injustice is perpetuated and justified by some. It is almost as if human rights and social justice were in short supply with not enough to go around, resulting in the need to compete for scarce goods. Sometimes property rights are defended as more important than human rights. It is a kind of schizophrenic value orientation, manipulated to suit institutionalized and personal prejudices.

Two additional influences during the past 20 to 30 years should be mentioned. One is the American tendency to measure the Negro against the experience of the Irish, the Italian, the Polish, the German, the Scandinavian, and other immigrant groups to this country. The comparison is not realistic. In addition to the reasons we cited earlier reflecting how the Negro's situation has been different from immigrant groups, there was also the pattern of European ethnic minorities protecting themselves by the use of machine politics in the big American cities where they settled.[2]

The other influence pertains to the rise of industrial unionism during the 1930s. The late George Blackwood of Boston University identified five patterns that were to be important later in The Movement for Negro civil rights that developed out of industrial unionism in the 1937–41 period:

1. A reliance on mass action—huge meetings, sit-ins, massed picketlines, coordinated demonstrations.

2. The rise of new, young, idealistic leadership which became symbolic of radicalism to many conservatives.

3. Vocal sympathy from liberals, tempered with some criticism about tactics.

4. A plunge into politics, culminating with the CIO-Political Action Committee.

5. The galvanizing of old organizations into broadening scope and creased vigor. ["Civil Rights and Direct Action in the Urban North"]

In 1941, the threat of a March on Washington led by A. Philip Randolph, a labor leader as well as a civil rights militant, was a significant omen of what was to follow some years later. So it was that the black militant of the 1960s probably learned from 1930 industrial unionism that the great American middle class becomes disturbed by militancy and especially by violence, and that it tends to regard them as Communistically inspired simply because the status quo is upset. Social revolutionaries are prepared to live with this.

Nonviolent, Direct Action

It was during World War II, concurrent with the transition for the Negro already described, and concurrent also with the initiation of the earliest programs in police-community relations as we now know them, that the Congress of Racial Equality (CORE) was founded. This was the first group dedicated to nonviolent, direct action for civil rights.

In 1947 several CORE members, including Bayard Rustin, were arrested and served time in North Carolina as a result of an attempt to test the Supreme Court's ban on segregated interstate travel. This was a forerunner of the so-called Freedom Rides of a few years later.

In the early 1950s the main thrust of civil rights activities was legal and political action, spearheaded by the National Association for the Advancement of Colored People (NAACP). A climax was reached in May 1954 with the Supreme Court's decision in the school desegregation cases. (*Brown et al vs. Board of Education of Topeka et al, 347 U.S. 483*). Charles Silberman (*Crisis in Black and White*, pp. 287, 288) contends that this decision overturned Plessy v. Ferguson (1896) in one sense, but in another sense it did not. Contrary to the claim of some critics who said that the 1954 decision relied on a psychological or sociological finding that segregation is harmful, the decision actually rested on a *legal* finding that segregation is inherently unequal. In effect, the Court declared that whether or not segregation is harmful is beside the point, and that the Constitution guarantees every citizen equal treatment under the law regardless of whether inequality is good or bad from a sociological or psychological standpoint.

It gradually became apparent to many Negro leaders in the years immediately following the 1954 decision that legislative and judicial action was proceeding on the basis of the most conservative interpretation of "all deliberate speed." Not only was there stubborn resistance in the South, but economic and social progress for the Negro in the North was painfully slow. Along came the Student Non-Violent Coordinating Committee (SNCC or "Snick"), and the Southern Christian Leadership Conference (SCLC), headed by Dr. Martin Luther King. Sit-ins, street marches, demonstrations, and Freedom Rides became the new tactics of The Movement. The Montgomery bus boycott in 1957 dramatized the emergence of nonviolent, direct action—not new in history or in application in other spheres, but new in its specific application to civil rights in America. Some observers date The Movement from this point.

It is important to understand what was happening at this time among whites. Robert B. Mills of the University of Cincinnati, in his paper, "Police-Community Relations: A Psychologist's Viewpoint," refers to the pre-1957 period when issues of racial equality had been mainly the concern of only a handful of white liberals and "progressives."[3] The bulk of the white community had been untouched by these appeals. Race relations tended to be seen as largely a Southern problem; Northern whites smugly pointed to the "wider opportunities" available to the Negro migrant to Northern cities. Civil rights action was defined as efforts to win more freedom *for* the Negro. The passivity of the Negro in his own behalf was assumed.

With the Montgomery confrontation, however, it began to appear that the Negro had found a tactic that was destined to revolutionize the civil rights scene. It came alive with the bus-boycotters wearing blue-

and-white crosses captioned, "Father, forgive them." The fear was gone; Negroes began to walk straighter. It was now a matter of doing for themselves and beginning to discover an unprecedented answer to the question, "Who am I?"

Subsequent sit-ins in Greensboro, Atlanta, Birmingham, and elsewhere fueled the fires of inspiration. Protest demonstrations spread across the nation; in 1963 alone, at least twenty-eight Northern and Western cities had some type of major racial demonstration. Police forces in many places were harried and harassed; cities not actually tested by demonstrations nonetheless worried about them. People lay prone in front of trucks, went limp when ordered to move, climbed construction cranes, chained themselves to equipment, and passed out leaflets galore. Another climax was reached with the March on Washington of August 1963, a gigantic exercise in symbolic unity for civil rights forces, with the endorsement of a sympathetic President in the White House. Police-community relations programs suddenly gained high priority.

Silberman's analysis (pp. 141, 142) is that the Freedom Rides and various other types of demonstrations were important for Negro morale, but the effectiveness of their impact tended to be exaggerated. There were highly significant gains for Negro self-pride, but not enough to conquer widespread apathy or to stir millions of slum-dwellers to action. (The late Louis Lomax, a journalistic chronicler of The Movement, was puzzled by the paucity of the results.) Silberman believes that the protests were as important for whites as for blacks. The notion that most blacks preferred their subordinate status was shattered. Freedom Rides in the South could be blamed on Northern outside agitators, but Birmingham and Selma were something else. The depth of black discontent was evident, as well as the ease with which it could explode into violence.

John Morsell said in "A Rationale for Racial Demonstrations" that the essential fact about the demonstrations of the early 1960s was that they were *racial*. Whites were often involved, but The Movement was predominantly black in its fabric. Morsell added that the Negro was not particularly worried about white backlash. The reasoning was that it was better to be positively disliked and feared than to be overlooked and ignored. The real question was how long it would take the white majority to grasp the necessity for immediate change.

But whites, at least, were forced to express some kind of attitude or to take a position on what was happening, if only by their silence. Many previously unexamined feelings came under discussion. A considerable amount of white good will and idealism was activated that had previously been latent. But black militancy also triggered vociferous opposition, both from individuals and in organized fashion, e.g., a National Association for the Advancement of *White* People. In June 1964, Mills described the situation as follows:

I would interpret the predominant mood of the bulk of the white community as somewhat ruffled at present, but basically uncommitted to making any changes. A "wait-and-see" attitude appears to predominate; most white citizens are hoping that the whole thing will "blow over." This lack of willingness to do anything for or against the Negro unless prodded by an immediate threat has been characterized in uncharitable terms by some Negro leaders, but such an attitude is typical of the conservative middle-class community. The chronic question of the Negro civil rights advocate is: What does this thunderous silence from whites signify? . . . The way in which the Negro interprets this pregnant silence is crucial in determining what his next move will be. ["Police-Community Relations"]

Martin Luther King, unquestionably the leader of The Movement in the early 1960s, was a champion of nonviolent, direct action. Referring to the turbulent summer of 1963, King wrote:

With the dawn of 1963, plans were afoot all over the land to celebrate the Emancipation Proclamation, the one-hundredth birthday of the Negro's liberation from bondage. . . . But alas! All the talk and publicity accompanying the centennial only served to remind the Negro that he still wasn't free, that he still lived a form of slavery disguised by certain niceties of complexity. . . .

. . . .

Nonviolence is a powerful and just weapon. It is a weapon unique in history, which cuts without wounding and ennobles the man who wields it. It is a sword that heals. Both a practical and a moral answer to the Negro's cry for justice, nonviolent direct action proved that it could win victories without losing wars, and so became the triumphant tactic of the Negro Revolution of 1963. [*Why We Can't Wait, pp.* 10–14]

A Shift in The Movement

In 1964, Silberman wrote:

The protest movement will never be the same again. It is bound to become more militant; many of the Negro poor are intolerant of "moderation" and contemptuous of the doctrine of non-violence. . . . The growth of black nationalism is bringing to the surface the most fundamental questions of Negro goals. More and more Negroes are beginning to wonder if they really want to eat at the white man's lunch counter after all. [*Crisis in Black and White*, p. 144]

At exactly the same time, Morsell was saying:

It is perfectly logical and the height of good sense to hold that more radical measures, more direct confrontations, are doomed to failure because of the sheer numerical inferiority of the Negro population. The Negro cannot take on the white population, solely in terms of relative numbers, to say nothing of the infinite disparity in power and resources, and hope for success thereby. But if enough Negroes are convinced that they are not going to win anyway, many may be tempted to lose in such a way as to inflict the greatest possible loss upon the majority as well. ["A Rationale for Racial Demonstrations," p. 149]

President John F. Kennedy was pressing Congress for comprehensive civil rights legislation up to the time of his assassination in November 1963. President Lyndon Johnson maintained this pressure and announced the concomitant "War on Poverty" in January 1964. In March 1964, Malcolm X—having broken with the Black Muslims—made headlines with his declaration of intent to form a Black Nationalist Party "to pursue active self-defense against 'white supremacists'," even through violent means if necessary. Concurrently, there were Negro boycotts of schools in New York City, Cleveland, and other cities.

The chronology of pertinent events in 1964 was as follows:[4]

May 4	In a Gary, Indiana case, the Supreme Court left standing a lower court decision that school boards have no constitutional duty to end racial imbalance resulting from housing patterns. (Note: The Supreme Court's decision in the school desegregation cases was at this point ten years old.)
May 25	The Supreme Court ordered schools in Prince Edward County, Virginia, to reopen on an integrated basis.
June	The first group of college student volunteers arrived in Mississippi, to assist in a Negro voter registration drive in that state. Three civil rights workers were reported missing after release from jail in Philadelphia, Miss. They had been arrested for speeding and were released after paying a fine. FBI agents found the bodies of the three August 4, buried in a nearby earthen dam; medical examiners said that the men had been shot to death.
	The Supreme Court reversed the 1960 trespass convictions of 42 sit-in demonstrators in five cases in Maryland, South Carolina and Florida.
	A racial demonstration occurred in St. Augustine, Fla., led and eventually stopped by Dr. Martin Luther King when it became violent.
July	On July 2, President Johnson signed the Civil Rights Act of 1964, among other things establishing a Federal Equal Employment Opportunity Commission and a Federal Community Relations Service.
	A riot in Harlem protested the slaying of a young Negro by an off-duty police officer. Another riot developed in

the Bedford-Stuyvesant section of Brooklyn. A riot in Rochester, N.Y., was set off by a rumor that police had beaten a Negro man for molesting a white woman. The National Guard was called in.

August   Racial violence broke out in Jersey City, Elizabeth and Paterson, N.J.—and in Chicago and Philadelphia.

September Whites boycotted New York City schools to protest the bussing of students.

The FBI reported that it had found no evidence of central planning of the summer's riots; that they were not riots of race against race, but "senseless attacks on all constituted authority, led chiefly by teenagers and people in their early twenties, indicating an increasing breakdown nationally of respect for law and order."

This chronology suggests that 1963–64 was something of a turning point in the philosophy and strategy of The Movement. One could interpret it as evidence of growing impatience with legal and political action and by 1964, with the nonviolent direct action espoused by Martin Luther King. Those who later saw 1967 as the decisive turning point failed to take into consideration what appeared to be a developing pattern and sequence of events beginning three to four years earlier.

The Voter Registration Drive

The emphasis placed by The Movement in the 1960–64 period on Negro voter registration merits comment. Robert Lane estimated that in 1952, 35 percent of American Negroes voted, compared with 79 percent of whites (*Political Life,* pp. 235–244). In the 1960 election it was estimated that 60 percent of adult Negroes *in the North* voted (Gosnell and Martin, "The Negro as Voter and Officeholder"). This election seemed to signal the beginning of a new era in Negro political activity: a drive to gain their objectives by the use of the ballot. This strategy gained momentum in the subsequent period.

But there were handicaps. George Blackwood pointed out that transiency, a high degree of social disorganization, and lack of a strong sense of community attachment were characteristic of the Negro lower class. The relatively small Negro middle class provided little leadership in effective civic action. Northern cities and states failed to develop plans for training blacks and other urban newcomers in the intricacies of big-city living. The only instances of effective black political organization were in Chicago and Harlem, with Congressmen William L. Dawson and Adam Clayton Powell as the respective symbolic leaders. But by 1960 it was evident that Dawson was in increasing difficulty;

old-line politics was beginning to be seen as a species of "Uncle Tomism." Powell hung on a bit longer in Harlem because of his adroit shift to a more militant posture.

By 1963, as direct action techniques moved northward and westward, a more and more formidable white opposition emerged. Terms such as "white power structure" and "white backlash" came into wide usage. Northern whites who had been sympathetic to the Negro revolt so long as it stayed in the South were more skeptical of its merits in their own city or neighborhood. Blacks grew bitter as they realized that demonstrations seemed to be reaffirming a long-held Negro belief, expressed by C. Eric Lincoln as follows:

> The white man does not *know* the Negro, has never known him, and has never seriously undertaken to find out what the Negro is like as a person . . . For most of the history of biracial America, the white man has considered the Negro to be a different order of being altogether. ["Patterns of Protest"]

On May 25, 1963, the *New York Times* reported a meeting of Negro leaders with Attorney General Robert F. Kennedy. The tone of the meeting underscored the failure of white liberalism to understand and to adjust to what Blackwood called "the rising tide of racial conflict in the North." There were, to be sure, wide differences in philosophy among Negro factions, but the 1963 March on Washington symbolized a certain measure of basic unity, even to the relatively conservative Urban League. Some kind of mix between direct action and political action took shape as a general formula, with the 1964 political campaign especially underlining the latter. But mass militancy of the type represented by Malcolm X was increasingly popular among Negroes, and such organizations as ACT, RAM, and FREEDOM NOW made their appearance—and were more inclined to violence than Malcolm X ever was.

Black Nationalism

The militant groups rejected completely the possibilities of working within the American political system. They were dedicated to disruption of that system and unremitting warfare on the "white power structure," by violence if necessary. Meantime, old line organizations such as NAACP were still stressing registration and voting. Obviously, no one organization or sentiment could speak for all blacks at that or any other time, any more than one organization could speak for all whites. Yet there were men such as Malcolm X who came to represent a growing number of blacks at this time.

Malcolm X was a complex personality and a very important figure in the history of The Movement in this country in the 1960–65 period.

Prior to his break with Elijah Muhammad in March 1964, Malcolm preached the standard Muslim line: separation as the only way for the Negro to establish his identity and develop his own culture. It was a revival of the Marcus Garvey creed, complete with a genetic theory to support it. As M. S. Handler writes in the Introduction to *The Auto-biography of Malcolm X:*

> Malcolm appealed to the two most disparate elements in the Negro community—the depressed mass, and the galaxy of Negro writers and artists who have burst on the American scene during the past decade. The Negro middle class—the Negro "establishment"—abhorred and feared Malcolm as much as he despised it. [P. xii]

In the same book, the Negro actor Ossie Davis said this:

> Malcolm . . . was refreshing excitement; he scared hell out of the rest of us, bred as we were to caution, to hypocrisy in the presence of white folks, to the smile that never fades. Malcolm knew that every white man in America profits directly or indirectly from his position vis-à-vis Negroes, profits from racism even though he does not prac- tice it or believe in it. . . . You can imagine what a howling, shocking nuisance this man was to both Negroes and whites. . . . He would make you angry as hell, but he would also make you proud. . . . And you always left his presence with the sneaky suspicion that maybe, after all, you *were* a man![5]

Malcolm's attitude toward the white man changed considerably in the last year before his assassination on February 21, 1965, and this change was probably a key factor in his break with Elijah Muhammad. George Breitman (*The Last Year of Malcolm X*) has analyzed this change and pinpoints three aspects of it: a sharp decline in Malcolm's separatist black nationalism; a diminution of his antiwhite perspective— although he continued to view American society as institutionally racist; and the appearance of global elements in Malcolm's thought. Apropos of the latter, Malcolm undertook to convince black people in this coun- try that they, along with Africans, Arabs, Asians, and Latin Americans, had a common enemy: "the international power structure." It is not clear exactly what Malcolm meant by this, and Breitman's argument that Malcolm was leaning toward the international socialist movement is not convincing.

Handler believes that another reason why Malcolm broke with Elijah Muhammad was his growing doubt regarding the authenticity of Elijah's version of Muslim religion. Malcolm died still apparently feel- ing that he had not yet discovered true Islam. Handler concludes that it was Malcolm's intention to raise Negro militancy "to a new high point, with the main thrust aimed at both the Southern and Northern white supremacists."

The Widening Chasm

The 1964 political campaign uncovered strong popular feelings against black militancy. Silberman reflected that "the North is finally beginning to face the reality of race. In the process, it is discovering animosities and prejudices that had been hidden in the recesses of the soul" (p. 8) and went on to say:

> Myrdal was wrong. The tragedy of race relations in the United States is that there is no American Dilemma. White Americans are not torn and tortured by the conflict between their devotion to the American creed and their actual behavior. They are upset by the current state of race relations, to be sure. But what troubles them is not that justice is being denied but that their peace is being shattered and their business interrupted. [P. 10]

Silberman pointed to the question that black nationalists were raising: whether Negroes really wanted integration—whether they should "keep banging on the doors of a white society that much of the time seems determined to keep them out." Lorraine Hansberry (*Raisin in the Sun*), James Baldwin (*Nobody Knows My Name*), and Kenneth B. Clark (*Dark Ghetto*) were in the forefront of those asking this question.[6]

The chronologies that follow pick up the sequence of subsequent events.

Chronology of The Movement: 1965

January   The Selma, Alabama, voter registration demonstrations took place.

Federal indictments were secured against 18 men in connection with the 1964 killing of three civil rights workers in Philadelphia, Miss. (Later dismissed.)

February   Some 3,000 Negroes were arrested in Selma as they tried to register to vote. Dr. Martin Luther King was jailed there.

Malcolm X was slain in New York City.

March   The Supreme Court held that while the Constitution prohibits racial segregation of pupils in schools, it does not command integration.

The Supreme Court unanimously declared unconstitutional the Louisiana voter literacy test.

President Johnson called upon Congress for legislation to expedite registration of Negro voters.

Police harassed a racial demonstration in Montgomery, Ala., with cattle-prods.

25,000 white and black followers of Dr. Martin Luther King marched from Selma to Montgomery where Governor Wallace received a delegation, after two refusals.

Mrs. Viola Liuzzo, a white civil rights worker from Detroit, was killed near Selma.

President Johnson "declared war" on the Ku Klux Klan. The House of Representatives Un-American Activities Committee announced that it would investigate the KKK.

Dr. King called for a national boycott of Alabama products and for withdrawal of Federal support of Alabama aid programs.

April	The U.S. Commissioner of Education announced that all public schools must be desegregated by the beginning of the 1967 school year, or lose Federal assistance.
June	Mass demonstrations in Chicago protested the slow rate of school desegregation.
July	Demonstrations and violence occurred in Bogalusa, La.
	Dr. Martin Luther King led a Chicago protest of 10,000 marchers against de facto segregation of schools.
August	Riots exploded in the Watts section of Los Angeles; 35 persons died and $200 million in property damage resulted.
	The National Center on Police and Community Relations was established at Michigan State University.
	President Johnson established the President's Commission on Law Enforcement and Administration of Justice.
December	Three Klansmen were convicted of conspiracy by an all-white Federal jury in Montgomery, Ala., for the murder of Mrs. Liuzzo.

In chronicling these events in the civil rights field during 1965, one tries to avoid arranging things to fit a predisposed conclusion. Yet one detects a rather clear pattern of rising militancy in behalf of Negro rights. Street demonstrations were increasing in number and in fury as the status quo was challanged more and more vigorously, and these challenges were more and more vigorously resisted. While the South still appeared to be the main "arena" for action, there were significant happenings in the North and West—for instance in Chicago and Watts. The conviction of three Klansmen by an all-white jury in Alabama was another kind of important news.

Chronology of The Movement: 1966

February   The U.S. House of Representatives Committee on Un-
            American Activities cited KKK leaders for refusal to
            cooperate in the Committee's investigation.

March   Three Black Muslims were convicted of the murder of
            Malcolm X.

            A second riot erupted in Watts, with two fatalities.

April   Attorney General Nicholas Katzenbach announced a
            47% increase in Negro voter registration in the South.

            President Johnson proposed an open housing bill to
            Congress.

June   A White House Conference on Civil Rights called upon
            Congress for action in further civil rights legislation.

            James Meredith was shot while leading a "pilgrimage" in
            Mississippi. Some 15,000 joined in a march to Jackson.

            Violent riots by Puerto Ricans took place in Chicago.

July   CORE endorsed Black Power; NAACP rejected it as
            "separatist."

            Riots occurred in Brooklyn, Chicago and Cleveland as
            President Johnson pleaded for non-violence.

August   Dr. Martin Luther King was stoned while leading a
            march in Chicago.

September   An open-housing riot developed in Cicero, Ill., with the
            National Guard called in. Fifteen were wounded.

            Riots were set off in Atlanta and in Grenada, Miss., the
            latter in connection with school desegregation.

Plainly, the tempo of militancy was accelerated during 1966. The
split among Negro rights organizations on the issue of separatism became more open. The Puerto Rican situation in Chicago indicated that
other minority groups were beginning "to get the message" of rising
militancy.

Chronology of The Movement: 1967

February   President Johnson asked Congress for a Civil Rights Act
            of 1967, to end discrimination in housing, jury selection
            and employment.

            The report of the President's Crime Commission was pub-
            lished, with 200 proposals for improvement in the entire
            criminal justice system and in police-community relations.

April	The Southern Education Reporting Service announced an increase of 10 percent in school desegregation in eleven Southern states, but also an increase of 400,000 pupils attending all-Negro schools.
	Racial violence flared up in Nashville, Cleveland and Montgomery.
May	One was killed, two were wounded as the National Guard quelled a riot at all-Negro Jackson State College in Mississippi.
June	The Supreme Court unanimously declared unconstitutional a Virginia law forbidding marriage between whites and nonwhites, and indicated that similar laws in fifteen other states were void.
	A Federal District Court in Washington, D.C. ordered the city to end de facto school segregation.
July– August	The first of a series of major riots in American cities occurred in Newark, N.J. Some 26 persons died, 1,500 were injured, more than 1000 were arrested, and property damage of more than $15 million was incurred.
	Forty persons perished in a Detroit riot, 2000 were injured, 5000 were left homeless, and property damage exceeded $200 million.
	Serious disorders also erupted in Boston, Tampa, Cincinnati, Buffalo, Plainfield, Hartford, Waterloo, Minneapolis, Toledo, Cleveland, Waukegan, South Bend, Rochester, East Harlem, Englewood (N.J.), Philadelphia, Chicago, Milwaukee, Wichita, Pittsburgh, Providence, and New Haven; minor disturbances took place in a score or more of other cities.
	President Johnson appointed a National Advisory Commission on Civil Disorders (Kerner Commission) to investigate the causes of the riots and disturbances and to recommend programs to deal with the conditions causing them.
October	The Supreme Court let stand a lower court decision ordering immediate desegregation of schools in six Southern states.
	An all-white jury convicted seven men who participated in a 1964 conspiracy to murder three civil rights workers in Philadelphia, Miss.
December	Antidraft demonstrations were reported in New York City, Madison, Manchester, Cincinnati, and New Haven.

This was a year of unspeakable tragedy, of death, arson, and looting, and of searing, widespread violence. Plainly now, it was revolution—some said rebellion or insurrection. The signs had been there for some years; it was simply a question of the triggering by a combination of circumstances, often involving law enforcement officers.

It became apparent that Black Power militants were moving to the left, politically speaking, with some tinges here and there of anti-Semitism. There was also some evidence of rising black political effectiveness in such events as the appointment of Thurgood Marshall as the first Negro justice of the Supreme Court, the appointment of Walter Washington as mayor of Washington, D.C., and the election of Carl Stokes as mayor of Cleveland and of Raymond Hatcher as mayor of Gary. The mood of the summer of 1967 was expressed by one black woman: "The brother's got to take everything he gets. Whitey ain't about to get up off of anything unless you make him."

Militant blacks hailed the riots as the dawn of a new era in civil rights. Moderates were much less exuberant and, in fact, were gravely apprehensive that The Movement might be set back irretrievably as a result of the mayhem. A measure making it a Federal crime to cross state lines with intent to foment a riot was rushed through Congress, but later investigations disclosed that "outside agitators" had little to do with the disorders.[7]

Events in 1968

In a special message to Congress in February 1968, President Johnson outlined a series of proposals to deal with crime in the United States. His proposals included gun control laws and what later became the Safe Streets and Crime Control Act (Omnibus Crime Bill). Also in February, a Governor's Select Commission on Civil Disorder in New Jersey issued a 478-page report on the 1967 Newark riot, containing 100 specific recommendations for change in city government, housing, policing, municipal courts, welfare, employment, riot procedures, and antipoverty programs.

Later in the same month, the National Advisory Commission on Civil Disorders released a summary of its 1400-page report. Chief findings and recommendations were as follows:

This country is moving toward two societies, one white and one black.

White racism is the chief cause of Negro violence and riots.

Unprecedented funding and action are called for to heal the chief wounds—for example, creation of two million new jobs within 2 years; decentralization of city governments to make them more responsive to the people; a national system of income supplements based on need; new ventures in low and moderate income public housing; substantial improvement in police-community relations.

Chronology of The Movement: Remainder of 1968

April	The Supreme Court ruled that the Federal Government must pay more than a century's interest to the Peoria Tribe of Indians in Oklahoma on $172,726 it failed to pay the tribe in 1857 for land ceded by a treaty.

A sniper's bullet killed Dr. Martin Luther King in Memphis.

In the aftermath of Dr. King's assassination, racial violence occurred in 125 cities in 29 states and the District of Columbia, with more than 2600 fires causing property damage estimated at more than $45 million. King was in Memphis to help the cause of striking garbage collectors. More than 50,000 people—black and white—walked in his funeral procession in Atlanta.

President Johnson signed a new Civil Rights bill aimed mainly at housing discrimination. It also included a guarantee of broad rights to American Indians.

May–
June

Rev. Ralph Abernathy, successor to Dr. King, led the Poor People's caravans from all parts of the country to "Resurrection City," on the mall near the Washington Monument in Washington, D.C.

June

Senator Robert F. Kennedy was assassinated in Los Angeles.

President Johnson again asked Congress for tougher gun control legislation. He also appointed a Presidential Commission on the Causes and Prevention of Violence, under the chairmanship of Dr. Milton Eisenhower.

The Supreme Court, in a 7 to 2 ruling prohibiting racial discrimination in all sales or rentals of real estate, turned an 1866 civil rights law into a sweeping fair housing statute.

July

A small band of black nationalists fired rifles point blank at two policemen in a squad car in Cleveland. A four-hour pitched battle followed in which seven persons were killed. A full-scale riot ensued; the National Guard was called.

The National Advisory Commission on Civil Disorders issued a report stating that a majority of Negroes viewed urban rioting as a justifiable means of social protest.

August

The Poor People's Campaign moved to Miami to try to influence the Republican National Convention. Miami rioting killed three Negroes.

The Democratic National Convention in Chicago brought the police, National Guardsmen, and protesting youths into street confrontation, featured on national television.

December   A 233-page report entitled *Rights in Conflict* (the so-
            called Walker Report), issued by a special panel of the
            National Commission on the Causes and Prevention of
            Violence, scored the Chicago police for using excessive
            brutality and action tantamount to a "police riot" in
            handling the demonstrations during the Democratic Na-
            tional Convention.

This was the year in which the National Advisory Commission on
Civil Disorders pointed to white racism as the fundamental and primary
cause of violence and rioting. There were those who asked, what is
racism? At the 1968 National Institute on Police and Community Relations at Michigan State University, Don McEvoy of the National
Conference of Christians and Jews undertook to answer that question
and said, in the context of a lengthier statement:

> Racism in the United States is a cluster of attitudes that have evolved
> into a system. The system is based on the concept of the superiority
> of whites over blacks. It has been perpetuated by whites in order that
> they may maintain their economic and political control over blacks.
> ... This system has the power to enforce and perpetuate itself.[8]

McEvoy went on to reflect upon the growth of pride in being
black. Separatism merely avoids the real issue, he said, which is the
question of learning to live together cooperatively in a pluralistic, democratic society. Black racism, he added, can be just as chauvinistic and
just as insidious for "the good society" as white racism, understandable
though it may be as defensive behavior.

The Movement in 1969

This was the year of miracles: man set foot on the moon, the New
York Jets won the Superbowl football game, and the New York Mets
won the World Series! But in the civil rights field, events continued in
a melancholy vein, with only a few heartening developments.

January saw Richard M. Nixon inaugurated as our 37th President.
In the same month, the National Commission on the Causes and Prevention of Violence reported that an ever-increasing percentage of crime
was being committed by youths. Nearly 5,000 students in London
demonstrated against British discrimination toward nonwhite immigrants. It appeared that The Movement had gone international, which
should have surprised no one. Racism is hardly a unique American
phenomenon.

February brought serious racial demonstrations at the University
of Wisconsin and at Duke University. Campus unrest reflected a con-

fluence of student concern regarding racial issues, the war in Southeast Asia and related matters such as ROTC programs and the draft, and an awakening of interest in ecological and environmental conditions. At the end of the month, on the first anniversary of its report, the National Advisory Commission on Civil Disorders warned that little perceptible progress had been made in changing national priorities in the manner recommended by that panel.

A Federal report in March indicated that the War on Poverty had fallen considerably short of its goals. The National Guard was called into Chicago in early April as violence erupted on the anniversary of the death of Martin Luther King. Memphis was placed under curfew. Clifford Alexander, Jr., resigned as chairman of the Equal Employment Opportunity Commission, protesting lack of support from the administration. Harvard University was the scene of violent student unrest. The Cornell University administration capitulated to black student demands involving alleged unfair treatment of five Negro undergraduates.

In May, Negro militant leader James Forman interrupted a service at Riverside Church in New York and demanded that churches and synagogues pay $500 million to Negroes as reparations for years of maltreatment. City College in New York was closed as black and white students fought a pitched battle. Negro civil rights leader Charles Evers, whose brother, Medgar, had been shot down several years earlier, was elected mayor of Fayette, Mississippi, defeating the white incumbent.

The National Commission on the Causes and Prevention of Violence warned in June that legislation punishing rebel students or colleges for campus disorders would be ill-advised. This report also stated that the police had become a "self-conscious, independent political power." The Reverend Ralph David Abernathy was arrested during a violent strike by 200 black hospital workers in Charleston, S.C. In August, the Justice Department filed suit against the state of Georgia to compel school desegregation.

September saw racial disorders in Hartford, Conn., and in Camden, N.J. The U.S. Commission on Civil Rights declared that the administration was backing a policy of retreat in racial desegregation. The next day, the administration replied that more would be accomplished in this matter in the ensuing two years than had taken place in the previous fifteen years.

The Supreme Court asserted in late October that school districts that had not yet racially desegregated must do so immediately. It seemed to be the ultimate interpretation of "all deliberate speed." In a November report, the National Commission on the Causes and Prevention of Violence concluded that violent crime was a phenomenon of urban America and warned that U.S. cities could soon become places of terror interspersed with armed fortresses. Harvard University suspended 75 black students in December, after they seized a dean's office and other areas in a demand for more black construction workers on campus. In its final report, the National Commission on the Causes and Prevention of Violence called on the Federal Government to reorder its national priorities and spend a minimum of $20 billion a year on domestic programs to cope with social problems.

Chronology of The Movement: 1970

January   As thirty Mississippi schools began to end their dual school systems, under Federal Court order, many white parents shifted their children from the integrated schools in predominantly black areas to private, all-white schools.

The Internal Revenue Service received orders from a panel of three Federal judges to cease the practice of granting tax-exempt status to segregated private schools.

The Supreme Court ordered fourteen school districts in the South to integrate some 300,000 pupils by February 1, reaffirming its 1969 "desegregate now" ruling.

Citing "more than 100 attacks on police by black extremists" in the second half of 1969, FBI Director J. Edgar Hoover warned against "hate-type" organizations such as the Black Panthers. Hoover noted a changing pattern of racial turmoil, from "large-scale riots of previous years" to "attacks on police officers and disturbances in high schools and even elementary schools." He scored the growth of revolutionary militancy among student agitators.

February   The February 1 deadline for total desegregation of southern schools set by the Supreme Court was defied by officials of twenty districts in Alabama, Georgia and Mississippi. A dozen Southern senators demanded that the new Federal school desegregation guidelines be applied to northern as well as Dixie schools, or be abandoned altogether. Pontiac, Michigan, was ordered by a Federal judge to integrate its schools at all levels by the fall of 1970.

Two Southern governors (Georgia and Louisiana) signed into law bills that would bar bussing of pupils and teachers to integrate schools in these states.

After five days of deliberation, a Federal grand jury found the defendants in the turbulent 21-week trial of the "Chicago 7" innocent of conspiring to incite riots during the 1968 Democratic National Convention, but convicted five of crossing state lines with intent to incite riots.

Pre-trial hearings for 13 Black Panthers, charged in April, 1969, with plotting to bomb public places, possession of illegal weapons, attempted murder and attempted arson, got under way in New York Supreme Court.

A black protest demonstration occurred at Amherst College.

Three white Detroit policemen and a black private guard were acquitted in a trial on conspiracy charges dating back to the Algiers motel incident during the Detroit riot of July, 1967.

March

A Lamar, S.C., white mob attacked buses taking 39 black students to a newly integrated high school.

The leveling of a townhouse in New York City's Greenwich Village was the first of six destructive explosions in a span of seven days which spotlighted a nationwide rise in terror bombing.

In Maryland, two black militants were killed in the explosion of a car, an incident tied to the H. Rap Brown case.

President Nixon instructed the Justice Department to enforce "at once" the Supreme Court's desegregation decrees.

April

Millions of Americans participated in antipollution demonstrations to mark Earth Day.

Yale University witnessed a sympathy strike for Black Panthers awaiting trial for the murder of a fellow Panther in New Haven. The strike virtually shut down regular classroom activity for ten days.

Anti-ROTC protests at Stanford University were climaxed by fires which destroyed scholarly work valued at $100,000.

The National Guard was called to quell disorders on the Ohio State University campus, with 20 wounded and 600 arrested.

Black and white youth touched off violence in River Rouge, Michigan, with fire-bombing and looting threatening to overflow into Detroit. Riot police with fixed bayonets patrolled the streets.

May

Four young people died from National Guard gunfire at Kent State University as they participated in a campus peace demonstration. More than 400 colleges and universities suspended classes in the first general student strike in the nation's history. Anti-war forces demonstrated in Washington, 100,000 strong.

Ten days later, two students were killed and ten wounded at Jackson State College in Mississippi in an encounter with city and state highway patrolmen.

Construction workers in Manhattan turned on student protesters near City Hall and beat them up. The "hard hats" had their parade in Washington later in the month.

Kenneth A. Gibson, a Negro city engineer, was elected mayor of Newark, N.J.

Rev. Ralph Abernathy led a "march against repression" across the state of Georgia.

The conviction of Black Panther co-founder Huey P. Newton on charges of voluntary manslaughter was overturned by the California Court of Appeals.

California's striking grape pickers won their first big contracts with two major growers.

June
President Nixon named a Commission headed by former Pennsylvania Governor William Scranton to study campus violence.

July
The Department of Justice disclosed suits against school districts in several southern states refusing to desegregate.

The FBI branded the Black Panther party as the country's "most dangerous and violence-prone extremist group." The Weatherman faction of Students for a Democratic Society was described as "a principal force guiding the country's violence-prone young militants."

Racial riots flared in small cities through July: Asbury Park, N.J., Michigan City, Ind., New Bedford, Mass., Lawrence, Kan., New Brunswick, N.J. Sniper fire killed two Chicago policemen.

A Federal grand jury in Detroit indicted 13 members of the Weathermen on charges of conspiracy to commit bombings through a nation-wide underground of terrorists.

Cesar Chavez and the AFL-CIO United Farm Workers Organizing Committee signed contracts with 26 more major grape growers in California.

August
An explosion at the University of Wisconsin demolished a building, killing a scientist and injuring four other persons.

Southern schools resumed classes quietly, many in newly integrated districts.

A series of bombings occurred in Minneapolis-Saint Paul. In the worst disorder in Los Angeles since the 1965 Watts riot, several hundred Mexican-Americans rioted, with a newspaperman killed, sixty other persons injured, and 178 business firms looted or vandalized.

September   In a speech at Kansas State University, President Nixon deplored "the spreading disease of violence." The Presidential Commission on Campus Unrest warned of a rising "crisis of violence" on college campuses.

October   A report of the same Commission charged that the Jackson State College killings had been "completely unwarranted" —a case of "unreasonable, unjustified over-reaction."

A panel of three Federal judges in Buffalo, N.Y. struck down a 1969 New York state law barring the forced bussing of public school children to achieve racial integration.

The U.S. Commission on Civil Rights released a report highly critical of the failure of Federal agencies to enforce civil rights laws.

A series of riots took place in New York City jails, involving mostly Negro and Puerto Rican prisoners.

The Presidential Campus Unrest Commission decried the Kent State shootings as "unnecessary, unwarranted and inexcusable." An Ohio grand jury placed major responsibility on Kent's "permissive administrative policies."

Angela Davis, the black militant sought for two months for her alleged role in the killing of a California judge, was apprehended by the FBI in New York City.

November–   Replying to the Commission on Campus Unrest, Pres-
December   ident Nixon rejected the plea that he lead the nation back from the brink of social division. The President endorsed some of the Commission's recommendations but blamed campus disruptions on members of the academic community.

Chronology of The Movement: 1971

January   President Nixon invited 14 Soviet scientists to attend the trial of Angela Davis in response to a USSR request to "safeguard her life."

A Federal court in Montgomery, Ala., found a segregationist probate judge guilty of civil and criminal contempt of a Federal court order and sentenced him to a fine of $5,752 and a year's probation . . . for failure to include on the Greene County general election ballot the names of six black candidates.

A Federal grand jury in Harrisburg, Pa., indicted Fr. Philip Berrigan and 5 others for conspiracy to kidnap Presidential Aide Henry Kissinger and blow up heating systems of Federal buildings in Washington, D.C. to force an end of the Viet Nam war and release political prisoners. Seven others, including Fr. Daniel Berrigan, were named as co-conspirators.

James Carter called for an end of racial discrimination as he was inaugurated as governor of Georgia, succeeding segregationist Lester G. Maddox.

In New York City, Rabbi Meir Kahane, militant Jewish leader, was arrested for failure to appear on riot charges in connection with harassment of Soviet officials in protest of Soviet treatment of Jews.

A six day illegal wildcat strike took place of 27,000 PBA members in the New York City Police Department. They reported for duty in civilian clothes and refused to work because of a pay dispute.

Bureau of Labor Statistics announced an increase in unemployment in urban poverty areas from 5.5% in 1969 to 7.6% in 1970, and a rate of 35.8% among black teenagers.

U.S. District Court Judge William K. Thomas ruled illegal a report by the Portage County grand jury on the May 1970 disorders at Kent State University, and ordered the report destroyed, but did not dismiss the indictments of the 25 persons involved.

Supreme Court ruled that under the Civil Rights Act of 1964, employers cannot deny jobs to women with young children unless they deny work to similarly circumstanced men. It also ruled 6–3 in a New York case that state and local welfare officials could cut off benefits from recipients who refused to permit officials to inspect their homes.

February   Four days of race riots were ended by 600 National Guardsmen in Wilmington, N.C., after 2 persons were killed.

U.S. Census Bureau reports showed that the black population of inner cities rose during the '60's to the point that in addition to Washington, D.C., other cities were now more than half black, including Gary, Ind., Newark, N.J., and Atlanta, Ga. The reports also noted marked economic gains for Negro families, except for the ⅓ headed by a woman.

In Lamar, S.C. a grand jury indicted 22 whites for participating in riots during which 2 school buses were overturned.

March
The Weatherman underground subversive organization claimed "credit" for a bomb exploding in a women's rest room in the Capitol Building in Washington: $300,000 damage.

U.S. Department of Health, Education and Welfare reported that more than 10% of the population of the nation's 7 largest cities were on welfare. Boston had 15%.

University of Puerto Rico students rioted for independence at ROTC headquarters; 64 arrested and campus shut down.

Lt. William L. Calley, Jr., was convicted by court martial for premeditated murder of South Vietnamese civilians. In response to public outcry, President Nixon stated he would personally review the case.

Supreme Court held, 8–0, that employment tests which screen out Negroes and do not relate their qualifications to the work they seek are in violation of the 1964 Civil Rights Act.

April
A 2-week-long anti-war demonstration by 300,000 veterans and sympathizers in Washington D.C. and San Francisco was staged peacefully. Terminated by 5,000 police and 12,000 troops.

Captain Samuel L. Gravely, Jr., the only sea going skipper among three Negro captains, was made an admiral.

Supreme Court unanimously upheld the constitutionality of bussing, use of racial quotas, pairing of schools and zoning to end officially imposed school segregation and dual school systems.

May
Three Negroes (Dillard, Hamlet and Cartwright) were elevated to the rank of general.

A jury in New York City acquitted 13 Black Panthers on 156 counts of conspiracy to bomb New York police stations, department stores, etc., after a nine month trial.

Two New York City policemen were shot in the back in a Harlem ghetto (second such attack in 3 days) in what Commissioner Patrick Murphy called a plot.

The six month murder trial of Bobby Seale and Mrs. Erica Huggins, accused of slaying former Black Panther Alex Rackley, ended in a deadlocked jury.

Supreme Court affirmed a lower court ruling declaring unconstitutional a New York State anti-bussing law which said appointed school boards could not assign pupils to achieve racial balance without parental consent.

June

The last 15 Indians who had occupied Alcatraz Island in a protest were removed, after 19 months, to hotels in San Francisco.

Vernon E. Jordon, Jr., 35, director of the United Negro College Fund, was named head of the National Urban League to succeed the late Whitney Young, Jr.

Supreme Court declared unconstitutional 5–4 a Cincinnati law making it a crime for 3 or more persons to loiter in an "annoying" manner in public places, saying it was vague and infringed on assembly guarantees.

The Court ruled, 5–4, in a Jackson, Miss., case, that city officials may close public swimming pools rather than comply with a court order to desegregate them.

Chief Justice Warren E. Burger, in a dissenting opinion in another case, asked Congress to enact laws to prevent freeing criminals because police erred in their method of obtaining evidence. The law, he said, should penalize officers who violate the laws on obtaining evidence, but "no evidence otherwise admissible should be excluded because of violation of the 14th Amendment" (re: unreasonable search and seizure).

July

Huey P. Newton, co-founder of the Black Panthers, was freed after a second mis-trial.

Lt. William Calley's life sentence for murdering 22 Vietnamese civilians was reduced to 20 years by the Commanding Officer of the Third Army.

Charges of treason were filed (under an 1848 law) against blacks charged with shooting at the headquarters of the Republic of New Africa in Jackson, Miss., in which a policeman and an FBI agent had been killed.

August

In Chicago, State's Attorney Edward Hanrahan and 13 law officers were charged with obstructing justice in the investigation of a December 1969 police raid in which 2 Black Panthers were killed.

George Jackson, one of three inmates charged with the murder of a guard in the Soledad Correctional Facility in 1970, was killed in an alleged prison break at San Quentin Prison. Two trustees and 3 guards were also slain.

Stephen Bingham, 29, a lawyer suspected of smuggling a gun to Jonathan Jackson, 17 (brother of George), in the 1971 Marin County courtroom murder of a judge and 3 prisoners was charged with five counts of murder. (Three other prisoners escaped.)

September   At Attica Prison, more than 1,000 New York State troopers quelled a riot in which 1,200 prisoners held 38 hostages for 4 days. Nine hostages and 28 convicts were killed. Fatal injuries later brought the total deaths to 43, the bloodiest prison revolt of the 20th Century.

A follow-up of the 1968 Kerner Commission Report stated that if present trends continue in inner-city racial matters, "most cities will, by 1980, be preponderantly black, brown and bankrupt."

October   H. Rap Brown, black militant, was seized in a shoot-out (with 3 others) in the hold-up of a bar in New York. He had been on the FBI most wanted list since May 1970.

The Knapp Commission investigating the New York City Police Department began a public hearing revealing wide-spread corruption.

December   On the last day of the Knapp Commission hearings, New York City Police Commissioner Patrick V. Murphy said, "the courts must accept the giant share of the blame for the continual rise in crime." He added that the courts let too many criminals go free and give sentences that are too light; that of 94,000 felony arrests made by NYC police last year, "Exactly 552 went to trial. The rest were 'disposed of.' "
Presiding Justice Harold A. Stevens said, "What he should look at is the kind of arrests the police make." Hugh R. Jones, president of the State Bar Association said the real culprits are the city and state budget-makers who have "starved the criminal justice system."

The Present Outlook

It is always perilous to cast oneself in the role of prognosticator where human eventualities are concerned. Therefore, we will venture no predictions as to the course ahead for The Movement. Racial violence and rioting have become more sporadic and scattered, but it would be a grave mistake to interpret this as a sign of any lessening in the pressures to move on expeditiously with the task of eliminating second-class citizenship in all of its manifestations. It appears that strategies and tactics in the civil rights field are shifting in tune with world and domestic political and social happenings.

An example of what this means is afforded by the seemingly more and more common employment of modified guerrilla tactics in pressing the cause of minority rights. The bombing of carefully selected "establishment" buildings is one aspect of this, as other issues are merged with that of race. While the FBI is cautious about charges of a general conspiracy, there surely have been conspirators at work with carefully calculated "hit and fade" activities that harass, irritate, annoy, frustrate, and generally "bug" the apparatus of the orderly society. Black Power, as represented particularly by the Black Panthers and their contemporary counterparts, has raised troublesome questions that are not easily shrugged off. Perhaps the central question has become separatism versus integration. While the Black Panthers may not be regarded as fearsomely as they once were, what they symbolize cannot be ignored.

It has been suggested that militant blacks now perceive major riots as basically self-defeating, tending to spark massive counter-violence and backlash. The burned-over areas of yesterday's riots are mute evidence of the futility of it all, as many see it. The destructive aspects of rioting are appalling, hitting especially hard at those whose despair is not alleviated by the discovery, in the aftermath of the violence, that they are completely "wiped out." This is not to say that riots have not had terrifying, attention-getting effects, and thus have been useful in a ghastly, cynical sense. But it is like making a case for the advantages of war.

Generalizing about black attitudes and intentions is an idle and risky pastime. Whitney Young often pointed to the depth and diversity of the black community. There are signs of a beginning, he said, in tapping "the immense pool of resources and shared desire for liberation that exists in the black 'family' ", with the prospect for more realistic and unified efforts in the future. Yet the cleavage between black separatists and black integrationists looms large and reflects the central issue with respect to The Movement in America today. It should also be noted that within each of these broad camps, there are sharp differences of view as to strategy and tactics.

Something of the drift of the situation may have been suggested by meetings of three black organizations in September 1970. The Congress of African People met in Atlanta, with hundreds of delegates. Convened by a divergent group of black activists and intellectuals, many of whom had participated in previous Black Power conferences, the meeting had the stated aim of providing "a functioning methodology for reducing the contradictions and artificial diversity of nationalistic theory." Much was said about "nation building," black self-determination, black self-sufficiency, political and economic autonomy. There was a professed intention to unite the black people of America, Africa, the Caribbean, Australia, Mexico, South America, "and all over the planet earth." Speaking at this meeting, the Reverend Jesse Jackson, then an

SCLC leader in Chicago, charged that integration was a white plot to destroy blacks.

The Black Panther Party's "Revolutionary People's Constitutional Convention" took place at the same time in Philadelphia. This group and the Congress of African People were split on several issues, the most important of which was that the Panthers were disposed to work closely with white radical groups. The Panthers denounced the U.S. Constitution as no longer serving the people. A new, model Constitution was drafted, to create what Panther leaders described as a socialistic government free of oppression. About one-third of the 6,000 delegates at this meeting were white, representing numerous radical organizations. One proposal was that minorities should be guaranteed the right to integrate, segregate, federate, or secede—as they pleased—"so long as no group oppresses any other group." Incidentally, one slogan of the conference was "The only good pig is a dead pig."

Meantime, CORE held its annual meeting in Mobile. "Desegregation without integration" was the theme, indicating that this organization had given up on integration as a method of obtaining black equality. CORE's proposal for schools was to create neighborhood districts, with blacks controlling in black neighborhoods and whites controlling in white neighborhoods. Voluntary transfers would be granted to pupils wishing to attend racially mixed schools. CORE Director Roy Innis continues to push the neighborhood control idea.

But the NAACP and the Urban League steadfastly maintain their allegiance to the goal of integration. One of the few voices raised at the Atlanta meeting in defense of integration was that of Whitney M. Young, Jr., executive director of the National Urban League. He told Congress:

> I believe that any time an educationally and economically disadvantaged group can be isolated, it can always be—and, without exception, has been—subject to gross discrimination, exploitation and oppression. White Americans who engage in wishful thinking that we are going to take them off the hook and solve their problems by all of us collectively moving to separate states, or leaving en masse for Africa, should be told loudly and clearly, "forget it." "We are here to stay, and in the process we are going to make this country live up to its Judaeo-Christian ethics and its democratic promise, or see it go down the drain of history as immoral and hypocritical, deserving of its fate." [*U.S. News and World Report,* September 21, 1970]

What has happened to the Black Muslims, pioneers in racial separatism? Their present track appears to be one of making blacks less dependent economically upon whites. They have purchased huge tracts of southern farmland and have plans to build a food-production system that will include meat-packing plants, canneries, distribution facilities, stores, and restaurants. Eventually, the Muslims hope to produce enough to feed one-third of all the black people in the country. Their motto is, "We don't want to be dependent on anyone but God." Yet there appear to be signs of upheaval within Black Muslim ranks. The struggle spilled over in Baton Rouge, Louisiana, in January 1972 with the shooting of two policemen and two young Muslims. The young dissidents in the organization seem to feel that it is too narrowly sectarian, inhibited, and insulated from other American blacks—so Paul Delaney speculated in *The New York Times* (January 21, 1972). Incidents in several cities suggested that the conservatism of the Black Muslims was being challenged internally.

Information concerning the Black Panthers has been difficult to come by. They answer questions about themselves by stating, "Those who know won't say. Those who say don't know." In a recently published book about the Panthers, Don Schanche suggests in the following passage that they have not given much thought to the society that will develop out of their apocalyptic concept:[9]

> It is as if the articulate Panthers are afraid to think beyond the destruction of the present system to the construction of a new system— because no matter what new system they are able to conceive, the old problem that gave birth to the old organization to begin with—racism— remains. [*The Panther Paradox: A Liberal's Dilemma*]

The central philosophy of the Panthers was expressed by their Information Minister, Eldredge Cleaver, from his African exile in 1969. As reported in *Time,* October 24, 1969 (p. 27), "Protests and demonstrations have exhausted themselves," he said. "The only response can be an escalation of violence itself. People who don't like that kind of talk go through long periods of re-evaluation. But there's nothing to re-evaluate—except the choice of weapons."

More recently, however, the Panthers have split into two or more factions, one led by Huey Newton, the other by Cleaver—apparently a right and a left wing. As *Newsweek* put it, "the party is gravely if not terminally ill." While its day as a national influence may well be over, remnants of it will probably survive, "to bedevil the cops and enchant the young here and there." And some other force of similar ideological and symbolic thrust will emerge.

In a special issue on "Black America 1970," *Time* (April 6, 1970) editorialized:

> The struggle between the races in America is indeed the struggle for the soul of a nation. Lately a lull seems to have descended on that struggle. . . . Yet this relative calm exists on the surface only: it is largely an illusion. Blacks are asserting a new sense of pride, self-reliance—and impatience. . . . It is not always easy for whites to realize that the violence of black rhetoric, the calls of "Get whitey" and "Kill

the pigs," spring from a deep wound caused by 3½ centuries of blatant injustice and from a feeling that polite, peaceable methods have not worked.

In early 1972, police in various cities had identified a Black Liberation Army, so-called, with tactics of mobility and anonymity and charged with numerous armed robberies and police slayings. Typical revolutionary behavior of the urban guerilla was a general characterization of this movement, and the police were having a difficult time gathering information about it. More people were asking whether there was a conspiracy of radical, youthful, terrorist organizations spreading around the world.

A National Black Political Convention was held in Gary, Indiana, in March 1972, attended by 8000 blacks. They represented a wide variety of political interests. They adopted an agenda calling for an independent black political movement, but were not specific as to how this was to come about. The trial and acquittal of Angela Davis over a 13-week period in the Spring of 1972 and her announced intention "to work for political freedom" were events pertinent to our interest in this chapter.

The Violence Phenomenon

Violence is not new in America. Both as an instrument of social policy and as an instrument for demanding change in social policy, it has a history. It was not invented by militants for the cause of racial justice in the 1960s, nor by people responsible for television programming. In various facets of American life—sports, for example—violence is highly institutionalized, legitimized, and made a central value of a psychologically and sometimes economically profitable cult. The literature dealing with violence is extensive and suggests how enormously complex a matter it is.[10]

With respect to the violence of the 1960s that was associated with The Movement, particularly in 1967–68, we have suggested that it was in the making for years. Harold Pfautz of Brown University has analyzed it as follows:

> ... [these] collective disorders are not race riots in the usual sense of the term but expressive insurrections, fed by the fires of aggravated frustrations, fueled by the colossal indifference of the majority of affluent dominant whites, and touched off by the growing vacuum of civic leadership and commitment to democratic values on the local community level. The shattering of the domestic tranquility, which is the bed-rock of any social life, attests not to the sickness of Negro Americans so much as it reveals the sickness of American communities. The violent outbursts are neither plots nor programs but indicators of

one basic fact—that no community can survive, can be a "Community," if literally thousands of its members, if proportions of its population ranging from 5 to over 50 percent, are literally outside its social system. ["The American Dilemma: Perspectives and Proposals for White Americans"]

The Report of the National Advisory Commission on Civil Disorders (the Kerner Commission), issued March 1, 1968, is an important document in the literature of urban violence in the 1960s. Many of its recommendations have yet to be taken seriously. There is no mystery, no shortage of informative studies about the violence phenomenon as related to The Movement. The "gut" question is the quality and measure of commitment to do what must be done to abolish the causes of violence. What is lagging is what Christopher Lasch has termed "a sense of injustice and of the indignities and humiliations which [white Americans] . . . have increasingly allowed themselves to accept as normal, inevitable, proper, and even 'moral' " ("The Decline of Dissent," p. 17).

The National Commission on the Causes and Prevention of Violence, established by the President in June 1968, compiled and published the most comprehensive data available on the subject (1969 Report, *To Establish Justice, To Insure Domestic Tranquility* and others).[11] The Commission suggested specific measures for better *control* of violence: that the nation double its investment in the prevention of crime and the administration of justice; that central offices of criminal justice be created at the metropolitan level to make all parts of the system function more effectively, and that private citizens' organizations be formed to work as counterparts of these offices; that public officials —including law enforcement officers—intensify their efforts to develop more effective tactics in handling both peaceful demonstrations and violent disturbances; and that a national firearms policy be adopted that would limit the general availability of handguns.

The Commission also made many recommendations aimed at removing the *causes* of violence: that young people must be given a greater role in determining their own destiny and in shaping the future course of our society; that aggrieved groups must be permitted to exercise (short of violence) their constitutional rights of protest and public presentation of grievances; and that the conditions of family and community life must be improved, especially for the poor in our cities. Numerous suggestions dealt with police and community relations, as did preceding Presidential Commissions. Some aspects of the reports of this Commission anticipated the later (Fall of 1970) findings and recommendations of the President's Commission on Campus Unrest. Incidentally, it may be noted that a favorite ploy of those who are upset by what such Commissions find and recommend is to attack the credibility of the panel.

Several University-based research centers focusing on violence have arisen in recent years. The best known of these is the Lemberg Center for the Study of Violence at Brandeis University, Waltham, Massachusetts. Its publications have been extremely helpful to students of the violence phenomenon. Case Western Reserve University in Cleveland also established a Civil Violence Research Center, and there are similar entities on other campuses.

The Law and Order Issue

A reply to the militant, gathering momentum in the 1960s, was a phrase that became a code for the politics of fear: law and order. But the full benefits of what this should mean—law for all and order for all—as with other benefits of American life, remained remote for millions of our people, such as poor blacks, poor whites, many Mexican-Americans, many Puerto Ricans, most Indians, some Orientals.

Former Attorney General Ramsey Clark observed:

> The demagogic phrase "law and order" may mean many things, but to most people today it signifies force, order as an end in itself, repressiveness . . . It divides black from white, young from old, rich from poor, educated from ignorant. It speaks of the horror of the criminal act while overlooking the greater tragedy: the innate capability of our people to commit crime. It somehow calls for force to prevent the act of crime while ignoring the heart prepared to commit it. [*Crime in America*]

Public concern about crime and violence is not only legitimate; it is the sine qua non of corrective social action. The rhetoric of politicians plays on this, but not necessarily with motives of social good. For example, the Organized Crime Control Act of 1970 contains a provision permitting judges to impose thirty-year sentences on anyone convicted of a felony if it is decided that the defendant is "a dangerous special offender." This is bad law, and it is questionable order. Another example: the District of Columbia Omnibus Crime Bill, now a law—widely publicized as "model" legislation regarding law and order—gives police the authority to search premises with a warrant, but without announcing their presence and demanding entry. This law also provides for preventive detention—the incarceration without bail of criminal suspects who appear, in the judgment of a magistrate, to be likely to commit further crimes if they were free.

In November 1970, Peter Schrag wrote in *The Saturday Review:*

> The cry for law and order has encouraged local prosecutors, police, and grand juries to crack down on dissenters, to intimidate unpopular figures, and to initiate criminal proceedings of dubious merit. Civil liberties organizations around the nation have noted sharp increases in the harassment of students, teachers, university administrators,

writers, black people, and other minorities. Dissenters are finding it
harder to get jobs or to keep them. . . . It is the poor who cannot
afford high-priced legal talent, cannot raise bail, and cannot defend
themselves against the intricacies of the legal process; it is the poor
who are more likely to be regarded as bad risks, as potential criminals,
and as "dangerous special offenders." But it is also the poor—and the
black—who are, and always have been, the special victims of local
police raids, of unexplained shootings, and of violent acts inside or
outside the station house. ["The Law-and-Order Issue," p. 26]

There is a clear implication in this of the confusion—to some extent deliberately nurtured—between crime and dissent. The assault seems
less directed against crime and violence than against those who challenge the status quo. As Schrag says, "the target is social and cultural
deviance, not criminality." The approach to our social problems becomes a matter of ascribing blame—"they did it, not us," or "this
problem was here long before we came into office"—rather than one of
serious efforts to deal with the basic causes of crime and violent behavior.
If some things in life are worse than poverty, we may list the costs of
order as an end in itself as one.

Without doubt, there have been unprovoked attacks on policemen,
and they appear to be increasing. This is a significant part of the price
for the law-and-order shibboleth, although it is not usually interpreted
in this way. More often, the statistics pertaining to attacks on police
officers are utilized as an argument for tougher law enforcement. This,
in turn, boomerangs in a rising count of terroristic assaults. That this
"revolving door" must be stopped is suggested in the following official
New York City Police Department figures, which may be considered
indicative of the increasing gravity of the problem nationally:[12]

Jan. 1 to Aug. 31		1970	1969
Policemen:	Killed	3	0
	Wounded by gunshot	34	11
	Cut or stabbed	44	33
	Bitten by humans	96	50
	Punched	217	250
	Kicked	154	54
	Struck with object	158	89
	Assaulted making arrest	152	101
	Miscellaneous injuries	130	3
	Totals	985	591

On June 1, 1971, it was reported that more than 100 police officers had been killed in the United States during the previous year and
more than 1700 had been injured in assaults and attacks. In 1960, 48
policemen were killed in this country in line of duty.

The historian Henry Steele Commager, writing in *The Saturday Review* (February 13, 1971), observed that the emergent violence of recent years is not acceptable either to an alarmed and frightened Establishment or to the victims of the Establishment who are no longer submissive. Commager went on to say that:

> ... now, too, official violence is no longer acceptable to its victims— or to their ever more numerous sympathizers: the violence of great corporations and of government itself against the natural resources of the nation; the long drawn-out violence of the white majority against Negroes and other minorities; the violence of the police and the National Guard against the young; the massive and never-ending violence of the military against the peoples of Vietnam and Cambodia. These acts can no longer be absorbed by large segments of the society. It is this new polarization that threatens the body politic and the social fabric much as religious dissent threatened them in the Europe of the sixteenth and seventeenth centuries.

Commager concluded:

> The most striking feature of lawlessness in America today is that it is encouraged by public examples. . . . While governments, corporations, and respectable elements in our society not only countenance lawlessness and violence but actively engage in it, violence will spread and lawlessness will flourish. We are betrayed by what is false within.

Other Minority Groups

Discussions of The Movement as it evolved in the 1960s tend to focus on events and activities highlighting the struggle for Negro rights and equality. For many people, "minority" is a synonym for Negro. We should be reminded, therefore, that other minority groups are also in the picture. What happens in the enactment of the social drama for blacks in this country carries with it implications and often direct action ramifications for Chicanos, Puerto Ricans, Indians, Americans of Oriental extraction, Southern Appalachian migrants and other "poor whites," and various ethnic minorities.

The Movement in recent years has spread to one or another of these groups. Cases in point include the Alianza Federal de Mercédes under the leadership of Reies Lopez Tijerina in New Mexico (the so-called Tierra Amarillo raid in June 1967, and the subsequent case of Valdez v. Black, civ. No. 7242); the Texas Rangers and union organization efforts (1967) in Starr County, Texas; the 1968 El Paso tenant movement, organized by MACHOS (Mexican American Committee for Honor, Opportunity and Service); the organization and ultimate success of the Farm Workers' Union in California, under the leadership of César Chavez; the efforts in many states, with only meager success, to improve the sorry lot of migrant farm workers; the rise of Brown Power. Unrest in other factions was revealed in the disturbances fomented by Puerto Rican militants in Chicago, East Harlem, and other cities where Puerto Ricans are the newest of the newcomers,[13] and in the Indian occupation of Alcatraz Island and periodic "thrusts" by tribes in northern New York state and elsewhere that dramatized the incredible plight of American Indians. Our national policy in Indian affairs was described by a Congressional committee in 1969 as "400 years of failure".[14] There was even an occasional eruption in the "Chinatowns" of San Francisco and other cities, which makes news when it occurs because of the common assumption (stereotype?) that Americans of Oriental descent are docile and nonbelligerent and "handle their own problems" without public furor.

The Movement encompasses all this and more. Many poor whites do not take to being called "hillbillies" or "hoosiers." Sometimes their treatment by "justice agents" leaves much to be desired. And of course there are unbarbered and unmanicured "hippies" among dissenting youth, about whom we shall have more to say in a subsequent chapter. Moreover, the women's liberation movement seems bent upon joining the ranks of the disaffected, and homosexuals have organized to take their place in parades and demonstrations. The Movement has assumed an astonishingly diversified "image."

A Concluding Thought

Writing in *The New York Times* (November 17, 1970) Terry Sanford, the president of Duke University and former Governor of North Carolina, observed:

> In putting down destruction, it is not appropriate to put down dissent. Suppression of dissent leads to destruction. Those who call for forcing students out of school, forcing peaceful pickets and protestors to disperse, forcing compliance with arbitrary rules, do not understand the problem. . . . Resolution of differences by the use of force is not a lesson we need in the world. Any bully can teach respect for force. It takes a much more sensitive touch to teach reliance on reason. Reason takes more patience, more love, and greater understanding. [P. 43]

Norman Cousins, former editor of *The Saturday Review,* struck a key point:

> The American people are in trouble today not just because of the severity of their problems, but because the yardsticks for measuring and dealing with change are breaking down. The need for change is not the main issue. The main issue is that too few are willing to stand by any governing principle having to do with change. The result is a bumbling amateurism in dealing with historical processes. Passion is a

valuable ingredient of change, but if it is detached altogether from knowledge and the making of objective judgments, the result is likely to be a bloody spew. ["Explanations and Excesses, p. 20]

Cousins added that pluralism in a society is infinitely desirable, but it is also infinitely difficult. The only way it can work—the only way a consensus society can function—is "by keeping the confusions and the combustibles apart. . . . The slaughter of innocents is what happens when know-nothingness and vengeance converge."

The ultimate protection against generalized violence is the particularized, individualized pursuit of justice. In Cousins' terms, we "must not be deflected from this purpose by those who attach fuses to grievances or dreams." Special dispensations for violence cannot be granted to any group. "People, whatever their reasons, can only be judged by what they do."

Notes to Chapter Eleven

1. *Report of the United States Commission on Civil Rights, 1959* (668 pages). The U. S. Commission on Civil Rights, speaking in the fall of 1970 through its chairman, Notre Dame president Father Theodore M. Hesburgh, stated that the government had virtually abdicated its responsibility in rights enforcement. In the spring of 1971, the Commission said that "the dinosauer has finally opened one eye," though it still found substantial "recession" in civil rights activities in some government agencies. The Commission was especially critical of a new home-ownership program for low-income families which had been used, so the Commission alleged, to perpetuate racial segregation in the suburbs. (*The New York Times,* May 11, 1971, and June 11, 1971.)

2. See James Q. Wilson, *Negro Politics,* particularly pp. 77–93. Also Harry A. Bailey, Jr., ed., *Negro Politics in America.*

3. Paper presented at an Institute on Police-Community Relations, held at Xavier University in Cincinnati, June 8, 1964.

4. Chronology adapted by Hoyt Coe Reed from *The World Almanac,* The Newspaper Enterprise Association, New York.

5. This commentary by Ossie Davis, *On Malcolm X,* appeared originally in *Grump* magazine.

6. See also Parsons and Clark, eds., *The Negro American,* and Fred Powledge, *Black Power, White Resistance.*

7. The 1967 riots were the backdrop for numerous studies, investigations, reports, manuals, and other publications, unanimously finding that social problems were at the base of the situation, and "something ought to be done . . . etc." Righteous wrath and indignation were everywhere apparent.

But as with well-intentioned New Year's resolutions, not much actually happened. See such works as Carmichael and Hamilton, *Black Power: The Politics of Liberation in America;* Tom Hayden, *Rebellion in Newark;* Paul Jacobs, *Prelude to Riot;* Lewis M. Killian, *The Impossible Revolution;* Louis Masotti, ed., *Riots, Violence and Disorder;* Cohen and Murphy, *Burn, Baby, Burn;* Morris Janowitz, *Social Control of Escalated Riots;* Hubert G. Locke, The *Detroit Riot of 1967.*

8. Papers presented at the 14th annual National Institute on Police and Community Relations, Hoyt Coe Reed, ed., May 1968. See also Whitney M. Young, *Beyond Racism.*

9. See also Eldridge Cleaver, *Soul on Ice,* and Study 5 (Part III), "The Black Panther Phenomenon," in Radelet and Reed, *Studies.*

10. For example, see Marvin E. Wolfgang, ed., "Patterns of Violence." Also Wolfgang and Ferracuti, *The Subculture of Violence,* and Hans H. Toch, *Violent Men.*

11. In addition to Commission reports listed in Works Cited, investigative reports for the Commission include one each on Chicago, Cleveland, Miami, Counter-Inaugural (January 1969), and San Francisco State College. Commission reports include a Progress Report to the President (January 1969), an Interim Statement on Campus Disorder, a Commission Statement on Firearms and Violence, and a Commission Statement on Violence in Television Entertainment Programs.

12. Data reported in *U.S. News and World Report,* September 21, 1970, p. 38. The International Association of Chiefs of Police, through its Police Casualty Analysis Program, compiles and maintains data of this type.

13. See Clarence Senior, *Strangers Then Neighbors: From Pilgrims to Puerto Ricans.* The heavy and continuous out-migration of Puerto Ricans to the mainland United States in the period 1946–64 left about 2 million on the mainland and 2.7 million on the island. In recent years, they have been returning to the island at a faster rate than they have been leaving.

14. Committee on Labor and Public Welfare of the U. S. Senate, *Indian Education: A National Tragedy—a National Challenge.*

Chapter Twelve

The Police and Minority Groups

During the past thirty years, The Movement in civil rights and race relations has had formidable effects on all the social institutions of our society. Its effects upon political institutions have been suggested, particularly when its thrust has been expressed in terms of power, changing the status quo, restructuring "the establishment," voting registration, "getting out the vote", and the like. Black businesses and industries attest to its effects upon economic institutions, and so does the emergence of tougher Fair Employment Practices laws. Its effects upon religious institutions have been spotty and erratic. Some religious bodies have earnestly endeavored to take a position in the vanguard of social change, while others are still debating the relative merits of admitting nonwhite and other "awkward" members or hiding behind a facade of ostensible openness in policy while actually discouraging the participation of "certain people." Our educational institutions became interested in intercultural or intergroup matters in the early 1940s, when the first specialized human relations workshops for teachers were held, coinciding with the earliest police training programs with a similar focus. Schools and colleges have been in the vortex of The Movement during the past thirty years, from questions of Fair Educational Practices legislation to power battles in our cities regarding administrative control and curriculum.

Certainly the media of public information have been caught up in The Movement one way or another: many would say not always constructively as a "monitor of social change," if this is a fair way of describing what one role of the media should be. More about this in Chapter Eighteen. Music and the arts, organized sports and recreation, and other leisure-time institutions also have had an up-and-down record relative to The Movement, with some of these demonstrating exemplary leadership for change while others are still engaged in fierce conflict or striving to duck the issue. Voluntarily joined civic-social organizations also have had a checkered record regarding civil rights questions; many of them skirt and dodge such matters at all costs. Others may be found anywhere in the spectrum of positions, from most open to most closed. Lively arguments still take place as to whether one should or should not join a club or society where one can be "among one's friends" and "with people of similar interests." The "black ball" and so-called "gentlemen's agreements" still carry special connotations in such circles.

As to the Police

Police work and other aspects of the administration of justice have also been vitally affected by what has been happening in civil rights and race relations. Some would contend that the police have been particularly hard hit, but this may be to measure the effects disproportionately by street encounters and risk of life and limb. To argue the point of "who has suffered most" is an idle rhetorical exercise. It is enough for our purpose to observe that The Movement has undoubtedly contributed substantially to widening the opportunities for police officers to demonstrate creditable professional behavior—or its opposite.

The first thing to be noted regarding police response to The Movement has already been indicated, that is, the development of specialized training programs to help in coping with new dimensions of the police task.[1] Police generally feel that they are not responsible for the conditions that have fomented the crisis in civil rights, yet they feel that they are expected to supply most of the solutions. They see themselves as easily available targets of abuse and criticism and as convenient scapegoats for all manner of social problems. In our big cities, which have become so heavily populated by blacks, and other minority groups, the police have more continuous contact with them than any other predominantly white organization. For numerous police officers, daily face-to-face transactions take place, involving—as Robert Mills spells it out—the adjudication of family disputes, personal counselling, making arrests, setting ground rules for future behavior, or simply passing the time of day with many black citizens.[2]

On the other hand, for most blacks, the white world remains rather remote and inaccessible. The white policeman has made his presence felt in neighborhoods where all or most of the residents are black. He is visible and he is *there,* and he is perceived as the custodian of "Whitey's law" and "Uncle Charley's system," indeed as the *personification* of that system. Therefore, the police officer—even if he is black (in which case he may be perceived as a "fink" or an "Uncle Tom")—takes the brunt of the frustrations, the anger, the hostility and bitterness vented by blacks over their lot. He is seen as a symbolic agent of patent injustice, a "kept man" of the system—clearly "the enemy"—never to be trusted under any circumstances.

This is, of course, a stereotypic view of the police. Evidences (and there are actually many) of compassionate, humanistic policing tend to be dismissed as rare exceptions. "Most all cops are on the take—or brutal—or inhuman—or . . . "! The apparent preoccupation of civil rights organizations with police conduct stems from the frequency of intimate contact between the police and the minority group community. There is an underlying implication that if the police and the criminal justice system cannot adhere to the equal protection principle, it is useless to talk about it in employment, education, housing, etc.

In short, the police officer is a convenient object of the displaced hostility of the minority group, however stereotypic the image may be. Much of the criticism so often directed against the police by minorities is really intended for the larger white community power structure, but it is *displaced* to a more readily available, identifiable target. This explains the sometimes irrational elements that appear in minority complaints against the police. As with any stereotype, there are fragments of truth and actual experience to bolster it. There *are* some crooked, or brutal, or inhuman policemen, and there *are* memories (or stories that are believed) of harrowing experiences with Southern—or Northern—"law men."

The police, on the other hand, do not enjoy having been drafted for front-line duty in the civil rights struggle. They often say that once again they are in the middle. However, a rather decisive factor that tends to warp many a big-city policeman's outlook on questions of Negro civil rights is the difficult and dangerous job of trying to contain what is erroneously referred to as "Negro crime." There is, of course, no such thing—any more than there is Jewish crime or Belgian crime or freckled-faced crime. There are crime-breeding social conditions that happen to predominate in areas where blacks and other minorities live in greater numbers. The elimination of these social cesspools is, as Mills observes, one way of explaining what The Movement is all about.

In brief, the racial theory of crime causation has long since been discounted and rejected by criminologists. But the policeman on a ghetto beat carefully counts those who give him a bad time. If most of the people living in the neighborhood are black, it follows that most of those who are troublesome to the police officer will be black. In due course, blackness itself becomes a reason for troublesomeness, in the reflex thinking of a harried officer. As an agent of a bureaucratic organization that tends, as with all bureaucracies, to deal with people and situations stereotypically, the officer comes to associate "cussedness" with skin color.

Dual Stereotyping

The police officer's perception of the community of the ghetto is as stereotyped as the community's perception of the police officer. The mutually reinforcing character of this dual stereotyping phenomenon is central in understanding police and minority group relations, particularly in big-city ghetto situations. It is reinforced by the fact that the policeman seldom himself resides in the area he polices. Police officer and civilian have little opportunity to get to know each other on a person-to-person basis. In fact, the very impersonality of the joint stereotyping is appalling: "Naw, I don't know his name, but he's a cop, and I hate cops!" And the reverse of this: "To me, he's just another nigger!"

Further, these stereotypes typically are subject to the self-fulfilling principle. If some blacks are viewed as furtive, the conduct of any black is seen as furtive; if some policemen are viewed as "Neanderthal," the conduct of any policeman is seen as such. On either side, attitudes are justified on the ground that "you can't afford to take a chance. It's better to be wrong a hundred times than dead once." On each side, the standard epithets are fired off: "police brutality," "nigger cutting," "uptight mothers," "black s-o-b's," and so on. Communication deteriorates to "shooting darts at one another from twenty paces." On the one side, there is agitation for establishment of a civilian review board or for neighborhood control of the police. On the other side, there is often an exceedingly defensive police reaction, rooted partially in long experience as society's favorite fall guy for social and moral bankruptcy.

The Issue of Brutality

The most emotion-packed complaint directed against the police is that of brutality. It may be well to deal with what is meant by the term "police brutality." Part of the problem is a matter of communication, in a certain special sense.

One meaning of brutality is its literal interpretation: the use of undue or unreasonable physical force in some aspect of police actions. Ordinarily, the police react to the charge of brutality at this level of definition. Usually they will respond by conducting an investigation and, more often than not, reporting that there is no basis for the charge. Then they are dismayed when the matter does not end there. They insist that brutality charges are exaggerated; that they are the "straight men" in a political game.

Another level of definition for police brutality is verbal or psychological brutality. The accusation is that an officer has insulted someone by calling him names, or by using derogatory language, or by calling a stranger by his first name, or by the use of the term "Boy." This is demeaning, therefore brutalizing. Police officers are often nonplussed by such criticism and will sometimes reply that they meant nothing by it. But words and language do betray our stereotypes.

A third level of definition for brutality may be the most significant. It pertains to the police officer as a symbol of "the establishment"—of the "white power structure"—of "Uncle Charley's system." The minority group member feels that he is a victim of systematic brutalization by this system, which attacks his very personhood. Thus, the policeman— as symbol of the system—is brutal because the system brutalizes.

In situations where brutality charges are made against the police, there is frequently a communication problem created by differences in the level of definition of the term. These situations are further complicated by emotional outbursts on both sides, by charges and counter-charges, and by media stories that often accentuate the negative. It is difficult to bring reason to bear on the matter and to get at the question of exactly what it is that is being contested. Policemen sometimes make the point that the public is quick to accuse an officer of brutality, but not so concerned when the officer is attacked, assaulted, insulted, spit upon, stoned, or killed.

The ticklish brutality question casts police and community relations at its worst. It is a symptom that something is seriously wrong in police-citizen transactions. Being philosophical about it is not very helpful, in the heat of the situation. After all, it is not very comforting to a hospitalized policeman, or to a hospitalized victim of a policeman's wrath, to be told that there was really nothing personal intended—that it was merely symbolic warfare, springing from dual stereotyping. As it is said, such an explanation is not acceptable as legal tender at the grocery store, however impressive it may be to academic yearlings. It does not pay medical bills.

There is no question that there are police officers for whom beating up or defaming people are grim means of job satisfaction. With some such officers, this may be why they joined the force; with others, it is more a result of what we have called occupational socialization. With some, it is plain fear, in the face of what may be termed "statistical danger"—a perception and interpretation of what seems necessary for survival. And it is true that the abuse and provocation absorbed by police in line of duty is little known and far from appreciated. The mendacity, defiance of law, family abuse, impulsive and immoral conduct, alcoholic and drug-addicted behavior, and other socially destructive acts that the policeman witnesses are more than a little discouraging to the maintenance of a balanced and constructive perspective about his job and about the people with whom he most frequently comes in contact. The warped and cynical attitude often evident in police officers who have long worked in the depressed areas of our cities is a great obstacle to their understanding of Negro civil rights problems and sympathy for the goals of social justice.

The real solution to the brutality problem is long-range, for it will be solved only when oppression and second-class citizenship have been abolished. But there are many constructive steps that can be taken in building good police and community relations, short of this ultimate goal, which will diminish the intensity of the emotional charges and countercharges. Heightened mutual trust between police and community can do much to reduce the number of instances where brutality insinuations are made. This is a tall order, given the status of the current distrust in various circumstances, and there are those who despair completely of any possibility of thawing the ice. But somehow ways must be found to encourage reason to prevail, or the "armed fortresses" warning of the National Commission on the Causes and Prevention of Violence will become reality. A first step is understanding what brutality charges really mean.

Chief Complaint of Minorities

It is commonly assumed that brutality is the principal complaint of minorities against the police. Several studies, including the Michigan State University survey for the President's Crime Commission in 1966, debunk this assumption. The most frequent complaint is permissive and differential law enforcement in areas where blacks and other minorities predominately reside. The chief grievance is inadequate police protection and services in inner-city neighborhoods. It is regarded by minorities as the worst form of racial discrimination.

The "expectation of unfair treatment by the police" ranks next highest among minority group complaints. Harassment and verbal brutality come next. Differential treatment in field interrogations, in such things as "stop and frisk" and "failure to move on" follow. Physical brutality rates next. Finally, there is resentment over what minority groups view as discrimination in police personnel practices—in hiring, promotions, etc. The point here is not that most police departments today do not want more minority group officers, but rather that existing policies and practices are weighted against the minority group applicant. Moreover, these procedures are often defended as "fair for everybody; after all, the majority have rights too!"

Kenneth Clark conveys something of the flavor of ghetto attitudes toward the police in the following interviews (*Dark Ghetto: Dilemmas of Social Power,* pp. 4ff.):

Man, age about 33:

> The white cops, they have a damn sadistic nature. They are really a sadistic type of people and we, I mean me, myself, we don't need them here in Harlem. We don't need them! They don't do the neighborhood any good. They deteriorate the neighborhood. They start more violence than any other people start.

Man, about 35:

> I think we should all get together—everybody—all get together and every time one draws back his stick to do something to us, or hits one of us on the head, take the stick and hit *him* on *his* head, so he'll know how it feels to be hit on the head, or kill him, if necessary. Yes, kill him, if necessary. That's how I feel. There is no other way to deal with this man. The only way you can deal with him is the way he has been dealing with us.

Man, age 21:

> Everything is a big laugh in this dump unless you kill a cop. Then they don't laugh.

Reflecting on these and other interviews, Clark writes:

> In a disturbing sense, there remains the possibility that homicide in the ghetto is consistently high because it is not controlled, if not encouraged, as an aspect of the total network of the human exploitation of the ghetto. The unstated and sometimes stated acceptance of crime and violence as normal for a ghetto community is associated with a lowering of police vigilance and efficiency when the victims are also lower-status people. This is another example of the denial of a governmental service—the right of adequate protection—which is endured by the powerless ghetto. [Ibid., p. 86]

Countercomplaints of the Police

The police also have their favorite complaints, directed against the minority community. The Michigan State University study found them to be the following:

1. Many policemen feel that the public is apathetic to their problems, and they have been abandoned in the "war against crime," particularly in the ghetto.

2. The police feel that most of the charges made against them by "vocal minorities" are patently unfair. In effect, policemen cry "foul"; they feel that they are being "had."

3. Many police officers strongly resent what they regard as the overemphasis on the rights of the individual at the expense of the rights of society.

4. The police are torn by uncertainty as to their role in today's society. Why, they ask, should there be cries for more civilian control of the police when the police are better trained, better educated, and more efficient than ever?

5. Many police officers express great concern over what they perceive as the "moral decay" of society. Their view of life places them on a collision course with segments of the population who see "the system" that the police represent as an anachronism.

In sum, most police officers tend to see themselves as "trying to do good," fighting sin, lawlessness, and evil. They feel hurt by the storm of criticism that breaks around them and by what they consider a "nobody cares" public attitude. In the ghetto, where social conditions are worst and where beleaguered minorities are most visible, a policeman may tend to see "these people" as the personification of all that frustrates and disturbs him. Both the policeman and the people feel powerless to change the conditions that basically make the police-community relationship so hostile, so sterile. They blame each other for their many problems and thereby freeze communication further.

We have mentioned the tendency to find someone to blame for problems seemingly too overwhelming to sort out piece by piece, with due attention to one's own responsibility. Writing in *The New York Times* (May 11, 1971), Russell Baker recalled the America of the 1930s when President Herbert Hoover was blamed for all trouble. In the 1940s, it was Germany and Japan that were blamed. In the 1950s, it was Communism. Nowadays, Baker thinks, the paranoia has metastasized: "everybody and everything is the cause of all the trouble." And indeed, the list of contemporary scapegoats is long: white liberals, hardnosed conservatives, black militants, hippies, Doctor Spock, unwashed bums, the Establishment, effete snobs, the military-industrial complex, the Eastern media, the FBI or the CIA, the new left, the Supreme Court, Mayor Daley, Ronald Reagan, deficit financing, Howard Hughes, Hollywood or Las Vegas, and lots more.

The truth is, as Pogo put it: "We have met the enemy—and he is us."

The Dirty-Workers

Several years ago, Lee Rainwater referred to "the revolt of the dirty-workers" in an article in *Transaction*. Borrowing from sociologist Everett Hughes, he pointed to the Nazi S.S. in Germany as a cadre that had carried out the dirty work of anti-Semitism while Germans in general were silent about what was going on in the concentration camps. Rainwater wondered whether something similar to this might not be happening in America today. Many white Americans feel that ghetto blacks and other minorities must be controlled and confined. These same Americans are ashamed and uncertain as to how this should be done, and they prefer to conceal from themselves much of the detail of how the doers of this dirty work—the police, the teachers, the welfare workers—actually go about their assigned tasks. Rainwater wrote:

As the ghettos in this country grow, a new dimension is added, a dimension of silence and ignorance about exactly what these functionaries are expected to do, and how in fact they do carry out society's covert orders to control and cool out those who must be excluded from ordinary society. If the teachers, social workers and cops were ever to spell out in detail what their duties are in order to justify their wage demands, they would threaten the delicate balance preserved by silence about their assigned dirty work—no one wants to learn that they [sic] are striking for "combat pay."

The dirty-workers [to quote Rainwater again] are increasingly caught between the silent middle-class, which wants them to do the dirty work and keep quiet about it, and the objects of that dirty work, who refuse to continue to take it lying down. Individual revolts confront the teachers with the problems of the "blackboard jungle," the police with the problem of "disrespect for law and order," and the welfare workers with the problem of their charges' feigned stupidity and real deception. These civilian colonial armies find their right to respect from their charges challenged at every turn, and often they must carry out their daily duties with fear for their physical safety. ["The Revolt of the Dirty-Workers"]

Some might feel that this is an overly harsh view of the situation. But there are harsher descriptions; for example, this by W. H. Ferry:

. . . let me show why we must have a police state. It is because we have run out of other remedies. . . . We simply do not know what to do about 25 million black Americans. It is only a little less true that we do not know what to do with our agitating children and hippies and other self-evictees of respectable white society. . . . As middle-class America looks across the tracks to blacktown, it does not understand what it sees there. But it is clear enough . . . that middle-class America does not see other human beings like themselves. . . . Blacks are never sufficiently grateful for the kindnesses and favors done them by whitetown.[3]

Hans Toch takes a similarly cynical position:

In general, police and blacks are obsessed with the need to instill respect in each other. For both, the demand for respect is for recognition on the basis of group membership rather than for a positive reaction to personal qualities. . . . For each group, the other symbolizes threats that lurk on every corner of the ghetto. The young black does not know how to react to police incursions, and the young officer feels helpless in dealing with difficulties posed by his tense encounters with hostile blacks. Each man comes to feel that he must rely on his group identification—badge or color—as a substitute for answers he cannot find in himself. . . . Neither party need conclude that it has to make the delicate judgments implicit in personal encounters: the matter is prejudged; two men approach each other, not as human beings but as uniformed members of military forces engaged in a doomed truce in a no-man's land. ["Cops and Blacks: Warring Minorities," p. 492]

A retired policeman, Professor William Brown, observes:

To the police, one of the most unsettling features in the police-black relationship is that the prescriptions which they were only recently given for establishing "community relations" are hopelessly inadequate for understanding, let alone dealing with, the problems created by the black activists. The police official who has determined (somewhat late and somewhat under pressure) to be fair and impartial is now willing to accept rational discussion of objectives, the setting of boundaries and all the other devices for the control of noncriminal civilian groups which seemed to be the answer to meeting the black protest movement only a few years ago. Having accepted the model of fairness, the police seem particularly disturbed by what they regard as the unfairness of the blacks. "What do they want?" "Why do they provoke, taunt, refuse to agree to reasonable regulations?" ["Mirrors of Prejudice," p. 498]

Former Detroit police commissioner George Edwards, now a Federal Court of Appeals judge, has observed that in the past, the police have rarely sought civilian assistance in any systematic way and least of all in those areas where the forces of law enforcement have been hardest pressed (*The Police on the Urban Frontier,* pp. 17ff. and p. 77). Judge Edwards believes that three factors have particularly complicated police and minority group relations "on the urban frontier": (1) The civil rights movement has decreased the blacks' tolerance of indignities inflicted by the police and greatly intensified the demand for equal law enforcement; (2) demonstrations, no matter how peaceful, require considerable police manpower to handle, with an acute sense of risk involved as policemen see it; and (3) every time illegal violence is employed, either by demonstrators or by the police, it increases the mutual animosity.

It will be recalled from our discussion in Chapter Six that the reciprocal attitudes and values of police and minority groups and what we called "the value gap" between them are complex questions, concerning which research data are just beginning to appear. Researchers at Michigan State University have concluded from their studies that the current mass protest by dissatisfied youth, militant blacks, and radical whites about such social values as *a world of peace* and *equality* reflects value patterns that are highly incongruent with predominant police value patterns. To illustrate this point, the research shows significant differences in respective rankings for *equality*. Police rank *equality* markedly lower in value priority than did a national sample of whites and far lower than national sample of blacks. The MSU researchers (Rokeach, Miller, and Snyder) rate this the most significant aspect of the value gap between police and policed, and in their words:

... given the especially large discrepancy in value for *equality* between police and blacks, it is hardly surprising that black residents of the ghetto will view policemen as enemies who are there to preserve "law and order," i.e., to preserve the conservative value pattern of a white power structure. ["The Value Gap Between Police and Policed"]

The Theory of Cognitive Dissonance

The theory of *cognitive dissonance,* first proposed in 1957 by Leon Festinger and elaborated in 1962 by Brehm and Cohen, is based on "the notion that the human organism tries to establish internal harmony, consistency, or congruity among his opinions, attitudes, knowledge, and values. There is, in short, a drive toward consonance among cognitions (*A Theory of Cognitive Dissonance,* p. 260). Festinger explains further that the relation between pairs of cognitive elements can be "irrelevant": i.e., they have nothing to do with each other and are therefore *dissonant;* or the relation can be "relevant" and therefore *consonant*: i.e., one element follows from the other. Thus, dissonance refers to the strain or tension between two items of knowledge, two attitudes, opinions, or values.

The concept of contra-cultural conflict and the concept of cognitive dissonance have much in common; the former is an example of the latter. Festinger identifies five general conditions under which cognitive dissonance occurs:

1. Dissonance almost always exists after a decision has been made between two or more alternatives.

2. Dissonance almost always exists after an attempt has been made, by offering rewards or threatening punishment, to elicit overt behavior that is at variance with private opinion.

3. Forced or accidental exposure to new information may create cognitive elements that are dissonant with existing cognition.

4. The open expression of disagreement in a group leads to the existence of cognitive dissonance in the members.

5. Identical dissonance in a large number of people may be created when an event occurs which is so compelling as to produce a uniform reaction in everyone.

The magnitude of post-decision dissonance varies with the importance of decisions, the relative attractiveness of alternatives not chosen, and the similarity of both chosen and unchosen alternatives. Festinger puts it this way:

> The magnitude of the dissonance resulting from an attempt to elicit forced compliance is greatest if the promised reward or punishment is either *just sufficient* to elicit the overt behavior or is *just barely not* sufficient to elicit it. [Ibid., p. 263]

The central hypothesis of the theory of cognitive dissonance is that "the presence of dissonance gives rise to pressures to reduce that dissonance,"[4] and that the pressure to reduce dissonance depends on the magnitude of the dissonance. Reducing dissonance calls for changing one of the dissonant elements of knowledge, opinion, attitude, or value; the addition of new, consonant elements to support the decision taken; or decreasing the importance of the dissonant elements of knowledge, opinion, attitude, or value.

What does this have to do with police relations with blacks? Strecher has analyzed its relevance very helpfully ("When Subcultures Meet"). He defines the concept of "culture shock," which has become familiar in training personnel for such overseas programs as the Peace Corps. In *An American Dilemma*, Myrdal described four stages in the culture shock syndrome (pp. 59–64):

1. A kind of "honeymoon" period, during which the individual is fascinated by the novelty of a strange culture. He is polite, friendly, etc.

2. The individual settles down to a long-run confrontation with the conditions of life in the strange culture and the need for him to function effectively there. He becomes hostile and aggressive toward the culture and its people. He attributes his difficulties to trouble-making on their part. He develops elaborate, stereotypic caricatures of the local people.

3. Here the individual (if he has survived Stage 2) is beginning to open a way into the new cultural environment. He may take a superior attitude but he will joke about local behavior rather than criticize it. He is on the way to recovery from shock.

4. The individual's adjustment is as complete as it can be. He accepts the other's customs as just another way of living and doing things.

Strecher's analysis traces the pattern in police interaction with lower-class Negroes. First, there was the exodus of millions of blacks from the rural South and their migration to the metropolitan areas of the North and the West. The social adaptation process, which might be called "survival techniques," produced black behavior patterns clearly *dissonant* with the conventional norms of the larger society—patterns that formed a distinctive poor-black, urban subculture. Cognitive dissonance exists in the lower-class Negro's simultaneous awareness of the conventional norms and the substituted norms by which he actually lives. He also realizes that his way of life does not work out nearly as well as those not living it say it does. So he rejects the conventional goals and legitimate ("responsible") ways of achieving them, and allies himself with other goals and means that bring his behavior and norms into consonance in his "world."

Of the policeman's side of the picture, Strecher says:

> Enter the policeman, who has problems of his own. He is recruited
> from the middle and working classes, and as a result of historical
> racial segregation patterns knows almost nothing of the Negro poverty
> subculture. His occupational socialization produces a self-conception
> centered upon crime-fighting and life-protection, and a set of sub-
> cultural perspectives which tend to reject all roles dissonant with his
> self-conception. . . . [In addition], the policeman who is assigned to
> work in predominantly lower-class Negro neighborhoods . . . experi-
> ences a culture shock reaction to social strangeness, loss of familiar
> cues and symbols, and his inability to interact spontaneously with the
> Negro residents. . . . It is natural for him to react to this uncomfortable
> experience aggressively.
>
> . . . .
> Lower-class Negro behavior is dissonant with the police view of social
> order, morality and propriety; the implicitly moralistic evaluation of
> lower-class Negro lifestyle by policemen reactivates for the Negro
> dissonance between behavior and conventional ideals, up to then re-
> duced by his subcultural solution. ["When Subcultures Meet"]

Two comments may be appended to Strecher's analysis. First, if
his linkage of concepts is valid, it has clear implications for programs to
improve police and minority group relations. If Strecher is right, it is no
wonder that so many such programs miss the mark. Secondly, although
his theory focuses particularly on police relations with lower-class Negroes, it is relevant also (with minor adjustments) for police interaction
with other disaffected groups.

The Extent of Dissonance

How serious is the dissonance between the police and lower-class
blacks? On the more or less positive side, Gary Marx reports in his
1967 study of the attitudes of blacks toward the police in four cities
that 64 percent of adult blacks in Chicago thought the police treated
blacks "very well" or "fairly well," as compared with 56 percent who
said this in New York City, 53 percent in Atlanta, and 31 percent in
Birmingham (*Protest and Prejudice*).

For perspective on the question of how great the dissonance, it is
useful to dwell for a moment on comparative opposites: black militancy
and white militancy. As we said in the preceding chapter, black militancy in the United States crystallizes in increasing dissatisfaction with
basic social institutions: the schools, political and governmental entities,
the police, the criminal justice "nonsystem." There is increasing Negro
unwillingness to accept the assumptions of white culture, white values,
and white power. The disposition toward militancy is especially pronounced among black youth who tend to view the more militant leaders

as heroic figures—for example, Malcolm X. More and more there appears to be a tendency among black militants to believe that change cannot occur substantially enough or fast enough within the existing system. They say, "Power is never relinquished voluntarily; it has to be *taken.*"

In the American historical tradition, white militancy is aroused when white factions rise up to defend home, family, or country against forces considered alien or threatening. Militancy of this kind has often assumed the form of direct vigilante action, in which racism and nativism join forces in intermittent reigns of terror against minorities and those considered "un-American." As so many writers have said, violence is embedded in our history, although most people today repudiate it. But white militancy today, directed against advances in black civil rights, is not simply the preoccupation of a relative handful of extremists. Its rhetoric makes demands for "law and order," and for doing something about "crime in the streets." It is a basic element in the separating force in our cities: increasingly militant blacks (and other minorities) versus increasingly militant white resistance.[5]

In this situation, the police officer—overworked, undertrained, underpaid, undereducated, and underappreciated—is caught between conflicting community pressures that make it next to impossible to function successfully in his expected role. Discord in police-community relations is a symptom of more fundamental problems: such things as poverty, discrimination, and a society's hang-ups in handling legitimate and socially healthy dissent. Little wonder, then, that the police and other "dirty workers" are voicing protest by such tactics as slowdowns, "Blue flu," unionization, lobbying, and other moves toward political power. The politicization of the police is quite understandable, if not altogether desirable. We shall devote more attention to this subject in Chapter Nineteen, for it has become a critical question in police and community relations today.

Seymour Lipset says that police "rebellion" is a response to their being faced with "confrontation tactics" by students and black radical militants, whose strategy is to enrage the police and provoke overreaction ("Why Police Hate Liberals," p. 82). This in turn can be exploited to the advantage of those intent upon disrupting, embarrassing, or overturning the existing "system." The militant philosophy views killing a policeman not as murder, but as a legitimate act of self-defense, under any circumstances. "A cop is *the enemy,* and the enemy must be liquidated."

Lipset believes that the tensions between the police and New Left student and black nationalist radicals are probably the most extreme example of deliberate provocation that American police have ever faced. He observes:

Police understand as normal the problems of dealing with crime or vice. They may resent violence stemming from minority ghettos, but this, too, is understandable and part of police work. But to take provocative behavior from youths who are socially and economically much better off than they and their children is more than the average policeman can tolerate. [Ibid.]

How intense is the feeling? Through the character, Ras the Exhorter, Ralph Ellison described it:

I ahm no black educated fool who t'inks everything between black mahn and white mahn can be settled with some blahsted lies in some bloody books written by the white mahn in the first place. It's three hundred years of black blood to build this white mahn's civilization and wahn't be wiped out in a minute. Blood calls for blood! You remember that. [*The Invisible Man*, p. 326][6]

Race Not the Decisive Factor

It is timely here to remember James Q. Wilson's point that race is not the decisive factor in current inner-city police-citizen embattlement. No doubt, he says, race makes the potentiality for dissonance greater, but he adds:

. . . if all Negroes were turned white tomorrow, this hostility—only slightly abated—would continue. Throughout history the urban poor have disliked and distrusted the police, and the feeling has been reciprocated; the situation will not change until the poor become middle-class, or at least working class, or until society decides to abandon the effort to maintain a common legal code and a level of public order acceptable to middle-class persons.

. . . .

One reason for the increasing complaints of "police harassment" may be that, in large cities, Negroes are being brought under a single standard of justice; one reason for the complaints of discrimination may be that this process is proceeding unevenly and imperfectly. As the populations of our large cities become, through continued migration, more heavily Negro, more heavily lower income, and more youthful, we can expect these complaints to increase in number and frequency, especially if, as seems likely, organizations competing for leadership in the central cities continue to seek out such issues in order to attract followers. [*Varieties of Police Behavior*, pp. 297–299]

The high visibility of the *black* poor exaggerates the policeman's distorted view. But Wilson's emphasis upon social class should not, of course, be interpreted as absolving police officers from accusations of racial bias. Having touched upon this question in Chapter Five, we will repeat only a few pertinent comments. Bayley and Mendelsohn reported in their Denver study (*Minorities and the Police,* p. 148) that little credence is given by policemen to charges that policemen treat minority people unfairly or improperly. Walsh found that police officers viewing their work as but a job were far more likely than those viewing themselves as professionals to claim that unequal treatment was the fault of the minorities themselves.[7] Some 85 percent of the "jobbers" thought this, of whom 62 percent believed that minorities actually enjoy more privileged treatment than they deserve. Yet 40 percent of the officers viewing themselves as professionals were willing to admit that the problems of police-minority relations were caused, at least in part, by police officers.

Westley, Kephart, and Skolnick found evidence of considerable racial prejudice among the police they studied.[8] But Skolnick observes —as we noted in Chapter Five—that from the point of view of the policeman, the term "racial bias" is not an accurate description of his attitude toward Negroes. In private conversation, many white policemen strongly express negative feelings toward blacks. But they do not admit to being racially prejudiced, (1) because one may hate somebody without being *biased* against him, and (2) because if a police officer admits to racial bias, it tends to make a scapegoat of him. He feels that he is no more prejudiced than his fellow citizens who are isolated from contact with Negroes.

Thus, by his standards, the policeman is not biased; he simply tells the truth. And he concludes that while he is no more or no less prejudiced than others, it is irrelevant anyhow, because it is his job to extend justice evenhandedly, no matter what his personal feelings. As a "professional," he sees his behavior as not necessarily governed by his personal attitudes. He has a job to do, and he must do it. In a predominantly Negro residential neighborhood, the officer sees his job as *combat.* From the vantage point, therefore, of both police officer and community, their relationship is warfare—enemy to enemy. But the policeman would insist that racial prejudice has nothing to do with it.

It is a curious jumble of human relations. Behavior by the policeman that is seen as bigoted by ghetto blacks is shrugged off by the officer as "just doing my job"—not bigotry, even though privately the policeman admits to racial prejudice. In effect, the officer is saying, "I may be prejudiced, but when I'm on duty, I'm fair—I treat 'em all alike, no matter what color they are." In like manner, a so-called crackdown by the police, in a high-crime area where the population is largely black, may be viewed by residents as racially discriminatory. But the police explain that it has nothing to do with race, that it is their job to contain crime, and that the residents are uncooperative.

What is the problem, basically? The problem is a complex of reciprocal "images," of mutually reinforcing stereotypes, of communication, and of environmental circumstances. Skolnick summarizes it well:

To the extent that police are bigoted and manifest prejudices in the daily performance of their duties, to the extent that they employ different standards, to the extent that they insult black people living in the ghetto, they receive the hostility and hatred of the black man in the ghetto. This hostility and hatred in turn, reinforces the policeman's bigotry, the policeman's hatred, the policeman's fear, and the social isolation of the policeman from those black citizens with whom he must come in daily contact. ... Thus, as social conditions prod the black man into increasingly hostile responses, the police are on the receiving end and are themselves tempted to respond with renewed hostility. ["The Police and the Urban Ghetto," p. 9]

Police Concept of "Animals"

James Walsh devotes attention to the police officer's concept of "animals."[9] To the policeman this concept covers a variety of persons but centers especially on those with whom, as Walsh puts it, "very little likelihood of a positive outcome faces the officer as he sets out to handle a family dispute, to face a mentally disturbed person, a belligerent drunk, a neighborhood quarrel in which the police must play 'umpire,' or the known cop-fighter."

The heart of the policeman's trouble with what he calls "animals" is in what he sees as the "can't win" nature of the encounter. If the officer physically abuses a citizen, he faces criticism and possible counterattack, probable insolence, and the chance of enhancing the standing of the "animal" in the eyes of the latter's peers. If on the other hand, the officer avoids forceful and aggressive tactics, he subjects himself to the insults of the "animal," possible jeers and taunts of bystanders, and in the eyes of the officer, loss of respect on all sides, most importantly from his fellow-officers.[10]

Walsh found that a high proportion (80 percent) of the police officers who strive to be professional felt that physical force was most apt to be used by an officer when he was dealing with an "animal." Adding to the officer's resentment was his expectation that the "animal," if arrested, would soon be released by the courts and returned to the street to give the officer further trouble.[11] This is "dirty work" that the police wish they could escape but know they cannot and becomes a contributing factor in their cynicism, as pointed out by Niederhoffer.[12]

Race and Crime

Several aspects of the relationship between race and crime call for analysis. One is the question of racially delineated crime statistics, which is part of the difficult general problem of criminal statistics.[13] Police tend to view racial and ethnic delineation of such data as an aid in the investigation of crime and the apprehension of suspects. The dangers that social scientists see in this practice grow out of correlating race with criminal behavior, as suggested by the notion of "Negro crime." A widely accepted myth in popular belief is no less a potent factor in distorted communication simply because it is a myth (President's 1966 Commission report, *Field Surveys V*, Chap. VII).

Not only is there overwhelming scientific evidence that races as such do not have a propensity toward crime, but there is considerable data to substantiate that criminal acts are predominantly *intragroup* and *intraracial*. Wolfgang and Cohen (*Crime and Race*) have brought together much information on this matter and point out that "when crime and color converge, the person is in double jeopardy." They say further that:

> To the visible badge of color is added the label of criminal, reinforcing attitudes of prejudice and compounding acts of discrimination. . . . What is most regrettable is that many people—partly from exaggeration of a few facts, partly from a readiness to believe—strongly associate the two factors of color and crime. . . . The private citizen, clinging to a false premise, is soon beset by a host of false fears and driven to hasty reprisals that damage society's efforts to integrate community life. [P. 3]

This is the danger of the "crime in the streets" spectre. It is not that street crime may not actually be increasing strikingly; it is rather the implied association of race and crime, in stereotypic terms. To paraphrase Mills, something much more sophisticated than the shotgun collection of statistics by race is needed in order to pinpoint the social cancers that produce crime and related problems.

Demonstrating how pernicious is the direct association of race and crime, Kephart's 1952 study (*Racial Factors and Urban Law Enforcement*) of a thousand white policemen in Philadelphia found that these officers overestimated the percentage of arrests of blacks in their districts. The higher the real arrest rate of blacks, the greater was the overestimation. Actually, about 70 percent of all persons arrested were blacks, but estimates by white officers averaged over 95 percent.

Another illustration of the point is the police saturation of some predominantly black neighborhoods. This may well produce a larger number of arrests of blacks. But it is not so much the behavior of blacks that produces the higher crime rate as it is the increased police activity that results in more arrests. Corresponding results might occur in circumstances where all the variables remained the same except for the color of those residing in the area.

Yet there is an undeniable paradox in this matter. Although the practice of employing racial designations in crime records poses problems, it is defended in another sense. The key consideration may be the proper and discreet *use* of such information. As Wolfgang and Cohen put it:

As long as segregation and discrimination persist, and the struggle for more participation in society continues, there may be some utility in the statistical designation of race, simply to keep an accounting of social problems and to measure the progress of change in the economic and political status of minority groups. [*Crime and Race*, p. 9]

However, three additional considerations that have important bearing on this practice are:

1. There is a great need to re-evaluate the methods of crime data collection and presentation, a need that is now rather generally recognized by criminologists.

2. Police administrators should realize that certain types of statistics that are administratively, operationally, or analytically useful need not necessarily be made a matter of random public reporting.

3. The average policeman is not an anthropologist. Even if he were, could he be sure of his judgments as to who is Chinese or Japanese, Indian or Negro, Puerto Rican or Mexican? What anthropologist would support this lumping together of race and nationality? What about blacks who have passed as white—by the thousands? How black is black, how white is white? If a person is mulatto, is his crime to be recorded as half white and half black? The absurdities multiply as analysis of the question deepens.

Police Protection and Crime Statistics

We asserted above that criminal acts are known to be predominantly *intragroup* and *intraracial*. This reflects well-known information regarding the victims of crime, substantiated by President Johnson's 1966 Crime Commission and by the Kerner Commission.[14] The problem of violent crime is, in large part, a problem of crimes committed by Negroes against other Negroes in the ghetto. The President's Commission on Crime in the District of Columbia found that 85 percent of the murders, 79 percent of the rapes, and 84 percent of the serious assaults in Washington were perpetrated by Negroes against Negroes.[15]

As Bruce Terris points out in "The Role of the Police", the crimes reflected in these statistics occur in areas where police and community relations are poorest. And as we have said, the chief complaint of minority people against the police in big cities is "lousy service in our neighborhood." These factors merge into a pattern. There must be some constructive breakthrough in it, not only if there is to be any improvement in police and community relations, but also if there is to be any significant progress in coping with "the crime problem" where it is statistically at its worst. Indeed, the improvement of police and minority relations is the only route that offers any hope of ameliorating some of the toughest aspects of the social malignancy of crime.

In too many places, crimes committed by blacks, with other blacks as victims, are considered less serious than crimes committed by whites against whites or by blacks against whites. Crimes committed by whites with blacks as victims also tend to be considered less seriously. As John Dollard declared more than 30 years ago:

> The formal machinery of the law takes care of the Negroes' grievances much less adequately than that of the whites, and to a much higher degree the Negro is compelled to make and enforce his own law with other Negroes. ... The result is that the individual Negro is, to a considerable degree, outside the protection of the white law, and must shift for himself. This leads to the frontier psychology ... [Such] condoning of Negro violence ... may be indulgent in the case of any given Negro, but its effect on the Negro group as a whole is dangerous and destructive ... So long as the law does not take over the protection of the Negro person, he will have to do it himself by violent means. [*Caste and Class in a Southern Town,* Chap. XIII]

To do something about serious crime in predominantly black neighborhoods where blacks are so often the victims looms as a logical goal of constructive efforts in police and community relations. Crime prevention and crime control for neighborhood and community stability should be the main objective; the improvement of police-citizen relations may well be a dividend of such efforts. Roy Wilkins, executive director of NAACP, believes that at least part of the Negro community is ready "to blow the whistle" on the robbers, muggers, and knife-wielders. He has said that crime control becomes a real possibility as soon as law-abiding Negroes, always in the vast majority, take an active role against crime and criminals.[16]

In discussing this situation, Robert Pearman, a reporter for the Kansas City, Missouri, *Star,* observed ["Black Crime, Black Victims"] that the cries of moderate Negro leaders for better police protection are tempered by ambivalence. They want stronger police protection, but they also want more humane police treatment. Pearman quotes Kansas City Police Chief Clarence Kelly, who is said to doubt that there is any conscious lessening of effort on the part of police officers because of race or economic status. Kelly is reported as conceding that what may have an effect is a feeling among officers of "what's the use, this can only cause trouble. ... there is always the threat that the victim either won't prosecute or that the officer himself will be charged with misconduct." Kelly is described by Pearman as deeply disappointed that Negro businessmen and moderate leaders, themselves often victims of crime, have not "stepped forward with a plea for good law enforcement."

Wolfgang and Cohen conclude their analysis of race and crime with a poignant paragraph:

> Thrust any child, white or colored, from the womb to a world that offers the rewards of status and success. With a moat of discrimination, cut him off from the mainland so that there are few or no opportunities to achieve those rewards. Let him continue to wish for the same things the mainlanders desire, but make him move around much more, lose a father to death or desertion, and a mother to work and dependency. Give him less knowledge to absorb, less money than the mainlander receives for the same tasks. Surround him with examples of unlawful achievers, and make him fight to protect the mainland without fully participating in the rules to govern it. Shorten his length of life, expose him to disease, treat him as if he were biologically inferior and call him nasty names to convince him of it. Even if the mainlanders value the service he gives them and the feeling of importance his contrast offers, he is lost. [*Crime and Race*, pp. 101, 102]

Social Change and Crime

In a discussion of social change and the association of race and crime, Frank Remington begins with this statement:

> In a period of rapid social change, it is important to ask how an officer can steer a course of neutrality if he cannot rely upon the principle of full enforcement of the law against all citizens, regardless of social or racial status. The difficulty of the task makes it tempting for police to pretend that the problem does not exist, or that the responsibility is not theirs, a common and understandable public attitude of many police officials today. ["Social Change, the Law and the Common Good"]

Remington turns to a consideration of assaultive conduct. He says that race is a very convenient way to classify the statistical incidence of assaultive behavior, even though it is apparent that social and cultural factors are causal, not race. But statistics for the real causes are said to be "not workable." Remington believes that the police should assume the initiative in setting a law enforcement policy that distinguishes between serious and nonserious assault on the basis of factors other than race. It will be difficult, he admits, but "trying is certainly better for the community and, in the long run, for the police than is falling back on the easy alternative of claiming full enforcement, and administratively relying upon race as a simple, readily available indication of behavioral differences."

Remington cites aggressive, preventive patrol as an example. It is, as we have noted, a police practice usually confined to high-crime areas, commonly districts where the majority of residents are members of minority groups. It is acknowledged that the easiest and most practical classification is geographical-racial. To devise an alternative policy is difficult. But aggressive, preventive patrol raises serious questions about the validity of police actions; for example, street searches, which are frequently illegal. Remington views such procedures as self-defeating for the police.

These are surely not simple questions. But Remington offers some possible guidelines:

1. Police insistence that police illegality is essential for adequate law enforcement is self-defeating; inevitably, it places police in conflict with minority groups, and it perpetuates the common belief that police authority should be drastically limited because they will abuse whatever authority they are given.

2. Police insistence that their responsibility is to fully enforce the law perpetuates a myth that is impossible of achievement, and undesirable if it could be achieved.

3. In the development of law enforcement policy, race ought, wherever possible, to be rejected as a basis of classification. The factors which cause crime are non-racial. We must get on with the difficult task of developing classifications that are based upon more salient factors. [Ibid.]

Police Leadership

Remington is not alone in his plea for more police leadership and responsibility in social and civic policy.[17] David Bordua developed the same thesis in a paper, "Comments on Police-Community Relations," prepared for the National Advisory Commission on Civil Disorders. He believes that the problem of race relations in the United States is only secondarily a police problem and only secondarily a problem that can be dealt with by improving this or that aspect of public administration. The problem, Bordua contends, is basically political in the larger sense, and its long-run solution will require political action to provide equal opportunities for blacks and to improve the competitive abilities of disadvantaged blacks.

The full entrance of blacks into civil society means, Bordua continues, that they become legitimate claimants to protection *by* the police as well as protection *from* the police. The balance between these is hard to strike, but Bordua thinks that this goes to the heart of the issue in police relations with blacks. Until recently, in many American cities—not all of them in the South—a priority mission of the police was "nigger control." Police maintained good relations with the white community by being tough on blacks. But now, as blacks become more civically and politically significant, they demand that they be heard and that they too be seen as part of a "community" to which the police must "relate." Actually, Bordua observes, there is some evidence that blacks sometimes have a better relationship with the police than they do with other segments of civil order. In many places, it is possible for a Negro to be treated decently in a station house, but not to be allowed at all in the local country club!

As we noted in Chapter Two, Bordua calls for the police to be "out in front, showing the way" in race relations: in effect, to join the civil rights movement. He thinks this would be truly professional demeanor requiring "principled norms of conduct," as against being guided by subgroup prejudice. Bordua joins Remington in saying that "this isn't easy." He goes on to suggest some possible guidelines for police recruitment and training and in departmental policies and procedures:

1. As community managers and monitors of social change, the police should enforce the law as vigorously as possible, but short of the point where vigorous enforcement produces more strain than the system can stand. (This means that the police ought to be as much concerned about the social and civic state of the ghetto as they are about the crime rate therein.)

2. The vulnerability of the police as the symbolic repressive agents of society must be decreased, one way being for the police to exert pressure on other agencies which now shrink from the "dirty work" of exerting authority. Bordua asserts that American society has a long history of abandoning the police and, in effect, segregating them from the rest of the social order.

3. Communication *to* police about the ghetto should be improved, as should communication *between* police and ghetto residents. *Communication is often best when communication per se is not the manifest aim of a program.*

4. Police should increase the amount of supportive service that they perform. (This guideline reveals Bordua's concept of the police role in today's society—obviously not a "traditionalistic" concept.)

The Minority Group Police Officer

The black minority and other minority groups are seriously underrepresented in the personnel of virtually all police organizations in the country. There is widespread concern about this among police administrators and civil rights agencies, who try to cope with the situation by imposed formulas or gimmicks that for the most part fail to produce the desired result. The outlook is that the solution of this problem will be long-range and largely dependent on social change in a far broader context than police administration.

Police departments today are, of course, generally required by law to operate on the basis of a merit system in employment and per-

sonnel practices. However, the general complaint of police administrators with respect to minority group applicants is that not nearly
enough are qualified. On the face of it, this is a plausible and defensible
administrative posture, widely assumed in various facets of public
affairs and usually crowned with the statement, ". . . and we certainly
can't *lower* our standards." Getting qualified applicants of whatever
color or background for police work today is something of a challenge,
and the difficulty is much more acute in the case of the black applicant,
or the Puerto Rican, or the Mexican-American, etc. What is the
problem?

It is astonishing that there should be so much apparent difficulty
in understanding what the problem is. The factors explaining it are
fairly obvious. Yet various recruitment campaigns and promotions are
mounted in a manner to suggest that the instigators really believe that
such things as television and radio spots by "famous names" and bill-
board posters will get the job done. There is consternation when these
ploys simply do not work.

As with any other problem, solutions must be meshed with
causes. What, then, are the causes of the problem of underrepresentation of minority people in police agencies? Following is an outline of
some of the more important considerations:

1. Minority group applicants have not in the past been particularly
    sought in recruiting efforts by police agencies.

2. Minority group young people have not viewed police work as an
    attractive or inviting career because they see police organizations
    as predominantly white, English speaking, etc., and also because
    what they have seen of what police do, in so-called high-crime
    neighborhoods, hardly elevates their estimate of the occupation.

3. In the minority group community, especially in low-income areas,
    to aspire to be a police officer is frequently to be regarded by
    one's peers as "selling out to the enemy"—as a "fink" or a traitor
    or an "Uncle Tom." One pays a high price for such aspiration.

4. The above point suggests the difficult problem of marginality—
    for example, for the black police officer.[18]

5. The complex question of qualifications for police work is cur-
    rently undergoing re-examination and re-evaluation. What should
    it take to qualify? The qualities that are most useful in today's
    police function may not be measurable in such terms as years
    of formal education, or how tall a man is, or what he weighs, or
    how sharp his eyesight. The important question is, what are the
    relevant qualifications? We too easily succumb to doing it the
    easy way: for example, requiring more formal education, which
    we equate with "elevating standards." Assumptions of this type
    urgently need rethinking, to reveal the superficiality of the admin-
    istrative stance: "We can't get enough qualified applicants"; "We

can't lower our standards"; etc. White, middle-class bias taints much that we are doing and saying about this.

6. Many minority group people have reason to doubt that they are really wanted in police agencies, because they have reason to know that there is considerable racial prejudice and discrimination therein.[19]

7. As a result of past educational discrimination and given present civil service-type "merit examinations" for police service, minority people are in fact at a disadvantage in the educational require-ments. Also, since many such testing instruments are tilted by culture and social class and weighted with paper-and-pencil and reading skills, minority people are further handicapped.

8. For *social* rather than racial reasons, numerous young Negroes—again as an example of the typical minority group situation—have a criminal record, making them technically ineligible for police service. This, too, calls for a good deal of re-evaluation, with more careful attention to the individual applicant rather than reliance entirely on broad, "no-exceptions," bureaucratic, "pro-grammed" classifications.

9. Attitudes within police organizations toward minority group per-sonnel often create problems internally, a significant factor in the difficulty of *retaining* such personnel even when initially secured. One indication of this is the development of "defense" organiza-tions to protect the interests and rights of minority group police officers—for instance, the Guardians, the National Society of Afro-American Policemen, the Council of Police Societies, Of-ficers for Justice, etc. Their purposes are more serious than fraternity and fellowship. There is one theory that some of the negativism among police rank-and-file directed against actual or prospective minority group colleagues is grounded in the self-image problems of some policemen. They fear, for example, that police work will increasingly come to be regarded as what they call "nigger work." It should also be noted that there is an attitude sometimes evident in the white community (and occasionally in the black community) to be contended with: that "a black cop is not a real cop."

10. Many educationally better-qualified Negroes are taking positions in business, industry, and the professions rather than in public service simply because salary and other financial and social in-centives are far better.

There is no question that the minority group policeman is a very important figure in police and community relations. His lately acquired importance is a telling symptom of the gravity of police and minority group polarization. It is probably true that there is a resultant "counter-momentum"—a tendency for police departments to expect too much from the minority group policeman, almost to a point of suggesting that if only there were enough black police officers, all problems of police-black relations would evaporate. Some black policemen may be able to do certain things better than some white policemen in a predominantly black neighborhood—but the same thing is also true in a predominantly white neighborhood. In the long run, it may increasingly come to be recognized that blackness or whiteness is not a very important determinant of an effective policeman. It comes down to individual traits of personality, sensitivity, attitude, knowledge, and the like. Some black officers do not know the culture of certain black neighborhoods. Some black police officers are rougher in black neighborhoods and are despised more by the residents than are white officers.[20] At the present time, it may well be that the importance of the black police officer on the police and community relations scene is mainly symbolic. This in no way detracts, however, from the fact of his importance. On the contrary, it underscores again the community leadership opportunity of police and criminal justice agencies, as Bordua says, to show the way in race relations.

Other Minorities

As in the preceding chapter, we have tended in this chapter to focus on the Negro as our example of minority group. It should be emphasized, however, that much of what we have said applies as well to other groups. Yet the difficulty with such a statement is that it is too general; it conveys an impression of uniformity, of alikeness, when in fact we mean *similarity* allowing for some *uniqueness.*

Take, for example, Spanish-speaking Americans. Puerto Rican citizens of varying skin pigmentation are one subgroup. But not all Puerto Ricans can be lumped together either. And then there are the Spanish-surname people of the Southwest and other places throughout the nation, some of them migrant agricultural workers, others not. In their study of police and minority relations in Denver, Bayley and Mendelsohn say that people of Mexican-American (Chicano) heritage have in common the Spanish language, a historical tradition, and a sense of cultural uniqueness (*Minorities and the Police,* p. v). The authors go on to observe that Negroes participate to a greater extent than the Spanish-named in the culture of America; blacks generally do not, for example, speak a different language; it is their distinctive physical appearance that sets them apart. To complicate things further, there are, of course, many Spanish-speaking blacks of Latin American background.

The Denver study reflects some differences between Negroes and the Spanish-named in many facets of police and community relations as measured in the study. For example, the Spanish-named were twice as critical as Negroes of the job done by the police in their respective neighborhoods. Over twice as many Spanish-named claimed that they or someone in their family had been badly treated by the police. A recently published study by the U.S. Commission on Civil Rights cites many serious problems in the treatment of Mexican-Americans in the Southwest by the police and other justice agencies.[21] It should be noted that location and culture affect these matters; Denver may be one thing, Los Angeles or Santa Fe another.

The point is that minority groups are not all alike in every respect, and one should flatly reject the notion that "if you've seen one, you've seen them all." There are, of course, certain problems that are common to minority groups, as earlier indicated when we defined the concept—for instance, sociopolitical powerlessness. Our centering upon the Negro group assumes that there are some common attributes in police and minority group relations, *not* that there are no important distinctions. In *The Police and the Community: Studies* (Radelet and Reed), Part III presents several different studies of police-minority relations: one dealing with Southern Appalachian mountaineers, one with black, teen-age gangs, one with the Mexican-American, and one with the Black Panthers. We might well have included several more, dealing—for instance—with white, dissident youth, or with Puerto Ricans in East Harlem, or with the Omaha Tribal Council of Indians in western Nebraska. There would be elements both of commonality and of uniqueness in all of these studies.

Certain white minorities are also struggling for acceptance in this country. As Paul Mundy has said, "The third generation remembers what the second generation would like to forget, namely, his ethnic identity." Various ethnic groups in major cities are demanding a voice on boards and commissions to influence such matters as curriculum content and choice of history books in schools. Italian Americans are acting to eliminate the stereotypes they find offensive. Many police officers come from ethnic white minority group backgrounds, and ethnically based clubs and societies of policemen are common in our larger cities. There are still a few places, too, where religious cleavages are strong within police organizations. The Knights of Columbus and the Shriners are still prominent in police circles and have considerable influence in some quarters.

Other Criminal Justice Components

We have discussed some of the implications for the police of The Movement in civil rights and race relations. What about other parts of the criminal justice system? A more thorough consideration of these appears in Part Four. But as to the specific question raised above, the courts may be taken as an example. How the judicial apparatus

acts in time of civil crisis is an important test of a society's capacity
to uphold democratic values and protect civil liberties (Skolnick, *The
Politics of Protest*). During urban disturbances in the late 1960s and
early '70s, defendants were deprived of adequate representation, subjected to the abuses of overcrowded facilities, and held in custody by
the imposition of high bail. These measures, taken under the duress of
mass arrests and ostensibly for the prevention of further disorders,
amounted to preventive detention and the suspension of due process.[22]

Skolnick points out that the inability of the courts to cope with
civil emergencies results in a decline in respect for legal authority.
Demonstrators and militants have come to believe that legal institutions
serve only the powerful and are incapable of remedying social and
political grievances. Skolnick thinks the crisis in the courts is due to
three factors:

1. The quality of justice in the lower criminal courts during routine
   operations is quite low.

2. In response to community and political pressures for immediate
   restoration of order, the courts tend to adopt a police perspective
   or "riot control," becoming in effect an instrument of social control
   relatively unrestrained by conditions of legality.

3. The courts are not suited to the task of resolving the political conflicts which occasion civil crisis and mass arrests. [*The Politics of
   Protest*]

Skolnick is especially concerned that the trend toward devising
"emergency measures" does not become routinized as the main social
response to crises that go deeper than the need to restore order.

In Conclusion

So much has been said and written in the past few years about
urban crisis, and indeed specifically regarding police relationships with
minority groups, that any overview is necessarily limited to a selection
of points and issues. We have not "touched all the bases" in this
chapter, surely, but we have mentioned some of the more important
considerations, with the hope of stimulating further thought and discussion.

There remain several matters, however, that merit more extensive
analysis: collective behavior and civil disobedience; police-youth relations, student unrest, and campus disturbances; and citizen complaints
and the police. These will be dealt with in the next three chapters.

A final point with reference to the police and minority groups
is stated well by Bayley and Mendelsohn:

The police are important for minority people not just because of what they do but because of what they are. Minority people recognize that other problems must be solved if substantial improvements are to be made in the quality of their lives. Yet what they experience at the hands of the police is of enormous emotional significance. It symbolizes for them the backhanded treatment they receive from society as a whole. The police are the ubiquitous, public, authority-laden symbols of their own second-class citizenship. Upon them is vented the accumulated frustrations of lifetimes of inequality and subservience. . . . In sum, the position the police occupy in the minority world is only partly a result of what police do in that world; more importantly, their position is a function of fundamental emotional judgments made by people subjected to pervasive deprivation and inequality. This being the case, substantial improvements in police-minority relations cannot be expected solely as the result of changes in police policy and behavior. It will be necessary to change their symbolic status as well, and that is a function of a total system of majority-minority relationships. [*Minorities and the Police,* pp. 141, 142]

Notes to Chapter Twelve

1. An informative reference in this regard is *Guide to Race Relations for Peace Officers,* a training guide prepared in 1946 (reissued in 1952) by Davis McEntire and Robert B. Powers for the Office of the Attorney General, State of California. Republished in 1958 under the same auspices, with the title *Guide to Community Relations for Peace Officers.*

2. Robert B. Mills, *Police-Community Relations: A Psychologist's Viewpoint.* Paper presented at an Institute on Police-Community Relations, held at Xavier University in Cincinnati, June 8, 1964.

3. W. H. Ferry, "The Police State, American Mode." Starr King Commencement Speech, Unitarian Church of Berkeley, California, October 10, 1969.

4. Compare Festinger's theory with that of Morton Deutsch regarding conflict resolution, discussed in Chap. IX.

5. For discussion of this issue, see *The Politics of Protest.* A Staff Report to the National Commission on the Causes and Prevention of Violence, prepared by Jerome H. Skolnick. Note especially Chaps. 4, 5, 6, and 7.

6. As a further pertinent note, *The New York Times* reported in the fall of 1970 (November 29, p. 32) that the Miami, Florida, Police Department, under Chief Bernard Garmire, conducted a project attempting to find out what engenders fear and hatred of blacks among white policemen and how deep these emotions are. The study was being done with the help of several social and behavioral scientists and a grant from the Law Enforcement Assistance Administration, U.S. Department of Justice. One preliminary

finding of the study is that service in the ghetto itself hardens the attitudes of the white policeman and "inculcates bigotry toward Negroes." Fear is strong among white policemen working in the ghetto, the study indicates, and they liken their job to military combat. Such emotion is likely to cause overreactions.

7. James Leo Walsh, "The Professional Cop."

8. William A. Westley, "Violence and the Police"; William R. Kephart, *Racial Factors and Urban Law Enforcement;* Jerome H. Skolnick, *Justice Without Trial.*

9. Walsh, "The Professional Cop."

10. See Study 3 (Part III), "The Police and Black Teen-Age Culture" (in Radelet and Reed, *Studies*), which deals with black teen-age gang members and the police.

11. A similar conclusion is reached by Reiss and Bordua in "Environment and Organization: A Perspective on the Police."

12. Arthur Niederhoffer, *Behind the Shield,* Appendix. See also Study 3 (Part II), "Profile of the Police Subculture," in Radelet and Reed, *Studies.*

13. See Gilbert Geis, "Statistics Concerning Race and Crime."

14. See, for example, Chap. 8 of the report of the National Advisory Commission on Civil Disorders.

15. Report of the President's Commission on Crime in the District of Columbia, pp. 42, 44, 54, and 78. (Quoted by Bruce J. Terris in "The Role of the Police.")

16. Quoted by George C. Edwards, *Police on the Urban Frontier,* p. 77 ff.

17. Remington and his colleague at the University of Wisconsin Law School, Herman Goldstein, presented their case for this in their draft of what became Chap. 2 of the *Task Force Report: The Police,* among the publications of President Johnson's Crime Commission.

18. Effectively analyzed by Nicholas Alex in *Black in Blue.* As he says, it is in effect *double* marginality: the black policeman cannot escape his racial identity while serving in his official role. But in the black community, he cannot be a simple human being—he is always a cop. (*"Oreo"*: black on outside, white on the inside.)

19. See the Crime Commission's *Task Force Report: The Police,* Chap. 6, pp. 167–175; also the Commission's *Field Surveys V,* pp. 19, 20 (Michigan State University). See also the 1968 report of the National Advisory Commission on Civil Disorders, pp. 165, 166. So-called Cadet and Pre-Cadet programs today, frequently aimed particularly at minority youth as young as 14–15 years of age, strive to overcome these long-standing doubts and suspicions regarding police work.

Paul Delaney reported in *The New York Times* (January 25, 1971) that drives to recruit more black policemen had failed in many cities. But a few cities have been relatively successful. By August 1970, 35.9 percent of

Washington, D.C., policemen were black, as compared with only 17 percent 4 years earlier. Chicago had 16.5 percent black policemen in January 1971, an increase of about 300 men in four years. In Atlanta 28 percent of the force are black. In the New York City Police Department, only 7.5 percent are black, but in the City's Housing Authority and Transit police organizations, the percentage of black officers is much larger—more than 50 percent. About 12 percent of Detroit police officers in January 1971 were black as against only 2 percent in 1960.

Figures for other cities, all as of January 1971: Los Angeles 5.2 percent; Milwaukee 2.3 percent; Charlotte 4.5 percent; San Francisco 4.8 percent; Dallas 1.9 percent; New Orleans 6.1 percent; Boston 2.1 percent; Miami 10 percent; Hartford 12 percent. In Philadelphia the percentage of blacks on the force declined from 20.8 percent in 1967 to 18.6 percent in 1971.

20. It is an interesting question for discussion to consider why this seems to be the case.

21. U. S. Commission on Civil Rights, *Mexican Americans and the Administration of Justice in the Southwest*. See also Study 4 (Part III) in Radelet and Reed, *Studies*.

22. Substantiated by both the Kerner Commission and the Violence Commission.

Chapter Thirteen

Collective Behavior and Civil Disobedience

Collective behavior is defined by sociologists as relatively unstructured social behavior—such as that occurring in crowds, riots, revivals, and even sometimes with rumor and fads—which is not fully controlled by cultural norms. It brings into play emotions and unpredictable personal interaction.[1] For obvious reasons, collective behavior is of major concern to the police.

Casual Societal Groups

There are many different classifications of societal groups. Some groups are established, some are casual. Examples of the former are vertical and horizontal groupings, in-groups and out-groups, primary and secondary groups. Casual groups include crowds, mobs, and assemblages. Then there are related types of group behavior such as social movements, social epidemics, fashions, fads, and crazes.

A *crowd* is a temporary gathering of people engaged in some type of collective behavior, ranging from casual strolling to a riot. It differs from an *aggregation,* which is simply an assemblage of individuals in spatial proximity. In a crowd, the individuals are also in psychological contiguity. Crowds often begin as aggregations, evolving through an interactive process known as *circular stimulation.* This means the reciprocal stimulation of individual emotions, causing behavior responses that are less deliberative and less critical than would normally be expected. As a result, members of a crowd are apt to act under the influence of commonly felt emotion.

An *audience* is a type of crowd responding primarily to a single source of stimuli while engaging in only minimum social interaction. Thus, in an audience, there is little circular stimulation. Attention tends to be focused on a performance of some kind rather than on other crowd members. A *mob* on the other hand is a type of crowd with a purpose, often contrary to law, often highly emotional, and with a sense of anonymity. A mob is sometimes characterized as an *acting crowd,* with considerable circular stimulation and an aggressive attitude toward a common object. It feels bound to no convention or rules and acts solely on the basis of aroused feelings. Collective excitement submerges critical and deliberate conduct even more than in a crowd.

The element of psychological suggestibility present in a mob easily leads to violence. There is even a tendency, as in lynch mobs, to hold violence justifiable, so intense is the feeling about righting a supposed wrong. Cowards feel brave in a mob. A *riot* is mob behavior that erupts into public violence, tumult, and disorder. In their study of the 1943 race riot in Detroit, Lee and Humphrey said:

> Riots are the products of thousands upon thousands of little events that have affected the habits and emotions of thousands upon thousands of people, both future rioters and future innocent bystanders. [*Race Riot,* p. 5]

William E. Dowling, Wayne County prosecutor at the time, described that riot in the Detroit *Times* (July 17, 1943):

> The Sunday night of the riot, a gang of colored boys and girls ranging from 13 to 20 years went to Belle Isle with the expressed purpose of driving the white people from the island. They started out, knowing that 85 percent of the approximately 100,000 people on the island were colored, and beat up a white boy.
>
> Next, they attacked a man and his wife who were eating a picnic lunch. They went on around to the bridge and one of the colored girls was pushed into a white girl who was accompanied by a sailor. A fight followed and it spread across the bridge.
>
> One of the colored boys raced downtown to a club and had it announced over the public address system that a Negro woman and her baby had been thrown into the river.
>
> Then it started. By 4 a.m., 400 stores owned by whites in the colored district had been wrecked, looted, pillaged and destroyed. A street car had been stopped and 50 white factory workers were taken out and beaten. It was 5 a.m. before the whites started to retaliate.[2]

Many might quarrel with this version of what happened, on the grounds that it is biased. But in a mob and riot situation, there are no completely trustworthy observers. Objectivity is lost in the stampede. Power and righteousness are felt to abide in the surge of the impassioned mob.

The art of crowd control is important to the police. Typical tactics include directing attention away from the common objective, efforts to divide members of the crowd physically and psychologically, and attempts to divert the leaders so as to dilute their integrating influence. The primary aim is to relieve the emotional tension caused by circular stimulation.

Related Group Behavior

A *social movement* is a collective attempt to bring about a change in existing practices or institutions. The Womens' Liberation Movement is an example. It implies dissatisfaction with some phase of existing social organization.

Fashion is a movement characterized by vertical ascent or descent through social classes. It is imitation throughout a social structure of a particular "elite," as to clothing, manners, art, or ideas. Distinction, novel experience, and conformity are among the motivating forces.

Fads, crazes, and *social epidemics* are types of fashion movements. They are usually more eccentric than fashion, more localized and of shorter duration, and pertain to frivolous things, not of great importance in total culture.

Herbert Blumer pointed out long ago in "Collective Behavior" that the members of a social movement often have high morale, dependent on belief in the absolute rightness of their purpose and in the possibility of ultimate attainment of their goal. It takes on the character of a sacred mission. Often the members of a social movement see all opposing forces as evil. "If you're not for us, you're against us!" The objective is so right and necessary that it cannot possibly fail. Parades, rallies, and "pep meetings" provide ceremony and ritual and help enhance the feeling of being a select group with a "manifest destiny." A feeling of personal expansion comes from association with others (rapport) in the movement. Sometimes special uniforms, slogans, hymns, and gestures help "turn people on."

The Police and Collective Behavior

We tend to think of police action in collective behavior situations in terms of protecting society against excesses such as disorder, pandemonium, violence, and sometimes unlawful activity. Just as important, however, are the activities of groups engaged in nonviolent demonstrations which are not illegal, but which nonetheless require police action to protect the demonstrators in the exercise of their rights—to assembly, to free speech, etc.

Police, of course, are sympathetic with the philosophy that the best way to deal with a riot is to prevent it. Therefore, the so-called "triggering incident" comes in for considerable attention today in police training. It is recognized that the triggering incident is the culmination of what is usually a long series of events, occurring in a social situation that is clearly inflammable. But the incident that sets off the conflagration may be quite innocent and have no direct connection with the real issue. Many police departments have had to confess: "We looked for something to happen here, and instead of that, it happened way over there, where we least expected it!"

In "The Police and Community Conflict," William Brown emphasizes that a major disorder is almost always the culmination of a building-up process. Planning for control of disorder, he says, is based on a combination of conventional police mobilization tactics and *an understanding of the community.* Tension control measures include:

1. Receiving and evaluating reports of tension.

2. Getting background; fact finding; area surveys.

3. Diagnosing the problem (identifying causes).

4. Setting up programs to relieve tension that stress *communication* and *interpretation*—the two basic processes in police-community relations.

The prevention of riots is not the responsibility of the police alone. A just social order for all is the ultimate answer, and in this goal the entire community and society have their most important responsibility. Law is based on the behavior of individuals, not groups. A police officer arrests only individuals who violate the law. This is one reason why group behavior is difficult for the police to handle. Nelson Watson put it this way:

> Police cannot take into court a whole group and present evidence against them en masse. If the police are unable to identify and arrest individual violators and present evidence of the specific violation, case by individual case, all they can do is suppress the violence. It is inevitable that in large-scale disorder many violations of the law will go unpunished. This makes it doubly important to devise preventive programs involving all interested segments of the community. ["Group Behavior and Civil Disobedience"]

Watson further pointed out that police methods in dealing with collective behavior situations will vary by circumstances, time, geography, area in a given community, the socio-economic and cultural variations among people, and other such conditions. He emphasized the importance of flexibility in police policies and operational procedures in heterogeneous, social-conflict-laden communities, whose problems he pinpointed as follows:

> Since many lower-class persons are unskilled and are poorly equipped educationally, the most important fact of life for them is the means of obtaining the necessities. For many, existence is a series of crises or emergencies in which food and shelter are principal concerns. The net result is that satisfying their basic needs for the moment demands such a large proportion of their physical and psychological resources that they are unable to devote adequate time to the development of the symbolic skills so important in today's complex society. Their survival problems are much closer to them than those of the more affluent in our society. [Ibid., p. 109]

Watson concludes that police approaches to the control of crime, violence, and disorder must be designed to match the varying psychological and sociological circumstances of the people involved. This is the principle that we enunciated earlier: that dealing with people in their individuality does not easily submit to mass-oriented, bureaucratically processed classifications, and "no exception" practices. A school system, a university, or a police department cannot be administered in this way in today's American society without encountering turbulence. The evidence of this is widespread. No one should make his case for democracy on the basis that it is necessarily efficient or tidy.

Symbols and Symbolic Behavior

Crowds, mobs, and social movements often employ various types of symbols and symbolic behavior. Mentioned earlier were parades, rallies, uniforms, slogans, hymns, and gestures. We have such terms as "soul brothers" (and sisters!), "soul food," and other evidences of a nomenclature and language that has developed as part of the subculture of The Movement in civil rights and with youth.

Symbols and symbolic behavior are endemic to collective behavior. They represent an effort to structure disorganized situations in some small degree, a way for participants in social movements to communicate with each other in a rapport-building manner and to impart a sense of common cause. The same thing occurs, for basically the same reasons, in all subcultures, including that of the police. Incidentally, rumor serves something of the same purpose: to share a "hot tip" is a way of enhancing fraternal feeling, although it may well backfire.

Symbols are what Watson calls "rallying points" in collective behavior situations. Signs on business places reading "Blood-brother" have a special meaning. The term "nigger-lover" has a symbolic and emotion-charged connotation. A swastika, a Confederate flag, a white-sheeted figure, an elevated black clenched fist, the V-sign, and various obscene gestures carry strong emotional undertones that can quickly arouse people to irrational responses, particularly in group settings. Demagogues play on these feelings skillfully and manipulate gatherings in support of their particular purposes, which are sometimes socially questionable.

Because symbols are by their nature premised on stereotypes ("substitutes for thought," Walter Lippmann said), they are of dubious value in intergroup relationships. To illustrate, we may return momentarily to police-black relations in the ghetto. The police officer is seen as a *symbol* of "the system." The Negro is seen as a *symbol* of lawlessness and social irresponsibility. "The system" (or "the Establishment") is itself symbolic and stereotypic terminology. So is "lawlessness and irresponsibility." So is "white, middle-class power structure." So is "hippie." So is "Fascist pig." So is "Amerika." And so on.

Symbols are mechanisms of irrationality. They are dysfunctional in genuine human relatedness because they encourage categorization of people and events. Their utility in collective behavior situations is ephemeral. To speak against symbolism in human communication is, to be sure, pitting oneself against impossible odds. Where would modern advertising be without it? So let us concede that symbolism is here to stay. Just as one might ask, "Are there not *good* prejudices?", one may say there are unquestionably *good* (or in any case harmless) symbols. While rationality is of the essence of humanity, it is universally regarded as such a bore!

Social Response to Collective Behavior

Studies of collective behavior and its implications for the police have been done on a massive scale in recent years. Some of these study reports are public property, easily accessible to those who ask what causes such behavior and what can be done to prevent it from getting out of hand. One example is the study done in 1967–68 by the National Advisory Commission on Civil Disorders, whose report is prefaced by this statement from President Lyndon Johnson:

> ... The only genuine, long-range solution for what has happened lies in an attack—mounted at every level—upon the conditions that breed despair and violence. All of us know what those conditions are: ignorance, discrimination, slums, poverty, disease, not enough jobs. We should attack these conditions—not because we are frightened by conflict, but because we are fired by conscience. We should attack them because there is simply no other way to achieve a decent and orderly society in America ...

The President might well have added that this is the only ultimate solution for problems of police and community relations.

Another study of collective behavior in America was conducted in 1968–69 by the National Commission on the Causes and Prevention of Violence. This Commission declared:

> In our judgment, the time is upon us for a reordering of national priorities and for a greater investment of resources in the fulfillment of two basic purposes of our Constitution—to "establish justice" and to "insure domestic tranquility."

Still another study of collective behavior was made in 1970 by the President's Commission on Campus Unrest, which asserted:

> Too many Americans have begun to justify violence as a means of effecting change or safeguarding traditions. We believe it urgent that Americans of all convictions draw back from the brink . . . Students who bomb and burn are criminals. Police and National Guardsmen who needlessly shoot or assault students are criminals. All who applaud these criminal acts share in their evil. We must declare a national cease-fire.

In an analysis written for the National Commission on the Causes and Prevention of Violence, Jerome Skolnick states that collective behavior has come to mean the behavior of outsiders, the disadvantaged and disaffected (*The Politics of Protest*, Chap. IX, pp. 251–264). "Panicky" and "crazy" are terms usually reserved, he says, for social movements and insurrections. Skolnick questions typical governmental responses to civil disorders, which—he claims—have historically combined long-term recommendations for social change with short-term calls for better strategy and technology to contain disruption. He offers five reasons for so questioning:

1. As the Kerner Commission stressed, American society urgently requires fundamental social and political change, not more firepower in official hands.

2. We must set realistic priorities. We must carefully distinguish between increased firepower and enlightened law enforcement.

3. Police, soldiers and other agents of social control have been implicated in triggering and intensifying violence in riots and other forms of protest. A non-lethal weapon is still a weapon, and it does not solve social problems.

4. Riots are not merely pathological behavior engaged in by riff-raff. Neither are they "carnivals." They are spontaneous political acts expressing enormous frustration and genuine grievance. Forceful control techniques may channel grievances into organized revolutionary and guerrilla patterns.

5. In measuring the consequences of domestic military escalation, we must add the political and social dangers of depending on espionage

as an instrument of social control, including its potential for eroding constitutional guarantees of political freedom.

Skolnick further observes:

If American society concentrates on the development of sophisticated control techniques, it will move itself into the destructive and self-defeating position of meeting a political problem with armed force, which will eventually threaten domestic freedom. The combination of long-range reform and short-range order sounds plausible, but we fear that the strategy of force will continue to prevail. In the long run this nation cannot have it both ways: either it will carry through a firm commitment to massive and widespread political and social reform, or it will become a society of garrison cities where order is enforced with less and less concern for due process of law and the consent of the governed. [Ibid., Summary, p. xxvi][3]

Police action is unquestionably an important aspect of social response to collective behavior. Jerome Hall recalls that the *posse comitatus* is historic in our culture ("Police and Law in a Democratic Society"). But Hall reminds us that a critical situation provides an excellent opportunity to actualize the ideal of self-policing. He points out that several hundred citizens were deputized as peace officers in the 1919 Harlem riots, and voluntary service by socially-minded white and black citizens—to help "cool it"—has often emerged in civil disorders.

The gravity of mob disorder is reflected in the prohibition under criminal penalty of two less serious situations that tend to culminate in riot—unlawful assembly and rout. While it is generally true that preparation to commit a crime is not a crime, this is not true with unlawful assembly or rout, in which the incipient stages of riot are recognized and prohibited.

Hall makes this point:

The police are familiar with arrest for assault and battery and for disorderly conduct, but they have ignored other available controls and legal measures which can be taken before crimes are committed or before serious aggressions occur. First among these is the peace bond, used in family disputes and in rural areas, but ignored as a control of incipient symptoms of serious disorder. . . . There are other noteworthy legal controls which were designed to check criminal conduct in its incipient stages. At common law a threat, privately made, was not criminal unless it amounted to extortion. But under many statutes a threat uttered publicly in conditions tending toward a breach of the peace is "disorderly conduct," as is insulting, profane language in public. More serious is the common law crime of solicitation or incitement to commit a crime, and incitement to riot is one form of that offense. Conspiracy extends incipient criminal behavior to the conduct of two or more persons; there are reported cases where convictions of conspiracy to commit a breach of the peace were upheld. [Ibid.]

The police should, of course, be familiar with these and other possible legal controls. But the greater wisdom is knowing when and how to apply them. A well-intentioned police action to maintain or to restore order, with no more than good intention going for it, has been known to result in volcanic violence and disorder.

Civil Disobedience

Collective behavior often reflects noncompliance with generally accepted norms. One of its methods or strategies may be civil disobedience: the deliberate violation of a law, or of a regulation having the force and effect of law believed to be immoral or unjust. It is a deliberate challenge of civil authority, with the expectation of incurring sanctions, by persons whose convictions (conscience) compel their loyalty to what they see as a higher order of authority. It is not anarchy—not utter rejection of all authority—but a choice of authority priority.

Acts of civil disobedience are usually engaged in by relatively few people, a small minority raising its voice against a prevailing and generally accepted norm or practice. Civil disobedience challenges what the majority deems acceptable, and puts the social conscience to a test. Little wonder, then, that acts of civil disobedience are repugnant to many people. The police are especially disturbed by civil disobedience, one reason being that it puts them squarely in the middle between contesting moral positions on what is usually an emotionally charged issue. The national poll of police opinions conducted by the International Association of Chiefs of Police in 1969 showed that nine out of ten police officers disagreed with the proposition that a person has a right to deliberately disobey a law that he believes to be immoral or unjust. About the same proportion believed that persons who deliberately violate the law to attract attention to their "cause" should be arrested, searched, and booked in the same manner as other violators [Watson and Sterling, *Police and Their Opinions,* p. 59].

Discussion of the sticky topic of civil disobedience in conferences on police and community relations has been known to become so dominated by feelings as to produce a recommendation that all civil disobedience should be prohibited by law! As Watson observes, this is equivalent to insisting that it is illegal to do anything illegal. To alleviate some of the tension, some important distinctions should be made in any discussion of civil disobedience. To begin with, it is not always a question of deliberate violation of a law. It may be a protest against something required or prohibited by a given law. It may also be a way of protesting a court order. It may be more a matter of taking issue with the way a law is enforced than with the substance of the law itself.

Other distinctions are in the domain of logic. Is civil disobedience illegal? Obviously it is, most of the time. (It could be a protest against a policy, rather than a law.) Is civil violence illegal? Yes. But civil disobedience is not necessarily civil violence, and the latter is not necessarily civil disobedience. Not all illegal acts involve violence, nor is all violence illegal. It is surprising how frequently discussions of civil disobedience bog down in exactly such seeming minutiae, which on closer examination draw important distinctions.

Another distinction was advanced by John Morsell of NAACP, who stated in 1964 that a restaurant sit-in or a freedom ride were *not* acts of civil disobedience ("A Rationale for Racial Demonstrations," p. 148). He argued that these actions were based on the premise that exclusion from a licensed public facility on the ground of race was a violation of constitutional right. If these acts violated local laws, it was the local laws, not the freedom rides or sit-ins, that defied the law of the land. A school boycott, on the other hand, is civil disobedience. But the boycott of a business firm accused of discriminatory hiring practices is not civil disobedience, for there is no law requiring anyone to buy in that store.

Watson ("Group Behavior," p. 112) described the relationship between civil disobedience and collective behavior as "disorderly fallout." He pointed out that most law enforcement is done by the people, not by the police. It is a matter of law observance by most of the people, most of the time. In connection with civil disobedience, however, even when the plan and intentions of the participants are peaceful, there is sometimes a pattern of nonparticipants becoming involved with participants emotionally, and then physically. Suddenly and spontaneously, there is disorder and violence. The police must move in to protect property and persons of whatever persuasion, participants and nonparticipants alike.

Many law enforcement officials feel that a tragic result of civil disobedience is to encourage in young people an attitude of general disrespect for the law and for all public authority. Yet this is largely speculative and as Watson said, evidence is lacking to prove that there actually is such a transfer. In fact, there is a counterargument that acts of solemn and considered civil disobedience actually cultivate greater respect for *just* law.

Watson added a further point:

> The object of civil disobedience is to call attention to a condition which the participants want to have changed. Naturally, the more widely and dramatically the acts are publicized, the better for the purpose. Unfortunately, this publicity often makes the police look bad, especially if violence breaks out. And not only that, it also gives the officers a lot of hard and unpleasant work to do. And not only that, the cases are often dismissed and the officers then feel that their work was all for naught. So I think we can conclude undeniably that civil disobedience is quite unpopular with the police. [Ibid., p. 113]

Philosophy of Civil Disobedience: Thoreau and Gandhi

It should be evident from what we have said so far that civil disobedience is truly a complicated subject. It deserves study far beyond superficialities. While we cannot devote exhaustive attention to it, some further probing of it seems appropriate.

Henry David Thoreau and Mahatma Gandhi are generally thought of as leading philosophers of civil disobedience. Gandhi tested and changed his ideas on the subject time after time in the course of a lifetime of experiences; Thoreau spent one night in jail and telescoped his thinking into one great essay, *On the Duty of Civil Disobedience*. The following is an attempt to chart a comparison of some of the main ideas of the two (adapted from Raghavan N. Iyer on "Gandhi" and Harry Kalvin, Jr. on "Thoreau," in *Civil Disobedience*):

A Comparison of Philosophies

Thoreau	Gandhi
We should be men first, and subjects afterward. Undue respect for law is dangerous.	The State at no time can claim inalienable, unchallengeable authority for itself or its laws so long as it is essentially a coercive agency, even with the tacit consent of most of its citizens.
There is a need for confronting the tax-gatherer in other contexts.	Only the citizen is a moral agent who can appeal to his own conception of moral integrity and truth against the authority of the State. But only if the means one employs are non-coercive. If he employs coercive means, he puts himself on the same plane as the State.
As for adopting the ways which the State has provided for remedying the evil, I know not of such ways. They take too much time, and a man's life will be gone. I have other affairs to attend to. I came into this world, not chiefly to make this a good place to live in, but to live in it, be it good or bad. A man has not everything to do but something; and because he cannot do **everything,** it is not necessary that he should do **something** wrong.	The citizen's obligation to the authority of the State depends upon the extent to which the laws of a State are just and its acts non-repressive. Submission to the State is a price paid for an individual's personal liberty, but it is always a conditional price.

A Comparison of Philosophies (continued)

Thoreau	Gandhi
The State has no real utility. In fact, I pity it because it does not know friend from foe. The State does not have a decent, civilized purpose. To go to jail is a way of withdrawing from it. Jail is the only proper place for the just man.	Every citizen is responsible for every act of his government. A truly just and democratic State deserves active loyalty, but the citizen always retains the right to disobey particular laws that he regards as unjust and repressive.
I do not wish to be the agent, through the State, of an injustice to another, or to pursue a neutral life that lends support to the State in some sense.	The very notion of authority implies that the individual is an author and is morally autonomous in some sense; otherwise authority cannot be distinguished from force or power.
Any action to which a man adheres as a matter of conscience should be constitutionally immune from the power of the majority.	Non-violent means is essential in legitimating the right and doctrine of resistance.
Even voting **for the right** is doing nothing for it. (One must do more.)	The validity of one's appeal to one's conscience is wholly independent of social recognition.
	There is a form of resistance compatible with respect for law and order.
Civil disobedience is a form of political action. Going to jail is a means of communication, with some hope for its public effectiveness.	Non-cooperation and passive resistance are distinct from civil disobedience; the latter is a last resort by a select few—a deliberate breach of immoral statutory enactments where one invokes the sanctions of the law and invites penalties and imprisonment.
	Civil disobedience presupposes the habit of willing obedience; if a man is not respected generally as law-abiding, his act of disobedience is less authentic.
	Civil disobedience is despicable if it is a mere camouflage for some other goal or end, such as a cover for concealed violence.

A Comparison of Philosophies (continued)

Thoreau	Gandhi
There are times when the injustice is so great that a calculus of consequences of civil disobedience is not required—no possible consequences out-weigh the obligation to resist the injustice.	The civil resister is not an anarchist; he wishes to convert, not to destroy. True civil disobedience is reluctant, it is defensive, and very rare in the well-ordered State.
	Mass civil disobedience in the pure sense must be spontaneous, not organized, not manipulative.
Thoreau offers no theory on the propriety of accepting punishment. He just goes to jail because there is no apparent alternative. It is, with him, a matter of indifference, because in going to jail one is really free.	The prerequisites for civil disobedience include concern for the justice of the cause; strict non-violence in thought, speech and deed; the capacity and willingness to suffer; moral discipline; humility; and above all, self-purification by good works among the people on behalf of whom one offers resistance.
	A movement undergoes five stages: indifference, ridicule, abuse, repression and respect. If a movement breaks up at the fourth stage, it never was genuine.

It is evident that Thoreau's arguments were not analytically strong. But Gandhi recognized—as University of Chicago law professor Harry Kalven has pointed out—"that the power of civil disobedience was that it did not use entirely rational persuasion but a symbolic behavior, because there is a more immediate means of moving a person than simple rational argument."

A Question of Law

Consider what is most often challenged by an act of civil disobedience: the law. The standard definition of law is familiar: it is a rule of reason directed to the common good and promulgated by proper authority. There are questions inherent in each part of this definition. Is a given statute truly *a rule of reason?* Who determines this? By what special insights? By whose reason? Is a given statute truly *directed to the common good?* Again, who determines this? By what standards? And so on. Is a given statute truly *promulgated by proper authority?* From whence does this authority spring? Divine right of kings?

Scott Buchanan of the Center for the Study of Democratic Institutions reminds us that there are those who take seriously the theory that law-makers *discover* rather than make law, finding that genuine law is what the people *ought to want* (on "Martin Buber," in *Civil Disobedience*). This means that such things as justice, peace, freedom, and order are *discovered* as products of continuing dialogue among people of diversified background, interests, and perceptions—and this is what "the consent of the governed" in democratic, pluralistic nations should ideally achieve.

Buchanan borrows from the theology of the late Martin Buber, who set out to show how the Old Testament—the Torah—could be interpreted as a continuous dialogue between the people and God. It was through this dialogue that the Jews became the chosen people, "the people of the law." The law was not imposed by a tyrannical God, for the people talked back to Him. Buchanan concludes that the Torah is "the demonstration in dramatic form of the doctrine that law is a teacher." The law, therefore, is not dogma; it is "a question to be pursued."

Such a conception of law has weighty implications for one's perspective on civil disobedience. This is not to suggest that *any* act of protest, purportedly for "good cause," is ipso facto justifiable. But it should be apparent from our consideration so far that civil disobedience is a complex matter, in any given instance. As Buchanan observes:

> In grammatical terms, laws are obviously imperative sentences; they are, in positivistic terms, commands issued by an authority to be obeyed by subjects on pain of punishment. But if the subjects are free persons who can object, talk back, and disobey, there is at least a moment when the law is a question.... If the moment is extended, there will be an argument with many more questions, questions about the jurisdiction of the law, about the meanings of killings, stealing, lying, and adultery, about the purpose of the law and the common good. These are familiar questions in the courts and *mutatis mutandis,* for the legislature and the executive. In fact, whenever the law is in operation, it is itself a question and is up for questioning. [Ibid.]

This is not a new doctrine, nor was it invented by Buber. It is prominent in Plato, and Gandhi lived it out. Our First Amendment freedoms of speech, press, assembly, and petition are important as individual rights. But under this concept of the law, these freedoms become the "apparatus," so to speak, of the continuing dialogue, by and through which laws are learned and understood and by which—as Buchanan says—laws "become imprinted in the habits and hearts of the citizenry. *They are the means by which the laws are continually improved and adjusted to change.*" Clarence Darrow, the famous criminal lawyer of the 1920s, referred to the law as "like clothes. They should be made to fit the people they are meant to serve."

It may be appended that the current social agitation for civil rights and for peace is greatly concerned with questioning laws and policies. How else is law to be learned, in the free society? To say that this perspective on law makes it no easier for a police officer to deal with a limp civil disobedient is, indeed, to speak the truth. However, there is a certain social and moral drama in what the officer does under such circumstances, and how he does it, for in effect *we are learning law by acting out justice or injustice in the streets.*

Rationale for Civil Disobedience

Challenges to government, law, or policy are inherently threatening and invariably produce questions as to the authenticity, sincerity, or morality of a given action. How can "the real thing" be tested or evaluated? What are the conditions that distinguish ordinary infractions of the law from civil disobedience? "If everyone were to disobey the law, the results would be disastrous; consequently, nobody has that right." True or false?

Such a question goes to the heart of the civil disobedience quandary. Perhaps we can untangle a few of the knots. To repeat a point made earlier, there are many popular misconceptions of civil disobedience. It should be recognized that many protest actions are not civil disobedience. Some, in fact, are civil *obedience*—for example, distributing literature, parading with a permit, voter registration programs, teach-ins, and picketing with a permit. Another point: civil disobedience is not antilaw; it is in the democratic tradition, and in the sense of conceiving of the law as a question, perfectly compatible with the dignity of law.

From the point of view of simple morality, the question of testing a civilly disobedient action may be approached in a manner similar to the question of a "just" war. Some of the queries in such an approach would be:

Is the issue truly a grave matter? (One does not commit an act of war or an act of civil disobedience frivolously.)

Have all other reasonable, feasible, possible, conceivable means of resolving the issue been explored?

Is the act merely an excuse for violence—as Gandhi put it, "a camouflage" for some other purpose? (Does the act have an ordinary criminal intent?)

Is the act a chosen course, not accidental?

How clear is the purpose? (To call public attention to injustice, to bring about a change, etc.) Is there a reasonable chance for success in achieving the purpose?

Is one prepared to accept the consequences of the action? (One should not be surprised if one is arrested and jailed.) What harm may come to other parties as a result?

It is interesting to set these questions beside the conditions delineated by Sidney Hook (compare also with Gandhi) under which individuals—on ethical grounds—may refuse to obey a certain law:

1. It must be non-violent, peaceful not only in form but in actuality.

2. Resort to civil disobedience is never morally legitimate where other methods of remedying the evil complained of are available.

3. Those who resort to civil disobedience are duty-bound to accept the legal sanctions and punishments imposed by the laws.

4. Civil disobedience is unjustified if a major moral issue is not clearly at stake.

5. Where intelligent men of good will and character differ on large and complex moral issues, discussion and agitation are more appropriate than civilly disobedient action.

6. Where civil disobedience is undertaken, there must be some rhyme and reason in the time, place, and targets selected.

7. There is such a thing as historical timing. Will the cumulative consequences of the action, in the current climate of opinion, undermine the peace and order on which other human rights depend? ["Social Protest and Civil Disobedience"]

Martin Luther King in his *Letter From Birmingham City Jail* (April 16, 1963) wrote pertinently in this passage:

You may well ask, "Why direct action? Why sit-ins, marches, etc.? Isn't negotiation a better path?" You are exactly right in your call for negotiation. Indeed, this is the purpose of direct action. Non-violent direct action seeks to create such a crisis and establish such creative tension that a community that has constantly refused to negotiate is forced to confront the issue. It seeks so to dramatize the issue that it can no longer be ignored. . . . I have earnestly worked and preached against violent tension, but there is a type of constructive non-violent tension that is necessary for growth. Just as Socrates felt that it was necessary to create a tension in the mind so that individuals could rise from the bondage of myths and half-truths to the unfettered realm of creative analysis and objective appraisal, we must see the need of having non-violent gadflies to create the kind of tension in society that will help men rise from the dark depths of prejudice and racism to the majestic heights of understanding and brotherhood. So the purpose of the direct action is to create a situation so crisis-packed that it will inevitably open the door to negotiation.

Still in the same vein, J. L. LeGrande lists the following basic tenets in "Nonviolent Civil Disobedience and Police Enforcement Policy":

1. Governmental laws and societal practices may be evil.

2. Every individual has the right and duty to evaluate laws and practices in order to establish their moral propriety.

3. After determining that laws or practices are evil or unjust, an individual is morally obligated to resist their imposition.

4. When the traditional legal remedies have been exhausted or are ineffective, the individual must employ disobedient behavior to dramatize the injustice before society.

5. The violation or disobedience must be public and non-violent.

6. The individual must be willing to accept the legal penalties or social criticisms that follow as consequences of his acts.

Harrop Freeman of the Cornell University Law School puts it this way (in *Civil Disobedience,* pp. 2–10):

1. Civil disobedience is a recognized *procedure* for challenging law or policy and obtaining court determination of the validity thereof.

2. Theories of *jurisprudence* recognize the propriety of non-violent challenge to law or policy.

3. The *obligation to obey the law* is not absolute but relative, and allows for some forms of non-violent challenge.

4. Protests and civil disobedience should receive *protection under the First Amendment.*

5. Even if the act of protest or disobedience is found to be a technical violation of law, the purpose of the disobedience should in some instances *cause the punishment to be nominal.*

Freeman adds some helpful comments. He says that if civil disobedience were never justified, it would deaden moral and democratic sensitivity and prevent legal change. He points out that many laws are disobeyed in that they are simply ignored, without any active concern by the State. As to the argument that it would be disastrous if everyone disobeyed the law, Freeman calls this an illogical deduction from the specific to the general. The civil disobedient does not urge disobedience of all laws. He does not argue that one disobedience justifies all disobedience.

On this point, Richard Lichtman offers the following observation:

The civil disobedient can meet the argument that general civil disobedience would produce undesirable consequences only with the
counter-argument that this prospective evil is less compelling than the
gross brutality or injustice against which the act of disobedience
protests. And so, in fact, all such dissenters have contended, from
Socrates to Gandhi, that in view of the malignancy of the world, their
act of defiance is a necessary course. [In *Civil Disobedience*, p. 16]

Freeman poses the key question: how far is a society willing to go
in the latitude it permits for dissent? The minimum level is tolerance,
or forebearance without approval. As Judge Learned Hand put it:
"Liberty is so much latitude as the powerful choose to accord the
weak." A somewhat greater indulgence would be at the level of peaceful coexistence, as in Immanuel Kant: "Every action is right which, or
according to the maxim of which, the freedom of will of each can co-
exist with the freedom of everyone according to a general law." A third
level identified by Freeman is that of simple charity: love the person,
even if one disapproves of his folly or errors—and try to convert him, as
in Wordsworth: "By discipline of time made wise, we learn to tolerate
the infirmities and faults of others." At a fourth level, according to Freeman, a society might say that the individual has a *right* of dissent (and
of civil disobedience) because of the advantages to society of free and
open discussion.

Other Interpretations of Civil Disobedience

Other views of the conditions or prerequisites for civil disobedience are instructive. Bayard Rustin, who has worked in civil disobedience movements on every continent, asks these questions of the
civil disobedient:

1. Are you attempting to break a law or are you attempting, rather,
   to adhere conscientiously to a higher principle in the hope that
   the law you break will be changed and that new law will emerge
   on the basis of that higher principle?

2. Have you engaged in the democratic process and exercised the
   constitutional means that are available before engaging in the
   breaking of law? (Is what you perceive so monstrous that you do
   not believe there is time for dealing with it by constitutional
   means?)

3. Have I removed ego as much as it is possible to do so? (Or do I
   just want to get my picture in the paper?)

4. Do the people whom I ask to rebel feel there is a grievous wrong
   involved?

5. Am I prepared cheerfully to accept the consequences of my acts?

6. Am I attempting to bring about a new social order by my rebellion, or a new law that is better than the one that now exists? (Clarity of purpose). [In *Civil Disobedience*, p. 11]

Rustin says that a seventh question springs from Kant's categorical imperative: Would the world be a better place if everybody, not just in my country and not just those who are black, but everyone in the world did likewise? (What happens to war if *everyone* burns his draft card?)

Rustin's six-point rationale for civil disobedience is also of interest:

1. Civil disobedience in a democratic society is sometimes the only instrument left to dramatize the injustice that has been hidden and to bring it to the surface.

2. Civil disobedience insures religious and civil liberty as nothing else can.

3. Civil disobedience can create and establish just law when legislatures are not necessarily prepared to do it.

4. Civil disobedience forces the implementation of law that is on the books, but which, for a number of reasons, is ignored.

5. No society is safe which does not attempt to curtail civil disobedience but in which there are not individuals who will engage in it.

6. Civil disobedience often affects and directs court decisions. [Ibid., p. 12]

Another approach is taken by Richard Wasserstrom, formerly of the Stanford Law School, later dean of arts and sciences at Tuskegee Institute (in *Civil Disobedience*, pp. 18, 19). He contends that an act of civil disobedience, as differentiated from other acts of protest, must involve *disobedience of the law,* with no fudging. If an act is performed under a claim of ultimate constitutional right, it is not civil disobedience. On this point, Wasserstrom disagrees with Freeman.

Secondly, Wasserstrom stresses that the act must be one of *civil* disobedience. This means that it requires nonviolence. Force may sometimes be necessary to overcome oppression, but this is not civil disobedience. Thirdly, an act of civil disobedience must be a public rather than a private act, because its primary function is educative. Willingness to suffer legal punishment as a consequence of the illegal conduct is implied. Also implied is the necessity for prudent choice of technique and integrity of purpose. Civil disobedience involves strategy as well as moral conviction. Sincere belief alone does not justify the employment of this particular pedagogical device.

It is evident that there are some common denominators in the thinking of all whom we have quoted. However, as Wasserstrom indicates, there is no set of mechanical rules by which to determine when disobedience of the law, and particularly civil disobedience, is justified. Neither is there in any other sphere of morality.

Some Concluding Comments

Joseph Sax, professor of law at the University of Michigan, writes in *Saturday Review* on what he calls "the miracle of prosecutorial discretion," which produces or ignores criminality virtually at will. The law, he contends, is so vast in its technical coverage and so open-ended in its possibilities for interpretation by police officers, prosecutors, and judges that "it becomes almost meaningless to talk about civil disobedience as if there were conduct which 'the law'—as some external force—declared illegal." It is no easy task, Sax continues, "to make lawyers peek out from behind that supposedly value-free facade, 'the law', and begin to talk about unjust laws and unjust administration of the law; but out they must come and face the reality of prosecutorial and judicial discretion."

Sax wryly observes:

> Nobody is opposed to civil disobedience; people simply want the laws that they deem important to be vigorously enforced and those they consider unfair to be ignored. Most motorists consider the idea of a speedtrap outrageous, but rarely complain when policemen conceal themselves in public washrooms to ferret out homosexuals. The annual antics of American Legion conventioneers are viewed as harmless enough fun, but let political protestors go out in the streets and all the rigors of the law relating to trespass, obstruction of traffic, and disturbing the peace are suddenly remembered, whereupon we are solemnly told that acquiescence in illegality is the first step on the road to anarchy. ["Civil Disobedience: The Law Is Never Blind."]

There may be those who would say that we have slanted our discussion of civil disobedience.[4] While we would argue this point—our sources agree on some aspects of civil disobedience and disagree on others—there is an obligation of fairness to all sides on a subject so charged with feeling and so open to dialogue.

Following, then, is a series of excerpts from an article by Chicago attorney Morris I. Leibman, whose position may be summarized thus: the crowning achievement of the American Constitutional system has been the development of the "law society." But today this society is threatened by organized and deliberate civil disobedience justified by concepts that are semantic traps. The only enduring method of realizing the goals of those who engage in civil disobedience is the use of society's means for orderly change. In Leibman's words:

No society can give its citizens the "right" to break the law. There can be no law to which obedience is optional, no command to which the state attaches an "if you don't mind."

No individual or group at any time, for any reason, has a right to exact selfdetermined retribution. All too often, retaliation injures the innocent at random and provokes counter-retaliation against those equally innocent.... The only solution is the free and open-law society.

... Those who reject our legal methods and choose terror, force, violence, hate and bigotry only play into the hands of the international Communist conspiracy. I wish it were possible to have the ideals of justice and freedom in all their perfect form at this moment. But the cry for immediacy is the cry for impossibility. What is possible is to continue patiently to build the structures that permit the development of better justice.

We must be for equality under the rule of law. We can only be for freedom under law, not for freedom against the law. We must avoid unreal questions, e.g., is justice more important than order, or vice versa? Order is the *sine qua non* of the constitutional system.

I cannot accept the right to disobey when the law is not static, and effective channels for change are constantly available. Our legislatures have met the changing times and changing needs of our society, and our courts need not apologize for their continued dedication to the liberty of all men. Our law is not only a guardian of freedom, but the affirmative agent for freedom.

Civil disobedience is an *ad hoc* device at best, and *ad hoc* measures in a law society are dangerous. It is at best deplorable and at worst destructive. ["Civil Disobedience: A Threat to Our Law Society."][5]

Concluding our discussion of this important topic, we repeat the observation that no comprehensive, general formulas are going to resolve the infinitely varied questions that arise in connection with dissent, protest, and civil disobedience. As we have said, distinctions must be made in the kinds of actions that fall into these categories. The central question is that of the justice with which the law is enforced. Sax sums it up well:

A public less bedazzled by the mystique of "the law" and more willing to look through to the question of *justness* will inevitably be strengthened in its ability to impose upon public officials pressure to be less (or as the case may be, more) vigorous in seeking to attribute criminality to particular kinds of conduct. ... To abdicate that responsibility is only to begin the march in law-abiding lockstep toward moral oblivion. [*Saturday Review*][6]

What we are seeing in street demonstrations today leaves many observers questioning that the traditional theoretical-ethical consideration of civil disobedience is relevant. The fine-line distinctions of scholarly analysis seem far-fetched to a policeman facing an unruly mob bent on blocking a street. These circumstances are hardly conducive to philosophical "navel-gazing," the policeman might suggest. And one would be inclined to sympathize with the officer's position. But somewhat parallel circumstances have failed to discourage inquiry into the ethics of war. Scholarly perspective requires, after all, stubborn and persistent endeavor to deal rationally with behavior, and especially in circumstances where action or reaction may be regarded by some as irrational. To this end, theory and philosophy are essential, even when somewhat provocative.

Notes to Chapter Thirteen

1. Definitions used in this discussion are from *Vocabulary for Sociology* by William J. Goode. Deviant behavior is defined as action that violates a group norm or rule.

2. Stephen Slingsby, in an analysis of the Detroit riot of 1967 ("Militants vs. Traditionalists: The New Power Struggle for the Uncommitted"), distinguishes among *militants, traditionalists,* and *survivalists* in the riot situation —borrowing a typology first used by Nathan Cohen in his study of the 1965 Watts riot in Los Angeles. Slingsby said that the survivalists are alienated from urban living in every respect except "making ends meet" somehow. They believe that change cannot be effected in anything beyond one's self. The militants and traditionalists vie for control of the survivalists. Community self-regulation is the only possible buffer response, Slingsby argues, or "the next cities in which such a holocaust occurs will have to learn for themselves all the lessons that those in Watts, Newark, and Detroit should have learned for them."

3. See also Carl Bakal, "The Failure of Federal Gun Control."

4. See also Abe Fortas, *Concerning Dissent and Civil Disobedience.*

5. For those who may regard this as an "extremist" position, attention is invited to another article: Earl F. Morris, "American Society and the Rebirth of Civil Obedience."

6. Some useful guidelines for the police are suggested by Raymond M. Momboisse, "Demonstrations and Civil Disobedience."

Chapter Fourteen

Youth
and the
Police

A recurrent theme in police-community relations is that there are *particular* problems in the police relationship with youth, with the poor, and with minority groups. When these three variables are combined, the relationship problems are frequently at their worst. Our focus in this chapter will be on youth and the police. Again, this is a subject about which there is an abundance of material and some noteworthy emergent research.

Basic Considerations of Police-Youth Relationships

At the outset of a consideration of police-youth relations, several assumptions are apparent. For instance, it is given that we are especially concerned with youthful attitudes in their crucial period of "jelling," although we will give some attention to both younger and older youth. The junior high school age (11–15, approximately) seems to be especially interesting in the matter of attitudes toward all authority systems. It is further given that youthful attitudes toward the police are a specific of more general youthful attitudes toward authority systems and figures. It is also given, as an assumption not yet adequately tested by research, that youthful attitudes toward the police may vary according to the age and probably the sex, the socio-economic status, and the racial-ethnic background of particular youth. And it is given, finally, that police attitudes toward youth will also vary by circumstance and situation and tend to be in a reciprocal relationship with youthful attitudes toward the police.

Many would hold that reciprocation in the attitudes of youth and the police is one of the key elements in police and community relations. Better police-community relations in the future depend heavily on today's work in police-youth interactions. This work is too often interpreted to mean merely the prevention of juvenile delinquency, or police handling of the delinquent, or the functions of a specialist juvenile unit in a police agency. It is not our intention to turn our discussion in the direction of another analysis of delinquency and what the police should do about it. There is, however, a systemic aspect to our subject, in the sense suggested in Chapter Four, that relates to *attitudes*. Consequently, we are interested here in the social institutional (systemic) influences that bear on attitudes—family, school, religions, etc.

Attitudes Toward Authority

Recall what we said in earlier chapters about the development of attitudes toward authority. We discussed the process of *socialization* and its effects on the self-image and the key question of identity: who am I? We said that the manner in which authority is imposed upon the child early in life sets a pattern for how the child will view people in authority later in life. Without getting into the relative merits of "discipline" and "permissiveness" in rearing children, we will look at some underlying reasons for the changing attitudes toward authority and social controls and the changing role and functions of social institutions. Their relevance to the present subject requires repetition of several points made earlier.

In a simple, homogeneous, folkway society, where primary group restraints are strong, attitudes toward authority are simple and efficient because there is only one significant code or norm of behavior. Nonconformity in such a society is rare, and when it appears, the sanctions for it are immediate and often quite harsh. On the other hand, in a complex, heterogeneous, rapidly changing society, there are many dissonant attitudes toward authority, and social controls are correspondingly numerous and intricate. In such a society, there are many competing codes or norms of behavior, with mass appeals from many directions.

Plainly, the necessary balance between liberty and authority is much more difficult to achieve (because consensus is more difficult to achieve) in the urban, industrial, mobile, bureaucratic society than it is in the rural, agricultural, stable, folk society. There is also the apparent fact in today's situation that more people insist upon having something to say about issues and questions of liberty and authority. Kenneth

Boulding has observed that as the powers to control men have increased (big government, big business, etc.), the *authority* to do so is under increasingly severe challange.

What about change in the social institutions that have such a vital influence on attitudes and behavior—including, of course, attitudes toward authority? Consider, for example, the family of yesteryear in just one respect: it was multifunctional as to social, economic, religious, and educational requirements, as compared with the family of today. Or take what a man did for a living. Once, work in our society was a moral calling, a way of life and an important means of self-identity. Today one specializes, works as a cog in a bureaucracy, or loses his identity on a production line. Yesterday, government was a local affair centering in the town-meeting and the citizen felt that he had voice and vote in decision making. Today, decisions are made remotely, by "experts." Further, education beyond the early grades was once regarded as the privilege of a few rather than the expectation of most young people. And so on.

What then, in the kind of society ours has become, is the "proper" attitude toward authority and authority figures? Who decides this and how, and on the basis of what standards? Who is really to say that today's youthful attitudes toward authority are worse—or better—than yesterday's? If one contends that today's youth have less respect for law and authority than yesterday's—and that this is bad—it may reveal more about the values of the contender than it does about the values of youth.

Probing Deeper into Youth Attitudes

An eminent child psychologist, Cornell University's Urie Bronfenbrenner, writes that children *used to be* brought up by their parents. He asserts that de facto responsibility for upbringing has shifted away from the family to other settings in society where the task is not always recognized or accepted. As Bronfenbrenner states it:

> While the family still has the primary moral and legal responsibility for developing character in children, the power or opportunity to do the job is often lacking in the home, primarily because parents and children no longer spend enough time together in those situations in which such training is possible. This is not because parents don't want to spend time with their children. It is simply that conditions of life have changed. ["The Split-Level American Family"]

Professor Herbert Wright and his associates at the University of Kansas have systematically compared the daily life of children growing up in a small town with the lives of children living in a modern city or suburb. The differences are sobering. Bronfenbrenner points to how little we know about the influence of the peer group—or of television, for that matter—on the lives of young children. As for adolescents, James Coleman's studies have been helpful. Some of his conclusions were:

> The aspirations and actions of American adolescents are primarily determined by the "leading crowd" in the school society. For boys in this leading crowd, the hallmark of success was glory in athletics; for girls, it was the popular date.
>
> Intellectual achievement was a secondary value. The most intellectually able students were not getting the best grades. The classroom wasn't where the action was.
>
> Home background was the most important element in determining how well a child did at school. This was especially true for Northern whites, applied to a lesser degree to Southern whites and Northern Negroes, and was actually reversed for Southern Negroes, for whom the characteristics of the school were more important than those of the home.
>
> Such items as per pupil expenditure, number of children per class, laboratory space, number of volumes in the school library, and the presence or absence of ability grouping contributed little to the child's intellectual achievement. Teacher qualifications were more important. But the most important factor was the pattern of characteristics of other children attending the same school. If a lower-class child had schoolmates coming from more advantaged homes, he did reasonably well; if all the other children came from deprived homes, he did poorly. But the performance of advantaged children remained unaffected. Good home background appeared to be the difference. [*The Adolescent Society*]

It may be added that a number of studies show that peer pressure to engage in aggressive behavior is very difficult for teen-agers to resist in American society.

The general conclusion to be drawn from such references is that "school culture" and "peer culture" (and probably "television culture") have become exceedingly important influences on youthful behavior and attitudes—probably more important, by and large, than "family culture" or "religious culture." What are the implications of this for youthful attitudes toward the police? In the schools, we find what is called "citizenship training," concerned with the preparation of citizens for participation in democratic society—what social scientists call the *political socialization process*. There are numerous indications that this process, which is actually of lifelong duration, is not being managed very well in our society. Witness, for example, the proportion of people who do not vote in general elections. Witness the ignorance of the public

in police and governmental matters. Witness what Fred Inbau in "Lawlessness Galore" calls "the philosophy of irresponsibility and unaccount-
ability."

Generally speaking, there is widespread indication of rather adverse youthful attitudes toward the law, law enforcement, and law
enforcement officers. Studies bear this out, subject to variations by
specific age (the attitudes of grade schoolers are generally more favorable than the attitudes of high schoolers), race, socio-economic status,
etc. Police officer attitudes toward youth are also interesting to analyze;
for example, Reiss reported in his study for the President's Crime Commission (1966) that eight out of ten police officers interviewed in
Boston, Chicago, and Washington, D.C., saw juveniles as harder to
deal with today than when they started their careers as officers (Field
Surveys III, Vol. 2, Sec. II, p. 83). These policemen saw juveniles as
changing mainly in that they are more aggressive, defiant, and rebellious,
show less respect for law and authority, and that they (the juveniles)
are more aware of the restrictions that have come to be applied on
police conduct. There was some evidence that officers sometimes exacerbate their relations with juveniles by treating them with less civility than
adults, and more often as "nonpersons."

Bayley and Mendelsohn reported in their Denver study, *Minorities
and the Police* (pp. 45, 46), that policemen immediately think of two
groups in which they feel there has been a noticeable decrease in respect for the police in recent years: teen-agers and minorities. Some
14.5 percent of the officers interviewed in that study thought that teen-
agers have a *particularly* unfavorable view of the police. These officers
felt that children under twelve were the most favorably disposed; teen-
agers not in college the least well disposed; and college students somewhere in between.

Political Socialization

We have said that youthful attitudes toward the police are part of
a larger context of attitudes toward authority and political institutions.
So-called citizenship training in schools is a program in political socialization based on the assumption that attitudes can be stabilized so that
authority is obeyed because citizens learn to accept political institutions
and leaders (including policemen) as possessing legal and rightful
power. Laurence Kohlberg speaks of the person's *internalizing* the
values of the society in a sequential development ("Moral Development
and Identification in Child Psychology"). From their intensive political
socialization study of a large sample of public school children, David
Easton and Robert Hess concluded:

> Every piece of evidence indicates that the child's political world
> begins to take shape well before he even enters elementary school and
> it undergoes the most rapid change during these years . . . The truly

formative years of the maturing member of a political system would seem to be those years between the ages of three and thirteen. ["The Child's Political World"]

Much citizenship training in the primary grades in this country has been in the form of patriotic rituals and rather superficial civic instruction (see Fred I. Greenstein, *Children and Politics*). Relatively few experimental programs at this level have departed from the usual pattern. In Los Angeles, an exception to this has been the *Patrolman Bill program,* which reinforces civics lessons on safety, responsibility, law, and law enforcement. Robert Derbyshire studied this program, with some interesting results ("Children's Perceptions of the Police").

Derbyshire hypothesized a greater degree of antipathy toward police on the part of pupils of low socio-economic backgrounds, and a positive change in perception of the police on the part of those low socio-economic status pupils who took part in the Patrolman Bill program. Third grade public school pupils from three divergent ethnic and social class categories were asked to draw pictures of the policeman at work, as an art class assignment. One low socio-economic status group from Watts was asked to draw the pictures two weeks prior to Patrolman Bill's visit and on the third day following his visit. Each picture was then evaluated by four independent raters on a seven-point scale for the degree of aggressiveness, authoritarianism, hostility, kindness, goodness, strength, or anger expressed in the picture. An additional rater, working separately, performed an item analysis of police task performance on the basis of the picture's content. Comparison of ratings yielded no significant difference between the item analysis and the evaluation by the four raters on the entire field of the picture.

From the results, the image held of police behavior fell into four categories:

Aggressive: fighting, chasing, shooting

Assistance (with negative overtones): unloading a paddy wagon, searching a building, in a car with prisoners, giving traffic tickets

Neutral: walking, riding in a patrol car, directing traffic

Assistance (with positive overtones): talking with children, giving directions

In the pre- and post-test group, there was a significant shift from responses in the neutral or negative categories to the positive assistance image, which tended to verify the hypothesis that "personal contact with policemen under informal, nonthreatening conditions significantly reduces children's antipathy." Significant differences also appeared between the three highly diverse groups tested: one predominantly black and of low socio-economic status; one predominantly Spanish-speaking and of low socio-economic status; and one suburban, middle-class, white. The group from Watts expressed less antipathy toward the police after the Patrolman Bill program than was originally expressed by the most positive (white, middle class) group. Whether similar gains would hold with children of other ethnic or socio-economic backgrounds is uncertain. Just how permanent is the attitude change resulting from the program is another question, but Derbyshire cautions that ". . . experience of others who have researched attitudes and attitude change suggests that changes of this nature last only until further negative experiences."

A program similar to Patrolman Bill called *Officer Friendly* was initiated in Chicago elementary schools (along with a companion program called *Our Firefighter*) in 1966, financed largely by the Sears Roebuck Foundation. This program was subsequently launched in a number of other school systems throughout the country. The stated goals of the Officer Friendly program[1] are:

1. Providing the opportunity to develop understanding of the rights, responsibilities and obligations of living in the modern urban environment.
2. Developing rapport between the child and the uniformed officer.
3. Developing a wholesome image of the police department (and other public service agencies) in the mind of the child.
4. Reinforcing basic rules and regulations which govern experiences and activities within the child's environment.
5. Promoting interest in establishing goals and seeking positive and immediate ways of building toward their attainment.

The Officer Friendly program consists of three phases, encompassing an entire school year. The first phase is for orientation, wherein pupils and teacher become acquainted with the program by meeting Officer Friendly and by reviewing materials that lay the groundwork for Phase Two. The second phase is an instructional period in which Officer Friendly, the teacher, and the pupils participate in a structured teaching-learning experience in keeping with the purposes of the program. Phase Three is a reinforcement lesson and includes a merit award presentation conducted by Officer Friendly. At the conclusion of this final phase, all materials go home to be shared with family and friends, to acquaint those around the child with the program. The program is not an isolated unit but a resource unit to supplement the regular social studies curriculum. Unfortunately, the Officer Friendly program has not been evaluated in a manner comparable to the Derbyshire study in Los Angeles.

Other Pertinent Studies

With various associates, Robert Hess has inquired into early political socialization in a study of over 12,000 grade school children in four regions of the United States. Hess and Easton found that the phenomenon "most apparent to most children in the realm of politics" is the existence of an authority outside the family and school; this external authority is specifically represented in the Presidency and the policeman. The child becomes increasingly aware of other institutions of authority such as courts, Congress, and local elected officials as he grows older. Emotional rather than rational processes explain these cognitions of external authority; favorable feelings are developed, for instance toward the Presidency, long before concrete knowledge of it materializes.

Hess and Torney (*The Development of Political Attitudes in Children*) theorize that reciprocal role relationships are the key to political socialization, that the child learns to see his own behavior in relation to that of some other person or institution, and that role expectations are *learned*. The child learns the rights and duties of the individual in relation to the rights and duties of the system. As Hess and Torney see it, early political socialization begins with an attachment to the nation, which is stable, basic, and exceedingly resistant to change. Authority figures and institutions are perceived by the child as powerful, competent, benign, infallible, and to be trusted. Laws are just and unchangeable, with punishment inevitable for wrongdoing.

The child's points of contact with the system are persons—the President and the policeman. These later become institutions, abstractions, and the *roles* occupied by the persons. The points of contact—the President and the policeman—are also the visible authority figures, and compliance with authority and law is mediated through these figures. Hess and Torney point out that the family can also strongly influence attitudes toward authority, roles, and compliance. While the family and strong authority figures influence *attitudes,* the school appears to be the primary source for content, information, and concepts. For children of low socio-economic class status, it may be the *only* such source, as Coleman also concluded. The Hess-Torney study indicates that the school is a "central and dominant force in the political socialization of the young child," and that the period between grades three and five is especially important in acquiring political information.

Where and how, then, do significant attitude changes occur? First, Hess and Torney point out, there is a fund of positive feeling for the government, especially for the President, which extends to include law, as we have noted. Secondly, the child's socialization occurs through a "core" of respect for power wielded by authority figures, especially police. But some strain in this image gradually develops. While the school presents a positive image of the policeman, the child discovers early that the police have the duty, not only to capture lawbreakers, but also to *punish* lawbreakers. This discovery leads to mixed feelings about the police—a beginning in what we earlier identified as the adversary concept. There follows, thirdly, experience in compliant roles at home and school—and finally, normative belief that all systems of rules are fair (see Hess and Torney, HEW Report, 1965).

Easton and Dennis did some extensive work with political socialization data, especially as it relates to the police officer (HEW Final
Report, 1968). A free-drawing exercise was utilized as an exploratory
instrument in which more than 600 elementary school children drew
pictures of various authority figures. Evaluation of the pictures was done
on the basis of content; for example, whether the policeman was seen
as performing a protective, prohibitive, or punitive activity. Over 50
percent of the resultant drawings emphasized prohibitive or punitive
activity, which suggested that the policeman's capacity to direct and
punish emerged as salient to the child. The policeman also appeared in
the drawings as physically dominant, being drawn several times larger
than such comparison objects as an automobile or other people. The
policeman was also portrayed as physically and verbally active. Crime
detection and prevention activities seldom appeared in the drawings,
which suggested that the children were not aware of the police playing
such roles.

On a questionnaire rating, 78 percent of the second graders and
68 percent of the third graders thought the policeman "can make many
people do what he wants." Of the fourth graders tested, 66 percent
thought the policeman "can punish many people." Easton and Dennis
(p. 199) concluded that "the child is impressed with the presence of
a power over and beyond that of father or mother and one that even
parents, as potent as they may appear to the child, cannot escape."
Policemen are seen as the "seed out of which a sense of the legitimacy
of the authority structure springs." Through the policeman, the child
"is encouraged in the belief that external authority should and must be
accepted," which reinforces a similar posture he is earlier encouraged to
adopt toward the President and the government.

Lending further legitimacy to the policeman in the child's eyes is
the affective impression of benevolence and dependability. However,
these feelings were highly ambivalent, as indicated by the way the children rated the policeman on the questionnaire. For example, while 71
percent of second graders thought the police "would always want to
help me if I needed it," and another 14 percent said "almost always",
they rated the policeman very low in such statements as "I like him"
and "is my favorite."

The conflict here, according to Easton and Dennis (p. 217) is
between the punitive cognitive image and the affective impression of
benevolence and dependability. Nonetheless, they concluded that the
children in general had a fairly high level of respect for the policeman.

Moral Development

Laurence Kohlberg characterizes society as a system of defined
complementary roles, in a manner similar to that of Hess and Torney.[2]
In becoming socialized into the system, the child must implicitly take the

role of others toward himself and toward others in the group. These *role-taking* tendencies, representing various patterns of shared or complementary expectations, form the basis of all social institutions, according to the Kohlberg theory.

In the Kohlberg study, the moral development (attitudes and values concerning right and wrong, good and bad) of 75 boys was observed at 3-year intervals over a 12-year period. In addition, cross-cultural studies were carried out in several foreign countries. Kohlberg concluded that moral development is an invariant sequence of six stages, coming one at a time and always in the same order. This sequential nature of moral development did not vary by countries, therefore does not appear to be culture-bound. Only the *rate* of development varied.

The six stages may be classified at three levels: pre-conventional, conventional, and post-conventional. At the pre-conventional level (ages 4–10, with significant growth from age 8), "good" and "bad" are interpreted in terms of physical consequences regardless of human meaning or value, or in terms of the physical power of those who enunciate the rules and the labels of good and bad. Toward the end of this period, reciprocity develops, but on a pragmatic quid pro quo basis. At stage three (conventional level), "good" is what pleases or helps others and is approved by them; the child conforms to stereotypical images of what is majority or "natural" behavior.

Maintenance of the status quo is perceived as valuable in its own right at stage four. The post-conventional level is characterized by a major thrust toward autonomous moral principles with validity and application apart from the authority of groups or persons who hold them, and apart from the individual's identification with these persons or groups. Stage five is the "official" morality of American government as embodied in the Constitution, with a "social contract" orientation defining "right" actions in terms of standards critically examined and agreed upon by the whole society. Stage six is oriented toward decisions of conscience and toward "self-chosen ethical principles appealing to logical comprehensiveness, universality and consistency"—principles such as justice, the reciprocity and equality of human rights, and respect for the dignity of human beings as individual persons.

The development of attitudes and values appears to be related to cognitive development, with increasing differentiation and increasing integration at the various stages. Kohlberg theorizes that the reason for the invariant developmental sequence, regardless of culture, is that "each step is a better cognitive organization than the one before it." Each stage takes account of everything present in the previous stage, but the child makes new distinctions and organizes into a "more comprehensive or more equilibrated structure."

As an afterthought regarding programs of the Patrolman Bill and Officer Friendly type, it may be noted that we do not know enough about the role played by the "socializers"—teachers, policemen, and parents—and the extent to which such programs affect *their* attitudes. This would appear to be a *probable* correlative of the effects upon the attitudes of the children. It is surprising how much such programs often teach the socializers about political institutions; also, teacher and parent attitudes toward police, and police officer attitudes toward teachers and parents, are worthy of study, particularly as they might influence children's attitudes.

William Dienstein's work might be mentioned in this regard. He found something of the same conflict as Pfiffner did in the relationships among police, social workers, educators, and probation officers Dienstein's primary interest was in the causes of delinquency, and he concluded:

> ... while each agency is dealing with delinquency, and each may handle the same violator, their approaches to the same problem tend to take on polar aspects—control and punishment on the one hand, and treatment on the other—and they find no route to mutual understanding, communication, or cooperation. Working thus, at cross purposes, they cannot hope to succeed. ["Conflict of Beliefs About Causes of Delinquency"][3]

If these conflicting patterns and goals of behavior (in Pfiffner's terms, the police-rehab conflict) are based on significantly different interpretations of the needs and characteristics of youngsters themselves, the socialization process may be correspondingly unsuccessful. In short, it is possible that some of the ambivalence that develops in the attitudes of children toward the police and other authority figures may be due to divergent and conflicting values of the several occupations working with youth.

Other Pertinent Research

Other significant studies bearing on youthful attitudes toward the police give plentiful evidence that adults and youth are not in meaningful contact and that adults admit their inability to understand certain youthful behavior. Various analysts have identified a distinctive adolescent subculture, Franklin Patterson (*The Adolescent Citizen*) and James Coleman (*The Adolescent Society*) among them. We have already mentioned some of Coleman's thinking, to which may be added:

> With his fellows, he (the adolescent) comes to constitute a small society, one that has most of its important interactions within itself, and maintains only a few threads of connection with the outside adult society.

John Clark and Eugene Wenninger's findings regarding the attitudes of juveniles toward legal institutions support the notion of a general "anti-authority syndrome" on the part of juveniles and a common rejection and hostility toward certain juveniles on the part of parents, school teachers, and representatives of legal institutions ("The Attitude of Juveniles Toward the Legal Institutions"). Clark and Wenninger found that socio-economic class was not closely related to the attitudes of youth toward legal institutions. But there were notable differences in such attitudes in different communities they studied.

A Detroit study by William Wattenberg and Noel Bufé concluded that time spent by a police officer with youth is highly influential in favorably affecting the attitudes of youth toward the police and legal institutions ("The Effectiveness of Police Youth Bureau Officers"). Other studies—for instance, of the Youth Service Corps project of the Detroit Police Department, and of the "Positive Actions For Youth" project in Flint, Michigan—reach the same conclusion. But in the Detroit program, a significant percentage of the youths maintained a negative attitude toward policemen, including 10 percent who did not believe that policemen are necessary in society, and 12 percent who felt that policemen do more harm than good. David Krebs found a group of delinquency-prone youths who were not amenable to positive change because of a lack of relational ability in their personality background ("Perceptual Defense in the Delinquent Child"). (*See also* the study by Brendan Maher, and Ellen Stein, "The Delinquent's Perception of the Law and Community.")

Many empirical studies have dealt with intergenerational conflict. Gerald Pearson, for example, extensively discusses it in *Adolescence and Conflict of Generations;* he holds that the conflict arises from the emerging ego development of the adolescent in interaction with the older generation, which manifests stubborn resistance to the development of a personal identity and the assumption of adult roles by the adolescent. Amos and Washington discuss the differences between teachers and pupils in identifying student problems. In this study, "A Comparison of Pupil and Teacher Perceptions of Pupil Problems," teachers identified fewer problems as characteristic of students than did the students themselves and appeared especially unaware of the extent of student problems in regard to such matters as money, work, the future, and health and physical development.

Junior High School Youth

It was mentioned earlier that the junior high school or middle school age group (11–15) is widely regarded as especially relevant in the study of changing youthful attitudes toward the police and authority in general. Several notable studies with this focus have been undertaken. Robert Portune studied 1,000 Cincinnati junior high school students in what is generally regarded as the pioneer research of this type (reported in *Changing Adolescent Attitudes Toward Police*),[4] and he and his associates have continued to plow new ground in subsequent project activity.

His investigations provide evidence that the beat patrolman lacks clear understanding of adolescent behavior and, correspondingly, that adolescents appear to have little understanding of the police officer in his role. Portune writes:

> The obligation to develop favorable attitudes toward law enforcement is especially pressing in the junior high school. Junior high school students are in a transition period, breaking away from the opinions of mom and pop, trying to fit society to their own personalities and egos, developing their own attitudes toward the world around them. I think we have to catch them at this age. School people are more and more coming to the realization that early adolescence is a key period in life, especially with respect to attitude formation. Thus, with the school's growing responsibility for attitude formation and the junior high school youngster's growing importance, our target group seems well chosen.

> . . . .

> Perhaps there are isolated social studies programs in isolated school districts that concentrate on the particular institutions of law enforcement—perhaps there are programs designed to build favorable attitudes toward police—if so, such programs are not widespread, their development is often unscientific, their evaluation is questionable. It is in the approach to attitudes through attitude research that we hope to achieve our objectives. [Ibid.]

Portune found inconclusive evidence as to the effect of socio-economic level on attitudes of youth toward police. This coincides with the Clark and Wenninger finding. However, Donald Bouma (*Kids and Cops*) and his associates found—in studying junior high school youth in several Michigan cities—an inverse relationship between social class and antagonistic attitudes toward police among adolescents.

Relying considerably on Portune's work, Martin Miller and associates at the National Center on Police and Community Relations at Michigan State University conducted a study of Lansing junior high school youth in 1968. They developed a design for evaluation, in terms of attitude change among pupils, of a unit of instruction in citizenship education, placed in the curriculum of four Lansing junior high schools during the school year 1967–68. The actual instruction was handled by police-teacher teams over a period of four weeks for the entire unit. The evaluation design was a test-retest, longitudinal pattern with a control group provision. The instruments used included a general information sheet, the Short-Nye Self-Reporting Delinquency Scale (1958), the Portune Attitude-Toward-Police Scale (1966), the Clark Attitudes Toward Legal-Institutions Scale (1964), the Rokeach Value Survey (1967), and a sentence completion technique tailored for the project by the research team.

An indication of one aspect of the results of this study has been provided in earlier references to the values of police officers.[5] Beyond this, the MSU study found that the values of teachers and police officers who work with children come across "loud and clear" to the children and are reflected in children's attitudes toward what the study calls "compliance systems." The research also disclosed slightly positive changes in children's attitudes toward the police as a result of the instruction and suggested that the socio-economic background of the children did not appear to be a significant factor in these attitudes, although the MSU researchers agreed with Portune that the evidence was inconclusive.

Gang Attitudes

Gang culture and its indigenous attitudes toward police and legal institutions is a matter for special attention in the consideration of police-youth relations. We have suggested some of the flavor of this in various places in this text. A study of black, teen-age gangs appears in *The Police and the Community: Studies,* Part III (Radelet and Reed). Attention is also invited to a number of valuable works dealing with the gang.[6]

One aspect of the matter, strongly suggested by gang culture and previously mentioned, merits brief reconsideration in our discussion at this point, because it appears to be of such singular importance. The point is one analyzed by James Q. Wilson, Jerome Skolnick, and others. It pertains to the patrolman's "signals" of *danger* and *impropriety* in confronting a citizen. As Wilson puts it:

> The patrolman believes with considerable justification that *teenagers* [italics ours], Negroes, and lower-income persons commit a disproportionate share of all reported crimes; being in those population categories at all makes one, statistically, more suspect than other persons; but to be in those categories *and* to behave unconventionally is to make one a prime suspect. [*Varieties of Police Behavior,* pp. 40, 41]

As we have seen, this has to do with the patrolman's stance in "handling the situation" on the street. But as Wilson observes, from the standpoint of those who are "handled," it appears as license for the policeman "to speak harshly or discourteously, to search without cause, and to behave in a patronizing manner." And in the extreme case, it means actually to be manhandled physically. Resentment about this kind of treatment is likely to be keen among young men on the street, especially when they are associated in gangs.

Alvin Echols has pointed to a related aspect of the matter:

> Young people are rebelling against the hypocrisy of a society that sets certain values and then lives up to their opposite. Young black offenders can find few good examples inside or outside their community, while the conditions which make delinquent acts an attractive choice are created and maintained by the entire society. The strategy

set up by the society to contain black juvenile delinquency has three elements: the deadline—keeping blacks in black neighborhoods; vengeance—a judicial and confinement system that punishes and does not rehabilitate; and tribute—programs to buy off trouble temporarily. This strategy has worked only in the sense of making poor blacks the most frequent victims of black juvenile crime. The blame for the strategy's failure to reduce crime has been placed on the black culture rather than the society that devised the strategy and carries it out. ["Deadline, Vengeance, and Tribute"]

Disaffected Youth

This brings us to the matter of disaffected youth, particularly in the sense related to the civil rights movement of the 1960s. Youthful disaffection with "the Establishment" is, of course, not a new phenomenon, nor is it something uniquely American. But it did assume a character in this country during the past decade that was in some respects unprecedented. It surely has troubled many people, not least of all the police, who are invariably involved whenever *what is* comes under serious challenge by significant numbers of the population bent upon change to what they believe *ought to be*.

Recent years have seen an impressive assortment of studies, analyses, dissertations, and "pundit-ry" pertaining to the youth problem. Again, as with race relations, we seem to understand pretty well what the problem is. At least there is an abundance of plausible diagnostic theory. The difficulty, as with race, ecology, and poverty, is that we seek to solve the problem without seriously disturbing anyone or without changing the things that most desperately need changing. As Echols says, we mount programs to buy off trouble temporarily—programs that deal with symptoms rather than with causes—programs of the "too little and too late" variety.

When we speak of "the youth problem," what are we talking about exactly, and what has it to do with police and community relations? By and large, it appears that youth today—and we have in mind particularly youth of high school and college age—are better educated, more morally and politically sophisticated than past generations. Any such generalization will be questioned by some who may ask, for instance, "what do you mean by 'morally and politically sophisticated'?" Nonetheless, we will stand by the hypothesis, substantiated by evidences of the idealism of youth, as reflected in youthful participation in the civil rights movement, in antiwar protest, in ecological-environmental and Peace Corps programs, and in sundry activities that have prodded universities and other "Establishment" institutions to do some long overdue thinking, evaluating, and changing. We think this is moral and political sophistication, however erratic and amateurish.

As Skolnick says, such direct action by youth—with the increasing disaffection of student activists, their pessimism over the possibility of genuine reform, and frequent resort to tactics of confrontation—cannot be explained away as "hi-jinks", or as a matter simply of personality maladjustment, or of youthful intransigence ("boys will be boys," etc.), or simply as delinquency (*The Politics of Protest*, Chap. III). The ideology of youthful protest and activism has focused on several identifiable areas. One is clearly civil rights and race relations. Another is war —war in general in the case of pacifists, the war in Southeast Asia more particularly with youth who are not necessarily pacifists—Selective Service, ROTC, the "military-industrial complex," the Pentagon, etc.

Still another focus has been environmental and ecological problems. Women's liberation has attracted some youthful activists; a few have gravitated to organizations such as FREE (Fight Repression of Erotic Expression). Common ideological ground for all youthful activists has been villification of the "despicable" police. Campus encounters between the police and demonstrators have frequently been vitriolic, and sometimes intensely violent, and have tended to reinforce perceptions on both sides that aggravate tensions and make even minimal communication unthinkable. In such circumstances, the "generation gap" becomes a horrendous abyss. We quoted Seymour Lipset earlier in his characterization of these confrontations as "the most extreme example of deliberate provocation which the police have ever faced." Lipset elaborated:

> It is doubtful that the American New Left students will ever come to see the police in a sympathetic light, as exploited, insecure, alienated members of the under-privileged classes. As members of the first leftist youth movement which is unaffiliated with any adult party, they are unconcerned with the consequences of their actions on the political strength of the larger left-wing movement. To a large extent, their provocative efforts reflect the biases of the educated upper middle class. Lacking a theory of society and any concern for the complexities of the "road to power" which have characterized the revolutionary Marxist movement, they are prepared to alienate the police, as well as conventional working-class opinion, in order to provoke police brutality, which in turn will validate their total rejection of all social institutions. Hence, we may expect a continuation of the vicious circle of confrontation and police terror tactics. ["Why Police Hate Liberals," p. 83][7]

Campus Unrest

The Kerner Commission (National Advisory Commission on Civil Disorders) underlined the youthful thrust of the civil rights movement in the 1960s. According to this Commission, it was college student sit-

ins in the South during the winter and spring of 1960 that marked a decisive break with the past. Even though student demonstrations in the
South ended in what seemed to be failure in many cases, the participating youth "had captured the imagination of the Negro community and
to a remarkable extent the whole nation." The Commission went on to
say in its 1968 Report (p. 107):

> The Southern college students shook the power structure of the
> Negro community, made direct action temporarily preeminent as a
> civil rights tactic, speeded up the process of social change in race
> relations, and ultimately turned the Negro protest organizations toward
> a deeper concern with the economic and social problems of the masses.
>   Involved in this was a gradual shift in both tactics and goals:
> from legal to direct action, from middle and upper class to mass
> action, from attempts to guarantee the Negro's constitutional rights to
> efforts to secure economic policies giving him equality of opportunity,
> from appeals to the sense of fair play of white Americans to demands
> based upon power in the black ghetto.

The point is that the civil rights movement of the 1960s was
largely a *youth* movement. Studies of serious riot and disorder situations
in 1967–68 pointed out the high proportion of youth and young people
participating. The student movement in civil rights revolutionized the
existing structure of Negro civil rights organizations. For instance, the
organizing meeting of the Student Nonviolent Coordinating Committee
(SNCC), at Raleigh, North Carolina, in April, 1960, was convened by
Martin Luther King, but within a year this group considered King too
conservative and broke with him.

The President's Commission on Campus Unrest,[8] in 1970 in the
aftermath of the tragedies in the spring of that year at Kent State University and at Jackson State and the attendant student strikes and class
boycotts on many campuses, listened to witness after witness attribute
the main causes of student demonstrations and disorders to problems of
the larger society: the war in Vietnam, racial discrimination, poverty,
pollution of the environment, etc. This Commission carried on its work
under difficult conditions: a combination of intense emotionalism and
great complexity in the nature of the problem it was charged to study,
plus the coincidence of its investigations with an "off-year" national
political campaign. Chairman William W. Scranton warned that "playing
politics with the problems is to guarantee further alienation and radicalization of young people" (*The New York Times,* September 24, 1970,
p. 28). He may have had in mind the words of President John F. Kennedy, spoken to the Organization of American States ten years earlier:
"Those who make peaceful revolution impossible make violent revolution inevitable."

The general theme of the Commission's report on campus unrest
was that there is blame enough for all, and it appealed to all sectors to

join urgently in national reconciliation. As usual, there was an inordinate preoccupation, in the wake of publication of the Commission's Report, with ascribing blame for the problem: the President, the administration, "permissive" parents, university administrators and faculty, the students, the police, the National Guard, an apathetic public. Again, "to pin it on somebody" seemed to be more important than understanding the problem and taking steps to deal with it. So it is that existing divisions are aggravated.

The Commission recommended that police and National Guard forces be better trained to deal with campus disturbances in a firm but nonlethal manner. It also called for greater coordination between local, state, and college security forces and clearer guidelines for action in campus disorder situations. It held that those who commit criminal acts should be sternly prosecuted. It asked universities to spell out specific codes of permissible conduct and pleaded for more effective self-policing by faculty, students, and administrators. It urged more Federal support for higher education, particularly for Negro colleges. The nation's slow response to the issues of war and race, the Commission said, had contributed to the escalation of student disorder. Moral leadership from the President was cited as essential in preventing violence and creating understanding.

Clearly, the Commission on Campus Unrest repeated and emphasized points that had been made earlier by other bodies and sources. The conflict in cultures between the young and the old had been identified in many quarters. The racist character of American society had been rather thoroughly analyzed by the Kerner Commission. President Johnson's Crime Commission had been concerned about such things as the need for greater coordination and better training of police operations and personnel. The violence phenomenon had been the focal concern of another Presidential Commission. All of these Commissions had, in one way or another, pointed to the signs of corrosion in America's social institutions. In 1968, the Carnegie Commission on Higher Education had recommended increased Federal aid to colleges and universities with emphasis on equal opportunity for low income students, easing problems of minority students, and spreading the community college movement to all the states.

Indeed, in July 1970—several months before issuance of the report of the Commission on Campus Unrest—Presidential advisers Alexander Heard and James Cheek had called for greater awareness of student attitudes and more student participation in the formulation of foreign and domestic governmental policies. Their memoranda described the deep moral commitment underlying student revolt, its seriousness of purpose, and its sincere intent to eliminate what students believe to be weaknesses in American society. In effect, the Heard-Cheek message was this: our youth are trying desperately to tell us something of great importance; let us listen to them, and let us be guided by their counsel "as full-fledged constituents of government" (*Time,* August 3, 1970, p. 9).

The Heard-Cheek memoranda also spoke of four basic causes of "the communication problem" with college youth:

1. The President uses words that mean one thing to him and something different to many students.

2. What the President regards as successes, students often regard very differently.

3. To some students, the President appears not to understand the nature of the crisis that has come over the country.

4. The President and some students proceed from vastly different assumptions.
[*U.S. News & World Report,* August 3, 1970, pp. 28, 29]

It should be borne in mind that Heard and Cheek were special Presidential advisers; their recommendations focused on what they saw as a need for Presidential initiative in various facets of the situation.

In a survey conducted for the President's Commission on Campus Unrest by the Urban Institute, a Washington research organization, it was disclosed that:

Campus disturbances had occurred most often at large, eastern, liberal arts colleges with high admission standards and ROTC programs.

The three reasons most frequently cited by college administrators, faculty and students for campus disturbances were the war in Indochina, lack of internal campus communication, and the perceived unresponsiveness of the Federal government to domestic problems.

Only 22 percent of the smallest colleges reported incidents of any kind, compared with 60 percent for the largest colleges.

Violent incidents and incidents of all types occurred about twice as often in liberal arts colleges and those with relatively high spending per student, compared with other categories. [*The New York Times,* November 5, 1970]

Few observers analyzed the situation as astutely as Terry Sanford, president of Duke University and former governor of North Carolina. To the quotation from a statement by him that we cited in Chapter Eleven, we may now add:

This college generation needs no apologist. These students are more closely allied than we might realize with that remarkable group of men who rethought all prior concepts and precepts of government, and then produced our Consitution nearly two hundred years ago. Their instincts are humanitarian. They are convinced that the individual is the denominator that counts. They take their freedoms very seriously, although sometimes a little too self-consciously. In the students' rethinking of our institutions and society, we may all be the beneficiaries. [*The New York Times,* November 17, 1970, p. 43]

Crisis of the Universities

What campus unrest during the past few years has done to the colleges and universities is a topic about which much has been said and written. The nature of the new crisis of the universities is suggested by Notre Dame's president, Father Theodore Hesburgh in an address to the Notre Dame faculty:

> . . . young people in the universities do not realize how much the university depends upon the support of the larger surrounding society. Even less do they understand that when their frustrations about the problems of the larger community lead them to act in anger and, at times, with violence, there is only one normal response from that larger community, namely, counterviolence and repressive action. [*The New York Times,* October 17, 1970, p. 29]

Father Hesburgh further stated that some punitive legislation against faculty and students had been considered in the summer of 1970 in almost every state—about half of which had been enacted into law. The resignations of a number of college presidents had been forced, and some presidents simply quit because of what they felt was the hopelessness of their responsibility. Both Federal and state programs of support for higher education had been reduced or tied to impossible conditions. Private colleges and universities were finding it increasingly difficult to hold the support they had, much less to augment it. Father Hesburgh concluded:

> Maybe the university is the only place on earth where we can bridge the generation gap by common moral concern on the part of young and old, faculty and students. Granting that students are often naive in their concern for instant solutions to very complicated problems, granting their addiction to absolute black and white judgments in matters that are often very gray, granting their lack of a sense of history, their rupture with tradition, and their inability to appreciate experience and competence, they still are concerned and are unafflicted by the anomie that is the cancer of so many of their elders. [Ibid.]

Issues of academic freedom, the politicization of the university, and latitude for political dissent are at the center of the higher education maelstrom. Generally, however, many academicians believed that student protests had breathed refreshing life into the campus—

> . . . forcing changes that, in retrospect, are clearly valuable but might not have come for years without student pressure. Most believe, too, that campus violence can be isolated and checked if not entirely eliminated. But educators are acutely aware that the colleges and universities have barely begun to deal with their momentous problems

of money, size, structure and curriculum. And even should they solve these internal difficulties, they would still face the external problems of society that are essentially beyond their control. If universities are social barometers, they are surely predicting storms ahead. [*Newsweek,* June 15, 1970, p. 72][9]

One further reference may be of interest. In the early Fall of 1970, the results of a study of the attitudes of almost 7,000 junior and senior high school students in Greater New York and Philadelphia were announced by the sponsor, the Center for Research and Education in American Liberties, Teachers College, Columbia University. This study, done with a grant from the U.S. Office of Education, found that most student unrest *at the high school level* is not basically over racial and national political issues. This marks a difference between high school and college unrest. More than 50 percent of the high school students surveyed stressed issues of school governance and individual rights as sources of conflict (*The New York Times,* September 22, 1970, p. 29). These high school students reported that 68 percent of their "hang-ups" were with persons in authority, and only 20 percent with their peers. The Columbia University researchers concluded:

> In all schools, in the urban ghetto and suburbs, the incidents of conflict reported by students involve school governance. Of all American institutions, it is particularly ironical that the one institution charged with the mission of teaching democracy is usually perceived by the student as one that leaves him powerless.

Grayson Kirk, president emeritus of Columbia University, expressed concern for the widening gulf between scientists and humanists in modern society and, at the same time, for the growing cleavage between the university world and the Government:

> Somehow, because our universities and our Government are ever more interdependent, campus rifts between radicals and conservatives and between the humanities and the sciences must be diminished. Interference by public authorities in university affairs ought to be limited to support for the academic authorities in their efforts to free the campus from disorder. Our universities are too important to be allowed to suffer from the activities of a small group of men who seek to distort the spirit of a university and who, in their mistaken efforts, have been allowed to benefit from the healthy tradition of academic tolerance. ["Limits of Academic Tolerance"]

Some Causes and Remedies

As a result of studies we have so far noted, the broad aspects of campus upheaval have become rather familiar. But more specific diagnosis of the causes may be profitable. Kenneth Keniston of Yale University emphasizes the need for dealing justly with student grievances. (Keniston and Kerner, "The Unholy Alliance Against the Campus").[10] He thinks that student activism is here to stay, and we should become reconciled to it. He urges the establishment of new codes of student government, reflecting joint efforts of students, faculty, and administration.

Keniston has stressed that the overwhelming majority of campus protests in recent years have been peaceful, orderly, and clearly within the boundaries of dissent protected by the First Amendment. Violent and disorderly protests have been the exception, not the rule. However, he points out that these campus protests have been increasingly concerned with social, political and off-campus issues; that where violence has occurred, it has become increasingly intense; that students show diminishing confidence in the ability of established institutions to achieve social changes that students consider increasingly necessary; and that there are emergent radical student elements quite willing to use violence systematically.

These are the reasons, Keniston believes, why the impression has been created that an ever-larger proportion of campus protest involves illegality and disorder—these factors, plus the rhetoric of politicians and selective reporting by the mass media. As a result, the issue has been typically oversimplified. The vast majority of American students have been caught in a pincer movement between the extreme left and the extreme right, while remaining committed to peaceful dissent.

Keniston thinks that extremist critics of campus discipline, both of the right and the left, are incorrect. As a rule, campus officials have dealt quite firmly with violent, illegal protests, with only a few, media-dramatized exceptions. Neither does he agree with those who say that student demonstrators have been coddled by civil authorities. Police, he says, have overreacted far too often, but this has scarcely been the norm. The evidence is to the contrary. Also incorrect, Keniston asserts, is the extremist charge that faculty members indoctrinate students with revolutionary or violent ideas. The study by the Carnegie Commission on Higher Education found that faculty people are generally conservative, defending institutional neutrality and strongly opposed to disruption and violence. Just as false is the charge by the radical left that higher education indoctrinates students with a military-industrial, racist-imperialist mentality. Again, Keniston cites contrary indications.

Finally, Keniston discounts with well-documented argument the charge of extremists that the universities have been politicized. He says, rather, that the greatest danger of such politicization today comes from a public rapidly being persuaded that universities are centers of sedition and causes of unrest. Another danger would be that there might develop on American campuses "a climate of opinion so unanimous that active discussion of some issues would be effectively silenced."

Keniston concludes his analysis with three points:

Campus protesters tend to be better students than non-protesters.

To bar the protest-prone from campuses would deprive society, in addition to being illegal. Peaceful protest and non-violent dissent are essential to the vitality of this nation.

Higher education must be reformed to serve society better, not destroyed as a scapegoat for national problems.

Another view of the campus scene is that of Sidney Hook of New York University. He rejects the notion that campus peace depends on solving the nation's problems. He told the President's Commission on Campus Unrest that:

There will always be social and foreign policy problems in an open society of uncoerced opinion . . . so that we are confronted by [the prospect] of unending academic violence if we accept this view. [*The New York Times,* August 7, 1970, p. 30][11]

Hook contends that students have no more right to coerce a university than trade unionists or farmers have to coerce their adversaries. He sides with Keniston in advocating a strengthened system of campus government and spells out a plan for an academic court to hear cases and impose sanctions in matters of faculty-student discipline. Hook's ideas on this were widely circulated, at the behest of President Nixon. In the event of campus disruptions, Hook recommends a corps of student-faculty marshals—and if this is not enough, court injunctions. If an injunction were disregarded, civil officials should then enter the case, accompanied by student-faculty marshals, with force kept to a minimum.

In 1970, Hook initiated an organization called "University Centers for Rational Alternatives," comprising some 2,000 faculty members at about 200 colleges and universities, whose objective is to put the Hook recommendations to work on campus. Hook's philosophical foundationstone is the preservation of academic freedom. Politicization of the university would seriously erode this, Hook believes; hence, his stress on handling protest and dissent peacefully, within an internal disciplinary-governmental system on each campus.

Hook's colleague at New York University, Ernest Van Den Haag, in "America's No. 1 Dilemma," explained general unrest that pervaded America in 1969 as the result of the erosion of authority in our social institutions—homes, churches, government, and especially schools and colleges. Van Den Haag has this to say about the stance of "student rebels":

. . . in a democracy the law is ideally the expression of the majority's will. Opponents are allowed opportunity to change the law peacefully—

that is, by persuading the majority to their own view. But to give opponents the right to achieve by violence what the unpersuaded majority rejects is to give the minority the right to impose its will on the majority. The situation can only lead to tyranny by the minority, for the minority cannot keep itself in power and impose laws that the majority does not want except by oppression and restriction of the majority's freedom. [Ibid., p. 39]

Leo Rosten ("Who Speaks for the Young?") places "the young and their problems" in a perspective that would please many observers. His first point is that the vast majority of America's young do not support self-selected "spokesmen." Militants, they claim, do not speak for them. The so-called "generation gap," Rosten contends, is much smaller than we assume. Samuel Lubell's interviews show that only 10 percent of college youth are in disagreement with their parents. Cynicism, Rosten says, is much more a problem of the young than of the old. Money and affluence do not hamper happiness, except among masochists. If stereotypes and status symbols are to be condemned, Rosten wishes to point out that they are most conspicuous among the young.

Rosten further states that the system has legal, flexible, peaceful (albeit slow) methods by which it can be changed. If "the pigs go, who will protect the youthful revolutionaries from the wrath of [their] opponents, many of whom are as violent and sadistic as [they]?" Not all the faults and misery are in "the system." Some of the sources of discontent surely fester within young people, Rosten declares, through youth's inevitable frustrations and sense of inadequacy, and concludes:

I find it tragic to see students rampage like mindless buffaloes. It is heartrending to see "mind-freeing" drugs induce a premature senility. I think obscenity is neither art, liberation nor "honesty." ("Hypocrisy" is often only gentleness, compassion, decorum.) It is mindboggling to see yammering young herds lockstep to the tyranny of gurus who say "Do your own thing," but mean "Conform to our eccentricities."

Tune in to truth. Turn on—to free yourself from the platitudes, the hysteria, the delusions of your sad and (I think) sick "spokesmen." [Ibid., p. 18]

The Fall of 1970

The Spring of 1970 having been as turbulent as it was on American college campuses—with the tragedies of Kent State and Jackson State, and widespread student strikes and class boycotts—anxious educators wondered, in September, what the new academic year would bring. A total of 524 institutions had experienced disruptive protests during the 1969–70 school year, with 14 deaths and more than $9 million in property damage.

There was hope for comparative calm. Mass violence often has a traumatizing effect for a period of time, when its cost has been calculated and its horror more rationally realized. Also, many students had come out of the previous spring's upheavals with the conclusion that they had been manipulated by extreme radicals. There were signs that these radicals were quarreling among themselves. Their motives began to look more like commotion than reform. Further, important changes had been instituted in many colleges, to meet legitimate student complaints and to improve communication between students and officials. College administrators had learned something about how to deal more sensibly and sensitively with student grievances, and campus security arrangements had been considerably improved.

Moreover, some faculty members, after a summer of meditation, came to recognize that academic freedom and intellectual pursuit require a peaceful, noncoercive environment. For example, the president of the American Sociological Association, Reinhard Bendix of the University of California, addressing the annual meeting of that association in Washington in early September, criticized those who would "turn the nation's universities into convenient battle-grounds." The function of a university, he said, is to produce knowledge; "political problems are for politicians to solve" (*The New York Times,* September 1, 1970, p. 20).

Another factor was the passage by 32 state legislatures, during the Summer of 1970, of laws dealing with campus unrest, all punitive in some sense. Some universities had adopted student conduct codes or guidelines. In late September, President Nixon asked Congress to authorize prompt Federal intervention in cases of bombing or arson on college campuses, and requested 1,000 additional FBI agents to intervene in campus disorders. This marked a shift in the President's position, which had previously stressed mainly the responsibility of school administrators to maintain campus peace.

The report of a special task force of the National Education Association summed things up pretty well:

> A revolution in rights has begun throughout our society during the last decade. Those who claim rights are being required to recognize the rights of others. A man's right to control other men is being challenged. A man's right to make his own decisions and act on them is being recognized and exercised ... Out of the struggle, a more balanced concept of rights is emerging. [Fred M. Hechinger, *The New York Times,* July 12, 1970]

Public disenchantment with militant, radical youth was evident in the Summer and Fall of 1970. Politicians, sensing this during the off-year election campaign, rallied around opposition to violence and

destruction and dedication to firm action against campus "hijackers."
While wooing potential 18-year-old voters, the political strategists expressed indignation against campus agitators and college officials who
tolerate "anarchy." One senator, long a champion of youth, spoke of
"the folly of undisciplined radicalism."

Some colleges—and even a few high schools—granted "political
vacations" to enable students and faculty to join in campaigning during
the weeks immediately prior to Election Day, 1970. The Princeton-
based "Movement for a New Congress" claimed to have more than 400
chapters in 22 states. But many students and many more academic officials discouraged the recess plan as fundamentally inconsistent with
institutional neutrality. A good many seemed to feel that not much
could be done in politics, that violence wouldn't work, and that no other
viable options were available or feasible. The Students for a Democratic
Society and the "crazies" were having serious survival problems, done in
by indigenous radical splinter groups—from the Marxist Progressive
Labor faction to the notorious Weathermen—and also by their own
political immaturity.

The radical gap left by the demise of SDS was filled to some extent by the "communes," "collectives," and "cadres." There seemed to
be as much or more attention to self-rehabilitation as there was to the
cause of peace or to "bagging" ROTC. A survey during the Summer of
1970 of fifty colleges and universities by the League for Industrial
Democracy found that what was once a more or less unified movement
with uniform goals, following a widely accepted leadership, had become
a melange of grouplets, projects, and styles "with no shared sense of
direction, and very often with profound and even bitter internal differences" (*The New York Times,* August 26, 1970, p. 22). There were
many bomb threats in and around schools and colleges during the Fall
of 1970, and a few actual explosions—the most serious having occurred
in August at the University of Wisconsin. By and large, however, the
threats seemed to be far more a matter of harassment by pranksters and
practical jokers than they were inspired by radical student elements. (It
is easier, of course, to say this in retrospect than it is at the point of
administrative decision whether or not to order a school closed in the
case of a bomb threat.)

In late November 1970, an assemblage of students, street people,
revolutionaries, faculty members, and assorted curiosity-seekers took
place at the State University of New York in Buffalo (*The New York
Times,* November 22, 1970, p. 51). The week-long activities included
poetry readings, films, talks, puppet shows, and "spontaneous outbursts"; it was called "The New Nation Celebration." While its adver-
tised purpose was to "help fuse together all aspects of revolutionary
culture—spiritual, political and social," only about a dozen hands went

up when the throng was asked how many were "really politically active."
Allen Ginsberg appeared more as an entertainer than as a guru of the
college generation.

Campus Mood in the Fall of 1970

The 1970 election period taught student political volunteers some
important lessons. The Movement for a New Congress had avoided rash
predictions about what would be accomplished. What actually happened
was approximately an even distribution of what, by their standards,
were wins and losses. As a result, opinion was divided as to whether the
effort had been worthwhile. On the positive side, it could be said that
the number of student volunteers equalled the number of volunteers of
all ages working in the usual off-year election. For them, the experience
of practical politicking must have had some value, including perhaps the
recognition that change under the political processes of our system is
neither cheaply nor cataclysmically won. Many students would retort
that they already knew this, and that it was one reason for their skepticism about these processes.

It may be that a goodly number of college students who participated in the spring demonstrations did not bother to vote, though they
were eligible, in November. As James Reston wrote in *The New York
Times*:

> Somehow, the students seem more interested in the personalities rather
> than the problems of American politics. They seldom express any
> allegiance to either major political party, have very little to say about
> any of the Democratic party's Presidential candidates, but say a great
> deal about President Nixon and Vice President Agnew, most of it
> critical and some of it unpublishable.
>
> In short, for the moment, a lot of them seem to be saying that national
> politics is not very relevant to their lives, but they are muttering about
> it rather than shaking their fists and spoiling for physical confronta-
> tions, as they were last spring. ["Student Involvement or Detach-
> ment?"][12]

David Broder of the *Washington Post* (December 4, 1970) wondered whether the students, in the Fall of 1970, had not reverted to the
style of the 1950s and become members of a new silent generation.
However, the mood of students was difficult to read—and it is notori-
ously erratic. An American Council on Education poll of more than
180,000 freshmen entering 275 private and public colleges and universities in September 1970 disclosed that:[13]

> Two out of five believed that marijuana should be legalized. This com-
> pared with one out of four a year ago, and one out of five two years
> ago.

Three out of five thought colleges are too lax in dealing with student protests. Fewer than half thought so four years ago.

Only 3.1 percent identified themselves as far left, 33.5 percent as liberal, 17.1 percent as conservative, 1 percent as far right. But 45.4 percent listed themselves as middle-of-the-road.

Only 39.1 percent listed "be well off financially" as an important personal objective, compared with 43.8 percent in 1966.

Clearly the American college campus today is a dynamic place where attitudes are extremely fluid. The school year ending in June 1971 saw little on the college campus scene to compare with the previous year. While some campuses continued as centers of turbulence, and there were sporadic, serious incidents of disturbance and even of violence, the general demeanor and mood was peaceful (some might say "resigned") and intent upon academic goals rather than political activity. But every professor in every classroom, as well as every student, was influenced by the background of embattled and somewhat defensive academe. Old ways in the faculty-student relationship were everywhere being assessed and in many cases being recast. And the end was not in sight.

The same generalization may be applied to the school year ending in June 1972, with the exception that flair-ups occurred on many campuses in May, following the mining of Haiphong harbor. But the memory of campus events of two years earlier prompted many peace demonstrators to wonder whether anyone was listening—or really cared.

The Hip Scene

Rock festivals attracting 300,000 people! Love-ins, Be-ins, Happenings! Grass—acid—speed! These are among the popular associations with "the hippies"—the ultimate dropouts, a subculture of tuned-out youth who call themselves freaks and are in some respects more alienated than the Weathermen. It is a worldwide assortment of aimlessly wandering, uprooted, ridiculed, scorned, indolent young people.

What is a hippie? One may find them anywhere: not only in Taos, New Mexico, and in the Haight-Ashbury sections of many American cities, but in Amsterdam, Rome, Vienna, Paris, London, Bonn, Geneva, Johannesburg, Tokyo, Saigon, Bangkok, Ottawa, Mexico City, Santiago, Spain's Ibiza Island, and even in Moscow. As a derivative of "hip" or "hep," the term has apparently been in use since about 1915. The dictionary refers to a "hipster" as "in the extreme, one who has removed himself from commercial, material, political, and all physical and intellectual reality, intensely believing in and protecting only his true, non-emotional, non-social, amoral identity."

Newsweek (July 27, 1970, pp. 22–24) described the hip scene as follows:

> Far out. Hundreds of hitchhiking freaks with beards, back packs, guitars, flutes, wild hair and dogs—the Panzer troops of the Age of Aquarius . . . The Straights pretend not to see them, or shout, "Go to work, you creeps." But the drug-age nomads don't work much. They exist by panhandling, signing up for food stamps or selling a little dope. They stay stoned all day on weed, hash, acid, mescaline, cocaine, and uppers and downers; they crash at night in ditches, woods, churchyards, empty buildings or on the beach. . . . The authentic year-round road freak typically is about 19. He dropped out of school—and life—after he finished high school, or maybe just before. Most of his kind come from middle-class backgrounds. Boys outnumber girls, two to one. Some pair off more or less monogamously; others take their sex as casually and as transiently as a puff of grass. Everybody shares everything: dope, food, pennies. . . . And everybody keeps moving. The freaks, when they hitchhike, aren't heading anyplace in particular—just looking for a place to get it together.[14]

They challenge the pretenses, the conventions, and the values of the "mainstream." But by and large, they are peaceable "flower children," not inclined to "rip things up." Occasionally, however, they become serious police problems; for example, in connection with immense gatherings at rock festivals, or in pandering dope or stealing to get the wherewithal for it, or in connection (rarely) with sex competition. At the extreme fringe of hippie subculture, there exists a sometimes maniacal, sometimes cultishly demonic type, seeing themselves as sane as society is insane, devoted to a curious combination of demigod charisma, witchcraft, voodooism, and far-out supernaturalism. Needless to say, they are of special interest to the police, for mass-murder or mass-mayhem are not beyond them.

As A. C. Germann points out in "The Hip Scene: A New Community," any police agency wishing to understand and communicate with all segments of the community must learn to understand and communicate with those whose creed is "violence is out; love is in!" The hip community, Germann goes on to say, is irreverent toward "the Establishment" and toward the police, "its blue-frocked representatives." He identifies other distinguishing marks of the subculture: romantic idealism; folksongs with social messages; rock music that is sensuous and rasping; ballrooms that "blow the mind" with sound amplification and strobe lighting; boutiques with posters, incense, jewelry, and buttons; psychedelic or hallucinogenic drugs and marijuana.

There are some similarities to hobo culture and some differences. There are some similarities to the motorcycle culture and some differences. But college students who are characterized as "hippies" are really not, for there is more to hippie subculture than dress and appearance.

One important difference is that college students who "look like hippies," although sometimes close to "dropping out," have not yet done so. Generally, too, they are more serious in their purposes than true hippies. It should be noted, however, that there are thousands of true hippies gravitating to university communities throughout the country, even though they are not students. They bring along some political and social problems that the already troubled college towns do not welcome (*The New York Times,* November 10, 1970, p. 1). The resultant tensions are somewhat similar to those created when hippies in number "take over" sizeable sections of big-city business or residential areas.[15]

In the college communities, the hippies are a disparate crowd, sharing a rejection of middle-class values and—despite their disdain for formal education—an affinity for the relaxed atmosphere of college campuses. Some of them are college dropouts. They like the company of disaffected students who are not quite as far out as they are and from whom they are indistinguishable in dress and mannerisms. All of this causes some problems for police, universities, and communities. "Neighborhood workshops" and sensitivity sessions are being tried in a few places in the hope of providing some communication breakthroughs. But the basic problems of the young people involved are agonizing as they try to "do their thing," somewhat outside of an engulfing system. As Germann says of them:

> The unanswered question is whether a negative, defiant, voluntary poverty can be transformed into something positive, productive, useful and rewarding . . . The *problem* is how to actualize their potentialities for positive, productive, and useful lives without destroying personal integrity and valid values. It would seem necessary that parents, teachers, religious leaders, governmental representatives and research scientists begin to assess the hip scene with serious attention—and to no less degree should the police professional ["The Hip Scene," pp. 44, 45][16]

Dope and Drugs

Dope and drug addiction is not, of course, a problem exclusively or necessarily of youth or of the hippie subculture. And it is not our intention here to canvass this vast and complex subject and all that has been written and said about it in the growing anxiety of recent years. However, certain aspects of drug culture are of deep concern in police and community relations. The basic problem for the police is how to deal with elements of clashing moral positions in the community, corresponding divisions of opinion as to what the criminal code should say about it, and increasing numbers of "nice families" in the community with "hooked" members. For the police, it is the old story of trying to find community consensus where there is none. It becomes a question of, to use Banton's terms, police authority as against police power. The problem is further complicated by the connection with organized crime because of the illegal suppliers of drugs. The plain fact is that doing something about street crime in our cities today means most of all doing something about hard drugs.

A good beginning is to try to understand what is happening and why, and there is a monumental literature to refer to for help in this. Taking drugs is a species of "cop-out," a form of social escapism, like alcoholism. For some addicts, it is a kind of ultimate rebellion that supplies boldness for new acts of rebellion requiring special courage, as well as dedication, to perform (Horace Sutton, "Drugs: Ten Years to Doomsday?"). Yet, we should be wary of single-track explanations. People take drugs for all sorts of personalized reasons, and in this sense there is no such thing as "*the* drug problem." As Sutton puts it:

> Not merely a youthful frivolity to be equated with the roarings of the Twenties, not just the trappings of a new world order, not only the enlightened way of life of an untethered generation, the drug epidemic may be the shadow of an end-of-the-century plague. It may also be only one part—the more visible part—of a larger set of socio-medical problems: suicides and alcoholism as well as narcotism, in which few medical advances have been made. Society is reacting strongly against drugs (which in New York accounts for only one-sixth as many deaths as alcoholism) because it afflicts the young and the innocent and breeds crime. [Ibid., p. 61]

To say so little about dope and drugs may be of little utility, especially as this issue promises to figure so prominently in police and community relations in the immediate future; indeed already does so. Quite frankly, it is too complex a subject to deal with adequately in a comprehensive text of this nature. Like organized crime, it is so central an issue in the transactions of police and policed—and yet so seemingly sinister and bewildering—as almost to defy the possibility of resolution. We leave to others the specific, probing analysis that this subject so urgently and desperately needs.

The Message for the Police

In this chapter, our chief aim has been to bring about better understanding of the problems of today's youth and to identify some aspects of the situation that apply to police-youth relations. In summarization, we have a substantial assist from Joseph Kimble, former Police Chief in Beverly Hills, California, now teaching at the State University of New York at Stonybrook, Long Island.

In an insightful article, "Night Thoughts of a Police Chief," Kimble refers to "the anguished protestation of modern youth . . . largely directed against the ideology of extremism in *either* sector [the radical

Right or the radical Left]." It is also directed, Kimble notes, "against the silent, ambivalent middle that by default perpetuates the extremes." The majority of American youth, he says, are protesting "the addiction to uncompromising viewpoints." They are protesting "an unhealthy obsession with the past, with self-indulgence and self-hypnosis." They are protesting "inertia, indifference, and the compromise of integrity for the sake of expediency."

It is unfortunate, Kimble continues, that youth's protests generate overreaction in some quarters, even when not accompanied by violence or unreasonable conduct. This is so because it is always unfashionable in any society to question the status quo. The motives of those who protest become automatically suspect. Kimble enumerates some of the "urgent messages being semaphored" by youth today to the law enforcement field:

> Young people view traditional law enforcement in a nontraditional way. They view police as a threat, as too conservative, too resistant to change. They hear the police side of drugs and other issues, but they have access to bodies of knowledge that provide different and sometimes better answers.

> Some youth question the honesty of a few police agencies in that their response to certain community problems is thought to be biased. For example, do the police have one code for the majority and another for minorities? Are observed acts inconsistent with official policies? Are too many police agencies operated on the military general staff concept? Young people understand the need for a redefinition of police role and a new kind of policeman.

> It is reasonable to say—and it is often said—that the police *shouldn't* be expected to deal with broader community problems; but in fact they are forced to do so because the community as a whole chooses to pretend that the problems don't even exist. The police have been asked to practice medicine without a license—a license the community has failed to issue in terms of support and involvement.

What do young people want of the police? Kimble responds:

> [Their] expectations include the enforcement of law in a legal, ethical and humane fashion, by officers with a broadened social outlook and an awareness of the changing world around them. They envision qualified and positive leadership, directing an organization composed of individuals who care about other people, individuals who are emotionally, intellectually and morally competent to deal effectively with the complex problems of this society. Young people want law enforcement that is contemporary and constitutional. [Ibid., p. 492]

And what do young people want of the American public? Kimble replies that he hears youth pleading that America should at last acknowledge its basic problems, as a first step in finding solutions.

A Final Thought

One blanket adult charge against youth is "irresponsibility." All minorities tend to be so branded. One is led to wonder about the meaning of responsibility, and how it is taught or caught or somehow acquired. We have had a little to say about this, in this and in earlier chapters, as we dealt with the formation of attitudes toward authority in the very young. The dictionary says that responsibility is the quality or state of being responsible, as in moral, legal or mental accountability, reliability, trustworthiness.

It appears, then, that responsible action involves decision making, often regarding moral questions. This implies, in our kind of world, deliberate choices that must be made from among alternative behavior patterns. To do this is "better" (more responsible) than to do that. Why? How does my decision to do this rather than that affect others? Why does this matter? It is a bit like a police officer deciding on what constitutes "probable cause" or a "reasonable search" or "undue force." How is this learned, or taught, or imparted—this exquisite gift of "responsible" behavior?

The answer is that it is acquired by *practice*, by *experience*, by *training* in decision making, and *by being expected to live with the consequences of the decisions one makes*. The latter is the hard part, especially where youth are concerned—in their relationship, for instance, with parents—and admittedly there must be some limit to how far the consequences aspect should be pushed. All we are saying is what has been said better by many others: children (youth) learn responsible behavior by participating in the process of reaching decisions that affect them, as nearly as possible (depending upon age, maturity, etc.) with full voice and vote. This is a simple version of what the so-called "authority crisis" between young and old seems to be all about. Put another way, we may ask: why should a youngster want to become an adult (a *responsible* adult, mind you) when he is given all he wants, right now?

Archibald MacLeish is one of those who makes the point better:

Only when freedom is as human as humanity is free can a nation of men exist. Only when the balance between society and self is both harmonious and whole can there truly *be* a self, or truly a society. ["Trustee of the Culture"]

Notes to Chapter Fourteen

1. *Officer Friendly* Resource Unit, 1968. Available from the Sears Roebuck Foundation, Skokie, Illinois.

2. Laurence Kohlberg, "Moral Development and Identification in Child Psychology." Also by the same author, "The Child as Moral Philosopher."

3. On the same theme, see James J. Brennan, "Youth and Police."

4. Robert G. Portune, "Attitudes of Junior High School Pupils Toward Police Officers; Police-Juvenile Attitude Project: Preliminary Report"; University of Cincinnati, unpublished manuscripts, 1966. *Changing Adolescent Attitudes Toward Police* by the same author is a complete report of the project and includes a recommended model program.

5. Rokeach, Miller, and Snyder, "The Value Gap Between Police and Policed." See also Martin G. Miller, "Socialization and the Compliance System: An Attitudinal Study of Adolescents, Their Teachers and Police Officers." Unpublished Ph.D. dissertation, Michigan State University, College of Social Science, 1971.

6. See Werthman and Piliavin, "Gang Members and the Police"; Frederick M. Thrasher, *The Gang: A Study of 1,313 Gangs in Chicago;* William Foote Whyte, *Street Corner Society;* Block and Niederhoffer, *The Gang: A Study in Adolescent Behavior;* David J. Bordua, "Delinquent Subcultures: Sociological Interpretations of Gang Delinquency;" Cloward and Ohlin, *Delinquency and Opportunity: A Theory of Delinquent Gangs;* Albert K. Cohen, *Delinquent Boys: The Culture of the Gang;* David Matza, *Delinquency and Drift;* Short and Strodtbeck, *Group Process and Gang Delinquency;* Irving Spergel, *Racketville, Slumtown, Haulberg: An Exploratory Study of Delinquent Subcultures;* Lewis Yablonsky, *The Violent Gang;* and Dorothy Campbell Tompkins, *Bibliography on Juvenile Gangs in the United States Since World War II.*

7. For an extreme view of the gravity of the polarization described by Lipset, see Jerry Rubin, *Do It!* Also Cohen and Hale, *The New Student Left.*

8. The Commission's 1970 report, *Campus Unrest,* includes special reports on Kent State University and Jackson State College, together with an extensive bibliography.

9. See also such books as *The Battle for Morningside Heights: Why Students Rebel,* by Roger Kahn, and *Remembering the Answers: Essays on the American Student Revolt,* by Nathan Glazer.

10. See also Kenneth Keniston, *The Uncommitted: Alienated Youth in American Society,* and by the same author, *Young Radicals.* As an illustration of a trend, the Academic Council at Michigan State University, previously an all-faculty group with 3 students as nonvoting members, now has 31 undergraduate and graduate students as full participating members.

11. See also Sidney Hook, *Academic Freedom and Academic Anarchy.*

12. With passage of the 26th Amendment in July 1971, granting the 18-year-old franchise, the resultant political effects will be interesting to watch.

13. Quoted by Vincent J. Burke in the Los Angeles *Times,* December 26, 1970. Also relevant to this discussion is *The Greening of America: How the Youth Revolution Is Trying to Make America Livable,* by Charles A. Reich. A Louis Harris survey of youth (aged 15–21) opinions on a broad range of social questions was reported in *Life,* January 8, 1971, pp. 22–30.

14. See also Lewis Yablonsky, *The Hippie Trip,* and by the same author, "Hippies: Their Past and Their Future."

15. For discussions of the implications of the hippie take-over, see various articles in *Transaction,* April 1970.

16. See also Hans Toch, "Last Word on the Hippies." Toch sees two positive themes running through hippie life. One is what he calls "chronic passivity in relation to the stream of life." The other is irresponsibility, freedom from obligations: "Don't do it if it doesn't groove ya'." Toch believes that many people can project into the idealized hippie their dissatisfactions with their own lives and with our imperfect social structure. As he puts it, "the hippie hangup redirects attention from individual and social problems whose solution is difficult, to pseudo-problems that require no consuming commitment."

Chapter Fifteen

Citizen Complaints and the Police

When Sir Robert Peel said that the police are the public and the public are the police, he was saying something important about accountability for police actions. We have noted that policing in democratic society is a public, political function. The police are at least theoretically answerable to the public for their every move. Ultimate responsibility for police activity resides in the community. Such authority as the police have is delegated to them by the body politic, exactly the point Banton had in mind in his distinction between police authority and police power.

The police are seldom questioned when they operate in a manner clearly supported by community consensus; their *authority* is recognized and generally accepted. But when they operate, as they sometimes must, in a manner involving their *legal power,* and where community consensus is questionable, there may well be citizen complaints. As Banton puts it, power is not necessarily morally rightful. Authority, on the other hand, includes a moral element. If someone has power over someone else, he can force a certain action; if someone has authority, his commands will tend to be obeyed voluntarily ("Social Integration and Police").

Under social circumstances, therefore, in which authority systems and authority figures are challenged—and questioned especially as to the arbitrary exercise of power—it is predictable that police conduct will come under closer scrutiny by the public. This is what has occurred in recent years. Logically, police behavior will tend to be particularly scrutinized by elements of the population (generally speaking, the powerless) who are insisting more and more emphatically that they be counted as part of the community to whom the police are accountable. For the police are expected to serve *all* the people, as with any public institution. The matter of citizen complaints directed against the police has become a major issue in police and community relations in recent years, and a great deal of feeling about it has been aroused in many places. The subject has been heatedly debated by both police and community elements and it is important that we analyze it.

Setting the Stage in Citizen Complaints

One's opinion on questions pertaining to complaints against the police will, first of all, probably be governed by a certain philosophy. We have already stated our belief, for instance, that the police should be held accountable to the public for their behavior, with no equivocation or "gamesmanship" about it. We have asserted that this should mean *all* of the public, the powerless as well as the powerful. We have implied that we believe, with Banton, that police activity should be based, insofar as possible, on the moral authority of the office, rather than solely on its legal power. We have earlier acknowledged the difficulty in today's American society of securing the minimal community consensus without which the moral authority of the police may be repeatedly questioned and challenged.

So much, then, as a beginning of a philosophy regarding citizen complaints. Now to add to it.[1] Traditionally, the administrator of a police organization has the responsibility for supervision and discipline of personnel. This administrative prerogative is conditioned to some degree by public opinion—in a vague, general way. It is somewhat more specifically and directly influenced, at the municipal level, by city councils, commissions or other legislative bodies, by mayors, city managers or other executives, and by police or public safety boards, commissions, civil service bodies, etc. It is a general working principle to keep interference with *proper* administration at a minimum. Questions are sometimes raised as to what "proper" may mean. Efficient administration is not necessarily effective administration from the point of view of community relations. Efficiency may become an end in itself, which "dehumanizes" administration and creates serious internal or external problems. Police *effectiveness* in social control is closely linked with their moral authority; it is dependent in large degree on community cooperation. A key question is, how to "channel" grievances constructively and positively, inside and outside the department?

In this context, by a "complaint" we mean a grievance. In police vocabulary, there is some semantic difficulty with the term. When a citizen calls to charge that his neighbor is disturbing the peace, in many departments the call is recorded as a complaint. The complaint is against the neighbor, not against the police. This is not our meaning in this chapter. We mean a grievance of (1) a departmental employee against the department; (2) a departmental employee against another departmental employee; (3) a citizen against the department; or (4) a citizen against a police officer. Hence (1) and (2) are *internal* complaints, while (3) and (4) are *external*.

We believe also that there is a direct relationship between the number and type of external complaints and the level of public confidence in a police organization. As a general rule, in a community where there are numerous complaints against the police and accompanying clamor for establishment of a civilian review board or some other external mechanism for control of police behavior, there are police-community relations problems and other problems of a more basic nature. The clamor is typically a telling symptom. But the likelihood is that whatever mechanism is proposed for dealing with complaints, it would do little or nothing about the real difficulties.

The Police and Complaints

In arriving at some principles for dealing with complaints, the following points need consideration:

1. A starting point in any police agency honestly and sincerely intent upon dealing constructively with public complaints is to recognize that some citizens truly believe that some policemen do sometimes mistreat some citizens. Incidents happen often enough to make the belief plausible. To respond to this with a heated, "It's a damn lie," is worse than no response at all. The belief that it does occur is real to some people, and the mistreatment itself may be. So how are mutual trust and confidence to be developed? This is the decisive question. Certainly it cannot be done through mutual excoriation.

2. Walter Gellhorn of the Columbia University Law School poses these basic questions in "Police Review Boards: Hoax or Hope?" *Should* the police control police? *Can* the police control police? If the answer to the first question is "yes," then it is clear where the burden of proof lies with respect to the second question.

3. Initiative for improvement of complaint procedures should come from police administrators, ideally in circumstances where it is not likely to be interpreted publicly as defensive or reactionary, or as "crisis-oriented," or as an opportunistic "gimmick" to relieve political pressure.

4. If persons who believe they have been treated unjustly have no forum which they trust to explore their claims, their attitude of distrust is never dispelled.

5. There is an inconsistency between police lamenting, on the one hand, the apathy of the public regarding problems that loom large for the police, and on the other hand resisting the right and obligation of citizens to complain about what they perceive as improper police conduct. However negative a citizen complaint may be initially, it is a way by which the citizen has his say about governmental service and *participates* in democratic political process. With a *positive* police philosophy regarding complaints, the matter can often be turned to positive good for police service and for police and community relations. Some complainants may eventually become staunch allies of the police and valuable contributors to worthwhile programs and projects, as experience shows. This is a point on which Gellhorn elaborates:

. . . if the police authorities are to earn the public's approval of their stewardship, they must themselves be willing to do the job they are unwilling to allow others to do in their stead. This does not mean upholding every charge against a subordinate; accusations are easily made, not easily proved. It does mean that the authorities must be wholeheartedly interested in exploring complaints—just as interested, indeed, as are the complainants in having exploration made. The suspicion of whitewash, of unwillingness to expose wrongdoing because of a misguided sense of loyalty, will not die speedily. It rests on too much disillusioning experience in days past. If, however, the police begin to make frank disclosure of how they have acted on each complaint and what they have found; if they are willing to allow the complainant to comment and make further suggestions should he care to do so; if they are prepared to subject their completed work to examination by an external critic; if, in sum, they cease thinking of themselves as a brotherly band beleaguered by citizens (and, of course, other hostile forces) and start thinking of themselves as public servants within a specialized law administration organization, the gap between them and the community they serve should begin to close. [Ibid.]

In this passage, Gellhorn presents a philosophy for dealing with complaints that is in keeping with truly professional public service. There is more to it than merely the "machinery" for handling complaints. There are implications for administrative policies, for organizational planning, for public information and interpretation, and for the training of police personnel. Indeed, there are implications for governmental administration in a broader context than the police department. It is hard to see how a police organization could operate with one philosophy in this matter, while the larger governmental system of which it is a part operates with an opposing philosophy.

The Ombudsman

Gellhorn recognizes this larger context of complaint philosophy. He has become well known in this country as a leading proponent of the "ombudsman" plan for dealing with citizen grievances against any branch of governmental service, including the police. Gellhorn thinks that an official with authority to examine the entire range of municipal administration "holds more hope for the future than does a special tribunal for trying citizens' complaints against individual policemen." The ombudsman approach does not single out the police department for special treatment. Gellhorn further observes:

> It does not remove from police hands the power to direct, judge, and discipline the staff members whose actions have been challenged, but —as in the case of other departments—leaves to the professionals the job of appraising fellow professionals. . . . Far from opposing this concept, policemen should find in it much to welcome. The Scandinavian countries and New Zealand have already put it into practice with good results.[2]

The ombudsman is a highly placed functionary authorized to inquire into the merits of any citizen's grievance about official actions or failures to act. He then recommends, but may not command, whatever action he thinks is suitable in the light of his investigation. The ombudsman is in effect, an appellate office. It is by no means a substitute for complaint procedure within, for example, a police department, to deal with internal or external grievances. Experience with the plan in other countries shows that it has done much, as Gellhorn states, "to reinforce citizens' confidence in public administrators by showing the flimsiness of accusations that had at first seemed grave." While the ombudsman plan has been tried in several places in the United States in the recent past, it has not as yet had sufficient testing to establish its practical feasibility and merits. Some American universities are experimenting with it in terms of due process in handling complaints of students, occasionally of faculty members, and potentially even the complaints of administrators.

The Control of Delegated Power

The ombudsman procedure is premised on realization of a broad problem of government that has been of concern from the beginning: how is the use of delegated power to be controlled? Because the police have a particularly strong delegated power, the problem with them is especially sensitive. Control of their behavior most frequently becomes a matter of public contention under circumstances in which confidence in them is uncertain. Monrad Paulsen, one time colleague of Gellhorn's on the faculty of the Columbia University Law School and presently Dean of the Law School at the University of Virginia, refers to the "anarchistic strain in all of us" ("Police Conduct and the Public"). He observes that Americans like to "manipulate law and legal roles," as witness old movies about police and law enforcement that often contain "wink situations." Paulsen says that "our habit of following the rules only when a policeman is looking over our shoulder has contributed to mistrust of authority and mistrust of legal process."

This attitude, Paulsen believes, is further embellished by stereotypic perceptions of the police officer as a "tough bully-boy," and by the fact that "we have given the police a job to do, but we haven't told them what the rules are." As an illustration, the Supreme Court upsets convictions because the police work is held to be unconstitutional and thus places the police in a bad light. The police are in effect held accountable on a Monday for violation of a rule established on Monday that—it is decreed—should have guided their conduct the previous Saturday. This is the type of thing that is sometimes apparent in citizen complaints against the police, and it is the type of thing that at least partly explains why so many policemen are "up-tight" on the subject of complaints.

The issue has broader implications than for police alone. John Herbers reported in *The New York Times* (November 27, 1970, p. 1) that tenants of public housing were rebelling in several cities across the country against what they considered to be paternalistic, arbitrary policies of housing management, ranging from unfair eviction to imposition of ugly decorating schemes. In some cities, tenants were being given some voice in management, and complaints had correspondingly declined. The Federal Department of Housing and Urban Development had also proposed a standard lease and grievance procedure. There was news also of the accomplishments of such organizations as the Metropolitan Tenants Organization and Tenants United for Fairness.

How is the use of authority to be controlled? *Quis ipsos custodes custodiet?* Who will watch the watchers? The late Stanford University Law Professor Herbert Packer has analyzed this basic question, asserting that "the trouble that the police and the rest of us are now in is largely the result of our improvident reliance on the criminal sanction to perform a lot of messy social tasks for which it is not especially suited" ("Who Can Police the Police?").[3] Packer asks what business the Supreme Court has, trying to educate or discipline the police. He suggests that this is happening because no one else is doing it. Who else could? The police themselves might do it, but they have not. Most of the professional progress in police work in recent years, Packer feels, has been in reducing corruption and in increasing efficiency. While these are certainly worthwhile achievements, "the revolution in rising expectations among urban minority groups and the due process revolution in the courts will not be satisfied with efficiency."

Who else might police the police? Legislatures might do it and Packer contends that such bodies are best suited for it—far more so than the courts—and he indicates why he believes this. But the fact is, he continues, that legislatures have utterly abdicated this responsibility. Packer thinks that the Court's performance in the criminal procedure area has been increasingly unsatisfactory as its constitutional interpretations have become more legislative in tone. Along with Paulsen, he questions whether the familiar sanction against the police represented by the exclusionary rule of evidence is adequate. Incidentally, Paulsen defies anyone to try to explain that rule to a European, "lest he be committed as a lunatic." The exclusionary rule seeks to discourage police misconduct by the method of failing to convict persons who have been the victims of such misconduct. It also frees the malefactor so he may try again to victimize some innocent person. It does not compensate the victim of police misconduct. In short, it has little to commend it, Paulsen argues, though conceding that it has probably had some small impact on police procedures.

Both Packer and Paulsen think that the question of sanctions is basic, and they entertain parallel notions as to what "the stick" might be. Packer suggests that one possibility might be the right to file suit against the governmental unit that employs the policeman, accompanied by provisions for recovery of minimum or fixed damages, counsel fees, and the like. The strategy would be "to build respect for due process into the policeman's model of efficiency. The policeman who persistently violates the norms costs his employers money and is therefore seen as inefficient."

The Civilian Complaint Review Board

Another possibility considered by Packer, Paulsen, and Gellhorn is some kind of administrative complaint and review structure aimed at making the internal process of police discipline more responsive to values other than efficiency. The so-called civilian review board is what Packer calls "a crude model" of what might be designed. However, none of these three analysts is enthusiastic about the civilian review board. Paulsen refers to endless public debates and bitter political infighting, such as that in New York City several years ago which focused on the question of whether there should be civilian participation or civilian domination of a complaint review board.[4] Paulsen and Gellhorn object to such review boards, even with civilian participation, and favor the ombudsman plan, for similar reasons:

1. Experiments with review boards in Philadelphia, Rochester, N.Y., and a number of other cities have not been very successful. There were problems of publicity, of staffing, of budget, and of limited powers. In Philadelphia, the police department conducted investigations, raising doubts as to the independence of the board. In Rochester, the board was confined to dealing only with complaints of brutality. In both places, litigation by policemen's organizations brought injunctions, keeping the board from functioning.

2. Review boards may "soothe but bring no lasting relief." Stronger medicine is needed to cure community ills. Mere palliatives cannot contend with discrimination and poverty.

3. The review board symbolizes and assumes conflict between the poor and public authority. Moreover, it singles out the police for special blame and overlooks the existence of closely allied official activities.

4. The review board system presupposes a polarization, the complainant on one side and the accused policeman on the other. This makes for burdensome procedures, simply because of the adversarial nature of the proceeding. This in turn tends to discourage the expression of grievances, or turns the proceedings into acrimonious exchanges when grievances are "processed." It leaves complainants wondering if the ordeal is worth the effort.

5. The problems brought to light by a review board may be such as to require upper level administrative action in a police agency. A review board (as contrasted with an ombudsman) will probably not have sufficient "clout" to persuade administrators to effect such changes. Moreover, the desirable administrative changes may well pertain to a larger context of public service than merely the police department.

William Brown has said that the review board proposals do not go far enough.[5] Such a view, by a retired New York City Police Inspector, was news at the time Brown expressed it—in the aftermath of the controversy over the review board question in New York City during the Summer of 1965. Brown stated that a bureaucracy in a democracy should be responsive to the needs of even the poorest and least vocal of those it serves. Therefore, he continued, not only conscience, but also good administration calls for the establishing of some mechanism that can assure any person aggrieved by official action a chance to be heard, and to know that his complaint will be listened to with respect and by a power able to correct wrongful administrative actions or positions. Brown delineated some important requirements for an adequate review system: honest and competent administration, concern for due process, provision for appeals, a positive philosophy to correct rough spots in a system, and clearly stated functions of the review process.

Brown contended that the civilian complaint review board does not meet these requirements. It is too much a symbol of the antagonism between police and minority groups. It tends to widen the communication gap rather than to narrow it. It diverts attention away from more fundamental and broader issues. Something more is needed, Brown concluded. He advocated serious consideration of the ombudsman system.[6]

The ombudsman system, it should be repeated, is not a substitute for resolute police administration that is intolerant of offensive conduct by policemen. As Gellhorn puts it:

The behavior of policemen is not a great force of nature beyond human control. If superiors from the top of the chain of command to the bottom are determined to correct subordinates, if they themselves are held accountable for inexcusable failures to detect and discipline offenders, they can eliminate much of the behavior that now brings police establishments into disrepute. . . . The police *can* control the police.

. . . .

What is needed at this point is not a further institutionalizing, through a civilian board, of the notion that a complaint signalizes a dispute between two individuals alone. What is needed, rather, is acceptance of the view that a citizen's complaint about a policeman, just like a citizen's complaint about any other public servant, deserves the attention of superior administrators who are intent upon reducing irritations and improving services. If anyone believes that the responsible superiors have not given the desired degree of attention, an outsider's inquiry becomes desirable. The issue then presented is not the guilt or innocence of a particular public servant, but the probity, efficiency, and policies of those who have weighed citizens' allegations about shortcomings or misdeeds. These are to be judged by a review of what the superiors did, not by a trial of what the subordinates are accused of having done. Persons who wish to protest about police operations should indeed be able to bring their protests before a competent authority wholly outside the Police Department. But this should not operate to supplant the Police Department as the primary investigator and decider of charges against its members. ["Police Review Boards: Hoax or Hope?"]

To this Packer adds his main point, one which Skolnick, LaFave, Remington, and others have also stressed:

The aggressively interventionist character of much of our criminal law thrusts the police into the role of snoopers and harassers. There is simply no way for the police to provide so much as a semblance of enforcement of laws against prostitution, sexual deviance, gambling, narcotics, and the like without widespread and visible intrusion into what people regard as their private lives. Ideally, the police should be seen as the people who keep the law of the jungle from taking over. . . . it is only when the police are seen, as they are in our society, as the guardians of conventional morality and ideological purity that such a slogan ["Support your local police"] could become as emotive and divisive as that one has. [*The Limits of the Criminal Sanction,* p. 283]

In short, the best procedures for handling citizen complaints against the police will still leave the more basic task of evaluating a criminal code that insists upon putting policemen in indefensible positions where citizen complaints are inevitable.

Recommendations of Presidential Commissions

Several special Presidential Commissions during the 1960s had something to say about the matter of citizen complaints against the police. In its general report, *The Challenge of Crime in a Free Society* (p. 103), the President's Commission on Law Enforcement and Administration of Justice (1966) recommended that every jurisdiction should provide *adequate* procedures for full and fair processing of all citizen grievances and complaints about the conduct of any public officer or employee. Under the heading of "Insuring Fairness," the *Task Force Report: The Police* (pp. 193–204) of the same Commission discusses in some detail internal procedures within a police organization, handling internal investigations, citizen complaints, external review, court appeals, civil remedies, civilian review boards, and the ombudsman system.

A more concrete case analysis of the functioning of the grievance systems in the San Diego and Philadelphia police departments is provided in Field Surveys IV, *The Police and the Community* (Vol. 1, pp. 167–175; Vol. 2, pp. 195–284), of the same Commission. This includes a thorough description and evaluation of the Philadelphia Police Advisory Board, originally called the Philadelphia Police Review Board, created in 1958.

The National Advisory Commission on Civil Disorders (Kerner Commission) expressed particular concern in its 1968 Report (pp. 151, 152) for opening channels of communication between government and urban ghetto residents. It recommended establishment of joint government-community Neighborhood Action Task Forces and formal mechanisms for the processing of grievances relating to the performance of city administration. The Commission did not specify the form of such mechanisms, but did identify certain criteria of "adequacy":

The grievance agency should be separate from operating municipal agencies.

The grievance agency must have adequate staff and funding to discharge its responsibilities.

The grievance agency should have comprehensive jurisdiction, bringing all public agencies under scrutiny.

The grievance agency should have power to receive complaints, hold hearings, subpoena witnesses, make public recommendations for remedial actions, and in cases involving law violation, bring suit.

The grievance agency should be readily and easily accessible to all citizens.

Grievants should be given full opportunity to take part in all proceedings and to be represented by counsel. Results of investigations should be reported to grievants and made public. Expanded legal services should be made available to ghetto residents in various types of legal-aid-to-the-poor programs.

The Kerner Commission emphasized that making a complaint should be easy and convenient. The procedure should have a built-in conciliation process to attempt to resolve complaints without the need for full investigation and processing. Excessive formality should be avoided. Since many citizen complaints pertain to departmental policies rather than individual conduct, information concerning complaints of this sort should be forwarded to the departmental unit that formulates or reviews policy and procedures. Information concerning all complaints should be forwarded to appropriate training units so that any deficiencies correctable by training can be eliminated.

The National Commission on the Causes and Prevention of Violence stated emphatically in its 1969 Report, *To Establish Justice, To Insure Domestic Tranquillity,* that aggrieved groups must be permitted to exercise their constitutional rights of protest and public presentation of grievances ("Summary," p. 10). To enable the less affluent to obtain effective and peaceful redress of grievances, this Commission recommended additional steps to meet their needs for legal assistance and encouraged state and local jurisdictions to experiment with the establishment of grievance agencies to serve all citizens.

The President's Commission on Campus Unrest said in its 1970 Report that the most urgent task for government must be to restore faith of Americans in their government, in their fellow citizens, and in their capacity to live together in harmony and progress (pp. 215, 202–206). This Commission recommended reforms in the governance of institutions of higher education to include special attention to such things as:

Increased participation of students, faculty, and staff in the formulation of policies.

Procedures for dealing with grievances, to insure that such are promptly heard, fairly considered, and—if necessary—acted upon.

This Commission went on to declare that many grievances are legitimate and correctable, but even when they are not—even when they are but a pretext for disruption—they often arouse emotions that are more than ephemeral. Within the limits of practicality, every complaint should be investigated and answered by as informal a process as may be appropriate in particular instances. Unwarranted charges should be repudiated, policies misunderstood should be explained, unfounded rumors should be dispelled, and facts should be provided.

The same Commission observed that campus grievance committees generally have not worked very well. Problems with such committees have been the polarization of their members, a tendency to handle grievances on the basis of policies rather than merit, and slowness of response. Variations on the ombudsman system have also been tried on some campuses. To be successful in such circumstances, the ombudsman must have both great autonomy and the support of top university administration. He must not be penalized by the administration if his findings and recommendations embarrass university leaders. Some institutions have appointed special student affairs administrators or advisory bodies to act as liaison between students and administration.

Definition of Complaints

Early in this chapter, we proposed a four-dimensional definition of complaints. Some aspects of it have been neglected in our discussion to this point. In complaints of departmental employees against the department, it is usually "unfair practices" that are involved. The belief is growing that a police department has an obligation to provide suitable channels through which all employees may offer criticisms and recommend changes, without peril. Much more attention must be devoted to this than in the past. Police unionization is gaining in strength and in political power, indicating the need for administration to be genuinely concerned for the welfare of all personnel. We shall have more to say shortly about internal control mechanisms. Even the military services are currently devoting unprecedented attention to internal grievance procedures.

The second type of complaint that we earlier identified—that of a departmental employee against another departmental employee—includes complaints made by a superior officer against a subordinate, those of a subordinate against a superior, and those of an employee against another employee of equal rank. The Michigan State University study for the President's Crime Commission indicated that while police departments respect the right of superiors to voice complaints against subordinates, there is rarely any established procedure for complaints of subordinates against superiors, or of employees against employees of the same rank. The importance of providing suitable machinery for these types of complaints cannot be overstressed. So-called police scandals frequently occur in circumstances where subordinates fear reprisals if they attempt to complain formally about superiors. Military-type organization has fostered this atmosphere. Formalized complaints of employees against other employees of equal rank often result also in subtle (and sometimes not so subtle) recrimination against the complainant.

In the third category of complaints—that of a citizen against the department—are such charges as unfair, discriminatory, improper, or inefficient practices on the part of the police organization. Sometimes departmental policies are questioned, and re-evaluation is the prudent response. An applicable administrative principle is the recognition that policies in a police organization are not solely the possession and private domain of police administrators. The very nature of this type of complaint calls for public airing.

The fourth classification of complaints is the most common—that of a civilian against a police officer. These are allegations that an individual officer or group of officers has committed some act or omission that violates either the law or departmental policy. The most frequent complaint of this type, studies show, is discourtesy. The use of unnecessary force is second in frequency, and mishandling a traffic ticket is third. Contrary to popular impressions, Negroes are not disproportionately represented among complainants. But a high proportion of complainants are of lower socio-economic class background.

Of the four types of complaints described here, the latter two types are especially important in terms of community relations. However, this in no way minimizes the need for establishing sound procedures for handling all four types. Any of the four can, at a given time and place, create serious administrative problems. The community often displays a fickle attitude in the way it views complaints. It may focus on alleged discrimination in police hiring or promotions today and on alleged corruption or abusive tactics or some form of favoritism in personnel assignments tomorrow. What a given administrator considers unimportant may suddenly emerge in public attention as a matter of great importance—or vice versa. The wise administrator will "go with the punch" in such a manner as not to ignore or belittle what any element of the community thinks is important. At the same time, he must try to persuade the community not to ignore or belittle what may well be more important, long-run considerations—the "win a battle but lose the war" kind of thing.

The Special Case of Brutality

In Chapter Twelve, we devoted some attention to the matter of police brutality. We were particularly interested at that point in the various definitions of the term and the inherent communication difficulties. It should be stated again that police brutality is the most explosive and most disputed claim made by minority groups against police officers.

Generally speaking, the police definition of what constitutes brutality is narrower than the definition of those community elements who are most likely to make such charges. All agree, however, that the use of unnecessary or unreasonable physical force constitutes brutality. The argument on this point tends to focus on what constitutes unnecessary or unreasonable force. As to so-called verbal brutality, some police officers have trouble understanding why calling a Negro "Boy" should be regarded as brutal. Police officers are inclined to doubt that unaffected citizens in the community would consider this brutality. But studies show that this police assumption is largely erroneous (Field

Surveys V, President's Crime Commission, p. 151). Less than a third of the police officials canvassed in one national survey felt that such things as sarcasm, ridicule, curtness, and disrespect should be considered brutality. But more than half of the Caucasian community leaders and almost three-fourths of the Negro community leaders thought so.

There has been a tendency for police officials to assert that brutality charges are seriously exaggerated. They point to statistics compiled by the FBI that record a very small number of convictions. But the U.S. Commission on Civil Rights has cited the inadequacy of the salient Federal statute for handling flagrant cases of brutality.[7] J. Edgar Hoover admitted the ineffectiveness of existing procedure for dealing with charges under this statute. Incidentally, there is nothing in the statute that can be construed as covering *verbal* brutality.

In any case, the important consideration is whether significant numbers of people *believe* that police brutality, however it is defined, really occurs. There is abundant evidence that such a belief is fairly widespread, especially among the poor and minority groups. It is an aspect of their generally unfavorable attitude toward the police. Moreover, there is evidence of sufficient actual incidence of police brutality, physical and verbal, to lend credence to the belief and fuel the conclusion that brutality is more common than it really is. Such is the stuff that nurtures distrust of the police—and reciprocally, prompts many police officers to distrust "rabble-rousers" in the community. The policeman says, "They're just out to get us, that's all." The poor black says, "Those fink bastards lie in their teeth."

It appears that disrespect and verbal abuse constitute the type of police brutality that requires the greatest attention today. Physical beatings have not disappeared completely, but they are rarer than was the case some years ago. Verbal attacks, on the other hand, are rampant in police-citizen encounters, almost always two-way to be sure (citizen assaults against policemen, as we have noted, is an increasingly grave problem), but verbal affronts are especially offensive when employed by "professional" peace-keepers who personify the majesty of the law. Frequently, "communication" between police officer and citizen is in the rhetoric of racism. And verbal abuse can quickly become physical abuse, as we noted in our discussion of collective behavior.

Verbal brutality involves questions of policy and supervision. Superiors in a department will say that they do not condone such behavior by a patrolman or a subordinate officer. Too often, sanction stops there. If questioned about this, the superior may cautiously refer to the police union, suggesting that disciplinary action for such a "minor offense" might bring down the wrath of the union—which begs the question as to who should exert discipline. Thus it is that an administrative-supervisory quandary develops, a position that is extremely vulnerable from several standpoints, including the possibility that the union might *support* appropriate disciplinary action in clear-cut cases.

Many departments have little in the way of statistical data related to brutality charges. In regard to the use of excessive physical force, the Michigan State University study for the President's Crime Commission had access to records in five major cities, which—if accurate—revealed odds that an officer would be accused of using excessive force once in every 18 years in City A, once in every 30 years in City B, once in every 19 years in City C, once in every 23 years in City D, and once in every 29 years in City E (Field Surveys V, p. 168). There was some evidence that citizen complaints increase as public confidence in the police increases, at least in the short run. This is the kind of thing that makes the criteria of *good* police-community relations difficult to define.

One of the decisive factors influencing public trust in procedures for handling brutality and other complaints is the outcome of internal investigations in police agencies. Suspicion is frequently aroused that such investigations are "whitewash jobs," with a low percentage of sustained charges, a correspondingly small proportion resulting in disciplinary action, and a general tendency to "sweep it under the rug" when there is evidence to support the complaint. Sometimes a local newspaper will "turn the heat on" in such circumstances, at the risk of straining police-press relations and inviting an accusation of "sensationalism," "yellow or inflammatory journalism," or "muckraking." And it should be said that the newspaper is not always well informed in such situations, to put it mildly.

In any event, the statistical and records-keeping variances and discrepancies and inadequacies in records in many departments and between departments highlight the general problem of sloppy handling of citizen complaints. The orientation of too many police agencies toward complaints is negative rather than positive. They see it as threatening, as something that must be "headed off at the pass" at all costs. Sometimes this attitude seems to prevail even in otherwise relatively progressive police organizations. This stance is, of course, understandable in an elementary human sense. But it is also, in part, a carry-over of a past when it was considered administratively useful to perpetuate a certain mystique about the daily happenings in a police station.

Such an attitude toward citizen complaints obviously boomerangs in lessened trust and confidence in the police, reflected in movements to establish some form of stronger exterior control over their behavior. Thus, as police officials insist that the police *should* control police conduct, it must be clearly demonstrated, to the satisfaction of all community "audiences," that the police *can* control police conduct. To the extent that this can be achieved with a *positive* orientation wherein citizens are persuaded to feel that their complaints are, in effect, contributions to better police service for all, much of the rancor associated with the matter of complaints can be eliminated.

A Critique of Existing Control Methods

It may be helpful to enumerate some of the main criticisms that have been leveled against existing control methods and procedures. These are necessarily generalizations with no particular place or police department in mind; the criticism may not be valid in specific cases, but it holds often enough to justify its inclusion here:

1. Insufficient sophisticated training of police officers, both pre-service and in-service, in the subject matter of human relations.

2. Ineffective administrative policies and supervision relative to police misconduct.

3. Serious credibility questions regarding internal discipline and investigative procedures.

4. Inadequate statistics, data retrieval systems, and record-keeping relative to citizen complaints.

5. Deficiencies in public information and interpretation regarding complaint procedures. Closely allied with this is an attitude toward complaints that is reflected in making the procedure overly formal, unduly difficult, inconvenient, embarrassing, or even legally foreboding for the complainant, e.g., the use of lie detectors.

6. Numerous police agencies have no established pattern of complaint procedure, handling same in a haphazard manner—for example, the chief of police deals with all complaints personally, or he assigns an officer to investigate when he thinks the charges warrant.

7. Too often, the complainant is not advised of the disposition of the case.

8. Few departments provide for systematic, periodic evaluation of their complaint procedures, with or without provision for public participation in such evaluation. The latter is highly recommended.

Having listed some of the principal criticisms of existing complaint procedures, it is well also to list some of the emergent positive features:

1. Many police departments see it as the duty of any and every police officer to be a complaint hearer, either by way of supplementing the activity of a special unit or in some cases as a "better system" than that represented by a special unit. (The latter is open to argument.)

2. Commendable due process provisions applying both to the complainant and to the accused, in hearings conducted as part of investigations into serious charges, are increasingly evident.

3. Provision in complaint procedure for appeals to a next higher level, if desired, is no longer rare.

4. Some form of external *advisory* group for internal investigative units exists in many departments. Admittedly, there is considerable variation in the actual influence of such advisory forums, and some question as to whom they represent.

5. The secretive "climate" that has tended to surround complaint and investigative procedures in the past is slowly evaporating.

6. Many departments are moving away from complicated, "red tape" procedures that scare away complainants. The widespread use of standard, simple, mail-in complaint forms (pioneered by the Oakland, California, Police Department) is indicative of this trend. It should be noted, however, that efforts to assure a dispassionate inquiry into a complaint and at the same time to safeguard the rights of an official whose occupational future may be at stake, may have the unintended effect of discouraging the expression of grievances.

It should be added on the positive side that an increasing number of police agencies are taking steps to remove the basis for each of the eight criticisms earlier listed.

Evaluating Complaint Procedures

We have mentioned the need for systematic, periodic evaluation of complaint machinery. What guidelines or checkpoints may be suggested for this purpose? Depending on local community and departmental variances, the following questions may be helpful (MSU study report, Field Surveys V, pp. 228–229):

1. Is there policy or law requiring that all complaints reported be recorded at a central point to insure proper data retrieval?

2. Is there policy or law that prohibits employees from attempting to discourage any civilian from making a complaint?

3. Does the department make conscious efforts to cause complainants a minimum of inconvenience and embarrassment?

4. Is the machinery for hearing and processing complaints fair, impartial and objective?

5. Is the machinery adequately publicized and interpreted so that all citizens know of it and can get further assistance if they need it?

6. Are all complaints adequately investigated?

7. Are there reports to the party making the complaint so that he is aware of developments from the time he makes the complaint until the time of disposition?

8. Does the department have a reputation for integrity with the entire community? (Do all members of the community consider it *their* police department?)

9. Is there an avenue for formalized appeal of police decisions or findings?

By obtaining responses to these questions from randomly selected citizens, the police administrator will acquire a fairly reliable gauge as to the adequacy of complaint procedures. The ninth question, of course, takes procedure outside the department—to a police or safety commission, to the city council, to the city's community relations commission, to an ombudsman, to the prosecuting attorney, or to the courts.[8]

Control of Internal Complaints

The aforementioned checkpoints pertain to the external complaint —those of a citizen, directed against the police department or against a police officer. For internal complaints—those of an employee against the department, those of a superior officer against a subordinate, of a subordinate against a superior, or of an employee against another employee of equal rank—some checkpoints may also be suggested, again subject to local variances:

1. All employees must be held strictly accountable for their behavior.

2. Supervision is the crucial function relative to internal (and external) complaints. The supervisor must have authority commensurate with responsibility. But if supervisors abuse this authority, they should be held strictly accountable. Guidelines are useful in prescribing and proscribing supervisory responsibilities.

3. Administrative directives should clearly delineate the rights and responsibilities of employees at every level in the department. Such policies should also clearly indicate available grievance and appropriate disciplinary procedures. Top administrators in the department should not be handling minor rule infractions while line supervisors are handling more serious matters.

4. Administrators also should have authority commensurate with their responsibilities. As a general rule, this includes discipline to the point of terminating an officer's service, subject only to the limitation of advisory consultation with the chief executive of the particular governmental jurisdiction, and the right of appeal by the officer to a civil service or other board of review. The latter should *not* have the power to overrule the police administrator, but only to review the administrative action and to make their findings public.

5. Members of the organization at all levels should know that they can call attention to the improper conduct of other employees without incurring organizational penalties. Indeed, this should be made clear in departmental regulations.

6. Some method or system of staff inspections should be routine, with reports made directly to the chief administrator.

7. Some sort of internal staff unit for the investigation of charges of employee misconduct is desirable in departments of sufficient size to justify it. The Michigan State University study report suggests the duties of such a unit (Field Surveys V, President's Crime Commission, pp. 235–242).

8. Departmental trial boards can be administratively advantageous in departments of appreciable size. Important features of such boards are suggested in the same study report (pp. 243–245).

The importance of carefully defined, widely disseminated, and adequately interpreted employee grievance procedures should be emphasized again. Due process provisions of such procedures should be loud and clear.

Some Additional Observations on Complaints

There are a few points to be added on this extremely important matter of complaints. One is the observation that a patrolman on the street is something of a neighborhood ombudsman. Unless there is reason for an individual officer to be avoided, people will tend to look to him for information, direction, assistance when in trouble, a helping hand in rain or snow, a listening ear in frustration, some friendly counsel, or referral to the agency or persons appropriate to a particular need. If the officer turns them off or turns them away, many people have no idea where they may find assistance. Police officers on street duty are accustomed to hearing complaints about many things. Most of the time, they are able to offer something: a suggestion, a word of advice, a cautionary note, a bracing thought, an encouraging idea. The best of police-community relations is not done through big projects, committees, and programs. It comes down to the one-to-one contacts of a police officer and a citizen.

In our discussion of discretionary use of police power in Chapter Five, we referred to the central question of police accountability. We quoted Albert Reiss in his delineation of the possible options in this regard. He acknowledges that a system of external review creates problems, especially when there is review of an individual's performance within an organization. This form of accountability, he points out, interferes with both institutionalized forms of professional control of practice and with organizational forms of control to protect its boundaries. Public school teachers in this country, when faced with the same kind of question, formed professional organizations that have resisted school board review "on professional grounds." The police have lacked extralocal, line, professional organization, although there is currently a beginning of movement in that direction.

Regarding the ombudsman system, Reiss has this to say:

> Without doubt, attempts to institutionalize the role of ombudsman in
> American society would encounter considerable resistance, particularly
> from lawyers and judges, who perhaps have been most exempt from
> public scrutiny among the professionals in the United States (unless it
> be physicians). Quite clearly also, their resistance would be stipulated
> on "professional" grounds of competence to control practice. Since
> police in the United States are inextricably linked to the system of
> criminal justice, they are inclined to regard with cynicism a civic
> accountability system of their organization that exempts the office of
> public prosecutor and jurist. But they are more vulnerable to client
> claims. Unlike the lawyers and social workers in the criminal justice
> system, their claim is based primarily on local police organizational
> control or police malpractice, rather than on professional association
> control of malpractice. ["Professionalization of the Police," p. 223][9]

The Question of Community (Neighborhood) Control

In tune with Reiss, James Q. Wilson maintains that:

> . . . though the [civilian review board] issue is passionately debated, it
> is not clear that, however it is resolved, it will have much effect on the
> *substantive* police policies that are in effect—partly because some are
> not "policies" at all but styles created by general organizational ar-
> rangements and departmental attitudes, and partly because grievance
> procedures deal with specific complaints about unique circumstances,
> not with general practices of the officers. [*Varieties of Police Behavior,*
> pp. 229, 230]

The question of control of the police tends to revolve around
what has happened, under duress of social change, to the idea of *local*
control. In the big, heterogeneous, impersonal, bureaucratic, insensitive
city, "local" is a euphemism. The question of "who's in charge?" of the
police, under such circumstances, may become a matter of long-range
skirmishing with distant, remote, forbidding, somewhat mysterious
forces "downtown." If one is poor and powerless and resides in a
ghetto, it is like trying to deal with a foreign power via diplomatic
gibberish. Under such circumstances, one wishes that there could be a
truly local, neighborhood police, close enough to be held fully accountable to residents of the neighborhood for all activities and services.
Precinct stations might serve this purpose, were it not for a tendency
to handle complaints at that level by saying, "We're sorry we can't
help. We take our orders from headquarters."

As we have seen, the issue of control is complicated by the conditions that make the management of conflict the policeman's most important task. It is a task that is more difficult in places where conflicting
behavior norms and values are most evident and where attitudes and

behavior deviate the most from the standards of "nice, white, middle-class folks." This describes a social milieu in which the bases of political power are apt to be shifting, with social groups splitting, coalescing on new issues, and polarizing in a struggle for power. Eleanor Harlow describes the situation as follows:

> Because what the police should do and how they should do it cannot be standardized for every situation, they are required to decide for themselves, often instantly and in a hostile environment, not merely what is "legal" or illegal, but what is right and wrong, what is "order" and when does order become "disorder," what is an "antisocial" act within a given context, and what behavior can be considered "disturbing" to society. These are issues which social scientists and lawyers might be hard put to answer and over which different groups and individuals certainly would disagree. The police cry that no matter what they do they are criticized is valid, and probably necessarily so. In a situation of competing and conflicting values and norms, someone is going to feel that police interference was unnecessary, morally wrong, inadequate, illegal, discriminatory, badly undertaken, or unjust. ["Problems in Police-Community Relations," p. 19]

One Side of the Argument

Those who advocate steps to restore community or neighborhood control of the police obviously begin with the assumption that the police in the American metropolis are no longer under civilian control; that is, democratic public control. For them, it is a question of how to make the police more responsive to the needs of all groups in the community. The feeling is that the police increasingly control themselves, in a manner irrelevant to community needs and wishes. In this sense, the police are seen as having become "too damn independent," and with the rise of police unions, the speculation is that they are likely to become even more so. The argument is that such things as psychological screening of police recruits, human relations training, and "all the talk about police professionalization" have not worked to restore civilian control of the police—that in fact, the gap between policemen and civilian is greater than ever.

What to do? Arthur Waskow of the Institute for Policy Studies in Washington has identified three possible directions:

1. Formal restructuring of metropolitan police departments into federations of neighborhood police forces, with control of each neighborhood force in the hands of neighborhood people through elected commissions.

2. Creation of countervailing organizations (in effect, "trade unions" *of those policed*), responsible to a real political base, able to hear grievances and force change.

3. Transformation of the police "profession" and role so as to end the isolation of policemen from the rest of the community, thus to establish *de facto* community control by chiefly informal means. ["Community Control of the Police"]

The first of these alternatives, Waskow explains, would be institutionalized by the election of neighborhood or precinct police commissions which would (1) appoint high-level precinct officers (perhaps with the approval of metropolitan headquarters, the mayor, or a civil service commission); (2) approve the assignment in the precinct of new policemen and be able to require transfers out; (3) discipline officers, perhaps with the concurrence of a city-wide appeal board; and (4) set basic policy on law enforcement priorities in the neighborhood.

Those fostering such an arrangement feel that it would respond to the allegation that no great metropolis can be democratically governed from City Hall. Secondly, they feel that it responds to the concentration of blacks (and other minorities) in certain neighborhoods and allows for police service fitting the needs of particular parts of the city, just as presently exists in suburbia. Policemen might even be required to live in the neighborhood where they work, although this could be difficult to enforce.

To those who object to this proposal on the grounds of "hot pursuit" considerations, it is said that such difficulties already exist across police jurisdictional boundaries. Similar practical solutions can be worked out. Moreover, it may even be possible to visualize a single metropolitan police organization of diverse and largely autonomous neighborhood forces: a confederation of sorts, organized, perhaps, in the pattern of the national police system of England. And it is added, there is really nothing new about the idea of different systems of policing from neighborhood to neighborhood; it already exists in metropolitan areas, *defined by the police rather than by the public.*

Certain aspects of police organization would, under this proposal, continue to be handled at central headquarters: records, finger-printing, radio communications, certain specialized squads, training, planning and research, crime in the business district, and the like.

As to the second proposal—the control of the police through countervailing power—a few experiments have been attempted. The Community Alert Patrols in Watts (and counterparts elsewhere) and the Community Review Board established by the Mexican-American community in Denver are examples. So-called Citizen Observer teams also come to mind. These are to be carefully distinguished from civilian review boards; the main difference is in the effort to mount independent political power to confront that of police forces, without utilizing a quasi-judicial model (Waskow, p. 5). Political pressure comes, rather, through appeals to public opinion.

One advantage of the countervailing power approach, Waskow points out, is that it can be undertaken without the agreement of those in power. Another is that it is not necessarily anchored in a neighborhood. A third point is that, in the short run, it is wiser to organize the powerless to *oppose* police power than it is to organize them to *grasp* it —lest the recognition of need for drastic social change in other spheres be stultified. Moreover, "the enemy" is seen as not only the formal police command and its ties with the metropolitan power structure; it is also the informal police subculture, with its "blue curtain" political power through unions and fraternal associations.

The third option identified by Waskow—transformation of the police "professional" and role—would require, he believes, the radical *deprofessionalizing* of some police roles, particularly on-the-street, peace-keeping functions. Waskow foresees much of this type of police work being performed by nonsworn personnel, not carrying arms, and dressed in an unmilitary style uniform. Such personnel would live in the neighborhood where they work. Waskow's description of these peace-keepers is similar to that of the community service officer depicted by the President's Crime Commission, sometimes called paraprofessionals. The main point, for Waskow, is that such personnel would be the most visible "policemen," and would be perceived by residents in any neighborhood much more as "our police," thereby establishing informal control. This plan also splits police work into distinct roles, which Waskow feels is one of its strengths.

We may suggest parenthetically, however—reflecting our opinion —that Waskow seems to underestimate what is involved in on-the-street order maintenance. He says that this role is not a highly technical or specialized one, but depends rather on "a fairly widespread and certainly nonprofessional skill in conciliatory human relations." We think this point would draw an argument from many policemen, including even some policemen who heartily dislike "calming people down." One line of the argument would probably be: "How educate an escaping armed robber so he will refrain from shooting the peace-keeper officer, not knowing that the officer isn't a *real* policeman?" There has been a recent instance or two in which black community service officers of a police department were shot to death by snipers in a predominantly black neighborhood. This is certainly not an argument against the judicious use of paraprofessionals. But to draw a parallel, in the use of teacher aides in urban public schools, the aide is most effective when paired with a knowledgeable, experienced teacher.

Waskow's sympathy for neighborhoood control is representative of a significant feeling in numerous large cities about both schools and police. The central issue is political power, and conflict is inevitable no matter which option (or combination of options) materializes. Waskow concludes, with reference to the police:

. . . it is hard to see how democratic civilian control over a staff of armed men who are widely believed to hold a monopoly over legitimate violence and who are well organized in a separate subculture and a strong political force can be re-established without intense political conflict. [p. 7][10]

Another Side of the Argument

James Q. Wilson presents another side of the argument in "Controlling the Police."[11] What is involved, he says, is two competing models of how best to maintain order. One model—held by police officers generally—is what may be called *institutional*. In this view, law must be strictly enforced and with special vigor in those areas where community and familial norms appear weakest. Furthermore, according to this model, high-crime or high-disorder areas offer too many temptations for corruption to police officers, best controlled by centrally directed police activity. Moreover, insuring due process of law requires administrative regularity, strongly enforced departmental rules, and central authority.

Opposed to this is what Wilson labels the *communal* model. This position begins with the observation that most police work is concerned, not with serious crime, but with regulating public conduct. Wilson refers to this model as, in effect, "suburbanizing" the central city; that is, permitting each neighborhood (usually defined along lines of class and race) to determine its own style of police service by a system of participatory democracy.

Wilson sympathizes with the objectives of the communal model but questions the means, for these reasons:

1. A central city cannot be fully suburbanized because it is, by definition, *central*—a place where many competing life styles come into frequent contact. It is here that the deepest social cleavages exist.

2. Therefore, giving central city neighborhoods control of the police risks making the police power an instrument for interneighborhood conflict. It might well put the police "at the mercy of the rawest emotions, the most demágogic spokesmen, and the most provincial concerns." The possibility of a small, self-serving minority seizing control of the police (or the schools) would become "very great indeed."

Wilson points out that these are arguments against plans *to disperse the authority* that governs the police, not against ways to *decentralize the functions* of the police. The latter tends to strengthen local units; the dispersal of authority, in contrast, tends to weaken them. As Wilson phrases it: "Precinct commanders in a *decentralized* department would have greater freedom of action and more control over their patrolmen; precinct commanders in a *dispersed* department would surrender that control to whatever constellation of political forces the neighborhood might produce."

Wilson opts in favor of what is, in effect, Waskow's third alternative: an approach to the patrolman's work in terms of role definition emphasizing order maintenance functions, which would have the effect of bringing the officer closer to the people in a neighborhood, even to the possible requirement that the officer live in the neighborhood. But Wilson does not seem to share Waskow's view that the patrolman's function in this respect are less than professional. Wilson further observes that "a community concerned about lowering its crime rates would be well advised to devote its attention and resources to those parts of the criminal justice system, especially the courts and correctional agencies, which—unlike the police—spend most of their time processing (often in the most perfunctory and ineffective manner) persons who repeatedly perpetrate these crimes."

To those who defend the communal model for police control on the grounds that it avoids the "middle class bias" of the legal code and of moral order, Wilson retorts that if this means a concern for the security of person and property and a desire to avoid intrusions into one's privacy and disturbances of one's peace, it is not clear why this is a bad thing. If on the other hand it means a dislike for eccentric dress or manners, the term "bias" is aptly chosen.

Another objection Wilson has to the communal model is that it fails to provide for social class differences within a given neighborhood. For example, middle-class blacks now often live close to lower-class blacks. How can one style of policing in such a neighborhood be satisfactory for both? There are presently complaints about "a single standard of justice" on a community-wide basis; why would it be more acceptable on a neighborhood basis?

An Issue in Suspension

It is apparent that the issue of community control of the police revolves largely around the question—again—of role definition. If the major function of the police in big cities is conflict management, as most analysts claim, there will be inevitable disagreement (therefore complaints) as to what should be done, how, and to whom. Until the poor become middle class, as Wilson puts it, the question of control of the police (and of the schools) will continue to be a hotly contested political issue.

However, much can be done to "cool it," short of turning to a plan for control that may succeed only in aggravating tensions because it copies on a smaller logistic scale what is presently wrong with the system on a larger scale. The principal objective is to develop conditions in which the police are truly responsive to the needs of people residing in particular neighborhoods, so as to encourage perceptions of the police as "our police." As the needs and life styles of people differ from community to community and neighborhood to neighborhood, so the style of policing should differ. There appears to be no reason why this objective cannot be achieved under centralized, imaginative, truly professionalized administration—and all that this implies for policies, supervision, planning, recruitment standards, and training of personnel.

Police administration in some large cities today is proving that it can be done. And in such cities, it is amazing how little talk there is of civilian review boards and community control of the police—except perhaps in "pockets" of a metropolitan area where a relatively small, independent police agency is being maintained by antediluvian politicians. "Neighborhood" control in such circumstances might well be directed to the common good—at least temporarily, even if it leads to some political 'head-rolling"—as a means of furthering the concept of centralized metropolitan or regional police administration. This can be done in a way that preserves, and in fact cultivates, the equally important goal of making the police officer *part of,* not apart from the neighborhood or community he serves.

Community control, of course, poses drastic challenges to the political (and economic, for power flows with access to the tax base) status quo. In the case of public schools in many large cities, the idea is vigorously opposed by many professional educators and politicians who see it, quite naturally, as a threat to their "turf." Advisory councils, on the other hand, are not threatening because no shift in authority is involved. One way or another, community involvement is "the name of the game—with schools or police—and controversy on this issue has become an urban commonplace.

Notes to Chapter Fifteen

1. An important reference for this chapter is Chap. 4, entitled "Police Conduct and the Public," of *Field Surveys V* (Michigan State University) for the President's Commission on Law Enforcement and Administration of Justice. This part of the Michigan State U. survey report was prepared by John E. Angell, then a member of the faculty of the (then) School of Police Administration and Public Safety at Michigan State. He is now Coordinator of Education and Training for the Dayton, Ohio, Police Department.

2. See also the following additional works by Walter Gellhorn: "Administrative Procedure Reform: Hardy Perennial"; "Protecting Citizens Against Administrators in Poland"; "The Swedish Justitie—Ombudsman"; *Ombudsmen and Others: Citizens' Protectors in Nine Countries;* "The

Norwegian Ombudsman"; *When Americans Complain: Governmental Grievance Procedures.*

3. See also by the same author, *The Limits of the Criminal Sanction.* Also see Herman Goldstein, "Administrative Problems in Controlling the Exercise of Police Authority."

4. See Algernon D. Black, *The People and the Police.* Also Dan W. Dodson, "Police and Community Relations as a Political Issue."

5. William P. Brown, "The Review Board Proposals Do Not Go Far Enough." Paper presented at the 71st National Conference of Government held in New York City, November 17, 1965.

6. Brown cited Albert H. Rosenthal, "The Ombudsman—Swedish Grievance Man"; Donald C. Rowat, "Ombudsmen for North America"; Martha P. and Andrew N. Farley, "An American Ombudsman: Due Process in the Administrative State"; Kenneth C. Davis, "Ombudsman in America." See also Donald C. Rowat, ed., *The Ombudsman: Citizen's Defender.*

7. *United States Criminal Code* (Title 18), Section 242.

8. One possibility regarding such appeals is described in Study 6 (Part III), "A Model for Handling Citizen Complaints," in Radelet and Reed, *Studies.*

9. For a study of the grand jury in California as ombudsman, see Bruce T. Olson, "Ombudsman on the West Coast." See also the following works: William H. Hewitt, "New York City's Civilian Complaint Review Board Struggle"; Lee P. Brown, "Police Review Boards" and "Handling Complaints Against the Police"; I.A.C.P. Position Statement on Police Review Boards; Whisenand and Felkenes, "An Ombudsman for Police"; and Stanley V. Anderson, *Ombudsman for American Government?*

10. A proposal inspired by the Black Panthers that would have turned the Berkeley, California, Police Department over to neighborhood control was on the ballot for public referendum in Berkeley in November 1970. The Acting Chief of Police referred to the plan as "unworkable." But more than 15,000 people signed the petition to put the matter on the ballot. The referendum was postponed to the April 1971 municipal election, when the proposal was roundly defeated. But the membership of the city council was "liberalized," and there was speculation that the police department was sure to feel some effects. In New York City, Mayor Lindsay proposed in June 1970 that 62 neighborhood governments, along the lines of community planning boards, be set up throughout the city. Subsequently, the proposal was aired and debated at numerous public hearings.

11. Also in James Q. Wilson, *Varieties of Police Behavior,* pp. 284–299.

Summary
of Part Three

Our general purpose in Part Three has been to consider some of the more striking sociological aspects of contemporary problems of police and community relations. We began by alluding briefly to the standard sociological classification of the various patterns of group interaction called *social processes:* cooperation, competition, conflict, acculturation, and others. We were especially interested in the measures by which a society brings its individual members and subgroups into sufficient conformity to permit the survival of the society. These measures are referred to by the collective term *social control,* and law is its most obvious form. Therefore, the vital functions of law observance and law enforcement are universally recognized.

Social change, however—especially in its effects upon group interaction in modern society—has radically transformed social control. One way of explaining current problems in police and community relations is by discussing the relationship between social change and social control. To ask what has happened to *community* is another way of suggesting the same thing. Unquestionably, social control has become infinitely complicated. We illustrated this by describing current population trends in the United States the increasing concentration of our people in big cities; the movement of people outward, from central city to suburbs; and the qualitative nature (in the human relations sense) of the suburban movement. We analyzed in particular how the latter trend has affected black people in the metropolis, caught up for the past two generations in adjustment to urbanization. We devoted special attention to the so-called culture of poverty. These are crucial matters in police and community relations, given what is known about the reciprocal attitudes of police and minority groups, and of police and the poor.

The Movement in civil rights and race relations in the United States since World War II was our next consideration. We chronicled the main events, including the emergence of nonviolent, direct action under Martin Luther King's leadership; the rise of black nationalism, spearheaded especially by Malcolm X; and the urban catastrophes of the past few years. The issue of racial integration versus racial separation was examined, along with the violence phenomenon symbolized by the "law and order" undercurrent of the 1970 political campaign.

Many people tend to equate police-minority group relations with police-community relations. We earlier noted a distinction, saying among other things that one is an important part or aspect of the other. So we devoted a chapter to analyzing the relationship of the police with minority groups specifically. We saw the base of the problem as one of power: the police as symbolic agents of the *powerful* elements, legally required to serve *all* the people, interacting with the *powerless* —many of whom are black or of other minority groups, and many of whom, white or black, are poor. The dual stereotyping and displaced hostility in this interaction were pointedly emphasized. Many views would hold that efforts to improve police and minority group relations in the 1960s amounted only to a "holding action," with little effect on the real problem.

"Brutality" is the emotion-packed charge often directed against the police by the powerless. It is not usually defined with great care; we characterized three levels of definition for the term by way of suggesting one of the communication obstacles. We delineated some of the most frequent complaints and countercomplaints of the police and minority groups. Has society at large made "dirty workers" of the police, with their main task that of controlling those who do not share equitably in society's largesse?

The black and police subcultures were next compared through the effects of the sociopsychological concept of *cognitive dissonance*. The dissonance is great indeed. But it was observed that race itself is much less the decisive friction factor than is social class. The association of race and crime lends itself to facile statistical classification, bolstered by perpetuated stereotypes. It is easier to refer to "Negro crime" than it is to develop classifications reflecting the fact that the causes of crime are nonracial.

We then posed a revolutionary question: can the police lead the community in race relations? Can they be "monitors of social change" in their main job of social conflict management? By any contemporary barometer, the police officer of minority group background will be of great strategic importance. But such officers have been difficult to recruit. We reviewed ten reasons for this. We concluded the chapter with a brief consideration of police relationships with other-than-black minority groups and of the manner in which the civil rights movement has affected other-than-police components of the criminal justice system.

Social upheaval in urban America in the 1960s was manifest in various forms and degrees of collective behavior: crowds, mobs, symbols, social movements, riots, etc. We referred briefly to such phenomena, noting their special importance to the police, and we touched on social responses to the collective behavior associated with The Movement. We considered civil disobedience as a particularly sensitive aspect of this matter. We distinguished what it is from what it is not, compared the ideas of Thoreau and Gandhi on the subject, explored the meaning of law, and reviewed the approach of various writers to the conditions for moral justification of civil disobedience.

The Movement in race relations and civil rights in the 1960s was in considerable degree a *youth* movement. The reciprocal attitudes of youth and police are of special interest in the study of police and community relations. The roots of youthful attitudes toward authority systems and authority figures (e.g., the police officer) are established, as we saw in an earlier chapter, in the political socialization processes experienced by individual children. We referred to a number of studies dealing with this subject, including several focusing on the junior high school age level, which is thought to be a particularly important age group in attitude research of this type.

We alluded to the special nuances of police-youth attitudes in the context of teen-age gangs and "disaffected" youth. The college scene was our next consideration; we moved from this to hippie subculture; and thence to a passing comment regarding dope and drugs. The chapter ended with an indication of the implications for the police of contemporary youth culture.

The issue of citizen control of the police was our central concern in the final chapter of Part Three. We analyzed several questions that arise in the matter of complaints, internally within a police agency, and externally when a citizen lodges a complaint against the department or against one or more of its personnel. We recommended a positive philosophy for dealing with complaints of all kinds. We applied this philosophy to a critique of existing complaint procedures in police agencies, one conclusion being that so-called civilian review boards are not generally "the answer," and we defended this position. We suggested that the Scandinavian ombudsman system merits much more testing in this country, for it appears to have much to recommend it as an appeals entity. We identified criteria for evaluating the adequacy of both external and internal complaint mechanisms. Finally, we discussed the pro and con of community control of the police at the neighborhood level—a concept that is also a controversial issue in school administration.

What are some of the "benchmarks" of the *specific* problems of police and community relations, particularly as to minority groups, the poor, the "disaffected," the powerless? The following may be suggested, to be placed side-by-side with the more generalized points enumerated in the Summary for Part Two:

1. The stereotype held by minority groups of the police officer as a symbolic agent and representative of the powerful, therefore "the enemy"—a matter of displaced hostility.

2. The counterstereotype in the image the police officer often entertains of the minority group; for example, the idea that crime is racially caused.

3. The problem of value gap and cognitive dissonance indicated in a comparison of police subculture and that of poor blacks, and the accompanying communication chasm.

4. The underrepresentation of minority groups in the personnel of police agencies.

5. The inadequacies of citizen complaint procedures in the matter of public control of police behavior.

6. Special problems for the police in dealing with civil disobedience.

7. Problems for the police associated with youthful attitudes toward authority.

8. The "dirty worker" public image of the police.

9. Deficiencies in police recruitment standards and in police training, especially pertaining to the conflict management aspects of police work which have become so important.

10. Police administrative and supervisory "traditionalism" in failing to see police and community relations as basically a *management* concept.

To set the stage for Part Four, we may say that there are four subjects in the purview of this text that merit more attention than we have devoted to them to this point, though all have been mentioned more than once. These are:

1. Relationships within the criminal justice system between the police, prosecution, and the courts.

2. The special problems of community relations for corrections agencies.

3. Police-press relations—in the broader sense, relations between the criminal justice system and the media of public information.

4. The police and their political-governmental relationships.

Part Four comprises chapters dealing with each of these four subjects.

Part Four

Special Considerations

Chapter Sixteen

Police,
Prosecution,
and the Courts

We have referred more than once to the fact that the police are part of several overlapping social systems, one of which is called the *criminal justice system*. We defined a *social system* as a pattern of continuing social relations among individuals or groups. A social system, then, is presumably an harmonious arrangement intended to bring order out of confusion, an interacting or interdependent group of factors and functions forming a unified whole. This definition clearly contains an idealistic element: that a social system integrates predominantly positive, or "good," relations into its components, else it may not function well as a system. No serious relationship problems should be present within an authentic, properly functional social system.

But social systems are, after all, human inventions relating people in various parts of a process. A given social system is more or less functional depending upon the quality of these relationships, in exactly the same way as a community or a large police department (both complicated and multiple social systems in and of themselves) are more or less functional as measured against their purposes. Hence, the relationships within the criminal justice system—between police and prosecutor, between police and the courts, between prosecutor and courts, between police and corrections, between the courts and corrections—are highly important aspects of what we mean by *community relations* in the major theme of this book.

Since the criminal justice system in the United States is a vast and extremely complex phenomenon, our discussion of it requires some limitations. We will look at part of the system in this chapter, and part in the next. An avalanche of literature deals with the system—descriptively, analytically, and, in the recent past, more and more critically. We will not attempt to recapitulate much of this here. However, we will stress that a considerable part of what is dysfunctional in the criminal justice system has to do with relationships among its components, and between each of these components and the larger outside community. Therefore, in discussing the internal and external relationships of the criminal justice system, we will be considering matters at the center of its deficiencies. In short, we contend simply that the paramount problems of the criminal justice system are largely and fundamentally *relationship* problems. Consequently, their solution requires improved relations, both as means and as end. This is the central thesis of this and the following chapters.

Criminal Justice as a System

We have already raised a key question: Is our criminal justice system really a system? There are those so convinced that it is *not* that they refer to it, unapologetically, as a nonsystem. Basically, they have relationships in mind. As an example, Robert H. Scott, director of the first National Institute on Police and Community Relations at Michigan State University in 1955, clearly implies that a social system is more or less functional, therefore more or less truly a system depending upon the quality of relationships (coordination) observable in the system:

> The administration of criminal justice, viewed as a totality, may seem to be a continuous and coordinated process. However, when examined at close hand, serious gaps and barriers become apparent. Inconsistencies inhibit cooperation; chasms cut communications. The process of criminal justice becomes a series of segments, separated from each other by differences in philosophy, purpose, and practice. Moreover, the segments themselves are often characterized by internal conflicts and confusion. The blanket of the administration of justice, when seen at close range, becomes a patchwork quilt. ["Problems in Communication and Cooperation"]

Scott is among many who are saying that our criminal justice system today does not score very well in its intent to be a coordinated whole bent on a unified purpose. It is, to this extent, a system in search of systematizing.

Identifying the Problems of the System

What are the main problems? Scott identifies them as follows:

1. Problems of the age of the offender. These include questions of procedure, questions of due process, and questions of custody or treatment.

2. Problems of the so-called youthful offender, lying athwart the fields of juvenile delinquency and adult crime, thus of the dual processes of juvenile and adult justice.

3. Problems of judicial process in the disposition of felonies and misdemeanors. A particularly thorny problem is the county jail—where treatment programs are rare, where secure storage is regarded as more important than treatment, and where many persons are confined for long periods before they have been found guilty of any crime. In short, there is no coherent system of justice for the adult offender; rather there is one system for the misdemeanant and another for the felon.

4. Problems of different and, to some extent opposing, philosophies within the system, particularly in functions and goals: i.e., court decisions upholding due process that restricts police powers; punishment vs rehabilitation (or custody vs treatment) of offenders; conflicts arising from overspecialized functions and poorly defined roles.

5. Problems of conflicting theories in the causes of, and responsibility for, crime. One theory emphasizes societal and environmental factors, another, individual choice; and there are other, in-between theories.

6. Problems of professional education in the criminal justice field. This reflects the basic questions just suggested: goals, roles, functions, specialization, theories of crime causation, etc. Teachers tend to perpetuate their insular interests and approaches. Truly systemic perspective that is *problem-centered* rather than agency-bound or too narrowly professional is difficult to come by. Stereotyping, defensiveness, and scapegoating abound within the system. Ties to community agencies such as education and welfare are often not effectively established or coordinated. In short, our approaches to crime and delinquency prevention and treatment frequently fail because they tend to deal with the problem in fragments, compartments, pieces. The critical test of a criminal justice system is the degree to which it succeeds in coping with the crime phenomenon as a *totality*.

Scott's analysis is a good beginning in pinpointing the relationship problems of the system. Elmer H. Johnson, formerly of the Center for the Study of Crime, Delinquency and Corrections at Southern Illinois

University, has examined the dilemmas in contemporary law enforcement and concludes that they are traceable to relationship problems among law enforcement programs ("Interrelatedness of Law Enforcement Programs").[1] Johnson begins his analysis with the police role question, observing that to deal with criminals depends largely on suppression and control measures oriented to viewing the offender as an enemy. But most of the patrolman's time is spent at tasks of social-behavioral and political matters that do not lend themselves to suppressive measures. Therapeutic and preventive ideologies are favored in these latter tasks (shades of Pfiffner's terms again); Johnson states that "the tasks of greatest quantitative importance involve the officer in problems for which he is inadequately equipped to deal and which involve the police agency in ideological conflicts."

Johnson points out that one response to this problem—as we have seen—is the view that the police should be limited to dealing with "real" crime.[2] Johnson refers to this as a "cops-and-robbers" model of law enforcement, conducive to a "barracks" mentality among police officers. (Pfiffner calls it an *equitation complex.*) It is based upon the adversary concept of police-citizen relations. It "assumes falsely that sharp delimitation of function will free law enforcement from the dilemma of being compelled to frame policies while overtly denying that police executives have the obligation to assume policy-making responsibilities" (Johnson, p. 510).

Johnson argues further that limiting police responsibility to dealing with "real" crime "ignores the fundamental fact that law enforcement operates within a larger social sphere requiring coordination of police actions with the working of the other social institutions of the community." This point is crucial, for in effect Johnson is declaring that a narrow definition of police role as "crook catcher" tends to isolate the police from the community and its social and political structure. It therefore exemplifies the fragmented, compartmentalized approach to crime and order that Scott points to as one of the chief problems of the criminal justice system.

Interrelated Efforts of the System

The necessary interrelatedness of efforts to deal with the crime problem, Johnson continues, may be seen in three references:

1. The various aspects of the work of a typical police agency should form a cohesive whole. This requires considerable managerial skill in a large agency. The misuse of specialization can, for instance, jeopardize the sense of interdependence that binds the employees of the agency into a common effort.

2. Historically, police agencies in this country have been tied to local governments. The fragmentation of government has created a frag-

mentation of law enforcement agencies and of law enforcement perspective. But crime is not "structured" in such a manner. The fragmentation of crime control agencies makes coordination on a metropolitan, regional, or national scale difficult. This was a major emphasis of the President's Crime Commission in 1966 and has more recently been stressed by the Law Enforcement Assistance Administration.

3. Police work is but one phase of the overall social control system of a society or community. Various social institutions join in this responsibility. The quality of interrelatedness among these agencies and institutions is therefore of vital importance.

Johnson refers to the police agency as a social institution in these terms:

> The ultimate purpose of criminal law and law enforcement is to lend support to the network of social institutions which maintain order and regularity in the human relationships within the community. Each social institution consists of a number of culturally defined behavior patterns, closely related to each other, which are transmitted through the generations to afford a set of expectations whereby the behavior of individuals is made consistent with the particular social purposes served by the particular institution. [P. 512]

A police department depends upon and must cooperate with other social institutions. Police work cannot be a thing apart. But some forces and factors, as well as organizational and professional chauvinism tend to work against cooperation and coordination. Johnson identifies some of these influences:

> Policemen as specialists in law enforcement, implying that the average citizen (like other social institutions) is free of the obligations, held earlier in history, to participate actively in police work.

> A police bureaucracy in a semimilitary model, which favors the development of organizational loyalty surpassing loyalty to the total community served by the organization. The police subculture, as with any subculture, tends to separate policemen from the larger community.

> Activities that make the patrolman "a manager of human relationships similar to a social worker," when he really wants to be thought of primarily as an opponent of criminals. Again, this role predicament generates in many police officers an attitude of resistance to activities that might be interpreted as social work. Building and maintaining cooperation with other agencies and institutions is often interpreted in this way.

> A social institutional crisis characteristic of communities generally, in part because of the rising discontent of the powerless and "dis-

affected." Increasingly prevalent demands for reform of familiar institutional arrangements make the police and the criminal justice system a favorite target, a scapegoat for general social and moral default. But at the same time, the police are expected to control the unrest, the agitation, and the disorder that more frequently mark demands for change. In this sense too, the police are placed in a peculiar pincers— a position not conducive to cooperative relationships in the community. They are at once the agents of a holding action against change in the status quo; and at the same time they are symbols of what is regarded by the reform-minded as most needing change.

The interdependence of social institutions that causes the imperfections of one institution to spread to another. Take, for example, the relationship of the police with the courts. The separation of powers is pregnant with potential conflict on such issues as admissibility of evidence, methods of interrogation, status of confessions, and use of force. Also, tension develops in the relationship because the courts determine disposition of cases, thereby creating a test of the "success" of police work which the police cannot control. As Johnson says: "Critics of the courts charge that police are being handcuffed. Critics of the police contend court control is required to prevent police lawlessness. While the debate rages, the failure to establish effective policies leaves an institutional vacuum" (p. 513).

The organization of police for street work, making them more likely than social service agencies to contact the "hard-to-reach." Thus, the police are drawn into this institutional vacuum, as Johnson puts it, "because they deal with the problems of the poor and ignorant which other agencies are not anxious to serve."

To quote Johnson again:

In urban ghettos, the flight of "respectable" people to the suburbs, and the erosion of social institutions, have left the police the major representative of middle-class values among a population of socially and economically underpriileged people. This pattern is consistent with the tradition of assigning the police those tasks disgusting to others.

The police are handicapped in serving these needs because of the lack of an effective functional division of labor among the social service agencies for specialized emergency services. The lack of an integrated system forces the police to provide services, although the social service agencies do not regard their work as legitimate. [P. 514]

The Police Concept of Relations

Given these considerations, it becomes clear why the police often adopt a "concept of relations" which means, in effect, "help us do our job, *as we see it.*" Intended, as Johnson points out, to preserve the status quo for the police department while other agencies and institutions do all the changing, this concept is not conducive to cooperative problem-solving in the community. It is, rather, a concept in which ballyhoo, press agentry, propaganda, and whitewashing are apt to be featured. The police are cast in these activities as the father who knows best, trying to deal (alone) with wayward children. This paternalistic attitude is particularly aggravating to minority groups, because it is patronizing and counter to the sense of identity inculcated by the current movement.

The police have no monopoly on this inner-directed pattern of thought regarding relationships. It is matched, for instance, by the attitude of many public school professionals. "Yes, cooperation with other community agencies is good and necessary. But it must be on our terms. After all, we are professionals, and we know best." Organizational, institutional, and professional chauvinism has many faces; that the criminal justice system has its fair share of it is hardly headline news. Yet in times of unusual social instability, myopic functional rigidity and stubborn conformity to old ways hardly contribute to enlightened community services, nor the development of coordinated, cooperative efforts to deal with problems that can be dealt with in no other way. Johnson's conclusion is a crisp summary:

> ... the dilemmas faced by the police executive stem from the interrelatedness of social institutions, all of which are undergoing a crisis. Because the ultimate significance of police work is its contribution to the social order, law enforcement is affected by any condition affecting the social order. The final solution of the dilemmas of the police awaits resolution of the institutional crises encountered by the community as a whole.
>
> Because law enforcement is largely a local matter, the reform of inadequacies of local government is a vital prerequisite. Because of the inherent linkages between law enforcement and the judiciary, the possibilities of revision of police procedures will depend on the outcome of changes in the procedures of courts. The place and function of the police must be determined clearly with an integrated system of social service appropriate to the needs of the particular community. Because the adversary role characteristic of the contemporary policeman does not lend itself to social service functions, a new role is likely to emerge in the case manager model wherein the police agency provides emergency services and acts as a referral agent within a more specifically articulated system of social service agencies. [P. 516][3]

Initiative is needed for change. When police problems are said to be aspects of broader systemic and social institutional pathology, the police may conclude that nothing can be done about their problems until something happens elsewhere. So why do anything?

While ultimate, general responsibility for operating a police department and coordinating the broader criminal justice system lies in the community, leadership and initiative must come—if it is to come at all—from the police and other professionals in the system. The community must be educated and stirred to understand what needs to be changed. The police at the same time should demonstrate the type of leadership for change that is sensitively tuned to community needs. In other words, the educational process is a two-way street. Leadership is an abstract and malleable concept sometimes interpreted to mean maintaining the status quo: to continue doing the wrong things, more and more efficiently. As we have said before, police leadership in these times includes educating the community in what it *ought to want*. In this fashion, communication may be encouraged that will legitimize the need for change in the system, although not solely on the terms of the police, nor of any other one party, special interest, or faction.

A Geopolitical Approach to the Law

John Pfiffner speaks of a "geopolitical approach" to law observance.[4] A generalist public administrator heading a police agency, he contends, must be concerned with recreation, housing, welfare, health, and other specialties, as much as law enforcement. Such an administrator sees police problems as interacting with other functional specialities. Again, *coordination underlies administrative process*. Pfiffner argues that overall policy formulation, "global" strategy, and coordination are essential in dealing with the problems of crime and delinquency in urban society; and for this approach he applies the term *geopolitical*. His is surely not a lone voice. He joins Johnson in observing that the agencies dealing with law enforcement seem so overwhelmed with the enormousness of their tasks "that all they can hope to do is maintain a holding operation—keeping a finger in the dike to hold back the flood." Pfiffner describes a general systems approach to crime and delinquency which combines coordinated planning, goal setting, policy delineation tied in with community ethos, and extensive research.

This theme appears repeatedly in Pfiffner's writings. He is an unabashed proponent of what he calls "aggressive cultivation" of police-community contacts. Crime and delinquency are problems, he insists, that call for systemic and cross-systemic perspective. For examples, what may be learned from medical and psychiatric therapeutic teamwork in community mental health; from industrial management group dynamics, learning theory, and planned change; from human ecologists on the effect of changes in social or physical environment upon attitudes and behavior; and even from military government (perhaps as suggested by John Hersey in *A Bell for Adano*), on whose attitude toward the civilian community Pfiffner says, "Certainly the military precedent in embracing social science research as an integral phase of military operations should be canvassed by the police."

Pfiffner has frequently referred to the opposite value orientations of *police types* and what he calls *rehabs*. Scott may have had this in mind when he spoke of "philosophical conflicts" within the criminal justice system. Pfiffner believes that a therapeutic team approach to police work with juveniles has emerged. At first, serious conflict often occurred between custodial security people and the therapists, and it still occurs in many institutions where new concepts of treatment have not taken deep root. But he thinks the policeman-specialist in work with juveniles is more and more "evolving a therapeutic component, with a community orientation."

The Police-Prosecutor-Court Relationship

So far, our discussion in this chapter has taken a broad view. Now we focus on the police-prosecutor-court relationship. Ramsey Clark's recently published broadside *Crime in America* is more diffuse than focused, blasting slums, poverty, racism, overpopulation, unemployment, ignorance, ill health, bad housing, unreliable crime statistics, organized crime, drugs, guns, undertrained and underpaid police, confused police jurisdiction, inadequate and underpaid prosecutors, imprudently picked judges, court delays, antiquated and overcrowded jails and prisons, seriously deficient rehabilitation facilities and procedures, and insufficient recourse to science in crime detection and the study of criminal behavior.[5] Clark is also critical of capital punishment and the suppression of dissent.

Clark believes in local law enforcement. He calls for closer ties between police and community, especially the youth of the community. Whereas district attorneys are politically elected or appointed, Clark advocates their being drawn from a career service without political recommendation. Techniques must be devised for clearing court dockets more quickly, for continuing legal education of judges, and for better ways to select them. The criminal code should be constantly revised. Probation and parole must be vastly improved, with rehabilitation as a clear goal; job training, work release, halfway houses, and pre-release guidance centers are essential. Preventive detention—jailing the accused until his trial on the ground that his prior convictions make him a bad risk—is inconsistent, Clark believes, with the presumption of innocence; and he further contends that interim hearings would clog the courts even more. Clark likes the indeterminate sentence, because that seems to him the only treatment concept that is consistent with the goal of rehabilitation. The bail system, Clark holds, actually deprives poor people of their liberty although they are not yet convicted of a crime.

In reviewing Clark's work, Isadore Silver concluded:

> The crucial questions are whether a modern society can depend upon a criminal justice system—even a perfect one—to maintain a viable

Social and Moral Order, whether the very concept of "criminal justice" (and how that term grates upon the ear) is meaningful, and
whether we have the knowledge and means to find creative alternatives
to *any* criminal justice system. Would Clark's estimable—and often
courageous, though traditional—reforms really "create a wholesome
environment" and eliminate or significantly reduce what we choose to
call "crime"? Do all societies need a concept of "crime" to define
themselves, and can modern societies afford such a concept? We—
and I include myself as well as Mr. Clark—being good Americans, do
not often choose to face those questions. We, liberal and conservative
alike, cannot be but losers because of such failure.[6]

Irving Reichert, who is associated with the Continuing Education
of the Bar program at the University of California at Berkeley, also
contends that the center of our criminal justice problems is philosophical.[7] Argument rests, he says, on whether it is better that some guilty
men go free to endanger the community, than it is to have all men live
in fear of the state. The founding fathers of our country opted in favor
of freedom. But this did not settle the debate, a debate that becomes
particularly sharp in times of increasing lawlessness. Reichert points out
that the present period is certainly not the first in our history when this
argument has been especially fierce. One constitutional lawyer has
asked, when *wasn't* there a crime crisis? But this point is hardly reassuring, and surely not intended to engender complacency. Yet, in perspective, neither should the Bill of Rights be repealed.

The Voices for Reform

The voices for radical overhaul of the criminal justice system are
legion. That substantial change must be wrought appears to be a virtually unanimous verdict; exactly *what* changes, and *how* they are to
be made are continuing questions causing much disagreement. Presidents of the United States over several decades have called for reform.
President Nixon has said, for instance, that ways must be found to clear
the courts of an endless stream of so-called victimless crimes, such as
minor traffic offenses, loitering, and drunkenness cases. He has advocated other steps to expedite criminal process, for example, a requirement already copied by several states from the British system: that
accused persons be brought to trial within sixty days.

Chief Justice Warren Burger has called for the establishment of a
national clearing house for states to pool their ideas on reforming the
court system. He has said that the American system of criminal justice
"in every way . . . is suffering from a severe case of deferred maintenance." The American Bar Association and various associations of
police, prosecutors, and judges have been saying similar things for years.

The Chief Justice's ideas were not long in catching on. A National Center on State Courts was established in June, 1971. The ABA immediately picked up the Burger theme for upgrading legal education and for regulating lawyers' conduct. Congress moved more slowly on the suggestion of the Chief Justice to create a judiciary council. His dissenting opinion in a 1971 case brought the so-called exclusionary rule into question. "For more than 55 years," he wrote, "this court has enforced a rule under which evidence of undoubted reliability and . . . value has been suppressed and excluded from criminal cases whenever it was obtained in violation of a defendant's Constitutional rights." This rule does not deter improper conduct by police officers, contended the Chief Justice, nor does it serve the cause of justice.

Mr. Burger went on to suggest a solution that would punish both the constable and the criminal. He proposed legislation that would compensate defendants whose rights have been violated, while providing that "no evidence, otherwise admissible, shall be excluded" from a criminal trial "because of violation of the Fourth Amendment," which protects against illegal search and seizure.

In another 1971 decision, the Chief Justice voted with the 5–4 majority and wrote the majority opinion. This decision held that a statement of confession inadmissable as evidence in court because the suspect had not been warned of his rights could nonetheless be used in court to contradict the suspect's on-the-stand testimony. The court minority saw the decision as a major break with the 1966 *Miranda* decision, later admitted for review.

President Johnson's Crime Commission accomplished the most thorough and comprehensive analysis to date of all aspects of the criminal justice system. This was its essential task; its recommendations were numerous, more or less innovative regarding specifics, and to the present time still largely ignored. There is no scarcity of information about what is wrong with the system.

The Kerner Commission report (pp. 194, 195) also had much to say on the subject. Its recommendations merit summarizing:

> That communities undertake, as an urgent priority, the reform of their lower criminal court systems to insure fair and individual justice for all. The 1967 report of the President's Commission on Law Enforcement and the Administration of Justice provides the bueprint for such reform.

> That communities formulate a plan for the administration of justice in riot emergencies. Under the leadership of the organized bar, all segments of the community, including minority groups, should join in drawing up such a plan. The plan should provide clear guidelines for police on when to arrest or use alternatives to arrest. Adequate provision must be made for extra judges, prosecutors, defense counsel,

court and police personnel to provide prompt processing, and for well-equipped detention facilities. Details of the plan should be publicized so that the community will know what to expect if an emergency occurs.

That existing laws be reviewed to ensure their adequacy for riot control and the charging of riot offenders, and for authority to use temporary outside help in the judicial system.

That multiple-use processing forms (such as those used by the Department of Justice for mass arrests) be obtained. Centralized systems for recording arrests and locations of prisoners on a current basis should be devised, as well as fast systems to check fingerprint identification and past records. On-the-spot photographing of riot defendants may also be helpful.

That communities adopt station-house summons and release procedures (such as those used by the New York City Police Department) so that they are operational before emergency arises. All defendants who appear likely to return for trial and to refrain from renewed riot activity should be summoned and released.

That recognized community leaders be admitted to all processing and detention centers to avoid allegations of abuse or fraud, and to reassure the community about the treatment of arrested persons.

That the bar in each community undertake mobilization of all available lawyers for assignment to ensure early individual legal representation to riot defendants through disposition, and to provide assistance to prosecutors where needed. Legal defense strategies should be planned and volunteers trained in advance. Investigative help and experienced advice should be provided.

That communities and courts plan for a range of alternative conditions to release, such as supervision by civic organizations or third-party custodians outside the riot area, in preference to relying on high bail to keep defendants off the streets. The courts should set bail on an individual basis and provide for defense counsel at bail hearings. Emergency procedures for fast bail review are needed.

That mass indictments and arraignments be avoided, and reasonable bail and sentences be imposed, both during and after the riot. Sentences should be individually considered and pre-sentence reports required. The emergency plan should provide for transfer of probation officers from other courts and jurisdictions to assist in the processing of those arrested.

The American Law Institute has given impetus to the reform of criminal codes through its Model Penal Code, produced after a decade of sustained labor. In numerous states, movement toward reform of the criminal code has frequently bogged down in legislative parrying over controversial features.

The Advisory Commission on Inter-governmental Relations (ACIR), comprising twenty-six governors, mayors, judges, city and county executives and presided over by Chairman Robert M. Merriam, adopted at its meetings of September 1970 and January 1971 an extended series of recommendations dealing with state-local relations in the criminal justice system. The Commission's recommendations included the following:

1. The Courts.

   That each state establish a simplified and unified court system, abolish or overhaul justice of the peace courts, compensate judges by salary rather than by fees, and require judges to be licensed to practice law.

   That all courts in each state be subject to administrative supervision and direction by the Supreme Court or Chief Justice in that state, toward the end of uniform rules of practice and procedure.

   That all states provide an administrative office of the state courts.

   That state and local governments adopt a merit plan of selecting judges, and that judges so appointed be required to submit themselves to voter approval at an election at the end of each term.

   That states require judges to retire at seventy, and that all judges devote full-time to their judicial duties.

2. The Prosecution

   That states strengthen state responsibility for prosecution, by enhancing the attorney general's authority to oversee the work of local prosecutors and empower the Supreme Court of the particular state to remove a prosecuting attorney pursuant to prescribed procedures and safeguards.

   That states centralize the local prosecution function in a single office responsible for all criminal prosecutions.

   That states require prosecuting attorneys to be full-time officials and that their jurisdictions be redrawn so that each is large enough to require full-time attention of such an official and provide financial resources to support this office.

   That states pay at least 50 percent of the costs of local prosecuting attorney's offices.

   That states enact legislation authorizing prosecutors to bring indictments through either grand jury or information procedures. Grand juries should be used primarily in cases of alleged official corruption or extraordinary public concern.

3. The Defense Counsel for the Indigent

   That each state establish and finance a statewide system for defense of the indigent, making either a public defender or coordinated assigned counsel service readily available to every area of the state.

4. The Police

That all local governments in metropolitan areas assure the provision of full-time patrol and preliminary investigative services to their residents. County governments should assume this responsibility where necessary, charging costs to local governments. Where the county does not assume these services, the state should mandate consolidation of police services in metropolitan jurisdictions which do not provide basic police services directly or through interlocal agreements.

That counties be empowered and encouraged to perform specialized, supportive (staff and auxiliary) police services for constituent localities in single county metropolitan areas, e.g., records, communications, crime laboratory, etc. In multicounty or interstate metropolitan areas, states should encourage appropriate area-wide agencies to perform such services, e.g., regional criminal justice planning agencies, councils of government, etc.

That states authorize or encourage the creation of specialized police task forces to operate throughout multicounty and interstate metropolitan areas, to deal with extra local and organized crime.

That states enter into interstate compacts giving carefully circumscribed extraterritorial police powers relating to "close pursuit" of felonious criminal offenders and to geographically extended powers of criminal arrest.

That state governments improve the capabilities of rural police systems.

That states consider granting the appropriate state law enforcement agency a full range of statewide law enforcement powers and removing geographic limitations on the operation of such agency. Further, that an appropriate state agency be encouraged to provide centralized records and crime laboratory services to all local agencies within a state, that a uniform intrastate and interstate crime reporting system be established and that all local agencies be required, on a periodic basis, to report all felony arrest and identification records to the state agency.

That where needed, the office of sheriff be placed on a statutory rather than on a constitutional basis.

That states give metropolitan counties the option of assigning basic responsibility for countywide police services to an "independent" county police force under the control of the county chief executive or county board of commissioners.

That states abolish the office of constable and transfer its duties to appropriate lower court systems.

That states abolish the office of coroner, with the duties accruing to an appointed local medical examiner and to the local prosecuting attorney.

That states create Councils on Police Standards to develop and maintain minimum standards for police selection and basic training.

That state legislatures revise their criminal code to better define the scope of discretionary police activities—particularly as to arrest powers, search procedures, and interrogation practices. States should also enact legislation providing comprehensive tort liability to protect state and local police from tort action arising out of legitimate use of discretionary powers.

That states modify existing laws which restrict local chief executives from appointing local police chiefs from the ranks of any qualified applicants and which restrict local police chiefs from appointing division heads and assistants reporting directly to them. States should also modify veterans' preferences and state civil service regulations which limit unduly or otherwise restrict the selection, appointment and promotion of qualified local policemen.

5. The Agencies

That local criminal justice coordinating councils be established in jurisdictions having substantial administrative responsibility for at least [two] of the major components of the criminal justice system. The work of such councils should be coordinated with the Law Enforcement Assistance Administration (LEAA) regional criminal justice planning agencies.

That state and regional criminal justice planning agencies and local criminal justice coordinating councils take primary responsibility for improving interfunctional cooperation in the state-local criminal justice system.

That because a workable partnership between police and community residents is necessary to effectively prevent crime, local governments should substantially increase their efforts to involve citizens in the law enforcement and criminal justice process through the establishment of police-community relations machinery and programs.

The principle of *systemic interrelatedness* is an underlying theme of these recommendations.

Some progress has been made in the establishment of local and regional criminal justice coordinating councils. The President's Crime Commission in 1966 encouraged such organizations in its recommendations. Both the National Advisory Commission on Civil Disorders and the National Commission on the Causes and Prevention of Violence spoke in the same vein, and the Omnibus Crime and Safe Streets Acts of 1968 and 1970 stimulated national, state, and metropolitan organization in such a pattern, e.g., the New York City Criminal Justice Coordinating Council.

Pilot Programs for Reform

Such sweeping recommendations for reform centering on the interdependence of the components of the criminal justice system are plainly important in setting goals. The system so desperately needs reform that only those who are reform-minded should be encouraged to begin careers in any phase of it. But progress toward reform is so slow as to discourage all but the extraordinarily persevering. The LEAA has aroused hope for a quickening pace, but there is little in the record to date to lead one to expect that the changes most urgently needed will occur without great toil and turmoil.

One organization that has earned wide respect in the criminal justice field in recent years is the Vera Institute of Justice in New York City. This institution has conducted a number of pilot projects, carefully assessing the strengths and weaknesses of specific experiments for changing parts of the system. It was established in 1961 as a private institution financed mainly by foundation grants and some government funds, and has concentrated especially on the relationship of criminal justice administration and the poor, primarily in New York City.[8]

The Vera Institute has identified particular problem areas and has designed experimental programs aimed at benefiting both the defendant and the relevant criminal justice agency. Its first project was bail reform; the second, a police summons project. By way of illustrating the Vera approach to bail reform, a defendant had been required to remain in jail awaiting trial if he could not make bail. The costs to himself, to his family, and New York City were substantial. From 1961 to 1964, with the cooperation of the courts and other agencies, Vera experimented with a different approach that incorporated interviewing and gathering information about the defendant, his job, his family situation, and such. Vera than recommended release without bail of certain defendants; under the experiment, 3,505 persons were released and only 56 willfully failed to return to court. In the fall of 1964, the city Office of Probation took over the program for the entire city. Later, similar bail programs were initiated in numerous other cities, and the project was also influential in the drafting of the Federal Bail Reform Act of 1966. Vera moved on to an experiment with release at an earlier stage in criminal process by providing for a police summons at the time of arrest, in the case of certain misdemeanors. This also turned out to be a successful experiment, widely emulated.

Jameson Doig of Princeton University has identified the main features of the Vera approach in "Police Problems, Proposals and Strategies for Change":

Sufficiently extended involvement in the project to provide a reasonable test

Manpower to conduct the project, at Institute expense

Acceptance of responsibility for possible failure

Careful evaluation of what occurs

Building support for an idea in the face of hostile or luke-warm reception

Working in close cooperation with operating agencies and securing the full support of top city administrators

An unusually able staff, building on the prestige of past successes

Vera has moved on to such projects as testing alternatives to arresting skid-row alcoholics, experimenting with a juvenile center in Brooklyn on ways of handling juvenile offenders, and assigning a Community Service Patrol Corps in Harlem. With continuing assistance from the Ford Foundation and other sources, the Vera Institute currently is interested in such experimental projects as—

Continued development of techniques for eliminating unnecessary court appearances by police officers and civilian witnesses.

Development of a pilot program to provide employment opportunities for offenders (including drug users) who have not been able to hold regular jobs.

Organization of programs in high-crime neighborhoods to train and use local residents to perform quasi-police, quasi-probationary, and quasi-adjudicatory services.

Development of methods for evaluating judicial prediction of a defendant's dangerousness and for increasing the accuracy of such judgments.

The Vera approach is not, of course, a panacea for all problems in the criminal justice system. But it does show ways in which change can be introduced, not painlessly perhaps but with minimum political risk to those for whom such considerations are vital. State criminal justice planning agencies might well consider the Vera plan and strategy, as LEAA's National Institute of Law Enforcement and Criminal Justice seems to have in mind.

Another organization with considerable influence in the field is the National Council on Crime and Delinquency, a nonprofit citizen organization supported by contributions from United Funds, foundations, business corporations, and interested individuals. The NCCD was founded in 1907 and has a membership of approximately 60,000; its chief interest is the rehabilitation of juvenile and adult offenders. On a community, statewide, and national level, NCCD works to develop effective juvenile, family, and criminal courts; to improve probation, parole, and institutional services and facilities; and to stimulate community programs for the prevention, treatment, and control of delinquency and crime. The Council—

offers direct consultation and makes studies of correctional services as practical guides to action.

develops professional standards and guide materials for use by judges, correctional workers, and laymen.

drafts model legislation and gives legal advisory service to legislative committees, courts, bar associations, correctional agencies, and citizen groups.

conducts an annual national conference on crime and delinquency, organizes training institutes, stimulates professional training for career service in probation and parole, and assists in conducting merit examinations for the selection of professional personnel.

publishes literature and serves as a clearing house for information about correctional work, maintains an extensive library, stimulates research, and provides technical data to public information media.

Relationships Within the System

In an earlier chapter, we referred to several factors that tend to engender relationship problems within the criminal justice system between the police, prosecution, the courts, and corrections. Certain of these problems may be mentioned again at this point. For example, some recent decisions of criminal and appellate courts defining the limits of interrogation, search of the person and property and the seizure of evidence, and of the use of force have been seen by both the police and the courts as limiting discretionary decisions. The clear implication of such court rulings is that the police must be subject to the authority of law, the prosecutor, and the courts, or to the authority of some type of civil procedure for external review.

As Reiss and Bordua and others have pointed out, this comes down to a jurisdictional dispute, within the system. It is at times a matter of professionals (lawyers and judges, presumably) seeking to restrict the powers of "would-be-professionals" (the police), as Reiss puts it; and conflict is therefore inevitable. Through arrest, the police introduce suspects into the system, but the power of assessing outcome of arrest as well as of police procedure resides with the prosecutor and the courts. This makes conflict endemic in the system. Reiss summarizes the problem:

Whenever a number of roles are involved in making decisions about the *same* case, problems of overlapping jurisdiction and rights to make the decision arise. Where professionals are involved, there will be competing claims to professional competence to make the decision. The role of the patrol officer, occurring as it does at the lowest rank order in the decision-making system, makes his role most vulnerable to counterclaims to competence, and least defensible. Paradoxically, however, it is the officer's original decision that controls whether law enforcement and criminal justice agents can process the decision at all. He has the broadest possible range of discretion and jurisdiction, and therefore of possibilities for the exercise of "professional" judgment, but the most vulnerable position in the system of law enforcement and criminal justice for restricting his jurisdiction. ["Professionalization of the Police," pp. 221, 229]

Paradoxically, Reiss observes, what the police want clear, the courts want to leave open. And what the courts want clear, the police want to leave open. A result of this is described by Reiss and Bordua:

> . . . dilemmas in defining success are partially resolved by the development of a complex bargaining process between police and prosecutors, the shifting of departmental resources in directions of maximum payoff from a conviction point of view, the development of a set of attitudes that define the police as alone in the "war on crime," and the elaboration of success measures that do not require validation by the courts. ["Environment and Organization," p. 36][9]

The pertinent points, then, as seen by Reiss and Bordua are these: the police are hedged in by officials whose formal discretion is greater than theirs. Although the prosecutor and the judge are traditional figures, the system has come to include probation officers and juvenile court people, with whom the police must also bargain. And in this bargaining, the police are dealing with role incumbents who are potentially hostile to the police. Thus, "in the system of maintaining law and order, other people have the law and the police get stuck with the order" (ibid., pp. 38, 40).[10]

To understand this is to understand something of the basis for antagonism that arises between the police and the prosecutorial-judicial components of the system. As an aside, Harold Pepinsky of the University of Minnesota has speculated that noncompliance of police with the *Miranda* rule of the U.S. Supreme Court has been motivated more by the desire of the police to develop and to maintain a stable identity, as individuals and as a group, than by any fear of harm to society, as, for instance, the view that the rule has resulted in the guilty going free. ("A Theory of Police Reaction to Miranda v. Arizona"). Pepinsky states that the obtaining of confessions specifically, and the interrogation process generally, serve to create and to stabilize this individual and group identity of police officers by establishing the police as followers and upholders of societal norms. In this process, in fact, the police define who does and who does not live up to the norms, and thereby seek to define the norms themselves. If this is so, Pepinsky argues, police cooperation in upholding the constitutional rights of suspects under interrogation can only come with reinforcement of a sense of normative consensus among the police. This has important implications for police attitudes and underlying motivations; and indeed for the goals of social control, generally, in free society.

The Scapegoating Charge

Yale Kamisar, professor of law at the University of Michigan, has said that some police officials have been inclined to blame court decisions for the crime increase because they fear that the public will blame the police.[11] So it goes. When *Newsweek* published an excellent feature on the justice system (March 8, 1971), a letter to the editor held the legal profession responsible for "the mess." Another letter asked, "Why don't the police put a stop to it?" Still another letter pointed to "soft" probationary procedures as the cause of "all the headaches." One stated that the increase in crime was all due to "prosecutors still wet behind the ears." It was the typical gamut of scapegoating, what Kamisar calls "a mood of irritated frustration with complexity." Police who deeply and rightly resent being made the scapegoats have few qualms about making the courts the scapegoats.

Kamisar points out that neither the police nor the courts can control the social factors that influence crime. But the answer, he says, is not in permitting the police or prosecutors to engage in unreasonable searches and seizures, or to ignore the exclusionary rule. He suggests Pepinsky's point, which Skolnick and others have also stressed: the extent to which the notions underlying the Fourth Amendment (using the exclusionary rule as an example) can be integrated into the policeman's value system. More than one political scientist has ruminated on the seeming erosion in political liberty that sometimes is held justifiable in the name of public necessity. This is what we mean when we stress the goals of social control generally. Scott and many others have indicated that our problems in criminal justice reflect irreconciled philosophical differences regarding ends and means. Scapegoating is one symptom of this. Repeating James Q. Wilson's way of putting it: some persons feel strongly that crime must be stamped out even at some cost in the erosion of civil liberties while others feel just as strongly that civil liberties must be safeguarded even at some cost in crime.

In short, the larger and more fundamental problems we face in criminal justice are embedded in the broad context of Constitutional government. In a 1965 speech to a police administrators' Institute in Los Angeles, UCLA Professor of Law Arvo Van Alstyne summarized the matter:

> Law enforcement, to be effective, requires an exercise of power; and the kind of power that must be exercised goes to the ultimate extreme, including the power to take human life itself. All exercises of power, however, have the potential capacity to destroy liberty, since power must be wielded by men, and men, by hypothesis, are imperfect creatures. Therefore, liberty requires law enforcement to preserve the public peace, which is essential to enjoyment of liberty. It also requires that law enforcement be limited and restricted to prevent its being exercised in such a way as to destroy liberty.

The Open Lines of Communication

If this is an acceptable way of describing a central paradox of our criminal justice system, then a question of perspective ought to be in the forefront. This is our primary concern, keynoted by the Scott and Johnson commentaries. Carl Hamm, a retired Milwaukee police captain, later on the staff of the International Association of Chiefs of Police and now of LEAA, has considered the matter in perspective:

> The criminal justice system within the United States is essentially an aggregate of bureaucracies which, collectively, are alleged to serve the needs of the community and the "client" (traffic violator, misdemeanant, or criminal) in a society with a mixed bag of values, morals, laws, and regulations and a conglomerate of standards for their application. Pluralistic planning, or advocacy, is the combination of opposition, confrontation, approval, and modification of official planning or action in accordance with the wishes of the ward, neighborhood, block group, or participant within or affected by the plan, regardless of whether involvement is through choice or circumstance. ["Pluralistic Planning Within the Criminal Justice System"]

Pluralistic planning! It provides, Hamm explains,

> . . . for the complainant to be not only heard, but heeded, and further, to receive a response. A glimpse of pluralistic participation may be seen in the traditional administration of the English village by a triumverate composed of the clergymen, the constable, and the physician. Its modern counterpart is apparent in many boroughs within the Greater London Council: still a triumverate, it consists of the police station, health clinic, and social services. . . . Thus, one of the largest cities in the world has neighborhood soccer fields, borough events, local health and social services, and its own police station, whose staff reside within that precinct or borough. [Ibid., p. 402]

Hamm concludes with the point that community participation and pluralistic planning (systemic or *geopolitical* planning) require an open line of communication between citizens and public officials. This is what we mean by perspective; the essential principle Hamm pinpoints applies to relationships within any social system—including the criminal justice system. Without it, there is simply no system.

Systems Analysis and the Police Department

How can this principle be made to work in the world of social reality? To reply to this question with a concrete illustration, we refer to what is called *systems analysis, systems research, operations research,* or *systems engineering.* The concepts involved are not new, but application in recent years of this functional emphasis has burst upon military operations, transportation, education, economics, and other social systems, stimulated and facilitated enormously by computer science and technology. Alfred Blumstein in "Systems Analysis and the Criminal Justice System" explains that systems analysis focuses successively on:

1. A particular *system*–a collection of people, devices, and procedures intended to perform some function.

2. The *function* of the system–the job it is supposed to perform.

3. *Measures of effectiveness*–the measure or calculation of how well alternative system designs perform the function.

4. *Alternative* system designs–the comparison of designs.

5. A *mathematical model*–a means of calculating the measures of effectiveness associated with each alternative system design.

Impressed with the possibilities of such an approach to the police department of a large city, or to the criminal justice system more generally, some police departments are well along in applying it to crime control. But of course, the police departments and the criminal justice system have other functions that raise different issues. Blumstein believes that the mathematical model is the most useful contribution of systems analysis:

> In its pure form, systems analysis is supposed to provide quantitative comparisons of the consequences of alternative decisions, in terms of both cost and effectiveness. These comparisons, however, are rarely sufficient for making most decisions, since the qualitative value considerations are usually at least as important as those that can be quantified. But by putting numbers on the measurable aspects of a question, the debate no longer need center on those questions, as it now so often does. Then the public debate and the administrative decisions can focus on the critical questions involved in the weighing of conflicting social values. [Ibid., pp. 94, 95.]

Perspective, then, is a basic tenet of systems analysis that places important but narrow questions in a broader systems context, ordinarily difficult to do because of the complexity of a given system. But by looking beyond the limited question, considerations previously ignored ("It's their problem, not ours"), or tranquilly accepted ("We do only what we are told"), come into focus. For example, Blumstein asks:

> What is the impact of higher arrest rates on the corrections process and on future crimes?
>
> What is the impact of community-based corrections on both the near- and long-range crime rates?
>
> What is the impact of non-bail release on the rate of guilty pleas and on court workload?

Would it be more economical to add court resources to cut the court backlog and reduce the cost of detention while awaiting trial?

What will be the effect of providing free counsel more widely on correctional work-loads?

Questions of this type call for interactions among all parts of the criminal justice system, between it and other social systems, and between it and various community groups. Such questions require *wholeness* of perspective—the combined views of all concerned groups. Ideally, such interactions will force an assessment of goals, roles, values, alternatives, and other elements upon which improvement depends. For example, with crime control as the focus, how can the system reduce crime? Crime might be reduced by intense policing. But at some point, intense policing is socially objectionable. Too much crime control may be oppressive, too little may be anarchy. At what point is it too much or too little? Judged by what criteria? And so on. Other examples: What effect have longer prison sentences on crime control? Who can be rehabilitated and by what kind of correctional treatment? *Who* are the people deterred from committing *what* crimes by *which* procedures of the criminal justice system?

Systems analysis can provide data to make the discussion of such questions more productive. The clashes in differing values will still persist, and working consensus will still be the hard-to-secure reward. But discussions (dialogue) and transactions enlightened by factual information on *quantitative* questions are much more likely to result in breakthroughs on *qualitative* questions. Another way to say this is in problem-solving terms: data obtained via systems analysis can be of great help in getting problems more adequately defined, in ways that many diverse "audiences" can accept. Problem-solving efforts in community relations frequently bog down at this first step. Systems analysis can be a strong ally of *pluralistic planning in solving* problems, both in and out of the criminal justice system.

Study 1, Part Four, in *The Police and the Community: Studies* (Radelet and Reed) describes how one constellation of the system—the police-prosecutor-court relationship with respect to the juvenile offender —is supposed to work, and some of the problems that arise in this relationship.

The Issue of Overcriminalization

One of the more heatedly debated issues in select circles of the criminal justice field today is a matter to which we earlier alluded—what is called *overcriminalization* or *legal moralism*. Is the criminal sanction being employed too widely in cases where it is ineffective or inappropriate, thus debasing its effectiveness in cases where it might be more applicable? This is one of the briar-patches of conflicting values in goals, roles, etc. We will not settle this argument here, but some consideration of the issue is in order.

Many states and the Federal government have been critically reviewing, and in some cases revising, their substantive and procedural criminal codes. We have mentioned the American Law Institute's Model Penal Code. A National Commission on Reform of the Federal Criminal Code has completed a 336-page report containing a proposed new Federal Criminal Code, some sections of which are considered radical in some quarters. For instance, the Commission recommended the abolition of capital punishment, an easing of curbs on marijuana possession, and outlawing private ownership of handguns. No revised criminal code gets through a legislative body without reverberations sometimes approximating an earthquake.

President Johnson's 1966 Crime Commission observed that most of the cases in the criminal courts consist of what are essentially violations of moral norms or instances of annoying behavior rather than of dangerous crime (*The Challenge of Crime in a Free Society*, pp. 126, 127). Almost half of all arrests were said to be on charges of drunkenness, disorderly conduct, vagrancy, gambling, and minor sexual violations. The Commission said that such behavior is generally regarded as too serious to be ignored, but its inclusion in the criminal justice system creates problems. The investigation and prosecution of such cases ties up police (investigation itself is frequently "impractical") and clogs courts at the expense of their capacity to cope with more serious crimes. Sometimes attempts to enforce these laws are degrading or embarassing for the police and raise troublesome legal questions for the courts.

Occasionally the enforcement of these laws, the Commission continued, has been unhappily associated with police, prosecutor, or court venality and corruption, leading to general disrespect for law. Arrest, conviction, and jail or probation rarely reform persons who engage in these kinds of behavior ("victimless crimes"), nor do they appear to deter potential violators. Continued reliance on criminal treatment for such offenders probably blunts community efforts to create more appropriate programs for the alcoholic, the homeless, the compulsive gambler, or the sexual deviant.

At the heart of some of the predicaments in which the criminal law finds itself has been the too ready acceptance of the notion that the way to deal with any kind of reprehensible conduct is to make it criminal. This is the crux of the issue generating widespread debate currently, with marijuana use or possession, homosexuality, and abortion having been added to the list of behaviors in question. Some argue that lowering the criminal bars against such behavior may be interpreted as license to engage in it. Others maintain that the limited tool of criminal law will work better against the most dangerous and threatening kinds of crime if it is confined to the kinds it can deal with most effectively. That criminality and immorality are not identical is an underlying assumption. The Crime Commission settled for stating the issue and urged weighing carefully the kinds of behavior that should be defined as criminal.

Skolnick regards overcriminalization as a significant element in police-community relations.[12] He holds that the enforcement of conventional morality typically produces two closely related consequences. One is a more threatening environment for the policeman. The other is the development of organizations for purveying forbidden goods and services. Legal moralism, Skolnick asserts, undermines the moral authority of the criminal law. He quotes an FBI agent's remarks to the President's Crime Commission:

> The criminal code of any jurisdiction tends to make a crime of everything that people are against, without regard to enforceability, changing social concepts, etc. . . . The result is that the criminal code becomes society's trash bin. The police have to rummage around in this material and are expected to prevent everything that is unlawful. They cannot do so because many of the things prohibited are simply beyond enforcement, both because of human inability to enforce the law and because, as in the case of prohibition, society legislates one way and acts another way. If we would restrict our definition of criminal offenses in many areas, we would get the criminal codes back to the point where they prohibit specific, carefully defined, and serious conduct, and the police could then concentrate on enforcing the law in that context and would not waste its officers by trying to enforce the unenforceable, as is done now. [*Task Force Report: The Courts*, p. 107]

> If we could assume [Skolnick adds] that we actually live in a society whose citizens subscribe overwhelmingly to a similar morality, *conventional* morality would indeed be, as the term suggests, *customary* morality. All evidence, however, is to the contrary. We are a nation of diversity, of ethnic differences, of regional differences, of rural-urban differences, of generational differences. We cannot coerce an entire nation to virtue as virtue is defined by those holding political power at any given time. [*Professional Police in a Free Society*, p. 16]

University of California law professor Sanford H. Kadish writes in a similar vein:

> Excessive reliance upon the criminal law to perform tasks for which it is ill-suited has created acute problems for the administration of criminal justice. The use of criminal law to enforce morals, to provide social services, and to avoid legal restraints on law enforcement, to take just three examples, has tended both to be inefficient and to produce grave handicaps for enforcement of the criminal law against genuinely threatening conduct. In the case of morals offenses, it has

served to reduce the criminal law's essential claim to legitimacy by inducing offensive and degrading police conduct, particularly against the poor and the subcultural, and by generating cynicism and indifference to the criminal law. It has also fostered organized criminality and has produced, possibly, more crime than it has suppressed. Used as an alternative to social services, it has diverted enormous law enforcement resources from protecting the public against serious crime. Finally its rise to circumvent restrictions on police conduct has undermined the principle of legality and exposed the law to plausible charges of hypocrisy. Pressures to criminalize persistently block practical assessments of what the criminal law is good for and what it is not. Studies of the sociology of overcriminalization offer a means of understanding, and perhaps, to some degree, of controlling, this unfortunate phenomenon. ["The Crisis of Overcriminalization"]

In a definitive book on the subject, Herbert L. Packer of the Stanford University Law School took the same position as Kadish and Skolnick (*The Limits of the Criminal Sanction*).[13] The book probes the rhetorical question: How can we tell what the criminal sanction is good for? Packer's analysis is highly systematic, beginning with the query: What are we trying to do by defining conduct as criminal and punishing people who commit crimes? To what extent are we justified in thinking that we can or ought to do what we are trying to do? Is it possible for us to construct an acceptable rationale for the criminal sanction enabling us to deal with the argument that it is itself an unethical use of social power? And if it is possible, what implications does that rationale have for the kind of conceptual creature that the criminal law is?

Packer proceeds from a discussion of such questions to others equally fundamental. For example, what do the rules of the game tell us about what the state may and may not do to apprehend, charge, convict, and dispose of persons suspected of committing crimes? Finally, Packer argues that we have over-relied on the criminal sanction and that we had better start thinking about how to adjust our commitments to our capacities, both moral and operational. In sum, Packer's thesis has to do with the uses of power:

> The criminal sanction is at once prime guarantor and prime threatener of human freedom. Used providently and humanely, it is guarantor; used indiscriminately and coercively, it is threatener. The tensions that inhere in the criminal sanction can never be wholly resolved in favor of guaranty and against threat. But we can begin to try. [Ibid., p. 366]

Related Problems of Criminal Justice

The President's Crime Commission, observing that the courts do not work perfectly—even within their limitations—and never have, named many problems of criminal procedure as well as of substantive criminal law. There are judges who misuse power. There are prosecutors and defense counsels who resort to obfuscation and chicanery. The sheer volume of cases alone, particularly in urban courts, has brought about problems that could be solved only by informal, invisible, streamlined administrative procedures for handling offenders. Prosecutors and magistrates dismiss cases; as many as half of those arrested are dismissed early in the process. Prosecutors negotiate charges with defense counsels to secure guilty pleas ("plea bargaining"); and a high percentage of convictions result from the guilty pleas of defendants, rather than from trial. But even though these negotiations avoid costly, time-consuming trials, their lack of judicial consideration of an offender or his offense causes problems.

The lower courts—the courts that dispose of misdemeanor cases or "petty offenses" and that often process the first stages of felony cases—are especially in serious trouble. Such courts process the overwhelming majority of offenders. The President's Crime Commission was not the first nor will it be the last august body to be "shocked" by what it saw in the lower courts:

> [This Commission] has seen cramped and noisy courtrooms, undignified and perfunctory procedures, and badly trained personnel. It has seen dedicated people who are frustrated by huge case loads, by the lack of opportunity to examine cases carefully, and by the impossibility of devising constructive solutions to the problems of offenders. It has seen assembly line justice. [*The Challenge of Crime in a Free Society,* p. 128][14]

Convinced that a central problem of many lower courts is the gross disparity between the number of cases and the personnel and facilities available to deal with them, the Commission specified some associated problems and then concluded, as the Wickersham Commission had said thirty years earlier, that the best solution to the problems of the lower courts would be the abolition of these courts. Short of this, it recommended that:

> Felony and misdemeanor courts and their ancillary agencies—prosecutors, defenders, and probation services—should be unified.

> As an immediate step to meet the needs of the lower courts, the judicial manpower of these courts should be increased and their physical facilities should be improved so that these courts will be able to cope with the volume of cases coming before them in a dignified and deliberate way.

> Prosecutors, probation officers, and defense counsel should be provided in courts where these officers are not found, or their numbers are insufficient.

> The States and Federal Government should enact legislation to abolish or overhaul the justice of the peace and U.S. Commissioner systems. [Ibid., pp. 129, 130][15]

Of the Commission's many more recommendations for criminal process and procedure generally, one in particular merits elaboration here.

Legal Services for the Poor and Powerless

How does the criminal justice process look from the vantage point of the poor and powerless? We earlier discussed the attitudes of minorities toward the police. What about their point of view toward other parts of the system?

Concern about such a question originated with the birth of democratic government. In the United States, this concern appears to have become increasingly compelling in recent years. It has been integral to The Movement in civil rights and the "War on Poverty." The issue, simply stated, is to see to it that *everyone*—including the poor, the powerless, the black as well as the white, the nonreligious as well as the religious, the unbarbered as well as the barbered—receives fair and equal treatment in the processes of criminal justice. This hub of the relationship between government and the individual is the essence of the free society. The ultimate test of the entire system rests in what Edward Bennett Williams calls *one man's freedom.*[16]

Organized legal aid for the indigent has grown commendably during the past decade. Through leadership, responsible research, unprecedented resources, and broad objectives, such organizations as the American Bar Association and the National Legal Aid and Defender Associations,[17] the Vera Institute, the National Committee For Public Justice, the Legal Services program of the Federal Office of Economic Opportunity, and Legal Aid societies in many cities have all made notable contributions.[18]

Poor people are prone to legal trouble. Bewildered and bemused by legalities they face daily as parents, consumers, tenants, recipients of public assistance, and accused offenders, they are often defendants, rarely plaintiffs. When the late Senator Robert F. Kennedy addressed the University of Chicago Law School May 1, 1964, he said: "The poor man looks upon the law as an enemy, not as a friend. For him, the law is always taking something away."

A National Conference on Law and Poverty, held in Washington, D.C., June 23–24, 1965, summarized the main features of the problem (Patricia Wald, *Law and Poverty:* 1965):[19]

> Poverty takes its toll in deteriorating human relationships. Poor families account for a disproportionate share of mental illness, alcoholism, drug addiction, illegitimacy, desertion and juvenile delinquency. Wife beating and child abuse are more frequent among the poor. Neglect

proceedings are typical. All of these matters have legal assistance implications.

The greatest material need of the poor is decent shelter. The poor inhabit the slums, and slum housing is not cheap. Welfare recipients spend the bulk of their allowances for rent and utilities, depleting food funds. Housing code violations are commonplace. Generally speaking, the legal rights of tenants in these circumstances are not well protected. Fundamental revision of antiquated landlord-tenant law is needed.

Impoverished minority groups face legal obstacles arising from discriminatory practices which intensify their need for legal help. The right to equal opportunity must be tortuously defined by lawyers and courts in a variety of contexts.

In consumer purchasing, the poor are often the victims of easy credit, high prices, legal threats, repossession, garnishment or its threat, and sundry unethical practices. Legal counseling is a much needed resource for the poor, and it is a practical way of imparting consumer education.

For many of the poor who are recipients of welfare assistance (somewhere in the neighborhood of 10–12 million people), the welfare system is a maze of bureaucratic "mumbo-jumbo," full of technicalities incomprehensible to anyone lacking legal training.

The poor form the overwhelming percentage of the criminally accused. This speaks for itself in terms of its legal aid ramifications.

Poverty breeds mental illness. Mentally ill patients frequently require legal assistance to protect their rights.

The same report states that the poor man is ruled by a legal system that he neither understands nor trusts. Often, the poor do not know that a lawyer can help. Or they do not know where or how to secure legal help. Or they find the lawyer too remote. Or they are afraid of reprisal.

Despite the advances made in legal services to the poor in recent years, the needs still far exceed what is available. Legal aid lawyers individually decide which cases to accept. Sometimes legal aid facilities shun publicity for fear of being taxed far beyond resources. Some organizations bar applicants by overly strict eligibility standards. Many legal aid offices exclude certain types of cases: e.g., divorce, adoption, bankruptcy, civil mental commitment, etc. To overcome the general indictment "too little and too late," a program of legal assistance for the poor should meet these qualifications:

1. Legal services must be accessible.

2. Legal services must be independent.

3. Legal services must be integrated with nonlegal services.

4. Legal services must be comprehensive.

5. Legal services must include preventive law, i.e., educate the poor to seek advice before crisis arises.

6. Legal services must be available to all who cannot afford to pay. [Ibid., pp. 64–67]

Many states today have a system by which counties compensate attorneys who represent indigent criminal defendants in the courts. The basic methods used include the following:

1. Assigned counsel
   The judge appoints individual lawyers from private practice on a case-by-case basis. Compensation is based on a predetermined fee schedule or an hourly rate.

2. Public defender.
   One or more salaried lawyers devote all or a substantial portion of their time to the defense of indigents.

3. Private defender.
   Like the public defender, the private defender's office consists of one or more salaried attorneys who devote all or a substantial part of their time to the defense of indigent criminal defendants. But it is organized as a private association and is governed by a board of private citizens.

Each of these methods has its advantages and disadvantages.

The President's Crime Commission made some pertinent recommendations:

> The objective to be met as quickly as possible is to provide counsel to every criminal defendant who faces a significant penalty, if he cannot afford to provide counsel himself. This should apply to cases classified as misdemeanors as well as to those classified as felonies. Counsel should be provided early in the proceedings and certainly no later than the first judicial appearance. The services of counsel should be available after conviction through appeal, and in collateral attack proceedings when the issues are not frivolous. The immediate minimum, until it becomes possible to provide the foregoing, is that all criminal defendants who are in danger of substantial loss of liberty shall be provided with counsel.

> All jurisdictions that have not already done so should move from random assignment of defense counsel by judges to a coordinated, assigned counsel system or a defender system.

> Each state should finance assigned counsel and defender systems on a regular and statewide basis. [*The Challenge of Crime in a Free Society*, pp. 150–153]

Both the Kerner Commission and the National Commission on the Causes and Prevention of Violence voiced strong support of programs expanding legal services to the poor. The commissions placed major responsibility for the leadership of such programs with the local bar association, and urged that law schools allow advanced students to provide legal assistance as part of their professional training, a recommendation that had also been made by the 1965 National Conference on Law and Poverty. In 1961, the Ford Foundation made a substantial grant to the National Council on Legal Clinics (comprising the American Bar Association, the American Association of Law Schools, and the National Legal Aid and Defender Association) "to promote law school legal clinics and internship programs in the administration of justice" (Wald, p. 90).

In the category of the powerless are the innocent victims of crime. Since they, too, need help, it is appropriate to mention here the programs for compensation from public funds that numerous states have enacted. And, like Great Britain, New Zealand, Canada, Australia, and Sweden, Congress appears to be moving toward making a nationwide program for compensating victims.

Troubles in the Legal Services

Legal services for the poor invariably encounter obstacles. By way of suggesting some of the problems:

> On September 22, 1970, *The New York Times* reported [page 34] that representatives of leading lawyers' organizations had started a fight against a proposed regionalization of the Federal program of legal services to the poor. The director of the Office of Economic Opportunity contested the position that such regionalization would emasculate the program. Some months earlier, private lawyers' groups had successfully joined with OEO to defeat a Congressional effort to give a veto power over Legal Services programs to state governors.

> As of December, 1970, the OEO Legal Services program had grown to $60 million, employing 2,000 lawyers in almost every state. It was handling over a million cases a year at a cost to the American taxpayer of $58 per case. But politicians and bureaucrats at various governmental levels were seeking to choke it off.[20]

> In February, 1971, George Washington University announced the discontinuance of its Federally funded Urban Law Institute, described as the most effective clinical law education program in the country. The University gave as its reason the belief that its law school students should not practice law. The Institute had been involved in several controversial cases in Washington, D.C. The director of the Institute charged that the University had succumbed to political pressure, and added that it was part of a pattern of opposition against successful legal

programs for the poor across the country. [*The New York Times,* February 22, 1971]

In the same month, the Supreme Court agreed to decide the question of whether poor persons prosecuted for petty offenses (misdemeannors) must be offered free legal counsel (New York *Times,* February 23, 1971, p. 21). The Court had ruled eight years earlier that poor defendants were entitled to free counsel in felony cases (*Gideon* v. *Wainwright,* 1963). Of the eight million annual arrests for non-traffic violations, more than half are thought to involve poor people accused of petty offenses.

In March, 1971, a bipartisan group of 98 senators and representatives proposed that the embattled Federal Legal Services to the Poor program be permanently insulated from political pressures by the creation of an independent National Legal Services Corporation, to be funded by Congress and operated by an autonomous board of public and private members (New York *Times,* March 18, 1971, p. 24). The Corporation would supplant and greatly enlarge the OEO Legal Services program.

Controversial Issues in Field Practices

There are five issues of police field practices that are apt to incite lively arguments in police and community relations discussions, and that also peculiarly test the police-prosecutor-court relationship. These issues are (1) entrapment, (2) so-called stop-and-frisk, (3) so-called preventive detention, (4) so-called no-knock, and (5) the use of firearms by the police. A brief analysis of each of these issues is relevant here.

Entrapment

When, in order to make an arrest, police or other law enforcement officers, or agents working in their behalf, encourage the commission of a crime, this practice is known as *entrapment* (Sagarin and MacNamara, "The Problem of Entrapment"). Generally, it is frowned upon by American courts and has, in fact, been regarded as sufficient defense if there is good reason to believe the crime would not have been committed had it not been for such encouragement. The American Law Institute and the American Bar Association have each proposed a code of criminal justice administration that condemns police entrapment, without unrealistically opposing the use of informers.

The courts have argued that the law sullies itself when it induces someone to commit a crime. Further, the law should not act so as to tempt anyone, nor in such a manner as to invite blackmail, extortion, and bribery. Entrapment has been defended in cases involving illegal purchases and sales (narcotics, liquor, pornography, etc.); in prostitution and homosexual cases; and in political cases involving strikes, civil rights, antiwar and black militant actions and student unrest. Sagarin and MacNamara contend that entrapment "constitutes a threat to the democratic process, tending to discredit otherwise legitimate social protest and to stay the hand of social change (Ibid., p. 363ff). Quoting former Chief Justice Earl Warren, "the function of law enforcement does not include the manufacturing of crime." They suggest guidelines for the use of undercover agents in crime detection in legitimate ways that would not constitute entrapment:

1. The weak, the impressionable, and the psychologically or otherwise temptable should be protected by society, not drawn into a criminal web.

2. Law enforcement agencies should employ ethically impeccable standards.

3. The use of the *agent provocateur* threatens the democratic process and discourages legitimate social dissent and protest.

4. Entrapment, encouragement, informers, and stool pigeons create many problems that may be worse than those they are intended to solve, e.g., the shake-down, blackmail, the frame-up, and bargain-counter justice.

Stop-and-Frisk

Several recent statutes and court decisions—the most noteworthy of which are the New York state Stop-and-Frisk law, the Uniform Arrest Act, and the Model Code of Pre-Arraignment procedure—have given police the authority to use force in the practice of stop and frisk and to detain persons for investigation on grounds of less-than-probable cause. Stop-and-frisk legislation is applicable in two distinct situations: in cases of so-called preventive criminality, where an individual's demeanor and the accompanying circumstances justify a suspicion that he is about to engage in criminal activity; and in instances where the aim is to allow the patrolman to conduct an "investigation" of a person he suspects has committed a crime.

Stop-and-frisk legislation has its roots in vagrancy and loitering statutes, and is subject to many of the same Constitutional and practical limitations. The Fourth Amendment provides the principal constitutional standard which this type of legislation must meet. If the necessary detention is considered an arrest within the meaning of this Amendment, any such police activity without probable cause will be unconstitutional. Lack of clarity in the distinctions between a detention and an arrest, and between a frisk and a search, render the regulatory statutes difficult to administer.

Society must run the risk of antisocial behavior in the interest of preserving the freedom of the individual. Further, the benefits resulting from the detention and frisking of suspicious persons may well be outweighed, as we have suggested earlier in this text, by an increase in tension between police and citizens, particularly citizens who are members of minority groups. In cases where authority is granted for apprehending persons suspected of having committed a crime, the present standard of probable cause should be retained. And forcing the police to conform to this standard will encourage improvement in methods of investigation (John Duffy, "Stop and Frisk: A Perspective").[21]

Preventive Detention

In late July, 1970, President Nixon signed into law the District of Columbia Crime Bill. This bill contained several controversial sections, among which was the provision that judges would be allowed to jail defendants considered dangerous to society for as long as sixty days before trial. This clause was widely attacked as unconstitutional, and also criticized for its unsubstantiated assumptions, namely: (1) that the persons arrested for dangerous or violent crimes have a high propensity for arrest for subsequent offenses of a serious nature; (2) that when persons who are arrested for serious felonies are re-arrested, it will be for an equally serious charge; and (3) that judges can accurately predict those who will be dangerous if released.

The National Council on Crime and Delinquency took a position of policy opposing such legislation for these reasons ("Preventive Detention: A Policy Statement").[22]

1. Such legislation substitutes a presumption of guilt for a presumption of innocence.

2. Such legislation probably violates the Constitutional right to reasonable bail.

3. Such legislation contains an inherent danger of practical abuse. For example, there is an element of prejudice to defendants who are needlessly detained.

4. Such legislation undermines needed reforms in the system, by accepting pretrial detention because of the court's failure to provide speedy trials.

5. Typical preventive detention proposals provide for complex procedural safeguards which, if observed, would constitute a great additional burden on the courts.

6. Analysis of the data shows that the amount of dangerous crime prevented would at best be very small, whereas the damage to many nondangerous defendants and to correctional systems would be considerable.

NCCD recommends the following procedures, in lieu of preventive detention (*ibid.*, pp. 2, 3):

1. Priority in trial should be granted upon the request of a prosecutor, in accordance with previously established court rules, without review by a judge.

2. The criteria and procedure should be formulated in any jurisdiction by the prosecutor, working with the court administrator, either a state administrator or an administrator for a district of general jurisdiction, and the controlling rules should be promulgated by the court.

3. Under these rules, crimes for which priority may be requested should be specified (a) by the nature of the crime charged, and (b) by elements that would be significant in identifying both dangerousness and likelihood of repetition.

No-Knock

Another controversial provision of the 1970 District of Columbia Crime Bill permitted police to obtain search warrants under which they could enter premises without announcing themselves if notice was likely to result in the destruction of evidence, to endanger the life of a policeman, or to permit an escape. This clause is popularly referred to as *no-knock*.

Again, this section of the bill has been harshly criticized on moral, practical, and policy grounds, and less so on Constitutional grounds. Some critics claim that many judges grant search warrants almost automatically, and that there is no reason to think that they will not also grant no-knock permission in the same fashion, particularly in narcotics and gambling cases. The Comprehensive Drug Abuse Prevention and Control Act of 1970, signed into law by President Nixon in October of that year, provided for search warrants which specifically allowed enforcement officers to enter, without notice, premises to be searched if there were probable cause to believe that the property sought would be destroyed or that notice would endanger someone's life or safety.

Some critics of the no-knock clause speculate that its actual effect may be to make the enforcement of narcotics laws more difficult because it encourages violators to resort to underground tactics. Clearly necessary are some guidelines aiming at control of the possible misuse of the no-knock procedure. Some states, with New York again leading the way, had moved to statutory enunciation of such guidelines as early as 1964.[23]

Use of Firearms

Various presidential commissions in recent years—on crime, civil disorders, violence, and campus unrest—have had something to say about the use of firearms by private citizens, especially handguns. The push for Federal and state controls has been pronounced, in the face of strong opposition by influential groups. Many progressive police administrators have joined in the plea for domestic disarmament.

Advocates of disarming the police, however, have been far fewer, and police officials themselves almost unanimously reject such action. The subject quickly generates highly emotional outbursts in this country, an interesting contrast with the situation in England—which has been a model for so much of American police organization and procedure but where the cultural milieu is admittedly different. For the present, at least, it appears that we must settle for sane firearms policies for all law enforcement agencies, such as the guidelines recommended by the President's Crime Commission (*The Challenge of Crime,* pp. 189, 190):

1. Deadly force should not be used against any suspect unless the arresting officer's safety or the safety of someone else is endangered.

2. Such force should never be used on mere suspicion that a crime has been committed.

3. Policemen should not fire on felony suspects when lesser force could be used.

4. Warning shots should never be used.

5. Any force, including deadly force, can be used by policemen to protect themselves or others.

6. Detailed written reports should be required on all discharges of firearms.

Many police agencies operate with more stringent regulations than these, as a matter of policy.

In Conclusion

This has been an extended chapter, touching upon selected aspects of the complex relationship of police, prosecution, and courts. The problems in this relationship reflect problems in the criminal justice system itself, which have been widely discussed by many observers in recent years. We have not undertaken to summarize this discussion, being content to highlight a few issues that seem particularly important.

We have asked what it takes to qualify as truly a system. We believe this has a good deal to do with a principle of interrelatedness, of interdependence—a basic principle running through all that we have said about police and the community. We identified some of the main factors which make criminal justice process dysfunctional as a system, stressing what we called "a concept of relations." We reviewed various approaches to the systemic reform that seems more and more to be a common commitment of partisans of every vintage, although there is much disagreement on *how,* and some disagreement on *what.* We spoke of the merits of a pilot program tactic for reform, exemplified by the Vera Institute in New York City.

Next, we considered more specifically some of the main burdens on the relationships of police, prosecution, and the courts. As a strategy for coping with these problems, we hit upon pluralistic planning, and noted how systems analysis can significantly help provide data to define problems and facilitate discussion.

Our attention then turned to what Professor Herbert Packer calls "the limits of the criminal sanction"—what is generally referred to as overcriminalization or legal moralism. This is the use of the criminal code to make a crime of everything people are against. Our difficulty in distinguishing between what is suited and what is ill-suited for criminal law complicates community relations for the entire criminal justice system. Related to this are procedural problems, such as volume of cases, plea bargaining, misuse of judicial power, etc.

We are especially interested in the question of legal services for the poor and powerless, our assumption being that one man's rights are as important as any other man's. Poor people are prone to legal problems, we observed, and, while acknowledging that notable progress has been made in legal services for the poor in recent years, we also noted that there is a long way still to go, and some signs of political opposition to going too far too fast. Finally, we reviewed briefly five controversial issues that merit attention in any contemporary text of this nature: entrapment, stop-and-frisk, preventive detention, no-knock, and the use of firearms by policemen.

A fitting close to this chapter is provided in a statement by President Nixon in his address to the National Conference on the Judiciary, meeting in Williamsburg, Virginia, March 11, 1971:

> Throughout a tumultuous generation, our system of justice has helped America improve itself; there is an urgent need now for America to help the courts improve our system of justice. . . . What is needed now is genuine reform—the kind of change that requires imagination and daring, that demands a focus on ultimate goals . . . The ultimate goal of changing the process of justice is not to put more people in jail or merely to provide a faster flow of litigation—it is to resolve conflict speedily but fairly, to reverse the trend toward crime and violence, to reinstill a respect for law in all of our people.

Notes to Chapter Sixteen

1. See also the same author's *Crime, Correction and Society.*

2. See, for example, Patrick Arthur Devlin, "The Police in a Changing Society."

3. See Fig. 2–2 in Study 1 (Part II), "The Structure of the Community," in Radelet and Reed, *Studies.*

4. John M. Pfiffner, *Needed: A Geopolitical Approach to Law Observance.* Pfiffner's term implies systemic perspective. See also Howlett and Hurst, "A Systems Approach to Comprehensive Criminal Justice Planning," and Klein, Kobrin, McEachern, and Sigurdson, "System Rates: An Approach to Comprehensive Criminal Justice Planning."

5. Ramsey Clark, *Crime in America.* From a review by Francis T. P. Plimpton, appearing in *The Saturday Review,* November 28, 1970, pp. 35–37. In a review of the same book, appearing in *Commonweal* (March 19, 1971, pp. 41–43), Isidore Silver, chairman of the Department of Government and Economics at John Jay College of Criminal Justice in New York City, writes:

   > As Clark and virtually all commentators have often noted, the primary function of the policeman is not to apprehend offenders or investigate crimes but to provide certain community services not obtainable elsewhere. . . . At best most of our Nation has a part-time police force dealing with a random and distinctly minimal segment of criminal activity. . . . In perspective, it is as if all concerned tacitly agreed that the "system" is an evil in itself and one which should enmesh as few as possible. A skeptic might conclude that "criminal justice" is only minimally concerned with "criminal" conduct and only accidentally involved with "justice."

6. Ibid., Isidore Silver.

7. Irving Reichert, in a speech to an Institute on Police-Community Relations held at the University of San Francisco, January 31, 1966. A spirited debate of the issues by a distinguished panel appeared in *Playboy,* March 1966, "The Playboy Panel: Crisis in Law Enforcement," pp. 47–58 and 143. See also *The Center Magazine,* May–June 1971. The entire issue is devoted to "Crime and Punishment in America."

8. For a description of the Vera Institute approach and its early projects, see the testimony of the Institute's executive director, Herbert Sturz, before the Ribicoff Committee (U.S. Senate, Committee on Government Operations, Subcommittee on Executive Reorganization), *Hearings: Federal Role in Urban Affairs,* Part 13, pp. 2,740–57, 89th Congress, 2nd Session (U.S. Government Printing Office, Washington, D.C., 1967). For more recent reports, contact the Vera Institute directly. See also Jameson W. Doig, "Police Problems, Proposals, and Strategies for Change."

9. In July 1971, New York City Police Commissioner Patrick V. Murphy announced initiation of a Criminal Justice Bureau within the department,

to monitor the performance of district attorneys and the courts in an effort to improve the control of crime. A similar Bureau exists in the Washington, D.C., police department.

10. See also V. A. Leonard, *The Police, the Judiciary and the Criminal*. Also *Model Rules of Court on Police Action From Arrest to Arraignment*, 14 proposals by the Council of Judges of the National Council on Crime and Delinquency, 1969. For a general reference, see Smith and Pollack, *Crime and Justice in a Mass Society*. Another pertinent work is Richard Quinney, ed., *Crime and Justice in Society*.

11. Yale Kamisar, "On the Tactics of Police-Prosecution Oriented Critics of the Courts." For an opposing view, see Fred E. Inbau, "More About Public Safety v. Individual Civil Liberties."

12. Jerome H. Skolnick, "The Police and the Urban Ghetto." Sydney Harris wrote in his syndicated column (February 8, 1971): "We try to turn all matters of private conscience and personal conduct into a 'law' in the U.S., and then we complain that there are 'too many laws' and that they are 'poorly enforced.' Naturally, when everybody is being censorious, we have an abundance of censors and a wholesale violation of these unenforceable edicts."

13. See also Edwin M. Schur, *Crimes Without Victims*.

14. For a more thorough discussion of plea bargaining, see Arthur Rosett, "The Negotiated Guilty Plea."

15. So much has been written and said about court reform that the subject is discussed here with a brevity out of keeping with its importance. The entire machinery of justice is so understaffed, underfinanced, cumbersome, and politically inspired that expediency has become its handmaiden. But speeding up judicial process is at odds with some of the strategies of "trial lawyership." There is considerable sentiment favoring adoption of certain features of the British system; for example, the magistrates courts, non-unanimous verdicts in jury trials, the relative ease of obtaining bail and its much less formidable monetary element, the method of screening out frivolous appeals, and—as we have noted earlier—the refusal of British courts to exclude evidence obtained through improper police methods. Yale law professor Alexander M. Bickel is among those asserting that we "overuse criminal law as an instrument of regulation and the civil law suit as the basic, all-purpose instrument of social and individual justice" (*The New York Times*, October 22, 1970). Federal legislation as proposed by President Nixon to eliminate unnecessary delay between arrests and trials would require the trial of Federal criminal suspects within 60 days, except in well-defined exceptions. There is bipartisan support for this legislation, but much less so for pre-trial detention extending to all Federal judges the power that Congress granted in the District of Columbia, effective in February 1971. Many police officials feel that certainty of punishment is the most important crime deterrent and that the overwhelmed courts have made a farce of this idea (*U.S. News & World Report*, January 31, 1972). See such additional

references as Leonard Downie, Jr., *Justice Denied: The Case for Reform of the Courts;* Stephen Gillers, *Getting Justice: The Rights of People;* Wasserstein and Green, eds., *With Justice for Some;* Jack D. Douglas, ed., *Crime and Justice in American Society;* and Robert Paul Wolff, ed., *The Rule of Law.* As to the shifting pendulum of the U.S. Supreme Court, see Arthur J. Goldberg, "On the Supreme Court," and "The Supreme Court: End of an Era."

16. Edward Bennett Williams, *One Man's Freedom.* Also see "What's Needed to Speed Up Justice?"; an interview with Edward Bennett Williams, *U.S. News & World Report,* September 21, 1970, pp. 94–98.

17. See Don Hyndman, "The Rule of Law in the Republic."

18. For an article on the Legal Aid Society in New York City, see *Life,* March 12, 1971.

19. Patricia M. Wald, *Law and Poverty: 1965.* Ed. by Abram Chayes and Robert L. Wald. Prepared as a working paper for the National Conference on Law and Poverty, under the cosponsorship of the Attorney-General of the United States and the director of the Office of Economic Opportunity, Washington, D.C., June 23–25, 1965.

20. Terry Lenzner (former director of the OEO Legal Services program), *The New York Times,* December 15, 1970, p. 45. See also *The National Observer,* March 8, 1971, p. 5

21. See also the President's Crime Commission *Task Force Report: The Police,* pp. 38–41.

22. The Board of Trustees of the National Council on Crime and Delinquency, "Preventive Detention: A Policy Statement." In the next chapter, we state a particular qualification to our stand on preventive detention.

23. In New York State, Section 799 of the Code of Criminal Procedure, as amended.

Chapter Seventeen

Corrections and Community Relations

This chapter deals with the corrections aspect of the criminal justice system. Just as there is an abundance of literature dealing with problems of the police and other facets of the legal system, so the writings about the problems of correctional programs fill many library shelves. It seems that although we know pretty well what the problems are, the debate is endless on what to do about them.

No attempt is made here to recapitulate any appreciable portion of what a great many analysts have had to say about correctional maladies. Rather, the highlight will be certain problems that seem particularly salient from a community relations standpoint.

The Correctional Process

Historically, society has sought to deter crime through punishment and to redress wrongs against itself by exacted penalties. The role of criminal law has been to moderate vengeance and to protect the accused against unjust punishment. The development of modern corrections is the attempt to introduce treatment into that process with the goal of changing the attitudes and behavior of the offender. As Richard A. McGee, former director of corrections for California, describes it in "The Administration of Justice: The Correctional Process":

This chapter is coauthored by Robert H. Scott. For information regarding Mr. Scott, please refer to the end of the chapter, page 468.

Man has never been pleased, in his saner and more thoughtful moments, with what he has had to do to carry out the sanctions of the penal law. And from the very beginning, this great new Republic of ours in the western hemisphere has generally frowned upon brutal, savage and unnecessarily severe punishments. . . . Since America has prized liberty so highly, it is only natural that it has always seemed to our leadership that the rightful punishment of an offender who has the high privileges of citizenship in a democracy should be the loss of his liberty. [P. 417]

McGee lists several crucial questions that hinge on the idea of institutional confinement as a correctional procedure:

1. How much liberty should be taken from a man's life for one offense compared with another?

2. Which is the greater offense against society: the deed for which an offender is imprisoned; or the long imprisonment with the intention of eventual release but no preparation for that release?

3. How do we measure the waste of penal servitude in lost labor and human resources, and in the cost of operating custodial institutions?

McGee comments on the basic causes of the prison maladjustment that would exemplify the last question: inadequate financial support; official and public indifference; substandard personnel; enforced idleness; lack of professional leadership and professional programs; excessive size and overcrowding of institutions; political domination and motivation of management; and unwise sentencing and parole practices.

While this speaks to only one side of *adult* correctional pathogenesis, it suggests something of the fundamental enigma of corrections and community relations. It is at once alike and unlike the enigma of police and community relations. Just as "the community" has conflicts in what it expects the police to do, so it has conflicting ideas on what it expects of corrections. Is it a matter simply of punishing the offender for his wrongdoing? Or is it a matter, as McGee says, of exerting "every known skill we possess to bring about psychological and social changes in and with the offender, aiming at rehabilitation and acceptable adjustment as free and responsible persons?" Actually, the juxtaposition of punishment and rehabilitation is an oversimplification—a point that we will take up later.

For centuries, punishment was considered the dominant purpose in dealing with the offender. He was required to "pay his debt to society." Beyond temporary control, this emphasis produced little more than hostility, perversion, and dehumanization. It certainly did not appear to have a deterrent effect upon criminal behavior. Indeed, one could argue that penal servitude itself was and is a significant cause of crime and other socially deviant activity. The distinction between punishment and penalty has never been clear. Emphasis shifted (at least in

lip service) a century and a half ago to the reform of the offender—
reform by means supplementary to incarceration itself—as a correctional
objective. Today, most professionals in the corrections field maintain
that while convicted offenders must be controlled, they must also, as
McGee states it, "be trained, treated and readjusted to the fullest extent
to which our knowledge and resources permit."

McGee contends that rehabilitation as the primary aim in correctional process has never been fairly tested.[1] Some reasons for this are:

1. The initial costs of such programs appear high.

2. Even if money were provided, skilled professional workers are too
   few.

3. Rehabilitative programs have been confused in the public mind
   with laxity or softness.

4. Quantitative tools have been lacking to test adequately the effectiveness of programs. Correctional research in rehabilitative techniques has been scant.

5. Where political influence has dominated correctional administration at the local and state levels, it has stultified the development
   of enlightened, sustained leadership in the field.

McGee is one of many observers who feel that the correctional
process is especially vulnerable to criticism where the short-term
offender is concerned:

> The petty offender is not so much a menace to society as he is an
> expensive nuisance. We seem to have hung our hope over these many
> decades on the idea that if we harass these people enough, and throw
> them into jail often enough, and float them from town to town, that
> sooner or later they will see the light and become honest, upright
> citizens. Those of us who are in this work, whether we be police,
> correctional workers, social workers, psychologists, psychiatrists, or
> what-not, know that we are merely chasing this problem through a
> revolving door. [P. 419]

Probation and Parole

Several forms of correctional treatment carried out by means of
community resources, have emerged in the nineteenth and twentieth
centuries. The central idea, referred to in the corrections field as
community-based correctional treatment, is that certain convicted
offenders may, under some circumstances, be controlled and rehabilitated without being institutionalized. One form of this idea is *probation*:
supervision under prescribed conditions in lieu of institutionalization,
with the provision that if these conditions are violated the offender may
then be committed to an institution. Another form is after-care supervision, commonly called *parole* for the adult offender. Parole may be
defined as supervision in the community following a period of institu-

tional experience, under prescribed conditions which, if violated, may result in the subject's being returned to an institution as a parole violator.

The arguments for one form or another of community-based correctional treatment are economically and socially impressive. The theory of probation and parole has few critics. Rather, sharp-eyed analysts point to what they perceive as shortcomings in the administration, the judgmental features, and the supervisory aspects of these programs. Corrections professionals themselves are concerned with the inadequacy of standards to guide the courts in selecting persons for probation and to guide parole boards in selecting persons for release from institutions. Concern is also shown for the size of caseloads for probation and parole officers that makes effective supervision impossible, and for the absence of even minimal professional standards in many jurisdictions.

Probation and parole operate on the assumption that multiple community resources are available to assist in rehabilitation. For example, it is of cardinal importance that suitable employment be found for probationers and parolees. This requires the understanding cooperation of employers and labor unions. Sometimes clinical services are necessary for the emotionally maladjusted. Frequently, family and marital counseling are urgently needed. Police in the community must be close allies in the probation or parole processes, to avoid compromising the objectives. Social agencies and welfare and religious organizations are indispensable members of the community team, if these correctional measures are to work properly. Probation and parole failures are often the result of community indifference and inertia.

A great deal of public misunderstanding—and plain ignorance—confounds release procedures from correctional institutions. Many people seem to prefer ignorance to understanding the correctional processes, and especially that part having to do with jails and prisons. Lee Rainwater's reference to the police, school teachers, and social welfare workers as "dirty workers" might well include corrections personnel. And as he says, "the silent middle class wants them to do the dirty work and be quiet about it" ("The Revolt of the Dirty Workers"). In a comprehensive national study of American corrections in 1967, the report of President Johnson's Crime Commission said:

> Corrections remains a world almost unknown to law-abiding citizens, and even those within it often know only their own particular corner. [*Task Force Report: Corrections*, p. 1]

Goals in Corrections

The question of goals has been pivotal to many of the problems in the corrections field. We might say that there is a kind of "hawk" and "dove" philosophy as to ends and means in this field, with shades of opinion between these extremes, just as there is regarding other issues in human affairs. As usual, the clash might be easier to reconcile were it not that there is something to be said on each side. The Crime Commission recognized this in a notable statement pertaining to goals in corrections:

> The task of corrections therefore includes building or rebuilding solid ties between offender and community, integrating or reintegrating the offender into community life—restoring family ties, obtaining employment and education, securing in the larger sense a place for the offender in the routine functioning of society. This requires not only efforts directed toward changing the individual offender, which has been almost the exclusive focus of rehabilitation, but also mobilization and change of the community and its institutions. And these efforts must be undertaken without giving up the important control and deterrent role of corrections, particularly as applied to dangerous offenders. [Ibid., p. 7]

That we would underscore the emphasis in this statement upon the *community* aspects of correction should be no more startling than recognition of the connection between social forces and crime, systematically revealed in many studies dating back to those by Clifford Shaw, Henry McKay, et al., in the 1920s and by other authors more recently.[2] Theories of social causation for crime that undergird the emphasis on reintegration in corrections have parallels in other fields, for example, mental health. Treatment of the mentally ill has shifted significantly in recent years from institutional to community bases, and social psychiatry has become a professional specialty that is wigwagging messages to corrections as well as to other fields. It is no longer unusual to discover those who see police and community relations as a problem in community mental health, or what today is sometimes called *ecological psychology*.

The President's Crime Commission pointed out that there is also a parallel in education. In an earlier era, slow learners were considered lazy; they were kept after school, birched, or rapped on the knuckles. Later, counselors and clinical workers were introduced into the school system to treat the problems of individual students. Today there is concern also for community factors, such as family disorganization, poverty, and racial discrimination, as influences upon scholastic motivation and achievement. New directions in correctional treatment today are not much different from these parellel developments. It is apparent that the mobilization of community institutions and resources necessary for anything approaching adequate community-based correctional treatment is a far larger task than corrections people alone can accomplish. Clearly, it requires broad social interests, among which the prevention of recidivism is an important byproduct. Evidence that these ideas are not purely utopian is provided by a good many current experimental programs. The Crime Commission cited and described some examples.

The issue of correctional goals is not simply whether the methods amount to "coddling," but whether they ultimately make the community more stable (healthier) by reducing the incidence of crime. The rehabilitation of offenders is a sensible way to go about doing this. Varying degrees and periods of incarceration is a sensible way to deal with certain offenders. Deterrence and control remain legitimate correctional functions. *The problem is that research and evaluation have so far not been nearly sufficient to establish what methods work best for particular offenders.* As the Crime Commission stated it:

> It is no more logical . . . to suppose that various methods operate with uniform effect in deterrence than to suppose that any sort of rehabilitative treatment will work with all sorts of offenders. . . . For the most part, the choice of methods can be made meaningful only at the level of specific types of offenders and individual cases. [*Task Force Report: Corrections,* p. 16][3]

As we focus on community participation in correctional processes, some of our basic assumptions should be stated:

> It is "the community" that defines crime, through the instrument of law.

> The community also establishes priorities regarding crime—that is, the police, prosecutor, courts and corrections constantly study fluctuating community attitudes for what laws are to be enforced and how, which offenders should be prosecuted, the type and severity of court sentences, and other related matters.

> The community encourages *overuse* of the law as a device for ostensibly solving social problems. As a result, the criminal code becomes a focus of continuing contention among clashing moral positions, inducing factionalism and divisiveness and corroding the common unity of true community. Ideally in a pluralistic society, the criminal code should reflect maximum possible consensus.

> The inappropriate use of the law (trespass, loitering, creating a nuisance, etc.) as a weapon against minor displays of social and political dissent or unpopular causes clutters the criminal justice system with so-called political criminals and invites dissenters to dramatize the consequent embarrassment of the system by assorted antics of disruption, unruliness, and theatrical displays—an extension of the previous point.

> The metropolitan areas where most of our people reside are polyglot amalgamations, with differing notions of law, crime, and enforcement. One police system (or one corrections system) may have great difficulty in its readings on what "the community" expects, because there

is no clear consensus of expectations. Within a single state correctional system, for example, there must be considerable accommodation for differences in court sentences for identical offenses. Corrections professionals are often plagued with such inequities. In an individual case, there may be various reasons for the apparent inequity, and the ambivalence of community attitudes is often one of these reasons. More will be said on this point shortly.

Along with several types of contemporary social and political dissenters whose views are too extreme for "the community" to tolerate without legal sanction, the "clients" of a correctional system also include those who have gone beyond the limits of what society will tolerate in hedonistic or erotic behavior. Legally sane, such persons are sometimes called "kooks" or "eight-ball Willies." Prison populations include also, of course, some incorrigible "hardrocks", and a wide variety of other types. If one is to speak seriously of a prison as a kind of community, the polyglot nature of its population must be understood.

The correctional philosophy of the issue is not institutional *versus* community-based treatment. It is, rather, a matter of blending these approaches generally, and of choosing the most suitable and sensible approach for each individual.

Talk of reform in corrections is always current. It is prevalent in sociopolitical phenomena, therefore prevalent in newspaper and magazine fare, radio and television documentaries, and among the program themes of such organizations as the League of Women Voters and other groups concerned with a fair system. Perhaps in the present era of seemingly heightened sociopolitical sophistication regarding many· long-festering social malignancies, we will at last begin to deal with corrections more responsibly. But cynics doubt it.

Some improvement appears to have occurred in recent years in public attitudes toward parole, evident, for instance, in employment opportunities for parolees (Federal bonding has helped here). But when a parolee is implicated in a serious crime, the entire correctional system is called into question. A parole system functions within rather tightly defined boundaries. In many states, judges set minimum sentences; the law sets the maximum. Once a judge sets a minimum, it is not easily changed. Parole boards have only the flexibility in this respect that individual judges are willing to grant, and some judges are more than a little adamant. The Olympian problem of parole is in knowing when to grant it.

Only 15 of the 50 states have specific statutory qualifications for members of parole boards. In 23 states, there are no requirements of character, education, or experience for persons appointed to parole boards. Lack of statutory or policy requirements does not mean that those appointed are necessarily short on relevant competence or experience. Yet the President's Crime Commission rightly pointed out the political and other abuses that still exist in some places in appointing parole board members.

Corrections and Community Relations

Let us now consider more specific problems of corrections and community relations. Some of these have already been mentioned, but a more systematic delineation is in order.

Problem Areas

1. Conflicting community expectations. The dissimilarities of various groups within a society foster dissimilar and conflicting ideas about the services that should be rendered by a public institution. We have already examined the implications of this point for the role of the police in today's society. Similar problems have developed in corrections that are caused by conflicts in what society expects from correctional services.

Due process (i.e., principles that limit governmental power to deprive a person of life, liberty, or property) is hardly new in the criminal justice system, but recent years have seen a special emphasis upon it well known to prosecutors, the courts, and the police, and lately evident in the field of corrections. At the same time, public concern about crime and order has increased. The implied conflicting community expectations are, as we have noted, a particular thesis in the writings of James Q. Wilson and Jerome Skolnick. Law-and-order proponents argue that too much stress on due process "handcuffs the police"; the civil libertarians say that law-and-order is simply fascist shorthand.

Some policemen, who tend to view probationers and parolees as "poor risks," or "born losers," sometimes feel frustrated "when justice is not done"; they are impatient with what they see as "clemency," "leniency," "soft-headedness" and the like. On the other hand, policemen often take a more lenient view of suspects who "cooperate" with the police; and of disposition of offenders by means of the negotiated plea—the so-called trade-off or copped plea. Corrections people may feel a particular case is a bad risk for society, while, under various pressures, prosecutors and judges may opt for a negotiated plea. Then, "to balance things off," the court may specify a substantial minimum, for example, a sentence of four and a half to five years, which lessens the chances for parole. Such practices engender conflict *within* the criminal justice system.

Another illustration of conflicting expectations is afforded by the punishment-versus-rehabilitation and custody-versus-treatment dichotomies. An example is provided in the following report from Minnesota (though surely this is not a one-state dilemma) following an attempted prison break by six inmates of the Stillwater prison in February, 1970:

> The inmates' main complaint was that the prison administration was not interested in rehabilitation. . . . Public reaction to the Stillwater incident seems to indicate an increasing impatience with the concept

of rehabilitation. State correction officials, however, contend that adequate rehabilitation programs cannot be carried out under the present system, which still stresses security at the expense of rehabilitation. The treatment staff at Stillwater alleges that its programs are impeded by old-line guards, protected by civil service, who actually work against rehabilitation.

The state corrections administration recognizes the difficulty of implementing progressive programs within the existing systems of huge, archaic prisons like that at Stillwater. It is seeking community correction centers, better education and training programs for inmates, and more contacts with the community to ease the prisoner's transition back to society. But without public support, it is unlikely that the legislature will endorse such programs. [*NCCD News,* May–June 1970][4]

2. Prevention of anomie. The punishment-rehabilitation dichotomy is complicated by a third element. By the penalties it exacts for crime, society maintains basic standards and upholds societal norms. When the power of social rule over individuals weakens, a state of "normlessness" is brought about. This state has been defined by the French sociologist, Emile Dirkheim, as *anomie.*

We have noted that the criminal justice system must take punishment into account, in the sense of just retribution and not simply vengeance; and also the rehabilitation of the offender, looking toward his eventual return to the community. Now we see that the system must also take into account a third element: the prevention of normlessness —anomie—in a society. The consideration of anomie is illustrated by the weight that a parole board may ascribe to whether an inmate's crime has been "shocking to the conscience of society." Neither punishment nor rehabilitation may serve this end.

The public becomes frustrated at the apparent failure of social institutions to prevent crime. But as Michael Meltsner has put it, ". . . in the criminal process, it is generally only the correctional system, not the courts or the police, that has the capacity—and a small one at that—to rehabilitate and reform. At a time when crime is a matter of great public concern, the role played by the correctional system in determining whether offenders become useful citizens or recidivists is critical" ("The Future of Correction: A Defense Attorney's View"). The same writer observes that the correctional process is perhaps most dangerous when it justifies itself as acting in the best interests of a defendant. The fact is that we do not really know enough about the effects of what we call treatment, in corrections, to predict what may best serve his interests.

3. Differentiation in correctional treatment. Political regimes often protect themselves against whatever they determine to be excessive dissent, by the use of their characteristic methods of dealing with it. We have touched on the problem this produces for the criminal justice system in its handling of current social unrest. Corrections is deeply implicated in this problem because it must deal with the casualties of social conflict. The crux of the issue for corrections is the question of how to differentiate among several types of prisoners who may commit identical crimes for different reasons. For example, to burn Selective Service files is arson. So is burning a supermarket in a riot. So is pyromania. So is arson for profit. The difficulty for correctional administration is to match the treatment with the individual problem, mindful that a central purpose in correctional treatment is to change anti-social attitudes and behavior to pro-social.

The standards for determining whether an individual's attitudes and behavior are sufficiently advanced in "treatment" to make him "a good risk" for release should, ideally, reflect societal norms. But when —through social upheaval—the norms become upset and society's distinctions between "anti-social" and "pro-social" behavior becomes ambiguous, how is corrections to draw a clear distinction between the two? If rehabilitation implies some sort of behavior norm as to what is anti-social and what is pro-social, whose behavior model is to be taken as anti-social? and whose taken as pro-social?

Again we see the basic problem of conflict in what the community expects from the criminal justice system. For the police or for the courts, the problems caused by this conflict are substantial. For corrections, they are even more formidable.

Political radicalization is becoming more commonplace in American prisons, meshing—as Tad Szulc has noted in *The New York Times*— with the growing opinion among prisoners and outside radicals, including ideologically motivated lawyers and criminologists, that most crimes committed in the United States, particularly by minorities and poor whites, are essentially "social" and "political" in nature. This is so, the argument runs, because such crimes derive from sociological and political conditions. But there is a counterargument from those who say that a George Jackson is not so much a political prisoner as he is simply a menace to the rights, the property, and the lives of others who must be protected by whatever means are made necessary by the actions of the inmate.

4. Social work influence. A fourth problem has to do with social agency activities. Where *treatment* of juvenile and adult offenders begins, the criminal justice system comes face to face with social work. Probation and parole in particular, but institutional rehabilitation programs as well, reflect considerable social work influence, observable in the professional training of corrections personnel. Philosophically, social work tends to view crime (and therefore correctional problems) as a social defect arising out of conditions of deprivation, neglect, abuse, and the like. There is, of course, much to be said for this view, and for the perspective that it suggests for *treatment*. However, corrections also has a responsibility for societal protection and security, that carries connotations of control and restraint of offenders. The field of corrections, then, is oriented toward the demands of society as well as the needs of the offender. For this reason, social work should not have an exclusive role in corrections. Corrections is an interprofessional, interdisciplinary field in which social work surely has a vital part to play, but its role should not be extended to the point of dominating change and improvement in a correctional system, with the assumption that social work "has all the answers."

5. Need for independent professionals. In some states, corrections —historically dominated by custodial goals—has developed into a monolithic bureaucracy. In other states, it is fragmented and piecemeal. It has had a quasi-military character analogous to the police, with less flexibility than social work. Its professional organizations often function in a manner suggesting "company unions." Internal criticism has been rare, and outside intervention even more so. What corrections needs is a solid body of independent professionals exercising a critical effect on the field, a kind of enlightened lobby of correctional personnel. To supply this need, the National Council on Crime and Delinquency is attempting to break the bureaucratic pattern with state-level, citizen-participation councils. We shall have more to say shortly about the influence this could have in changing public attitudes toward corrections.

6. Lag of the law. Another problem may be referred to as "lag of the law." We have alluded to the political dynamics of law-making and law-enforcing. Complex legislative and judicial processes are basically responses to public opinion, to the readiness of a substantial number of people to accept concepts and changes. Corrections is the last part of the criminal justice process to be scrutinized by the courts and by legislative bodies, because public pressures prescribe higher priority for other aspects. This is another way of saying that community relations is a particularly difficult task for corrections. Only recently has there been some sign of movement toward analysis of the correctional process *per se,* illustrated by the national conference on corrections summoned by President Nixon in December, 1971.

7. Due process. The recent tide of emphasis upon due process in corrections is not in itself, of course, a problem in community relations any more than for the police "to give a suspect his rights" under the *Miranda* rule. Some police officers and corrections workers see this as a long overdue movement in what they deem the right direction. The *problem* is that not all police officers or corrections workers see it this way. Nor does "the community." To cloud the corrections picture further, an outsider's assumption that the "doves" (treatment-minded personnel) approve of it turns out not to be so at all. Some "hawks" defend due process beyond what some doves are willing to concede. These doves see "too much due process" or "too many legalisms" as inimical to treatment procedures. They hold that lawyers should not be permitted to invade the domain of professional correctional treatment; that to do so restricts the discretionary flexibility that correctional professionals should have. Yet some of the doves in corrections tend to be pretentious in their claims for pet rehabilitation techniques that may be unduly manipulative and may therefore violate due process, and, furthermore, are open to question because of inadequate substantiation as to their effectiveness. In a community relations sense, the argument here is another commentary on the freedom-and-order teeter-totter.

This chapter focuses upon adult corrections for several reasons. First, the juvenile court came into being at the turn of this century and emphasized protection of the juvenile. Second, the system of juvenile justice encompassed concepts of special handling by police and corrections as well as the court.

However, due process is receiving increased attention in juvenile court. It now appears that protection sometimes results in depriving the juvenile of important rights accorded adults. Kent v. United States [383 US 541, 1966] scrutinized the circumstances under which a juvenile may be waived to an adult court.

A recent Michigan Supreme Court case, People v. Field, (July 26, 1972) declared unconstitutional the statute permitting the waiver of juveniles over the 15th birthday to adult court as lacking standards for determining whether to treat a juvenile as an adult.

In re Gault [387 US 1, 1967] held that the Juvenile Court in the case under appeal had denied: notice of the charges; right to counsel; confrontation and cross examination of witnesses; privilege of self-incrimination; transcript of proceedings, and appellate review.

This awareness of due process and the rights of the offender, now being emphasized in the field of corrections, developed somewhat earlier in other branches of criminal justice,[5] as illustrated by the following:

A prisoners' labor union has been formed at Green Haven Prison in New York State, petitioning for recognition as executive bargaining agent for the inmates.

Minnesota has established an ombudsman for the corrections system.

The Supreme Court has ruled that state prison officials are subject to damage suits by inmates who are mistreated or arbitrarily punished without a hearing. (*Sostre* case, on appeal from New York State, March, 1972.)

On June 29, 1972, in *Morrisey* v. *Brewer, Warden,* the United States Supreme Court overturned a U.S. Court of Appeals ruling that parole was only "a correctional device authorizing service of sentence outside the penitentiary." The Court spelled out requirements for parole revocation as (a) a preliminary inquiry near the alleged violation to determine whether there was probably cause to return the violator to prison; (b) a parole violation hearing in which the alleged violator was entitled to notice of the charges, witnesses for and against, and a written statement as to the evidence relied on and reasons for the decision. The Supreme Court specifically declined to consider the question of counsel and went on to say that it was not creating "an inflexible structure for parole revocation procedures."

Clearer delineation, as for instance in New York State, of the conditions under which the board of parole or courts of sentence must restore the voting rights of convicted offenders, and the conditions under which convicted offenders do not lose their right to vote. Indeed, a Bill of Rights for prisoners has been advanced by the Correctional Association of New York (*NCCD News,* May-June, 1971).

The American Friends Service Committee, in a District of Columbia study of communication between prisoners awaiting trial and their attorneys, recommended certain minimum standards to safeguard the integrity of rights to such communication (ibid.).

In a February, 1970 speech to the National Association of Attorneys General, Chief Justice Warren E. Burger urged the states to develop some simple methods for hearing "promptly, fully, and fairly" the grievances of prisoners, and pointed out that the Supreme Court has overturned many state court convictions on the ground that individuals sentenced to prison had been denied their constitutional rights. The Chief Justice was also highly critical of delays in court process (*NCCD News,* March-April 1970).[6]

Petitions by inmates of jails and prisons to civil rights agencies, pleading for investigation of alleged discrimination and other violations of civil rights, are not uncommon today.

While parole is discretionary (except where denial is wilful or capricious), the trend today is toward making the actions of parole boards *visible and accountable.* Once parole is granted, it cannot be withdrawn without due process. In January, 1971, the New York State Court of Appeals ruled that parolees have a constitutional right to have their attorneys present at hearings weighing revocation of their paroles (*NCCD News,* March-April 1971).[7]

The principle that inmates are not rightless is also being increasingly recognized in the policies and practices of correctional administrators. Once, when a prisoner was charged with an infraction of institutional rules, he was brought before a disciplinary board for a hearing, without an advocate. Nowadays there are prisons where an advocate system has been carefully developed to speak for the accused, although there are those who question the extent to which this is actually the case.

8. Concern for victims of crime. An extension of the prior point, this point pertains to the opinion that criminal justice has become too much concerned with the rights of the suspect and the convicted

offender and not sufficiently concerned with the victims of crime. Former Attorney General John Mitchell and the late FBI Director J. Edgar
Hoover have been among those who have called for "better balance in
the scales of justice." A growing number of states are enacting laws
providing for victim compensation, and Senator Mike Mansfield has
proposed legislation to compensate victims of criminal violence through
a Federal Violent Crime Compensation Commission (*NCCD News*,
March-April 1971).[8] Lag of the law is evident in a number of serious
loopholes in criminal law that operate inequitably in favor of offenders.
Several examples may be cited:

> The system of concurrent sentences in some states may not provide
> society with the protection it needs against the habitual offender.
> Sentences are often concurrent for a series of offenses committed prior
> to conviction as well as for those committed while on bond or proba-
> tion. An individual convicted of stealing fifteen cars could receive the
> same sentence, in effect, as an individual who steals one car. A cure
> for this problem would be to retain the minimum sentence but make
> the maximum cumulative to a reasonable limit. In its proposed Model
> Penal Code, NCCD sets this limit at thirty years, for the so-called
> dangerous offender.

> The mentally retarded person is not very well cared for by mental
> health programs, and even less so by the criminal justice system. A
> person with an IQ of, say, 50 may be held criminally responsible, and
> such persons clog our correctional institutions where adequate treatment
> programs are lacking.

> There is a question regarding "good time off" for dangerous offenders,
> the so-called sociopath who is not legally insane. Here again NCCD
> recommends a 30-year maximum sentence. The fear of the public in
> such instances is real and must be recognized. While in general prin-
> ciple we side with NCCD and with others who have been critical of so-
> called "preventive detention,"[9] there is a side of the matter that is
> strikingly revealed in the case of the dangerous offender. Bail is a
> matter of money, usually no hurdle for such offenders. Release on
> personal recognizance is frequently a sensible course, but it is not the
> answer with the dangerous offender who may be a psychopathic rapist,
> even though legally sane. Preventive detention merits consideration in
> such circumstances, provided that it is "tied up tight" with guidelines,
> limits, and procedural safeguards. The NCCD argues that this would
> place a further burden on the courts, that it would be unwieldy and
> costly—if used often. Probably so, but we would counter that it should
> *not* be used extensively; that its use should be confined to cases of
> "clear and present danger" to society.

A further point relative to concern for the victims of crime relates
to what we have said in an earlier chapter on the subject of victimless
crimes—overcriminalization, legal moralism, etc.[10] Certain crimes with-

out victims should be eliminated from the criminal code. And we may add that statutes pertaining to so-called nuisance offenses (loitering, trespass, disturbing the peace, etc.)—generally vague, legal catch-alls— should be revised and tightened to fit with current social realities. The point is this: due and proper concern for the victims of crime should include efforts to prevent the criminal code from being used inappropriately, prejudicially, and prohibitively where conduct may be morally or socially repugnant but does no apparent harm to society.

Statistics of the FBI reveal that the total number of arrests in the United States in 1970 was 8,117,700, of which 1,551,300 (19 percent) were for the seven "index crimes": murder, rape, robbery, assault, burglary, larceny, and auto theft. The total number of arrests for victimless crimes was 3,962,700 (49 percent of the total), itemized as follows:

Drunkenness	1,825,500	22.5%
Disorderly conduct	710,000	8.7%
Narcotic drug laws	415,600	5.1%
Liquor laws	309,000	3.8%
Runaways	232,700	2.9%
Curfew & loitering	129,600	1.6%
Vagrancy	113,400	1.4%
Gambling	91,700	1.1%
Suspicion	83,500	1.1%
Prostitution	51,700	0.6%
Total known victimless crime arrests	3,962,700	48.8%

9. Changing values. The cue to the problem here is again social change. Change—in the sense of the apparent functional deterioration of social institutions in the urban milieu that have traditionally had a stabilizing influence upon behavior—has had, not surprisingly, a traumatic effect upon corrections. Diagnostic evaluations of offenders frequently resort to such terms as "hedonistic," "sociogenic," and "addicted." Changing sexual mores lead some people to refer to a "moral vacuum," and society's concern for the prevention of anomie comes into focus. Sadism, brutality, and violence have their shadows in correctional institutions. In point of community relations, there is widespread public indignation with provocative displays of rebellion against society's most cherished values, the flaunting of obscenity and such. However, most of the Establishment finds it difficult to distinguish between Easy Riders and Hell's Angels. They tend to lump the two together into one stereotype, from such symbols as dress and hair-styles. The blind, unreasoning fear in such community attitudes must be reckoned with by realistic criminal justice professionals. Corrections cannot say simply that "the public is stupid." Public anxiety is real, and the partnership between corrections and community is not facilitated by scorn or ridicule toward situations of common bewilderment.

10. Simplistic approaches. Simplistic approaches, a phenomenon not unique to corrections, is another problem. One form of it is the "there ought to be a law" syndrome, about which we have previously commented. Another form of it is the "every man is an expert" approach, with everyone plugging his own pet remedy for complex social and personal pathology in a dearth of balanced, coordinated, interprofessional and interdisciplinary planning and production. Chief Justice Burger has hit a proper keynote (*Time,* March 2, 1970) in calling for a thorough rethinking of the American concept of justice:

> We find lawyers and judges becoming so engrossed with procedures and techniques that they tend to lose sight of the purpose of a system of justice. We should stop thinking of criminal justice as something which begins with an arrest and ends with a final judgment of guilt. ... Few things characterize our attitude toward prisoners and prisons more than indifference and impatience with the failure of the prisoner to return to society corrected and reasonably ready to earn an honest way in life. A large proportion of criminal offenders are seriously maladjusted human beings. And those who are not maladjusted when they go in are likely to be so when they get out.

11. Prison and jail reform. No list of corrections problems can omit the chronic one of the need for prison and jail reform, sometimes referred to as "the badlands of corrections." Richard McGee (p. 418) refers to the county jail as the "lowest form of social institution on the American scene . . . often more destructive than corrective." *Commonweal* magazine (February 26, 1971) refers to "these sinks of despair and breeding ground for still more crime and violence." A national jail census was conducted by the Federal government on March 15, 1970. On that day, there were 4,037 jails, in which 160,863 people were incarcerated. Some 500 jails still in use were built in the nineteenth century, and six in the eighteenth, the oldest one in use since 1705. One-quarter of all jail cells are more than fifty years old. On the day of this 1970 census, *some 83,000 (52 percent) of those held in jail had not been convicted of any crime.* Although 65,000 people were serving sentences in local jails, 10,000 of them for a year or more, most jails are equipped to do nothing but hold them behind bars for the duration of their sentences. Of the 3300 jails in large communities, 85 percent have no educational or recreational facilities of any kind. About half lack medical facilities, and about one-fourth have no facilities for visitors. In many of these institutions, the mentally disturbed, the hardened criminal, and the confused adolescent, the serious offender as well as the petty offender—and overlapping these types, the tried and the not-yet-tried—are lumped together, often under conditions of overcrowding, filth, and degradation.[11] The plight of our jails (with a few notable exceptions) illustrates the patchwork-quilt approach to corrections and dramatizes the problems of our parallel but separate systems for attempting to treat felonists and misdemeanants. It also drearily illustrates the existing state of affairs, resistance to change, and intransigent, county-level, political entrenchment.

The regional jail concept looks like a step in the right direction but, by and large, the jail is an excellent place for community endeavor to concentrate in the corrections field—with prisons not far behind. Upheavals, riots, and rebellions in prisons and jails in the recent past may be the wellsprings of hope for true reform. Unprecedented questions are being asked: for example, the extent to which the Bill of Rights applies to people behind bars; the Eighth Amendment's ban against cruel and unusual punishment; and whether people in jail awaiting trial should be given more or different rights from people in jail serving sentences. We commented earlier on the effects of a larger number of politically active, and angry, inmates in correctional institutions. Draft and drug offenses alone account for a sizable portion of this increase. It appears that the higher the proportion of "political prisoners," such as in New York and California, the more public attention is drawn to what goes on behind the walls. David Rothenberg, executive secretary of the Fortune Society, an organization of former convicts and others seeking to create a greater public awareness of the problems of penal inmates, may have said it all: "Government responds not to problems but to pressures."

12. Finances. Finally, but not least important, there is the problem of finances. Competition for the tax dollar being a main pressure point in political processes, we will settle for three observations:

> Prisons are at the lowest priority in public budgets and outlays.

> Treatment is expensive. But we continue to try to find cheap ways to do it; for instance, in saying that volunteers save money—a good thing is favored for the wrong reason.

> In correctional treatment, since we are still not sure of what works, requests for more dollars cannot be supported by adequate evidence that professional remedies are any better than popular, one-shot antidotes.

Coping With the Problems

Having recited and commented on a rather long list of corrections problems with particular community relations importance, something should be said about coping with these problems. We will suggest five general directions for coping and then pursue more specifically a sixth (probably no more important than the others, but too seldom analyzed).

1. Redesigning prisons and correctional systems. Some obvious things have already been stressed, such as the necessity for revising the criminal code, reforming jail and prison conditions, and discovering ways for expediting justice procedures without reducing due process. The Michigan Corrections Department has recommended remodeling and breaking up big prisons into smaller units, with a population limit of 600. Also recommended are better diagnostic procedures to determine where new prisoners are to be placed—to keep first offenders separated from confirmed criminals. Such proposals exemplify the possibilities in "inventing the future" of correctional systems. The state of Michigan is building a model, medium-security prison in Muskegon, with "a built-in capability to research" its problems.

2. Strengthening social and moral values. Not quite so obvious, perhaps, and considerably more elusive and difficult to deal with concretely is the matter of strengthening our social and moral fabric. Basically this is a question of values, a sensitive and amoeba-like subject. We have in mind especially values bearing upon leisure time, personal privacy, reducing emotional conflict in interpersonal relations, and such. We have in mind reducing social, economic, and political discrimination, and programs for eradicating poverty that transcend political partisanship. We have in mind a positive administrative philosophy in public affairs that rejects management by fiat in favor of policy making that genuinely involves people as full-fledged participants in the processes of government. To mention these things in these times may be viewed as preaching utopian platitudes (some simply call it "scripture"), but we do it without apology.

3. Improving corrections and rehabilitation processes. The Law Enforcement Assistance Administration of the United States Department of Justice and the program it currently and potentially encompasses represents a spectacular breakthrough in the cause of an improved criminal justice system, across the board. Premised as it is in large part on the work of the 1966-67 President's Crime Commission, LEAA promises a revolutionary departure from the patchwork approach. It seeks to deal with the criminal justice process as a whole by concerted efforts at the Federal, state, and local levels—and at some points by a *regional* perspective that transcends traditional political boundaries. It fosters a continuing, consistent, critical examination of the criminal justice process, emphasizing research, planning, and persistent efforts to elevate professional standards. The LEAA has considerable political visibility, it has money and, while it also has its weaknesses and limitations, it sees itself as a catalyst for change in the system. President Nixon, moreover, called a national conference on corrections in December of 1971 and promulgated a 13-point program for improvement, over a ten-year period, in "the American system for correcting and rehabilitating criminals."[12]

4. Increasing corrections research. Several times we have mentioned correctional treatment approaches that are not as yet proven. Exaggerated claims for this or that technique are common, as Chief Justice Burger has observed. Pointedly implied is the vast need for research in the corrections field. It has barely begun to develop. Research can be one way for correctional administration to improve communication with the public. In a time of societal emphasis upon rationality and science, why should so much of correctional practice be based on hunch, myth, misconception, irrationality, and untested rules of thumb?[13]

5. Developing community resources. Logically, coping with problems of corrections and community relations requires the mobilization of community resources. This was a major recommendation of the President's Crime Commission, and LEAA is pushing it currently. It is the foundation stone of NCCD's state citizen councils (in more than twenty states at last count), a program that has had the generous support of the Ford Foundation.[14] One important theme is a desirable blurring of the line between institutional and community treatment of offenders through such programs as work furloughs, educational work with inmates, and so-called halfway facilities. Increased use of probation and parole is clearly a part of this picture also. Elmer K. Nelson of the University of Southern California makes a good point:

> In moving toward the increased use of community treatment, many problems must be overcome, including a lack of research information on the effectiveness of particular techniques; resistance to needed changes on the part of traditionalist staff and organizational systems; the difficulty of creating new and noncriminal identities for ex-offenders; and the problem of drawing community institutions into the task. The national attention which has been focused upon the needs of the correctional field has created an unprecedented opportunity to bring new resources and methods to the solution of these problems. ["Community-Based Correctional Treatment"][15]

The use of volunteers is usually thought of as a part of the community resources in corrections or social work. We should repeat a point made earlier: volunteers are often misused as "cheap helpers" rather than as responsible partners. They should be carefully selected (*not* be people working out their own problems), systematically participating in a continuing training program, wisely supervised, and given particularized responsibilities as well as deserved recognition.[16]

Leadership in the Corrections Field

Having cited five general guidelines for coping with problems of corrections and community relations, we now deal with a sixth at greater length. This is the question of leadership by correctional professionals in helping the public (the community) to know and to understand "what it ought to want" in correctional programs.

Difficulties of Leadership Development

We may say at the outset that the development of such leadership is not a simple task. Some reasons for this have been suggested by other writers;[17] other reasons may be added:

> Corrections professionals are, as a rule, cautious, almost shy. Public attitudes toward corrections explain this, in part. The public seems satisfied with mere tokenism and doesn't seem to care whether treatment works or not. To look at correctional programs carefully would turn up so many inadequacies that professionals in the field doubt that they themselves could do what they would tell the public ought to be done. In effect, corrections personnel are afflicted with a group inferiority complex.

> The point at which some of the public do care about a correctional system is at the spreading belief that the system is failing, measured by such things as a particularly heinous crime committed by a person on probation or parole. What sometimes happens under such circumstances is that progressive steps in the field, of a type that moderate the revenge motive, are set back by what amounts to "backlash." Regressive steps are prompted by public turbulence. This is clearly not encouraging to forthright, progressive leadership in the corrections field.

> Again, the sticky question arises of what works and what doesn't work in correctional techniques and how success is to be measured. To what we have already said about this may be added the observation that the most promising programs are frequently expensive. Further, it should be observed that *scientific* tests of a program invariably fail to measure *humanitarian* efficacy.

> Conflicting aims and philosophies within the correctional field itself handicap community leadership by corrections personnel.[18]

> Criminals are disadvantaged persons. They have no lobby to intercede in their behalf with the bastions of power. In the competition for the tax dollar, prisoners are the last to be served. Even if conditions in prisons are recognized as bad, the political premium is on *control*. As with some other things, reform usually comes in the aftermath of riots and disturbances—a form of lobbying. It is a troublesome question to ask whether services available in a prison should be better than services available in the outside community. We have asserted that public attitudes toward corrections are extremely ambivalent. It is easier to help "the deserving poor." The criminal is viewed both as socially unworthy and socially dangerous. The Protestant ethic as well as the Mosaic code hold individuals responsible for their behavior, though conceding that environmental circumstances have some influence in the individual's choice of action. An eye for an eye . . . has a Biblical origin. Anthropology also conveys its lessons in retributive justice: if the tribe does not punish the transgressor, the gods will wreak vengeance on the tribe.

The political sensitivity of corrections has been mentioned. Prison reform is a favorite chant in political scandals, along with highway funds and police graft. During a nine-month period, September, 1969 through May, 1970, there were these headlines on the subject (*NCCD News*):

Oregon Correctional system reorganized; grouped with five other agencies directly under the Governor.

Sixty-three inmates at the Denver county jail asked the Colorado Civil Rights Commission to investigate their complaints of discrimination and civil rights violations by law enforcement and judicial officials.

New Mexico organizes first Department of Corrections as a result of legislation prompted by the state council of NCCD.

Four men are crowded together now in some small, close, and cluttered cells at the New Jersey State Prison. The cells are in a section of the prison opened in 1836.

Conditions at Auburn prison in New York state remain turbulent; some inmates have the idea that they are victims of a racist society, repressed by racist institutions.

West Virginia's old and dilapidated penitentiary has been the scene of fifteen violent deaths in the past three years: six slayings, five suicides, three poisonings, and one death by burning. A former director of corrections stated that he had visited some zoos that were cleaner and safer.

A University of Alabama Law Professor charges that the state's penal institutions neither punish nor rehabilitate.

Judge declares that many county jails in Iowa are "stinking dungeons where young prisoners are abused and contempt for society is nurtured." State correctional officials seek a major overhaul of the entire Iowa system of handling offenders.

Some 400 self-mutilations have taken place in Kansas State Penitentiary, in protest against the prison's new administration.

The State Senate Committee on Penal Institutions assailed New York City and upstate county jails as "more fertile breeding grounds for crime than the streets."

For over a year, the Ohio Department of Mental Hygiene and Corrections, in its news releases and publications, highly publicized an inmate training program that did not exist. A series of articles in the *Cleveland Press* regarding conditions at Ohio Penitentiary inspired a special legislative study of prison operation and the parole system.

In Tennessee, a State Senate Committee found that the Corrections Department's Division of Probation and Parole was headed by a director who was found guilty in four court-martial proceedings while in the Marine Corps and who, before appointment to his present position, made his living as a professional wrestler and barroom bouncer.

A former superintendent of a State Prison Farm in Arkansas was sentenced on a charge of brutality against inmates. He was found guilty of torturing prisoners with an old, crank wall-telephone used to send electrical shocks through their genitals.

Grand jury highly critical of conditions at Pendleton, Indiana Reformatory.

Any other corresponding period would produce a similar number and variety of conditions underlining the politics of corrections. It is a field in which survivors learn to play the game of political trade-off in harsh, pragmatic terms, and if they are idealists, as many correction professionals are, they learn to live with frustration, heart-rending disappointment, and tragedy.

Guidelines for Leadership

Leadership in community relations by correctional personnel, without which there is little hope for a brighter future in the field, can and must develop. For this, too, there are some suggested guidelines:

Correctional personnel should welcome and encourage broad, critical review of the entire corrections bureaucracy. Needed is continuing, sustained evaluation, planning and research; a way of removing politics from correctional work to a desirable, professional degree. This would educate the public far beyond ordinary public relations activity.

To clarify some implications of the previous point, corrections should promote the idea that professionalism and bureaucracy are not identical, and that they can be made compatible. Professional associations in the field of corrections should break away from the company union mantle and become more flexible within the system, that is, less rigidly intent on perpetuating existing practices. Professional schools for preparing correctional careerists, remembering that the public tends to turn to professional schools for *answers* and to bureaucracies merely for *explanations,* should recognize that their *critical* function is at least as important as their *educational* function.

Certainly training and professional standards in corrections must continue to be elevated, while emphasizing a more sophisticated and sensitive handling of inmates and probationers. The traditional distance between keeper and kept must be diminished. The movement toward upgrading correctional staffs, toward developing change agents in the system, is essential to reform and progress.

Overly rigid civil service and labor union requirements can conceivably be obstacles in the professional development of corrections personnel. There is no reason why professional associations and worker unions should not be able to co-exist, and indeed to complement each other. In fact, a union can be more inclusive in cutting across ranks and helping to unfreeze bureaucratic icebergs. But that a union and a professional association have different functions should be recognized and kept clear.[19]

Commissions or committees to look into corrections tend to focus on the particular rather than the general. The result is often to encourage the piecemeal, fragmented approach alluded to earlier, with each part of the system having its own goal ideas. A bar association committee for revising the penal code goes one way; an association of social workers goes another. The so-called Joint Commission on Correctional Manpower and Training, authorized by Congress in 1965, started with the particular and became general in its scope. It made sweeping recommendations, but was commissioned for only three years.[20] In May, 1970, the American Bar Association announced a nationwide citizen-action program to change public attitudes and seek reform of the American prison system. An ABA 18-member Commission on Correctional Facilities and Services was activated, headed by former New Jersey governor, Richard J. Hughes. As noted earlier, LEAA made a grant of more than $200,000 to the ABA for a Volunteers in Parole Program (VIPP), to enable hundreds of young lawyers to become part-time parole workers, under the supervision of experienced parole professionals. The project was designed for experimentation in eight states.

Wholeness of perspective is needed in dealing with the field of corrections and its community relations problems. The sheer enormousness of the problems suggests "biting off manageable hunks," but the problems must be seen in their larger context. Rehabilitation, for example, demands a complex of community agencies and services far beyond the field of corrections. The inter-organizational approach outlined by Elmer H. Johnson, referred to in the preceding chapter, is pertinent here. Corrections professionals should assist the community to go beyond the theory that to *name* the problem is in itself an important part of therapy. To name and to define the problem adequately is indeed, as we have seen, a crucial step for the community in solving the problem. But if this process sputters and dies at the problem identification stage, as often happens, nothing materializes to resolve the problem.

In its responsibility to inform the public, corrections would be well advised to stress the generic nature of the total field, rather than the public relations of any particular part of it. This follows from our previous point regarding whole perspective.

Corrections shares with other social institutions the challenge of recognizing the difference between the creative and the imitative, the need for prudence in knowing when to "maintain the status quo" as against "rocking the boat" (". . . giving me more probation officers won't do the job, but I need them so badly that I can't say this!"), and the delicate acknowledgment that what the public often gets is the reflection of a bureaucrat's judgment as to what the public wants, rather than what professionals in the system feel the public *ought* to want.

The fulcrum for change within correctional systems is *outside* the system. Therefore, corrections personnel must do more to discover how community and societal resources can be brought to bear on the problems of offenders, bearing in mind that *the community* is the corrective aspect of the correctional process.

Finally, corrections workers should keep their "client" relations prominently in the forefront of their attention. It is important to interpret to the client what's going on, and why—just as it is in medicine and police service. In corrections, it is not always easy to determine who the client is. There is some argument about this in other public services—in police work, education, welfare and health, etc. But in jails and prisons, few people perceive the client to be the prisoner. Most believe the client is society. This brings us back to the main question in corrections: What are. we trying to do? Most proponents of rehabilitation say that we are trying to obtain greater opportunity and development for the individual offender, thereby defining the client. Others maintain that rehabilitation programs should give added protection to the public, to protect the community from criminality. This is another way to define the client. In the final analysis, the argument may be futile, for the two sides may not really be talking about different goals. The one may well be a means to the other; more aptly, the relationship may be as the inside and outside of a water glass. What helps the offender protects the community.

Relations Within the Corrections Field

Much that we have said bears directly or indirectly on relationships within the field of corrections. The nub of the problem of corrections is conceptual, very much as it is with the police in their relations with the community. It comes down to the question of how the corrections worker sees his role. This calls for a bit more analysis.

Professional emphasis in corrections has lately been toward *treatment* of the offender. A utopian role conception portrays corrections workers using a variety of equipment and formulas to bring about remarkable reconstruction of "those who have gone wrong." A more realistic conception of role portrays them as social workers who are primarily trouble shooters and report writers. While the more sophisticated view—that of the corrections worker as an agent of change—is the dominant view in professional circles today, it is accompanied by a certain schizophrenic frustration on the part of the worker who knows that he really cannot do what he wants to believe he can do. Conditions in his milieu do not permit it. Societal attitudes do not permit it. In effect, the system in which he finds himself is counter-productive to his professional goals. The forces that would support him are so few, so scattered, so willy-nilly, that he feels compelled to vent his frustration and despair on some convenient scapegoat.

The result is that the corrections worker turns to damning "the system," the bureaucrats who run it, the society that tolerates it and "doesn't give a damn anyhow," the politicians who understand only the meaning of votes, the stand-patters in the system "who haven't had a new idea in thirty years," and the professional school faculty "who live in a dream world." But the corrections worker has some power within his immediate jurisdiction; and a man is never more dangerous than when he thinks he is being benevolent in the exercise of power—especially when he thinks he has "the answers."

Sometimes the correctional administrator who becomes the scapegoat of the correctional worker entertains no real hope that corrections can actually correct, but believes, rather, that the sooner an inmate can safely be released, the better will be his chances of recovery. Thus the practical-minded administrator who realizes the difficulty of securing additional resources, and distrusts the efficacy of what he has, may be more humane than the worker who insists upon conformity and participation in meaningless programs as the price of the inmate's freedom. Incidentally, the ostensible treatment process is likewise often subverted when the "client" for whom change is possible perceives the techniques to be a mirage and a fake.

But all the machinery of rewards and punishments in corrections reinforces conformity by convicted offenders, with the goals set by correctional workers. Prisoners are often forced to go through motions that have no meaning and to participate in programs that have no perceptible value for them. They do so because they believe their privileges and their ultimate freedom depend on it.[21]

Related to this is the conviction of some inmates that only poor people and other "rejects" go to jail or prison in the first place. Penal institutions have been largely class institutions; the current wave of agitation for reform no doubt reflects the fact that youth of upper- and middle-class backgrounds have recently tasted life behind the walls—on draft and drug charges and offenses related to civil rights and social protest activities. Criminologist Richard Korn spoke to this point in a paper prepared for the Joint Commission on Correctional Manpower and Training.[22] The notion that correctional treatment techniques amount to no more than "hocus-pocus" inspired by class-bound "do-gooders" is not conducive to a proper professional-client relationship.[23]

The predicament of the correctional worker, then, is one of role fostered by conflicting community expectations—something like the predicament of the police officer in today's society. Society resolves this predicament by seeking to sweep it under the rug; in the case of corrections, insisting that control and protection be paramount. While criminal law and procedure move perceptibly toward moderation of the revenge motive with convicted offenders, there remain those who see the convicted offender as fair game for revenge. It may even be, psychologically, a means of avoiding guilt feelings for a social disaster by self-congratulation that one has not himself served time.

Karl Menninger asserts that we *need* crime. It is similar to our need for the religious to be holy for us, heroes to be brave for us, and government officials to exercise power for us. As Menninger puts it:

> We condemn crime; we punish offenders for it; but we need it. The crime and punishment ritual is part of our lives. We need crime to wonder at, to enjoy vicariously, to discuss and speculate about, and to publicly deplore. We need criminals to identify ourselves with, to secretly envy, and to stoutly punish. Criminals represent our alter-egos —our bad selves—rejected and projected. They do for us the forbidden, the illegal things we wish to do, and like scapegoats of old, they bear the burdens of our displaced guilt and punishment. [*The Crime of Punishment,* pp. 153, 154]

Henry Wiehofen extends the point:

> No one is more ferocious in demanding that the murderer or rapist "pay" for his crime than the man who has felt strong impulses in the same direction.... It is never he who is without sin who casts the first stone.... A criminal trial, like a prizefight, is a public performance in which the spectators work off in a socially acceptable way aggressive impulses of much the same kind that the man on trial worked off in a socially unacceptable way. [*The Urge to Punish*]

To which Jim Castelli adds:

> Our need for criminals extends to our classifying a man as a "criminal" and abandoning him simply because he is accused; that is the largest reason why 52 percent of all inmates [in jails] in America have not yet been to trial and are technically, constitutionally innocent. ["The Year of the Prisons"]

When the viewpoint just cited is placed beside another perception of the matter—the demands of retributive jutice to which we earlier alluded—it is easier to understand why corrections is more prone to human error than any other aspect of the criminal justice process. A saving feature is that fewer clients are involved in this part of the process, as compared, for instance, with police "contacts." We have spoken of discretionary judgments by police officers on the street, pointing to these judgments as critical to the relationship of police and community. Now we point to the judgments, the human transactions, that are so much the substance of corrections. Who is competent to judge, to determine the time for release, and to stipulate the conditions that will help inmates to prepare for this time? What most harms human welfare: to neglect the prisoner and leave him to the tide; or, to try to help him by methods and programs so impoverished in dollars, creativity, evaluation, and other resources that no one really believes in their efficacy?

The Aim of Correctional Processes

Looking back over what we have said, several points deserve repetition, though perhaps in slightly different terms. Basically, there are two discernible views of correctional processes. One is to view a prison as a place of confinement and control; a security institution for the protection of society. Some consider this a harsh and inhumane attitude; but, remember, prisons were originally intended to be relatively more humane than other measures for dealing with criminals, e.g., banishment, torture, etc.

The second is to view a prison as a place for reform. Reform has always been more of an *external* than an *internal* process in corrections. Its chances depend upon what happens outside, rather than inside, the prison; in short, reform in correctional process is largely a *community* determination. Probation, for example, was originally a volunteer movement, pioneered by John Augustus. Halfway houses are emergent community resources, often initially operated by religious institutions. The challenge is to find the most favorable blend of custody and treatment in individuals. Today's *corrections specialist,* as found in pioneering programs in Michigan, finds his distinctive para-professional identity in this blend, a middleground between hawk and dove.

One is reminded of Daniel Glaser's reference to the positive impact—that is, the influence of each upon inmate attitudes and behavior—of two types of institutional personnel: the traditional corrections officer and the work supervisor or foreman (*The Effectiveness of a Prison and Parole System*). The inmate has been in frequent contact with both of these persons; the reasons for their special influence are speculative. In any case, the relationship here has been an easy one, though within certain limits, taken against what Gresham Sykes in *The Society of Captives* calls "the culture of the yard." The relationship has in the past been subjected to rather strict administrative controls, lest it be interpreted as fraternizing. Recently, however, this hard line has been modified, after recognizing that a practice that may be undesirable ten percent of the time may merit encouragement ninety percent of the time. The emerging corrections specialist epitomizes this changing philosophy by injecting a humanizing element in institutional treatment.

The importance of such an element is appreciated when we reflect on how and why the prison becomes so repressive, to the point of seemingly working against itself. With administrative caution and societal security always the paramount themes, rules are made progressively, first prohibiting this and then that, until the very things that could be effective correctional tools are prohibited without explanation. At present there is a countermovement to this, the *therapeutic community* developed by Maxwell Jones et al. that has become a household term in corrections today. The modern corrections specialist is, in this sense something of a therapist, working out in basic relationships with inmates. But more than conventional therapy is applied. The total institutional situation is used as a kind of garden plot, in which the individual's growth may be carefully observed, evaluated, and guided.

More needs to be said about volunteers and their role in correctional processes. There are several types of volunteers. One plays a specific, nonpolicy role, such as coach, referee, entertainer, or friendly visitor. Another skates on the edge of policy through questions raised in discussion groups, counselling groups and the like, which—in the partnership between the professional corrections worker and the volunteer—may emerge as questions or criticisms. Then there is the member of the community at large who serves either in an advisory or in a policy-setting capacity as a member of a board or commission; for example, trade advisory councils to help resolve employment problems for released offenders. In its best aspects, this exemplifies corrections and community relations.

Community relations committees have recently begun to appear in correctional settings. Prison administrators usually spell out very carefully the limits of their policy-making. Moreover, prison administrators tend to be wary of including inmates in institutional self-government; for instance, in prison councils aimed at sharing in making decisions or setting policy. Administrators are cautious and conservative because of a combination of forces inside and outside of penal institutions—forces that often appear to be allied, and threateningly radical. For instance, in the case of the new-breed political prisoners, it is assumed that they are somehow tied to Maoist terrorists on the outside. Forthwith, the correctional administrator opts "to keep the lid on" as best he can, in a situation that is always potentially explosive. The less settled the larger society, the more likely that its "garbage can"—the prison—will be edgy. While the disposition to administrative wariness is not something on which corrections has a monopoly, there are certain features of it in corrections which stand out in times of general social turbulence. Norval Morris, director of the Center for Studies in Criminal Justice at the University of Chicago, describes its distinctive nature in corrections currently:

> What happens is that the inmate invests ordinary criminal activity with the idea that he is part of political change. That way you end up with the absurdity that killing a policeman or robbing a store is somehow a political act. The common criminals have never been on the cutting edge of any revolutionary movement. Nor are they now. They are being used, and misused, by some elements of the New Left. But

it is important to understand how blacks come to see all of this. They see that prisons are disproportionately black and run by whites. They come to view the American prison system as meaning simply blacks locked up by whites. This is the kind of thing that feeds this rhetoric of revolution, and ultimately the violence. What we have now in our prisons is the fusing of the ideology of the political prisoner with the technology of the common criminal. It is an explosive mixture. ["Reform: It Must Come."][24]

In community relations terms, there is a kind of paradox in all this. Correctional endeavors desperately need community endeavor. But unsettled conditions and catastrophic happenings in prisons frighten the community away. There is, no doubt, such a thing in police and correctional work as the situation too awesome, too technically demanding, too harrowing to be left to anyone other than seasoned professionals. On the morning after the Attica uprising, the volunteers for work inside the prison included those who sought to exploit the situation to their particular advantage. And there were those who came to investigate, to study, or to minister to human needs. Those who did not come included some who were not so much frightened away as they were inclined to be "turned off" by such a tragedy and to interpret it as substantiating their conviction that a prison is a human waste-pile best kept out of sight. In any case, the effect—at least temporarily—is to curtail much of the community endeavor that the situation so urgently requires. The hope is always that such a public reaction will be short-lived.

Something like this also happens in the aftermath of urban riots. One of the difficulties with violence as an instrument for social change is that violence lacks control over what it may precipitate. It often begets reaction rather than action, risks brutalization, and degrades civility. As Anthony Lewis wrote in *The New York Times* (September 18, 1971):

> ... philosophers of liberal democracy argue that the only legitimate use of violence in an open society is to call attention to blocked political channels, to areas of official or public insensitivity. Once the fault has been dramatized, they would say, the political process must be left to correct it. That may be slow, but the attempt to force faster change by continuing violence or guerrilla tactics is likely to bring results worse than the disease.

A further point reverts to what we said earlier about the increased emphasis upon due process—the rules of fair play—in correctional procedures. As we observed, some correctional workers suspect that the stress on due process is an invasion by the legal profession of the domain of the corrections professional—something like lawyers pretending to be psychiatrists. It *is,* surely, the proper job of the lawyer to identify the points at which due process is abrogated or denied. The difficulty arises, however, when lawyers tamper with questions of sentencing, administrative and program decisions, and release, where it is important that they know considerably more than the average lawyer can know. Thus, a role is emerging for persons trained in both law and corrections to act as a buttress against interprofessional conflict.

This need for a buttressing profession suggests something about community relations that should be underlined. Frequently, the impression is created that good community relations is merely a matter of good will and cooperative effort. While good will and good intention are certainly valuable assets, responsible community relations also require *knowledge* and *understanding* of situations and problems. In short, interprofessional approaches imply mutual respect for what has to be *learned* in a given professional field. Law, for example, has traditionally been thought of in our society as fundamentally committed to fair play. Yet it is conceivable that the parole process can be made so legally complex and technical as to blur the distinction between one who has not yet been convicted of a crime and one who, having been convicted, is now a candidate for parole.

Parole violation raises another question. Parole is a privilege that can be granted or withheld. But once the prisoner has been granted parole, he may be said to have a vested right of which he should not be deprived arbitrarily and without due process. No one, for example, has an *absolute* right to a driver's license or to the practice of law, but *once these privileges have been granted* they cannot be denied summarily. Thus runs the emerging new theme in the parole field.

The central consideration is that of the rights of the parolee. Some of those who resist due process do so for fear that a parole hearing will become a repetition of criminal trial. There is a distinction—not clearly drawn currently—between what due process of law means in court activity at the point of criminal trial proceedings; what it means in parole board activity at the point of consideration for release from a penal institution; and what it means in a parole board hearing in the case of a returned parole violator. Such a distinction is important in countering simplistic for-or-against positions that block communication on questions that cry for vital differentiation.

The Impact of Social Revolution on Corrections

Earlier parts of this text have been devoted to various aspects of the social revolution of the 1960s pertaining to police and community relations. We have looked at the great changes in social ethics and modes of conduct that have shaken the state of affairs in sex, drugs, the gay culture, feminism, etc. in a variety of startling ways, and brought on new styles of dress, conversation, and demeanor. Much of the "swinging" behavior clashes with existing laws, and police as well as corrections personnel find themselves turning to criminal law as a means of forestalling change that is adjudged too drastic to allow by standards that they are sworn to defend.

In the forefront of the movement for change in social ethics are those whom we tabbed earlier as pro-social. The pro-social groups are challenging society to live up to its pronouncements, to bring its performance more in harmony with its proclaimed creed. The anti-social groups would overthrow existing values by any available means, even by violence, to correct the ills of society. Prisoners from both the pro-social and the anti-social groups, as well as other groups, many of them black, see themselves as victims of an unjust social and political structure and identify themselves as political prisoners.

That these crosscurrents inevitably accelerate to a point of collision is illustrated by the Soledad Seven in California and the Attica revolt in New York. A double-barrelled kind of action occurs: a takeover by rioting, seizing cellblocks, taking hostages, etc. from within a penal institution—which is not a new element in corrections—and a reinforcement by dissident elements outside the institution—which is the new development in corrections. The general social climate of war, airline hijackings, the kidnap-murder of a Canadian government leader, the seizure of hostages, bombings, bizarre Mansonian orgies, etc., is such that it would be surprising if the most violent of men—those in prison—did not react explosively. In this sense, Attica floodlighted the kind of violence that is increasing on the national and international scenes. What appeared to be reasonable concessions to the inmates were negated by two, thorny, non-negotiable items: the question of immunity for crimes committed, and the question of sanctuary and transportation to another country.

The community relations implications of the Attica phenomenon were both stark and subtle. To illustrate, Ramsey Clark wrote in *The New York Times* (September 30, 1971):

> Attica reminds us how quickly America resorts to violence and how little we revere life. We created the "Big House," knew of the inhumanity there and waited for the recurrence of death and destruction that was bound to come. When the crisis arose we accepted, perhaps wanted, official violence to smash the prisoners we hated and feared. . . . Attica shows again America's reliance on violence as a problem solver.

Writing in the same newspaper (October 7, 1971), California Governor Ronald Reagan expressed another view:

> Rhetoric to the contrary, a criminal who holds a knife to the throat of a captive is not an ambassador with diplomatic immunity. Unless we recognize this, if we accept the falsehood that violence, terror and contempt for the moral values of our society are acceptable methods of seeking the redress of grievances, then we will all become prisoners.

The Attica revolt and the issues raised are discussed by a panel of specialists in Study 5, Part IV, in *The Police and the Community: Studies* (Radelet and Reed).

Police and Corrections

Basically, the relationship between the police and corrections exhibits another role conflict. In the classic delineation of police responsibilities (protection of life and property, apprehension of criminals, preservation of peace, prevention of crime), the specific criminally related activities are investigation and apprehension. As we have noted, the police are confronted with a phenomenon in statistical attrition where crime is concerned.[25]

1. Only a certain percentage of crimes committed are detected.
2. Only a certain percentage of crimes detected lead to arrests.
3. Only a certain percentage of those arrested are prosecuted and go to court trial.
4. Only a certain percentage of those tried are convicted and sentenced.
5. Many of those convicted and sentenced plead guilty to a lesser charge.

By the time corrections enters the picture, either through imprisonment or probation, some policemen are already predisposed to feel that justice has not been adequately vindicated. Their view of corrections may be, "We catch 'em; you let 'em go!" To policemen who think in such terms, the increased use of probation, the indeterminant sentence, and the presumption of parole at some point are evidences of leniency. Some other policemen are not opposed to the principle of parole but think it is used too frequently, too lightly, and for the wrong people. In pre-sentence reports, it is not uncommon to find police recommendations strongly favoring incarceration in preference to probation, with longer minimum sentences suggested—an attitude revealed in the IACP national survey of the police and their opinions.

In criminal investigation work, the police logically tend to concentrate their efforts where the practical odds seem to point—the prior offenders. The data on such individuals is known—fingerprints, modus operandi, haunts and hangouts, and background. Add to this the considerations that those who have served time are seen as relatively poor social risks; prisons do leave disfiguring or crippling wounds.

The police view of probation and parole officers is ambivalent. Sometimes they are seen as allies, for instance, as sources of investigative evidence or information. At other times they are seen as fostering aims conflicting with police aims, for instance, premature release, "soft" treatment, and such. Generally, the police are more militarily organized and oriented than is corrections. In corrections, lateral movement of personnel is much more accepted than it is in police work. The police are "out-professionalized" by corrections, in that less educational preparation is required of the police. The policeman as pragmatist, often cynical, is apt to regard corrections people as naïve, as believers in rehabilitative fantasies that too often fail to work in the real world. As these police officers see it, to the extent that the corrections system fails, the police must handle the resultant problems and dealing with "hardened criminals" is difficult and dangerous.

These generalizations about the police and corrections must be qualified to allow for many shades of difference in individual opinions on both sides. Some probation officers still work at their job with surveillance as a primary orientation, although this is currently disappearing; similarly, there are police officers whose work, for example, with juveniles, would meet the highest standards of probation. Reciprocal stereotyping here does not make for any more positive relationships than in any other brand of we-and-they differentiation.

Another problem in the police-corrections relationship bears on the use sometimes made of individual parolees by the police. To assist the police in investigations, the parolee may be cajoled or frightened into the role of an informer or an undercover agent. Correctional workers generally take a dim view of this practice, for several reasons, one being that it tends to lead the parolee to believe that he should enjoy some special privileges not normally granted. Trust versus gullibility is an issue with a very fine line of distinction in correctional work. If cynicism gets to a point of blocking trust, treatment cannot work. But a realistic middle ground is difficult to find. Police are apt to see correctional people as a bit gullible for tending to rely too much on trust and, at the same time, the correctional worker may pin too much hope on the efficacy of the correctional process. Add to this the consideration that the police tend to see the public as the client and the criminal as the adversary; whereas the corrections worker tends to see the offender as the client, and those who would inhibit his release at the appropriate time as the adversary. Some corrections workers even see their role as a kind of police force within the institution—again a fading phenomenon, but not yet entirely eliminated.

Courts and Corrections

The criminal court and its ancillary functions powerfully affect corrections in many ways, some quite apparent, others less so.

The Prosecutor

The prosecutor must act with due consideration both for the protection of society and for the rights of the defendant as he approves arrest warrants; determines the category of crime with which the wrong-doer is charged; decides what cases to prosecute or drop (*nolle prose-qui,* more familiarly referred to as *nolle pros*); and negotiates guilty pleas. Although made with the approval of the judge, his decision may be the crucial one in determining whether the defendant is to receive probation or, if sentenced to confinement, is to go to a local institution or a state prison.

Setting bail is a matter on which the prosecutor may wish to present arguments to the court. Pre-trial confinement is a problem receiving particular attention. It burdens most heavily the young and the poor, for they are predominantly the ones who must idle away time awaiting trial in overcrowded cells, endangered by other inmates, while the prosperous, the respectable, and the organized crime offenders are enjoying the freedom provided by bail. In the attention currently focused on ways of releasing offenders awaiting trial, the long-known but little-used practice of release on recognizance has come into prominence. The Vera Institute made a study showing that selected offenders released on recognizance had a better record of appearing for trial than run-of-mill offenders admitted to bail.

The case of the parole violator has a special place in the prosecutor's decision on cases to be tried or dropped. A parolee who violates his parole by committing a new crime could serve the new and the old sentence at the same time. In fact, if the remainder of the first sentence exceeded the maximum of the new sentence, the new sentence would expire while the violator served the original. Under such circumstances, prosecution for the new sentence has little practical value. However, to prevent confusion or claims by the parolee that he was acquitted, the reason for not prosecuting the crime should be recorded. If this were done, the task of the releasing authority would be simplified and clarified; but the decision is the prosecutor's.

The prosecutor will often present a recommendation for sentence that sometimes reflects the views of the police as well. Probably the prosecutor does not often plead for leniency except where the offender has cooperated by turning state's evidence, by pleading guilty, or by assisting police through clearing cases.

Lastly, the prosecutor may make known to corrections his views on early parole. Occasionally he will intervene on behalf of an inmate who has assisted the prosecution; more often, if queried, he will leave the decision to the releasing authority. Frequently, too, he voices an objection to early parole.

Views concerning eligibility for parole vary widely among police, prosecutors, judges, corrections workers, and various segments of the public. Probation gains increasing acceptance, perhaps at the expense of parole, for the more promising cases are skimmed off, leaving a poorer residue. The differing views arise largely from the different roles played by the various professionals involved. Local courts, prosecutors, and police serve as a check upon the centralized parole process. The courts say that the standards of the community against the violator must be stoutly maintained, and those who threaten it must be kept out of circulation through substantial sentences. Negotiated pleas may result in heavier minimum sentences (presumably to counterbalance the shortened maximums), leaving less flexibility for parole. Some courts are reluctant to lessen the minimum by early paroles, perhaps distrusting parole "leniency", or prison population pressures. Authorities responsible for release, in turn, chafe against the inflexibility that curbs the release of inmates whose attitudes have changed and who lose ground when confined too long after adjustment begins to take place. Parole boards, from the state's vantage point, are confronted with the paradox of disparate sentences from different courts and communities.

Since the *Gideon* v. *Wainwright* decision (372 U.S. 335, 1963), the right to counsel of indigents accused of serious crime has become well-nigh universal. That right has been extended to parole violators charged with minor offenses, for whom a conviction would automatically revoke their parole. Further extension of the right to counsel appears certain, for misdemeanors as well as for felonies.*

On July 26, 1972, the Michigan Supreme Court held in *People* v. *Tanner* that a sentence of 14 years, 11 months to 15 years was an indeterminate sentence as provided by law. The Court did not adopt the American Bar Association's standard of a minimum of no more than one third the maximum. Instead, it specified that a minimum of more than two-thirds would *not* be an indeterminate sentence. The Court opined that with good time allowances, its rule reasonably approximated the ABA standards.

Ultimately, executive clemency is the means of overruling the decisions both of the courts and the authorities for release. Even here, such clemency is modified by statute and usually requires investigation and recommendation by the parole board. In all circumstances, chief executives move with caution, conscious of community sentiment, the inequity of the offender's position, and the inequity of continued guilt.

The Sheriff

The sheriff is an arm of the court as well as a law enforcement officer. In addition to his enforcement duties, he is custodian of those awaiting trial and those serving a jail sentence. We have noted the antiquity of many jails and the inadequacies of the jail system. The fact remains that the sheriff is the local penal administrator; and no system of corrections is complete without recognizing the part played by local correctional facilities. Prolonged confinement in overcrowded facilities

---

*Now extended to *any* offense the penalty for which includes confinement. (Angersinger v. Hamlin, U.S. Supreme Court, June 12, 1972).

with little or no program is an injustice, especially so since it falls with greater frequency upon the young, the indigent, and the minority group member.

The Judge

The trial judge not only presides—he decides. His assurance that guilty pleas are properly and fairly given; that charges are correctly drawn; that only proper evidence is received; that juries are correctly charged; and that verdicts are consistent with the weight of evidence is crucial to the administration of justice. To the community, the essential features are often blurred by what may seem excessive technicalities that defeat justice. The right of the public to know and the right of the defendant to be tried by court and jury rather than by the press are somewhat inconsistent, as we shall see in the next chapter. Witnesses and jurors alike may be frustrated by harassment and delay. All these people are part of the nontechnical community at large, whose confidence in justice is corroded by overtechnicality or eroded by delay.

The scales of justice are not evenly balanced. In the defendant's favor rests the formidable weight of reasonable doubt. To it are added the weights of protection against unlawful search and self-incrimination. Add to these fundamental legalities the problems of time-consuming jury selection, the technicalities of motions and pleas, and the formal rules of evidence. These are the fine meshes through which the defendant's guilt is screened. A prosecutor is not to be blamed if he argues against probation and for a stiff sentence. The police officer whose professional investigation convinces him of a guilt that cannot be proven beyond a reasonable doubt may feel an understandable frustration when, thwarted in telling what he knows, he sees the guilty set free. Nor is the community at large immune to such feelings of frustration.

Recent years have increased the tendency to protect the rights of the accused. This tendency, coupled with the fear of crime in the streets, has produced community reaction to what it considers soft treatment, "bleeding hearts," and "do-gooders." And tensions increase as disorder accompanies rapid social change.

Corrections System

When the verdict is in, or the guilty plea accepted, the work of corrections begins. The blindfold is removed from the eyes of justice and she sees the defendant for what he has been and what he may become as the probation officer presents the facts of the defendant's background in the pre-sentence investigation. The judge selects the means most likely to produce good results for the community as well as the offender. It is in the sentencing process that the trial court stands on the border of corrections. Here, in felony cases at least, the court usually has available a probation officer. The latter develops the pre-sentence investigation—the social and criminal history and a suggested disposition. A variety of sentencing patterns exist, and alternative dispositions are increasing; but basically, it is the judge who determines whether a defendant will go to prison and, if so, for how long. And the pre-sentence investigation is his principal tool for making his decision. The investigation, in addition to the information on the defendant's background, reflects community attitudes, including the views of the prosecutor and often of the police.

The traditional confidentiality of the pre-sentence investigation is now being challenged. Several jurisdictions are giving defense counsel access to that report in the sentencing process, in order to increase the chances for fairness. However, those who seek to preserve confidentiality fear that reprisals may result and sources of information dry up if the details of the report are made public. If the defense counsel has access to the report, the responsibility for protecting confidential portions of the report will be increased.

The probation officer is a direct corrections arm of the court. It is he who supervises the offender and initiates violation hearings. The adversary process should not intrude here. The defendant should be entitled to an advocate, a counsel for defense, who will point out any deficiencies in the report and argue for any favorable dispositions, e.g., probation instead of imprisonment. But in doing so, the defense counsel should remember that the question of guilt has already been decided.

The appellate court, the court of last resort in criminal justice, determines the rules by which the system operates. These rules are made in individual cases, but the merits of the person is not the point—the *principle* is. Thus, a persistent or even a dangerous offender may be the occasion for a sweeping reform in the criminal law. Miranda was a burglar, not a respected citizen, but his case became a legal bench mark for protection against self-incrimination.

An appellate court decision does not permit administrative problems as an excuse for denying improvements in the administration of criminal justice. The legal principle embodied in the case is the overriding consideration. The administrator must clean up the havoc that the hurricane of a decision may wreak. New resources may be required, legislation enacted, or even constitutional amendments sought. The appellate court is not indifferent to the problems created, but does not permit them to thwart justice.

The increasing interest of the court in the corrections process has already been described. The emphasis has been upon due process in parole violation procedures. There is presumably a delicate and intricate interplay among the various forces in criminal justice agencies. Instead of being defensive about the role of corrections, and instead of resisting interference with correctional procedures, the corrections professional would be well advised to be the one to inform the other criminal justice agencies, in particular the courts, of the deficiencies of his own field so that the courts, especially, can be cognizant of the better as well as the poorer correctional practices. Moreover, corrections should set its own house in order and not leave it to the courts to do so.

Unresolved Problems of Corrections

In a scatter-fire way, we have touched on a number of unresolved problems in corrections. The challenge is not to find problems in this field, but to find agreement on the solutions. A lengthy chapter, replete with talk about problems in a system, should come to a point of summary. In no particular priority, then, here are summarized the main unresolved problems.

1. The need for coordinating branches of the correctional system. Far greater coordination is needed throughout the correctional process: between state and local factions; between the police and courts and corrections: between the machinery for dealing with felonies and that for dealing with misdemeanors; and between all these and the community. The objective in this is *not* to create another super bureaucracy, but to move toward a true system—an integrated mechanism like a watch, with each part having a distinct function, interrelated with all others.

2. The need for equalizing rights in the jail-bail system. The person awaiting trial is subjected to the inequities of the jail and bail system, the so-called economic basis of justice; and the degradation—especially when one has not yet been found guilty of a crime—of confinement. The jail is aptly called the No. 1 corrections problem.

3. Reconciling the rights of offender and community. The increasing attention to *due process* in the field of corrections has pointed up our failure to reconcile the protection of society with the rights of the individual offender. Maintaining order and control among dangerous men and women in a prison, while at the same time recognizing and respecting their rights as persons is difficult, perhaps impossible. Sometimes the imposition of intricate legal and judicial machinery under these circumstances actually has the effect of sabotaging correctional treatment, as lawyers invade a territory in which they are professional strangers.[26]

4. Improving evaluation procedures and techniques. As in other fields, corrections suffers from *a deficiency of evaluation* of the results of its efforts. Much more attention has been devoted to person-keeping than to record-keeping. What works, for whom? Because we can prove so little about correctional methods, we have an over-supply of unfounded claims for one technique or another, of professional guesswork, and of tokenism. We are not sure what personnel and resources are needed to do a job so haphazardly defined. Consequently, there is a lack of candor in relations between corrections and the public. Failure is camouflaged as something for which neither corrections nor the community is to blame.

There are signs that the LEAA, the NCCD, the American Correctional Association, and the Presidential Crime Commissions, old and new, are pressing for much more sophisticated evaluation of correctional activities.

5. Balancing public security with offender rehabilitation. The problem is finding a suitable *balance between societal security and the fantasy of correctional treatment.* This is probably the most fundamental problem of corrections. To believe that much of a positive rehabilitative nature can take place within the confines of the fortresses called prisons is an illusion, no matter how enlightened the institution. But the problem is more complicated than could be solved by abandoning custodial institutions.

There are many ways of stating the interlocking requirements for correctional improvement. One way is to say that it has not been established that more humane treatment of criminal offenders will persuade them to turn away from crime. Gilbert Geis has pointed to a salient comparison:

> Our prison policy, then, is much like our Vietnam policy. We are too timid, too intelligent, too civilized, too aware of the possible dangers involved to carry through an all-out campaign so ferocious that it might conceivably, at least in the short run, bring about our triumph over defined enemies. Fighting, instead, a war incapable of achieving the goals we have set for it, we compound viciousness with futility.[27]

Geis goes on to observe that existing therapy programs in prisons prompt the inmate to invent "problems." This is so, Geis contends, because the solution of real problems takes longer than of counterfeited ones, and so prolongs confinement. Consequently, inmates quickly learn to "cooperate" with treatment techniques "while [scorning] the therapist for his naïveté if the therapist is taken in by the sham."

The Fortune Society's David Rothenberg puts the matter bluntly:

> Conceptually, prisons are all the same and do not work. A man cannot be punished and rehabilitated simultaneously.... Our prisons take men and women who have committed a crime and mold them into criminals.... Prison is the only business that can succeed by its own failures. It needs men returning to its fold so it can perpetuate itself. Whether the prison can change a man's life-style in a positive manner is not the prison's concern. It must maintain security and preserve

itself. . . . Our need for vengeance is sometimes greater than our need for solving problems. ["Prison is a Real Education," New York *Times,* December 3, 1971][28]

Rothenberg adds a key point: we should not be boxed into a single punishment concept for all men. This idea might stimulate improvement but not the answers to all problems. In the aftermath of the Attica tragedy, there has been discussion of establishing *maximum-maximum* security prisons for prisoners adjudged to be chronic troublemakers and incorrigibles. The proposal sparked mixed reactions from corrections officials, one view being that it might produce "political concentration camps." But New York State nonetheless seemed to be heading toward such a max-max, despite concerted opposition.

Consensus is nevertheless growing that prison sentences, except for persistent and dangerous offenders who must be locked up to protect society, are close to useless and at the same time very expensive. Yet, public opinion being as it is, more intelligent measures are hard to introduce unless they provide—and are seen to provide—some elements of justice, tangible and moral or psychological, for the victims of crime and for society itself. There must be *some* retribution for breaking the law, but not necessarily institutional confinement (Alfred Friendly, *The Washington Post,* September 18, 1971).

6. Inmate participation in prison governance. Some worthwhile results are showing up from greater responsible inmate participation in self-government. The problem is to diminish the fear of loss of control by custodians, which can paralyze the constructive progress. Inmates generally (with exceptions that must be provided for) will respond far more positively to such governing opportunities than is widely assumed.

7. Locking up prisoners at night. *Too many prisons lock up* (in their cells) *too many prisoners at night.* This pattern must be changed. There is no reason to perpetuate the pattern of the treatment staff going home at 5:00 P.M., when the custodial staff takes over. It is allegedly a matter of convenience and economy which should be examined carefully, for it creates unnecessary program constriction.

8. Curbing abnormal behavior. A prison is an abnormal social environment. Small wonder, therefore, that inmates find outlets in deviant and devious ways. The problems of *homosexuality, drug addiction, and alcoholism* inside prison walls beg for more imaginative approaches than have so far been tried.

9. Equalizing applications of the law. Corrections is often blamed unfairly for the problem of *inequity in sentencing.* In fact, the corrections problem here is that it must cope with such widely diversified judicial interpretations of what constitutes equitable application of the law. The indeterminate sentence is coming under increasingly heavy criticism in several states, particularly California, which pioneered legislation on it in 1917 and enlarged it into a total system in 1942. Such a sentence is designed to prevent courts from imposing harshly unequal penalties for similar crimes to avoid fixed penalties under an inflexible penal code, and to insure that release reflects the readiness of the offender to re-enter society. Critics of the indeterminate sentence charge that a prisoner languishes behind bars for years beyond the date when he normally could expect parole, for such things as minor infractions of prison rules, attitudes considered negative by correctional authorities, or a lack of interest on the part of the inmate in so-called rehabilitation programs. Such prisoners are said to be ripe for bitterness, frustration, violence, and rebellion.

10. **Developing ancillary services.** More effective *ancillary services* such as mental health and other social services for the convicted offender are needed. The community is where corrections takes place, not the prison. A prison is not a hospital; it is more like the contagious disease ward of a hospital, where the contagion is the main reason for confinement.

11. **Theories of crime causation.** Too much taken for granted is the theory of social-cultural causes for crime, long championed by Frank Tannenbaum, Clifford Shaw, and other pioneers in the scholarly study of crime causation. To keep this theory prominently in mind is especially important in the circumstances of contemporary value conflicts in such matters as drugs. But no single theory is sufficient in undertaking to explain contemporary crime, and the theory of individual "cussedness" should not be entirely scorned.

12. **Defining and dealing with criminal responsibility.** Unresolved also are the problems of dealing effectively with the *mentally retarded* offender and the *sociopath*. Both are in a kind of limbo between mental health and corrections, with the question of criminal responsibility for behavior too hazily defined by law. New programs are badly needed, combining the wisdom of mental health, education, and corrections.

13. **Expanding flexibility in sentencing.** Experience in several states points to the need for greater flexibility in sentencing convicted offenders.

14. **Financing correctional programs.** Finally, the unresolved problem with which to begin and to end any such listing is that of competition for the tax dollar. So long as corrections remains at the bottom of the budgeting totem pole, talk of reform and more enlightened correctional processes remains simply talk.

Current Directions in Corrections

The current churning of our culture affects corrections in several ways. First, the civil rights movement has forced increased emphasis upon due process in criminal justice, and most recently in corrections.

This emphasis may further relax unreasonable restrictions on the personal freedoms of inmates: may allow, for examples, uncensored mail (already a practice in Michigan and elsewhere); receipt of publications heretofore deemed unsuitable by cautious officials; and much greater freedom in styles of hair, beard, and clothing.

Second, the rapid rise to power of ethnic minorities in the wake of civil rights advances is bolstering strenuous efforts to recruit minority group members for corrections work. Similarly, black inmates are receiving courses in black history and culture. Other ethnic groups are also becoming conscious of their identity and special needs. Unfortunately, new racial consciousness has created new racial tensions.

Third, contemporary patterns of individual expression, illustrated by idiosyncratic styles of dress, behavior, and doing one's own thing, changing standards of censorship, and new sexual mores are rearranging traditional views of propriety. Who can say how much this has affected current proposals to eliminate victimless crime or sexual activity between consenting adults from criminal codes? Some corrections workers, oriented toward traditional values, see the increase in crime as growing from a prevailing attitude of "permissiveness" and the decline of moral values. Casual freedom, idleness, and wanderlust are seen as promoters of decadence. Such concerns can provoke overreaction and the pursuit of secondary or even irrelevant causes of crime. The result can be meaningless cures for nonexistent diseases and further separation of cultures.

The American Friends Service Committee, in *The Struggle for Justice,* proposes several changes,[29] including the following:

- Abolishing indeterminate sentences
- Reducing the number of crimes (eliminate "victimless crimes")
- Applying criminal law uniformly
- Making treatment programs voluntary
- Recognizing prisoners' human rights and civil liberties
- Enlisting the community in the reintegration of prisoners

Others, such as the National Council on Crime and Delinquency, would also abolish such victimless crimes as drunkenness, prostitution, drug addiction, gambling, and homosexuality, and concentrate resources on crimes against other persons and their property. Still others criticize the heaping of penalty on penalty until the result can be measured in sentences hundreds of years long.

Tragedy spotlights needs. Reforms follow. Some are placebos, others untested theories. Many prescriptions are good but insufficient, others are unrealistic, some even harmful. "Yesterday's wisdom is today's common sense and tomorrow's folly," said an East Lansing clergyman in a recent sermon. But alas the memory of the public is short and its fancies are fickle. The professional bureaucrat is forced to hitch the team of theory and practice and drive it down the road of the future. Let us see where some of the recommended routes might lead.

Eliminating the Indeterminate Sentence

Often bitterly criticized by inmates, the indeterminate sentence is seen by them as a device for authorities to lengthen prison terms at their own discretion without possibility for challenge. The inmates' demand is for fixed sentences.

Let's take a look at the pros and cons. The opponents of the indeterminate sentence argue that uncertainty of the length of the sentence constitutes cruel and inhuman punishment. Behaving himself ever so correctly or engaging in programs ever so diligently, the inmate cannot be sure what behavior will result in his release. Opponents argue further that decisions are arbitrary, biased, and unfounded.

Arguments for the Indeterminate Sentence

It is a commonly held thesis that an inmate's good conduct in prison does not mean good behavior in the community. The conception of paying a debt to society has two fallacies: first, under this theory, punishment becomes a "pound of flesh"; second, the penalty, exacted in terms of time incarcerated, becomes the factor that permits the inmate to ignore the need for change. The penalty is seen as part of a calculated risk. Readiness for release becomes irrelevant. And how is the penalty fixed? Clearly, by the criminal code. Yet the code cannot predict human behavior, or evaluate change, or differentiate among persons who commit similar crimes. In short, the fixed sentence makes individualized treatment impossible. The result of eliminating the indeterminate sentence would be a procrustean bed stretching the sentence of the less sophisticated offender and shortening the term of the experienced sophisticated one.

What would be the effect of the determinate sentence upon plea bargaining? Again, one can postulate that in many cases the degree of the crime admitted to the court would be the reverse of the criminal experience of the offender. As often happens, the question is better than the answer and raises issues that need more careful responses than so far proposed.[30]

Making Treatment Available But Voluntary

Several criticisms are leveled at treatment in correctional institutions: first, that treatment is inadequate; second, that results are not well observed or reported; third, that effects upon post-release behavior are unpredictable; finally, that an individual is forced to "knuckle under" by submitting to an invasion of his privacy as a person. He should, according to this theory, be able to choose between seeking such treatment or having his parole status determined without it.

Much more is needed by way of treatment—both in quantity and in quality—for which more money is essential. More careful evaluation of such treatment is indispensable. The voluntary nature of such treatment cannot be answered by a simple yes or no. Some kinds of treatment are more necessary than others. The child molester, the sadistic rapist, and the narcotic addict require treatment. If the offender will not accept it or cannot benefit from it (or cannot demonstrate change by other means), the alternative may be continued confinement. The chronic alcoholic, fraudulent check writer who says, "I have made up my mind not to drink and therefore need no therapy," may choose to refuse, but an early parole may be denied.

The willing cooperation of a man in treatment is surely preferable to pressured acquiescence. Mandatory treatment is not only undesirable, it is often ineffective. Just as the appendicitis patient may refuse an operation although the consequences seem certain death, so may the prison inmate refuse treatment in some program that seems essential, although he may lose his chances for parole.

Recognizing the Human Rights and Civil Liberties of Prisoners

Courts are now turning attention to the penal process. Once convicted, with appellate procedures exhausted, the probationer, prisoner, or parolee have been largely without redress within the legal limits of sentence, provided Constitutional rights were not denied. Now the corrections system is being called into account at many points. The confidentiality of the pre-sentence investigation is under challenge. How can a convicted person defend himself against unknown charges or unfavorable opinions obtained from undisclosed persons? Must a prisoner accept all administrative decisions about his care, custody, and treatment with no possibility of examination by an independent body? Is the decision of the releasing authority immune to inquiry? Can a parole once granted be revoked without a hearing? Are attorneys or witnesses, or both, to be permitted at parole interviews? Is a corrections agency obliged to provide the treatment that has been diagnosed as necessary? These and other questions are emerging—some, especially in the parole revocation process, have already been adjudicated in important aspects. Visibility and accountability, to use Fred Cohen's phrase, are new words in the lexicon of corrections.[31]

These changes are warmly welcomed by not a few corrections workers and greeted with caution and skepticism by others. Two observations seem relevant. First, skeptics fear that a judicial review of administrative decisions would paralyze the system and prematurely free dangerous criminals. This fear seems excessive. The alternative is to leave decisions unexamined and unchecked. Procedures can be developed that will safeguard prisoners' rights without defeating good administration. The court is simply examining the reasonableness and legality of administrative decisions.

Second, lawyers need to develop greater expertise in corrections matters. A parole violation hearing is not the place to re-try questions of guilt or innocence earlier determined by a court. Moreover, lawyers need to develop canons of ethics that apply to the confidentiality of information, such as those contained in a pre-sentence investigation. By so doing, the lawyer can defend his client against unjust or unfounded speculations without revealing their sources. Moreover, the offender whose status is the subject of an appearance or inquiry is entitled to know the factors considered in arriving at a decision. How else can he effectively plead his case or know how to correct his deficiencies? Admittedly, skill and will are required to achieve just decisions, which also serve the goals of treatment without undue encumbrance or delay.

Enlarging the Role of the Community for Returning Prisoners to Normal Life

Community rehabilitation assistance—already begun in important areas (community corrections centers, to name but one)—is urgently needed.[32] The blurring of the distinction between the prison and the community is manifested in work-release programs, furloughs, and overnight visits by inmates' spouses. These important steps are present now in token form. They should be expanded to meet the needs of inmates in all jurisdictions.

But the role of the community should be seen in broader terms. Crime is a violation of community. The idea of *community* presupposes commonly held goals, an openness, and an interrelatedness. Interrelatedness assumes equal respect for the rights of others. Criminal law is based upon consensus. The essence of criminal law is the invocation of sanctions. When the fabric of society is ripped by dissension, or when a substantial minority disagrees with a criminal sanction, self-enforcement breaks down and law is either unenforceable or ignored.

Basically, then, criminal law *is* community relations. Criminal justice is the process by which those who violate society's minimum standards are identified, penalized, and redirected. It is the *community* that must open its ranks to the violator if he is to be restored to full membership.

Notes to Chapter Seventeen

1. William Raspberry of the Washington *Post* refers (October 29, 1971) to "the counterproductive ambivalence involved in simultaneous punishment and education." But he goes on to reflect that separation of the two functions introduces special problems as well. See, for example, Study 5 (Part 5), "Assessment of Attica: A Symposium," in Radelet and Reed, *Studies.*

2. For example, Shaw, McKay, et al., *Delinquency Areas:* Sutherland and Cressey, *Principles of Criminology:* Cloward and Ohlin, *Delinquency and Opportunity.*

3. Some students of correctional process claim that the very concept of rehabilitation (treatment) is unwarranted. They reject the idea that persons who commit crime are "sick" and therefore in need of "treatment" that will "cure" them. Some say that rehabilitation is more cruel than punishment and call for an unapologetic system of punishment for crimes committed. In this way, an inmate would know exactly what is required of him.

4. *NCCD News,* May–June, 1970; a publication of the National Council on Crime and Delinquency. See also Karl Menninger, *The Crime of Punishment.*

5. See, for example, Milton Burdman, "The Conflict Between Freedom and Order." Also Paul A. Thomas, "New Pressures in Corrections."

6. Rules for so-called speedy trial have surfaced in several states, requiring that all state courts dismiss criminal charges against any defendant who through no fault of his own had not been brought to trial within 6 months of his arrest. See Robert L. Simmons, "An Answer to Trial Delay," for a suggested method of using video tape for taking testimony from witnesses in court.

7. See also Fred Cohen, *The Legal Challenge to Corrections,* p. 37. Also Marvin E. Wolfgang, "Making the Criminal Justice System Accountable," and National Council on Crime and Delinquency, "A Model Act for the Protection of Rights of Prisoners."

8. *NCCD News,* March–April, 1971. In the 18th century, Cesare Beccaria made a fatal error in overlooking or ignoring the victims of crime by assuming that only an injury to states results from any given criminal act. This oversight was written into Anglo-American jurisprudence. Now concern is beginning to appear for the victim.

9. Refer to our discussion of this in Chap. 16. The position taken by the National Council on Crime and Delinquency on preventive detention appears in *Crime and Delinquency,* January 1971, pp. 1–8. During the first 10 months of its operation (beginning February 1971), the District of Columbia preventive detention procedure was sought in only 20 of some 2000 possible cases, as shown in a study done jointly by the Vera Institute of New York and the Institute of Criminal Law at the Georgetown University Law Center (*The New York Times,* March 14, 1972).

It would appear, therefore, that preventive detention in this situation has not been a decisive factor in controlling crime. However, its proponents claim that the main problem is that the procedure had not as yet been reviewed by the Supreme Court; thus, that prosecutors, defense attorneys, and judges are "afraid" of it.

10. See Chap. 16. The position of the National Council on Crime and Delinquency on victimless crimes is stated in *Crime and Delinquency,* April 1971, pp. 129, 130.

11. See Law Enforcement Assistance Administration, U.S. Dept. of Justice, *National Jail Census, 1970;* National Criminal Justice Information and Statistics Service, Series SC-No. 1, February 1971, U.S. Government Printing Office, Washington D.C. Popular periodicals have made much of the jail and prison reform issue; for example, Ernest Havemann, "The Paradox of the Prisons," *Life,* September 14, 1970, p. 85 ff.; "Prisons in Turmoil," *Newsweek,* September 14, 1970, p. 36 ff.; "U.S. Prisons: Schools for Crime," *Time,* January 18, 1971, p. 45 ff.; and Ronald L. Goldfarb, "Why Don't We Tear Down Our Prisons?" *Look,* July 27, 1971, p. 45 ff. (based on a book about the American corrections system, by the same author, published by Simon & Schuster, Inc.) The Young Lawyers' Section of the American Bar Association has made overhaul of the American penal system its top priority. One of its projects, funded by LEAA, is called "Volunteers in Parole" and enables young lawyers to become part-time parole workers under the supervision of seasoned parole professionals. In October 1970, *The New York Times* reported that disturbances in New York City's prisons during that month constituted the most serious crisis Mayor Lindsay had faced during his tenure in office. But the same newspaper had reported essentially the same problems on December 27, 1954.

12. *NCCD News,* January–February, 1970. As this is written, LEAA seems to be in turbulent political waters, with evidence of serious problems in numerous states. Some of these problems were predictable; anyway, many LEAA-fostered ideas are essentially sound. For political balance: President Nixon's National Advisory Commission on Criminal Justice Standards and Goals shows promise of adding impetus to the cause of change in the criminal justice system, in the pattern of President Johnson's Crime Commission.

13. See *Crime and Delinquency,* January 1971. This entire issue is devoted to articles about research in the corrections field.

14. See *Citizen Action to Control Crime and Delinquency,* a publication of the National Council on Crime and Delinquency, 1968.

15. Many halfway houses are anathema to neighbors, who allege that they depreciate property values and tend to increase crime in the neighborhood. A community should be carefully prepared for such a facility.

16. Two apparently successful programs fitting this description are outlined in Study 2 (Part 4), "Misdemeanant Probation," in Radelet and Reed, *Studies.* See also the report of the President's Task Force on Prisoner

Rehabilitation, *The Criminal Offender—What Should Be Done?*, especially Part 4, which pertains to noninstitutional community corrections. Some innovative and promising programs in youth corrections at the Minnesota School for Boys at Red Wing and at the Robert F. Kennedy Youth Center in Morgantown, W. Va., are described in *Juvenile Justice and Corrections*, Part 4, Third Report by the Select Committee on Crime of the U.S. House of Representatives.

17. See *The Annals*, January 1969. The theme of this issue is "The Future of Corrections."

18. Many examples of this could be cited. An interesting one is described by Elmer H. Johnson in "Report on an Innovation—State Work-Release Programs."

19. In March 1970, corrections officers in New York City staged a work slow-down to compel the city to hire an additional 800 officers to relieve what they contended was an intolerable workload. Under a state law that bars strikes and slowdowns by government employees, a court order prohibiting the slowdown was issued. A statement from the mayor's office criticized the tactics of the corrections officers, pointing out that the city intended to hire 150 additional officers the following year and was in the process of transferring 2500 sentenced prisoners from city jails to state penal institutions. Reported in *NCCD News*, May–June, 1970.

20. As with all short-term Commissions of this nature, the fulfillment of its recommendations was left to "fate," often a word meaning dust on the shelf. This Commission was headed by James V. Bennett, former director of the U.S. Bureau of Prisons; NCCD director Milton G. Rector was chairman of the board. Its final report was issued in November 1969; its numerous impressive publications may be secured from the American Correctional Association, Woodbridge Station, P.O. Box 10176, Washington, D.C., 20018.

21. This point is one that was particularly dramatized in the Attica, New York, prison tragedy of September 1971. Anthony Lewis wrote in *The New York Times* (September 18, 1971) that "it is too easy to say that violent tactics can never be justified. When the channels of access to political influence are open to everyone in society, then violent means cannot be justified. But is there such a perfect society anywhere?"

    George Jackson had put it this way: "Every revolutionary theoretician and psychiatrist accepts as elementary the tendency of violence to turn inward when the oppressed can find no externalization, the 'collective autodestruction' phenomenon."

22. Available from the American Correctional Association, Woodbridge Station, P.O. Box 10176, Washington, D.C. 20018.

23. See *Soledad Brother: The Prison Letters of George Jackson*.

24. The syndicated columnist, Ralph de Toledano, wrote in October 1971 that he had a document in his possession proving that the Attica riot was "the

opening gun of a national campaign built around the demand that by July 4, 1976, all of the prisoners in all U.S. prisons must be released and the prisons abolished." (Lansing, Michigan, *State Journal,* October 12, 1971.)

25. See Jerome H. Skolnick, *Justice Without Trial,* chap. 8. See also the chart of the criminal justice system on pp. 8, 9 of the President's Crime Commission report *The Challenge of Crime in a Free Society.*

26. Sol Rubin argues that statutes are needed in the correctional field that recognize substantive rights of persons who have been convicted and subjected to correctional treatment and that maintain those rights by effective procedures placing specific responsibilities on corrections administration and subjecting the discharge of those responsibilities to court review. See "Needed—New Legislation in Correction," *Crime and Delinquency,* 17, no. 4 (October 1971): 392–405.

27. From a review of two books in *Saturday Review,* December 11, 1971. (The books: Robert J. Minton, Jr., ed., *Inside: Prison American Style;* and Levy and Miller, *Going to Jail: The Political Prisoner.*) John Galliher argues that part of the difficulty is that "we have been attempting in a feeble manner to implement more change among inmates than is reasonable or fair." See his "Training in Social Manipulation as a Rehabilitative Technique."

28. Arthur Waskow argues (*Saturday Review,* January 8, 1972, pp. 20–21) that we should forget about reform—that it is time to talk about abolishing jails and prisons in American society. Where do we put the prisoners? "Having no alternative at all," he contends, "would create less crime than the present criminal training centers do. The only full alternative is building the kind of society that does not need prisons."

29. A "Citizens Lobby for Penal Reform, Inc." was formed in Kansas City, Mo., in September 1971 by a group of concerned citizens. Another development of interest is Project STAR (Systems and Training Analysis of Requirements for Criminal Justice Participants), a four-state undertaking funded by LEAA and conducted by the American Justice Institute, of which Richard A. McGee is president. The project is designed to research and define the role requirements of different sectors of the total criminal justice system. Some 3500 members of all major sectors of the system are being asked to report their perceptions of members of each other sector. Educational and training requirements for the entire system will eventually be developed, with demonstration projects mounted to meet these requirements.

   Another AJI current project proposes a nonprison rehabilitation plan for young offenders in the age group 17–24. Its aim is to keep young offenders out of a prison system. McGee admits that the toughest problem with such a project is community acceptance.

30. A draft report has been prepared for the Special Committee on Prisons and Corrections of the State Bar of Michigan by Bruce Kahn, a postgraduate student at the University of Michigan Law School. This report con-

tains a brief but thoughtful critique of the indeterminate sentence structure and suggestions for modification that merit careful study. What Kahn proposes could retain the advantages of the indeterminate sentence concept while reducing certain disadvantages.

31. Cohen, *The Legal Challenge to Corrections;* see also NCCD's "A Model Act to Provide for Minimum Standards for the Protection of Rights of Prisoners."

32. See the monograph series on crime and delinquency topics of the National Institute of Mental Health; for example, *Community-Based Correctional Programs: Models and Practices.* In the same series is *Crime and Justice: American Style,* by Clarence Schrag, which is a comprehensive overview of literature and research bearing on the entire criminal justice system. Also see "Prison Story," a special issue on the punishment of crime, Boston *Globe,* Sunday, April 9, 1972.

The co-author of this chapter is Robert H. Scott. A native of Albany, New York, Mr. Scott graduated from Yale University in 1931, where he majored in English. He then earned the LL.B. degree in 1934 (later J.D.) at Albany Law School, Union University. While practicing law in the ensuing years, he served for a time as justice of the peace and as a special probate judge. As an Army officer during World War II, his principal assignment was as Chief of the Department of Law and Administration, Provost General School. In 1948, he moved to Michigan State University as an associate professor in the School of Police Administration and Public Safety, and in 1955 directed the first National Institute on Police and Community Relations. He shifted to the Michigan Department of Corrections as director of its Youth Division and was appointed Deputy Director for Program Services of the Department in 1966. On six months' leave from the Corrections Department in 1969, he carried out a charge from the governor to develop the office and staff, and a statewide master plan of regional operations, as acting director of the Michigan Commission on Law Enforcement and Criminal Justice, the state planning agency under provisions of the Federal Omnibus Crime Act of 1968. Returning to the Corrections Department, he was appointed a member of the State Parole Board, remaining in this capacity until December, 1973, when he retired. He is currently on part-time appointment as a professor in the School of Criminal Justice, Michigan State University.

Chapter Eighteen

Police-Media Relations

Relationship problems between governmental bodies and the media of public information are endemic to democratic societies. Conflict of interest is embedded in this relationship, and it is perfectly normal and generally healthy in terms of the common good. If the newspapers and other media were not "policing the police" and other governing factions; if they were not channeling information and interpreting the communication between criminal justice agencies and the public, they would be shirking a vital responsibility and would be open to serious criticism.

The Complicated Relationship of the Police and the Media

The relationship between a police organization and newspapers or television stations is so complicated that strong feelings and positions can crystallize on either side. The cultivation by the police of good relations with the media is an important means of good public relations by keeping the public informed of what is going on in a police department, and why. But where a police department hedges on publicity, or where a newspaper or other medium seemingly violates what the police view as the ethics or ground rules of reporting crime news, then problems arise.

Such a clash occurs most frequently when the police deem it necessary to withhold information from the media. This happens in the very nature of police work—for example, in the course of a manhunt, a criminal investigation, or a "crackdown,"—whenever the release of certain information threatens police objectives. Thus, it is not *always* in the best interests of either the police or the public that the police tell all they may know about a given case. Administrative judgments on withholding such information are occasionally questioned by the media, and their questions transmitted to the public—to the possible disadvantage of the administrator. Because he cannot explain his decision without disclosing information that he believes is best withheld, his "no comment" may be translated as administrative pugnacity or evasiveness.

This dilemma of police-media relationship is a typical one in police administration. The media side may also face a dilemma. A newspaper and a radio or television station are ordinarily profit-making enterprises. They also have responsibilities to the public interest. Whatever dilemma arises from these conflicting objectives is reconciled by the decisions of those who rule such enterprises and is recognized by the public only in somewhat detached notions as to what constitutes a "responsible" newspaper or television station. Public tastes and tolerances in such a matter are as varied and fickle as in the choice of toothpastes. Clearly, the public interest is not always best served by the profit-making policies or practices of the media. Among other things, this principle of the public interest might—more often than it does—call into question a newspaper's use of such treacherous euphemisms as "the public's right to know" in a manner suggesting as impregnable a right as that of life itself. From time to time, one suspects that the newspaper is really using an excuse for doing, in the name of the public interest, what best serves its profit motive.

So we have a dilemma on the police side of the relationship, and a dilemma on the media side. And as Winston Churchill might have put it, we also have a conundrum within the dilemma. For the newspaper, in a highly competitive market, often finds its premium story to be what the police (or the prosecutor, or the court) are reluctant to disclose. The ramifications of the dual dilemma and the conundrum constitute the essence of the problem of police-media relationships.

The Disclosure of Information

The broader issue in police-media relations, however, is a conflict as old as democratic government; and it is also a current one. Simply stated, it is the question of accessibility of information about government operations. As John Steele stated it in *Time* magazine:

This conflict often pits the President and the Executive Branch against Congress, regulatory agencies against consumer interests, bureaucrats against environmentalists, Congress against the voter, the courts against the bar and, at times, the news media against all of them. ["The People's Right to Know"]

With respect to what he called "a current cliché from the political lexicon—the people's right to know"—Steele observed:

The Constitution, as it happens, does not provide for any such right. The courts, moreover, have never interpreted the First Amendment—which prohibits Congress from abridging freedom of speech or the press—as requiring the Government to make unlimited disclosures about its activities. [Ibid.]

Steele further asserts that an uncurbed right to know eventually collides dramatically with what might be called the right *not* to know. Many historians, philosophers, political scientists, and even a few journalists have conceded that there must be some limit to the right of the public to have information about government. As James Russell Wiggins, former editor of *The Washington Post,* put it: "We can give up a little freedom without surrendering all of it. We can have a little secrecy without having a Government that is altogether secret. Each added measure of secrecy, however, measurably diminishes our freedom."

So the question is, how much secrecy? Under what specific conditions, and by whose judgment, may government officials operate "on and off camera"? Inquisitive newsmen as well as inquisitive Congressional and private investigators have turned up some appalling incidents of bare-faced news control by government in recent years. No one seems to be willing to confess that he knows much about criteria for such control. In fact, sometimes the justification for secrecy seems to be no better than apathy or red tape, or a splendid evidence of the effectiveness of special interest lobbies and pressure groups. Congress has not done much in legislating about the disclosure of official information in the public interest. The Freedom of Information Act of 1966 has been an inadequate measure to cope with the problem, for it exempted such areas as national defense and foreign policy. A congressional study reported that the media made little use of it during the first four years of operation, although commercial interests did.

The media, of course, are not immune from criticism either. Being at times too considerate of the sensibilities of government officials who try to manage the news is one such criticism. The abuse of trust where privileged information has been made available has also occurred. For instance, liberties are sometimes taken with informational release deadlines: "Not to be released prior to 12:01 a.m." on such and such a date. And more serious breaches of confidence occur, under competitive duress. So it is that we have another two-sided street here, calling for *balance* in carefully and painstakingly worked out groundrules and guidelines, while recognizing that excesses on either side threaten rights best safeguarded by a kind of constructive, creative tension in the relationship. In a nutshell, things can get too "chummy" in the relationship as well as too adversarial.

In a recent article, Daniel P. Moynihan, adviser to three Presidents, contends that the relationship between the Presidency and the press is changing because of five conditions:[1]

1. The journalistic tradition of muckraking—the exposure of corruption in government or of the collusion of government with private interests—while still very much alive in the reportorial spirit, is giving way to what Lionel Trilling calls "the adversary culture" as an element in journalistic practice. Common to both, however, is a mistrust of Government.

2. Journalism has become, if not an elite profession, then at least a profession attractive to elites. The political consequence of the rising social status of journalism is that the press grows more influenced by attitudes genuinely hostile to American society and American government.

3. Washington reporters depend heavily on more or less clandestine information from Federal bureaucracies which are frequently, and in some cases routinely, antagonistic to Presidential interests. When the bureaucracies think their interests are threatened, they often turn to the press. Both bureaucrats and journalists "stay in town"; Presidents come and go.

4. Questions of objectivity are often raised in reporting the statements of public figures. While the tradition in journalism is to print "the news," whether or not the reporter or the editor or the publisher likes it, there is a rub when it comes to a question of whether an event really is news—or simply a happening, staged for the purpose of getting into the papers. The issue, then, is: what is journalistic objectivity, and what is merely an excuse for avoiding judgment? If it becomes clear that someone is lying or "playing games," why print it—or at least, why print it on the front page?

5. Finally, and most important, there is the absence in American journalism of a professional tradition of self-correction—a mark of any developed profession. Honest mistakes ought to be seen as integral to the process of advancing the field. But journalism will never attain to any such condition.

Moynihan summarized his views by saying that he wished to emphasize two points: (a) that in the eyes of the media in a democracy, it is hard for Government to succeed, even when it has indeed done so; and (b) the conditions are thus set for protracted conflict in which the Government "keeps losing." And this, today, Moynihan believes is a serious matter of national morale. By way of resolving the issue, he calls for a better balance. He seems to admit, implicitly, that there is another side to the argument, but he does not spell it out. Perhaps, he says, some sort of national press council would help, of a type earlier proposed by Norman Isaacs, a working journalist; and even earlier by Robert M.

Hutchins and his Commission on Freedom of the Press. But Moynihan backs off and says that such a council would be the wrong thing to create in this country at this time; there is, he believes, "a statist quality" to many of the existing press councils abroad. He thinks the American press should become much more open about acknowledging mistakes. As for Government, he observes that misrepresentations of Government performance should never be allowed to go unchallenged:

> The culture of disparagement that has been so much in evidence of late . . . is bad news for democracy. . . . Where is . . . socially responsible criticism to come from? Or rather, where is it to appear in a manner that will inform and influence the course of public decision-making?

Government Power vs. Media Power

Clearly, then, the relationship of the police and the press is an aspect of the larger skirmish pitting the power of government against the power of the press. Both sides in this continuing battle plead for "better balance." But spokesmen for each camp, like Moynihan, seem to want the balance to be in their favor. Again, "We want to cooperate —but on our terms."

The depth of the issue today is great indeed. While government (the police and the criminal justice system are particular targets, but not by any means the sole ones) appears to be more than ever the object of public criticism, the news media also seem to be under attack as never before. Generally, the charge against the media is bias. The specifics vary. The poor and the nonwhite accuse the media of unfair treatment. Minorities have long since had their own newspapers, magazines, and network stations, as have the alienated groups with their underground press—and these media are especially critical of the police. Blue-collar descendents of European immigrants are saying that they do not get fairly treated by the media. Young radicals proclaim that the popular media distort their image. The police often accuse the media (as in Chicago in August, 1968) of "tilting" the news, and sometimes of "stoking the fires of unrest." The National Commission on the Causes and Prevention of Violence stated that "a crisis of confidence exists today between the American people and their news media." Other Presidential Commissions in recent years have not heaped praise upon the media. On the contrary, the Kerner Commission, for example, devoted considerable attention to media reporting, charging that the media had failed to communicate adequately on race relations and ghetto problems, and had failed further to bring more Negroes into journalism.

In short, the so-called credibility gap in the relationship between government and citizens seems to be matched by the credibility gap between the media and "the masses" (Mark Arnold, "The News Media —Besieged by Critics"). One explanation for the gap is the growing political polarization of the nation. People "strike out," as Mark Arnold phrased it, "at the messenger who delivers the bad news." Another explanation is distortion of the news by the media—through editorial bias, economic or political pressure, etc. Still another explanation is the charge that the media have not adapted well to the times, and that they have failed to identify for themselves a constructive role in interpreting current social change and social conflict. Newspapers are, however, moving away from the "shotgun" approach—the front-page buildup, with splashy pictures and boxscores of the latest riot news. Dramatic but meaningless predictions have also largely disappeared. But serious problems remain. Glaring instances of inaccuracy, exaggeration, distortion, misinterpretation, and bias still occur in all types of news media, as pointed out by the U.S. Commission on Civil Rights. (*Civil Rights Digest,* Volume 4, No. 1, Winter, 1971).

Unquestionably, there is an element of Americans viewing the news more and liking it less. There is also the element of enormous power, wielded by approximately 1750 daily, 578 Sunday, and 8000 weekly newspapers, 150 general editorial magazines, 6400 radio stations, and 840 television outlets. The wear-and-tear of competition, increasing publication and circulation costs, the frantic pace of life, and probably growing public disenchantment with the quality of news reporting are among the factors influencing the media. Politicians, in typical action, have moved with what they perceive as a rising tide of criticism directed against the media, and have sought to exploit it for their own political advantage.

Some observers who see these signs as threatening the survival of a free press point to various indications of what they interpret as government intimidation of the media. There is concern about the apparent fact that distrust of the media increases with education and income level. We have discussed at length the police role predicament in today's society. The media also have a pressing role dilemma, implicit in our reference to the conundrum within the dual dilemma. They are expected to stand apart from the society, in a kind of dispassionate, objective, watch-dog fashion despite their other role as members of society, with their own intrinsic pressures and prejudices. To this extent, the similarity in the role predicament of police and press is striking. There are also some differences.

The Balance of Power

It is not unusual for Big Power economic or political encounters to ignore largely the interests of third parties. Labor-management strife is one illustration. The Cold War in international relations was another. Big Media vs. Big Government appears to be another. The third party, generically, is the public, directing accusations of a credibility gap against both media and government. Where there is power, there is always the question of control; in this encounter, control of the media by the government, or control of the government by the media. Put another way, the ultimate conflicts of interest must be controlled through a negotiated balance of power, lest the conflicts destroy the system or the society.

Since this discussion pertains to the police-media relationship, it may seem to be ranging pretty far afield, but in fact we are very much on target. The point bears repeating that the contact of patrolman and newsman on the street or in the stationhouse is a microcosm of a larger, complex issue, an issue that is very hot in our time.

In a recent book, *The Best Cause,* John Hohenberg refers to the tendency in public discourse to blame every problem on "a crisis of confidence" in the institutions of democratic society. Under these circumstances, he says, ". . . when it is difficult for either the governors or the governed to find anybody, outside each other, to blame for their troubles, a certain amount of critical fallout is bound to descend on the press." Some of this is due, Hohenberg asserts, to the independent newspaper's contention that it is the principal common medium for discourse between the American government and the American people. Therefore, when the communication channels get clogged, the medium must be prepared to take some of the blame.

> What it all comes down to, in reality [Hohenberg continues] is whether the daily newspaper, as presently constituted, is capable of publishing the news at the same time it is trying to get at the truth. The public, as is evidenced by the widespread use of the phrase "newspaper talk," long ago recognized that the two functions were not necessarily identical. . . . Of course the truth is hard to come by in the complicated modern world. But neither the elite of democratic governments nor the paladins of the press can shrug off public dissatisfaction by pleading that the job is difficult and perhaps even impossible to do to everyone's satisfaction. Two thousand years ago, nobody was satisfied, either, with Pontius Pilate's crafty evasion, "What is truth?" ["The Free Press IS on Trial"][2]

The historical spectre of media power in this country is conveyed through dim memories of William Randolph Hearst and the Orson Welles portrayal of *Citizen Kane.* However, John Tebbel expresses doubt that the power of the press today is a matter of such personalities as Lord Thomson of Fleet Street (who is virtually unknown to most Americans of any age, yet who owns many newspapers in America), or Arthur Ochs Sulzberger, president and publisher of *The New York Times,* or Samuel I. Newhouse, a retiring figure known to few outside the industry. John Tebbel thinks that Robert R. McCormick and Roy Howard were the last of the "press lords" ("Press Power Revisited").

Newspapers today derive their power, Tebbel believes, from what they print. Gone is the day when a publisher and his paper could be a decisive factor in political fortunes; political editorials are read and heeded only where a paper's constituency is already largely in agreement. But this does not mean, Tebbel cautions, that newspapers are without any political influence. They do provide a sounding board for many viewpoints, and they do help to crystallize public opinion on the important issues of the day. Government would hardly be so concerned with the media if the assumption were that the media have little influence with voters and taxpayers. The danger, in Tebbel's view, is this:

> . . . the press might slip into the unrestrained advocacy [which makes] it a mere propaganda instrument and therefore utterly unreliable as a purveyor of news . . . Just as the idea of a university as an instrument of social change instead of an intellectual laboratory is being widely advocated, so too can we expect a further steady push by those who insist that a newspaper should have the same kind of public utility. . . . More and more, the real power of the press today emerges as a conveyor of information that government and others would like to withhold from the public if that were possible, so that they might exercise their own power without undue interference. . . . The public frequently does not agree with the information the newspapers provide, but that is immaterial. What is important is that the information is provided, without interference, so that the public can interpret it, argue about it, and act upon it if it chooses. That is, and always has been, the true mission of the press in our kind of democracy. [Ibid., p. 54][3]

Bias and the Media

Charges of bias invariably come from those who disagree with a position taken. Thus, a biased editorial or a biased study is one whose conclusions or recommendations are unacceptable to oneself. The ultimate absurdity is reached when an investigation is conducted by, let us say, a committee or commission of "impeccable credentials" to determine whether there is bias only to have its report branded as "biased."

What are some specifics of the charges of biased reporting directed at the media? We cannot offer an exhaustive listing, nor do we argue the merits or demerits of any of these allegations; but the following are indicative of current charges:

> Reporters today are disproportionately "dogmatic liberals" with a strong "leftward bias" and "a set of automatic reactions" that incline them to "oversimplify" the news. As a result, U.S. journalism is out of touch with the American mainstream.[4]

> The media are unduly subservient to the pressures of advertisers.

> The media are unduly subservient to the pressures of politicians.

> Local media depend too much for news coverage and editorial position on hookups with national networks.

The media all but ignore stories that challenge their basic editorial positions on favored candidates or proposals.

The media use chauvinistic criteria in judging what is news.

The media stress spot reporting, usually confined to the unexpected or the unusual. They neglect "perspective" reporting. (Example: the 5 percent of students who riot on campus is news; the 95 percent who do not is perspective.)

The media emphasize tragedy conflict, disorder, the bizarre, etc., in their reporting and tend to neglect joy, cooperation, peace, good works of ordinary people, etc. The media are more interested in problems than in solutions, destruction rather than construction, reaction rather than action, fights rather than civil dialogue, irresponsibility rather than responsibility, and so on.

The media distort by telling only part of a story, by promoting a particular viewpoint, or by slanting a story by headlines or by position in the paper.

The Kerner Commission said that the media made a real effort to report factually the 1967 disorders, but had failed to report adequately on the causes and consequences of civil disorders and the underlying problems of race relations. Racial bias in one form or another is a frequent criticism of the media.

Media reporters sometimes side with protesters and demonstrators, thereby embarassing the police and making the police task more difficult.[5]

Sometimes the media *stage* news events.

Interpretive reporting tends "to widen the credibility gap," merely revealing the prejudices of the reporter.

The media are fascinated with glitter and glamor at the expense of significance.

The media often label people with convenient, stereotypic terms.

Such a litany of allegations against the media may strike some readers as bias in itself. Although the subject is touchy enough to set off such responses the list is given here to further discussion in particulars, rather than in generalizations.

By way of swinging the pendulum of the discussion, let us turn again to John Tebbel for a look at the other side. He muses that critics of the press are usually just as wrong in their complaints about what the papers *do* print as they are about what they think *ought* to be printed. As he states it: "Critics in high places, particularly, make generalized assertions of no validity whatever as though they were fact" ("The Stories the Newspapers *Do* Cover")

Tebbel conducted a modest sampling of prominent dailies across the country, deliberately excluding New York and Washington papers (lest the survey be considered biased!), to determine what, if any, basis in fact there was for some of the main criticisms. He found the charge that the front pages are filled with crime and violence was without factual basis. So was the charge that the papers feature mostly local news. So was the charge that newspapers don't print good news, or that they are filled with trivialities. So was the charge that the papers offer only the publishers' opinions. It is now common, Tebbel found, for newspapers to present a broad range of opinion in the editorial section, often spread across two facing pages. Tebbel also discovered that the papers he surveyed run many nonviolent stories about nonviolent people preoccupied with worthwhile, nonviolent activities.

Someone would no doubt suggest that Tebbel is a biased reporter who set out to prove what he already believed. Perhaps our discussion would be more productive if again we turn to a concrete case.

The Rights of the Reporter

While there are those always willing to cheer for the "adventurer" who takes on "the stiff-necked" media in "open combat," there are also those who take a dim view of such things as the use of government subpoenas to uncover sources of press information about radical organizations, or the infiltration of the Saigon press corps by military agents posing as newsmen, or the use of a Congressional subpoena to persuade a national television network to submit any and all material connected with the production of a documentary "that provoked Big Brother in Washington," as one newsmagazine put it. An excellent case in point was provided in a situation with *The New York Times* reporter, Earl Caldwell.

The trouble began in October, 1969, when four Chicago newspapers, NBC News, and *Time, Life,* and *Newsweek* magazines were subpoenaed to produce files, photographs, film, and even reporters' notebooks on a four-day rampage by the SDS Weathermen in Chicago (*Newsweek,* February 16, 1970, pp. 55, 56). In early February, 1970, CBS News disclosed that it had been subpoenaed for all film that had been shot for a program on the Black Panthers. Then the government ordered Caldwell, who was also black, to surrender "all notes and tape recordings" of his interviews with Black Panther leaders, in particular an interview with David Hilliard, who was charged with threatening President Nixon's life.[6]

So the issue was joined: freedom of the press, resting on protection of confidential information and sources; and the obligation of every citizen to serve as a witness in support of law and judicial process. But in this case, the issue was complicated by the outrage of newsmen at the sheer number and catchall nature of the subpoenas ("fishing expedition"), and further by the application of such governmental tactics to newsmen covering the politics of protest and violence. The CBS network pleaded that what may have been orthodox procedures for news-gathering years ago were obsolete today. When, for example, a news source is a pot-smoking young activist who confidentially outlines his plan for a rally that may produce violence, the newsman's duty is not so clearly apparent, whether or not he sympathizes with the source or the cause. But prosecutors and defense counsels for indicted activists have learned that newsmen often possess vital information. As *Newsweek* stated it (February 16, 1970):

> Hauled into court under a subpoena and threatened with contempt proceedings if he doesn't talk, the newsman finds himself caught between the law, his professional ethics and his responsibilities as a citizen. ... Only thirteen [seventeen, as of May 1971] states have statutes protecting a reporter's confidential relationships, and attempts to get such a nationwide law through Congress have failed.

The *New York Times* initially provided legal counsel for Caldwell. Attorney-General John Mitchell announced that some of his subordinates had gone too far and that he would meet with the offended editors and try to work out a mutually satisfactory set of ground rules. Caldwell's trial in San Francisco Federal District Court was pressed, although the court stipulated that Caldwell could not be compelled to disclose confidential information from his interviews with Black Panther Party leaders "unless the government could prove there was no other way of obtaining the same information on a matter of 'national interest'" (*Newsweek,* May 11, 1970, p. 74). Caldwell appealed, but at this point the *Times* indicated that it would not take part in the appeal.

In November 1970 the Ninth Circuit Court of Appeals quashed the Federal subpoenas that had been served on Caldwell and vacated a contempt-of-court citation against him, and in so doing sharpened the focus on a journalist's hitherto ill-defined privilege under the First Amendment. In its decision, this Court said:

> The very concept of a free press requires that the news media be accorded a measure of autonomy. To convert newsgatherers into Department of Justice investigators is to invade the autonomy of the press by imposing a governmental function upon them. To do so where the result is to diminish their future capacity as newsgatherers is destructive of their public function. ... The need for an untrammeled press takes on special urgency in times of widespread protest and dissent. In such times, the First Amendment protections exist to maintain communication with dissenting groups and to provide the public with a wide range of information about the nature of protest and heterodoxy. [*Newsweek,* November 30, 1970, p. 87]

Caldwell had been prepared to go to jail. His own lawyers held that his chances of acquittal were poor. The general principle enunciated by the court in this particular case would have to be developed in later cases. From a journalistic vantage point, the decision was a landmark. But it was not the end of the case. In May, 1971, the U.S. Supreme Court agreed to hear a further appeal in the case, pressed by U.S. attorneys wanting the court to compel Caldwell to testify. In June, 1972, the Supreme Court ruled, in a 5-4 decision, that journalists have no First Amendment right to refuse to tell grand juries the names of confidential sources of information given to them in confidence. But it could be predicted that the matter would not be allowed to rest at that.

At the annual meeting of the American Society of Newspaper Editors in the spring of 1971, they discussed the need for national legislation to protect reporters from court procedures aimed at forcing them to disclose news sources. Particular alarm was voiced regarding the recent "epidemic" use of the subpoena (Richard L. Tobin, *Saturday Review*, May 8, 1971, pp. 45, 46). It was charged that "lazy law enforcement types" were using the subpoena to try to force the press to do their investigating. Attorney-General Mitchell was commended for his efforts to develop guidelines.[7] But most people at the convention still thought that freedom of the press was in grave jeopardy, under the threat of the subpoena. The problem of television and radio newsgathering was considered especially acute because they operate under government licensing. Richard L. Tobin wrote in *Saturday Review*:[8]

> As every newspaperman knows but won't always admit out loud, protection of a source of news can be used as an excuse or a crutch or, worse, to rationalize a point neither necessarily true nor useful to the general public. ... All the same, despite an occasional racket, such as the hiding behind the shield of news source immunity by an amoral journalist, the ASNE's drive for a Federal law to protect reporters from court procedures trying to force them to disclose their sources of news does make sense professionally. For if every legitimate source of information knew that he or his journalist friend might be hauled into court for questioning, or even jailing, not many headlines would be written or broadcast except for cut and dried events covered in routine fashion, and the traditional investigative role of the press would fade forever.

Commonweal commented:

> The public information media are a long way from perfect, and nothing should be allowed to obscure this fact. But there is nothing wrong with the press and television that can be cured by the heavy hand of Washington either, and this is an even more basic truth. [May 7, 1971, p. 206]

The case of the Pentagon Papers in mid-1971 went to the heart of the issue. As Jude Wanniski put it in *The National Observer* (June 21, 1971):

... the disclosures leave in their wake a host of far-reaching inquiries about the nature of government itself; about the war-making power of the Executive Branch in a representative government; about the methods of decision-making; about the inherent strain in a super-power democracy between the need for an informed public and national security requirements for secrecy in foreign affairs.

Free Press and Fair Trial

The issue we have been discussing has been, at times, dramatically portrayed in cases where questions of free press versus fair trial have been highlighted. There is a long legal history to this issue in this country for which an extensive bibliography exists.[9]

President Johnson's Crime Commission declared that newspaper, television, and radio reporting are essential to the administration of justice. Reporting maintains the public knowledge, review, and support, said the Commission, so necessary for the proper functioning of the courts. Critical inquiry and reporting by the media on the operation of the courts can prevent abuses and promote improvements in any part of the justice system. On the other hand, a fair jury trial can be held only if the evidence is presented in a courtroom, not in the press, and only if jurors come to their task unprejudiced by publicity. The Commission recommended the setting of standards for releasing news:

> Police, prosecutors, bar associations, and courts should issue regulations and standards as to the kinds of information that properly can be released to the news media about pending criminal cases by police officers, prosecutors, and defense counsel. These regulations and standards should be designed to minimize prejudicial statements by the media before or during trial, while safeguarding legitimate reporting on matters of public interest. [*The Challenge of Crime*, p. 138]

The differences of opinion regarding live televising of trials find many lawyers who are opposed on the ground that "the search for truth is difficult enough without putting it on stage" (Edward Williams, "What's Needed to Speed Up Justice?"). Canon 35 of the *Canons of Judicial Ethics* of the American Bar Association bases its ban on the filming of judicial proceedings on a fear that cameras, cables, lights, and technicians might constitute an intolerable courtroom distraction that could influence the behavior of participants in a trial and affect its outcome. Only in Texas and Colorado [as this is written] have supreme courts overriden Canon 35 to allow cameras in the courtroom, if both the presiding judge and the defendant approve. In March, 1970, a Denver judge permitted National Educational Television to film the entire trial in the case of The City and County of Denver v. Lauren R. Watson, a six-hour production (*Newsweek,* March 30, 1970, p. 59).

In Michigan, the state Supreme Court has recently adopted a revised code of ethics that forbids the release to the press of statements by attorneys and prosecutors that might influence the outcome of pending cases. The change in the lawyer's code of conduct, the first since 1935, reduces 47 canons into nine restrictions on press coverage of criminal trials:

> . . . Statements cannot be made concerning the identity, testimony or credibility of a prospective witness.

> . . . Statements cannot be made concerning the results of any tests or the objection of the accused to submit to examination or tests.

> . . . Statements cannot be made revealing the prosecutor's opinion as to the guilt or innocence of the accused.

> . . . Statements cannot be made concerning the character or prior criminal record of the accused.

> . . . Statements cannot be made concerning the possibility of a plea of guilty or to the acceptance of a lesser charge.

In addition to the restrictions set by the court, the American Bar Association accepted a provision that requires attorneys and prosecutors to provide the name, age, residence, occupation, and family status of the accused, and any information necessary to aid in the apprehension of the accused or to warn the public of any danger he may present if not apprehended.

Violence and the Media

As chairman of the 1947 Commission on Freedom of the Press, Robert M. Hutchins said that "the relative power of the press carries with it relatively great obligations." Many people today are gravely concerned about what they regard as the failures of our social institutions, and among them are many who point to the media as a prime example and the chief cause of much that has seemingly gone wrong with other institutions. Sex, sadism, and violence in magazines and newspapers, on the radio and television, and in the movies are often pointed to as symptoms of deteriorated values and coarsened public taste. Individuals and agencies disagree widely and sharply about the effects of certain subject matter—for example, of violence on television—upon children and adults. The protest against violence on television—clearly related to so many manifestations of the violence phenomenon on the social scene (civil disorder, crime, delinquency, etc.)—became organized in the 1960s.

We observed earlier that violence has been prominently ingrained in the American *ethos* from the beginning of our history. The encounters between the early settlers and the Indians were hardly a form of nonviolent social protest. The "winning of the West" was not inspired by a philosophy of live and let live. The games we played as children could not be blamed on television, for there was no such thing, but the silent and later sound movies most vivid to us prompted our quarrels about who would be Tom Mix, Buck Jones, John Wayne, or Tim McCoy. And it wasn't a tea party that we had in mind; we sometimes used "bee-bees" in our air rifles, and we weren't hunting for sparrows!

Graphic violence abounds in great literature. In nature, it is an important part of life. In human affairs, so is evil. But if evil or violence are featured, emphasized, held up as models of behavior in a multitude of ways, there will inevitably be social agitation for controls of one kind or another, premised upon concern for society's survival. Sesame Street forthwith emerged and joined Captain Kangaroo on television in a tone of sensitivity, gentleness, compassion, loving understanding of living things, and not least of all, of self and other people. For this, too, is telling it like it is. As Margaret Culkin Banning has put it:

> We need candor. But we should not confuse frankness with only the uncovering of lewdness, violence, and despair. Frankness should also expose loyalty, gentleness, courage, and love for they too exist and have a right to be shown on the screen and in the pages of books.[10]

Eliot Daley, speaking as a parent, zeroed in on television violence with the observation that the *average* child sees 12,000 TV deaths before he is fourteen years old.[11] What is real to these children? Daley asks. Far too many programs, he believes, convey the idea that the manipulation of persons through deceit, guilt, pseudohumor, or brute force is legitimized by the eventual getting of one's way. Small wonder that today's children are masters of manipulation. Daley thinks that the underlying difficulty for most young viewers is that programming directed at them is really adult fare presented in juvenile dialect. But children have not tested enough reality in the world at large to be able to put cartoon violence in a context where it can be funny.

> Ordinarily, [says Daley] the young viewer watches virtually in vain for *alternatives* to a violent expression of hostility or aggression. None are needed apparently, since there is a seemingly limitless warehouse of willing victims and an incredible quality and variety of violence. Worse, there is a total tolerance and total absence of condemnation of violence. Not a voice is raised to suggest the limited appropriateness of violence as a human-relations skill. . . . Nowhere does the violence-as-a-problem-solver thesis come a cropper.

The National Commission on the Causes and Prevention of Violence (1969) concluded that television was loaded with violence; that it was teaching American children moral and social values "inconsistent with a civilized society." The Commission marshalled some frightening statistics to bolster this charge, and contended that the vast majority of experimental studies bearing on the question have found that observed violence stimulates aggressive behavior. The Commission was careful to point out that it did not see television as a principal cause of violence in society. But it is, the Commission insisted, a contributing factor. Television entertainment based on violence may be effective merchandising, but it is, the Commission opined, "an appalling way to serve a civilization—an appalling way to fulfill the requirements of the law that broadcasting serve the public interest, convenience and necessity."[12]

The Commission approached the question of television violence with great care, at pains not to make television a scapegoat. It recognized that violence is a complex phenomenon, with complex causes.

A Task Force Report of 613 pages, prepared for the same Commission under the direction of a former Justice Department attorney, Robert K. Baker, and a Seattle sociologist, Sandra J. Ball, was entitled *Mass Media and Violence*. Published in January 1970, the report did not have the endorsement of the full Commission. This study contended that the news media in general contribute to violence in America by failing to report thoroughly on the social problems that lead to disorders, violence, and confrontations. This, in effect, repeated what the Kerner Commission had said. The Task Force Report described the news media as oversensitive to outside criticism and then continued:

> The news media can play a significant role in lessening the potential for violence by functioning as a faithful conduit for intergroup communication, providing a true marketplace of ideas, providing full access to the day's intelligence, and reducing the incentive to confrontation that sometimes erupts in violence. That is a subtle and uncertain mission.

Sometimes, said the report, the press is overly blamed for violence. Some groups do use the media to exploit their goals. But it should be remembered, the Task Force observed, that violence is not necessarily aimed at gaining media attention. Further, groups engaging in violence are likely to have their message lost because of the media tendency to focus on the violence to the exclusion of the message. Moreover, the resorting to violence is often a political instrument, used to provoke the police, and as in the case of campus disorders—to incite to radical action large numbers of students sympathetic to the New Left goals who would ordinarily reject New Left tactics.

The Task Force recommendations included more self-examination by the media, more interpretive reporting on social ills, tighter guidelines for the coverage of disorders, the establishment by news organizations of internal appeal boards to hear citizen complaints about coverage, better relations between the press and minority groups, and a press council independent of the media and government set up as a public watchdog for all news outlets. The report concluded:

> The last generation of reporters concentrated on reporting objective physical happenings—telling the reader what he saw with his own eyes and heard with his own ears. The next generation must con-

centrate on describing what somebody else thinks. . . . The government can no more legislate good journalism than it can legalize good manners. More important than the adoption of specific suggestions is that each news organization make an independent determination of what is significant.

The Police-Media Relationship of the Future

To blame the media alone for violence, riots, and civil disturbances makes no more sense than to blame the police. Occasionally, under particular circumstances, imprudent or even unethical media (or police) action may trigger mayhem, but usually the causes go much deeper. Hatred and hopelessness are not manufactured by the media nor by the police, though they may play a part. Who trusts whom? This is a key question in a social milieu that reveals its attitudes by the commonplace use of such terms as "watchdog," "bullshit," "Orwellian," and "conniving bastard."

As we said at the outset of this discussion, the fundamental issue is as old as the free society. Alexis de Tocqueville referred to it this way:

> In this question, therefore, there is no medium between servitude and license; in order to enjoy the inestimable benefits that the liberty of the press ensures, it is necessary to submit to the inevitable evils that it creates.

Are the media more the builders or the disrupters of democracy? Sometimes one, sometimes the other. Just like police departments, they make mistakes. Who trusts whom? Frank admission that none of us are omnipotent is a good beginning, if one is intent upon improving relationships with anyone.

We have suggested the complexity of the causes and effects of the violence phenomenon. Likewise complex has been the evolution of the government-media relationship in our society. Police-press relations is one among many vessels on a currently turbulent lake. The TV program, *The Selling of the Pentagon,* and the Pentagon Papers, were sails on another boat on the same lake. Government surveillance by means of wiretap is another large vessel that includes in its cargo a variety of governmental activities calculated to cope with dissent, protest, and revolutionary plot, at a time when such social swells are pervasively rocking the boat. Free press and fair trial is another substantial craft on the same lake. So is the protection of privacy and, at the same time, the protection of the rights of reporters and the public in handling police information, the news.

For the policeman, these big issues are telescoped in matter-of-fact questions. For example, he asks: If only a small part of the allegations about violence that have been made against television are valid, why is it that anyone would seriously suggest that policemen should be disarmed? Why should a police officer put his life on the line as a first tentative step in a grand strategy of defusing our society? It's not unlike international disarmament. Who takes the initiative? Where and how does the building of mutual trust begin? Not with crooks, surely. But just as logically, then, not with "crook catchers" either.

So it is that we eventually come to the kind of question that policemen, newsmen, and many others can study together. What produces violence or crime or social revolution in the first place? Not the police, alone—nor newsmen, alone—nor anyone else, alone. And so on. One risks maudlin homiletics and oversimplification by drawing out such reasoning endlessly.

Much can be done to establish police-media relations on a mutually beneficial plane, despite (or better, because of) the inevitable conflict of interests. Every urban police agency and local media have worked out a modus operandi, more or less effectively, in the form of "ground rules," "working principles," "guideposts," "guidelines."[13] The President's 1966 Crime Commission implied that the police-press relationship may thrive better when cooperative efforts have a specific focus—organized crime, for example, about which the Commission recommended, among other things:

> All newspapers in major metropolitan areas where organized crime exists should designate a highly competent reporter for fulltime work and writing concerning organized criminal activities, the corruption caused by it, and governmental efforts to control it. Newspapers in smaller communities dominated by organized crime should fulfill their responsibility to inform the public of the nature and consequence of these conditions. [*The Challenge of Crime*, p. 208][14]

Some may disagree with the details of this recommendation, but the basic message of police-media cooperation is clear. Their mutual stake is the survival of free society.

Notes to Chapter Eighteen

1. Daniel P. Moynihan, "The Presidency and the Press." (Excerpted in *The National Observer*, March 29, 1971, p. 22.)

2. See also Harry S. Ashmore, "Government by Public Relations."

3. Bill Moyers, press aide to President Johnson and former publisher of *Newsday*, thinks that the indiscriminate use of so-called backgrounders is one important source of the government-media relationship problem (*The New York Times*, January 6, 1972):

> The backgrounder permits the press and the Government to sleep together, even to procreate, without getting married or having to accept responsibility for any offspring. . . . In the end very little will

change. The Government will go on calling backgrounders as long as the Government wants to put its best foot forward. Reporters will be there to report dutifully what isn't officially said by a source that can't be held officially accountable at an event that doesn't officially happen for a public that can't officially be told because it can't officially be trusted to know. But don't quote me on that.

4. Howard K. Smith, ABC newsman, as reported in *Newsweek*, March 9, 1970, p. 84.

5. See, for example, Donald Myrus and Burton Joseph, *Law and Disorder: The Chicago Convention and Its Aftermath,* 1968. See also *Dissent and Disorder,* a report to the citizens of Chicago on the April 27 Peace Parade, prepared by an independent investigating committee, Edward J. Sparling, Chairman, August 1, 1968. Also Carolyn Jaffe, "The Press and the Oppressed," Parts 1 and 2.

6. The charge against Hilliard was dismissed in early May 1971 because of a "technicality" in the use of wire-tapping by the Government to secure some of the evidence.

7. As reported in *The New York Times,* August 13, 1970, p. 23, from a Speech by Attorney-General Mitchell to the House of Delegates of the American Bar Association, meeting in Saint Louis, August 10, 1970.

8. See also Richard L. Tobin, "Reporters, Subpoenas, Immunity, and the Court." Also Nat Hentoff, "A Deepening Chill."

9. For a representative reference, see Siebert and Hough, *Free Press and Fair Trial.* See also Study 3 (Part 4), "The Free Press—Fair Trial Issue," in Radelet and Reed, *Studies.*

10. Margaret Culkin Banning, "Sex and Violence in Movies, Books, TV—Helpful or Harmful?" *Family Weekly,* January 11, 1970.

11. Eliot A. Daley, "Is TV Brutalizing Your Child?" *Look,* December 2, 1969, pp. 99, 100.

12. As reported in *U.S. News & World Report,* "TV Violence: 'Appalling'," October 6, 1969, pp. 55–56. Also as reported in *Today's Education,* journal of the National Education Association, December 1969, pp. 52, 53. See also Charles U. Daly, ed., *The Media and the Cities,* the University of Chicago Center For Policy Study.

13. For example, the New York City Police Department, as described by the present Commissioner, Patrick V. Murphy (when he was Deputy Chief Inspector in 1965), to the National Institute on Police and Community Relations at Michigan State University. (In Brandstatter and Radelet, eds., *Police and Community Relations: A Sourcebook,* pp. 435–440. See also C. P. Corliss, *Guideposts to Reporting Spot News Happenings in the Los Angeles Megalopolis.* Printed by Butler Data Systems, Hawthorne, Calif., 1969.

14. For a series of articles of a more "nuts-and-bolts" nature regarding police-press relations, see "Guidelines" in *The Police Chief* 39, no. 3 March 1972): 62.

Chapter Nineteen

The Police and Their Political Relationships

In Chapter Four, we spoke of several interlocking social systems involving the police. We have already discussed the criminal justice system and the social institutional system. Now we will look at the political-governmental system.

In the first chapter of this text we said that, in democratic society, policing is a public, political function. This statement has implications inviting more explicit attention—another aim of this chapter.

What the police are, what they do, and what is expected of them, how well or how poorly they fulfill these expectations, what can be done to improve police services: these are, in considerable measure, political questions. They are also in some sense sociological, social psychological, and economic questions, depending on the eye of the beholder. Historically, however, policing has tended to be viewed primarily as a political institution, inextricably tied to the function of governing, to the executive responsibility for enforcement of laws enacted by legislatures and interpreted by courts. Given this orientation, it is surprising that police and community relations programs have devoted so little specific attention to the political aspects of policemanship.

Politics and the Police

One reason for this seeming oversight has undoubtedly been confusion from such slogans as "Take the police out of politics" or "The police must not play politics." If the slogans are interpreted to mean partisan political activities, or using a police department and police officers as a pawn of political machines and political bosses, or as instruments of political chicanery of one kind or another, then such slogans are quite sensible. To make a police agency part of a political spoils system exemplifies this meaning of political policing.

In another sense, however, the police have a perfectly legitimate, respectable, and indeed indispensable political role to play. Because of a public confusion about politics and the police, discussion of this respectable interpretation of the matter has been almost entirely avoided. This reluctance may trace back to some extent, to the use of the police by political regimes to enforce their own perpetuation of political power. This tyrannical use of police force has not been unusual in political history, and still happens today in so-called police states. However, it is time to stop thinking of the police and their political relationships as a hushed and clandestine activity.

With direct reference to police and community relations in the vein just mentioned, the well-known attorney, William M. Kunstler, has suggested the centrality of a political interpretation:

> You must start from the premise that the role of the policeman in any society, ancient Greece as well as modern New York City, is to preserve a non-political law and order.... So as long as we have government and we have to have policemen, we can only ask that they be non-political. Now, they are not non-political, which is the tragedy of it all. Policemen, like other people, are the victims of a system that utilizes them and other mechanisms to play political roles, to persecute people, not for the commission of crime, but because they are dangers to the community.... They find themselves, and I'm sure many don't want to be in that position, in the uncomfortable position of doing what they know in their hearts is wrong, morally wrong, ethically wrong, because it is the way to keep the job and do what they think society expects of them. And they are right. That is what society expects of them.
>
> So my basic complaint is not with policemen.... My real grievance is with the society that demands that police officers be, not upholders of law and order in the classical sense, but upholders of the political system, and opponents of any threat to that political system.[1]

This is a point of view that strikes at the essence of policing, understood as a *political* function. The question Kunstler leaves unanswered is how is it possible pragmatically, in a pluralistic democracy, for the police to be nonpolitical? We might just as well recommend that presidents, governors, and mayors should be nonpolitical. The key political question so far as the police are concerned is this: What does and what does not constitute legitimate, functional, publicly beneficial political activity by the police?

To ask this question is to call for some carefully drawn distinctions. And there is no readily available formula for doing so. Mostly, the distinctions must be hammered out in the crucible *of the political process itself,* but a few have been previously suggested. Politics, for instance, is not the same as government. Politics is the process by which power is acquired, transferred, and exercised upon others. John Pfiffner adds that politics is the process by which contesting forces vie for favorable outcomes on decisions. Thus, power (politics) and authority (government) are not identical. Nor are policy (the product) and politics (the means) synonymous.

The Role Question Again

Inescapably, this talk of distinctions takes us back to the questions of police role. As earlier implied, and as James Q. Wilson emphasizes repeatedly, the role question is at heart a *political* question. Police officials count votes, just as Supreme Court justices do. Consensus is a political phenomenon. Westley, Sterling, and others tell how police officers size up their reference groups and reach decisions to act this way rather than that way, depending upon how they weigh factors of influence and power in the community. We have quoted the British Royal Commission in its statement regarding the process of seeking and securing middle-ground positions when faced with alternative extremes. To survive as a police administrator requires deft political skills.

Wilson recognized early in his studies of the police that political arrangements made the choice between professionalism and fraternalism difficult, likewise the question of relative emphasis between the law enforcement role and the order maintenance role. He has pointed out also that prosecutors and courts are heavily influenced by political considerations and, as we have seen, are much involved in bargaining over charges and sentences.[2] These are thoughts that make patent nonsense of the simplistic observation that the police must be nonpolitical. Wilson puts it this way:

> The American police officer finds himself today on the grinding edge between the need to maintain his authority on the street and the increased community pressures against that authority. A police force may improve greatly because of professionalization, but if at the same time the popular image and authority of the police officer have deteriorated, the two changes may cancel each other out, producing no net gain in police morale and creating a continuing police problem. In order to maintain morale, the officer may have to rely increasingly on police doctrine, a perhaps exaggerated conception of the rightness of what he is doing, and a contempt for both the criminal and

hypocritical noncriminal elements of the population. Under such pressures, it is not surprising that many police officers have shown themselves amenable to extremist political positions. ["Police Morale, Reform and Citizen Respect," p. 161][3]

In the matter of the police role predicament, Wilson's is mainly a political analysis. In his consideration of three styles of policing (watchman, legalistic, and service), he states that the particular style that prevails in a particular community is not explicitly determined by community decisions, although a few of its aspects may be so determined. In Wilson's language, "the police are in all cases keenly sensitive to their political environment without in all cases being governed by it" (*Varieties of Police Behavior,* p. 230). He goes on to say that the police do not distinguish to any great extent among issues that are actually quite different in principle, whether it be a city manager's efforts to "reform" the department, a councilman's efforts to name a new deputy chief, or a civil rights organization's efforts to establish a civilian review board. All such issues are interpreted by policemen as a struggle by "outside forces" for control of the department.

Wilson's general conclusion is that understanding the political life of a community will not provide an adequate explanation of existing police policies. To a considerable extent, such policies are left to the police themselves. Many segments of the community apparently prefer not to support their interests unless a "crisis" develops that affects their particular interest. There may be public pressure for the police to "do something" about some problem. But *what* to do and *how* to do it is left to the police:

> ... police work is carried out under the influence of a *political culture* though not necessarily under day-to-day political direction.... with respect to police work—or at least its patrol functions—the prevailing political culture creates a "zone of indifference" within which the police are free to act as they see fit.
>
> The most important way in which political culture affects police behavior is through the choice of police administrator and the molding of the expectations that govern his role. [Ibid., p. 233][4]

In sum, Wilson's position is that the community ("political culture") influences law enforcement in a broad sense, but this influence is ordinarily indirect and indecisive. Many people feel that any kind of enlistment with the police spells trouble.

Styles of Political Policing

Even to mention "political policing" may be anathema in some circles. Having suggested, however, that there is a legitimate and necessary affiliation of police and politics, it may be possible to distinguish among several styles of political policing:

1. *Partisan*. The police "playing politics" in the narrow, *partisan* sense, using the police agency as part of a spoils system or as a tool of a political machine, etc. This is what is usually suggested by the term "political policing," with accompanying implications of corruption. The Wickersham Commission had this in mind when it spoke of "taking the police out of politics."

2. *Cultural*. A *cultural* style of political policing by enforcing local *mores* enshrined in ordinances or statutes, no matter what the law may be at a higher level. This is close to the interpretation of the police position that Kunstler evidently has in mind, that is, that the police are dupes to whatever the dominant political influence may be in a community, no matter how wrong it may be when judged by other standards. Styles 1 and 2 of political policing are often closely associated—"two horns of the same devil"—both strongly suggesting corruption as measured by professional criteria. Yet Wilson is not so sure that professionalism is in every way superior to what he calls "systems" policing (*The Police and Their Problems*).

3. *Fraternalistic*. The political power of police line organizations in direct political action, such as lobbying and what they call "job actions," including the union movement that has developed out of fraternalism. The caption *Blue Power* has become a label for it.[5]

4. *Administrative*. A police administrator playing a perfectly legitimate political role so that organizational goals in his department can be realized. It pertains to relationships with decision-makers in government: mayors, city managers, city councils, etc. It pertains to influencing public opinion so that important gains can be made in the quality of police work. We called this *community leadership* in an earlier discussion, and it is pertinent here. Not only is there nothing wrong with this type of political policing, it is integral to effective public administration.

Thus, we have four distinguishable types of police-political relationships, the first two of clearly questionable character, a third still very much in the testing stage, and a fourth seemingly beyond question. A closer look at the latter two may be useful.

Administrative Styles

A good example of the administrative style of political policing is described in Chapter Two of the *Task Force Report: The Police* of the 1966 President's Crime Commission. The Commission pointed to the increasing need for a deliberative planning process for developing policies to guide and control police officers in dealing with the wide variety of situations that require the exercise of some form of police authority. The Commission observed, however, that police administrators have been generally reluctant to develop policies for dealing with crime and potential crime situations. Several reasons for this were suggested, all with political implications (p. 17).

The Commission emphatically recommended that the police must assume a larger role in the development of law enforcement policies:

> The "administrative process" and administrative flexibility, expertise, and, most important, administrative responsibility are as necessary and as appropriate with respect to the regulation of deviant social behavior as they are with respect to other governmental regulatory activity. This seems perfectly obvious. Yet the common assumption has been that the police task is ministerial, this perhaps reflecting an assumption that administrative flexibility and "the rule of law" are inconsistent. This assumption seems invalid. The exercise of administrative discretion with appropriate legislative guidance and subject to appropriate review and control is likely to be more protective of basic rights than the routine, uncritical application by police of rules of law which are often necessarily vague or overgeneralized in their language. [Ibid., p. 18]

Mature participation of police, as a responsible administrative agency—along with prosecutors, legislatures, and courts—in the development and execution of enforcement policies is clearly political policing in a certain sense, and largely unprecedented. But few police executives would counter that the recommendation is ill-advised, inappropriate, or untimely. That it is a complex responsibility requiring widespread changes in police leadership, personnel, training, and organization is pointed out at some length by the Commission in such charts (ibid., p. 26) as that on the following page.

The Political Issue: Power

Government, the function of political institutions, is the exercise of power. The police are regarded by the community as an instrument of this power. The problem of police and community relations, simply stated, is that some people are dissatisfied with the manner in which the police use power. This defines the problem in political terms, but we should be mindful that there are also sociological, psychological, and other complementary definitions of the problem. The issue most controversial in police and community relations is that of police power and police restraint. As various observers have said, the means required to achieve police goals may conflict with conduct prescribed for the police as legal actors. Some argue for more power and freedom for the police to operate, in a loose construction of the law, as we have seen. Others argue for more control and restriction to compel the police to function under a strict construction of the law.[6]

The essential *political* issue, then, in the relations of the police with the policed in a democratic society is the balance of power and restraint. As Frank Remington has remarked, this issue is particularly difficult for governmental agencies such as the police, who find them-

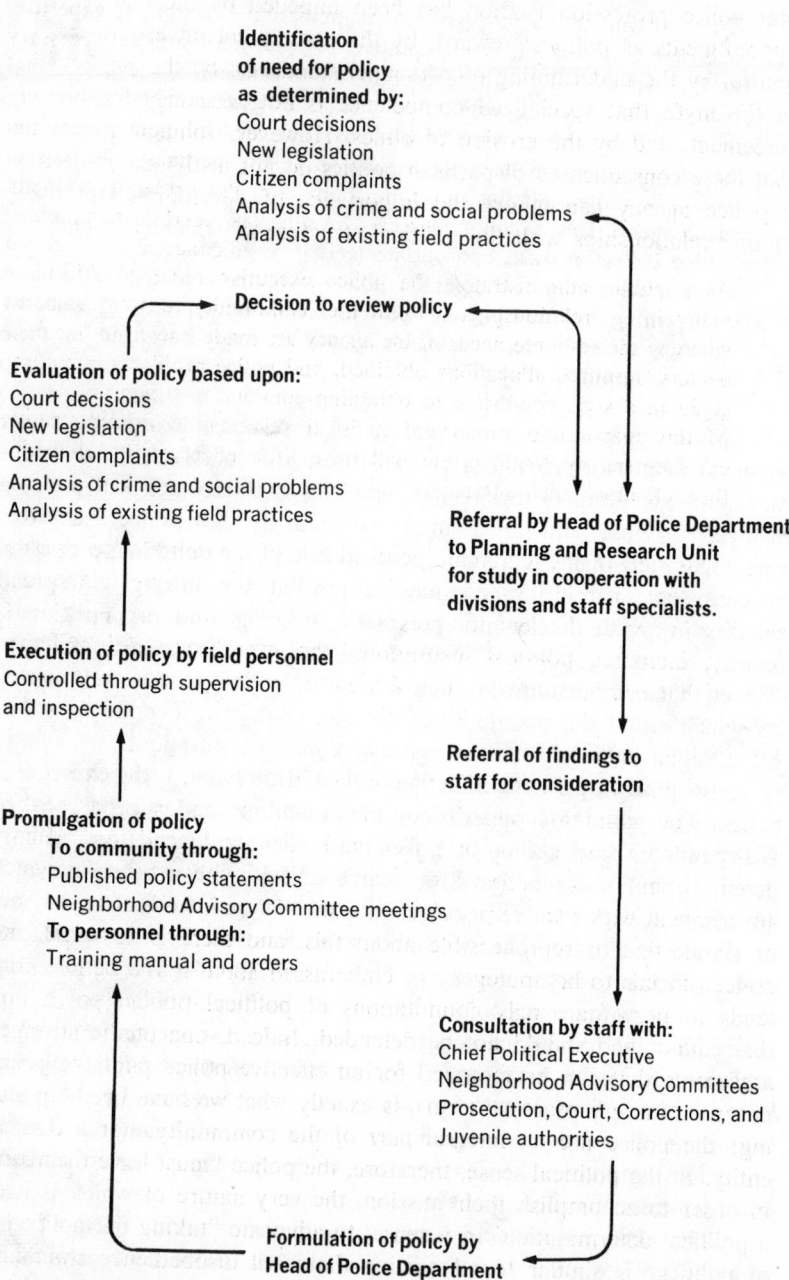

FORMULATION AND EXECUTION OF POLICE POLICY

**Identification
of need for policy
as determined by:**
Court decisions
New legislation
Citizen complaints
Analysis of crime and social problems
Analysis of existing field practices

Decision to review policy

Evaluation of policy based upon:
Court decisions
New legislation
Citizen complaints
Analysis of crime and social problems
Analysis of existing field practices

**Referral by Head of Police Department
to Planning and Research Unit
for study in cooperation with
divisions and staff specialists.**

Execution of policy by field personnel
Controlled through supervision
and inspection

**Referral of findings to
staff for consideration**

**Promulgation of policy
To community through:**
Published policy statements
Neighborhood Advisory Committee meetings
To personnel through:
Training manual and orders

Consultation by staff with:
Chief Political Executive
Neighborhood Advisory Committees
Prosecution, Court, Corrections, and
Juvenile authorities

**Formulation of policy by
Head of Police Department**

selves caught between those who desire change and those who resist change. ("Social Change, the Law and the Common Good," pp. 235, 236). Elaborating on the legitimacy of the police administrative-political role, Elmer H. Johnson ("Interrelatedness," p. 510) asserts that police professionalization has been impeded by the conferring of appointments as political reward, by the consequent uncertainty of job tenure, by the undermining of personnel standards, by the preservation of the myth that specialized competence is not necessary for law enforcement, and by the erosion of ethics. However, Johnson points out that these consequences of partisan politics do not justify the belief that a police agency can ignore the importance of developing and maintaining relationships with the political structure of which it is part:

> As a public administrator, the police executive must be skillful in maintaining relationships within the community power structure whereby the resource needs of his agency are made known to decision-makers, resource allocations obtained, and police problems communicated in a style conducive to obtaining community support. In terms of this responsible version of political skill, the limitation of law enforcement to "real" crime will have little effect toward reducing the difficulties encountered by the executive. [Ibid., pp. 510, 511]

This view of the legitimate political role of the police administrator is consistent with Johnson's emphasis upon the interrelatedness of police work with the activities of other social institutions in the community, including political institutions, that we discussed in Chapter Sixteen. One implication of such a view of police-political relations is recognizing that the possibility of change, of reform in policing and in the criminal justice system, is basically a *political* question.

In plain language, effective police (or public) administration depends on winning support for needed resources and needed changes. It depends on vote-getting in legislative bodies. It depends on "selling" people, often in competition for scarce dollars with other agencies of government, with relative priorities at stake. There is nothing mysterious or clandestine or reprehensible about this, and there is no reason for police officials to be apologetic or embarassed about it. To be defensive tends to perpetuate ugly connotations of political policing of a type that cannot and should not be defended. Indeed, one of the strongest arguments that can be mounted for an effective police public relations program, in very practical terms, is exactly what we have been suggesting: the police are an integral *part of* the community, not a discrete entity. In the political sense, therefore, the police "must have the votes" in order to accomplish their mission, the very nature of which is itself a political determination. In a sense, to advocate "taking the police out of politics" is similar to advocating that civil disobedience should be declared illegal. As the saying goes, "there's no way . . .!"

Several undercurrents in this discussion may be detected. One is Banton's distinction between police power and police authority. Chester I. Barnard (*The Functions of the Executive*, pp. 163–169) drew the same distinction when he said that "authority becomes viable only through the acceptance of those exposed to it." Another point is equally basic: empirically, politics and administration are inseparable.[7] Still another point: politics and power go together, remembering the definition of politics that was given in the opening paragraph of this chapter.[8] Floyd Hunter referred to power as a necessary function of society and defined it as the actions of some men going about the business of moving other men to act in relation to themselves or in relation to organic or inorganic things.[9] Power centers on decision making, said Hunter, and seeing to it that things get done that are deemed necessary to be done—"power functions" that are delegated to specific persons.

The Classical Theory of Police Organization

John Angell is interested in the translation of theories of power, politics and public administration to police organizations.[10] He observes that the structures of most modern American police organizations are rationalized, hierarchical arrangements that reflect the influence of classical organizational theory as delineated by Max Weber.[11] The salient features of these structures, Angell says, are these:

1. Formal structures are defined by a centralized hierarchy of authority.

2. Labor is divided into functional specialties.

3. Activities are conducted according to standardized operating procedures.

4. Career routes are well established and have a common entry point; promotions are based on impersonal evaluations by superiors.

5. Management is conducted through a monocratic system of routinized superior-subordinate relationships.

6. Employee status is directly related to their positions (jobs) and ranks.

Angell believes that these characteristics result in a firmly established, impersonal system in which most of the employees and clients are *powerless* to initiate changes or to arrest the system's motions. He raises serious questions on the adequacy of this bureaucratic model in the modern police agency. It creates problems, he contends, in police and community relations, in employee morale, and in communication and control—all of which is documented by the President's Crime Commission. The concern of police administrations for efficiency and economy (a basic goal of classical organization theory) has caused some lack of concern for certain side-effects detrimental to community relations. Moreover, Angell feels that classical organization concepts do not facilitate adequate flexibility in policy—with which to meet legitimate needs and values of particular subcultures or groups, for instance. Angell has another criticism, similar to a J. Q. Wilson point:

> Classical theory also supports police reformers who insist that police departments be isolated from politics. As police departments become more refined and move nearer their goal, they move further away from another basic goal of democracy—guaranteeing every citizen access to and influence with governmental agencies. Under a highly developed police bureaucracy, nearly all citizens view their police department as essentially beyond their understanding and control. Where the police department is a highly-developed, traditional bureaucracy, its structure and its philosophical underpinnings will eventually cause the organization to become socially irrelevant and ineffective. This situation, in turn, will have a profoundly damaging effect upon police and community relations.[12]

Angell argues further that the classical organization model appears to support a perpetual state of low morale among employees of bureaucracies. Weber himself condemned this aspect of bureaucracy. Angell points to increased police activism and the police unionization movement as indicative of this problem. He predicts that these are trends toward employee engagement in decision-making processes (widening the power base) that are unlikely to cease.

Another Angell argument against classical bureaucracy is its long-recognized problem of internal communication and control. The chief administrator seldom gets a true picture of what is going on in the department. The assumption that formal authority to command can force compliance from subordinates is everywhere being questioned today. As Chester Barnard put it, "authority rests with subordinates rather than with the supervisor."

The Environing System

Reiss and Bordua consider the "environing system" of the metropolitan police. They say that the central meaning of police authority itself is its ability to "manage" relationships. This is their description of police-community interaction in pragmatic, political terms:

> Directing traffic, investigating complaints, interrogation, arresting suspects, controlling mobs and crowds, urging prosecutors to press or drop charges, testifying in court, participating with (or battling, as the case may be) probation officers in juvenile court, presenting budget requests to the city council, pressing a case with the civil service commission, negotiating with civil rights groups, defense attorneys, reporters, irate citizens, business groups, other city services, and other police systems—even such an incomplete list indicates the probable values of a perspective that emphasizes transactions and

external relationships. The list also indicates something else of considerable significance. All of these transactions can be and often are antagonistic ones. ["Environment and Organization," p. 26]

Reiss and Bordua further reflect that modern metropolitan police agencies exist only because communities are legally organized. In effect, the police are called upon to *mediate* between the urban community and the legal system. The legal system is organized politically into larger or smaller, more or less centralized, units. Powers of government are separated or combined in various patterns of local, state, national units, and the police are organized accordingly.

This describes rather starkly the police-governmental (political) linkage. Some of the questions that we have discussed in earlier chapters have their foundation in this linkage: for example, the position of the police in the legal order, that is, their relation to prosecutors and the courts; police administrative strategies in manipulating the image of crime in the community and measurements of the "success" of the police; and problems of internal relations and morale in police agencies brought about by either or both of the factors just mentioned.

Reiss and Bordua conclude their analysis with a consideration of civil accountability, command, and control in police organizations, in a manner paralleling Angell's approach. They refer to police literature stressing command as the basis of control. In Weberian terms, the police department "as an order" is legitimated by the principle of command, with a correlative attitude required by those subject to it. Commitment to obedience, in this sense, is a sign of membership. The classical status reward is honor. Joining these segments of classical administrative theory, Reiss and Bordua emerge with this synthesis:

> In the case of the American municipality, police chiefs . . . are politically accountable officials who ordinarily stand or fall with the fortunes of their civilian superiors. . . . Given the often controversial nature of police work and the often irrational and unpredictable nature of political fortunes in municipal government, the American police chief who is responsible to a politically elected official comes close to the position of a "patrimonial bureaucrat," in Weber's terms. His tenure as chief, though not necessarily his tenure in the department, depends on continuing acceptability to the elected official(s). [Ibid., p. 52]

Given strict accountability [Reiss and Bordua continue] plus insecurity of tenure, we can expect a kind of obsession with command and a seemingly irrational emphasis on the twinned symbols of the visibility of the commander and the obedience of the force. Some of the rhetoric of command in the police literature likely arises from an attempt to protect the chief by the compulsive effort to overcontrol subordinates, almost any of whom can get him fired. This amounts to saying that as civil superiors increase the formal accountability of the police chief *without changing* the tenure features of the role, the increasing bureaucratization of the police stressed by J. Q. Wilson leads to the development of an organization animated by a principle of the commanding person. This "personalized subordination" to the hero chief can become an operating, if not a formal, principle of organization. [Ibid., p. 53]

Reiss and Bordua add that increased professionalization can be an accommodation to such a situation, aimed not at control of the force but at control of the mayor by changing the grounds of accountability. Perhaps it is difficult, they conclude, to have a professionalized police without having a professionalized mayor.

Relations Between Police and Local Government

The Reiss-directed University of Michigan study for the President's Crime Commission considered the police and their relations with local government and its legal system (Field Surveys III, Vol. 2, Sec. II, pp. 94–109). Police officers in the cities studied were asked about their views of the efforts of local government to deal with crime. Most officers did not believe that their local government had done much, although Chicago officers were far more supportive of the job that local government had done to deal with crime than were officers in Boston and Washington, D.C,

Four of every ten officers believed that local government had made it harder for the police to do their work. However, only 20 percent in Chicago believed this, while half the officers in Washington D.C. believed it, and 30 percent of Boston officers. The police officers complained that local government interfered with police powers and that officials were too critical of the police department.

The Hatch Act of 30 years ago, severely limiting the rights of Federal employees to engage in political activities, was subsequently copied at the state and local levels and applied to police officers, along with other governmental employees. But the Blue Power movement in recent years has challenged such restrictions on police political activity.[13] The history of the restrictions goes back many years, embedded in civil service reforms aimed at flagrant abuses arising from political patronage. The Hatch Act was a 1939 chapter in this history. Its coverage was expanded in 1940. Strict rules grew out of major scandals of the past. But by 1966, the appointment by Congress of a Commission on Political Activity of Government Personnel was a tipoff that the pendulum had begun to swing. Yet most police departments today still retain many restrictions on political activity by policemen.

In a recent survey conducted by the University of Wisconsin Extension, it was found that 89 percent of the middle-sized communities surveyed (37 cities responded) imposed some kind of restrictions on

the political activities of their police, as detailed in the following table
from "The Police and Partisan Politics" (Hamann and Becker):

Restrictions in Effect	*Percent*
No restrictions whatsoever	3
No political activity during working hours only	16
Cannot campaign for a candidate for *municipal* office on his own time	61
Cannot campaign for a candidate for *county* office on his own time	53
Cannot campaign for a candidate for *state* or *national* office on his own time	50
Cannot contribute to campaign funds for *municipal* candidates	45
Cannot contribute to campaign funds for *county* candidates	42
Cannot contribute to campaign funds for *state* or *national* candidates	39
Cannot engage in *any* political discussion	34
Cannot engage in political discussions on *local* matters	29
Cannot run for municipal office	50
Cannot run for county office	34
Cannot run for state or national office	29

The report points out that the restrictive rules were originally
created for a legitimate purpose. The report recommends that some
restrictions on the political activity of police officers should be retained,
and it explains at some length why this is deemed wise. However, the
report goes on to recommend some relaxation in rigid limitations of
police political activities, in the light of changing social conditions. A
compromise between two extremes appears to be the prudent course,
leaving the difficult task of spelling out specifics to local and state jurisdictions. There is no reason why police officers should be emasculated
citizens.

Fraternalistic Style

Our discussion so far has centered on the case for a legitimate,
inevitable, and socially desirable police administrative-political role, in
line with the fourth of the several styles of political policing that we
earlier identified. Our attention now turns to the third style, which we
labeled "fraternalism." While style four is mainly administrative, style
three pertains primarily to the political activities of police line organizations: Blue Power. The politicization of the police, in this sense, is a
phenomenon of increasing importance, and in some respects we would
say that it is as legitimate, as inevitable, and probably as desirable in the
long run as is style four of political policing. It is epitomized in the
police unionization movement that has grown out of fraternalism. Prob-

lems arise, however, when excesses occur in police activities of this nature; the difficulty is in varying notions of what constitutes "excess."

Jerome Skolnick has analyzed the political complexities of the police at some length (*The Politics of Protest,* pp. 201–217). The policeman in America, he says, is overworked, undertrained, underpaid, and undereducated. Moreover, his job is increasingly difficult, forcing him into the almost impossible position of repressing the demands of various groups for social and political change. In this role, he is unappreciated and at times despised. His difficulties are compounded by a view of social protest that gives little consideration to the effects of such factors as poverty and discrimination, and all but ignores the possibility of legitimate social discontent. This view invariably attributes mass protest to a conspiracy instead, promulgated by agitators, often called Communists, who mislead otherwise contented people. To the extent that this view exists among the police, it leaves them ill-prepared to understand or to deal with dissident groups.

Consequently, Skolnick avers, many police officers are increasingly frustrated, alienated, and angry. They are turning to militancy and political activism: Blue Power. They are protesting. Police slowdowns and other such actions ("blue flu"), often of questionable legality, have been directed toward material benefits, or changes in governmental policy ("take the handcuffs off the police"), or changes in internal organizational procedures. Direct police challenges to departmental and civic authority have followed recent urban disorders, and criticisms of the judiciary have escalated to "court-watching" by the police. What were once strictly or largely police fraternal associations have become more and more potent political organizations, more and more in the character of unions, more and more vociferous toward police management and municipal management on questions of power and control.

In short, the police are emerging as a self-conscious, independent political force. In many cities and states, the police lobby has become quite influential. Yet courts and police are expected to be neutral and nonpolitical, lest public confidence in the legal system be impaired. When Blue Power is coupled with police violence in handling mass protest, the projected image becomes a matter of grave concern for some elements of the citizenry. References to "a police state" become audible as illustrated by the following from W. H. Ferry:

> It is instructive to note the extent to which this power already is beyond the control of elected officials. This power appears more and more to reside in the police trade unions—the police benevolent and fraternal organizations. These unions are increasingly dictating to mayors and police commissioners what the police will and will not do: the weapons they will use, the circumstances under which they will use them, the methods to be employed with suspects or crowds. In many cities, the police are already in a state of near revolt against

their elected superiors, and this mood is encouraged by the police unions. It need scarcely be said that these unions are conservative and self-interested. These organizations naturally favor strongarm over non-violent methods, direct action against conciliation, station-house confessions to the laborious job of proving criminal acts, the judgment of the man on the beat over the judgment of his civilian superiors. . . . I hazard the opinion that these unions will prove the most intractable and dangerous to the general welfare of any in the nation's history.[14]

Ferry is not generally antiunion in his socio-political views. But he surely takes a strong position toward police unions—some may say too strong—and his is by no means a lone voice expressing concern—not so much about police unions *per se* as about manifestations of police power that provoke the ugly epithet "Police State."[15] As another example, Edgar Z. Friedenberg, professor of education and sociology at the State University of New York in Buffalo, wrote in *The Nation:*

. . . the law enforcement process is thought of as democratic, as more democratic than the law itself, since the courts are dominated by smooth-tongued lawyers, while the police represent—and indeed, act out—the anxieties and sentiments of the populace as well as, and often rather than, the commands of the law. Where the two are in conflict, the police remind individuals that they have overstepped the social norms. The victims may win on appeal, but it takes a decade and costs a fortune. Police action, rather than conviction in court, is the real sanction.

To criticize law enforcement as a social function, rather than to direct one's complaints to specific abuses, is therefore to challenge the democratic process itself. The socially acceptable response, instead, is to say that the law should be changed, but the police must be obeyed till it is. In practice, even this is more than an angry and hostile community will often tolerate. ["Hooked on Law Enforcement"]

Similar Views

In the same vein is the viewpoint expressed by Ed Cray, who has been associated for some years with the American Civil Liberties Union in Southern California:

From city to city, the authority of elected officials varies inversely with the control maintained by ranking police officers. . . . In the face of threats, real and imaginary, the police have openly girded themselves with a newfound armor—political influence, supported by public fear of rising crime rates and ghetto rebellion. . . . Law enforcement is testing its political muscle, emboldened by the easily sensed mood of a public demanding domestic tranquility at any price. The police claim they can provide instant peace of mind—the slogan is "law and order" and until their campaign collapses in futility, they will muster ever greater support. And with that support, the police will push even harder for complete control of law enforcement. ["The Politics of Blue Power"]

Many policemen react to such statements heatedly, accusing the authors of sharp-tongued extremism. Balanced perspective may be aided by recalling what retired New York City Police Inspector William P. Brown has said about the pressures that have moved the police toward "their own councils"—which we cited in an earlier chapter. In the same article, Brown wrote:

The police administrator . . . must ask the more difficult questions of how one deals with political realities, how one controls the police themselves in trying to effectuate a humane and yet practical policy of enforcement in such delicate areas as those involving race relations. ["Mirrors of Prejudice," p. 500]

While he was on leave from his position as an Indiana University associate professor of police administration, serving as Commissioner of Public Safety in Utica, New York, Hillard Trubitt analyzed the situation in a somewhat broader context in "Going by the Book." The police in a community, he said, are usually mirrors of the entire local government approach to city problems. It is true, he continued, that the police traditionally rely on old, established methodology and doctrine not geared to contemporary problems. But generally the police are no worse in this regard, and sometimes they are much better, than "their parent governmental entities" in their failure "to perceive the difference between form and substance." Trubitt maintained that the essential problem is an overregard for procedural regularity and not enough regard for the primary objectives. As he put it, "the goal of police service is peace and order, not bureaucratic game playing."[16]

The politicization of the police is not confined to the organizational citadels so often associated with it in the popular mind: the Fraternal Order of Police, the Policemens' Benevolent Association, and the like. Racial and ethnic police organizations such as the Guardians Society have also become more political-power minded, though they were this to some extent initially, by their very rationale. Political and social polarization on racial or ethnic grounds exists *within* big city police forces—hardly a startling statement. As a matter of fact, some think that as the numbers of black and other minority policemen grow, internal tensions within urban police agencies will be exacerbated. While it is difficult to imagine that in the near future such organizations as the Guardians will gain the membership strength to become bargaining agents, unquestionably they will make their political influence increasingly felt.[17]

This minority grouping within the police world evidences the same political *savoir-faire* observable in the Congressional Black Caucus, comprising thirteen black members, all Democrats, of the House of Representatives in the 92nd Congress. A few years ago, such a development would have been unthinkable. Washington *Post* reporter William Raspberry commented that this Black Caucus represented something truly special and unprecedented in the realm of national politics. It was, he said, a recognition that black people face some rather special problems, for which they should have "special interest" representation. At the same time, however, it was also a recognition that to work for the best interests of black people does not necessitate working *against* the best interests of white people. A Congressional Black Caucus, or black mayors of large cities, require political coalitions with whites in order to build the consensus that makes social problem-solving possible. Chicano political and social action organizations have also multiplied rapidly in recent years.

The Conservative Side

How sharp the political cleavages are within police ranks was reflected in the 1971 fifth anniversary issue of a publication of the American Federation of Police, headquartered in Florida, which describes itself as a national, fraternal association of law enforcement officers. The AFP is not a union, it insists, but "a dynamic force in professional law enforcement . . . dedicated to pursuing higher standards for lawmen through legal means, not strikes." The goals of the AFP for 1971–73 include:

1. Urging that all appointments as Chief of Police be nonpolitical, protected by civil service status in all cases.

2. A national standard for the selection and training of all police officers, with minimum pay required, tied to the cost-of-living index.

3. A review of the billions being spent by "administrators" in crime fighting, to be sure the funds are used as Congress intended. Pay increases for patrolmen should bring minimum wages to $12,000 in 1971, to $13,200 by 1972, and to $15,000 by 1973.

4. An increase in the police forces of all cities that will meet the alarming crime rate. De-emphasize the waste represented by "public or community relations" so that enforcement and crime prevention can return as the main duties of a police department, since criminals cannot be stopped with the game of "musical chairs" now called "community relations."

This is an appealing platform for many policemen, yet one that would cause some officers to seek organizational affiliation elsewhere. Policemen may be no more politically monolithic today than any other occupational group. Skolnick has pointed to conservatism as the dominant political and emotional persuasion of the police. In the mid-sixties, there were allegations that the John Birch Society had strong support and sympathy among the police. Various observers including Seymour Martin Lipset, as we noted earlier, have suggested a strong right-wing "tilt" in police circles. On social and political issues, Watson and Sterling (*Police and Their Opinions,* pp. 78–85) found that the police do tend somewhat toward a conservative position, but it is by no means as consistent, as extreme, nor as "all-of-a-mind" as some observers have suggested. Lipset also makes this point:

> In evaluating the disposition of the police to participate in the radical right, it is important to note that only a minority of the police are involved in most communities. Most police, though relatively conservative and conventional, are normally more concerned with the politics of collective bargaining, with getting more for themselves, than with the politics of right-wing extremism. ["Why Police Hate Liberals," p. 81]

If we grant the apparent propensity of the police to support right-wing political activities and to opt for status quo conservatism, it should be kept in mind that any such generalized description of so large an occupational group is subject to the perils of any generalization. Many policemen do not fit the description, and one might even hazard the prediction that the socio-political views of police officers in the future will be increasingly varied.

Police and Unionism

The movement of the police to form unions has been part of the broader surge of unionization of municipal employees. Police unions existed prior to 1960, but recent years have witnessed their unprecedented growth, coupled with increased legal recognition of their right to exist and to bargain collectively. Hugh O'Neill of Columbia University writes:

> One of the most important developments on the urban political scene over the last decade has been the rapidly increasing strength and militancy of municipal employee unions. These organizations have become new centers of power in the cities. They have used their power to influence not only the terms and conditions of employment, but major policy decisions as well. And with increasing frequency they have demonstrated the effectiveness of their "ultimate weapon," the disruption of vital municipal services.[18]

Historically, the American Federation of Labor had not been eager to organize police unions because the police were considered enemies of organized labor. The AFL changed this policy in 1919, probably influenced by the success of British police unions. The Boston police strike occurred in September, 1919, and was broken by Massachusetts Governor Calvin Coolidge and the troops he summoned. For a time, police unionism was thereby wiped out. Then a period of several decades followed when police organization assumed the form of benevolent and social societies; but even these were prohibited in some places.

With the Roosevelt era, the American Federation of State, County, and Municipal Employees (AFSCME) came into being. Police unionism still remained dormant, however, until the 1940s. By 1944, the AFSCME was reporting locals, made up entirely of policemen, organized in 28 cities. By 1946, this had become 49 locals, but still represented only a minor number of police departments. In the 1950s, public employee unions, plagued by the Communist bugaboo, went through a period of growing pains. But the 1960s brought a great surge in the unionization of public employees.

Late in the sixties, an AFL-CIO committee recommended that a national police union be chartered. In November, 1969, representatives of police organizations from 12 cities met in Omaha and drafted a constitution for the International Brotherhood of Police Officers. This constitution contained a no-strike clause, but as one official of the new group remarked, "a job action is not a strike" (*The New York Times,* November 3, 1969).

The AFL-CIO Executive Council was in no hurry to decide whether to charter the new union. The president of the National Fraternal Order of Police, which does not see itself as a union although it negotiates contracts, declared that policemen should not be permitted to join a union. President George Meany of the AFL-CIO announced that the labor federation would not issue a charter for a policemen's union unless there was a showing of widespread national interest. But the Omaha-drafted constitution of the fledgling organization was nonetheless approved by 75 delegates attending a May, 1970 convention in Washington. Still another organization, the International Conference of Police Associations, met in St. Louis in December, 1970, with leaders of 135 local police associations attending. In addition, there were rumors that the Teamsters might decide to enter the police unionization field, which seemed to be rapidly assuming the character of an Hobbesian "war of all against all."

Public employee unions generally have become more aggressive in recent years, the teacher unions for example. Strikes of independent police organizations occurred in Vallejo, California, in 1967 and Youngstown, Ohio in 1968. And "Blue Flu" became a common "job action." The six-day New York City police strike of January, 1971 further dramatized the new aggressiveness, with firemen and sanitation workers poised to join hands with the police "wildcatters." It signalled a bold, new willingness of municipal workers to turn to their ultimate weapon, graphically punctuating the fiscal predicament of many a metropolis as well as sharp differences among police union members, in strategy and tactics. O'Neill adds a significant factor:

> The final source of aggressiveness among municipal unions that might be mentioned is the generally militant attitude that in the 1960's seemed to be part of the national character. When acts of civil disobedience become everyday occurrences, the fact that public employee strikes are illegal is not enough to prevent them. When society as a whole becomes politicized, public employees become willing to take advantage of their monopoly in the provision of vital public services to achieve political ends that appear to them every bit as vital. This development has added a new and difficult dimension to the business of governing cities.[19]

With the advent of the 1970s, several points seemed to clear with respect to the unionization of public employees:

1. Collective bargaining in public service was an established institution.

2. Strikes by public employees seemed less and less earth-shaking.

3. State regulatory laws, such as the so-called Taylor Law in New York State, designed "to protect the public against the disruption of vital public services by illegal strikes, while at the same time protecting the rights of public employees," appeared to make grievance arbitration commonplace while at the same time reducing the instances of work stoppage.[20]

4. Federal statutes might eventually cover all public employees, allowing for state and local variations.

5. Successful adjustments were being discovered between civil service and collective bargaining.

6. Public administration in this new era required unprecedented professional competence.[21]

In a refreshing article that appeared in *The Police Chief* in mid-1971, Dayton (Ohio) Chief of Police Robert Igleburger and his associate, John Angell, asserted that police administrative opposition to police unions had become pointless ("Dealing With Police Unions"). Police executives are faced, they said, with the necessity of dealing with such organizations in good faith. They advocate a flexible managerial philosophy and skills, illustrated by the systems concepts of Talcott Parsons and Edward Shils (*Toward A General Theory of Action*). This theory portrays an organization as a cluster of interacting positions and roles, defined by reciprocal behavior expectations. The essential task of the administrator is the intermediary role, to facilitate role consensus among supervisors, middle managers, the employee union, and the city administration.

Emphasis in such an intermediary role is upon the necessity for flexibility, willingness to modify and redefine position, and to consider alternatives. In short, the administrative role—according to this theory—requires positive *political* skills and strategies. Igleburger and Angell bring this principle to bear upon the specifics of policy development, staff development, the establishment of an information system inside and outside of the department, the setting in motion of truly effective grievance procedures, the process of negotiation in itself, and the implementation of the contract after a settlement has been reached. Their article concludes on this note:

> In dealing with the union, the administrator must insure his employees and their union fair treatment and due process, but he must also be concerned about protecting the interests of citizens, legislators, his supervisors, and his managers. To adequately fulfill these obligations, the chief must view himself as an intermediary between these various significant groups and individuals who are concerned with the outcome of the collective bargaining process. A prerequisite to the competent fulfillment of this position is a realistic approach to collective negotiations through the use of rational techniques and strategies.[22]

The techniques and strategies of police unionization and politicization in recent years have been well described by various authors.[23]

Neighborhood Government

In Chapter Fifteen, we discussed the question of neighborhood and community control of the police, a discussion that is relevant in the context of our discussion in this chapter. The basic issue is how to govern the urban monstrosity. Is a New York City or a Los Angeles governable under today's conditions? How is big-city government to be made responsive to the needs of the governed? Whose police department (or school system) is it, fundamentally? Accountability and credibility are the current code words.

Such questions are clearly political. A public administrator might say that the big puzzle is how to decentralize functions or services while maintaining necessarily centralized authority—which is the way James Q. Wilson states it. Neighborhood meetings in which mayors, city managers, and councilmen "go out to the boondocks" to "mix with grassroots people" have become commonplace. Neighborhood advisory groups for various municipal departments—schools, police, parks, sanitation, and others—are no longer novel. Pertinent questions to ask regarding such groups are, Who sets them up? Who determines their membership? Who belongs, and whom do the members represent? What real power or influence do they have?

The key idea is *control*—political control. And in a democratic society, political control is a relative thing, with many built-in safeguards against its becoming absolute. This means that political control is divisible: it comes down to such questions as how much, by whom, and subject to what review. In the typical metropolis, a maze of governmental boundaries criss-cross the city—police districts, school districts, sanitation districts, health, zoning, planning, fire—all different—some political, some administrative, some simply historical. This is further complicated by recent Model Cities areas, urban renewal sections, task force zones, economic opportunity pilot neighborhoods, and what have you.

How far should we go with neighborhood government in large cities? If government becomes more splintered and fragmented than it already is, what about the efficiency of its "delivery system," its services to its clients? If 62 or 122 neighborhood police departments were to be created in New York City, how would they cope with crime and disorder that are not so neatly arranged? It would seem that if the desired goal is more citizen participation in decision-making and policy-setting in a police department or a school system ("responsiveness"), complete administrative autonomy at the neighborhood level is not the best way to achieve it. In fact, administrative trends in police work today run counter to such fragmentation.

Citizens should certainly play a stronger role in influencing police organizational goals, policies, and procedures. But because police work is increasingly a professional art calling for special training, experience, and knowledge, important distinctions must be drawn between the police role and the citizen role in the partnership we have been emphasizing. Granting that "community control" is being adversely exploited as a slogan in social revolution today, it may be that its best argument is not in the possibility that it may really happen—although the Berkeley, California referendum in April, 1971, was certainly instructive in this regard but in the reminder that change of some sort is needed in present structures and ways of doing things. Somehow these social structures, exemplified by police departments and school systems, must be "tuned in" to a greater extent than they have been to all segments of the community they serve. Bureaucracies tend to avoid making "controversial" decisions, if possible; more localized accountability means that agencies will be watched more closely and their actions will, therefore, be more responsive to community needs.

John Angell has shown that the major pragmatic question for a police administrator, from a professional and ethical standpoint, is to whom or to what should he be responsive. Angell analyzes police administrative responsiveness to judicial influences, public influences, legislative influences, and organizational influences and suggests some guidelines for administrative survival in each of these references:

> Responsiveness in the final analysis is an expected and legitimate means of accumulating and maintaining power in a democratic society, and a police administrator must learn to use it effectively. What does it matter if he organizes his area of responsibility in perfect com-

pliance with the classical theory [Weberian], if in the process he does not properly respond to the public and its values and, as a result, loses its confidence and support? He may be successful when evaluated in the light of classical organizational theory, and yet a failure when evaluated on his ability to meet public expectations. These latter criteria may have the most important effect on his ability to remain in his position. ["Responsiveness—An Obligation"][24]

Justice and Politics

In Study 1 (Part Four) of *Studies* by Radelet and Reed, we have outlined the typical practices and suggested some of the problems of the juvenile justice system. The problems of the juvenile justice system[25] are almost overwhelming, and at least one recent work has defined the issue in unequivocal political terms, thereby illustrating what we seek to convey:

> A central difficulty is that of introducing into law enforcement and the administration of justice a real, not hypothetical, balance of power between individuals who are on the receiving end of justice and the officials who administer it. The crucial task will be that of building a public policy which both recognizes and understands the inherent conflicts of interest between those groups and collectivities in society against which the law is enforced and those in whose name and for whose benefit it is enforced. [Martin, Fitzpatrick, and Gould *The Analysis of Delinquent Behavior*]

One of the authors of the foregoing extract, John Martin of Fordham University, presents the same thesis in another publication (*Toward a Political Definition of Juvenile Delinquency*). The real problem, he says, lies in the very way the institutions of the juvenile justice system are organized, in the specification of their goals, and in the manner in which they function. Far more is entailed than crowded court calendars, huge caseloads, legally trained judges, the lack of trained caseworkers, and lack of money. Martin writes:

> Much more crucial to a fuller understanding of the situation is an appreciation of the narrow ideological and theoretical foundation upon which the juvenile justice apparatus rests. The system is grossly conservative in that it accepts little or no active responsibility for winning social justice for the children with whom it deals. It remains wedded to the idea that what is wrong in delinquency is limited to that which is presumed to be wrong with the youngster himself or with his family. [Ibid., pp. 1, 2]

While Martin is speaking in a particular way of the juvenile justice system, his language seems to encourage the same description of the criminal justice system in general:

... far deeper organizational difficulties also exist which may prove to be far more significant than any of its other characteristics for understanding the unfairness and injustice which taint the system. Essentially the problem boils down to this: When decisions about the lives and careers of powerless people and their children are made by a large and remote bureaucratic system, which by design has made very little provision for establishing a balance of power between the two camps, unfairness and injustice inevitably follow. [Ibid., p. 2][26]

Martin is not content with generalized criticism. He examines specifically what he perceives as the central imbalance of power inherent in the system. He recognizes and documents the point that sociopolitical power has long been acknowledged as a useful line of analysis in describing delinquency. But he contends that it has not been expressed emphatically enough in recent treatises, which have tended to stress an *order model* of society, as distinct from a *conflict model*. Martin asserts that perhaps the outstanding characteristic of the juvenile justice system is that it is constructed on order model lines, reinforced by the ideology, theory, and treatment ideals of the mental hygiene movement, "with scarcely a thought given to the consequences of the political imbalances which may flow from such arrangements."

If the issue is, as Martin argues, essentially political, then the remedies must also be politically realistic: the vote, the ability to use the vote in an organized manner, and the ability of groups to influence political decision-making processes. Historically in the United States, the Irish and the Italians—to mention two ethnic examples—have demonstrated how political power can be exercised effectively. The black and Spanish-speaking groups are showing signs of learning this lesson, although with some handicaps that earlier "newcomers" did not have. (The Indians on Alcatraz knew the technique but are hardly newcomers!) In any case, the common ground in political terms between Martin's conception of powerlessness as it relates to the justice system, and the typical analysis of powerlessness as it pertains to racial and ethnic injustice is noteworthy. To illustrate this point, take the Stokely Carmichael-Charles Hamilton delineation of the necessary preconditions for a successful political coalition (*Black Power*):

1. The recognition by the interested parties of their respective self-interests.

2. The mutual belief that each party stands to strengthen its self-interests by joining with others.

3. The acceptance of the fact that each party has its own independent base of power and does not depend for ultimate decision-making on a force outside itself.

4. The realization that the coalition deals with specific and identifiable, instead of general and vague, goals.

The common ground should not be startling. The politically powerless, both in Martin's terms and in the terms of Carmichael and Hamilton, are predominantly the same people. What we have done is merely to lace together, in stark political terms, the threads of our discussion in several earlier chapters.

Freedom and Order

In the same fashion, it may be useful to tighten the issue by pulling together some further strands of prior study. In the rhetoric of political philosophy, the fundamental issue is individual liberty versus collective security, the eternal freedom-and-order seesaw. To be concrete about it, we may cite a recent commentary by the syndicated newspaper columnist, Sydney Harris. He holds that the most dangerous and widespread fallacy of our time has been successfully prompted by the advocates of "police power." They have persuaded the public, Harris feels, that the "effectiveness" of law enforcement increases as "due process of law" is diminished.

Harris points out that this is not true, has never been true, and can never be true. The real effectiveness of law enforcement, he continues, depends upon two factors only: the degree to which the public respects the law, and the degree to which law enforcement officers perform their duties fairly and honestly. Crime rates, he says, are everywhere lowest where these two conditions obtain, and highest where they do not:

> Crime is lowest in those countries where the public knows that the police are not corrupt or the agents of political forces; where the administration of justice is swift, certain, and equitable; where police and prosecutors are not permitted to conspire in the withholding of evidence unfavorable to their case; where the poor defendant has as much pre-trial protection as the rich one.

> And crime is highest—as in the U.S.—where the opposite conditions are rife: where the police are regarded with suspicion and distrust; where the administration of justice is slow, capricious, and weighted heavily against the poor and the ignorant; where prosecutors are more concerned with "making a record" than representing the people; and where defendants who cannot make excessive bail are kept locked up for months. ["Police Power Not the Answer"]

Some may prefer Jerome Hall's formulation of it:

> This general problem has sometimes been formulated in terms of an *opposition* of values—security *versus* civil liberty. On the surface, at least, it may seem persuasive that if any and all controls and methods of securing evidence are used, order and security can be more effectively preserved. So, too, at first blush it seems almost axiomatic that

the exercise of liberty necessarily involves the risk of disorder. But if the inquiry is considered not abstractly, but with reference to our society, opposing security to liberty is irrelevant. Harsh methods of control and democracy are incompatible, so that the question becomes simply the survival of democratic society. Thus, the basic postulate: A democracy, like all other societies, needs order and security; but it also and equally requires civil liberty. ["Security and Civil Liberty"]

Our entire criminal justice system is a testing ground for the tension that must be maintained between freedom and order. It is not the only such testing ground, but the issue arises explicitly in rules applied to persons accused of crime and those "accused" of mental illness. The boldest statement of the case is that letting a murderer go unpunished is better than risking a socio-legal structure under which an innocent man may lose his freedom.[27] Concern is sometimes expressed that the protection of individual freedom may have come to outweigh the common good.

For example, Professor Fred Inbau of the Northwestern University Law School said this in 1961, and has frequently said the same thing since:

> We are not only neglecting to take adequate measures against the criminal element; we are actually facilitating their activities in the form of what I wish to refer to as "turn 'em loose" court decisions and legislation. To be sure, such decisions and legislation are not avowedly for the purpose of lending aid and comfort to the criminal element, but the effect is the same. It is all being done in the name of "individual civil liberties." ... We can't have "domestic tranquility" and "promote the general welfare" as prescribed in the Preamble to the Constitution when all the concern is upon "individual civil liberties." ... Individual civil liberties, considered apart from their relationship to public safety and security, are like labels on empty bottles. ["Public Safety v. Individual Liberties"]

Professor Inbau was speaking to the annual conference of the National District Attorney's Association. Addressing the same organization ten years later, Attorney General John Mitchell said:

> Thirty-seven years ago, Mr. Justice Benjamin Cardozo wrote an opinion which contained a memorable warning: "Justice," he said "though due to the accused, is due to the accuser also. The concept of fairness must not be strained till it is narrowed to a filament. We are to keep the balance true."

> Had this warning been more widely heeded, we would not be facing today a serious imbalance in the scales of justice. For as most of you are painfully aware, a preoccupation with fairness for the accused has done violence to fairness for the accuser. In the process, fairness as a concept has often been strained to a meaningless shred.[28]

A good way to sharpen one's perspective on the fundamental issue is to hear a different drummer. Here, then, is what former Attorney General Ramsey Clark has written on the matter; bear in mind that the issue is definitely not Republican versus Democrat:

> The dialogue over the proper limits of police action and barely relevant court rulings consumes most of the emotion and much of the energy that could be constructively used to strengthen the system of criminal justice. . . . The resulting diversion of attention, emotionalization of concern and polarization of attitude damage the system of criminal justice. Those who . . . protest their willingness—even desire— to sacrifice freedom on the altar of order add immeasurably to the burdens of achieving excellence in the performance of criminal justice agencies and commitment to eradication of the underlying causes of crime.

> There is no conflict [Clark concludes] between liberty and safety. We will have both, or neither. You cannot purchase security at the price of freedom, because freedom is essential to human dignity and crime flows from acts that demean the individual. We can enlarge both liberty and safety if we turn from repressiveness, recognize the causes of crime and move constructively. . . . The government of a people who would be free of crime must always act fairly, with integrity and justice. [*Crime in America,* pp. 251–254]

Peter Schrag, in an editorial in *The Saturday Review,* summarizes our view of the issue:

> . . . too many national politicians have welcomed the confusion between dissent and crime, and . . . through the crime issue, they have launched a coordinated and consistent assault, not on thieves, rapists and murderers, but on minorities, political critics, and the weakest individuals in the society. The target is social and cultural deviance, not criminality. . . . At the same time, disregard of the more fundamental causes of disorder and injustice is likely to exacerbate "crime" and produce pressure for still more repressive laws. The failure of the nation to support the most hysterical politicians of law and order in 1970 provides what may be the last and best opportunity for a reasonable discussion of the issues. If not, it could be the fire next time. ["The Law-and-Order Issue"]

James Reston of *The New York Times* refers to the security and freedom relationship as "an old cat and dog battle." In the clash of great principles of government, he writes, the ultimate answers emerge from human judgments—"all neither wholly false nor wholly true." The actors change in this ancient drama, from Jefferson versus Hamilton to the *New York Times* or the Columbia Broadcasting System versus the Pentagon or the Attorney General of the United States. The conflict seldom presents a clear-cut choice between what is right and what is wrong. More frequently, the choice is between "two honest but violently conflicting views about what would best serve the national interest," as Reston phrases it, to which we would add: . . . or what seems best to meet the demands of individual conscience or conviction.

Neither freedom nor security (order) can be absolute. As Clark says, these principles are interdependent in the service of justice. The art of governing in a democratic society, he argues, involves judgments that must be made. In theory, in any given judgment, voting produces two positions: winners and losers. In actuality, the process requires compromise, negotiation, accommodation, bargaining, coalitions, settling for part of the loaf, and all such strategies and tactics for achieving political consensus.

True, we "hammer out" decisions through processes that are sometimes brutal, sometimes contrived or manipulated, and more often than not inefficient. And we have reason to speak of "dirty politics." But political processes in the free society, with their goal of consensus in government, accurately reflect human relations. As in the family or in international relations, it is consensus that keeps things running. How to achieve it by means which weigh all views of an issue, while yet ultimately submitting to the necessity for decision-making, represents the true test of whether we can manage somehow to keep things running.

James MacGregor Burns decries the tendency to embrace "the curious notion that the goal of democratic politics is agreement, adjustment, harmony, unity." He sees the goal as that of locating disagreement. Writing in *The New York Times,* he says:

> For the ultimate tragedy of bipartisanship is the erosion of responsibility. Leaders compromise on policies rather than clarifying the alternatives. They claim to represent some fuzzy national interest rather than group interests or party factions. In seeking to represent everyone, the government may end up representing none. . . .
>
> Parties should divide over specific goals and principles. They should present sharper alternatives to the electorate, both in the platforms they frame and the candidates they offer. The opposition should oppose—not blindly oppose, but search for the areas of disagreement. The more the parties disagree over major issues, the more chance we have of achieving "government by the people." ["Consensus Politics? Not on Your Life"]

Notes to Chapter Nineteen

1. William M. Kunstler, speaking in New York City to a seminar of black and Puerto Rican policemen, sponsored by the National Conference of Christians and Jews. Quoted in *The Hot Line* (monthly publication of NCCJ), May 1971, pp. 4, 5.

2. James Q. Wilson, "The Police and Their Problems"; *Varieties of Police Behavior;* "Police Morale, Reform and Citizen Respect," p. 159.

3. See also, by the same author, *City Politics and Public Policy.*

4. An intriguing study of the politics in "the care and feeding" of big-city police administrators is provided in the New York City situation at any given time in recent years. As an example, one might select the circumstances surrounding the sudden and unexplained resignation in September 1970 of Police Commissioner Howard R. Leary (to take a civil position at a comparable salary), and his subsequent replacement by Patrick V. Murphy. From the mayor to the Patrolmen's Benevolent Association, the general reaction was "amazement" at Commissioner Leary's abrupt action. There seemed to be general agreement that he had been doing a good job in the vortex of great turbulence. Question: Were his reasons for quitting really so mysterious? What does an honest administrator do, in the face of seemingly overwhelming counterpressure?

    The point here is not to resurrect yesterday's police political cadavers, but merely to underscore Wilson's thought regarding police administrators and to cite one "case experience" among many possibilities for study by those interested in politics in the metropolis and its impact on police administration. Subsequent developments in New York City, such as the administrative actions of Police Commissioner Murphy and the findings of the Knapp Commission—and the reactions of the Patrolmen's Benevolent Association thereto—have further dramatized the political dynamics of police work.

5. See the President's Crime Commission *Task Force Report: The Police,* chap. 7, pp. 208–215. See also Study 4 (Part 4), "Blue Power," in Radelet and Reed, *Studies.*

6. Speaking on the topic "Police Education and Training" at a symposium at Tufts University on the subject of Law and Disorder, Professor Robert Sheehan of Northeastern University's Law Enforcement faculty said: "There has . . . been a traditional political resistance to educating the police. The root of this resistance lies deeply imbedded in what seems to me to be a prevailing, but rarely stated, political attitude that if the police are encouraged to become professional, and thus are made more effective, they will become a much less controllable arm of the executive branch of government and hence less amenable to the interests of political influence that almost always lead to partial rather than impartial enforcement of the law." Quoted in *Atlantic Monthly,* March 1969, p. 130.) A highly recommended reference is Morris and Hawkins, *The Honest Politician's Guide to Crime Control.*

7. Herbert A. Simon, *Administrative Behavior.* See also Mailick and Van Ness, eds., *Concepts and Issues in Administrative Behavior.*

8. Pfiffner and Sherwood, *Administrative Organization.*

9. Floyd Hunter, *Community Power Structure.* See also C. Wright Mills, *The Power Elite.*

10. John E. Angell, "Toward an Alternative to the Classical Police Organizational Arrangements: A Democratic Model." Unpublished monograph, School of Criminal Justice, Michigan State University, 1970.

11. See Max Weber, *Essays in Sociology.* Also Reinhard Bendix, *Max Weber: An Intellectual Portrait.*

12. Angell, "Toward an Alternative." See also Alan A. Atshuler, *Community Control;* and Milton Kotler, *Neighborhood Government.*

13. The constitutionality of a New York State law prohibiting policemen from engaging in political activities was challenged in the State Supreme Court by the Nassau County Patrolmen's Benevolent Association in the spring of 1969—another "sign of the times."

14. W. H. Ferry, "The Police State, American Mode."

15. See, for example, William W. Turner, *The Police Establishment;* and Ed Cray, *The Big Blue Line.*

16. See also Dye and Hawkins, eds., *Politics in the Metropolis.*

17. At a Philadelphia meeting in June 1971, the National Council of Police Societies, an organization representing 25,000 black policemen, voted to oppose using black officers as undercover agents to investigate politically oriented cases in black neighborhoods. The 220 delegates from 15 cities also agreed to support the formation of civilian police review boards and pledged to take action against any law enforcement officer who abuses any citizen. The organization also voted to encourage at least two years of college education for policemen, to favor human relations training for all police officers, and to oppose the indiscriminate use of stop-and-frisk and preventive detention laws. (As reported by the Associated Press, June 16, 1971.) See Alex Poinsett, "The Dilemma of the Black Policeman."

18. Hugh O'Neill, "The Growth of Municipal Employee Unions." A one-day strike in June 1971 of New York City bridgemen and some 6000 other municipal workers was referred to by a union official as the "biggest, sloppiest, nastiest" strike in the city's history.

19. O'Neill, p. 13. James Reston, writing in *The New York Times* (June 9, 1971), suggested that the strikes by municipal workers illustrated the utter fragility of the modern city. There are now, he said, about 13,000,-000 people in the United States working for the government at some level —almost 18 percent of the total work force. When force is used by public service workers to achieve their ends, it can paralyze an entire city. Reston argues that this is arbitrary power, the very thing unions were established to oppose in management. He quotes Edmund Burke:

> Men are qualified for civil liberty in exact proportion to their disposition to put moral chains upon their own appetites. Society cannot exist unless a controlling power upon will and appetite be placed somewhere, and the less of it there is within, the more there must be

without. It is ordained in the eternal constitution of things, that men of intemperate minds cannot be free. Their passions forge their fetters.

20. That the public employee unionization movement (and a countermovement to protect the public interest) is not confined to the United States was reflected by a new Swedish law in March 1971, which forced the end of a strike by key civil servants that had been under way since February 1. Parliament ordered all strikers to return to work and barred all strikes in Sweden for six weeks in order to give Government mediators a new chance to obtain settlements of wage disputes. Labor leaders saw it as an ominous sign for future labor relations. (*U.S. News & World Report,* March 22, 1971, p. 90.)

Pennsylvania has three public employee statutes on its books. One law authorizes bargaining and grants a limited right to strike to all public employees of the state, its counties and municipalities—except policemen and firemen. A second measure grants bargaining rights to municipal police and firemen, and also provides compulsory, binding arbitration of impasses. A third (and similar) statute covers municipal transit authority employees.

Conferences, seminars, and workshops sponsored by such organizations as the International City Management Association, the Public Personnel Association, and the Society for Personnel Administration indicate that so-called public sector unionization and collective bargaining are indeed very "live" subjects in contemporary labor relations.

21. Dissent took many forms during the 1960s, and public employee unions were not immune from it. See James P. Gifford, "Dissent in Municipal Employee Organizations." See also Ewart Guinier, "Impact of Unionization on Blacks."

Evidently the hard-won victories of police bargaining teams are not beyond some gentle needling from the ranks. *Vanguard,* a publication of the San Jose, California, Peace Officers Association, carried this portion of a letter from a member:

Another little item passed through in the bargaining session was that air-conditioning units were to be placed in police vehicles. Now this officer doesn't have air-conditioning in my privately owned car, not able to afford it, but understand to work properly, all windows in the vehicle must be rolled up. Great! This coming summer I guess many of the men will be patrolling around with all the windows up, unable to hear a cry for assistance, sound of a window smashed, the siren of another emergency vehicle on the run, etc. We'll be a lot less effective, but what matter. The press will stay in the uniform longer and no more unsightly sweat stains under the armpits.

This year's bargaining crew should implement the above breakthrough by requesting extra dark tinted windows on the cars so that we'll be less able to see any infractions being committed around us.

Also, how about trying to get the Department's phone number unlisted?

22. Igleburger and Angell, "Dealing With Police Unions," p. 55. Not all police or public administrators would subscribe to this sociological-administrative philosophy in dealing with unionization or other, essentially political matters. Some would tend to place greater stress on the dynamics of power manipulation and would refer to their approach as "more pragmatic." See, for example, Pfiffner and Sherwood, *Administrative Organization*, pp. 16–32 and chaps. 17, 18.

23. In addition to the several pertinent references already cited in this chapter, see Dan W. Dodson, "Police and Community Relations as a Political Issue"; Paul Chevigny, *Police Power: Police Abuses in New York City;* and Algernon D. Black, *The People and the Police*. A profile of Blue Power is given in Study 4 (Part 4) in Radelet and Reed, *Studies*.

24. The question of whether police officers should be required to reside in the community or neighborhood where they are assigned has been argued pro and con. In August 1971, the Michigan Supreme Court ruled that a Detroit ordinance requiring police officers to live in the city was legal. The Detroit Police Officers Association was unhappy about the decision.

25. Howard James, "Children in Trouble."

26. See also such articles as Michael Novak, "The Politics of Resentment," and Peter Freiberg, "Situation Ethnics."

27. Milton Burdman, "The Conflict Between Freedom and Order."

28. As quoted in *The National Observer*, June 14, 1971, p. 3. *Time* magazine (June 21, 1971) commented:

> The Warren Court's application of most Bill of Rights safeguards to all criminal defendants now seems as self-wounding to the nation's highest tribunal as it then seemed vital to American justice. By overlooking the real fears of a crime-ridden society, the court made itself a political target, which in turn encouraged police evasion of its rules, the very official lawlessness that it had aimed to curb in the first place.

Summary
of Part Four

The four chapters in Part Four come under the miscellaneous caption, Special Considerations. The first two chapters take up relationships within the criminal justice system: police-prosecutorial-court relations, and corrections-community relations. The next chapter is devoted to police-media relations, and the last chapter to police-political relationships.

We find that The police are part of several interlocking social systems. One of these, called the *criminal justice system,* is usually described as including the police, the prosecutor, the courts, and corrections, with other social institutions and agencies playing important auxiliary roles. Evidence is mounting that the criminal justice system in our country does not work very well as a system, that it may in reality be a nonsystem. Since any social system is a human invention relating to people in different parts of a whole process, its dysfunctionality invariably raises questions on relatedness, coordination, teamwork, meshing together, and the like.

If, then, the criminal justice system is to be characterized as in some measure dysfunctional, what are the main reasons for this? We identified a half dozen problems pertaining to:

The age of offenders

The youthful offender

The two-track, non-unified approaches to felonies and misdemeanors

The opposing philosophies (therefore conflicting goal delineation) among practitioners within the system

The differing theories of the causes and responsibility for crime

The problems of professional education and training

In the most general terms, coping with these problems requires that the criminal justice system be made to function more effectively as a system, another way of saying that relationships within the system, and between any and all parts of the system and the community served by the system, must be strengthened. Only an awareness of a concept of relations fitting such descriptions as inter-organizational, inter-group, inter-institutional, inter-professional and inter-disciplinary will enable us to deal with complex, interlacing problems—such as crime—in these times. The problems have a network of causes; their solutions require a network approach.

Looking specifically at police-prosecutor-court relationships, we focused on what we called *jurisdictional disputes*. Whenever a number of roles enter into making decisions about the same case, and professional competence vies in handling the case, conflicts occur in which a rather complicated bargaining (trade-off) process materializes within the system. In these cases, police are often viewed as less professional than other professionals in the system. Moreover, they are sensitive to being treated as adversaries by prosecutors and judges in trial proceedings, and to having no say about the disposition of cases that they themselves introduce into the system. Police express resentment sometimes by accusations that they are being "handcuffed" by certain court decisions, that their own rights are given far less attention than the rights of the accused, and that "no one cares about cops anyhow."

We reviewed some of the recommendations of the President's Crime Commission, the Kerner Commission, and of the Advisory Commission on Intergovernmental Relations on the operation of the criminal justice system. We referred to the noteworthy pilot projects of the Vera Institute, and to the purposes of the National Council on Crime and Delinquency. A broad perspective is needed and the need was illustrated by what we called *pluralistic planning* (John Pfiffner calls it a *geopolitical* approach) in dealing with the problems of criminal justice. *Systems analysis* is an example of how science and technology can contribute to systemic improvement in criminal justice.

A fundamental question to be faced in any study of the criminal justice system is the question of how crime is defined. What specific behaviors has our society proscribed in the criminal code? An improvident and excessive use of the criminal code to perform tasks for which it is ill-suited has created acute problems for the criminal justice system. One problem—the sheer volume of cases flooding the system—in itself contributes to the finger-in-the-dike mentality toward controlling crime and to the frustrations that lead to scapegoating, in and out of the system. Pressures to criminalize, to try to solve all problems by making this or that behavior illegal, persistently block objective assessments of what the criminal law is and is not good for. In short, overcriminalization strikes at the very roots of criminal justice-community relations tensions.

Next, we examined the class-bound nature of our criminal justice system through its attitudes toward legal services for the poor and the politically powerless. The poor are ruled by a legal system they neither understand nor trust, and we summarized some of the current efforts to alleviate inequities in the system, none of which can boast of smooth political sailing. Five issues in contemporary criminal justice-community relations are considered especially controversial: entrapment, stop-and-frisk, preventive detention, no-knock, and the use of firearms by police.

Corrections and community relations problems discussed here are no easier to solve than other problems we have considered. Stressing that it was the community endeavor in correctional process that was our special interest, we undertook a kind of annotated enumeration of a dozen problems and then suggested several guidelines for coping with them. One in particular—the development of corrections leadership—would go far to educate the community and elevate the standards of correctional programs. The need for far greater coordination throughout the correctional process will be aided by the development of relationships within the field of corrections, and between corrections and the police, the courts, and the community.

In the chapters dealing with systemic relations, much was said about public attitudes, public expectations, and public education. The role of the media is of obvious importance in such matters so our attention turned next to relations between the police (and other criminal justice agencies) and the media of mass communication and public information: newspapers, magazines, television, radio, motion pictures, and other specialized means. An element of inherent conflict of interest was observed in this relationship as we viewed the media in its watchdog function in democratic society. Helping "to keep the police honest" is a function with adversarial connotations; in this sense, it may be argued that the police-media relationship should not, ideally, be too buddy-buddy. Rather, it is a matter of making the relationship of agencies of conflicting interests as cooperative and mutually supportive as possible, by developing ground rules.

The broader, deeper issue in police-newspaper and criminal justice-media relations is Power vs Power—Big Government vs Big Media. This issue has been dramatized over the years by the clashing Constitutional principles invoked in free press-fair trial donnybrooks, and recently by the case of newspaper reporter Earl Caldwell, by the televised program, *The Selling of the Pentagon,* and of course by the case of the Pentagon Papers.

By what generally acceptable standards is media reporting to be measured and judged? What is bias? What is truth? Should a newspaper merely report the news or does it have some obligation to the public to seek out truth? What should be the role of the media in monitoring social conflict? What, for example, is the responsibility of the media in the violence phenomenon? These are a few of the difficult questions in the discussions of what amounts to media-community relations in today's society, a subject too rarely studied in all our preoccupation with other social relations.

Although policing is a public, *political* function in a democratic society, there seems to be some reluctance to talk about the police and their political relationships. The assumption in recent years has somehow been that the higher the degree of professionalism achieved by the police, the farther removed from political influence they will be. Thus, we hear slogans such as "take the police out of politics." Of course, in one sense, this idea of separating policing from politics is a very good thing, indeed. In another sense, it is pure hogwash!

We differentiated between four styles of so-called political policing. *Partisan* and *cultural,* which we abhorred; *fraternal,* which is still unsettled, and *administrative,* which we saw as inevitable, legitimate, and—at least potentially—constructive. A functional chart of the Crime Commission to reflect the workings of the political process in formulating police policy was presented. Most troubles in police and community relations arise from questions of control of police power—of holding the police accountable to *all* of the community—the powerless as well as the powerful—in what they do, and how they do it. Accountability is a political matter, and so is its complementary side in police and community relations: winning public support for what the police need in the way of resources to do their job, and for the changes that should be made in the way they go about doing it. The classical organizational and functional model of most police agencies is foreign to the principle of accountability to the community. Police responsiveness to community needs therefore requires that the classical administrative, quasi-military model undergo major modification.

How far should police officers be permitted to go in the realm of practical politics? Statutory and policy limits on this question are universal; the argument today is that these limitations may be too stringent. Police militancy at the line level is on the increase, and there is no sign that it will subside. Police unions are here to stay, and Blue Power mocks the diehards who decry "the politicization of the police." The big question is, will police unions and Blue Power become allied with the cause of criminal justice reform, and go beyond the immediate aims of financial and personal security and protection of police officers? Political cleavages also occur *within* police ranks, as exemplified by the various racial, ethnic, and religious societies and organizations that attract police membership.

The consideration of the police and their political relations takes us back again to the fundamental, everlasting tension between freedom and order. Such a question as this illustrates the point: How is power to be better balanced between those who administer justice and those who are its presumed beneficiaries?

Part Five

Programs

Chapter Twenty

Police
Training Programs

Every problem, no matter how difficult, has its solution. This is a belief thoroughly ingrained in the American ethos, a belief often noted by foreign observers, but one which has not always helped Americans to understand other cultures. Its somewhat jingoistic stance suggesting the firebrand football coach in his between-halves salvo to his team has a certain euphoric quality when applied to today's social problems.

Some people say that some of these problems have become literally insolvable. Their story is that there will always be poor people, physically and mentally handicapped people, dishonest and selfish and irresponsible people, bigoted people, ignorant people, "fatcat" people, scheming people, indifferent and apathetic people, people who will be people. And there will always be people who will insist, when such things are said, that it is *other* people that the observer has in mind! Some say that "people problems" are inevitable. Nothing much can be done about them, not even in resourceful, indomitable America. Oh, we *could* solve some of these problems if we really wanted to—but we don't really want to! Darwin was right; it's the survival of the fittest. Our problems have become too complicated, too expensive to solve.

Take, for instance, the problem of police-community relations. Some say that not much can be done about it. Cops will always be cops! Short of a revolution, nobody voluntarily gives up power. And *power* is the name of the game in police-community relations, according to this view. All the recent attention to police and community relations amounts to mere charades, "motion sickness," because nobody wants to do anything about what's really wrong. People can't be forced to love what they hate. And a lot of people hate cops! Or, there is the argument that those who hate cops don't believe in our system of government anyhow. So why worry about it?

The counterargument is, of course, that every problem, no matter how difficult, has some kind of a solution *provided* that enough people care and decide that change is necessary. It has been said with some insight that our problems are not nearly as insolvable as those who profit by perpetuating them pretend. How can people be motivated to care?

A text of this kind may tend to foster psychological doldrums because it piles on problem after problem and layer after layer of complexity by phrases such as "this problem is further complicated by . . ." or "the popular view of this situation is a gross oversimplification." We repeat and repeat that problems must be adequately defined, giving due weight to diverse viewpoints, if there is to be any hope for solution. Many people just aren't that much interested. They are impatient with the democratic problem-solving process; they want instant answers. They chant, "Why do we have to take time for all this folderol? Everybody knows what the problem is. Let's get on to the solution." They usually mean by this that they have their own solution, and they want others to fall in line with them.

So it goes. The pragmatists among us preach that problems are solved only to the extent that people feel like actual or potential victims of the problem and decide to do something about it. Differences are then reconciled and turned into assets, coalitions are developed, consensus is achieved. Plainly, this is a somewhat cynical view of problem-solving; in effect, it is a political approach in which such things as brotherhood, the Golden Rule, and saintly concern for others are "nice", but not particularly utilitarian. "It's dog-eat-dog in this world." "You can solve a lot of problems if you don't care who gets the credit." Or, "You can solve a lot of problems if you don't look too closely at people's motives."

Out of this hodge-podge of varying philosophies and rationalizations for solving or not solving social problems, what programs have been mounted in the cause of solving police and community relations problems? It is about thirty years since these problems first came into prominence and just over fifteen years since the big push in programs of this kind got under way. What has been tried, and how have these efforts turned out? This is the question for this and the next several chapters. Some typical programs are described in some detail in Part Five of *The Police and the Community: Studies,* by Radelet and Reed.

The best way to decide the value of a program is to analyze several types. This we will do, with only sufficient description to identify each one. Additional information regarding programs is available elsewhere, some of which we will mention as we go along. Critical observation is easier than systematic, scientific program evaluation. Of evaluation, there has been very little, and we do not presume that what we say here about programs is any nearer to true evaluation than the extent to which it may be a strong argument for it.

Types of Police-Community Relations Programs

It is generally assumed that programs and solutions for police and community relations problems are one and the same. There is reason to doubt that this is really so. Since programs of this kind have not, for the most part, been carefully evaluated—beyond the feedback that convinces program planners that their efforts are appreciated by the participants— we do not know very much about what happens as a result of well-intentioned program efforts. There is no harm, of course, in people feeling good about an institute they have attended. But does it make a difference in what they think and in what they do? This is, after all, the crucial question, and one not easy to answer in the typical police and community relations program. Thus we find that to equate programs with solutions to problems is too grandoise an assumption.

Another assumption has been that big problems require big programs for solution. Some critical examination shows us a sneaky half-truth lurking in this assumption, and it also contains a booby-trap. Sometimes in human relations, the programs become so complicated and so bureaucratic, so filled with "politicking," so much "busy work" as an end in itself, that we lose sight of the problem that the program was supposed to solve. We forget that simple, routine acts of policemen and citizens, on a one-to-one basis, still constitute the basic metabolism of police and community relations. As Norman Cousins, former editor of *Saturday Review,* once put it: "To hold out a helping hand to a fellow human being who is in need may not represent universal regeneration. But it does happen to be individual responsibility at its best."

Another important point has to do with the *process* of community problem-solving. As we have indicated, there is a good deal to be said for the idea that the process is in itself a significant part of the solution. A shorthand way to suggest this is to say that *community* is both an end and a means. We have noted that functional breakdowns in social systems are basically *interrelationship* problems. Such problems can be solved only by mending the relationships.

Do programs matter? Can programs be made to count? Unquestionably much depends on how the goals of a given program are set.

As an example, the aims of some so-called human relations training programs for police officers have been stated so as to suggest nothing less than haloed monks as the ultimate product. Or the stated purpose of a given institute on police and community relations gives aid and comfort mainly to those who believe in the possibilities of paradise this side of Valhalla. One of the problems of evaluating such programs is in the implied need to measure what cannot be measured. The objectives of programs should be realistically cast. To be ambitious is a virtue; to be unrealistically ambitious can be a mark of an imposter.

In our view, police-community relations tensions today may be alleviated substantially by programs focusing on any combination of these three goals:

1. Revision of the criminal code to reduce overcriminalization and legal moralism.

2. Modification in the organizational models of police and criminal justice agencies, in tune with community consensual role delineations, better to harmonize social control with social change, to improve responsiveness and community support.

3. Vanquishing racism of whatever color or auspices, along with its fellow travellers, poverty and powerlessness—the abracadabra of the "ins" and the "outs"—the police being *in,* and some citizens being *out.*

Plainly, these goals are broadly cast; no single program can or should encompass them. They are relatively long-range, for programs collectively. It is not racism in Afghanistan that we have in mind. It is the racism, the criminal code, the police organization as near to us as *Mytown, USA,* although in our world today, what happens in one part of it affects all the rest.

We shall consider, then, in this chapter and the two that follow, five types of programs in the police and community relations field:

1. Police training programs

2. Institutes and metropolitan programs

3. Police-school liaison programs

4. Public relations and public information programs

5. Selected, special purpose programs

The Scope of Police Training Programs

When we speak of police training programs, we mean systematic pre-service or in-service instruction for police officers in subject matter described by such terms as human relations, intergroup relations, interpersonal relations, police-community relations, police-minority group relations, race relations, the social psychology of police work, the sociology of the police, crisis intervention, social conflict management, and the like. As we explained in Chapter One, such instruction was the earliest type of police and community relations program to develop historically. We explained why this was so. And in *Studies* (Part One) by Radelet and Reed are several examples of such programs. Often instruction of this kind has been part of a broader police training curriculum; sometimes it has been designed as a separate training program in itself.[1]

The first question faced by police trainers in programs of this type is about objective. Is the instruction aimed at changing attitudes, or is it aimed at changing behavior—and is this really a tenable distinction? In concrete terms, is it proper to say to police trainees, "We don't care about your personal prejudices in racial matters. What we care about is that you *behave* as a professional policeman should behave, no matter what your personal attitudes may be"? This position, closely akin to the stance that police officers will enforce a law whether they personally agree with it or not, has been taken by countless police trainers. From the standpoint of the integrity of training and educational pedagogy, this question of attitude and behavior is tricky. To split the two may be opportunistic, short-run strategy; in the long run, as with a railroad track seen at a distance, it appears to fuse into a single rail.

An important pedagogical question is whether instruction in community relations is most effective if presented by separate courses and topics, or by integration into regular training courses and topics. This is an old question in the field, going back to early experiments with teacher training in human relations. The argument has never been settled. Probably the best answer is that a combination of both approaches is best: some aspects of the material should be taught separately, for instance, the psychological dynamics of prejudice and rumor; and other aspects should be integrated, for instance, in teaching police field practices. Closely akin to this, pedagogically, is the importance in training programs of clarifying basic conceptual confusions: for instance, the relationship of community relations and public relations; of community relations and race relations or minority group relations; and the distinction between *preventive* police work in community relations and *tactical* police work in handling civil disturbances.

Human relations training for policemen, as with school teachers and others, is not simply a matter of what is taught in a given curriculum, no matter how imaginative it may be in content or method. Ideally, it is an emphasis, an orientation in all aspects of the given organization or type of activity. A good teacher of astronomy can teach the subject with a human relations slant. Good teachers of police management courses can teach the subject similarly, espousing management theory that is human relations oriented.[2]

Techniques of Police Training Programs

The methods of police training in general have, until recently, relied heavily on traditional patterns: lecture, lesson plans, limited opportunity for questions and discussion. Today, however, police training seems to be gradually breaking away from the past and beginning to try techniques long since adopted in other spheres of educational endeavor. But these changes are not occurring without a good deal of kicking and screaming.

Training and educational methods are, of course, as important as informational (cognitive) content. Specifically, instructional techniques in human relations training for the police have suffered from a poverty of imagination, undoubtedly contributing to negative reactions by many officers to such instruction, although we shall shortly see other reasons, for this response. Police trainers have recently discovered teaching methods sharing affective as well as cognitive dimensions of learning, the significance of which we mentioned in Chapter Eight.

Projective educational techniques such as role playing illustrate this technique. Audio-visual aids of one kind or another facilitate learning by enhancing sensory input. Group discussion under skillful leadership can help to stretch social horizons and provide insight into other people's feelings and ideas. The late William E. Vickery explained how this was done by a teacher of eleventh-grade American history in an industrial midwestern city.[3] This class undertook a study of migrations, focusing on The Westward Movement. Half the class were migrants, mostly from the South. Many of these pupils were the victims of poor home backgrounds, economically impoverished. Other members of the class were established residents of the city, and reflected relatively better economic and educational opportunity.

The teacher sought ways to help these two groups of children work together productively. She decided to compare the experiences of families who took part in the westward movement with the modern migration in which half the class had participated. The class discussions revolved around four guiding questions:

1. What makes a family decide to pull up its roots and move?

2. What does a family leave behind that they miss? What are they glad to leave behind them?

3. What may happen to them on their journey?

4. When they get to their new community, what experiences are likely to help them feel at home there? What experiences may they have that make it hard for them to feel at home?

These questions and others that the children themselves suggested were applied first to the modern migration. The migrant pupils were living textbooks for their classmates. The exchange of both information and feelings increased the class members' understanding of and respect for one another, and at the same time developed a sound body of knowledge on the subject of migrations.

This story identifies a classroom method that many teachers today would label as old stuff. However, in the realm of police training and education, this method has only lately been discovered. Even the more progressive police trainers today are still not too sure about the use of short stories, novels, and plays to stimulate discussion, best used in unhurried small groups. Some might plead that "time doesn't permit all these educational frills—we need these police officers so badly that we must get them out on the street as rapidly as possible." No doubt, practical exigencies force lamentable compromises and short-cuts in the quantity and quality of police training. Yet it is hard to see that this makes any more sense than it would to short-circuit the professional preparation of doctors of medicine because their services are so urgently needed.

Role playing is a familiar projective educational technique that is no longer strange in police training. It requires acting a part in a spontaneous, unrehearsed "play." Participants can explore the consequences of various courses of action in a social situation, evaluate these options, and make choices among them, without becoming defensive about customary ways of behaving. It is an excellent technique in problem-solving discussions related to community action, following the familiar action-research steps: study, analyzing conditions, diagnosing causes, deciding goals for the program, and exploring various lines of action for reaching the goals; then deciding the line of action, taking it, and evaluating the results.[4]

Techniques and tools are closely related in educational methodology. In the early years of police training in human relations, tools were hard to come by. There were few publications and to find a suitable film was quite a task. It was 1962 before Charlotte Epstein wrote *Intergroup Relations for Police Officers,* which has become a standard basic text.

The pooled resource approach to police training is not new, although the idea is being given unprecedented impetus today in metropolitan and regional training academies. In the 1950s, when the community relations subject was struggling to get any attention at all in police training programs (it still is, in too many places!), creative planners such as the late Howard Devaney in New Jersey devised interesting ways to get the job done. Devaney conducted forty to fifty Police Institutes on Community Relations, as he called them, in that state over a period of ten years. A given police agency, in Elizabeth or Newark or Trenton or Paterson, would agree to host such an Institute, with the sessions usually taking place in a local high school, and the National Conference of Christians and Jews footing the bill.[5] As many as fifteen or twenty police departments within a radius of fifty miles would, by enrolling several men each in the Institute, build a class of approximately 75 trainees, all experienced policemen. Sessions would be held one afternoon a week for six weeks, three hours for each session, with each session featuring a single consultant-lecturer or a panel on a different facet of police and community relations. The usual format was an hour of presentation, an hour of discussion in small groups, and an hour of general feedback with the speaker or panel. Devaney was the coordinator-director of each Institute; as a retired policeman and former president of the state Policemen's Benevolent Association, he had considerable influence and became known as Mr. Police-Community Relations in New Jersey and up and down the Eastern seaboard.

More recently, with the help of a Federal grant, law enforcement agencies of Riverside County, California pooled resources for a 21-hour course in police and community relations along lines similar to the New Jersey pattern.[6] The basic idea has been copied in other places. Standardized, or packaged, training guidelines, lesson plans, and syllabi are much in demand but difficult to design because of variations including general local circumstances, problems, and police agency organizational patterns.[7] Again we may mention that the Radelet and Reed *Studies,* Part Five, includes a number of studies describing various types of programs.

The Evaluation

Our interest at the moment is in the techniques of police training programs. Teaching social science as such to police officers has its perils. For some years, the Chicago Police Department has systematically included it in its training program, using the services of sociologists, social psychologists, and political scientists from local colleges and universities. Including this subject in a police training program is no longer as novel as it was when that department initiated the practice. A 1970–71 in-service training project in the Muskegon (Michigan) Police Department, funded by a State Crime Commission grant, provided a short course in urban sociology for command and supervisory personnel as one of its several aspects. However, the project was more noteworthy for the evaluation design that it devised, as scientific an assessment of such a training program as has yet been developed.[8]

Also noteworthy is a doctoral study done by Dr. Geraldine Michael at the University of Missouri-Kansas City that analyzed the results of a general-education social science program for a police training unit ("Social Science Education for Police").[9] This program was based on six questions:

1. Do police officers make the most appropriate instructors for police training units?
2. Can the behavior of police officers in actual working conditions be predicted during training?
3. Are field supervisors' evaluations of officer performance of any utility?

4. Can the traditional norms and values of police officers as reflected in various reports and public complaints be modified by an overall program of classroom instruction and situational training?

5. Can a training program help reduce the widely noted difference between stated police philosophy and actual police officer behavior?

6. Can one obtain effective criteria for assessing a good officer?

This study recommended (1) that criteria be established for appropriate and inappropriate behavior by police officers, (2) that evaluating procedures for police officer behavior should be instituted that are continuous and constant and do not depend upon traditional field supervisor evaluations, (3) that the question of using only police officer instructors in training units should be systematically investigated, (4) that guidelines for recruitment, training and placement should be established, (5) that existing police-community relations programs should be carefully evaluated, and (6) that selective as well as general recruitment for police service should be initiated. Dr. Michael's comments in the report of this study conclude on this note:

> In retrospect, there is great promise in involving social scientists in studies such as this which use social science theories and principles. Many programs utilized for policy making and decision making which affect the general public are based on non-social science perspectives. There appears to be a real gap between utilization of social science information and planning, and policy making in the general community. Therefore, in this sense, this kind of an effort should encourage others to apply social science information to the generation of programs in other areas of criminal justice and law enforcement. [Ibid., p. 61]

Programmed Instruction

So-called programmed instruction involves a philosophy of education with a long history. In the past twenty-five years, it has been extensively used in schools, industry, and the military. It is being pushed currently by some police training leaders. Programmed instruction puts learning in an ordered sequence of stimulus items, each of which brings forth a specified response from the student (More and Nesbit, "Programmed Instruction for Law Enforcement").[10] The student is enabled to advance in small steps at his own pace, reinforcing his responses by immediate feed-back as to results. This leads the student from what he knows toward what he is expected to learn in a given program. The technique is better suited to some types of subject matter than to others; for example, mathematics is easily adaptable to programmed instruction. Social science material is more difficult to adapt to it, but it is being done successfully. Programmed instruction has its critics who scoff at "teaching machines" and such, but its possibilities in all phases of police training are beginning to be recognized.

Again, what is sometimes called situational training is not unique
to police instruction, but variations of it are being used in some police
academies. In college programs, it is referred to as work-study; and
Antioch College, in Ohio, is often pointed to as a model. Field training,
practicum, field trip observation, apprenticeship, internship, are all terms
and approaches sharing a common educational philosophy: to provide
some in-situation (on-the-job) learning experience for the student or
trainee "to teach them what it's really like." Professional and vocational
schools in particular are likely to use some techniques of this kind.

About 1960, Arthur Siegel and his associates in an educational
consulting firm called Applied Psychological Services developed a
human relations training program for the Philadelphia Police Academy
that, when compared with other programs with similar purposes at the
time, had some unique features. It was a blend of lectures: discussions
of case materials depicting real-life situations, role playing, and learning
by doing (Siegel, Federman, and Schultz, *Professional Police Human
Relations Training*). The program consisted of thirty instructional hours,
with a maximum of twenty students per class. A similar approach borrowing many of Siegel's ideas and materials was adapted to a Detroit
police training project in 1965.

Case analysis, or *situational analysis,* appears to be an especially
productive training technique in community relations. Experiments with
it are still too few, however, because it is regarded as too expensive and
too time-consuming; and requires instructional skills for its proper use
that are not thought to be widely available. The American Institutes of
Research and the so-called Quaker Project in Community Conflict of
the American Friends Service Committee have been among those fostering *critical incident analysis* as a technique in conflict management developed originally by Professor John Flanagan of the University of
Pittsburgh. Simulated situations enacted through role playing or on film
are among the tools of this approach, an approach that has several variations in the search for new and better ways of coping with embattled
urban relationships.

Crisis intervention and *conflict management* has in some places
become a way of referring to police training that in the past was called
human relations or community relations. This shift in terminology is
significant, but it is more than a matter of semantics. Current patterns
in the training of urban police officers *are* more sophisticated than those
of the past. To illustrate the point, consider the training aspect of the so-
called Community Conflict Program of the Dayton (Ohio) Police Department. This is one of the several pilot or demonstration agencies of
LEAA's National Institute on Law Enforcement and Criminal Justice.

In the Dayton Police Department, conflict management means not
only what police-community relations formerly meant, but even more.
A conflict management team in the department is responsible for func-

tions of public information, community affairs, community organization, and youth aid. The members of this team are specially trained, and they help in training officers assigned to each of the functions indicated. But an associated in-service training program engages all officers in the department. The topics in the curriculum include:

Police role conceptions and community conflict

The meaning of community organization

Working with neighborhood leaders and how to recognize them

Identifying the signs of social disorganization

Referrals to appropriate agencies

Communication "traps" in dealing with culturally diverse populations

Sensitivity Training

The very term *sensitivity training* is a sensitive issue in some police quarters, even to the suggestion that it is "inspired by the international Communist conspiracy and other enemies of the Republic." One is reminded of some of the patently ridiculous charges that were made against progressive education, so-called, when John Dewey and others first championed it, and what is sometimes heard today regarding the permissive rearing of children. Some say that these things aren't so bad . . . as long as one avoids using the prototype terminology. Sensitivity training itself, then, is okay as long as one does not call it that! Those who don't wish to be tainted by the term sensitivity-training, sometimes espouse "confrontation" or "encounter group" training instead. It is convenient that a precise, generally acceptable definition of sensitivity training has not been coined. One can be for it or against it, depending upon his own definition of it and how he gauges receptiveness to it in the immediate circumstances.

Sensitivity training involves learning that stresses the affective dimension: feelings are facts. It employs empathy-building, projective techniques more or less bordering on group therapy, depending upon variables in a given situation. Under amateur direction, it is certainly *not* therapeutic, and indeed may be a means of compounding problems. One difficulty is that too many amateurs and charlatans regard themselves as competent enough to sell their services as consultants to police departments, school systems, and community organizations, and then proceed to do much damage for which sensitivity training in general is blamed. Properly understood, this should be the business of reputable professionals only, who know *what* they are doing, and *why* they are doing it, and are able to explain it in simple terms to anyone asking questions.

While sensitivity training is comparatively new in the police world, its theory goes back some years in educational psychology. Kurt Lewin and Carl R. Rogers were among its poineers, and the National Training Laboratory in Group Development at Gould Academy, Bethel, Maine, has provided considerable national and international thrust for it. Terminology such as group dynamics, group-centered leadership, nondirective T-groups, and the unstructured agenda are endemic to the method. It should be emphasized that it is *not* group therapy because participants are not mentally ill people undergoing psychiatric treatment.

Sensitivity training for police officers and other citizens, as a technique to improve police and community relations, has been conducted in numerous cities in recent years. It has been fostered by various educational consulting agencies whose personnel often includes university professors, and by some college entities directly, all interested in sharing in the largesse of Federal and state grants recently available to police departments wishing to bolster their community relations programs. A fuller description of sensitivity training can be found in Study 4, Part Five in *Studies* by Radelet and Reed. The nature of the technique is such that it is difficult to describe in a manner that can be taken as fairly representative. Social-psychological game theory plays a prominent part in sensitivity training. One problem with game theory is the difficulty people have in transferring the lesson of the game to the rigors of emotion-laden problems of human conflict in the real world. The game tends to be more fun, and something of an escape mechanism.

Police Chief Fred Ferguson of Covina, California has been an enterprising innovator in his experimentation with several different kinds of sensitivity experiences in training personnel of his department. One project was known as *Operation Empathy—Skid Row,* in which Covina policemen spent a day or two playing the part of skid row inhabitants. Dressed accordingly, with shopping bags containing collected junk or a bottle of wine, they were sent into a community where they were unknown. Several were apprehended by police officers and learned swiftly how it feels to be a derelict on the receiving end of justice. Another well-known Covina training exercise put police officers in jail for a weekend in neighboring Riverside County and included being booked, fingerprinted, mugged, deloused, and dressed and treated as a jailbird.[11]

In Houston, Texas, a group of businessmen formed Community Effort, Inc., as a private funding agency for the Houston Cooperative Crime Prevention Programs. A program was launched using T-groups and such other sensitivity training techniques as role playing, role reversal, role mirroring, force field analysis, and the like.[12] Another of the early programs of this type, conducted in Grand Rapids, Michigan, was later copied in Lansing and other cities.[13]

The discovery of the emotions as a part of learning and the development of various types of laboratory-training approaches should not be sidetracked before there is a fair chance to determine their worth. The opposition to these approaches voices varied reasons, all the way from the charge that it smacks of therapy to the charge that it is brain-washing. Max Birnbaum has summarized the matter well:

> ... the most serious threat to sensitivity training comes first from its enthusiastic but frequently unsophisticated school supporters, and second from a host of newly hatched trainers, long on enthusiasm or entrepreneurial expertise, but short on professional experience, skill, and wisdom. What is needed today is a clearer sense of how sensitivity training developed, the varied forms it may take, and the results that can be anticipated in any given situation. ["Sense About Sensitivity Training"]

Psychological and Psychiatric Techniques

Attention to the part played by the emotions in the learning process derives, as Birnbaum stresses, from an educational model, not a therapeutic one. Neither school teachers nor police training instructors should be therapists. Sensitivity training may have useful shock value, but skilled direction must keep it from becoming merely the application of gimmicks in a highly charged area for the purpose of manipulating human behavior, or subjecting it to pseudoscientific testing and observation.[14]

There is, however, a proper place for psychological and psychiatric techniques in police personnel practices. Psychological testing and psychiatric evaluation of police candidates is no longer considered bizarre, and some departments have adopted continuous, in-service group psychotherapy, individual therapy interviews, and emotional stress evaluations of persons promoted to supervisory positions.[15] Much has been said about police officer over-reactions in tense community incidents, and about training policemen for "affective disengagement." Emotional equilibrium in police work is a treasure that can be discovered through the use of established technical methods under skilled professional guidance. If it is possible for the military services to prepare personnel to withstand prisoner-of-war brainwashing if captured by the enemy, it should be possible to prepare police patrolmen to withstand the indignities to which they are occasionally subjected. But the heavy punching bag in the precinct station may still be a good idea!

Behavioral Science in Police Training

We referred earlier to the question of whether police training should aim at changing attitudes or at changing behavior. In many training programs, this distinction is not drawn, and there is considerable interest in attitude change. Some examples will help to illustrate the point.

In the Police Department of Miami, Florida, a training project (cited in Study 6, Part Five in *Studies* by Radelet and Reed) has examined the psychological stresses of policemen and the extent to which the so-called ghetto effect contributes to these strains. The reciprocal and mutually reinforcing attitudes of white officers and black residents have been systematically analyzed in this project by a team of skilled behavioral scientists.

Another example was provided by Project PACE in San Francisco, under the auspices of the American Institutes of Research and directed by Dr. Terry Eisenberg. This project is described in Study 10, Part Five in *Studies* by Radelet and Reed. The central hypothesis tested in this project was that a comprehensive and long-range education and action program will induce and sustain socially desirable changes in *attitudes and actions* among police and citizens.[16]

Along similar lines, the conceptualization of the dynamics of negative contact situations should be mentioned, especially as developed by Professor Jack Kuykendall of San Jose State College. He describes it as follows:

> Police/minority group negative contact situations can be analyzed from the "power maintenance" function of police and the overt threats posed by a minority group in power challenges. Minority group segregation is a consequence of dominant group rejection and ingroup solidarity of minorities, and represents distinct boundaries of separation. Dominant groups also possess the power—economic, political and social resources—often sought by the minority group. ["Police and Minority Groups"]

Specialized Police Training Programs

Once the many general police training programs in human or community relations began to surface in recent years, some with a more specific focus followed. Examples include police-media relations; police-Indian or police-Spanish speaking or police-Puerto Rican relations; police handling of campus disorders; relationships within the criminal justice system; the police role in labor-management disputes; and police handling of the mentally abnormal. Occasionally, a plea has been made by special interests for police training in dealing with homosexuals and transexuals. Today some police departments also have squads or units specially trained to deal with family crises, consumer fraud, and landlord-tenant disputes, as part of a general administrative emphasis on conflict management.

One of the more interesting and positive ventures in specialized police training was undertaken in the New York City Police Department by Morton Bard and his City College associates to demonstrate the possibilities for preventing crime and promoting mental health in training police as para-professionals in family crisis intervention.[17] Policemen in big cities are quite aware of the considerable proportion of police work that revolves around marital fights. Often these fights are serious, with homicides and assaults not unusual—dangerous ground for the officer bent on pacification.

As a psychologist, Bard began with the conviction that policemen need training in how to handle these situations with techniques that are more likely to calm the parties than to provoke violence. Some eighteen policemen were selected in an economically disadvantaged, racially mixed (population 85,000) precinct and trained intensively for one month as crisis intervention specialists. They were then constituted as a unit, with officers working in pairs to provide 24-hour coverage by one radio car, for a twenty-two-month period. There were weekly on-campus consultations for the men of the unit, some individualized, some as a group. As Bard explains it:

> One of the major challenges in the experiment was to see if policemen could be made psychologically sophisticated and be given highly technical skills without in any way confusing them about their professional identity. Throughout, every effort was made to preserve their identity as police officers and to avoid converting them into psychologists or social workers. In fact, they functioned throughout the program as general police officers and served as specialists *only* when dispatched on a specific family disturbance. ["Alternatives to Traditional Law Enforcement"]

The project was carefully evaluated. Over the two years, the unit handled almost 1,400 interventions with 962 families. The community response, measured in various ways, was clearly positive. There was a reduction in assaults in the area as well. Bard opined that the success of the experiment pointed to workable alternatives to "the traditionally military-modeled crime combat organization of virtually all police departments." As he put it:

> The approach taken in our project can best be described as conforming to the generalist-specialist model. Each officer was a general uniformed law enforcement agent performing patrol functions in keeping with the responsibility to keep the peace and enforce the law. However, each officer had, in addition, a highly trained skill in family intervention which could be called upon when required. The men in the unit were, in effect, on-call specialists who could render with competence a service which is ordinarily regarded by most policemen as an unwelcomed nuisance and not "real" police work. [Ibid.]

Clearly, the Bard model can be extended into other important functional areas. The project made a telling point: better community relations is basically effected by better performance of expected tasks, much more so than by the time-limited palliatives of one-shot community relations programs.

Other police departments have profited from the New York City experiment. The Richmond, California department, for example, decided not to train specialists in family fights, but rather to provide training for the entire patrol division. The scheme was geared to Richmond's team-policing concept. The Uniformed Division was already subdivided into eight teams of ten to twelve men, which were of appropriate size for training. Each team was given approximately fourteen hours of in-class training along with a comparable time for outside reading. Assignments involving practice with the new skills supplemented the reading (Phelps, Schwartz, and Liebman, *The Police Chief,* July 1971). Similar approaches have been made in Oakland, California, and in Dayton, Ohio, among other cities. These two programs in particular are discussed further in Studies 5 and 11, Part Five in *Studies* by Radelet and Reed.

Another kind of specialized training is exemplified by the so-called Community-Police Relations Leadership Training Program in California. This too is described at greater length in *Studies,* Study 13, Part Five; but a summary of it may be useful here.

The California State Legislature, through action in 1968 and 1969, specifically charged the Commission on Peace Officer Standards and Training, part of the State of California Department of Justice, to develop and execute a statewide community relations program. After examining several proposals, this Commission selected three institutions (the University of California at Los Angeles, San Diego State College, and San Jose State College) to define and develop the programs. Each of these institutions offered the course three times during the 1970–71 fiscal year, with attendance limited to twenty students a session at each institution.

The major responsibility for program development was lodged with UCLA, under the direction of retired Los Angeles Deputy Police Chief, James G. Fisk. The three schools coordinated their efforts and followed the same general course outline. The institutes were designed especially for police personnel assigned responsibility in their agency's community relations programs. General police supervisors and community relations operational officers were also recommended for attendance. This program was directed toward specialized training for police officers and civilians assigned to departmental community relations units. Little of this type of special training is available at present.

The objectives of the California program were delineated as follows:

1. To impart to participants the knowledge and analytical skills to
    (a) Examine the responsibilities of law enforcement agencies during a period of rapid social change.
    (b) Assess the involving nature of the communities they serve in order to perform their functions effectively.

2. To develop and implement new approaches to community-police relations based on the knowledge, skills, and perceptions gained from attendance.

The syllabus for the program had four components:

1. Study of the various cultures in American society.

2. Study of the various roles of the police and the implications for interaction with many different subgroups.

3. Study of the forces producing, and the processes for accommodating, social change.

4. Evaluation as a continuing component.

The institutes are provided without cost to California police and sheriff's departments, other than the officer's time. All costs, estimated at $2,000 a student, are paid by the Commission (P.O.S.T.), including two round trips from the trainee's home to and from the institution.

Police Attitude Toward Training

Not everyone takes easily to education and training, police officers included. When the subject is human relations, those with experience in police training programs in human relations are prepared for special resistance, shown in various ways including occasional vehement attacks on the instructor and his ancestors. Trainee reactions are frequently so negative and hypercritical that the question arises whether there may be some reasons for it beyond what might be termed "normal bitching."

Psychologist Robert Shellow looked into this question a few years ago with policemen from the Washington, D.C. area who underwent special training for coping with anticipated travail in connection with the 1963 march on Washington ("The Training of Police Officers"). Shellow observed the pattern of grousing about the training, the trainers, the "agitators," and such, and checked to determine whether this verbalized resistance seemed to affect the later performance of the officers. His conclusion was that it didn't seem to. Rather, the men's performance suggested that the training had been effective, despite their negative verbalizations.

Harold Silverman reported no serious resistance to the human relations instruction he provided in the Dayton Police Department ("Police Attitudes Towards Community Relations Training"). But Arthur Niederhoffer pointed out that while students of police academy training may be oriented to the social and behavioral sciences, the rookie is introduced to human relations on the job by an older patrolman who presumably "knows the score" (*Behind the Shield*). Such informal instruction frequently erodes the idealism of the academy. You will remember that both McNamara and Sterling made a similar point in their studies of police recruits in training.[18]

In a 1970 doctoral dissertation at the University of California, Thomas A. Johnson reported his study (in the Denver Police Department) of police resistance to community relations.[19] Johnson shows that a direct relationship between the goals of a police organization and resistance to police-community relations is revealed in the enactment of a patrolman's role. Johnson contends that patrolmen enact their role more in response to the nature of a situation classified as emergency, than to a situation classified as criminal or noncriminal. What this means is that where organizational goals are broad and general, patrolmen perceive efficiency as the primary goal, often at the expense of community relations goals. Moreover, Johnson found that police administrators tend to minimize organizationally induced role conflict. As he says:

> ... as long as there continues to exist the basic incongruity in what policemen are recruited to do, and in fact rewarded to do for the actual work being performed, there will always remain as a constant factor a high degree of perceived role conflict by members of the organization and a concomitant degree of citizen alienation from both the organization and its personnel.

Johnson observes that patrolmen did not deny the importance of improved police-community relations. They simply did not conceive of it as part of their primary role. To them it was not *real* police work. It was Johnson's opinion that defects in the structure and organization of municipal police agencies led to the problem. The correction of these defects will, he thinks, make a significant difference in police officer attitudes and behavior. In a patrolman subculture within the larger police subculture, Johnson concludes, the norms, mores, and values of the patrolmen are frequently incompatible with the normative value structure of other components of the police organization. Not only does this help explain resistance to police-community relations, he asserts, but it also provides a framework to analyze the resistance of patrolmen to organizational change in general.

Negative police reaction to human relations training is also, in part, the harvest of unimaginative, unproductive instructional methods and techniques. As Donald Bimstein has written, effective police training cannot rely on procedures used successfully only with children ("Improving Departmental Training Programs"). The average police trainee is ordinarily a mentally and emotionally mature person. He has the incentive to learn more about his job, but not to the extent of withstanding a procession of lengthy and dull lectures on what he should do or believe. He is pragmatic in his desire for knowledge; he wants instruction that is clearly and concretely job-related. Lectures may provide valuable information, but as a pedagogic method, the lecture is a relatively ineffective way to influence attitudes or to teach skills and processes. The student must be more personally engaged—talking, questioning, practicing, suggesting, arguing, discussing, teaching—anything but passively auditing. Fortunately, more and more police training facilities are recognizing this elementary fact and moving toward improved methods of teaching. The need for improved methods is related also to the application of a need-determination process that more closely and realistically relates police officer training to identified organizational needs.[20]

Improved training methods are also placing more emphasis on the evaluation stage. Alert training instructors are keenly interested in feedback from trainees on the quality of the instructional and educational programs.[21] The LEAA investments in police training projects require increasingly careful, objective evaluation. The National Center on Police and Community Relations at Michigan State University completed a rather complex evaluation (mentioned earlier) of an in-service, human relations training program in the Muskegon Police Department, the report of which appeared in May 1971. Sketchily described, the main results were:

1. The training program failed to increase the percentage of police officers seeing their primary role as peace officers rather than as law enforcers.

2. The percentage of policemen indicating some negative feeling toward blacks slightly increased rather than decreased during the training period. The percentage of officers registering negative feeling toward Mexican-Americans decreased.

3. The training program substantially improved officer attitudes toward welfare and probation workers, slightly improved attitudes toward the county department of social services, and slightly worsened attitudes toward the antipoverty program.

Among other findings in the study were that more than three-fourths of the patrolmen and one-third of the departmental supervisors felt that they received little or no benefit from the classroom training sessions, which relied principally on lecture. The training program was designed and conducted by the state Civil Rights Commission. Initially, it was deemed to be a notch or two higher on a figurative ladder of sophistication than many similar current programs.

Pertinent here also is a recent study done by the New York City Police Department, the report of which has appeared as an LEAA publication, *Police Training and Performance Study*. This study adhered to training guidelines recommended by the 1966 President's Crime Commission and by the Kerner Commission, which emphasized especially the proper exercise of discretion, understanding the community, the role of the police, and the limitations of the criminal justice system. Reports of happenings and cumulative printouts of the 20th precinct in New York City, an experimental laboratory precinct, were examined in an effort to relate training to police work; and "public opinion" and "trait image" surveys of recruits, instructors, and experienced officers were administered. The ultimate aim was the structuring of a new training curriculum for recruits, followed by a carefully designed escort officer program. In effect, the study was a thorough evaluation of police training and performance in the Nation's largest municipal training academy.

The recommendations that emerged from the study, while covering a broad spectrum, merit summarizing:

Basic Police Commitments

A continuing commitment, explicitly embodied in a departmental directive, is necessary to assure the priority of uninterrupted training for recruits. Such commitment should recognize the importance of the total educational experience which will be provided to the recruit through the new curriculum.

Stability in the recruit-training cycle is essential if a police-civilian instructional staff is to be utilized. It is recommended that new recruits be phased into the academy in increments of approximately 500 every 10 weeks during a year, beginning July 1, 1971. This will require a commitment by budgetary authorities, without which the recruitment and maintenance of a dedicated and competent professional civilian staff will be impossible. Reasonable stability in the size of the new recruit increment is necessary to permit the escort training aspect of the new curriculum to be effective.

Recruit Training

In pursuit of excellence in the training of recruits, in terms of their ability to assimilate, personal attitudes, and specific shortcomings in basic written and spoken communication skills, the new curriculum, as a total educational experience is phased with continuing interaction of academy and field experience and is also supported by recommended new services, such as a counseling center and a remedial educational unit.

The intensification and humanization of the educational experience under the new recruit curriculum is accomplished by three units of field experience preceded and followed by recruit interaction. The group leaders and escort officers perform a crucial role in the educational process and will constitute a training team.

A team of civilian professional personnel, teaching behavioral and social science units as well as units in law, and civilian professional counselors will be added to the academy staff.

The law component of the recruit curriculum will be intensified by introducing mini courses which will cover selected aspects of the laws which are directly relevant to a patrolman's field duties. In order to effectively implement existing departmental policies, a course unit in criminalistics is included in the curriculum which will stress training of recruits in crime scene operations and practical criminalistics.

The use of dramatization and small group discussions as a technique for developing interpersonal skills and decisionmaking effectiveness is made a part of the recruit curriculum which will be implemented by a human skills training unit in the police academy, consisting of professionally trained civilians and police officers.

The physical training component of the recruit curriculum will consist of three phases—basic physical conditioning, physical training and police techniques, and unarmed defense techniques. The new 126-hour program will require less time than the current curriculum unit. The terminal nature of recruit physical training would be deemphasized as a matter of department policy, and incentives would be instituted to encourage physical conditioning throughout the police career. Physical training programs would be integrated with other facets of police training.

The recruit firearms training program will be revised from 56 hours spread over 16 weeks to 48 hours (40 hours consecutively in phase II of training and 8-hour refresher course in phase IV). The recruit will not be armed until he successfully completes a week of firearms training.

A substantial unit in the behavioral and social sciences will be taught by professionally trained civilians stressing a study of the urban environment, criminology, sociology, psychology, and the principles and applications of ethics.

Organizational Recommendations

It is recommended that a new position be created in the police department designated "Director of Education and Training." This position will be filled by a distinguished professional educator who will report directly to the chief of personnel and serve as his adviser on matters of education. The director will be responsible for effective development, and maintenance of educational standards throughout the department. He will advise and assist in curriculum development, teaching methods development, recruitment and selection of civilian staff engaged in teaching and support services. A member of the department will remain in the role of Commanding Officer of the Police Academy, also reporting to the chief of personnel, with, however, expanded responsibility, such as that which the escort training function will create. It is recommended that the rank of Commanding Officer, Police Academy, be higher than that of the incumbent, who presently holds the rank of deputy inspector.

Creation of the following units within the Police Academy is recommended:

    (a) Administrative unit;
    (b) Recruit class leaders unit—consisting of sergeants—assigned on a rotating basis to the group leader role;
    (c) Escort officers unit—consisting of patrolmen selected to accompany recruits during the field training phases of the recruit curriculum;
    (d) Behavioral and social sciences unit;
    (e) Human skills training unit;

(f) Police science education unit;
(g) Legal education unit;
(h) Physical training unit;
(i) Firearms training unit;
(j) Field evaluation unit.

Support services to the Police Academy will be established, consisting of: (a) Counseling center; (b) Remedial education unit; (c) Educational materials development unit.

All existing units in the Police Academy will be absorbed into the above structure.

A field training program designated as the "Escort Training Program" will be established, implemented, and staffed by carefully selected patrolmen, whose function will be to accompany, counsel, and guide the recruit during his field training periods.

A counseling service for recruits is to be a support service in the Police Academy, staffed by professionally trained counseling psychologists.

The establishment of a field evaluation unit at the Police Academy is recommended. This unit will have the continuing responsibility to evaluate the field phase of recruit training and to identify training needs in relation to performance. This unit will, where appropriate, undertake to monitor the opinion of civilians who have come in contact with police services. The work of this unit will be completely distinct from individual evaluation of personnel.

Inservice Training
The unit training program, essentially the only program providing regular inservice refresher training to the entire patrol force (aside from specialized training), will be improved and expanded. Therefore, priority will be given to unit training. Enhanced status will be given to unit training sergeants, who will be assigned to the Police Academy and detailed to field commands on a rotating basis. Training sergeants will participate in the production of unit training memos, telecasts and training bulletins, administration of the escort training program, and will accept greater training responsibilities. More training telecasts, more frequent training sessions and innovations in techniques of presentation are recommended. All members of the force will have access to printed materials.

Unit training sergeants will be rotated between the Police Academy (their assigned command) and the field command to which they have been detailed. When at the Police Academy, they will instruct in one of the training programs. They will serve on various committees, such as curriculum, training techniques, and policies, and will, while detailed to field commands, meet with staff currently assigned to the academy monthly.

A systematic and progressive set of educational requirements for all ranks is recommended, including a policy decision that officers eligible

for promotion should meet specific collegiate educational requirements. These requirements, in terms of academic degree achievement,
will be related to an extended and phased timetable. Specific incentives
are recommended.

Supplementary Recommendations
To introduce the utmost realism into training processes, particularly
for recruits, a simulated city street should be constructed, or acquired,
which will provide not only street situations for training, but also suit-
ably furnished rooms for the acting-out of decisionmaking situations.

Specific proposals in the area of programmed instruction and com-
puter-assisted instruction are recommended on an experimental basis.
It is anticipated that in these areas funding will be sought from appropriate agencies to permit the development of self-instruction materials
and techniques which will permit recruits, in appropriate course units,
to proceed to a differential speed in the learning process. The implementation of such developmental procedures will be a responsibility of
the educational materials development unit, which is one of the new
support services recommended for the Police Academy.

Summing Up

Police training programs in human relations (community relations,
intergroup relations, police-minority relations, social and behavioral
science) have suffered from certain shortcomings. Here is a summary
developed by the Urban Task Force in Pittsburgh:[22]

1. Imprecisely stated goals and unrealistic expectations.

2. Insufficient active support for programs and program goals on the
   part of high-ranking police officials. There has been much lip-
   service and not enough real commitment.

3. Failure to recognize that a training program requires bolstering in
   all aspects of organizational philosophy and role conception. Too
   often, human relations training (as with community relations
   units) has been window-dressing, quite detached from the main
   thrust of organizational priorities.

4. Lack of sophisticated educational methodologies.

5. Lack of on-going consultation between police officers and program personnel in planning and implementation—in short, poor
   feedback.

6. Little correlation of the curricula to the day-to-day realities of the
   police function, even in programs using more sophisticated techniques.

7. Insufficient means for the reinforcement of new learnings following the completion of training sessions.

8. Little planning for fitting human relations training (or other types of police-community relations for that matter) into changing police agency operations.

9. Little use of the research findings and observations that appear in studies of police work and police-community relations, including the pertinent recommendations of several recent Federal Commissions.

10. Basic resistance to organizational change, and undue devotion to practices and procedures geared to horse-and-buggy communities.

11. Insufficient community participation in planning and implementing training programs.

12. Lack of systematic evaluation of the results of training programs.

Writing in *The Police Chief,* Frank L. Manella of the University of Illinois speaks of the need in police training today for what he calls a fundamental philosophy of humanism. The Canon of Police Ethics, he says, embodies some of this philosophy. But what is needed, Manella contends, is a *Credo for Police Humanism,* which he delineates as follows:

1. I believe . . . in the essential dignity of every human being, no matter what their status or state in life. To those citizens having the most contact with the police, life has provided little opportunity and much disappointment. The test of this belief in human dignity depends upon my not becoming disillusioned or bitterly cynical toward people who exhibit weakness and inadequacy.

2. I believe . . . that people can change. They can change their attitudes, values, life styles, and philosophies. If I accept this assumption about human nature, then I can avoid the fallacy of personality fixation which tends to classify people as "good" or "bad" and incapable of changing behavior once a certain age level is reached. If I believe people can change, then rehabilitation replaces retribution as a solution to people problems.

3. I believe . . . People change People! Humans change only through the help of other humans. All police officers can become a force for purposeful human change—a force prepared to help man cope more effectively with his limitations, inadequacies, and strengths. Every police contact becomes an opportunity for developing a sense of "peopleness" moving policing forward as a positive feature of a governmental system which always places people first.

4. I believe . . . in the essential goodness of all men, who, if given a chance can attain that level of human potential with which they have been endowed. The police are a vital part of the chance they need. By crossing their lives, the police can be, and often are, a source of hope, help, and opportunity. ["Humanism in Police Training"]

Notes to Chapter Twenty

1. A panoramic survey of police training programs in the community relations field as of 1966 was provided in two reports of the President's Commission on Law Enforcement and Administration of Justice: *Task Force
Report: The Police*, pp. 175–178, and *Field Surveys V: A National Survey
of Police and Community Relations*, pp. 290–325.

2. If there still are skeptics who doubt that this can be done, or who seek
information as to the teaching skills required to do it, the literature of
intergroup education in schools dating back 20 years is recommended. As
one example, see Taba, Brady, and Robinson, *Intergroup Education in
Public Schools*. Several management theorists are especially helpful on this
point. For instance, there is Theory Y as contrasted with Theory X as developed by Douglas McGregor in "The Human Side of Enterprise," an
article in *The Management Review*, and in his book with the same title.
See also Keith Davis, *Human Relations in Business;* Rensis Likert, *New
Patterns of Management;* and Bennis and Slater, *The Temporary Society*.

3. William E. Vickery, "Educating Citizens for Democratic Intergroup Relations, 1960–1980." Similar concepts were applied in a Wilmington, Delaware, public schools project directed by Dr. Vickery over a 3-year period
and described by Muriel E. Crosby in *An Adventure in Human Relations*.

4. George A. and Fannie R. Shaftel, *Role Playing the Problem Story*. Also
Kurt Lewin, *Resolving Social Conflicts*.

5. In a sense, these Institutes were harbingers of mobile police training centers that New Jersey has pioneered in more recent years. See the article
"New Jersey's Mobile Police Training Centers" in *Police*.

6. Riverside County Allied Law Enforcement Agencies (Box 512, Riverside,
California) produced an informative manual describing this project, under the direction of Riverside County Sheriff Ben J. Clark.

7. An excellent example is No. 79 in the California State Peace Officers'
training series, *Police-Community Relations*, Bureau of Vocational-Technical Education, The California Community Colleges, Sacramento,
August 1968.

8. Knowlton W. Johnson, *Examining Behavior and Perceptions of Law
Enforcement*.

9. See also Paul F. Cromwell, Jr., "Training-Education-Community Understanding."

10. This article includes a helpful bibliography on the subject.

11. This course in Covina was devised and conducted by Creative Management Research and Development, a nonprofit organization. For information on the approach of another agency, Community Confrontation and
Communication Associates (Dr. Irving Goldaber, president), see Fletcher
Knebel, "A Cop Named Joe."

12. Johnson and Gregory, "Police-Community Relations in the United
States." See also L. Deckle McLean, "Psychotherapy for Houston Police."

13. The Grand Rapids project was conducted by Scientific Resources, Inc., of Union, New Jersey (Dr. Saul Pilnick, president), now defunct. A Washington firm, Leadership Resources, Inc., used some similar techniques in a training program in the Washington, D.C., Metropolitan Police Department. In the late summer of 1971, the Associated Press reported (Lansing *State Journal*, September 3, 1971) that U.S. Senate investigators were checking complaints from government employees that they were being pressured into joining race relations group encounters that "bordered on the invasion of privacy." HEW Secretary Elliot Richardson said the "workshops," for 2000 employees, were not considered to be sensitivity training. He directed that the sessions be made voluntary and that there be no effort "to control thoughts and emotions."

    For a critical view, see W. Cleon Skousen, "Sensitivity Training—A Word of Caution."

14. See M. Lakin, "Some Ethical Issues in Sensitivity Training."

15. For example, see Shev and Wright, "The Uses of Psychiatric Techniques in Selecting and Training Police Officers as Part of Their Regular Training."

16. Eisenberg, Glickman, and Fosen, "Action for Change in Police-Community Behaviors." See also Burton Levy, "Cops in the Ghetto." Also relevant is a series of three articles by William J. Mathias, "Perceptions of Police Relationships With Ghetto Citizens."

17. Thoroughly described in an LEAA report (*Training Police as Specialists in Family Crisis Intervention*), available from the U.S. Government Printing Office, Washington, D.C. See also Morton Bard, "Family Intervention Police Teams as a Community Mental Health Resource," paper presented at a symposium of the American Psychological Association 76th annual convention in San Francisco, September 3, 1968; Morton Bard and Bernard Berkowitz, "Family Disturbance as a Police Function," paper presented at the Second National Symposium on Law Enforcement, Science and Technology, Illinois Institute of Technology Research Institute, Chicago, April 18, 1968; also by Bard and Berkowitz, "Training Police as Specialists in Family Crisis Intervention," an article in *Community Health Journal*.

18. John H. McNamara, "Uncertainties in Police Work," and James W. Sterling, *Changes in Role Concepts of Police Officers During Recruit Training*.

19. Thomas A. Johnson, "A Study of Police Resistance to Police-Community Relations in a Municipal Police Department." Unpublished doctoral dissertation, University of California School of Criminology, 1970. See Bayley and Mendelsohn, *Minorities and the Police*, for further information on the same departmental situation.

20. See James H. Auten, "Determining Training Needs."

21. See, for example, Taylor and Kleberg, "A Decade of Police Training in Illinois."

22. Thanks are due to the Urban Task Force, Episcopal Diocese of Pittsburgh, for their help in this summary. See Parker, Reese, and Murray, "Authoritarianism in Police College Students and the Effectiveness of Interpersonal Training in Reducing Dogmatism"; also Bruce T. Olson, "Some Social-psychological Sources of Tensions on Police Basic Training."

Chapter Twenty-One

Institutes and Metropolitan Programs

The term *police-community relations* originated with so-called Institutes beginning with that at Michigan State University in 1955, and since then copied or paralleled in many similar endeavors across the country. Through the years, the National Conference of Christians and Jews has been the most active sponsoring and promotional agency for such programs. Although many programs have been local in focus, there have also been annually repeated Institutes at the state and regional levels. Today there are several national Institutes, although the one at Michigan State is no longer held. All of this has been discussed in Chapter One, including the purposes, assumptions, and key concepts of such Institutes. *The Police and the Community: Studies* (Radelet and Reed) describes the Michigan State model in some detail (Study 2, Part Five), and a continuing statewide Institute (Study 3) in Michigan which was initiated in 1970 as the Michigan State University National Institute was phased out.[1]

Key Ideas of Institutes

It will be recalled that an Institute on Police and Community Relations includes these main programmatic ideas:

1. Special human relations training for the police is vital. But police officers need also the educational experience of meeting with other

citizens of diversified backgrounds, to discuss issues and problems of common concern and to participate in teamwork approaches to solving these problems.

2. Crime prevention can be and frequently is the primary purpose of teamwork approaches. Mutual understanding and respect may be heightened as a by-product of such problem-solving efforts.

3. Coordination and cooperation within the criminal justice system may be encouraged as a result of such joint endeavors.

4. Tensions between the police and minority groups are basically manifestations of conflict in the relationship between the powerful and the powerless, in political and economic terms. Race in itself is merely a convenient label for deeper inequities. Therefore, real change in police-minority relations depends greatly upon change in the larger political, economic, and social spheres.

5. Change in police and community relations depends also upon sorely needed revisions of existing criminal codes—for example, the so-called victimless crimes. Change also depends upon considerable attention to the role dilemma of the police and other criminal justice agents, coupled with drastic modifications in the structural and functional organization of police agencies, to align them more closely with community needs in changing times. Two key items in this are responsiveness to the community and appropriate control of police behavior.

No single Institute can possibly throw a net over the scope of these ideas; as the saying goes, some of the notions are "loaded." But we can see that these ideas are not nearly so revolutionary today as they seemed even ten years ago. Gradually we are beginning to realize that there is much more to "good" police-citizen relations than mere public relations moves "to improve the police image," however important these may be. We are beginning to recognize that the ultimate goal is stable community life (a just social order) across the board, as the 1966 President's Crime Commission and later national Commissions emphasized. Such a goal, under current conditions, is quite beyond the reach of bumper stickers and law-and-order sloganeering.

We will confine ourselves at this point to a brief reference to some of the various police and community relations Institutes that have been held, and consider their strengths and weaknesses. Then we will analyze various types of metropolitan programs that are largely spinoffs of the Institutes.

Some Representative Institutes in Community Relations

An annual five-day Southwestern Institute on Police and Community Relations has been conducted each August since 1957, at Texas A. & M. University. Its design has resembled that of the Michigan State

Institute, though attendance has been limited each year to less than 100 police and community leaders from Texas, Louisiana, Oklahoma, and Arkansas.

An annual Northeastern Institute was held in various locations for some years and gradually became billed as a national Institute. It has recently been based in Point Pleasant Beach, New Jersey, or in Atlantic City, and has a specific theme each year; for example, in 1971 it was police-school liaison projects.

An annual four-day Rocky Mountain Institute is centered at Colorado State University, dating back to 1966. It deals especially with problems of police relationships with the Spanish-speaking minorities. Georgia State University also has an annual Institute dating back several years, concentrating on police training programs.

A Southeastern Institute, drawing attendance from eight states, was initiated in 1961 at Wild Acres, North Carolina, and repeated there for several years. A Florida statewide Institute has lately become a national Institute in Miami, and it too has a specific focus each year—in 1971, delinquency prevention and community relations in the administration of justice. Numerous programs in various parts of the country have had a similar theme. Years ago, the so-called Precinct Youth Councils of the New York City Police Department functioned with strong police-community relations purposes, tied in with delinquency control.[2] More recently, these groups have been renamed Precinct Community Councils and their activities now cover a wider range.

Many police officers from other nations have attended Institutes in this country. A United Nations Conference on *The Police and Human Rights* took place in Canberra, Australia about 1960.[3] In recent years, the Canadian Council of Christians and Jews has sponsored police and community relations Institutes in several cities in Canada, beginning with pilot conferences in London, Ontario. In 1958, a week-long Institute on Police-Puerto Rican relations was co-sponsored in San Juan by the Commonwealth and the University of Puerto Rico. Attending were police officers from 30 to 35 stateside cities to which large numbers of Puerto Ricans had migrated after the end of World War II. In the summer of 1972, Adelphi University and the NCCJ jointly sponsored a European Study Tour on Police and Community Relations that visited Germany, France, England, and Scotland.

Numerous statewide Institutes have interested personnel on the subject of police and community relations. Michigan's current program of this type has been mentioned. In past years, such Institutes were held at the University of Missouri, Portland (Oregon) State University, Delaware State College (Dover), the University of Maryland (Baltimore), Newtonville (Massachusetts) College of the Sacred Heart, St. Vincent's College (Pennsylvania), the University of North Carolina (Chapel Hill), Drake University (Des Moines), and at the University of Nebraska (Lincoln and Omaha). One year the Nebraska Institute focused entirely on police relationships with Indians of the Omaha Tribal Council in the western part of the state. State Institutes have also been held in Arizona, Connecticut, New York, Kentucky (now at Bellarmine College in Louisville), Oklahoma, and Virginia. The University of Alaska has had a summer seminar on the subject. Adelphi University on Long Island has had summer workshops of two to three weeks duration on the subject since the late 1950s. Samford University in Birmingham, Alabama, has sponsored a state Institute for the past several years.

A five-day Hawaii statewide Institute took place in Honolulu in July, 1967, with a staff comprising partly islanders and partly mainlanders, convened and coordinated jointly by Michigan State University and the Honolulu Police Department. A Pennsylvania Institute of the middle sixties involved a series of conferences beginning with a general assembly at the State Police Academy in Hershey, then a number of localized meetings throughout the state, feeding back in turn into another general session, all over a period of six months. In the Chicago area, a 1968 Institute focused on police-community relations in suburban communities and consisted of a series of weekly sessions over a three-month period. Something similar has been done in the Washington, D.C. area. Wisconsin had its first state Institute at the University in Madison in February, 1970, on the theme *Law Enforcement and Free Dissent: Challenge of the Seventies.* Ohio and California had northern and southern Institutes for some years. In southern Ohio, the University of Cincinnati and Xavier University took turns as the site; in Cleveland, John Carroll University provided the facilities. In northern California, it was the University of San Francisco that was host. In southern California, the University of Southern California, and the California State Universities at Long Beach and at Los Angeles took turns; several years ago, this became a national Institute, based initially at USC and held each June—at present at Kellogg Center-West in Pomona, California.

Related Institutes

Since the NCCJ has been a prime mover in all of these Institutes, it is of interest to scan the regional program manual of that organization for examples of related projects, mainly local:

In Albuquerque, police participated in a parent education project on the theme *Rearing Children of Good Will.*

In Baltimore, one-day Institutes were conducted on the theme, *The Role of the Individual in the Criminal Justice Process.*

In New York City, a weekend police-youth seminar was held at Fort Totten.

Westchester County in New York has an annual countywide Institute.

In Charlotte, North Carolina, police-community councils have been formed, with the majority of citizen members residing in low income areas.

In Chicago, the human relations training program of the Police Academy was thoroughly evaluated by a committee of 103 policemen and educators.

In Cincinnati, a Law Committee composed of two representatives from all public junior and senior high schools meets monthly at the Board of Education office to discuss youth and the law and to make recommendations to their schools.

In Fort Worth, Texas, encounter seminars were staged by Texas Christian University attended by ten police officers and ten members of the minority community.

In Indiana, a five-day workshop on human relations included 25 members of the supervisory staff of the state reformatory at Pendleton, in the aftermath of a serious riot. In Indianapolis, an Advisory Council on Public Affairs to the Department of Public Safety was formed.

In Kansas City, a three-day Metropolitan Police-Community Relations Workshop was held. Kansas City also has formed a citywide Study Commission on Community Involvement, primarily concerned with public schools but with potential for other matters.

A Los Angeles Metropolitan Area Council on Police-Community Relations was established five years ago and has 55 affiliated agencies, including 12 police departments.

Louisville has a Police Community Advisory Board.

In New York City, a three-day conference revolved around the theme, *The Black and Puerto Rican Policeman and His Community.*

An Oklahoma Police Community Relations Council is in operation, tied to the Oklahoma Crime Commission, which is the state funding agency under the LEAA.

Pittsburgh is forming a city-wide Police-Community Relations Coordination Council, with affiliated Precinct Councils.

Numerous cities report police-youth rap sessions of one kind or another.

Strengths and Weaknesses of Institute-Type Programs

Institute-type programs in police and community relations have had both strengths and weaknesses.

Strengths

Projects aimed at improving police and community relations have been promoted.

Some honest communication has occurred in these settings, with some genuine dialogue and telling introspection, some worthwhile ventilation of doubts and fears, interchange of ideas, empathy, etc.

Some responsible community action has resulted from these Institutes, implementing the principle of total community responsibility for stabilizing interrelations through joint thought and efforts to solve problems and to cope with crime.

Police have been helped to see the diversity of the community, and elements of the community have been helped to see the police in human terms.

Overt expressions of prejudice and of outright hostility have probably become less blatant.

The professionalization of the police as well as interprofessionalism have been encouraged, and to some extent have been more carefully analyzed.

Some impetus has been provided for analyzing interrelationship problems in a social systems perspective—for example, the context of the criminal justice system.

All of these statements are carefully qualified generalizations. There is ample substantiating evidence, though it has not been systematically nor scientifically gathered. The same may be said for what follows.

Weaknesses

These conferences, as do all conferences, revolve around the spoken word; and while talk is a form of action, many variables determine the degree to which talk helps to solve problems. Its value should not be lightly dismissed, yet sometimes mere talk may substitute for solving problems.

Who are the people participating in such conclaves? From what backgrounds do they come? For whom do they speak? Sometimes the participants are more academics than they are adversaries. Go-to-meeting people go to meetings; others stay home with the problems.

We know too little about what happens as a result of such Institutes. Evaluation of attitude and behavior changes has generally not been done—and it is extremely difficult to do.

Educational conferences rarely involve or produce a consensus commitment to political action aimed at correcting social problems. Resolutions are usually as far as they go, if that far, and often difficulties arise in continuity and follow-through. There is a window-display aspect of such conferences, perhaps with limited politically symbolic effect, but not always focusing on what is most wrong, what most needs fixing, for the tendency is to zero in on issues where power is not in contest, thus to avoid political realities. Exemplifying this is a failure frequently observable in academic civil rights discussions in recent years: failure to understand the real meaning of organized violence as a substitute for "normal" political process—in short, the dynamic relationship between violence and social reform (Howard Zinn, *The Politics of History*).

Extending this reasoning a step further, conferences dealing with social pathology provide a kind of psychological release valve for societal guilt. Burton Levy of Wayne State University has referred to police-community relations as "a million-dollar Brotherhood Week operation where the parties involved in the dispute are often not named, where the symptoms and causes are frequently not discussed, and where most of the participants are hostile and defensive."[4] Levy may overstate the case a bit, but he goes on to say that there are two key questions that should be discussed frankly in any conference designed to reduce the hostility between blacks and police:

1. What steps can be taken within the bureaucratic framework to ensure that the policeman on the street is more likely to take the proper action in contact with black citizens?

2. Given the historical relationship and experience, how do you convince the black community that law enforcement in that community is wholeheartedly attempting to be absolutely fair and nondiscriminatory?

Too many conferences of this nature fail to engage the participants meaningfully in determinations of what the program is to be. Program design often is an elitist function, and the participants do not identify with it as their handiwork or as meeting their particular needs.[5]

Current Metropolitan Programs in Community Relations

The idea for police and community relations programs with rather sweeping dimensions in numerous metropolitan centers was incubated in such Institutes, for example, the program in Saint Louis, Missouri, generally regarded as the pioneer of its type. It was conceived as a result of participation by a Saint Louis team in the 1955 National Institute at Michigan State University. But the patterns of metropolitan programs are many and varied today. Studies appearing in the Radelet and Reed *Studies* (Part Five) describe some of these programs—such as those in Saint Louis, Dayton, Oakland, San Francisco, and Chicago. These may be taken as indicative of the range of similarities and differences.

Lee Brown has classified police-community relations programs in large cities into four types ("Typology: Orientation of Police-Community Relations Programs"): (1) externally oriented, as exemplified by the Saint Louis approach, (2) youth oriented, as exemplified by the New Orleans program, (3) service oriented, as exemplified by community services programs in Winston-Salem, North Carolina, and in

Chicago, and (4) internally oriented, as exemplified by the program in Covina, California, which we referred to in the preceding chapter. Brown distinguishes these four types of programs as follows:

> Externally oriented programs are generally developed by specialized police-community relations units in a police department and are directed toward the general public or various enclaves in the community.

> Youth oriented programs are directed mainly at youth in the community.

> Service oriented programs are aimed primarily at the alleviation of social problems.

> Internally oriented programs are operated on the premise that every police officer is a police-community relations officer and stress officer-on-the-beat efforts to create good relationships.

The Saint Louis Model

The Saint Louis Metropolitan Police Department was the first in a major city to establish a police-community relations division, doing so in 1957, after two years of preparatory work in the department and in the community spearheaded by the National Conference of Christians and Jews and its Saint Louis director, Virgil L. Border. He was elected chairman in 1955 of the Saint Louis Committee for Better Police-Community Relations and is still chairman of what today is called the Saint Louis Council on Police-Community Relations. This is a voluntary, independent, self-constituted advisory body to the police-community relations division of the police department.

Each of the nine police districts has a police-community relations committee. A district police-community relations officer works with the district committee as the representative of the District Commander. The district committees function with a constitution and by-laws, elect their own officers, and conduct a variety of projects and activities through their subcommittees. Any citizen residing in the district may belong to a district committee. A Patrol Area Leader has membership recruitment as one important duty.

One of the primary functions of a district committee is to serve as base for receiving and referring citizen complaints directed against the police. But the primary purpose of the entire program is crime prevention: in effect, teamwork between police and citizens in projects and programs aimed chiefly at heading off crime and thereby maintaining more livable, stable neighborhoods. A half-dozen storefront centers of the police department scattered throughout the city provide a facility for residents to seek police assistance conveniently: bases for all manner of social services.[6] The police-community relations division of the police department is staffed by a combination of sworn and unsworn personnel

and is directly accountable to the Chief of Police and the Board of Police
Commissioners.

DIAGRAM OF A DISTRICT COMMITTEE

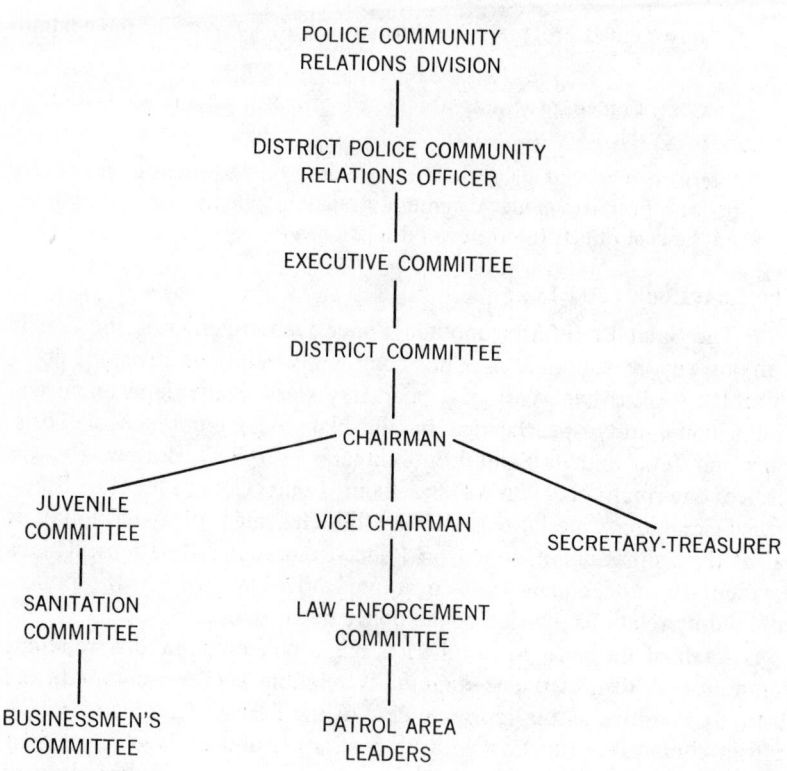

San Francisco

A police-community relations unit was established in the San
Francisco Police Department in May, 1962, adapting the Saint Louis
pattern. Subsequently, police-community relations committees were
activated in four districts, functioning with block committees rather than
with the Saint Louis-type subcommittees. Within five years after a very
promising start, the San Francisco program foundered mainly as a
result of cross-pressures within the department about the powers of the
central unit versus the powers of district commanders. While a modicum
program has continued to exist in San Francisco since 1967, it is no
longer rated as *the* program that it was for a few years.[7] A special
project aimed at improving police-community relations in San Francisco, called PACE, is described in *Studies* (Study 11, Part Five), Radelet and Reed.

Baltimore

Also following closely the Saint Louis blueprint has been the police-community relations division of the Baltimore City Police Department, activated July 1, 1966. This medallion conveys its central concept:

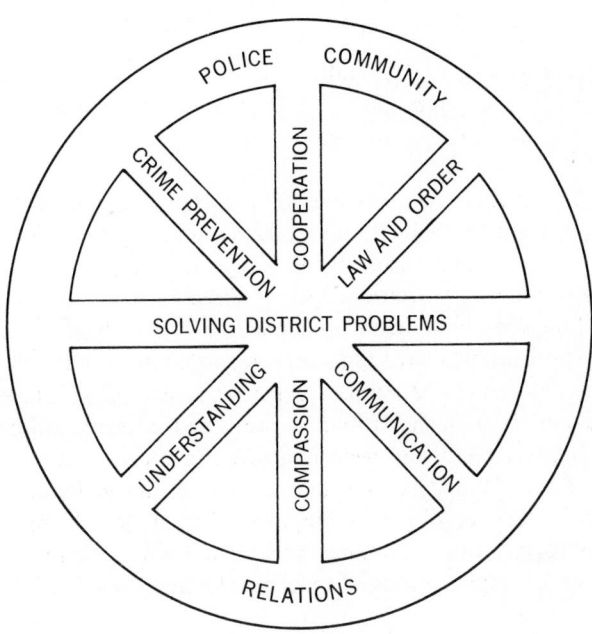

As in Saint Louis, there are nine district councils, each with functional subcommittees and an Executive Committee. Baltimore has also developed the storefront center program in high crime areas.

Washington, D.C.

A community relations division became part of the Washington Metropolitan Police Department in 1964. The purposes of the program are similar to those in Saint Louis, and storefront subcenters have also been established, in public housing projects. Before 1964, several district-level police-community relations committees similar to Saint Louis were operating but, more recently, activities have been undertaken by existing neighborhood and block clubs. There is also a Volunteer Aid program, manned by civilians in several precinct stations to provide information, and referrals for social services, and to help in precinct paper work. An OEO-funded, so-called Model Precinct project in police-citizen relations, begun in 1968, has provided the opportunity for experimentation with some of the projects which were continued, including the Volunteer project, the so-called Tension Area Patrol, Emergency Service Centers, and crime prevention clinics. This district has a board of citizens elected by residents to help acquaint the police with the special sensitivities of the black community. The Pilot District Project publishes a monthly Newsletter. The area of the program in Northwest Washington, comprises approximately 106,000 residents.

Cincinnati

Organization in Cincinnati is also based on district police-community relations committees, in the Saint Louis fashion.

New York City

The Precinct Youth Councils of the New York City Police Department predated the Saint Louis police-community relations program, yet shared some similar ideas. In recent years, the name of these precinct organizations has been changed to Precinct Community Councils and their functions have been broadened. Work with youth and community relations efforts have long been regarded as closely allied in this department. A Deputy Commissioner for Community Relations once functioned mainly as a departmental press and public relations officer, but the job description has been expanded in recent years.[8] The New York City Police Academy does an exceptional job in human relations training for police recruits. Commissioner Patrick V. Murphy is trying many ideas to improve community relations. Team policing experimentation is one example; testing the concept of the "resident patrolman" is another.

Chicago

A variation in the pattern of a police-community relations division in a big city police agency is observable in the community *services* division of the Chicago Police Department, a pattern described in Study 9, Part Five, of the Radelet and Reed *Studies.*

The Chicago Police Academy has greatly increased the time and attention devoted to sociological and psychological subjects in its basic training curriculum, largely provided now through the faculty of the Public Service Institute of the Chicago City College. In past years, faculty from Loyola University, DePaul University, and George Williams College helped with the program.

Chicago has a scheme of district police-community relations workshops that bring police and civilians together in regular, monthly educational endeavors. Sessions deal with a wide range of subjects, including burglary protection, shop lifting controls, explanations of various specialized units of the police department, operation and procedures of the juvenile court, bicycle safety, dangers of handguns, dangerous drugs, the canine corps, and the processing of arrested juveniles. A periodic newsletter, *Community Workshop Reporter,* is widely circulated and carries stories of the activities of the district workshops.

Citizen Advisory Committees

The programs mentioned so far revolve around the idea of citizen advisory groups of one kind or another, presumably supplying informational input for the police agency in community conditions and attitudes. These groups generally lack direct policy-setting responsibilities, but they are intended to influence policies and practices and help to guide police activities in a manner to keep the police tuned in to neighborhood needs. Further these groups fulfill an important function in a department's citizen complaint machinery, not because they are official adjudicating or investigating bodies but simply because many citizens use them as a convenient communication link with the Establishment. They help to establish the credibility of the police with the public. They help break down police isolation from the people they serve.

One problem with advisory committees is that they tend to attract "joiners" and often are dominated by persons who agree with the police or who do not cause trouble. Members are usually selected and invited to serve by police administrators and therefore it is unlikely that "troublesome" persons will get the chance. As William Brown puts it:

> Liaison should be established not with the people who like us, in particular, but rather with people who have the liking and respect of their minority associates. We want contact with the people who are the champions of the groups they represent, not our champions to them. ["The Police and Community Conflict"]

The President's Crime Commission (1966) made the same point:

> Persons who are hostile may be argumentative, disruptive, or otherwise difficult to deal with. Allegations may be made which are, or which appear to be, radical or irresponsible. However, this free discussion allows the committees to become vehicles for meeting conflict head-on in a controlled forum. The possibility of unpleasantness at a meeting is obviously preferable to leaving these confrontations to the streets. [*Task Force Report: The Police,* p. 157]

Another problem with advisory committees is that frequently they tend to avoid controversial subjects. Sometimes police participants have been known to walk out when such matters were introduced. This reduces the program to a sham, a mere game, granting that police officers, too, have their limits in how many insults and personal attacks they may be expected to absorb in one meeting! The point is that a history of poor relationships requires cool and civil temperaments and tongues on both sides if difficult problems are to be solved cooperatively.

Police-Community Relations Units and Storefront Centers

Common features of metropolitan programs are the police-community relations unit or division within a police department, and neighborhood storefront centers, usually in lower class, deteriorating, high crime areas. During the 1960s, these centers came to be looked on as standard earmarks of an urban police agency that was serious in its community relations purposes. The President's Crime Commission devoted rather enthusiastic attention to these features of a "good" program.

On the face of it, the logic of establishing such a unit in a department seems impregnable. We at Michigan State and in the National Conference of Christians and Jews championed it everywhere, for years. What we have come to recognize is that form is not necessarily substance. A police-community relations unit in a department, whatever it may be called, may make sense—but only under certain conditions. One condition is that such a unit should not be a facade for doing nothing about what most urgently needs repair. Another is that such a unit should not excuse personnel not specifically assigned to it from meeting their share of the total community relations responsibility. Some police-community relations units carry on a cornucopia of "busy work" activities involving many people in the community, but never really level with citizens about substantial issues. In effect, the unit joins the Establishment, for not to do so creates difficult problems within the department, or between the department and other governmental or community echelons. Everyone (well, almost everyone!) "on the inside" agrees that the unit is doing "very worthwhile work—if one goes for having social workers as cops, or vice versa!"

Semantics have figured in the matter because attitudes make important what a thing is called. As "police-community relations" has become old-hat and has declined in popularity, we begin to see departments moving toward such terminology as *critical incident* or *tension control,* or *conflict management,* or *crisis intervention.* It is no longer "community relations," but "community affairs" or "community involvement." The semantics have become more sophisticated and, in a few departments, so too have the working concepts, the functional charts, and the personnel deployment and training. But still, in too many departments, semantics is a means of deluding the public into believing that big things are happening when in fact "it's business as usual." In such departments, the byword with many policemen is, "I don't want any John Q. telling me how to do my job." A police-community relations unit in such a department, by whatever label, is mainly eyewash. And many groups in the community see it exactly so.

A word of sympathetic understanding is due the police officers who are assigned to police-community relations units. Attitudes toward them of some other officers in the department, including some at the supervisory and command levels, make their lot unhappy indeed. We alluded earlier to the relationship between such attitudes and the basic role predicament of the police. This may explain it philosophically, but it fails to provide much relief for the police officers who are victimized by this brand of internecine warfare. Their problems constitute another way of indicating that police-community relations units, as such, need to be more carefully evaluated than has been generally done to date. Their existence in a department does not mean that the department's community relations house is necessarily in order.

As for storefront centers, the idea again is certainly laudable. But again, there are divided opinions, with evidence to bolster both critics and supporters. As Glen D. King of the International Association of Chiefs of Police has astutely observed:

> Viewing . . . the storefront operation as basically a public relations activity will . . . likely doom it to failure. The police administrator must clearly distinguish between public relations programs, which are designed to interpret law enforcement programs and practices to the public, and community relations programs, which must be designed to provide an improved level of service. ["Storefront Centers"][9]

In short, a storefront center or substation can be as much a masquerade with the community as a police-community relations unit. The basic idea is sound; what matters is the way it is used.

Dayton and Oakland

Police departments in Dayton, Ohio, and Oakland, California, having had police-community relations units, have abandoned them in favor of more sophisticated nomenclature *and concepts*. Both are described in *Studies* (Radelet and Reed), Part Five. In our view, departments going in the direction suggested by the Dayton and Oakland approaches are coming closest to "where it's at" in police-community relations today. This does not mean that these cities are without problems—of relationships, of crime, or of social injustice and deprivation. It does mean that these departments reflect the best we now know about how to cope intelligently and professionally with these problems from the vantage point of the police. And both programs retain a great deal in the way of so-called traditional police-community relations activities.

Detroit

Perhaps no city in this country has devoted more attention to police-community relations in recent years than Detroit, particularly since the 1967 riot. Everything from block clubs to precinct councils to storefront centers, even to the somewhat distinctive Detroit Scooter

Patrol,[10] has been tried; and, since 1967, a combination of New Detroit, Inc., and the LEAA has made many dollars available for police-community relations undertakings of various types. Yet many people wonder whether the situation has improved.

A procession of surveys and investigations has produced evidence of abysmal social problems and of chronically strained race relations in this city. Studies of the police department have seemed to be as routine as roll calls. New Detroit and the Greater Detroit Chamber of Commerce have been among the influential bodies recommending *positive action programs* to improve police-community relations or the police department's services generally.[11] Many of the community betterment organizations have had a committee at work on police-community relations. A city-wide council on citizen-police relations exists, but it is viewed as the exclusive enterprise of the National Conference of Christians and Jews through its Detroit Round Table. Some feel that this council is not sufficiently action-minded. It is not always clear just what is meant by *action*.

The essence of Detroit's problem is that each of these many well-intentioned groups, all anxious to "do something"—and indeed, some with very solid accomplishments—have sought to mount a program on their own terms, each tending to see itself as "the coordinator" of activities. "Everybody wants to coordinate everybody else" is a typical expression of the matter. To be sure, Detroit does not have a monopoly on this kind of difficulty. But in Detroit, many worthwhile odds-and-ends and bits-and-pieces of programming for good police-community relations have had their usefulness somewhat blunted by the absence of a kind of master plan worked out cooperatively under some appropriate central, generally acceptable authority and initiative to put it all together.

Some of the resources for achieving such a goal in Detroit include the NCCJ city-wide Council; several Detroit teams participating in the statewide Institute; the resources of New Detroit, the Chamber of Commerce, and the UAW-CIO; a police department that has tried many ideas, such as the Scooter Patrol; a Civilian Complaint Bureau located in the downtown YWCA; an inventive recruitment scheme, recently initiated, aimed at more nearly equalizing the odds for minority group applicants to pass qualification hurdles; and, since April, 1970, a community relations bureau, and the efforts of the city's Interfaith Action Centers, NAACP, the Urban League, the Commission on Community Relations, and myriad other block, neighborhood and community-wide action groups and projects.

Some liabilities must be recognized also, among them the horrendous tax and budgetary miseries of a metropolis suffering acutely from suburbanitis; more than its fair share of white militant organizations; long-standing, indigenous control of the police department by old-line officers; and, since 1967 especially, free-wheeling purchase of handguns throughout the city by citizens bent on self-protection, unquestionably a factor in a soaring homicide rate.

Detroit is a checkerboard of good and bad in its police-community relations and in other attempts at facing social responsibility. It is like almost every other big city, where to speak of police-community relations is to isolate only a single prominent thread in a tapestry of predominant social immorality (William Serrin, "God Help Our City").

Crime-Buster Programs

Detroit is one of many big cities with a so-called crime-buster program. In Detroit, the current program is known as STRESS—meanthe "Stop the Robberies, Enjoy Safe Streets." It has been the subject of considerable controversy. Something similar to it, though by different names, exists in many cities, from New York City to Washington, D.C. to Philadelphia to Dade County, Florida, to Cleveland to Kansas City (Hot-Spot Squad) to Houston to Los Angeles. These programs operate through a presumably well-trained, well-selected unit of police officers designed to deal tactically with crime in the streets, that is, crime in the process of being committed. In Detroit, the unit focuses on robberies, using such techniques as decoy policemen.

These *Safe Streets* programs are open to the same questions that arise with saturation patrol in high crime areas. But the critics have been cautious, for they realize they are dealing with a mixed broth. Black citizens in big cities are interested in programs intended to contain crime in the neighborhoods where blacks reside in large numbers, simply because they are the chief victims of such crime. So they are inclined to be somewhat tolerant of experiments that show promise in this purpose, while at the same time retaining some skepticism. In the first eight months of the STRESS program in Detroit, eleven persons— ten of them black—were killed by STRESS units. One police officer lost his life, and 38 were wounded. Forthwith, the Michigan Civil Rights Commission threatened an investigation[12] and called for the program to be eliminated. Both NAACP and the Black Panthers agreed that STRESS tactics were unacceptable.

While feelings were strong on both sides of the matter, many citizens refrained from broadside condemnation of the program. In a few months, the Detroit squad made 1800 arrests of which almost half resulted in court action. But questions were raised about the use of police officers as decoys (entrapment), about standards of selection for officers (all volunteers) assigned to the program, about having more black officers so assigned, and about the nature of the special training and testing presumed for all officers so assigned.

With such titles as Operation Crime Stop, Stamp Out Crime (San Diego), and CHEC (Citizens Helping to Eliminate Crime), citizens are encouraged in many cities to assist the police directly in the apprehension of law-breakers and "suspicious persons."[13] For the most part, such programs rely upon the telephone (e.g., Dial-a-Cop). Critics of these programs refer to "vigilantism," to Orwellian connotations, and to the tendency for suspicious persons to be black, poor, young, "hippie-looking," and the like.

The hiring of private security patrolmen by residents of a particular block or neighborhood to protect life and property is increasing. These guards are civilians, usually uniformed but unarmed, and lacking police powers. Their mere presence is believed to have a deterrent effect on crime. Their main job is to telephone the police when necessary, and they are warned not to interfere in domestic quarrels.

Flint, Michigan, has a program called the Oak Park Patrol, in a high crime, predominantly black, area. It consists of a special force of thirty policemen, organized into 15 two-man teams, all of them rotating on their off days, at overtime pay. Half the teams work on foot, and half on motor scooters. They are instructed to stay so close to neighborhood matters that they must ignore routine police calls from other parts of the city. Even emergencies in Oak Park are handled by cruisers from elsewhere. Most of the men are college educated. Part of the patrol consists of uniformed interns, well known in the area because of past work as playground supervisors or work associated with the schools. The patrols are interracial. The program, funded by the LEAA, is said to have brought about a sharp decrease in major crimes and at the same time to have noticeably improved police-community relations.

Similar to the Flint program is the Safe Streets Squad in Dade County, established with an LEAA grant in December, 1970. Half of the 16-member squad are black, and all members are specially trained in community relations, family crisis intervention, and the "psychology of juvenile delinquency." A primary aim is the creation of better relations between police and youth; the approach to crime is more preventive than tactical.

The Roxbury section of Boston has a Tactical Patrol Force known as the Soul Patrol. The unit consists of 34 men, all of them black, operating in the high crime hours from 6:00 in the evening to 2:30 in the morning (*Newsweek,* January 3, 1972, p. 41). As with the Dade County Program, the Soul Patrol is an effort to combine effectively the objectives of crime control and good community relations. It is a matter of balancing the law enforcement and conflict management functions of the police, in tune with the needs of a particular community. Methods and techniques are therefore important; it is not simply a question of reducing crime at any cost and by any impulsive means.

Many inner-city residents are augmenting municipal and private policemen with a new activism all their own. Black citizens are organizing in many cities as militant supporters of law and order, to help their old nemesis, the police.[14] It may be found in Brooklyn's Bedford-Stuyvesant area, in the area of East 79th Street and Hough Avenue in Cleveland, in the third police district in Washington, D.C. (Citizens

Riders), in Chicago's second district, in the block-watchers project in Saint Louis, in Operation Get Involved in Dallas, in the Kansas City Central Council of 100, and in the growing watchdog phenomenon everywhere. A trained German shepherd or Doberman pinscher is a formidable ally in the cause of crime abatement, although the community relations aspect of it may be questionable.

Electronics help too in police-citizen cooperative crime control, as illustrated by the Community Radio Watch Program of Rochester, New York (Hal Wand, "Extra Eyes and Ears for a Police Department").

Some Other Large Cities

Certain features of police-community relations programs in other cities should be briefly mentioned. A principal goal of the program in New Orleans, for example, is to reach youth of the community.[15] Philadelphia has a long history of police-community relations programming, featured by such things as relatively early efforts to make human relations training for the police more effective experimentation with a civilian review board, a chief inspector for community relations in the police department's table of organization at a relatively early date, and a more recent rap session project including police officers and mental health social workers. Other aspects of the Philadelphia story have been described elsewhere.[16]

The Dade County Department of Public Safety in the Miami area has devoted considerable attention to its total community relations program, as have the Nassau County Police Department on Long Island, and the Los Angeles County Sheriffs Department. Study 6, Part One, in *Studies* by Radelet and Reed discusses police-community relations in Los Angeles. The LAPD is today engaged in more than 50 different programs that are classified as police-community relations. Dallas established a community relations division in the police department in 1968 and initiated storefront Community Service Centers, including a mobile unit. The division also has a program development section, one of whose projects is a Student-Police Council attracting students from each of twenty senior high schools. Another section of the division is called the Human Relations section, one of whose projects is a Rumor Control Center.

The Atlanta Police Department's Crime Prevention Bureau uses 50 community service officers from 17 to 21 years old as a police auxiliary. The youths come mostly from low income areas and might otherwise be unemployed. They help bring the police and the community closer together, and they are groomed to become regular policemen if they choose. These youthful subprofessionals had their predecessor counterparts in the so-called White Hats in Tampa and Dayton a few years ago, and in a pioneer experiment with subprofessionals in Richmond, California.

Smaller Cities

Cities of medium size have also made their mark in the development of police-community relations programs in recent years. Flint has had a comprehensive program in a department where 40 percent of the 375 officers have two years or more of college, and nearly half are enrolled in college classes.

Peoria, Illinois has developed a conscientious program in the past few years. San Jose, California has long been a leader in the field, as one of the three original LEAA Demonstration Cities, along with Dayton and Charlotte. Des Moines has stressed training and education of police officers and is striving for more of a community-interest program. Phoenix has had, in 1970–1971, a comprehensive Citizen Involvement Project in police-citizen dialogue, funded in part by LEAA.[17] (The program in Winston-Salem, is described in Study 9, Part Five, *Studies* by Radelet and Reed.)

Strengths and Weaknesses of Metropolitan Programs: A Summary

As our discussion has progressed, we have suggested some of the strengths and weaknesses of metropolitan programs in police and community relations. By way of concluding this chapter, it may be well to summarize.

Strengths (according to the advocates of such programs):

Have helped to build mutual trust, credibility, better communication, improved police intelligence with respect to community attitudes, and assisted the police in conducting investigations.

Have enlisted many citizens in partnership with the police in coping with crime.

Have improved police-public relations, especially with youth, and also police-media relations.

Have enhanced intercultural understanding and helped to reduce racism by forcing a re-examination of fundamental attitudes.

Have helped police liaison with many community groups, including extremist groups.

Have encouraged inter-agency and inter-professional cooperation.

Have improved police-school cooperation.

Have helped provide assistance for many people in need of jobs, health or hospital services, and many other needs, especially through storefront centers.

Have helped to control rumors.

Have helped to stabilize neighborhoods and to restore pride among residents.

Weaknesses (according to the critics of such programs):

Haven't done much to curb crime. (The problem is an old one in program evaluation: we don't know what would have happened if the program did not exist.)

Haven't gone much beyond window-dressing and public relations activities.

Haven't reached "the right people," "grass roots people," etc.

Haven't been supported by total commitment throughout police agencies. Regarded as a secondary function, too low in priority: "a necessary evil," "a pile of bull-shit," "not *real* police work," etc.

Lose sight of genuine police work. The problem is to maintain police identity and at the same time win the confidence of community groups. Deviation from standard police practices makes social workers out of the police—at least so the critics allege. Critics add that this isolates a community relations unit from the remainder of the department. (Jerome Skolnick, "The Police and the Urban Ghetto," pp. 15–17.)

Community relations workers in a police agency should not engage in formal complaint machinery or internal investigations. To do so turns them into "snitchers" and "head-hunters" and adds to their role ambiguity. (Theodore Rankin, "PCR—Fact or Farce?")

In addition, police intelligence should not be overemphasized in investigations, making stool pigeons out of citizens, jeopardizing the civil rights of informers as well as of suspects.

Should not cultivate only citizens who are already disposed to be friendly toward the police, sometimes for reasons of personal aggrandizement—as in the case of the typical "buff."

Should not operate with inadequately trained community relations personnel. As a simple example, many speak only English, and many of these do not understand the idiom of the streets and the ghetto.

Such programs attract those looking for a forum to vent their hostilities against the police.

Few *real* changes have resulted from the programs: policemen and police departments do not change much, many laws are still on the books that shouldn't be, and racism is still rampant.

It is untenable to sit in judgment on the merits of these plus-and-minus opinions and allegations. There are plenty of spokesmen, police, and nonpolice, for each point. Much depends upon what one wants to prove. If one is anti-community relations, he will find evidence for the weaknesses. If one is pro-community relations, he will find evidence for the strengths. As James Q. Wilson has observed, we are talking at and past one another, and the real issues are largely lost in rhetoric.

Notes to Chapter Twenty-one

1. Though produced in limited quantity and no longer available for circulation, *Proceedings* of each of the 15 national Institutes held at Michigan State University during the period 1955–1969 repose in the James J. Brennan Memorial Library of the School of Criminal Justice and in the Paula K. Lazrus Memorial Library at the New York headquarters of NCCJ. Although not connected directly with the Institutes, an interesting compilation of articles and papers was published in 1965 by the International Association of Chiefs of Police, called *Police and the Changing Community: Selected Readings,* edited by Nelson A. Watson.

2. See Lawrence W. Pierce, "The New York City Formula."

3. A *Proceedings* report of this conference was internationally circulated. The United States did not officially participate.

4. Burton Levy, "One Basis for Social Violence: Police-Negro Tensions," State of Michigan Commission on Civil Rights, undated monograph.

5. In his doctoral dissertation in the Department of Sociology, Washington University, Saint Louis, Mo., Victor G. Strecher discusses some of the merits and demerits of Institutes on Police and Community Relations: "Police-Community Relations, Urban Riots, and the Quality of Life in Cities," unpublished, 1968.

6. A number of articles describing the Saint Louis program in detail appeared in *The Police Chief* 22, no. 3 (March 1965). The March 1972 issue also contains a number of interesting articles on police-community relations.

7. See Jerome H. Skolnick, "The Police and the Urban Ghetto" pp. 14–22; Mary Ellen Leary, "The Trouble With Troubleshooting"; and Alvin A. Rosenfeld, "The Friendly Fuzz."

8. See Richard Dougherty, "Requiem for the Centre Street Mafia."

9. See also Ned O'Gorman, "Storefront."

10. See Morche and Colling, "Detroit's New Community Oriented Patrol"; Johannes F. Spreen, "Police Responsibility for a Community in Turmoil."

11. For example, the Report of the Police-Community Relations Project Committee of New Detroit, Inc., June 1970.

12. As reported by Agis Salpukas in *The New York Times,* December 14, 1971.

13. Indianapolis pioneered a program of this type called "Crime Alert," which has had considerable acclaim.

14. As reported by Edwin A. Roberts, Jr., in *The National Observer,* May 10, 1971. See also Victor L. Cizanckas, "Police Patrol for Black Americans."

15. See Sidney H. Cates III, "This Is Our Story" (mimeographed), New Orleans Police Department. See also "The Police and the Rest of Us," a citizens' report of the New Orleans Department of Police, prepared by the Round Table of Human Relations Groups, October 1969.

16. See *Field Surveys IV: The Police and the Community,* vol. 2, report to the President's Commission on Law Enforcement and Administration of Justice. Also Allen B. Ballard, "Police Working in the Neighborhood"; Harry G. Fox, "Preparing for Police Leadership in Community Relations"; and Fox and Margolis, "Rap and Rapport." Study 14 (Part 5) in Radelet and Reed, *Studies,* describes a North Philadelphia project.

17. "Citizen Involvement Program," a Police-Community Relations Project of the Arizona Region, National Conference of Christians and Jews.

Chapter Twenty-Two

Other Types of Programs

Among the types of programs designed for specialized service in the community are those for police-school liaison, public relations and information, and other special purpose programs.

Police-School Liaison Programs

Police and community relations programs and programs concerned with youthful attitudes and behavior are often thought of as synonymous. One reason is that the adult planners of such programs frequently regard "problems of youth" as a fitting subject for "interprofessional dialogue." Another closely related reason is the increasing incidence of juvenile delinquency and of crimes committed by young people. Still another reason is the hope that "things will be better in the future," in police-community relations and with respect to social problems in general, if we concentrate on proper teaching of today's youth. "They will do better than we have" is a typical expression of this theory.

Many programs and projects aimed at combatting or preventing youthful crime do have some dimensions of police-community relations. To the extent that the police are active in these programs, mutual objectives are not uncommon. Some police agencies combine police-community relations and youth services in one unit. A similar idea has inspired the community services or crime prevention units of other police agencies. Some departments feel that crime prevention is a more appropriate social responsibility for them than community relations per se. While this is fencing with semantics to some extent, one is well advised not to argue the point so long as the job gets done. Actually, the police have been engaged to a limited degree in crime prevention, and more in delinquency prevention programs, since the turn of the century. Juvenile aid units date back to the 1930s.

Among many types of programs of this general nature, one devised recently is called Police-School Liaison. The essence of it is to place a police officer on duty in a school. The idea dates back 20 years or so in England,[1] and about 15 years in this country. Flint, Michigan, is recognized as a pioneer developer of such a program, beginning in 1958.[2] Salient features of the Flint program are these:

> The police officer, called *police counselor,* is assigned to a junior or senior high school. He is also responsible for elementary schools in that area. (Flint public schools operate on a community school pattern.)

> The officer, in plainclothes, is not responsible for enforcing school rules and regulations. His main concern is with behavior of a pre-delinquent or delinquent nature. But he also exercises some secondary functions in career counseling, in rapping with students, and in helping to develop friendly attitudes toward police.

> Decisions to refer a case are made by a counseling team at the school, of which the police counselor is a member.

Rather impressive results, as represented by delinquency statistics, have been claimed for the Flint program, although there are those who remain skeptical. The plan has been imitated in numerous other cities, with some variations. Tucson, Arizona, for instance, adopted it beginning in 1963, with the officer stationed in school in full uniform—the idea being to encourage youth to see police officers as friendly helpers. The question of whether the officer should be in uniform has provoked much argument. In Tucson, the police officer alone makes the final decision on referrals of problem cases. The Tucson program was threatened by legal suit in 1968, the Arizona Civil Liberties Union charging that it was mainly a police intelligence operation, which deprived students of their civil rights.

Police-school liaison programs have both staunch advocates and strong critics. June Morrison lines up the arguments on each side as follows:[3]

Supporters of school-liaison programs point out:

> School administrators are generally favorable in their views of the program. So too are police administrators.

Police officers in such programs believe that goals are being met in a very satisfactory manner, in terms both of youthful attitudes and of delinquency.

Statistics seem to show that the program does make a significant difference in delinquency and youthful crime. While the results of program evaluations are circumspectly interpreted (and it is difficult to learn exactly what has been studied, by whom, and how), the statistical evidence of apparent success is persuasive.

Faculty and youth themselves are generally favorable in their views of the program. The same appears to be true with parents, though there are exceptions with all three groups.

Opponents of the programs claim:

Police officers in these programs are sometimes not adequately trained for their duties in school counseling.

The program injects primitive attitudes into the treatment of children.

Attitudes of youth toward police are not being changed in a positive direction.

The program takes manpower away from police activities that should have priority.

Interrogation and investigation by police officers in the program jeopardizes the civil rights of students.

Police officers are used as school disciplinarians, which should not be their function.

The program carries with it an Orwellian atmosphere of youth under constant harassment and surveillance. It establishes "a network of informers."

The program encourages the misuse of educational process for police purposes.

Some of the objections to the program can and should be met by procedural guidelines and safeguards, for example, in such matters as interrogating students and notifying parents. A central question in Police-School Liaison programs is again the question of role. To the extent that they are convinced that it pays off in helping to control delinquency and crime, police administrators are likely to be in favor of liaison programs. So the question is not so much whether the police ought to have a role in the programs as it is the ambiguity of the police officer's role in the school setting. Some of the forementioned arguments against the liaison-type program reveal other important points that should be resolved. One may well ask, for example, whether police officers in the school setting should be in uniform and whether they should be armed.

Defining the role of the school liaison officer means coming to grips with the central questions: What is it, exactly, that the police officer is there to do? Does a uniform—or a gun—contribute to this purpose? These are not easy judgments to make in our culture and society today, and the answers to these questions would probably differ according to particular community or neighborhood conditions and attitudes. The ultimate aim by one role definition is summed up in the Tucson statement of purpose:

> The School Resource Officer Program is a cooperative effort of the public schools and law enforcement agencies to develop an understanding of law enforcement functions and to prevent juvenile delinquency and crime.

If a community is to consider such a program, it would be well for all parties concerned to have the opportunity to speak their piece and to be fully informed about what is to be done, why and how, and with what procedural guidelines. This is not a matter for unilateral, arbitrary policy-setting by police or school administrators. Discussions leading to a decision should enlist the police, appropriate governmental leaders and bodies, juvenile court people, school administrators and faculty, certain social agencies, civil rights and due process organizations, students and parents, and every other interested citizen and group. The students and parents, who are pivotal figures in the aims of the programs, are most likely to be forgotten in this process. Initiators of the programs must take the time and the means necessary to ensure that the base of opinion and consultation is as broad as possible and that information about such programs where they presently exist is available for reference.

A national Institute on Police and School Liaison programs was convened under the sponsorship of the National Conference of Christians and Jews in Atlantic City, December 5–8, 1971. The participants in the Institute came from seventeen states and the District of Columbia. They represented all sections of the nation, from the East Coast to California and from New England to the deep South. The participants were police, educators, and high school students, plus a few additional persons who represented both public and private human relations agencies. A total of 185 persons took part in the deliberations.

The following is a resumé of the basic agreements hammered out in over 4600 man-hours of discussion in plenary sessions, task forces, and caucuses. Unanimity was not achieved on any issue, but broad areas of consensus emerged as follows:

1. As a matter of principle, it was agreed that the police do not belong in the schools. Their presence in the schools is viewed as indicative of the failure of the society at large to fulfill its primary obligations to its younger citizens. However, because the police *are*

serving in a variety of roles in many schools throughout the nation, the Institute turned its attention to ways in which their presence could be most creatively and constructively put to use.

2. Police should not be called to serve as school security guards, except in the most extreme emergency situations. The police should not be viewed as the first line of defense against disorder and should be called only as a last resort after all other measures have failed. After the emergency has abated, the police as an enforcement agency should be removed from the school premises as quickly as possible. Their continued presence tends to exacerbate the tensions they were called in to control, and inhibits an educational process.

3. On the other hand, the police would be welcomed into the schools by both students and administrators as liaison officers acting in an educational and counseling role. The Institute, therefore, recommended that all high schools seek to adopt a School Liaison Officer program.

4. The Liaison Officer should be an authorized, sworn member of the major law enforcement agency operating in the jurisdiction in which the high school is located. Under the command of either the Juvenile Bureau or the Community Relations Bureau of his department, he would be assigned to full-time duty working with students in cooperation with school authorities. It was emphasized that:

   a. The Liaison Officer should not be regarded as a law enforcer in the school. It was agreed, however, that if a violation of the law occurred within his immediate view, it would be necessary for him, as a police officer, to take appropriate lawful action. If a violation were to take place where he was not present, it would be preferable for the school authorities to determine, in consultation with the Liaison Officer, the proper course of action. If the incident is deemed to be one that the officer can deal with on a discretionary basis, he should do so. If there are grounds for legal custody, other police officers should be called in to make the arrest. While it must always be understood that the Liaison Officer is a police officer, his relationship with the students should not be jeopardized by giving them reason to believe that his role in their school is one of surveillance and enforcement.

   b. The Liaison Officer should not be called upon to take over the responsibility for maintaining discipline in the school. This is a task for the administration and the students themselves. Principals and teachers should not abdicate their responsibilities for order maintenance by calling on the Liaison Officer to enforce school policies and regulations. To do so would be to reinforce the already too prevalent image of the police as a repressive force rather than a helpful resource.

5. The visual image of the Liaison Officer in the school—how he should dress, whether he should be armed—was the subject of much thought and discussion. The final recommendations reflected mutual concessions:

   a. *Dress.* The majority preference was civilian attire for the Liaison Officer while on the job in the school, but many police officers felt that he should be in uniform. As a compromise solution, it was agreed that civilian dress with a sports blazer and an identifying pocket patch insignia would be appropriate most of the time, but that periodically, perhaps once a week, the Liaison Officer should wear his regulation uniform so that his identity as a policeman would not be lost.

   b. *Arms.* If the law or department policy required that all officers wear side arms, it was agreed that (1) when the regulation uniform was worn, the gun could be visible, and (2) when civilian attire was worn, the gun should be as inconspicuous as possible. The students and many of the police believed that, if possible, the weapon should be kept locked in the Liaison Officer's office during his period of duty on school property.

6. The role of the Liaison Officer was defined as combining three functions: counselor, resource person, and educational aide. The functions were outlined as follows:

   a. *Counselor.* Police, students, and educators alike felt that the Liaison Officer could make an important contribution as a resident friend, counselor, and listener to youth with personal problems. The role was likened by some to that of an ombudsman, to whom the students could turn for help and guidance.

   In this role, the Liaison Officer should cooperate closely with, and not conflict with, Authorized Guidance Counselors in the school. It was felt, however, that because most Guidance Counselors are so overburdened with testing, curriculum adjustment, and long-range planning for student welfare, they do not have the time to deal with the kinds of daily personal matters that the students might take to the Liaison Officer, and they would welcome help in this area.

   b. *Resource and referral.* The Liaison Officer should be well acquainted with the kinds of help available to young people with special problems and refer them to the local resources that can aid them in matters beyond his depth to solve. This helping function would frequently be on a "shared client" basis with the school Guidance Counselor.

   c. *Educational aide.* The Institute recommended that the Liaison Officer serve an educational function by helping to create and conduct courses of study designed to acquaint students with the American system of justice and the ways in which it operates on the local level and touches their lives.

These courses should be electives, but should earn credits. They should be developed cooperatively by the educators and the police and conducted under a team-teaching system. The courses should be designed to make use of a wide range of community resources and to put emphasis on group-process techniques, instead of lecture methods, with as much student participation as feasible.

7. With respect to the qualifications of the person for this kind of job, it was agreed by the Institute that:

   a. The Liaison Officer should have at least two years of college training or the equivalent experience.

   b. He should be a volunteer for the job, for only a man who really wants this kind of responsibility is qualified to handle it.

   c. He should receive specialized training both before and during the assignment, with emphasis on adolescent psychology.

8. Other recommendations pertaining to the Liaison Officer were the following:

   a. The students should be given a voice in the selection of the officer assigned to work in their school.

   b. Wherever feasible, it would be better if the Liaison Officer were a resident of the community in which the school is situated. The students, however, said they were more interested in the attitude that a man brought to his assignment than they were about where he lived. "We don't want a cop in the school; we want a friend. And if he's a friend, we don't care where he grew up," was the way one young man stated it.

   c. The Liaison Officer should have an office in the school and be available to the students on a daily basis.

   d. He should be considered a part of the educational team and be included in all faculty conferences and consultations.

   e. It was emphasized that beyond his regular duty in the school, the Liaison Officer should participate in extracurricular and community affairs and conduct regular meetings with parents, individually as needed and in groups.

9. The opinion of many of the Institute participants, cutting across police-youth-educator lines, was that the best Police-School Liaison program in the world would be worthless if the students' experience with the police outside the school setting contradicted the trust relationship established by the program. It was recommended, therefore, that *all police* working in the district in which the school is located be required to make periodic visits to the school and, under the aegis of the Liaison Officer, participate in "rap" sessions with the students. This kind of exchange, it was believed, would help to achieve better understanding on both sides.

10. All three groups attending the Institute—police, students, and educators—agreed that a Police-School Liaison Program should not be undertaken without adequate advance planning and delineation of goals and roles. Police, students, and educators should work together to establish the guidelines under which the program is to operate, and matters of student rights, educational prerogatives, and police responsibilities must be understood in advance by all concerned.

Other School Projects

There are many different types of police-school cooperative programs, as we have said. Some examples are driver education in high schools, traffic and bicycle safety programs, the Officer Friendly, Patrolman Bill, and other political socialization projects to which we referred in Chapter Fourteen. Add to these such activities as a Police-Community Relations Youth Council (Saint Louis), Teenage Traffic Court, Career Days, Operation Blue Star (Des Moines), Police Partners (Philadelphia), Teen Post and School Contact programs (San Diego), Police-Public School Cadet (Flint), Police Youth Service Corps (Pontiac, Michigan), police-junior aid programs, police cruiser tours (as described in Study 10, Part V, *The Police and the Community: Studies,* Radelet and Reed), shoplifting and theft prevention lectures, junior crime prevention projects, student symposia on law and order, youth protection instruction and narcotic education, and many more similar programs across the country.

The points brought out in the discussion of police-youth relations and attitudes in Chapter Fourteen are pertinent here. Following are brief reviews of some program experiments that relate to the subject:

Wayland, Massachusetts, a small (population 15,000), suburban, upper-middle-class community 20 miles from Boston, experienced a series of incidents that pitted high school students against police. In an effort to improve future attitudes and relations, rap sessions employing some sensitivity techniques were held between selected junior high school students and police officers. A careful evaluation of the project showed very positive results. (Meyer and Topham, "Sensitivity Training/Rap Sessions for Police and Pupils.")

The police-youth discussion group (or rap session) has many variations in many communities and traces back to a 1965 experimental project in Richmond, California. The youth attending are often "troublesome;" for example, lower-class black youth or youth on probation. Heated exchanges are common; a kind of modified group therapy takes place, aimed at reducing mutual hostility. Role-reversal techniques are often employed. (Gitchoff and Shope, "Kids vs. Cops.")

The Citizen and the Law project of the Los Angeles County Sheriff's Department is a good example of a political socialization project at the junior high level. The initial trial of the program was in Temple City, California. (Peter Pitchess, "Citizen and the Law.")

Another survey of attitudes toward police was conducted among junior high students of diversified backgrounds in Omaha, Nebraska, and reported in 1969 (Kuchel and Pattavina, "Juveniles Look at Their Police"). One interesting finding was the high percentage of students who said they would *not* like to be policemen.

In New York City, the Police Academy and the Board of Education teamed up in joint sponsorship of a seminar course (with increment credit) for school teachers, entitled *The Police Department and the Schools.* Police officers served as instructors in the course. It was an outgrowth of the 1964 so-called Kaplan-Lodge proposal, one recommendation of which was a course of this type, to broaden teacher knowledge and understanding of the police function and the methods employed and problems encountered in carrying out law enforcement duties. From its original enactment in 1965, the course was expanded and refined and made available to teachers throughout the city. (Lander Hamilton, "Collected Essays on the Police Function.")

A study of local police agency-school system interaction and cooperation in thirteen Illinois school districts revealed five major areas of concern in communications between police and school personnel: (1) juvenile delinquency detection, prevention and control, (2) traffic control on or near school property, (3) some aspects of safety education, (4) crowd control at large school functions, and (5) student/adult problems on or near school property. (Henry Midlander, "Communication Patterns: Police and Schools.")

Professor G. Douglas Gourley has conducted a three-week summer workshop entitled *Law Enforcement, Public Schools and the Community* at California State College, Los Angeles, for more than ten years. It was designed primarily for school teachers and administrators and consists of lectures in law enforcement and corrections, group discussions, and field trips. The agenda is unstructured, but typical subjects include juvenile crime and delinquency, police work with juveniles, vice, narcotics, criminalistics, the courts, probation, parole, and police-community relations. The workshop has generated substantial interest through the years, and evaluation discloses that it has produced significant attitude changes ("Workshop on Law Enforcement, Public Schools Reveals New Student Attitudes").

Whatever the means or the program, worked out with the collaboration of appropriate community groups, students, parents, and others, it is clear that school systems and police departments must get together in their common interests and purposes. Persons concerned with police-community relations and school-community relations have much to learn from each other, for there are parallels in their objectives. In the past, police and schools have tended to go their separate ways, each insisting that there be no "interference" with the other. While the need for clear role delineation for each institution becomes more

compelling as collaboration and cooperation increase, there is no justification in today's society for continuation of the separatist pattern
(James Kelly, "Schools v. Cops").

Law and Order in the Schools

Today's youth in large numbers do not conform to traditional
controls, in or out of school. Problems of discipline loom large in and
around classrooms, especially in the heterogeneous inner city. Teachers
and administrators from "good" backgrounds are faced with grave difficulties in understanding and adjusting to pupil behavior perceived as
antischool or antiteacher, if not antisocial. Some of this behavior is due
to personality and some to environmental factors, but there is little
question that it is sometimes technically criminal, sometimes dangerous,
and always frightening. Many school systems are therefore increasing
their protective and security personnel in order to enforce order and
discipline, and in so doing are encountering some negative community
reaction to "cops in the corridors."[4]

The maintenance of order is vital in a school setting. Wide agreement on such a generalization contrasts with wide disagreement on
what constitutes order, whether it is more or less important than (or
different from) freedom to learn, and in any case how it is best
achieved. To be specific, what difference may there be between the
school's approach to discipline and order with lower-class Puerto Rican
children and that of WASP, middle-class children?

> Many contemporary "disadvantaged" children, while feeling limited
> in upward economic and social mobility and limited in world-view,
> sense a greater freedom to express, and often act out, a generalized
> personal and collective rage at traditional and adult institutions. . . .
> The fact that must be dealt with is that if anger, hostility, frustration,
> or disenchantment are accompanied by invective or physical attack
> upon school personnel, fellow students, or property, the optimum
> atmosphere for teaching or learning rapidly deteriorates. [Wendell J.
> Roye, *Law and Order in Classroom and Corridor*]

Something must be done, then, to control bedlam and terror in
the school. It is to be hoped that this can be accomplished without
appreciably sacrificing teaching resources to monitoring resources.
How? More student participation in the governance of schools seems to
be part of the answer and more community participation in the governance of schools another. Programs that help to bridge the cultural and
social gulf between teachers and pupils are still another part of the
answer.[5] Improving the quality of instruction may help.

Ultimately, however, the question may be when to bring in the
police? First, we may say *certainly not until after a great deal of reflection by school personnel*. Calling in the police to handle school

disorder is very often an easy "cop-out," although it is conceded that community pressures sometimes force this action even when it is imprudent. Here again, a great deal of community education is required, preferably *before* a crisis develops. Panic takes over when a crisis occurs and impairs clear thinking. An increase in police or security personnel in schools does not really get at the base of the problem; it merely consoles those who are content to deal with symptoms. As Wendell Roye points out:

> Security forces secure, protect, monitor, control, intimidate, and repress. Remediation . . . is not the primary function of police, in hallways or elsewhere. . . . Employment of uniform, club, badge, gun, and the other paraphernalia of law enforcement to make teenagers walk straight and quietly down a school hallway is demeaning to the officer, insulting to the children and their families, and of questionable overall merit or effectiveness. Finally, uniformed guards in great number in a school are a clear indication that the institution is proceeding in fear and failure. [Ibid.]

This is not to argue that there is *never* a time and circumstance when a police officer is plainly needed in the school for the specific purpose of maintaining order or of invoking criminal process. But we believe that this should not be the first move when things get out of hand. One problem with the Police-School Liaison program, as we have stated, is the role ambiguity of the police officer in the school. Since he or she is on the scene and on the school staff, it is easy to rely on that officer as a kind of symbolic deterrent in disciplinary upheavals. The image of the officer then comes through to students as a bogeyman, rather than as a helper, counselor, confidant, and friend. To be sure, the officer must occasionally make arrests in the line of duty. Parents, too, must sometimes punish children. But few parents wish to be perceived by their children as mainly punishers. Punishment is not so much discipline—though it is frequently regarded as such—as it is a sign of the failure of discipline. Often enough, this is what has happened when a police officer makes an arrest. When he must do it in a school, a lot of things have apparently gone haywire.

School and police officials need to join in cooperative endeavors apart from dealing with crisis. Many school administrators think of calling the police only when events are beyond them. Many police officials think of preventive work in schools as "social work." Somehow, these attitudes must change. The appropriate time for school-police collaboration is in the absence of crisis, when joint resources can be brought to bear on the *prevention* of crisis. Such a strategy also helps to improve attitudes toward the police within the school, because the officer is more apt to be viewed as a helper, a colleague, a resource person, not as a disciplinarian, a punisher, a "pig."

Public Information and Public Relations

Police agencies today are doing many things for the purposes of public information and public relations—far more than ever before. Certainly this is necessary and important, but there is no escaping the truism that the best public relations is that of rendering good police service. In business and industry, a quality product is the best advertising. In police work, as in other kinds of public service, taxpayers measure quality by what happens when they need the service.

But in the case of the police, the taxpayer does not always *call* for the service. Sometimes it is thrust upon him. Even so, arresting an individual for just cause is regarded as a service to many. This is the idea of "the common good." But since most taxpayers are not quite so philosophical about it, the actions of the police become a target of public concern. As we have observed more than once, they *do* make arrests, they *do* put people in jail, they *do* sometimes inconvenience one's schedule. This makes public relations for a police agency a bit more complicated than it is for, say, a tourist bureau. With the police, there are similarities to public relations for medics and hospitals. The service provided may be a good thing in the long run, indeed even indispensable, but it isn't likely to get rave notices while the operation is in progress.

Because public ignorance and apathy with respect to police activities and criminal justice problems are generally acknowledged, public information and public relations efforts merit considerably more attention than has been assumed in the past. It is not merely the amount, but the *quality* of the public information and public relations endeavors that must be examined. As with railroad passenger service, the endeavors may be calculated to *discourage* public interest. Annual reports of police departments frequently appear to be so calculated, as we have noted. Indeed, there is even a theory that the police have not welcomed public attention because of a worry that it might expose widespread corruption. Yet it is interesting to study police officer rationalizations for corruption, which invariably implicate "the public." A companion theory, earlier noted, is the belief of some officers that professional policemen should not submit their deportment to review by uninformed, unprofessional citizens. Police resistance to public relations and public education tends to confirm the idea that they have something to hide, and to that extent makes the notion of a "professional" policeman ludicrous in the public view.

In Chapter Two, we listed some examples of the public relations and community service activities being carried on by police agencies. There is no need to repeat that listing, but we might well expand it.[6] One curious point regarding public relations for the police is the stress on selling police officers as *human beings,* which is clearly aimed at counteracting whatever tendency there may be for the public to see the policeman as repressive, punitive, and therefore *inhuman*. So public relations features "the human side" of the officer: most policemen are honest, trustworthy, empathetic, compassionate, helpful—and possess other such Boy Scout Law attributes.[7] Another public relations "pitch" proclaims that police officers are fair, firm, objective, courageous, not easily swayed, and vigilant in enforcing the law. There is just a trace of the superhuman in the image projected to the average citizen, who wants to believe that those who protect his life and property are a shade less susceptible to human foibles than he is.

The mixed role of the police is central to their public relations strategies. Depending on the audience, the images projected must truly be plural: the officer as helper, friend, and service-oriented in one projection; the officer as guardian, protector, and fearless enemy-of-crime-and-criminals in another projection. Police public relations must play to all audiences and their diversified expectations and "try to keep everybody happy." As a slogan, this is a pleasant somnambulant, so long as nobody discovers that the expectations are not simply diversified, but are to some extent *conflicting*. This is no great problem in a police department prepared to provide a diversity of services to meet these expectations and to project correspondingly diverse images in its public relations. But for a large city department set on a single style of service and a single image projection, some public relations difficulties are predictable. It is the same old point: pluralistic communities require pluralistic police services.[8]

The most elaborate public relations schemes and projects are no substitute for quality performance by the individual police officer in his contacts with clients. To emphasize the positive is another slogan but, with conscious effort, such an emphasis helps to cushion the negative and prohibitive in what a police officer must sometimes do.[9] Furthermore, television, radio, the newspapers and news magazines, departmental newsletters, advertisements, and the like, directed to public education and information, can be important instruments and allies of police public relations.[10] Public education in matters of great interest to the police depends to a great extent on the police taking the initiative. The case for recognition of the police as professionals rests significantly on the quality of their public educational efforts. A reverse aspect of this is education of the police by the various publics. A true professional is willing to listen as well as tell.

The policeman's uniform has come in for considerable attention on the part of the image-conscious in recent years. A number of departments have conducted experiments with a blazer-type uniform, designed to convey a "softer" image than that of the traditional military-type uniform. Role identity is again the key consideration. The experiments with the blazer dress in smaller cities seem to indicate that the public adjusts to it easier than do the officers themselves. If more evidence shows that the blazer reduces assaults on policemen, the transition may prove somewhat less traumatic for them.[11]

We have spoken of big-city police departments with community relations divisions or units, of other departments with a community services division such as in Chicago, and of still other departments with conflict-management divisions such as in Oakland and Dayton. The Indianapolis Police Department has a Public Affairs Branch headed by a Captain, as part of the Inspection and Training Division, replacing what was formerly a police-community relations unit. The Public Affairs Branch includes an Office of Public Affairs, PAL Club, and the Safety Education/Officer Friendly programs in the schools.

The Office of Public Affairs enlists the cooperation of all citizens in various departmental goals and programs. Teams of two officers each are assigned to specific areas of the city. Each team has the responsibility of listening to complaints and attempting to remedy the problem or channeling it to the proper authority. The team also furthers friendly relations with the community by personal contacts with residents, businessmen, and social agency personnel. Visits are made to clubs, parks, recreational areas and other youth activities and centers. The team also fills many speaking engagements. As part of its regular function, the Office of Public Affairs participates in the training program for police recruits.

The Police Athletic League (PAL) is organized as a club and is the department's best link with youth. Located throughout the city, PAL centers foster sports, contests, soap box derbies, dances, parties, summer camping, and other youth group activities. The Safety Education/Officer Friendly programs in the schools are also aimed at youth.

The Indianapolis Police Department conducts tours of police headquarters and puts on shows by an excellent motorcycle drill team. It sponsors an extensive antiburglary program called Crime Alert and a project in crime prevention in which marked patrol vehicles are issued to individual patrol officers on a 24-hour-a-day basis. The department owns a helicopter and a mobile-home type bus, which is used mainly for recruiting purposes and for small meetings with community leaders.

Special Purpose Programs

Some programs in police-community relations do not fit neatly into the categories we have discussed because they are designed to serve special needs in different communities. Following are brief reviews of some examples:

Several cities (San Francisco and Atlanta, among others) have assigned police officers to full-time duty in job opportunity and job training centers in economically depressed areas, with particular attention to assisting those released from correctional institutions in locating and qualifying for jobs—an aspect of OEO-antipoverty programs. Crime prevention is the rationale in such programs.

Citizen observer teams (e.g., Citizens Alert in San Francisco) have been tried in a few cities. These programs, which entail organized "bird-dogging" of police on duty, are not high in popularity with the police.

New Orleans instituted what was called The Police Foundation, an organization of local businessmen seeking to raise funds by public solicitation to help defray tuition costs for local police officers attending local colleges. New York City has recently announced formation of a local Police Foundation, also composed of businessmen, whose purpose will be to lend assistance in "streamlining" the criminal justice process. The Ford Foundation-financed Police Foundation operates at the national level, mainly as a catalyst for experimentation and change in police organization and practices. Several years ago, (then) Detroit Police Commissioner Johannes Spreen had some success with a campaign asking Detroiters to help their police by $1.00 contributions for new equipment.

Clergy-police relations have been brightened by such projects as a Philadelphia program in which clergymen of varying denominations rode the "red cars" with police officers on an 8-hour shift; by the 77th Street Interdenominational Clergy-Police Council that grew out of the 1965 Watts riot in Los Angeles; and by a clergy-initiated referral service in Washington, D.C., in which delinquent youth are sent to certain ministers for help in solving their problems. Church groups have also opened store-front clinics for narcotics addicts, halfway houses for released prisoners, have initiated such social services programs as FISH, and have been active in some communities in setting up crisis-counseling centers. In Pittsburgh and in fourteen other cities in the five jurisdictions of the United Methodist Church, someone in the local church started placing priority for church action in the relationship between the community and the police. The projects are linked together through the Board of Christian Social Concerns and the Womens' Division of the Board of Missions, with special funding from the Fund for Reconciliation. In each city, the task force is ecumenical. The National Council of Churches is field-testing a manual for local group action on law enforcement issues.

Mentioned earlier was the Houston Cooperative Crime Prevention Project, sponsored by a businessmen's organization called Community Effort, Inc. The program consisted of T-group and sensitivity training sessions, in six-week laboratory courses with meetings three hours weekly. The participants were police officers and community members, especially representatives of minority and dissident groups.[12]

Boston police districts have had community relations workshops similar to those in Chicago, sponsoring various programs such as helping applicants to prepare for police entrance examinations.

The effectiveness of group discussion in mitigating police-resident hostility in an urban ghetto has been studied.[13]

The National Association for Mental Health, Inc., publishes an excellent, succinct training booklet for police officers entitled *How to Recognize and Handle Abnormal People,* written by Robert A. Matthews, M.D., and Loyd W. Rowland, Ph.D.[14]

Relatively few police agencies have had notable success in efforts to recruit more black and other minority group officers. One exception is the Washington, D.C., Metropolitan Police Department, which has done relatively well in recent years in this respect. The New York City Housing Authority Police Department and the New York City Transit Police have substantial black representation, but it is said that this is because of their "lower" standards. As we have noted, this is a shibboleth that calls for closer examination. Generally, state police organizations have a poor record in representation of minority group personnel, and the story is no better in many municipalities. We discussed this at some length in Chapter Twelve.

The San Jose, California, Police Department uses public service time for regularly scheduled radio broadcasts to the 50,000 Mexican-Americans residing in that city, done in Spanish. The programs include information about the police and about various service agencies, including probation, parole, legal aide, state employment, and the like. (Donald and Cobarruviaz, "Eliminating the Language Barrier.")

Good police-community relations are effected not only by the initiative and activities of police agencies, but also by the initiative and activities of community organizations of many kinds. Illustrations: bicycle safety projects of service clubs; leaflet and poster projects; traffic safety and crime prevention films, speakers, panels, exhibits, fairs, billboards, etc.; home safety and pedestrian safety campaigns; drinking-driving-drugs programs. Several years ago, the Illinois Chamber of Commerce sponsored an excellent state-wide project dedicated to better police service and police-community relations.

In many cities, an elaborate rumor control network has been developed. In Los Angeles, for example, there is a police rumor control center in each of the 17 divisions.

In Atlanta, all new police officers are assigned to the Crime Prevention Bureau (another name for a police-community relations unit) for several weeks, until the Police Training school is ready to accept them. Young officers are sent into the community with experienced officers and familiarized with the people and their problems. Every policeman hired in Dayton begins as a community service officer, assigned so he will *not* be teamed with a veteran patrolman.

In St. Louis, the Police Junior Aide project is a coordinated effort of the Police Department, the YMCA, and the Metropolitan Youth Commission, dating back to the summer of 1967. Thirty-six boys, aged 14 and 15, were hired in poverty areas to work with the police in nondangerous tasks. Some of the boys were pre-delinquents. The program helped to curb delinquent behavior, but did *not* change the attitudes of the participants toward the police.

Increase in the incidence of conflict with the law on the part of Canadian Indians and Eskimos prompted a survey study by the Canadian Corrections Association (1967) to seek solutions to the problem. A selected field staff visited communities in urban, rural, and remote areas of the provinces. The law enforcement, judicial, and correctional processes were evaluated, as they related to these minority groups.[15]

The Positive Action for Youth (PAY) program has been operating in Flint, Michigan, community schools since the fall of 1966, with support from the Mott Foundation. The program involves male juvenile probationers, their peers, teachers, and parents, and offers group counseling, work experience, family counseling, supportive action, and individual counseling, directed to *all* family problems, not merely to the needs of the program participants. Somewhat similar are Youth Services Bureaus located in community centers, demonstrating that public and private organizations can cooperate to establish services for delinquent youth. (Michael N. Canlis, "Tomorrow Is Too Late.")

To improve the police officer's knowledge and appreciation of community relations and to demonstrate how the policeman can develop support from the community, the Community Relations Orientation for Police (CROP) program was established in Philadelphia. It provides training sessions and discussions of police-community relations goals and problems (Harry G. Fox, *The Police Chief,* June 1968).

A campaign of advertising and public relations to reduce the incidence of vehicle theft was initiated by the Los Angeles Police Department in 1966. (Thomas Reddin, "Operation Grass Roots.")

The Cincinnati Police Department has experimented successfully with a summertime Tension Alert Unit in its Community Relations Bureau. School Resources Officers, free for the summer, worked in teams of two, in uniform, walking the streets in heavily populated neighborhoods, talking to people and reporting any symptoms of potential tension or trouble. In New York City, the Preventive Enforcement Patrol (PEP) is a special squad of black and Puerto Rican policemen who live and work in Harlem, free from routine calls so they can concentrate on personalized preventive patrol.

An Institute centering on tensions between white and black police officers in large urban departments was held in Detroit in the spring of 1972, cosponsored by the Guardians Society, New Detroit, the Detroit Police Department, the Center for Urban Affairs, and the School of Criminal Justice of Michigan State University.

The Birmingham, Alabama, Police Department has a 23-page guidebook called *Answers To Issues,* covering in brief form many questions of police procedures.

An art exhibit in New York City's 32nd Precinct featured art work done by policemen and children of the neighborhood.

In Conclusion

A National Association of Police Community Relations Officers was formed in 1969, with membership comprising police officers working in this field and other concerned citizens. It is appropriate to conclude this chapter with this Association's statement of the objectives of a good police-community relations program from *Get the Ball Rolling:*[16]

1. To initiate continuing programs aimed at fostering and improving police services, communicating, reducing hostilities and ferreting out areas of tension and their causes in the total community.

2. To assist the police and total community in acquiring the special skills and knowledge to meet the pace of social change.

3. To assist in defining the police role in society.

4. To establish a reciprocal line of communication and responsiveness between the police department and the public.

5. To instill in every policeman the proper attitude toward, and appreciation of, good police-community relations.

6. To enhance the community's understanding of the functions of the police, and to aid the police in understanding the needs and aims of the community.

The Association goes on to say that the following should *not* be part of the objectives of police-community relations programs:

1. Police-community relations units should *not* serve as intelligence units of the police department, or work in an undercover capacity.

2. Police-community relations personnel should *not* be used as a tactical force in enforcement eventualities.

3. Police-community relations units should *not* handle matters normally assigned to an internal affairs unit.

4. Police-community relations should *not* be a "cooling" unit, acting as a pacifier between those in positions of responsibility and the community. It should pursue just and tangible solutions to problems.

5. A police-community relations unit should *not* be used as a vehicle of token appeasement for poor police practices.

The Association's central theme is this:

Those police administrators who fail to recognize the importance of police-community relations programs will fail to achieve what should be the ultimate aims of law enforcement.

Notes to Chapter Twenty-two

1. A Liverpool City Police Juvenile Liaison Officer Scheme was initiated in 1951 (*The Police and the Children,* Office of the Chief Constable, Liverpool, England, 1962). This program has been criticized on the grounds that the police officers assigned to schools have lacked training in social groupwork or casework, and that the police have injected punitive and inflexible attitudes into the treatment of children.

2. The Flint program is described in Study 4 (Part 5) in Radelet and Reed, *Studies.* The President's Commission on Law Enforcement and Administration of Justice, in its *Task Force Report: The Police,* describes many different types of school programs in which the police participate.

3. In our analysis of Police-School Liaison programs, we rely considerably on June Morrison of the Department of Public Administration, University of Arizona, in her article, "The Controversial Police-School Liaison Programs," which gives a comparison of various features of this type of program in selected cities.

4. In our discussion here, we rely heavily on Wendell J. Roye's work, *Law and Order in Classroom and Corridor.*

5. See Frank Reissman, *The Culturally Deprived Child.* Also Arthur I. Stinchcombe, *Rebellion in a High School,* and Education Advisory Committee of the National Urban League, *The Problem of Discipline/Control and Security in Our Schools,* Position Paper No. 1, 1971.

6. Lee P. Brown has provided a thorough descriptive listing of many types of programs in his *Police-Community Relations Evaluation Project.*

7. George H. Savord, "Selling Law Enforcement to Your Public." See also Jerry Marx, *Officer, Tell Your Story,* and Richard L. Holcomb, *The Police and the Public.*

8. Anderton and Ferguson, "Police-Community Relations Coffee Klatch Program."

9. John P. Howard, "Integrating Public Relations Training for Police Officers."

10. See Walter Grauman, "Lights! Camera! Action! The Role of Television in Law Enforcement," and Thomas J. Hardesty, "Ads for a New Image."

11. Richard H. Snibbe, "Police Visibility—Positive or Negative," and Victor Cizanckas, "Experiment in Police Uniforms."

12. See L. Deckle McLean, "Psychotherapy for Houston Police." See also Robert Liberman, "Police as a Community Mental Health Resource," and Sikes and Cleveland, "Human Relations Training for Police and Community."

13. Lipsitt and Steinbruner, "An Experiment in Police-Community Relations." See also DuBois and Li, *Reducing Social Tension and Conflict Through the Group Conversation Method,* and Burton Levy, "Cops in the Ghetto."

14. Originally copyrighted, 1954, by the Louisiana Association for Mental Health. The NAMH address is 10 Columbus Circle, New York, N.Y. 10019.

15. Canadian Corrections Association, *Indians and the Law,* (Survey), Ottawa, 1967, 67 pages, 75 cents.

16. A publication of the National Association of Police Community Relations Officers, Room 305, 100 Maryland Ave., N.E., Washington, D.C. 20002.

Chapter Twenty-Three

The Police Side
of Police and
Community Relations

The police side of the partnership with the community begins with *commitment*. It is frequently the integrity of the police commitment to meaningful community relations that is questioned by community groups —sometimes questioned even by police officers themselves when they ask, "Is the Chief really serious about this? Did he mean what he said in the speech he made last night?"

This is, of course, the question of credibility. Is it "for real"? The implication is that police officials sometimes behave as "politicians"— they say things for effect, without genuine commitment. It is suspected that there is a big gap between pronouncement and practice. It is even suggested occasionally that the police simply cannot be taken seriously as a force for change—certainly not for change of the proportions required to make a truly significant difference in police and community relations. Now and then the accusation is made that community relations is a kind of game for the police—more shadow than substance, "a necessary evil," and similar less-than-salutary characterizations. Basically, the issue is one of commitment.

The police declarations of commitment are generally very positive and sometimes even insightful. For example, the executive director of the International Association of Chiefs of Police, Quinn Tamm, writes:

The police chief who does not include a greater sensitivity to community needs as a part of his basic philosophy of law enforcement is now out of step with the times. . . . They [police-community relations programs] are beneficial insofar as they reflect a real desire on the part of the police to provide as great a level of service as possible to the citizen. They are useless to the extent that they attempt to distract attention from basically improper police practices in daily operations.[1]

Chief Howard H. Earle of the Los Angeles County Sheriff's Department, author of *Police-Community Relations: Crisis in Our Time,* observes:

Police-Community Relations is a field as rife with social dissension as any endeavor in the history of man. And whether they know it or not —or like it or not—peace officers spend a lot more time engaged in police-community relations activities than they suppose. [*Police,* September–October, 1969]

Commitment is always difficult to measure in human affairs. Perhaps it is sufficient to say that the police commitment to the principle of community relations ought not *ever to* be questionable, dubious, or a point of contention. There should be no hedging or ambiguity about it. Police work is utterly dependent upon community involvement, and this is a basis for commitment that cannot be halfhearted or equivocal.

Organizational Structure of the Police Department

With commitment established as of cardinal importance in what the police do, the next matter for consideration is organizational structure. However, tables of organization, with all the tidy blocks and lines connected on a chart, are less important in community relations than is what may be called *organizational orientation.* This is rooted in organizational commitment and the recognition that there should be community concern in every facet of the police agency.

Policy

Organizational orientation is reflected, first, in administrative policy. As we have said, community relations is, in an important sense, a management concept. An outside analyst would want to see, as the initial step in a departmental survey, what is "in the book" in the way of written rules, regulations, policies, general or special orders pertaining to community relations, human relations, working with community forces, cooperation with other social agencies, civil rights, and the like. One might expect to find such principles as these clearly enunciated:[2]

The personal conduct of each member of the department is the primary factor in promoting a program of desirable community relations.

Tact, patience, and courtesy shall be strictly observed under all circumstances.

A police officer is a public official representing all of the people. He
shall maintain a professional attitude and demeanor which will not in
any manner communicate any personal prejudices.

Superior officers shall by example demonstrate, and shall instruct subordinates in proper deportment and desirable attitudes in their dealings
with the public.

All people may have prejudices; however, a police officer must learn
to distinguish between his right to hold personal opinions as a citizen
and his sworn duty as an officer. While his right to hold his beliefs
as a citizen is inviolate, any manifestation of prejudice while acting as
a member of the Police Department cannot be tolerated.

When making a lawful arrest or authorized search or seizure, department personnel will use physical force only when the exercise of persuasion, advice, and warning is found to be insufficient to obtain
cooperation, and use only the minimum degree of such physical force
necessary on any particular occasion.

All citizens of this country, in keeping with our democratic processes,
are guaranteed certain basic constitutional safeguards. These safeguards will not be denied any citizen even though he has committed,
or is suspected of having committed, a criminal act.

Policies in a police organization ought to make clear what management expects from all employees.

Supervision

Policies and regulations in a police organization are only as effective as supervisors make them. So-called middle management is frequently singled out for special attention in police-community relations
programs because sergeants, lieutenants, and captains in larger departments possess crucial authority and influence with respect to the meaning and impact of high-level policies and pronouncements. In considerable measure, the entire "system" of police work revolves around
supervision. It is surely here that the community relations orientation
gets its decisive test. If the supervisory attitude is that "it's a lot of
crap," the ball game is lost with line personnel. Such an attitude is more
often conveyed subtly than explicitly, especially in organizations where
it runs counter to stated policies. Police officers do not find it difficult
to sense supervisory attitudes and priorities. They quickly learn how to
play the game in pleasing their immediate superiors. There is, of course,
nothing about this that is unique to police work.

In short, as V. A. Leonard has stressed, no organization can rise
higher than the quality of its supervisory personnel.[3] J. L. LeGrande has
summarized the matter in this way:

... strict autocratic leadership is a thing of the past—strict application of rules and regulations is giving way to situational leadership—and group leadership is eroding to a one-and-one relationship between supervisor and employee. Perhaps the most important thing for the supervisor to realize is that his role is constantly changing and that he has an obligation through constant self-evaluation and training to equip himself to meet it. ["Commentary on Police Supervision."]

Planning and Research

The modern police organization cannot avoid or neglect community and societal realities—the sociological, demographic, economic, and political influences that enter into the relationship of the police and the community and shape the attitudes of both. Some research is being done in this direction, but much more emphasis should be placed on planning and research functions as an integral part of the police organization. A better understanding of these influences may well have an important bearing not only on how the organization is structured, but on administrative philosophy, personnel recruiting policies, and what the role of the police officer should be.

Personnel Practices

It is equally evident that organizational personnel practices bear directly on community relations—in recruitment standards, training programs, promotions and other incentives, and in the placement of manpower and womanpower. We have insisted that much that police agencies now do regarding recruitment qualifications and the testing and measurement thereof badly needs re-evaluation, in the light of community relations as well as enlightened administrative considerations. The height, weight, eyesight, and I.Q. requirements, and the standard testing and measuring instruments and devices are presently under critical review. Traditional ideas and approaches are being challenged. Training programs dealing with the social psychology of policing are abandoning some of the "tried-and-true" nonsense of the past, in favor of more sophisticated, more productive content and methods. Similarly, the residuals of the "strong back and weak mind" legacy in recruitment standards are slowly—some would say, all too slowly—withering away. It may not be unrealistic to hope that certain principles of police recruitment will some day catch up to business and industry.

As part of the same dream, we might add the hope that some day the color of a policeman's skin will come to be regarded as quite irrelevant in recruitment, placement, and promotions. But unfortunately, that day seems still to be in an indefinite future, as in other fields of vocational endeavor.

The future has already arrived, however, in some aspects of police personnel practices. Psychological testing and psychiatric techniques in selecting and training police officers are no longer novel. The thought of lateral entry and placement in police organizations is coming in for some too-long-delayed study and even some moderate experimentation.[4] The techniques of police training are beginning to reflect awareness of situation analysis, role playing, and other empathetic instructional mechanisms, small group discussion, simulations to engender emotional control under stressful circumstances, and the like.[5]

Special attention should be devoted to the rewards and incentive system in a police agency. As this system is calibrated, so will be police officer performance. When community relations accomplishments by policemen are given equal and sometimes even greater weight than "good pinches" and traffic tickets in the dispensation of rewards, it speaks to the men in the ranks in a language they readily understand. It is a surefire way of reducing the number of uncomplimentary remarks about police-community relations, and it can have a substantial effect on organizational attitudes and behavior. Workers respond according to the incentives. This is a pragmatic slant on organizational goals when the goals are viewed as naive or too idealistic. The harvest in improved community relations is an important benefit in itself, and one that reflects the growth of police professionalism and eases the burden for beleaguered officers.

Other Considerations

Among other police functions which play an important part in community relations are complaint procedures—the process for handling grievances in a manner that contributes positively to organizaional integrity. We have devoted all of Chapter Fifteen to this subject, so important is it in our opinion.

Other vital elements in agency structure, with respect to community liaison, are the public information and public relations functions, which were discussed in Chapter Twenty Two. Not so readily apparent is the community relations dimension of the records and reports task. One example of a conflict in this area is resentment of racially delineated crime statistics.

A Detective Bureau may also have a community relations program. There may be fear on the part of the public that the program may be used for intelligence purposes. Then some citizens may say, "They're not going to use me as a stool pigeon." Still another consideration is a juvenile unit or youth division in a police department that can be a significant force in community relations, plus or minus, depending on its thrust.

The traditional military model of police organization is increasingly viewed today as anticommunity relations. The discussion often highlights the management efficiency of the military model and its lesser effectiveness in the area of community relations. Since this puts organizational structure to a functional test, we will turn next to functional considerations.

Functional Considerations

Looked at in functional terms, police relations with the community come down to one-to-one interactions between police officers and civilians. This is the ultimate concern of all programs, projects, units, and strategies. Individual reciprocal attitudes and behavior are of primary interest. Studying these attitudes sounds simple enough, but actually, as we have stressed, the interaction is often quite complex. The officer represents or symbolizes several social systems, lumped together in the stereotypic image labelled "the Establishment." He is a member of a social organization carrying with it some connotations of threat, fear, deprivation of freedom, suppression. As Michael Banton puts it:

> ... police-community relations cannot be properly understood unless the policeman's actions are seen as the actions of the members of an organization. It is the organization, and the pressures to which it is subject, which chiefly decide how the policeman will approach citizens. If there is substance in this interpretation, it is important to encourage research into police officers' conception of their proper role, into their sources of job satisfaction, and how they react to social changes. ["A Sociological View of Police-Community Relations"][6]

On the civilian side of the relationship, as Banton points out, the tone of police relations—for example, with minorities—is affected by the composition of the particular group and the sort of service expected from the police officer. The chief source of friction, he believes, lies in the discrepancy between the policeman's idea and the civilian's idea of how the relationship between them should be conducted. Should the civilian, particularly a civilian identified by the officer as "suspicious" or "potentially dangerous," act in a manner that the policeman interprets as a challenge to his authority, a minor incident may easily escalate into a very nasty situation.

Many students of police-community transactions have referred to this same point, as we have noted. Banton states it succinctly: ". . . in situations in which police officers believe the citizen is questioning their authority, they demand submission." Members of minority groups today find such submission difficult. They feel that they have too long submitted to "The Man." On the other hand, if the policeman takes a narrow view of his role, he is not inclined to give minorities any special consideration. There are clear implications in this for police training and command policies. Banton concludes:

> ... the police need training in this field in order to provide the minorities with a service equal to that which police provide for the majority. The ordinary police officer understands majority behavior and likely reactions because he is himself drawn from this section of the population. He needs additional training if he is to understand minority reactions and their implications. Some police officers resist this view and regard additional training as a form of special treatment instituted to

satisfy a vocal pressure group. Lectures about minority social patterns are easily interpreted as requests for discrimination against white people. . . . The implementation of the proposals for training therefore needs to be watched with special care, both to ensure that sufficient time is set aside in the curriculum and to monitor its effects lest it provoke a reaction which prevents the training from achieving its objectives. [Ibid.]

Police violence, as William Westley perceived years ago, has profound implications in a democratic society. It represents political autocracy, with all the horror that this conjures up in the memories of those who have experienced it, and those who know it only vicariously. Certainly the rising incidence of attacks on policemen must be condemned and stopped. But as Tom Wicker has said in *The New York Times* (October 25, 1970), ". . . neither that fact nor public concern about other forms of disorder justifies the police or any level of government in using whatever means they choose to maintain order." Wicker goes on to say:

. . . when authority itself is guilty of an unjustified and illegal act, it not only commits a crime, it brings the law and those sworn to uphold the law into the scorn and disrepute of those who ought to respect it. A law is not only broken but respect for *all law* is undermined. . . . nothing could contribute more to an *atmosphere of lawlessness* than a widespread belief that law enforcement officers themselves are corrupt or brutal or unjust, and that government permissiveness allows them to go unpunished for it—even encourages them. And it is in an atmosphere of lawlessness that violence is most likely to proliferate.

The Jackson State College tragedy of 1970 raised the question of whether police and their superiors holding political office are legally liable in quelling massive disorders. The law is clear on the matter of damage suits and prosecution against individual officers for specific charges, but the Federal judiciary is now being asked to rule on cases of alleged brutality by groups of officials and law enforcement officers on groups of people. The Attica prison riot and the 1971 May Day demonstrations in Washington raised similar questions: Can political office holders and police superiors be held accountable for the actions of their men? Can police and their superiors be held legally responsible for the lack of crowd control training, or the failure to adhere to training and procedures? Can some or all be held responsible even though no one officer can be identified as an assailant? The key point for the courts to decide is how much and what type of force is "reasonably necessary," under given circumstances.

Guidelines for police practices in today's urban "jungle" have been specified by many analysts in recent years.[7] The do's and don'ts of police handling of mass demonstrations and civil disobedience have been pretty well spelled out.[8] The community or societal responsibility for violence should be stressed more than it is. Take a matter such as firearms control, especially of hand guns. Many police officials have spoken for Federal legislation to control their use. The murder-by-gun rate in the United States is 35 times higher than that of West Germany or Britain, and more than 300 times higher than that of Japan—all strong gun control nations. New York Police Commissioner Patrick V. Murphy writes:

> Statistics reveal that about 25 percent of all violent crimes in the country involve the use of firearms. Furthermore, guns are the weapons used in 65 percent of all murders. Logic tells us that a decrease in the availability of guns would necessarily achieve a decrease in the number of violent crimes, and experience in the few areas where effective gun control has been enforced confirms this expectation. We cannot be equivocal with the present increase in violent crimes and the increase at an even more rapid rate of crimes involving guns. To control crime in this country, we must control firearms. ["Social Change and the Police"][9]

One of the trickiest issues sometimes raised is that police activities in community relations might be used for intelligence purposes. We have referred to this several times—for example, in our discussion of police-school liaison programs in Chapter Twenty Two. The intelligence function in police work has different meanings for different people, in and out of police organizations. Gathering information is undoubtedly a defensible police function, but the means employed to do this have legal and ethical significance. In a simple one-to-one relationship, if Person A becomes convinced that Person B is using ostensible friendship merely to "pump" him, the relationship obviously will not thrive. An element of mutual trust is involved in the sharing of information. If A is not sure that he can trust B, and if B has reason to believe that he cannot trust A, "intelligence" can be a contentious factor.

No one would question that the police must be as well informed as possible about what is going on in the community. Establishing communication with all groups and factions is desirable, but under some conditions it is difficult to do this, especially with groups that the police are anxious to know more about. At this point, more "traditional" intelligence techniques may be employed: undercover tactics, infiltration, sometimes even such methods as wiretapping, "bugging," etc. If the American Civil Liberties Union hears of it, "the fat may be in the fire." In an era of "extremist" groups, such developments are common.

Suppose that the group in question is antipolice as well as extremist by some standard. Suppose that many moderate citizens regard the group as a threat to civic harmony. Suppose further that the group is the object of rumors that it has "secret meetings," is "plotting revolution," or that it "carries on sexual orgies." All of these factors complicate police determinations as to proper and defensible intelligence: what to do and how to do it? There is no general answer that can be applied in all circumstances. But this much can be said: the more open and mutually trustful the communication lines, the less necessary will be resort to undercover means. The more truly the communication is two-way, the less likely one party will be to accuse the other of "using me as a stool pigeon" or "pumping me for information." Any police-community relations program characterized by community groups as primarily or exclusively designed for police intelligence purposes is in serious trouble. It is indefensible for a police organization to establish a police-community relations program with the chief purpose of counter-espionage. While a police administrator would not advertise such a purpose, it would not take long for community groups to perceive it.

What we have said about this issue is what prompts some job-hardened police officers to "turn off" the police-community relations advocates. "Naive," they say. "You can't handle some of these radical outfits with milk-and-honey approaches. They'll make you look like a fool!" The same officers express similar sentiments in referring to street encounters with "known hoodlums." It is a view that should not be shrugged off lightly. The "philosophers" must avoid being cavalier with the feelings of working policemen. Perhaps the best approach is to give any individual or group the benefit of the doubt, until there is good reason to resort to other tactics, but to do this with caution and with reasonable safeguards for personal and societal protection. In such situations, some ingenuity may also be helpful; unconventional tactics have been known to win many a tight ball game.

Something should be said about the rather-too-popular public administrative tactic of deluding or "snowing" the public and thereby dodging issues. For example, an accusation is made by, let us say, a public figure that the police are not doing very well in curbing the drug traffic or gambling. Forthwith, the police chief holds a press conference in which he vigorously denies the charge, citing statistics to show that the police department made X percent more arrests or conducted Y percent more "raids" this year than last year. The upshot of this defense is at least twofold: (1) It contributes to the defensive posture of the police, and (2) it fails to place the responsibility for the problem where it really belongs—with the community and its ambivalent attitudes about drugs or gambling.

Another functional consideration, and one to which we have devoted attention commensurate with its importance, is the effect of the police subculture on sound police and community relations. Captain Kenneth N. Fortier of the San Diego Police Department has ably analyzed this matter in "The Police Culture—Its Effect on Sound Police-

Community Relations."[10] He names a number of characteristics of the police subculture that tend to impede the community relations orientation:

1. The policeman has a propensity to cynicism. He sees the seamy aspects of life too frequently to be "a trusting soul."

2. His cynicism is reinforced by his superiors and fellow officers, and he comes to regard being "naive" as a capital shortcoming.

3. He comes to believe that the only persons who understand and support him are other policemen.

4. Policemen stick together; they coalesce. Sometimes they will even lie to protect one another. The sense of fraternalism is extremely strong.

5. Policemen tend to be very defensive. They tend to be hypersensitive to criticism. They argue, rationalize, seek scapegoats—perhaps because they are so often blamed for so many social problems.

6. Many policemen tend to restrict their intellectual development. They read little serious literature and recline in limited exposure to other viewpoints.

The antidote for these characteristics of the police subculture is in broadened perspective. Open and effective, broadly based community relations is the solution, directed toward gradual elimination of "tight little island" attitudes. Education and training are important in this process, especially when accompanied by other elements of progressive organizational orientation and administration.

Responsiveness and Accountability

The administration of police agencies is subject to four crucial influences: judicial, public, legislative, and organizational. Responsiveness and accountability are attuned to these influences. John Angell has suggested certain guidelines in each of the four spheres (*The Police Chief,* March 1969.) As to public influence, for instance, Angell speaks of the need for the police administrator to be flexible enough to change programs or redirect methods when community pressures indicate a need for such change. He should be prepared with alternatives in the event of public resistance to a particular way of dealing with a problem or situation. We quoted Angell earlier in his analysis of classical police organizational arrangements as related to public responsiveness.

All bureaucratic organizational structures have inherent problems of public responsiveness and accountability. The complicated structure itself is conducive to a hide-and-seek game of shifting responsibility from desk to desk and office to office. "Oh, that's not our job—you'll have to see so-and-so." People get tired of trying to chase down the ultimately responsible party. In large police organizations as in large universities, necessarily bureaucratic, it is presumed, because of "practical" considerations, responsiveness and accountability to the community must be explicitly and deliberately cultivated and emphasized in administrative philosophy and actions. These qualities must be made more than mere abstractions.

The interest in civilian review boards and "community control" in recent years is symptomatic of bureaucratic problems in this regard. At issue is the fuller development of constructive participation of citizens in public affairs, in the face of increasing bureaucratization, depersonalization, and mechanization of governmental institutions. The 1966 President's Crime Commission pointed to a lack of confidence in law enforcement agencies by a significant portion of the public as harmful to police attitudes and values as well as to citizen cooperation with the police.

Richard Chackerian and Richard F. Barrett of Florida State University have made a very helpful diagnosis of the matter in "Police Professionalism and Citizen Evaluation." They refer to attacks on the idea' of professionalization of the police, coming from several directions. One is the charge that professionalization "merely provides the conditions for the protection of the police, rather than insuring increased police commitment to equity and fairness in enforcing the law." James Q. Wilson's comment about protecting the practitioner from the client rather than the client from the practitioner will be recalled. The implication is that while professionalism implies the application of technical standards widely accepted in police circles, these standards need not be related to "the public interest."

Chackerian and Barrett also refer to attacks on police professionalism made by those advocating neighborhood control. They might well have added civilian review boards. The idea here is that equity and effectiveness in police service result in favorable citizen evaluations of the police. However, it is the socially homogeneous neighborhood that becomes the context for developing the specific standards of equity and effectiveness, rather than the police organization itself or a larger polititcal unit. Professional and community standards should be harmonized, and the uniqueness of neighborhood life styles must be taken into account. Chackerian and Barrett have validated the following hypotheses in their research:

1. High evaluations of police performance by citizens are positively associated with low crime rates, high arrest rates, and citizen perception of equity in law enforcement.

2. Professionalism is associated with low crime rates, high arrest rates, and citizen perception of equity in enforcement.

3. Professionalism is positively associated with high evaluation, but this association will be stronger in socially homogeneous communities than in heterogenous communities.

They go further in arguing also that evaluations of the police might be less a consequence of police effectiveness than an expression of an extremely diffuse sense of access to government. Their hypotheses in this respect are:

1. A high sense of access to government will be positively related to high evaluations of law enforcement.
2. Professionalism will be unrelated to evaluations if the effects of access are controlled.

It may be recalled that we commented earlier on the difficulty of distinguishing public attitudes toward the police from public attitudes toward government in general. Credibility—or the absence of it—is comprehensive.

Putting These Ideas to Work

Police departments in large cities (and in some small cities, too) are putting into operation the concepts we have discussed here. Robert R. Dempsey of the Legal Division of the New York City Police Department studied 46 police agencies in cities ranging in population from 125,000 to 8,000,000 and reported in "Police Disciplinary Systems" that all had established disciplinary procedures for processing complaints against officers. In January 1972, New York City Police Commissioner Patrick V. Murphy extended a year-old experimental neighborhood police team concept involving the "resident" policeman, assigned to duty in the precinct where he lives. Some harassment and abuse of the resident patrolmen subsequently developed (threatening telephone calls, for example), but it was announced that the project would continue.

Job analyses of police patrol work and evaluations of the field patrolman's function are beginning to appear (see, for instance, O'Neill and Bloom, "The Field Officer: Is He Really Fighting Crime?"). Studies of this kind promise to draw attention to the role question and will be important in police-community relations in the years ahead. As one example of changing roles, with the advent of seemingly more efficient patrol car operations, the patrolman on foot has come to be almost a vanishing breed. Today, however, foot patrol is being reassessed in the context of community relations and crime control. The concept of "selective patrol" has emerged, with patrol officers in one-man cars patroling their districts both in a car and on foot, relying heavily on modern two-way radio communication.[11] Closely related is experimentation with motor scooters—and in Baltimore, the police are trying bicycles (Edward L. Lee, "Back to Bikes for Baltimore").

The English social anthropologist Michael Banton has observed that crime prevention is a "sadly underdeveloped aspect of police work in many American cities."[12] He is not alone in this observation. In fact, a crime prevention thrust in police and community relations programs, though often clearly stated in program goals, has not generally taken hold. Richard Snibbe of the University of Georgia's Law Enforcement Training Center has formulated several relevant ideas in "A Concept for Police in Crime Prevention":

1. Although many factors leading to crime are beyond the control of the police, preventive policing must be based on those which the police can predict and influence.

2. Field situations, when analyzed as to causal relationships from which origins of activity are located, can provide the information base for preventive policing plans. The ability of the police to control physical and psychological environments can result in the reduction of predicted following acts.

3. Human behavioral descriptions and classifications of crimes will provide more useful information to the police than legal definitions.

The crime prevention and community service dimensions of police work are kindred activities. Both have been associated with the "social work" concept of the police role—not "real" police work. This text is dedicated to the need for readjustment in this absurd notion. Greater emphasis must be placed on community service as a legitimate goal of police organizations.[13] Doing so reflects the reality of community expectations and of what the police are actually doing most of the time.

David Bordua has called for an increase in the amount of what he calls "supportive services" performed by the police ("Comments on Police-Community Relations"). He advocates a more positive approach to customary nonenforcement or semi-enforcement services, the development of routinized large-scale services of a helping nature, which are at the same time highly visible (e.g., ambulance service), and the development of a more generalized public safety or protection service with police serving as a kind of ombudsman for the poor. The latter would include expansion of referral services, to link problems with community resources.[14]

Team Policing

Bordua recognizes that what he proposes calls for police organizational adjustments. He favors what he calls the Area Team, which would be responsible for public safety and order as well as most operations in a defined territory. The teams would be made up mainly of detectives, supplemented by Youth Officers, some patrol personnel, community relations people, and others. The basic operational idea would be to reduce the overreliance on patrol, to refine police information gathering, and to create a more sustained though less abrasive police presence. The concept implies more decentralization of operations than is prevalent now, but Bordua thinks that the values of central control should be coupled with decentralized initiative and interrank collaboration. The team concept presupposes, he says, a police controllable largely through training and commitment to mission.

Angell proposes a model police organization of three primary sections: general services, coordination and information, and specialized services.[15] All supervisory positions, as traditionally defined, would be abolished; military ranks and titles would not be used. He defines the control system as checks and balances in which one section of the organization would have authority in one instance, another section would have authority in another instance, and the third section in a third instance. The general services section would consist of teams of generalists decentralized to work in a small geographic area. The coordination and information section would be centralized and might even be regional or statewide. This section would encompass what are now called administrative and staff functions. The specialized services would contain those activities currently classified as line units, e.g., investigative, juvenile, and traffic functions.

Operationally, Angell's basic unit is one usually referred to as the generalist-specialist combination in team policing. In it he sees these expected advantages:

1. It should improve employee morale and effectiveness because it eliminates formally assigned supervision.

2. It gives citizens more influence in policy decisions. Because policies would be more flexible, it should provide more socially relevant police service.

3. It increases the professional standing of the generalist without damaging the status of the specialist.

4. It destroys the formal classical hierarchy and thereby provides employees with the authority and responsibility necessary for attaining professional status. It facilitates citizen involvement and organizational responsiveness.

Such a model presupposes substantial changes in management philosophy and in police training programs. Angell feels that the most important change necessary will be in attitudes—at all levels of the organization. Is it practical? The answer is that this basic design (with minor variations) is being tried in a number of police departments. Team policing tends to be differently defined in various places. In 1971, the Ford Foundation's Police Foundation surveyed team policing experiments in six cities: New York City, Detroit, Dayton, Syracuse, Los Angeles, and Holyoke, Massachusetts.[16] The survey report indicated that the Holyoke effort was "perhaps the most successful" in forming the basis for a new conception of police role.[17] The Palo Alto, California, approach to the same concept is reflected in the organization charts in Fig. 23–1.[18]

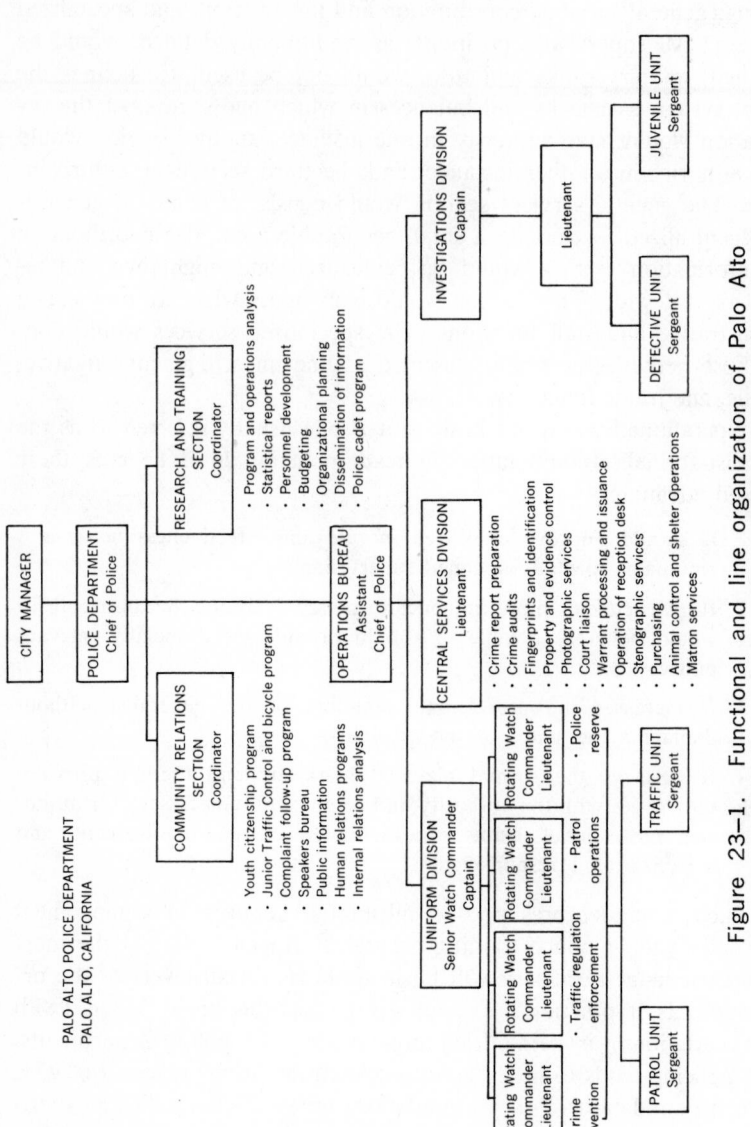

Figure 23–1. Functional and line organization of Palo Alto Police Department (courtesy of **The Police Chief**, in article by Leo E. Peart)

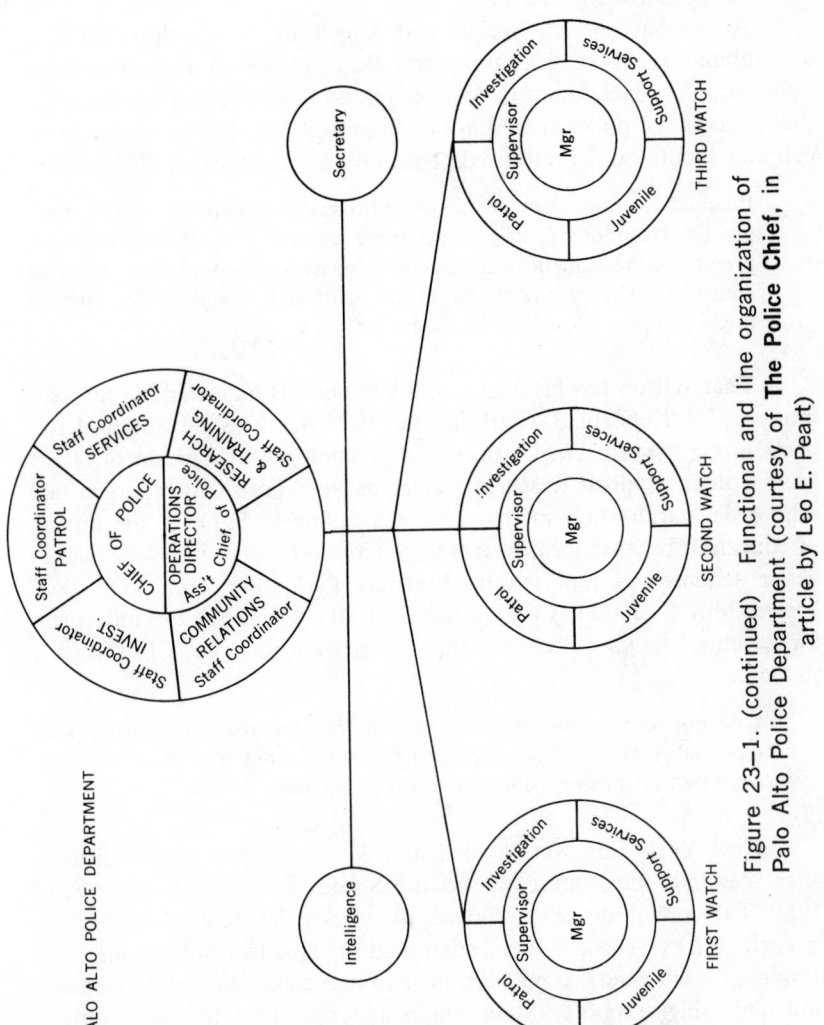

Figure 23–1. (continued)   Functional and line organization of
Palo Alto Police Department (courtesy of **The Police Chief,** in
article by Leo E. Peart)

Decentralization

Team policing and democratizing police organization are closely associated, conceptually, with functional decentralization of police work in metropolitan centers. The idea is similar to ·that advocated for the public schools, with the same rationale. It is synonymous with the concept of neighborhood control.

As we have noted, Bordua and Angell are among those favoring a combination of centralization and decentralization in metropolitan police organization. James Q. Wilson agrees, believing that the authority that governs the police should not be dispersed, but that police functions can and should be decentralized. This, he argues, is a vital distinction:

> Precinct commanders in a decentralized department would have greater freedom of action and more control over their patrolmen; precinct commanders in a dispersed department would surrender that control to whatever constellation of political forces the neighborhood might produce. ["Controlling the Police"]

That Wilson has his finger on a key point is indicated by the testimony of Dr. Kenneth B. Clark in May 1972, to the State Board of Regents in New York. Dr. Clark, noted psychologist and president of the Metropolitan Applied Research Center in New York City, charged that school decentralization in that city was failing to improve the quality of education because local boards were more interested in power than in better schools (as reported by Emanuel Perlmutter, *The New York Times,* May 8, 1972). Coming from a leading figure in the movement for decentralization of schools, this was newsworthy. Dr. Clark further stated:

> I do not see that we have kept—or the local boards have concentrated on—quality and methods for raising quality as much as they have concentrated on power, actions, control of finances.

New York City was divided into 31 community school districts after the State Legislature passed the School Decentralization Act of 1969. The community school boards are elected by the registered voters in each district. These boards, composed of unpaid members, have the power to select and assign personnel in the elementary, intermediate, and junior high schools within their boundaries. They also have power, within overall limits set by the Board of Education, over the allocation of virtually all funds spent in the schools. Dr. Clark did not recommend the abandonment of the decentralization plan, but he did urge that efforts be made to make it more effective as a means to improving educational quality. City School Chancellor Harvey Scribner said that the plan needed more time for proper testing. Mayor John Lindsay declared that the city's decentralized school boards had brought a new vigor to the whole process of achieving quality education—but it was too soon to make a final judgment.

In 1965, London decentralized its government, dividing itself into 33 separate "Londons" (Bernard Weinraub, *The New York Times,* March 23, 1972). The powers of the borough councils range from control of child welfare and health services to pollution control, street cleaning, and garbage collection. The Greater London Council has overall planning authority for the city. The idea is to make government as local as possible—to bring it closer to the people. The evidence is that the plan has worked quite smoothly, although there are still some fuzzy areas of unclearly defined power. Squabbles are settled by compromise or ultimately by the central government if necessary.

Until recently, public acknowledgement that a metropolitan police organization performed with a different style, depending on the particular precinct or area, was considered to be administrative suicide. But that this was actually so was generally conceded by a "So what's new?" Painstaking studies of what the police do and how they do it are now producing data substantiating the great disparity in neighborhood conditions within a single metropolitan organizational jurisdiction. In New York City, for instance, there are wide differences in the ability of individual precincts to arrest criminals. A *New York Times* study, reported February 14–15, 1972, by David Burnham, revealed that:

> In one Harlem precinct with 53,351 residents, there were 105 criminal homicides in 1971. In a precinct in Kew Gardens, Queens, with 162,802 residents, there was one homicide. For 1971, the homicide rate in Central Harlem was 328 times as high as the homicide rate in Kew Gardens.

> The robbery rate of the Manhattan West Side's 20th Precinct was twice as high as the East Side's 19th Precinct.

> The rate of reported burglaries was 31 percent higher in Greenwich Village than the average rate in eight of the city's worst slum precincts.

Such statistics require careful interpretation, surely, and any conclusion, as Director Henry S. Ruth, Jr., of New York City's Criminal Justice Coordinating Council said, ". . . raises far more questions than it answers." Aside from the speculation such surveys engender as to the causes of the findings, the case for diversification in police style from precinct to precinct, and perhaps even within precincts, is fortified. Simply in terms of deployment of manpower, the implications are obvious. The study also showed sharp police performance variations by precincts, measured by the relative success of the police in making arrests. But of course this is a precarious basis on which to judge police officer efficiency, because many variables must be considered.

Much can be done with the concept of functional decentralization in metropolitan police organizations, with a view to more effective service as well as improving police and community relations, at the neighborhood level. This is not a new discovery. The St. Louis district police-citizen councils were created for this purpose in 1956. It should be recalled that this program was primarily geared to citizen involvement with the police in crime prevention and neighborhood improvement, not simply to foster better relationships or to "elevate the public image" of the police.

The Table of Organization

Viewed in the context of community relations, what is the ideal table of organization for a police department? This is a question often asked but not easily answered. There are as many answers as there are particular situations, considering size of the department and numerous other factors. The organization plan of the Palo Alto Police Department shown in Fig. 23-1 is apparently suitable to their situation. The 1966 President's Crime Commission suggested the form shown in Fig. 23-2 for "a well-organized municipal police department" (*Task Force Report: The Police,* p. 47).

In the Syracuse, New York, Police Department, the basic unit of organizational structure is the Crime Control Team. The structure of the department is shown in Fig. 23-3 (from J. F. Elliott, "The Crime Control Team").

Whatever the organizational structure, this thought—well put by Robert D. Pursley—should be paramount in the planning:

> Under traditional police organization, it is the organization that molds the parameters of responsibility and action and the individual is required to fit, period! There exists absolutely no assessment of human resource potential available around which the organization is woven. Perhaps with the past calibre of personnel that was attracted to law enforcement the need for control and narrowly defined job description was the best arrangement; however, changes occurring today and in the near future will cause this type of organizational pattern to fail unless substantial, basic modifications are made. ["Traditional Police Department: A Portent of Failure?"]

Ultimately, the basis for sound police-community relations rests in organizational commitment, orientation, and functional thrust, not primarily in organizational structure.

The Police-Community Relations Unit

Many police organizations in recent years have made a police-community relations unit part of their structure. The Law Enforcement Assistance Administration has provided funds to accomplish this in many departments of varying size and circumstances across the country.

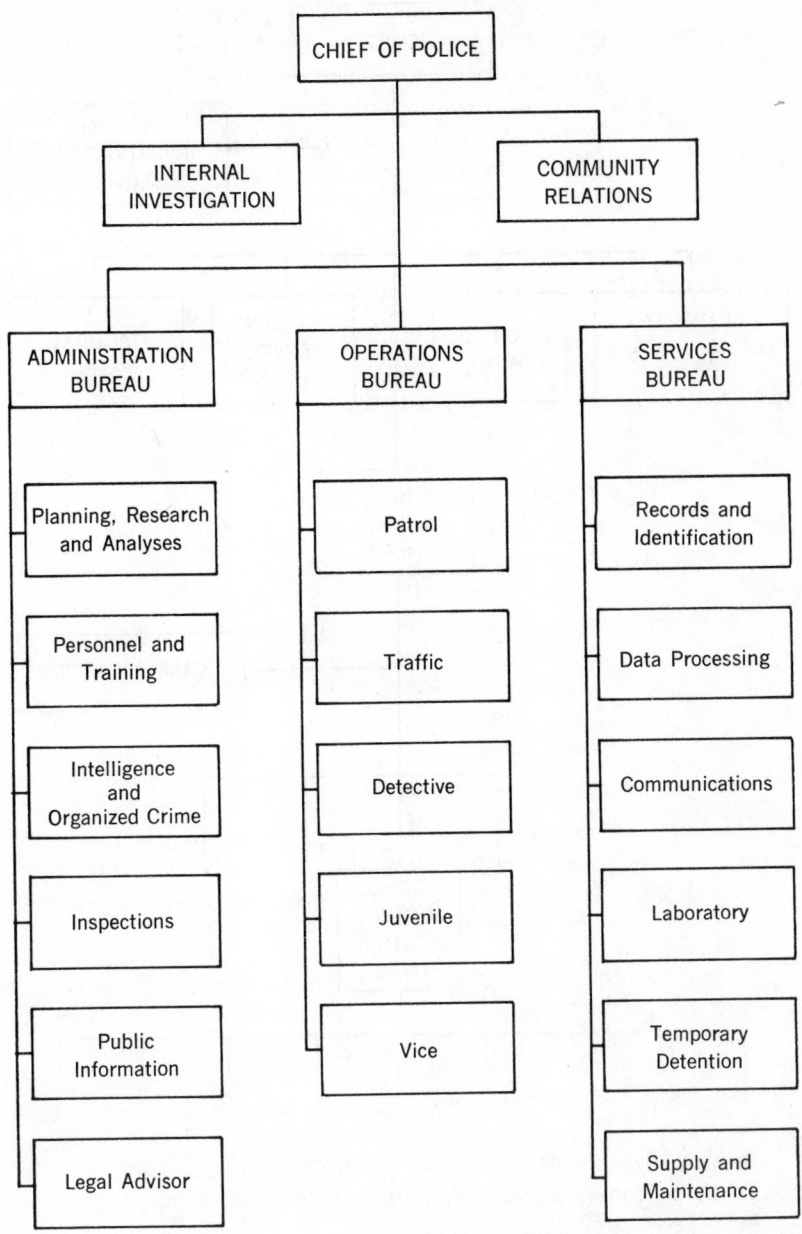

Figure 23–2. Model of a well-organized police department

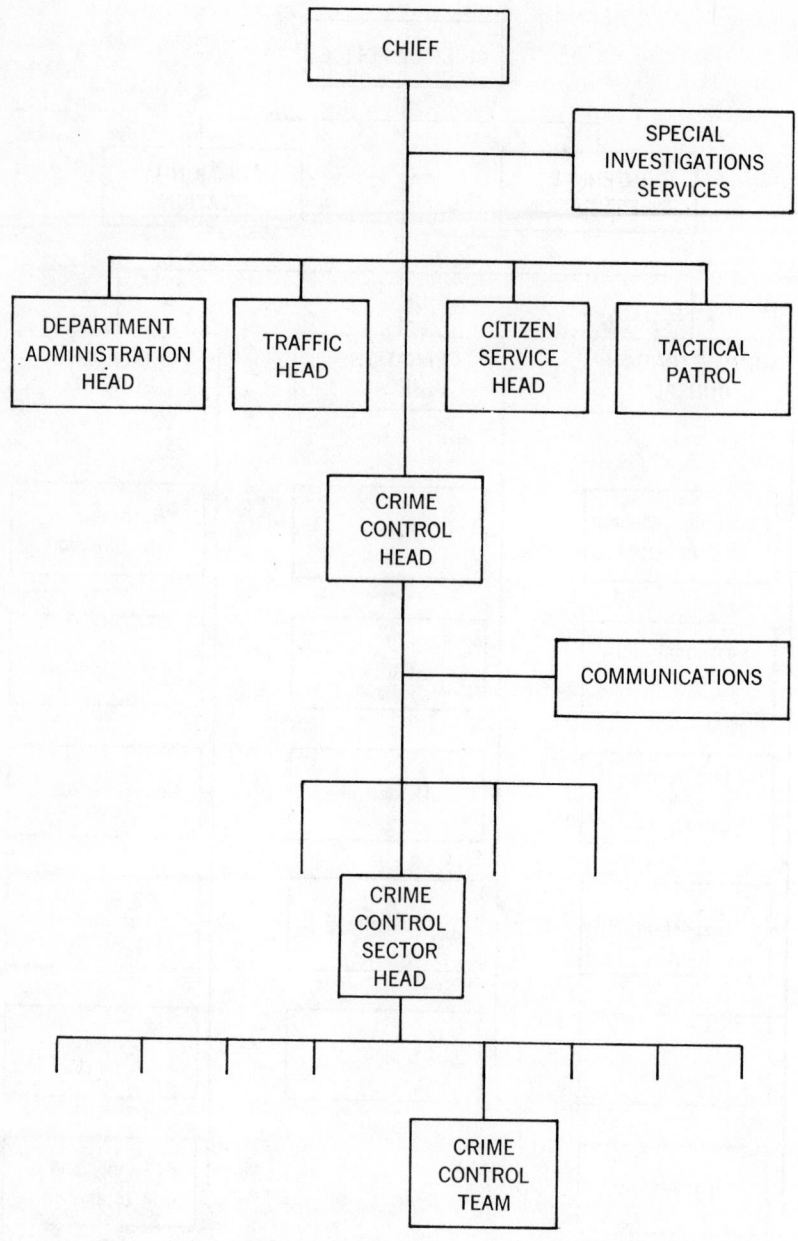

Figure 23–3. Organization Chart of Syracuse, New York, police department (courtesy of **Police,** in article by J. F. Elliott)

Specialists in the field of police and community relations have encouraged this trend. The titles and some other features of these units differ somewhat: Crime Prevention Bureau, Community Affairs Division, Community Services Division, Conflict Management Division, etc. But the essential idea is pretty much the same.[19] Recently, the term "police-community relations" has come to be regarded as old-hat in some quarters, and some critics newly arrived in the field have made strong indictments of the early approaches. New euphemisms such as "community involvement" are thought to be improvements on old ways of saying things.

By and large, however, the police-community relations unit in a police department has come into vogue, and something should be said for its advantages and disadvantages. One general criticism has been mentioned several times: such units are sometimes more form than substance, more interested in public relations gimmicks than in solid, issue-related programming, more devoted to political and administrative gamesmanship than genuine commitment—part of a strategy to divert public attention from what really needs to be done to effect significant change. The answer to this criticism is that the critics are sometimes correct.

Another related problem is in the negative attitudes of many men in the ranks toward the PCR unit and personnel assigned to it.[20] As we have said before, this hostility can be substantially reduced, if not eliminated, over a period of time by proper administrative tactics and community support. It should again be emphasized that effective community relations is a theme that should "orchestrate" the entire police organization, and not merely a special unit therein. This means more than the slogan "every officer a PCR officer." It means that every action in every part of the organization must be "community-conscious." Sir Robert Peel said it well: the police are the public, and the public are the police.

Earning Community Respect

It is certainly difficult to build a good relationship between police and community under circumstances in which the police are unworthy of public respect. Graft, corruption, and other illegal practices in police work are inevitably police-community relations concerns. And as the Knapp Commission has found in New York City, police corruption is certainly of current relevance. It ought to be a matter of concern in many cities, as Albert Reiss has suggested in *The Police and the Public*. He claims that extensive corruption exists in almost every major and many medium-sized police departments in the country.

Almost daily newspaper accounts of kickbacks, shakedowns, and perjury implicate policemen at many points on the map. Curiously, investigations are often inspired by newspaper or television allegations, as was the case with the Knapp Commission. The tie between police corruption and organized crime is widely recognized. Many observers believe that much corruption is still uncovered.[21]

What is not always so sharply stressed in publicity about police graft is its link with the community. Bribery of a police officer is an illustration. For every officer who is offered a bribe, there is a "law-abiding citizen" offering it. This does not, of course, excuse the behavior of the officer who accepts the bribe, but it does suggest that police corruption is a problem broader at its base than is usually assumed. Incidentally, it was reported that the New York City Police Department made 356 bribery arrests during the six-month period September 1971 to February 1972, as compared with 75 such arrests in the same period a year earlier (*New York Times,* April 5, 1972). Evidently some progress was being made in dealing with at least this brand of corruption in one important location.

Comparisons are often made between the American and British police. It is pointed out that 95 percent of the people in Britain respect their police and believe them to be honest, courteous, and doing a good job. As William V. Shannon has observed in "A New Look at the Police," a major reason for this is that the British police are not saddled with enforcing laws that are unenforceable.[22] Gambling is legal, homosexual relations between consenting adults in private is legal, abortions can be obtained free through the National Health Service, prostitutes are not arrested if they stay off the streets, and narcotics addicts are treated relatively leniently. In the United States, Shannon notes that "vice squad" has become "a synonym for payoff and potentially good policemen are demoralized by protection money flowing from illegal but enormously profitable gambling of all kinds." He concludes that "no real improvement in police performance is possible until Americans face up to this corruption and the double standard which produces it."

A similar view of the matter has been expressed by Richard Dougherty:

> ... New York, with its Broadway flair for public confession and self-flagellation, is not unique in the matter of police corruption. Indeed, it may be stated as an axiom that no illegal activity which is dependent on a sizable retail trade can operate in any city without the cooperation of crooked cops. However much the folks in Seattle, New Orleans, Philadelphia ... would like to think otherwise, so long as anyone can buy a drink after hours, put down a bet with a bookmaker, patronize a whorehouse, or buy narcotics, some part of what he pays will find its way into the pockets of police. ["The New York Police"]

There have long been those who have dismissed the problem of police corruption rather lightly by citing the old saw: there are a few rotten apples in every barrel. But there have also been those with a ready rebuttal. For instance, it has been pointed out that corruption cannot exist without the cooperation of the "honest" cop. The police—especially the patrolmen subculture, working as it does with respect to "covering up for your buddy"—are stacked against the honest cop informing on his crooked partner. Corruption cannot exist on a widespread basis without officers in general knowing about it. The honest cop can stop it. Unless and until he does, the plaintive cry from policemen that the reputation of all is being blackened by a few will not find many sympathizers.

In testifying before the Knapp Commission, Sergeant David Durk of the New York City Police Department said that he and Officer Frank Serpico knew nothing about corruption that was not known to every officer. Not to know was, they stated, to be either blind or incompetent. Durk went on to observe that, to him, police corruption was an attack on "a way of life, on the rule of law, and on the vocation of policing." The real price, he added, was "not free meals, but broken homes in dying neighborhoods, and a whole generation of people being lost." He concluded:

> Responsibility must also be fixed outside the Police Department, against all the men and agencies that have helped bring us to our present pass, against all those who could have helped expose the corruption but never did. Like it or not, the policeman is convinced that he lives and works in the middle of a corrupt society, that everybody is getting theirs and why shouldn't he, and that if somebody cared about corruption, something would have been done about it a long time ago.[23]

Bruce Olson has astutely observed that the proper study of mankind is its police.[24] He goes on to suggest that the proper study of the police needs more attention paid to intrinsic elements of the job; for example, the attitudes policemen have about their work. The police unionization trend is motivated by more than salary and other economic benefits. In what ways do police officer attitudes toward the job contribute to internal organization tensions, external community relations tensions, indeed to corrupt behavior? Olson feels that social science has neglected such questions, and professional police literature even more so. He reports on some modest research concerned with questions addressed to police officers:

1. What are the good things about this department?
2. In what way should the department be improved?
3. What do you think the citizens of your town want you, as a policeman, to do?
4. What do you think your job as a policeman is?

Integrity development has become a major theme in police training. An innovative workshop on the subject was launched in the 106th Precinct of the New York City Police Department in November 1971 (Doyle and Olivet, "Workshop in Law Enforcement Integrity"). The 6-month basic training program in that city's Police Academy now includes a 20-hour block of time on the subject. It is interesting that, until recently, corruption had never been mentioned in the academy program.

A further thought may be added on the subject of organized crime. Corrupt policemen unquestionably are caught up in the cobweb, but it is an exceedingly complex phenomenon, with many factors enmeshed in it. Hypocrisy in public attitudes about the activities on which organized crime thrives is at the heart of it. To make gambling illegal when so many people want to gamble is one illustration. As we have said, this kind of "double speak" is critical in understanding police-community tensions. One encouraging sign is the manner in which police operations across jurisdictional boundaries have been maturing in bringing coordinated efforts to bear on organized crime. It is an excellent example of what is possible through interrelated, concerted planning (see Dudley Gourley, "A Final Solution to the Problem of Organized Crime"). But even the most ingenious police efforts are laughed at by substantial segments of the public.

Further Personnel Considerations

There are three considerations in the area of police personnel management about which we want to say a bit more: the minority group policeman, policewomen, and recruiting standards.

Minority recruitment campaigns by big-city police departments in recent years have resulted in very modest gains in the number of black and Chicano policemen. At the same time, many interested applicants have not survived the civil service test and other qualification obstacles. Richard Margolis has observed that the problems associated with police minority hiring practices are less promotional than institutional.[25] New recruitment policies are needed, preferably shaped as much by minority communities as by police departments.

There is also the question of what minority group officers encounter once they are sworn. To gain ten black officers and lose seven by reason of internal organizational attitudes and practices is ramshackle progress. Sometimes these internal conditions are difficult for naive "outsiders" to comprehend. Not uncommonly, black officers are subjected to frame-ups and various kinds of calculated plots ("shaft") in relation to assignments, promotions, and other considerations. One wonders why they continue as policemen. To suggest that the situation is no worse than it is in other lines of work is hardly comforting. The point is that retaining minority group officers in police organizations is as important as recruiting them initially. As the nonwhite proportion of the population of many cities increases, it is logical to expect an increase in the proportion of nonwhite police officers. The resistance comes from white officers living in suburbia, but working in the inner city, who regard the black or Chicano officer as a threat. The "metropolitanizing" of police organizations would be a step toward curbing this particular brand of choosing up sides, but the inherent attitudes call for a multi-faceted approach. Black police officer organizations realize this and are planning their strategies accordingly.

The time has also come to take a new look at the policewoman. This is not the place to undertake a review and evaluation of the Women's Liberation Movement. But it is worth noting that even the FBI is now accepting applications from women for the position of special agent. This is one of many signs that the importance of women in law enforcement is beginning to be recognized. Women have been in police work in this country since 1893, but now at last there are indications of a broadening concept of their role. Particularly with respect to community relations, an increase in the number of women in police work—especially in the peacemaking aspects—should produce interesting results to be carefully analyzed and assessed. Will more women on the beat, for instance, mean less use of force by police? A few metropolitan police departments are presently looking for answers to such questions —Washington, D.C., as one example, where 100 women were hired in the Spring of 1972 for regular patrol duty.[26]

Recruitment standards in police work have special connotations when considered in relation to minority group (including women) applicants. Too often when an emphasis is placed on hiring minority groups there are allegations of "lowering standards," suggesting that the question is being viewed in a distorted (one writer calls it "Neander-thal") manner. On the other hand, there are encouraging developments too, as indicated in the following random sampling of recent reports:

> If the Supreme Court's ruling in *Griggs v. Duke Power Company* (915 Sup. Ct. 849, 1971) is applied to the police profession, havoc may be predicted in the recruit selection standards of police agencies unprepared to substantiate the relationship between the test instruments used and the officer's job. General intelligence tests are no longer regarded as trustworthy in predicting police job performance.[27]

> Five instruments were developed by the Educational Testing Service of Princeton, N.J., to be used in a study of the characteristics of 1300 applicants to the police civil service examination in New Jersey, over a four-month period in 1970. The performance of the pass applicants differed significantly from that of fail applicants on various items of each test of the battery.[28]

Several big city police departments—Houston and Philadelphia as examples—are reporting success with nineteen-year-old police officers.[29] The possibilities in cadet and pre-cadet programs have not as yet been adequately assessed—for example, in relation to minority recruitment.

A Rand Institute study of the careers of approximately 2000 New York City policemen found that many of those who received bad ratings during their probationary period later were accused of being corrupt, abusing citizens, and breaking departmental rules. Poor ratings in the Police Academy were "the strongest indicators of later poor performance," the report of the study stated. Older policemen with more education at the time of their appointment received a substantially smaller number of charges alleging abuse of citizens than younger, less educated policemen. Men who had been arrested for nonviolent crimes prior to joining the force were less likely than other officers to be later charged with false arrest, illegal search and seizure, and other instances of harassing citizens. (David Burnham, *The New York Times,* May 8, 1972).

In 1964, the Chicago Police Department, in cooperation with the Chicago Civil Service Commission, initiated a continuing research program on applicants for patrolman. The objectives were to study the characteristics of effective patrolmen, to upgrade the quality of recruits, and to validate the selection and evaluation procedures.[30]

Following in the path of the Chicago Police Department, the Detroit Police Department in 1971 began implementing a selection testing system designed to predict an applicant's performance as a police officer on the street. The tests measure an applicant's motivation, occupational interests, ability to size up a situation, aptitude in dealing with problems involving people, tolerance under pressure, personality and emotional adjustment, as well as basic intelligence. The test battery has resulted in the hiring of more minority candidates since a wide range of cultural factors are taken into account in the testing process.[31]

Some very promising work on the subject of recruitment standards is being conducted by the Professional Standards Division of the International Association of Chiefs of Police. Deborah Ann Kent and Terry Eisenberg of the staff of that organization have reviewed the pertinent research and literature on police selection and promotion (*The Police Chief,* February 1972), with these conclusions:

The quality of research on the subject, with a few exceptions, is poor.

The conclusions drawn in far too many studies border on charlatanism.

There is some evidence (though much more is required) supporting the potential value of some written objective tests, situational tests, and personal history data in predicting police officer performance.

The problem of criteria stands out as a major stumbling block to improved police selection and promotion procedures.

For all practical purposes, nothing is known about the effective promotion of police officers to higher ranks and/or different functional areas.

Job or task analysis has largely been either avoided or superficially addressed to date.

Effective selection and promotion strategies are severely restricted by virtue of the numerous and often contradictory roles and activities a police officer performs.

Police Unions

We have observed that police unions are increasingly a potent force in the politics of law enforcement. With respect to police and community relations, it is not yet clear which way these unions will go. It is no more clear what their effect will be with reference to police professionalism. Yet one thing is clear: police unions are here to stay, even as they pretend not to be unions. Line organizations of police officers have emerged as a formidable political power-bloc. How wisely and constructively this new-found influence will be used is still a question.

One is struck by the similarities in the patterns of diverse opinion that exist among policemen and among college professors as to whether unionization (of either) is a good thing. The majority of police administrators and the majority of college administrators take a dim view of the unionization movement. This is hardly surprising. It appears, however, that relatively few administrators of either type have had time to study the factors, in and out of their organizations, that have produced the unionization phenomenon. One might speculate as to the effect it would have if these factors were carefully identified and fashioned into administrative programs designed to cope with the needs and sentiments thus laid bare.[32]

Those who favor police unionization claim benefits for it in influencing judicial and legislative actions affecting police powers, in public information dividends, in promoting unity among officers and improving morale, and of course in making common cause regarding financial betterment. Few advocates of police unions are specific in what they think unions will do for professional growth in other than economic terms or in improvement of police service to meet community needs. The advantages of unionization are generally delineated much more in what it will do for police officers than in what it will do for society. What most needs to be shown, perhaps, is how the good of one may well be the good of the other. It is in this sense that police unionization poses a police-community relations puzzle, not as yet resolved.

Opponents of police unions claim that such organizations concentrate power into relatively few hands, that they increase the possibility of police strikes and "job actions," that unionization tends to deprive police administrators of essential administrative prerogatives and autonomy, and further that it alienates police and community. It seems clear that *power* is the key idea among both proponents and opponents, accurately reflecting social tides in the context of our times.

Saying this scarcely provides fresh insight, but it does suggest the practicality of thinking and speaking of police unions in *political* terms. For they are, at base, more political than economic entities, though the two strains are inevitably intertwined. Their rhetoric highlights such terms as votes, bargaining, coalitions, caucus, deals, contracts, job actions, "calling the shots," prime target, lobbying, and the like. This is a relatively new language in police work, and it is too soon to tell what it will mean. Police officers themselves are sharply divided on the matter, even those who pay their dues and are classified as union members. But they do tend to close ranks when a subject such as civilian review boards comes up. After all, "professionals" should have some autonomy and not be "bugged" by naive citizens. But then, why do "professionals" need a union? Is it to protect the practitioner from the client? If so, then who protects the client from the practitioner?

Portents for the Future

We have mentioned a number of recent developments in police administration and operations that seem to point promisingly toward more enlightened and far-sighted service to the community. It is appropriate that we conclude this chapter on a note of optimism for the future —heralded by these illustrative progressive rumblings, to be added to those previously cited:

> There is evidence that a bridge is at last being built between operating police departments (and other criminal justice agencies), and colleges/universities. More policemen with some college education is an important aspect of this, but there are other aspects—for example, various types of research and consultant activity, more astute dovetailing of police training and police education, and the work of such campus entities as the Harvard Law School Center for the Advancement of Criminal Justice.[33] LEAA and the Ford Foundation deserve special applause for their tangible encouragement of such developments, and other funding sources have also contributed.

> College-educated police officers should mean a new look at many traditional ways of doing things in police organizations. Some will write articles and books. Some will find themselves assigned to key positions—in personnel work, training, planning and research, and community relations. Some will be promoted to the supervisory and

administrative levels. Many will be committed to *change*—significant change.

In one particular facet of higher education alone (with no slight intended to other facets)—psychology—operating police agencies are reaping important rewards. Morton Bard's pioneer work with the New York City Police Department in family crisis intervention is one well known example. Hans Toch's research on violence prevention in the Oakland Police Department comes to mind.[34] Departmental consulting psychologists are common today.[35] Attitude measurement in connection with community relations programs, though extremely difficult to do, is being tried in various ways.[36]

Personnel incentive policies and career development programs that reward more insightful and understanding handling of clientele are emerging in the police world. Compared with business and industry, there is much catching up to be done in this regard. But there are promising beginnings.[37]

Metropolitan and regional approaches to criminal justice services and problems are unfolding, again thanks to LEAA stimulation. It is no longer novel in narcotics control, computerized information systems, communications, training, and planning. Crime control demands it. The regional concept is well-exemplified in the Dayton-Montgomery County (Ohio) Criminal Justice Pilot Program, with its research-demonstration-evaluation dimensions drawing on substantial professional experience in police, courts, corrections, and systems analysis.[38] There is also some stirring in multi-state projects such as Project STAR (System Training and Analysis of Requirements), seeking to define roles and goals of operational personnel in the criminal justice system. And Raymond Galvin is among a few visionaries inviting attention to the importance of cross-national and cross-cultural comparative study of police and criminal justice systems.[39]

It is a bit startling to realize that *planning* is a function so recently institutionalized in police work. Chief of Police E. F. Holladay of Monterey Park, California has asked a good question: Shall we continue to repair, or build a new house?[40] Wesley Pomeroy has posed some of the old and new questions in law enforcement administration that will be somewhat easier to deal with to the extent that research and planning help identify, analyze, and furnish clues for constructive steps.[41] One example of the possibilities is provided by the long-range planning design of the Kansas City Police Department.[42]

Closely coupled with the research and planning functions of modern police organizations is *systems analysis,* with its inherent unifying theoretical approaches to the problems that, as Bruce Olson has put it, "tear apart" any social system.[43]

Considerable attention has been directed in the past few years to the need for *legal advisers* for police agencies. Some pioneer work on this was done some years ago by Professor Frank Remington of the

University of Wisconsin Law School and Professor Edward Barrett of the University of California Law School. The New York City Police Department recently announced appointment of six young lawyers as civilian advisers at the divisional level.[44] These legal advisers will work in the field and in court, assisting police officers in such matters as how to testify, search and seizure situations, interrogation of suspects, etc. An American Bar Association committee recommended in the Spring of 1972 that police departments should make far fewer arrests and hire legal advisers to help shape law enforcement policy.

"Forward-looking" police administration is a value-laden idea in its definition, and many police executives might even be hesitant to be so described. Yet it does require courage to take positions which depart from long-accepted and generally unchallenged ways of doing things.[45] One veteran police officer puts it this way: "The trick is to effect the changes with reason, taking care not to be guilty of making changes only for the sake of change."[46] Former Oakland Police Chief Charles R. Gain is one of those who has consistently played the role of the administrative "change agent"—an "uncommon cop," in the terminology of one national periodical.[47] New York City Police Commissioner Patrick V. Murphy is another example, as suggested in his views regarding the manner in which he believes the civil service system has inhibited the promotion of strong leaders within police agencies. We have referred to Dayton Chief Robert Igleburger as another example, and there are others mentioned throughout this text.

Business and industry today are strong on what is called *future trend analysis*. Organizations such as the Institute of Life Insurance make much of it, for obvious reasons. It makes sense for police management to explore the matter of future outlook study, for reasons so apparent that the point need not be elaborated here.[48]

It is possible, perhaps, to cast the crucial question of police role too philosophically, too theoretically. James Q. Wilson recognized this when he decided to visit eight communities to observe first-hand how uniformed officers dealt with common offenses. He and other role analysts quickly realized that the exercise of discretion was a key factor in understanding, in practical terms, what police officers actually do. These analysts also see the exercise of discretion as important in the officer's own job satisfaction, as well as in the professionalization of police service.

Michael Banton says, therefore, that it is of the greatest interest to discover where the policeman gets his ideas about how he should exercise discretion. Banton thinks that these ideas come from the officer's training, from the courts, and *from the officer's participation in the community which he polices*. As Banton puts it:

The more a policeman is hindered from participating in the community, the less he will understand public sentiment, the less well he will exercise his discretion, therefore the more are members of the public likely to be irritated by his behavior, the more will they treat him differently in social contacts, the more isolated will the police become.[49]

Banton believes that internal relations in a police department are closely connected with external relations between police and public. In other words, problems of police-community relations are often an extension of relationship problems within police organizations. He is concerned about what he calls "a crisis of authority" in many large American municipal police departments, centering in the question of who shall define the police role. It is a struggle, as Banton sees it, between the "bosses" and the "men," the latter being represented by increasingly powerful police unions.

Behind the disputes in labor-management relations, he observes, is a difference of opinion as to what the job is all about. Men on the street think that the bosses are out of touch with changed circumstances. One difference of opinion pertains to the "war on crime," and it illustrates the point. The younger officers think it necessary to have as many men as possible in cars on the streets. To them, this is "real police work," much more exciting and "professional" than engaging in "a lot of do-gooding social work." But if the priority is to reduce crime, greater efforts by the police alone are not the major requirement. Rather it is a matter of training police officers to appreciate, Banton points out, "that one of the most important aspects of their job is encouraging public cooperation and eliciting information." The decisive insight is in recognizing the difference between a too-narrow or too-superficial perception of the job and a broad-based, community-oriented view of it. The internal division on this point, within police ranks, is projected today into problems of external relationships. It may well be the very heart of the police-community relationship situation.

The syndicated columnist, Sydney J. Harris, has Banton's analysis in mind, it appears, as he writes:

> Police officials will admit that public cooperation is the prime ingredient in the effectiveness of a police force. The people must recognize the legitimacy of the power they have delegated to the police; when they do not, civil order collapses and laws are broken without any sense of shame or guilt or indignation about lawbreakers.

> "All authority is moral," I began by saying yesterday. Nowhere is this plainer than in the performance of police duties and the public response. Crime will not drop—no matter what harsh Draconic measures we take—until and unless trust and respect for the police are restored in the slum communities. As always, this political problem rests on a moral base. ["Police Power Waning"]

Notes to Chapter Twenty-three

1. Quinn Tamm, "Editorial," *The Police Chief* 38, no. 3 (March 1971): 6. This entire issue is devoted to articles on police-community relations.

2. From *Special Order No. 33,* December 5, 1963, Los Angeles Police Department, W. H. Parker, Chief; and *General Order Concerning Civil Rights,* April 25, 1966, Chicago Police Department, O. W. Wilson, Superintendent. *The New York Times* reported (February 29, 1972) a new Master Plan for the New York City Police Department, containing more than 100 recommendations for policy changes, to be in effect by September, 1973. Many of the contemplated changes, originating with Commissioner Patrick V. Murphy, pertain to community relations—for example, that "better men" shall be assigned to the busiest precincts, and that racial prejudice in the ranks shall be diminished.

3. V. A. Leonard, *Police Organization and Management,* 1964, p. 196. See also Robert L. Brunton, "Supervision—A Major Problem for Police Departments."

4. Leroy A. Smith, "Lateral Entry: An Inside Job," and William H. Hewitt, "Police Personnel Administration: Lateral Entry."

5. For instance, see "Project CREM," *Police* 16, no. 6 (February 1972): 72. Also Donald A. Lund, "Confrontation Management."

6. A memorandum submitted to the Parliamentary Select Committee investigating relations between the police and Coloured immigrants, University of Bristol, England, March 1972 (unpublished).

7. For example, see Nelson A. Watson, "Developing Guidelines for Police Practices."

8. Raymond M. Momboisse, "Demonstrations and Civil Disobedience," and Harry G. Fox, "Demonstrations Demand Specialists."

9. See also Security Planning Corporation (Washington, D.C.), *Non-Lethal Weapons for Law Enforcement: Research Needs and Priorities,* a report to the National Science Foundation, March 1972.

10. Other references to the same subject have been cited in chap. 6. Pertinent also are such popular works as *The New Centurions* and *The Blue Knight* by Joseph Wambaugh.

11. James H. Crawford, "Combined-Selective Patrol," and James D. Bannon, "Foot Patrol."

12. Michael Banton in a letter to Louis A. Radelet, November 25, 1971.

13. Robert Wasserman, "Conflicts in Police and Community Relations Programming," National Center on Police and Community Relations, Michigan State University (unpublished monograph), 1967.

14. Professor Leon Weaver of Michigan State U. School of Criminal Justice has emphasized the public service represented by the participation of local police departments in civil defense, natural disaster, and man-caused disorder. See Paul M. Whisenand, "Municipal Police Services in a Disaster Preparedness Program."

15. John E. Angell, "Toward an Alternative to the Classical Police Organizational Arrangements: A Democratic Model." School of Criminal Justice, Michigan State University (unpublished monograph), 1970. The article describes Angell's model in considerable detail.

16. It should be noted that Angell was a consultant to the Holyoke Police Department and is a member of the Dayton Police Department.

17. Lawence W. Sherman, "A Comparative Survey of Team Policing." The Police Foundation (unpublished report), 1971.

18. Charts are from "Management by Objectives," by Leo E. Peart.

19. See Edgar Davis, "A Method of Approach to the Tasks of a Human Relations Officer," and Marshall E. Jones, "Police Leadership and Human Relations."

20. Lee P. Brown provides an able assessment of the problems of police-community relations units in *Police-Community Relations Evaluation Project.*

21. As reported by David Burnham in *The New York Times,* January 28, 1972. It was Burnham's revelations in April 1970 that led to the appointment of the Knapp Commission. Burnham was a member of the staff of the 1966 President's Crime Commission.

22. Relative to the British situation, *Newsweek* (January 24, 1972) reported that morale at Scotland Yard was at an all-time low—for several reasons quite familiar in the United States, including apparent corruption.

23. *The Hot Line* 4, no. 5 (February 1972). National Conference of Christians and Jews.

24. Bruce T. Olson, "Police Opinions of Work," and L. Craig Parker, Jr., "Self-Disclosing Behavior in Police Work." We have alluded to the manner in which the unexpected, innovative move can win many a ball game. Joseph F. Coates discusses the use of humor to reduce tensions in street demonstrations in "Wit and Humor: A Neglected Aid in Crowd and Mob Control."

25. Richard J. Margolis, *Who Will Wear the Badge?* (a study of minority recruitment efforts in protective services). In May 1972, a Federal judge ordered the Philadelphia Police Department to hire one black police officer for each two white officers hired. A social worker's experience in training a group of police recruits, many of them black, for the police department of a large eastern city is described by John J. Hughes in "Training Police Recruits for Service in the Urban Ghetto."

26. See Lois L. Higgins, "Historical Background of Policewomen's Service"; Gary R. Perlstein, "Policewomen and Policemen: A Comparative Look"; and *Time,* May 1, 1972, p. 60.

27. Stanley Vanagunas, "Police Entry Testing and Minority Employment." See also Margolis, *Who Will Wear the Badge?",* p. 14.

28. Leo S. Goldstein, "Characteristics of Police Applicants."

29. See, for example, Harry G. Fox, "Nineteen."

30. For fuller information see Spencer and Nichols, "A Study of Chicago Police Recruits."

31. *The Police Chief* 38, no. 11 (November 1971): 14.

32. John C. Meyer, Jr., "Both Sides Now: Police Opinions of the National Police Union." The distinction between a *union* and a *professional association* is not always clearly drawn. See also Goldner and Koenig, "White Middle-Class Attitudes Toward an Urban Policemen's Union."

33. See Joseph D. McNamara, "Profile: Harvard Law School's Center for the Advancement of Criminal Justice," and James P. Morgan, Jr., "Responsibilities of Universities to the Criminal Justice System."

34. Hans Toch, "Quality Control in Police Work."

35. See Martin Reiser, "Psychological Research in an Urban Police Department."

36. See, for instance, Clifford D. Blagg, "Improved Community Relations Via Attitude Quantification."

37. Note such articles as Rod Carpenter, "Psychology and Its Ever-Changing Ways"; Donald G. Webb, "Police Administrators and the Personnel Incentive Policy"; and Peter J. Pitchess, "Career Development for Professional Law Enforcement."

38. The first phase (July 1, 1970, to December 31, 1971) report of this project is available from Community Research, Inc., Dayton, Ohio 45402. See also R. T. Parsonson, "The Regional Trend in Law Enforcement. See also the editorial on regionalization in *The Police Chief* 38, no. 8 (August 1971): 8. Another useful reference is Kuykendall and Gould, "Cooperative Police Services."

39. Raymond T. Galvin, "Law Enforcement: A Comparative View."

40. In an editorial with that title in *Police* 13, no. 2 (November–December 1968): 1–3.

41. Wesley A. Pomeroy, "New Trends in Police Planning."

42. See Key and Warren, "Kansas City: Long Range Planning Program."

43. Bruce T. Olson, "Conflicts in Values in Criminal Justice."

44. As reported by Leroy Oelsner in *The New York Times,* May 16, 1972.

45. Several articles in *The Police Chief* 38, no. 1 (January 1971) illustrate the idea; for instance, the articles by former San Francisco Chief of Police Alfred J. Nelder, Morton Bard, J. P. Morgan, Jr., W. S. Robinson, Quinn Tamm, and David G. Epstein.

46. Kenneth M. Cable, "The Chief and the Community." Also pertinent are Quinn Tamm, "Objective-Performance Management Training," and Charles L. Newman, "Police and Families."

47. Norman Melnick, "Uncommon Cop" and "The Gain Mutiny."

48. L. L. L. Golden, "Alerting Management." See also Alvin Toffler, *Future Shock;* Guy Halverson, "You and Your Police"; and LEAA Report No. SD-D-1, *Criminal Justice Agencies in the United States, 1970.*

49. Michael Banton, "Authority and the Urban Policeman," unpublished monograph while a visiting professor at Wayne State University, Detroit, June 1971.

Chapter Twenty-Four

The Community Side of Police and Community Relations

Police officers participating in police and community relations work frequently feel that in these programs there is too much emphasis placed on the police responsibility and insufficient attention given to community responsibility. Program planners reply, often with more ardor than clarity, that it really is a two-way street, that law enforcement and keeping the peace truly are the responsibilities of the *total* community, but that there are special requirements of police leadership for several reasons, one of which is professional expectations. Moreover, there is the fact that "community" is not a single, manageable, reachable entity, but is rather a splintered conglomeration to which no one message will appeal.

To speak, therefore, of "community responsibility" for crime or for other social problems is actually to employ an almost meaningless generalization: what is everyone's responsibility is no one's. Programs to improve police and community relations or to contain crime (which may be, in large measure, one and the same)—must do a better job than this of fixing specific responsibility. How is this to be done?

We believe that much of the answer lies in the first step of the problem-solving process—that is, in how problems are identified and defined. In a word, more people of different backgrounds and ways of seeing things should have a fair, "unloaded" opportunity for input. The more people having that opportunity, the more likely it is that a problem will be defined so that people will identify it as *their* problem and share the responsibility of doing something about it. So it is that *the process* becomes as important as *the product,* and thus can constitute a large part of the solution.

Some Guiding Principles

Throughout this text, we have attempted to present some guiding principles for the development of effective programs in police and community relations. In the preceding chapter, we reiterated some key ideas bearing on police responsibilities. Now we shall undertake a similar review pertaining to broad community action, beginning with these basic points:

> Police-community relations programs should take into account (more than they have, to date) the practical political factors bearing on problems and the possibilities of resolution. The politics of PCR needs much greater emphasis.

> Improving the police image with various factions in a community may be a worthwhile secondary goal in programs, but it should not be featured as a primary purpose. Likewise, it should be recognized that the popularity of police officers, or persuading citizens to "like" policemen, are not program objectives of major importance, however gratifying they may be as spin-off dividends.

> Going back to the definition of community relations, the combination of public relations, community services, and community participation seems to be as viable a theoretical construction as ever, although one or the other will be stressed at a given time and place. But to hold that public relations alone is community relations is like saying that case work is all there is to social work.

> PCR programs have tended to appeal mainly to the "joiners," not unlike other community action endeavors. Yet it is not correct to say that "the wrong people are involved." It is not a question of "right" or "wrong" people. It is rather a question of discovering ways to hear the messages of those in a community who are not joiners—and who should not be compelled to join an organization or attend meetings as the price of being heard.

> Community elements must become much more articulate in their expectations of services from the police and assume a larger share in determining police role and such associated considerations as police policy delineation, structural and functional organization of police agencies, citizen complaint procedures, police recruitment standards, training content and methods, and the like. These matters must not be left solely to the discretion either of police and public administrators, or of police unions—by reason of community default.

It would help the police greatly if a larger community consensus could be secured as to which of two sometimes conflicting ends is to have priority: the protection of individual rights or the apprehension of criminals. The issue in this is not the propaganda line: "soft on crime." The issue is whether a free society is to become no more than a mere propaganda line.

Voices from the community are often quick to criticize police action when the action may deserve criticism. The voices should be just as quick to commend police action when it deserves commendation. If community-sensitive police behavior helps to fortify credibility and trust in "the system," then by the same token citizen assistance to a police officer helps to strengthen his or her belief in the integrity of civic responsibility. More than this, it restores an antique Anglo-Saxon principle that badly needs restoration.

Community forces should influence police organizations to confine the functions of police-community relations units (whatever they may be called) to identification of conflict, planning for conflict control, and public information. To mention one of the major abuses of this principle, such units should *not* be citizen complaint bureaus, nor carry on internal investigations in the manner of so-called "gumshoe squads." This is not to say that a citizens' complaint bureau may not be vital. It is simply a matter of keeping conflicting functions from snarling role definitions and job specifications, thereby contributing to everyone's confusion.

Again, it should be said that police and community relations as a field of study and social action tends to be thought of in too narrow terms. This is illustrated by the notion that it is just another name for public relations, by the notion that it means solely race and minority group relations, and by the tendency to isolate the police from the larger social systems of which they are part. The problems and issues in this field must be seen as pieces in a larger jigsaw.

No particular formula for good police-community cooperation can be applied in all communities. While there are general trends, problems and programs will have distinctive local features simply because the relevant conditions vary. "Package" programs are like nonprescription patent medicines.

Community leaders should recognize the important difference between an advisory body of citizens for a police department and a so-called civilian review board. It is not a question of one being better than the other. Each has a purpose, and each operates differently. A citizens' advisory committee is set up mainly to provide a police agency with information and recommendations, ideally reflecting as wide a spectrum of community opinion as possible. A civilian review board is an adjudicatory body dealing with complaints. It conducts hearings and functions in a quasi-judicial manner. An effective advisory group may help to make a review board unnecessary. But there are situations in which police relations with the community have deteriorated to the point where a review board is seen as "the only answer." In such an unhappy state of affairs, it will probably be discovered eventually that a review board doesn't do the job either.[1]

Many community organizations would be well advised to consider inviting police participation in their activities. Numerous groups have overlooked this, or have decided on their own that the police would not be interested. For some groups, this may be the case, but a principle of appropriateness should be applied. Interagency relationships are an integral part of police and community relations.

Education of school children in matters of law enforcement, legal institutions, social control and the police part in it, and problems of the criminal justice system is a very significant aspect of the total community task.

To be precise in goal delineation for a given program is as important as it is to be precise in problem definition. Neither of these is done very well in the vast majority of social action undertakings, and the results are correspondingly blighted. Example: why have this PCR project? Answer: to prevent riots. Nonsense! Too many things in community life today, having little to do with PCR, can conceivably trigger a riot.

Blaming the police for social problems takes many forms. Crime? Delinquency? Drugs? Zany behavior? Traffic congestion? The prevailing mood is to view these as "police problems"—"let the cops worry about it; that's what they get paid for!" How cope with such an attitude, widespread as it is? The answer is to widen and deepen community education and participation. How to do this?

Answers to the last question are the keys to community action. What is it that moves people to care? Various social organizers and planners have become more or less famous for their ideas on this question. Ralph Nader is a contemporary "institution" reminding us that most people will do almost anything to avoid making waves, and the late Saul Alinsky, widely known organizer of community action groups, said that middle-class Americans considered direct, controversial statements as "boorish and uncultured" (James G. Driscoll in *The National Observer*, January 29, 1972). Not to get involved in conflict or controversy has come to be regarded as a virtue. Yet Alinsky believed that conflict was the essence of a free and open society. It has been, he often declared, "the matrix of every new and good idea" in America. Alinsky's career was dedicated to organizing the "wave-makers," to create a unified force—he called it "fun," "adventure," "exhilarating"—and he wrote a book entitled *Revielle for Radicals*. The Naders and the Alinskys are not popular with the Establishmentarians; what they say is upsetting.

Community Action

It will be recalled that in Chapter Two we discussed the Sherif principle of superordinate goals as applied to community problem-solving. Police and community relations programs have sometimes been billed as "an interprofessional approach to community problems." The central idea has been explained by Robert Trojanowicz:

> One of the major considerations when attempting to initiate community development programs is to understand how two or more interest groups can have sufficient convergence of interest or consensus to agree on common goals which will result in program implementation. Each group involved and interested . . . must be able to justify and, hence, legitimize the common group goal within its own pattern of values, norms, and goals. ["Police Community Relations: Problems and Process"][2]

This theory, which has a long history in community organization and community development, lends itself nicely to police and community relations. The logical primary focus (convergence of interest) is the crime problem. Particularly in planning of prevention programs, this problem is a natural for community action. Approaches to it could help to heal relationship difficulties, not least of all those in community-police interaction. The possibilities are beyond calculation in inter-agency cooperation and coordination. As a monstrous social problem, crime makes interprofessional and cross-community action mandatory. Richard Myren has expressed the thought this way:

> . . . crime must be put into its context of general social deviance and the relationship of that deviance to conformity; criminal justice agencies, such as police departments, must be put into their context of the general criminal justice system; our criminal justice system must be put into its context of the general legal system; and the legal system must be put into its context of general social control mechanisms, both formal and informal. Failure to focus on context has led to distortions responsible for at least a substantial part of the difficulty that crime is causing in America today. ["A Context for Crime"]

Crime prevention through community involvement is a laudable slogan for a sound program in the community-police partnership (Norman Hardin, *Police,* November-December 1969). Some of the assumptions in such a program would be:

1. As Peel said, the general enforcement of community standards is conducted more by the community itself than it is by law enforcement officers.

2. Coordinated efforts to deal with complex problems require effective communication among the parties cooperating in the effort.

3. The different parties will have different experiences with the problem—therefore will tend to define it in somewhat different ways. Each party should have full opportunity for input.

4. Effective problem-solving through community action begins with education of the partners in the effort: fact-finding, surveys, research, etc. However, data collection should not become an end in itself.

5. It is appropriate for a police agency to play a pivotal role in coordinated crime prevention programs. In fact, this provides such agencies with the opportunity to work more than they usually do at their most neglected function, in the only way in which it can be done—in league with community institutions, organizations, and forces.

There is a popular American fable that money alone will solve most social problems. This delusion is currently being applied to the crime problem. There is no question, of course, that programs in criminal justice often starve for lack of adequate financing. Neither is there any question that the Law Enforcement Assistance Administration has helped substantially to meet this need. But because such funding is necessarily a political procedure, spokesmen for LEAA have tended to interpret results in such statistical terms as a reduction in crime rates. We have been told that helicopters, radio communication, and data processing systems help to reduce crime. No doubt these claims have some validity. The productivity of mechanical and electronic devices is easily measured. But the productivity of a neighborhood citizens' council in its efforts to stabilize family life is much more difficult to weigh. Politicians cater to a public that wants results interpreted in "hard and cold facts."

The point is that there is more to the crime problem than is represented "by bread alone." Unlimited LEAA funds and more street lights, more policemen, more police cars, more helicopters, and more "hardware" of other types are vain investments unless ways can be found to involve people of all kinds in understanding and combating crime. This is a hackneyed point, surely, and therefore it is commonly ignored. Can it be made to work? There is evidence to suggest that it can.

Take what is called community-based treatment in the corrections field. We discussed this concept at some length in Chapter Seventeen. Only a bare beginning has been made in exploring noninstitutional correctional programs as alternatives to incarceration. Community resources for such programs are only beginning to be identified and harnessed. The potential for interagency cooperation and coordination in such programs can only be imagined. What communities *are* doing is clearly far less than what they *can* do, or even what they *should* do (HEW Report, *Delinquency Today: A Guide for Community Action*). But there are signs that progress is being made in new directions in the field of corrections.

In Toronto, the 30,000 citizens of Police Patrol Area 5411 are having an opportunity to determine whether they can handle neighborhood crime better than can the police and the courts (reported by Frank Drea in *The National Observer,* June 10, 1972). An east-end neighborhood of 96 blocks, considered "average urban," has been chosen for testing new concepts in Canadian criminal law. The aim is to discover whether mediation and counseling can take the place of arrest and trial in dealing with certain minor crimes.

In the experiment, sponsored by the Canada Law Reform Commission—a governmental body—petty thieves can pay for what they steal instead of serving a jail term. Policemen turn over domestic brawls to be dealt with by neighbors and volunteers. The police continue to patrol and handle serious crimes. But by police decision, minor crimes are turned over to one of the project workers. One purpose of the program is to encourage citizens to say what they think the laws of the future ought to be. The program has other features underscoring the responsibility of "average citizens" to participate appropriately in coping with crime.

As a result of a combination of various police department measures and steps taken by other community agencies in Washington, D.C., an astonishing crime rate has been reduced dramatically in the past two years (Herbert Miller, "Reversing the Crime Trend"). A significant aspect is a narcotics treatment program heavily geared to methadone. A new approach to the problem of narcotic addiction became Federal policy with the passage of the Narcotic Addict Rehabilitation Act of 1966. Under the provisions of this Act, known as NARA, narcotic addicts are civilly committed to a Federal program that provides them with treatment, followed by supervised aftercare in their own community for up to three years.

An extension of the Federal policy encourages the development of community-based treatment and rehabilitation services wherever they are needed throughout the country. These services eliminate the need for narcotic addicts and other drug dependent persons to be hospitalized at great distances from home. They also offer addicts and drug users treatment, aftercare, and rehabilitation in their own communities; permit them to continue education or employment or resume it soon after treatment; and reduce disruptions in personal and family life.

Programs of this nature may seem at first glance quite far removed from police and community relations. But second thought suggests factors closely associated with crime, indeed with organized crime, and the clear implication of requiring community teamwork, along with participation of the police and other criminal justice agencies.[3] Police-community relations program planners have done far too little with this type of approach.

The 1966 President's Crime Commission generated some systematic and scientific studies of public attitudes toward crime. Information of this kind is in the long run nearer to the center of the target than is data revealing what burglar alarms apparently do to reduce crime. For it is public attitudes and beliefs about crime and its causes that weigh heavily in determining the feasibility of alternative methods of crime prevention and law enforcement.[4]

Leading figures in and out of police work continue to plead for more and better interagency cooperation and coordination in community action aimed at crime and other social problems. The yawning reaction is again, frequently, "So what's new?" A typical unarguable statement is this, by 1972 IACP President George A. Murphy, chief of police in Oneida, New York:

> The time for direct communication with our colleague agencies in the criminal justice system is now. We must meet and learn from each other. And together we can identify and act upon the common problems which confront us all. Through such interaction, we can forcefully meet the problems of antiquated laws, probation and parole inequities, poor enforcement, irresponsive institutions, and the myriad of other challenges that obstruct the war on crime.[5]

Another statement of the same position is:

> The uncertain future of justice may be illuminated by terminating criminal and juvenile justice provincialism and requiring systematic and cooperative planning by all agencies concerned with crime and the criminal and delinquency and the delinquent.[6]

There is no need to belabor the point. The need is for more dedicated *action,* community by community, to furnish abundant evidence that the pronouncements are not mere talk.

One noble effort to this end should be mentioned again. A National Alliance on Shaping Safer Cities, Inc., was established in 1971 at the initiative of the American Jewish Committee.[7] It brought together 57 national and regional organizations of varying ideological hues—from the Campfire Girls to the AFL-CIO, from NAACP and the National Urban League to the Southwest Council of La Raza, from the United Methodist Church to the Fortune Society. The central purpose of this organization of organizations is in coordinated, cooperative activities to reduce crime and the fear of crime. It deserves the fullest support.

Program Evaluation

All program planners and managers are haunted by the requirements of evaluation. Through the years, in police and community relations programs, evaluation has been conducted far more in quantitative
than in qualitative terms. How many institutes or workshops? How
many participants? How many cities or states represented? How does
this compare with last year and the year before that? How many re-
peaters? How many speeches to service clubs? How many church meetings? How many school visits? And so on.

Such information is not without value. But it can be deceiving.
It can lull programmers into false assumptions. It tends to emotionalize
and sentimentalize ideas as to what particular programs accomplish.
If people "feel good" or "get a lift," the conclusion is drawn that significant, lasting change has been activated. Most of the time, this is an
illusion. "Feeling good" about a program is quite acceptable. But if the
prime purpose is to change attitudes, or to induce behavior modification, or to inspire alterations in the organization of a police department,
"feeling good" may be a somewhat less than satisfying outcome.

One reason why qualitative evaluation of police-community relations programs has so rarely been done is that it is very difficult to do.
When program objectives speak of change in attitude or behavior,
checking the results is a task fraught with booby-traps. Perhaps the
most perplexing part of it, typical of all behavioral research, is the control of variables in before-and-after testing. But the difficulties in program evaluation begin earlier. In many instances the obstacle is in the
way the goals of the program are stated—if they *are* stated. The decisive question is whether progress toward the goal is actually measurable.
Often the "change the world" language employed by human relations
programs planners in goal statements leaves evaluators cold. Evaluation is often treated, under these circumstances, as a kind of frill
—an academic exercise. After all, it is said, "what we want is action—
not all this professorial gobbledygook."

Program evaluation is a big subject, and we must limit what we
say about it here.[8] But some "bare bones" points should be stated, and
a listing seems in order again:

> The first step in program evaluation is to identify the component
> parts of the evaluation process: objectives, programs, standards, and
> methods.[9] In effect, this can be translated as: What is it that the
> program is intended to accomplish? What is the specific substance
> of a program that it seems may achieve this (model)? What testing
> criteria will disclose the extent to which the program meets its objec-
> tives? What methods of testing (instruments) will produce the desired
> evaluation data?
>
> Evaluation should be built into program design and process, from the
> initial stage. It should be integral to the process, not an afterthought,

nor an end in itself, nor merely by way of succumbing to the pressure of funding agencies who insist on it. Ideally, evaluation "feed-back" should occur as the program progresses, rather than at or after its completion—the point being to try to improve productivity while there is still a chance.

In comparing two or more programs, it is obviously essential that the four parts of the evaluation process should be as nearly identical as possible. This is the important matter of control of variables, and it has other ramifications—for instance, if a comparison is to be made between programs in two or more communities, two or more neighborhoods or precincts, etc., the situations to be compared should be as nearly alike as possible. Frequently, a "control group" is incorporated in the evaluation—a place where there is no program—as a check against outcomes in places where there is a program.

Further, regarding comparative study, it should be noted that program features may vary—as, for example, in measuring the effects of alternative programs—but the objectives, the standards, and the evaluation methods should *not* vary.

Program evaluation should be related as closely as possible to the needs of practitioners in a given field. This means that, ideally, practitioners as well as theoreticians should learn to live with each other in joint planning of programs, with due attention to evaluation as part of such collaboration. In short, the ultimate measure of the worth of program evaluation should be *utility*.

Behind goal delineation in a given program lie certain values and assumptions which should be carefully and painstakingly examined for their "tilt." This is more difficult to do than to state the objectives. But the unstated values slant the objectives, and there is sometimes a great difference between the underlying values of the program "architects" and those of the program recipients. Unless such differences are carefully identified, evaluative research can be a nightmare.

There are various levels of program goals, such as short-range, long-range, immediate, etc. Effective evaluation requires that these be properly distinguished.

Program goals are, as we have said, frequently stated in global terms. They are also often stated in such idealistic terms as to be unmeasurable. Idealism á la "climb every mountain" is not to be faulted, certainly, but as with "feeling good," it complicates program evaluation. Human relations programs surely should have affective impact—some "emotional sock"—for as we have seen, attitudes involve strong feelings. Changing attitudes therefore means changing feelings. All of this is simply to repeat our earlier point: qualitative program evaluation in police-community relations is extremely difficult to do. Feelings are facts but they do not easily submit to measurement.

Fixing the target audience for a program is another vital aspect of evaluation. "Anybody can come" may be good public relations for a program, but it hardly facilitates evaluation. Who is to be affected by the program? Programs with "something for everybody" usually turn out to be disappointing to all.

Process evaluation is as important as content or methodological evaluation. To explain: a group begins, let us say, by identifying and defining a problem. It proceeds to a diagnosis of causes, thence to designing a program to remedy the matter. This program has a certain content and certain methods. But the best programs are not totally successful, and the worst may not be total flops. Which parts worked and why? Which parts failed and why? Process evaluation attempts to identify the conditions resulting in success or failure—what helped and what hindered.

There is a cost accounting aspect to program evaluation—the ratio between what was given up and what was gained—how much return for the investment made. "Cost" in this sense is not simply a question of money. It includes such considerations as time, energy, man-hours, psychic expense, even "emotional drain."

The public is a major hindrance in program evaluation. Reports that do not fit public biases are promptly blasted and laid to rest on the shelf. If a program is deemed by the public to do "good," contrary evidence is not apt to be welcomed.

Because politicians are responsive to public biases, and politicians sometimes influence funding agencies, the latter are not always friendly toward "objective" evaluation. Sometimes the sponsor of a program is eager for an evaluation, provided there is assurance that the results will support what he has already decided to do or has done.

Occasionally, evaluators themselves handicap their own efforts. There is such a thing as a *strategy* of effective evaluation, which avoids many of the common pitfalls. People feel threatened by evaluations of their performance. It is important that they be made to feel part of the process itself—in effect, so they may be assisted in discovering for themselves how performance may be improved. The more evaluation is self-oriented in this sense, the better.[10]

A police-community relations project based in San Francisco is described in *The Police and the Community: Studies* (Radelet and Reed), Study 11, Part Five. The final report of this project, called PACE, contained some assertions of interest to evaluators of programs in this field.[11] For example:

In effect, the term PCR is useless; it is useless operationally; it is useless administratively; and it is useless from an effectiveness point of view; for historical and contemporary evidence indicates that traditional PCR efforts have borne very little fruit in improving the police-community relationship.

People want respect and efficient service; nothing more and nothing less. Any police activity designed to achieve these objectives is very likely to meet with substantial success.

PCR programs that foster mutual respect and more effective crime prevention and control are appealing to those who historically and presently have rejected programs labelled as "PCR." They are appealing because they are responsive to the self-interest of both the police establishment and the white majority community.

The severe inequities that exist in law enforcement and the administration of justice system and the need for change are recognized and supported by [only] a small percentage of people. The majority of people feel no need to know more.

PCR has traditionally been defined in terms of police-minority relations, which is a limited and unrealistic definition.

Police departments and other city agencies do not *plan* but *react*—react to pressure.

Program "effectiveness," measured with relevant and meaningful criteria, is not a value endorsed by most people. Organizational survival and effectiveness often are clashing values, and survival usually wins.

Another project report of special interest in program evaluation pertains to the Washington, D.C., Pilot Precinct experiment mentioned in Chapter Twenty One (Rita Mae Kelley, et al., *The Pilot Police Project*). Following are some highlights from the report:

Police-community relations is a power relationship consisting of three interrelated dimensions: efficiency, responsiveness, and representativeness.

The conflict over how to improve PCR is often based on different judgments of how improvement can best be achieved. One group stresses greater professionalization of the existing police force; another group stresses changing police policies and structures to permit greater citizen participation in and control over law enforcement.

The essential problem is to determine which attitudes and behaviors of policemen are correctable by in-service training and which changes need to be made at a broader institutional and personnel level.

The community *must* be a core part of any effort to improve existing relationships.

Police officers are happier with training units stressing technical professional efficiency than they are with training units stressing personal responsiveness to citizens.

Efforts to improve PCR cannot be limited to bettering the quality of police services. PCR improves when local citizens not only have access to power positions vital to police selection and decision-making, but when they actually obtain some control over these two power dimensions.

The two project reports that we have summarized above imply: (1) that these projects were carefully evaluated and suggest the possibilities in future project research; and (2) that our discussion in Chapter Nineteen of the politics of police and community relations was quite pertinent. Many would insist that political and economic power is "the name of the game"—thus, police and community relations is simply the powerful versus the powerless. But no single-formula approach covers all the contingencies.

Innovative Thinking

In preceding chapters we have mentioned various innovative or progressive developments. Some that carry rather strong implications of community initiative merit emphasis here.

The term *paraprofessional* has come into wide usage in recent years in different fields of public service. In police work, in which the Richmond, California, Police Department pioneered the idea some years ago, a paraprofessional is a field employee not sworn as a police officer, but performing duties closely resembling and strongly supportive of those performed by officers. Paraprofessionals are employed by police agencies to do important community relations work, as for instance the civilian aides in Chicago's community services division. Often these aides fit the description of what is called a CSO (Community Services Officer), in the pattern suggested by the 1966 President's Crime Commission. The aides may be male or female, they may be younger than sworn police officers, they usually reside in the area in which they are assigned, and they usually reflect the racial and cultural characteristics of that area.

The paraprofessional is often assigned duties in community relations and community services that free sworn officers to concentrate on matters that only they can handle. This implies that what the paraprofessionals do is sometimes rather vaguely defined, though loosely classified as "social work." A common problem in departments with such aides is that community services tend to become too separated from the uniformed division. This plays into the hands of those inclined to solve the police role problem by turning over the "social work" functions to civilian aides, thereby splitting the police organization into incompatible camps.

Paraprofessionals can be a vital and significant force for helping to build and maintain police-community partnership *if they can be assimilated and accepted within police agencies*—in short, if compatability with sworn officers can be achieved. Essentially, this is a matter of spelling out as clearly as possible the differing but complementary functions of each, and demonstrating that teamwork is not only possible and organizationally desirable, but that it enhances personal values as well. The question of the precise differentiation between the duties of sworn officers and aides is one that may be answered somewhat differently in different situations. In any case, there should be community input on the question. One more point: the effective merging or integration, in functional terms, of the activities of sworn officers and those of paraprofessional civilian aides—within urban police organizations—may gradually make a separate and distinct community relations unit extinct.

Community service officers, unarmed and wearing a distinctive uniform, are thought to be of special advantage in dealing with street demonstrations, confrontations, and riots. Their principal task then becomes one of "cooling it" by the use of pacifying, mediating, communicating tactics. But again, this does not excuse sworn officers from meeting their share of the responsibility. In Miami Beach, preparations for the 1972 national political conventions included a 96-hour special training course at Florida International University for all of the 250-man police force of that city. It included such topics as the "history and contemporary modes of dissent" and "the philosophical foundations of the Bill of Rights" (*Time,* June 12, 1972, pp. 16, 17).

We mentioned earlier the question of civil liability for inadequate police training, which the Federal courts are exploring in the aftermath of the 1970 Jackson State College tragedy. The ancient common law rule known as the doctrine of sovereign immunity is rapidly disappearing in modern jurisprudence. This makes it imperative that police administrators be aware of what the courts are doing regarding the daily activities of police officers. For instance, in the use of deadly force, the responsibility for adequate training of officers in the use and care of firearms is quite clear, as are the civil liability traps for the unwary policeman and his employer. Other examples of issues that are particularly sensitive to court decisions are the misuse of arrest powers and malicious prosecution flowing from it; invasion of privacy; negligence in the reasonable protection of life and property, and negligence in the operation of a police vehicle. Little wonder that police departments are increasingly exacting in the legal training of officers and are moving toward more reliance on legal advisers.[12]

Along the same line, many police agencies today are experimenting with alternatives to traditional arrest procedures—with noteworthy community relations implications. Perhaps the best known experiment of this type is the procedure permitting officers to release misdemeanants at the scene of arrest if the surrounding circumstances indicate that there is no need to transport an arrestee to the police lockup for detention or to require posting of a bond. The traditional procedures are used only when the field release of the arrestee is adjudged to be inappropriate. This alternative procedure, endorsed by several Presidential commissions and now enacted into legislation in several states, is likely to spread. The results of the so-called citation procedure, to date, are encouraging. Continued evaluation of such experiments is urgently needed.[13]

We return again to the matter of crimes without victims. It is not a popular subject, but it has enormous police-community relations importance. Professors Alexander Smith and Harriet Pollack of New York City's John Jay College of Criminal Justice pinpoint the issue well:

> Possibly because we live in an era that has seen great changes in public mores in a relatively short time, we have too many laws that the police are attempting to enforce and the courts to handle that large segments of the public simply will not obey.... There is something very frightening to most people in advocating repeal of morals laws. It is as though, by advocating repeal, the conduct that heretofore has been forbidden is being endorsed. Nothing could be further from the truth. In repealing morals laws, the legislature is not proposing that people become immoral; it is simply declaring that the criminal sanction will no longer be used to enforce a particular mode of conduct.... The unpalatable truth is that passing a law does not mean that it will be obeyed or that it can be enforced. Conversely, the repeal of a law does not necessarily mean an increase in undesirable conduct. ["Crimes Without Victims"]

The Philosophical Arguments

Among the issues that evoke much philosophical discussion is the question of how dissent is being handled in our society. Some observers would hold that "mishandled" would be the better term. If the norm is efficiency, totalitarianism has all the better of it. But this is hardly a recommended model.

What behavior threatens the survival of a society? Does it, in fact, threaten—or is it simply the belief that it does that should prevail? How much freedom for individuality should be allowed in an ostensibly free society? Self versus society: there is conflict here that must, to some degree, be reconciled. Therefore, there is the need for mediating social control. Enter the police officer. As Joseph Grange asserts, "man needs society to survive, but he must reject its pressures to live in a genuinely human way."[14] He goes on to say that "the conflict between social order and creative individuality is solved by judging societies not by their capacity to repress individuality, but by their power to promote creative self-expression." This is a crucial difference between a *closed* and an *open* society. It need hardly be added that a closed society is sometimes called "a police state."

Occasionally, events occur that are reassuring to those concerned about our American capacity to deal liberally with dissent. Such events translate somewhat abstract principles into concrete demonstrations. An excellent illustration was the Supreme Court's June 1972 unanimous decision, declaring unconstitutional the Federal Government's practice of wire-tapping domestic radicals considered dangerous to the national security, without first obtaining court approval. From a court increasingly characterized as conservative, this decision was remarkable evidence of a growing national maturity in handling dissent, although not all observers would agree with the Court nor with our saluting it in this instance. Some liberals reacted with the prediction that it didn't matter what the Court said—wiretapping without judicial permit would continue.

Associate Justice Lewis F. Powell, Jr., wrote the opinion, saying in part (*New York Times,* June 20, 1972; *National Observer,* July 1, 1972):

> History abundantly documents the tendency of government—however benevolent and benign in its motives—to view with suspicion those who most fervently dispute its policies. The price of lawful public dissent must not be a dread of subjection to an unchecked surveillance power. Nor must the fear of unauthorized official eavesdropping deter vigorous citizen dissent and discussion of Government action in private conversation.

Dissent in a democracy carries with it connotations of *change,* of dissatisfaction with things as they are. Students of criminal justice today, as we have observed, are encouraged to become dissenters—"change agents," as it is said—and many students are inclined to be a bit nervous about what this may mean. The idea of change has not in the past been popular with police officers and other agents of criminal justice. And to be *leaders* in social change—to show the way in such matters as racial justice—has been regarded in law enforcement circles as a species of idiocy. This attitude is in itself changing, however indecisively. A good place to look for evidence of such change is in the legal profession.

A century ago, de Tocqueville declared that lawyers were "the American aristocracy." There remain some remnants of this elite, but by and large, the profession is in process of a severe shaking up, under pressure of countless indications of failure to meet its responsibilities. The new mood among many young lawyers was observable beginning in the summer of 1964 when some 400 law students and recently graduated lawyers went to Mississippi to defend civil rights workers who were enrolling Negroes as voters. The theme of the new mood is the use of the law to right all sorts of wrongs—for example, by use of the class-action suit.

Peter Vanderwicken describes the new mood:

> Opposition to the *status quo* is the common theme of all the young activist lawyers. Many of them outrage the established profession, for example, by wearing beards, body shirts, bell-bottoms, and boots on the job. And they are creating new—and sometimes bizarre—kinds of legal organizations.... Whatever else may be said about them, the young activist lawyers have struck a nerve. They are awakening a

sometimes complacent profession to its failures of commission and omission.

. . . .

Authority relations, which are consensual and informal, have been eroded and replaced by power relations, which are coercive and hence involve the law. The crisis has arisen in part because large institutions, especially government agencies, often appear unresponsive to changing public demands and cold to the complaints of those who feel they didn't get a fair deal by society. Disaffected citizens have found a voice in the activist lawyers, who have tried through legal techniques to force institutions not only to perform their stated functions better, but also to take on new and more extensive responsibilities for the public good. ["The Angry Young Lawyers"]

Such tremors in the legal profession are bound to have repercussions in public attitudes toward the law. As Vanderwicken says, "the activist lawyers are on dangerous ground. They are assaulting many of the basic customs and institutions of our society." Perhaps the legal system is being asked to do too much. The law has been traditionally perceived as a sacred network of interlocking rules, to hold life together. This is why civil disobedience, as we saw in Chapter Thirteen, and the idea of the law as a question are so disquieting. "The law is a jealous mistress and will brook no other."

The Yale Law School's Robert H. Bork writes:

There is abroad a feeling of disappointment with and about law, a suspicion that it may be weak and unsure. This feeling is particularly frightening because we turn increasingly to law as other supports seem to fail us. The legal establishment itself is uncertain. The signs are everywhere. ["We Suddenly Feel That the Law Is Vulnerable"]

Bork goes on to reflect upon what he calls the "imperialism" of lawyers, "priding themselves on their ability to ransack other men's specialties quickly and beat them in argument on their own grounds." The field of law, he asserts, possesses very little theory about itself. It borrows from the social sciences but has no discipline, no core of its own.

One aspect of the unease about law, Bork believes, is the tendency to use the law too much. It is not, he argues, an implement that can be turned to *any* purpose. It is now in danger of overreaching its capabilities. And there is, he adds, a limit to how much defiance of law a legal system can tolerate. When law is thought of as simply one element of power in a complex struggle, it denies to itself any unique claim to respect. It then becomes, Bork contends, "on a par with any other kind of force" and he goes on to say:

No society can be healthy and effective if all disputes are drawn into legal processes. The spread of law throughout human relations signals not only a decline in individual freedom but also a withering of community, traditional modes of accommodation, and informal authority. A healthy society requires that there be considerable play in human relations, a degree of trust in the good faith of others, confidence that things can be worked out tolerably, a willingness not to insist on every "right" one may think one should ideally possess, and a large amount of individual self-reliance. The attempt to define all the rights of individuals and to enforce them by legal processes signifies the diminution or disappearance of these virtues. [Ibid.]

Bork thinks that the increasing legalization of our culture is a sign of the deterioration of the culture and particularly of the breakdown of community. Human transactions that must more and more depend on "what it says in the by-laws," or on what is specified in the contract, or on "existing policy" are based, he feels, on mutual suspicion, distrust, and adversarial attitudes. The law cannot repair such a broken sense of community. Moreover, the trend toward legalization of everything requires time and energy for tending the legal machinery that would be better spent on other tasks. There may be areas in which a government of men rather than of laws is to be preferred, Bork concludes.

These are thoughts not for lawyers and legal scholars alone. There is something in this for both liberals and conservatives to contemplate, Republicans or Democrats. And in the sense in which the law is the foundation of the criminal justice system, with societal (community) attitudes as its "wet cement," the thought is certainly pertinent here.

The Current Scene

The current sociopolitical scene is in some ways not very promising for bettering police and community relations. The implication of Bork's view for the idea of community is one way to suggest this. Another route to a dark outlook is to consider what is going on in the political arena of public education. Politicians are running for cover on the busing issue, trying to dream up ingenious ways of speaking out of both sides of the mouth. Opponents of busing are solemnly professing their commitment to desegregated or integrated schools. Proponents of busing are just as solemnly professing that they are not enchanted with the idea of children riding long distances to attend classes in "dangerous" neighborhoods.

This is not the place to debate the busing question nor to invoke propaganda on either side. It is sufficient for our purpose simply to point to the parallel between metropolitan or regional public school organization and metropolitan or regional police/criminal justice organization. More than this, it is important to point out that the hub of the issue symptomized by the busing controversy is one with considerable police-community relations significance. Another way to suggest this is to refer back to Bork's point regarding the limits of the law. Stated more bluntly, the American experience with racial justice under law since the 1896 Plessy-Ferguson decision is demonstrative of the inherent limitations in setting behavior norms by legal edict and interpretation.

The cleavage in our society, of which the battle over busing is a symptom, seems to leave police-community relations as a flanking maneuver—a peripheral issue. And in a sense, it is. In another sense, however, the PCR issue is really the same issue. Are we going to live together or separately? What price community? This is the issue, not busing. If busing children is not the way, then what is? Suburbia may seem like escape from the problems of the inner city. But the unavoidable discovery is in learning that we cannot turn our backs on the responsibility for the problems.[15]

Looking Back

What should be coming through to "the community" these days is some understanding of how little "the criminal justice system" can do about crime, as one such social problem. This recognition is more important than identifying what should *not* be handled through this system, important though that is. As Professor James Vorenberg of the Harvard Law School—who directed the 1966 President's Crime Commission—has pointed out, it is this realization that results in turning attention where it should be: in broad terms, to community responsibility for crime *prevention*. Some say this is naive. But somehow Vorenberg does not seem naive when he writes:

> It is increasingly clear that the police, the courts, the prisons, and the correctional services generally are engaged in what, at best, is a holding action. . . . this means that until we are willing to give poor people a stake in law and in order and in justice, we can expect crime to increase. The best hope for crime control lies not in better police, more convictions, longer sentences, better prisons. It lies in job training, jobs and the assurance of adequate income; schools that respond to the needs of their students; the resources and help to plan a family and hold it together; a decent place to live; and an opportunity to guide one's own life and to participate in guiding the life of the community.[16]

Vorenberg is saying that social justice is the path to crime control. In "The War on Crime: the First Five Years," he looks back on the five years since the completion of the President's Crime Commission's work. He says that crime is unquestionably a far worse problem for the country than it was in 1967, and the criminal justice system appears even less capable of coping with it. He sees only faint signs of progress by the police, and this mainly in community relations. In correctional services, he points to a few promising developments, notably in community treatment of offenders. Perhaps here, he speculates, "the system's reaction to the slaughter at Attica" may be sounder ground for hope than the Crime Commission's manifold recommendations ever were. As to the courts, Vorenberg asserts that "the quality of the adjudication process seems clearly to have deteriorated over the same period." His conclusion is, to say the least, sobering:

> The Crime Commission's final conclusion was that "controlling crime in America is an endeavor that will be slow and hard and costly. But America can control crime if it will." At that time I thought there was hope for changes that would both strengthen the agencies of criminal administration and reduce the injustices that underlie much crime. I still do not believe that we have to settle for a society where we live in fear of each other. But today, I find it hard to point to anything that is being done that is likely to reduce crime even to the level of five years ago. [Ibid., p. 69][17]

We would add only that a supreme test of our efforts in police and community relations in the years ahead will be in the degree of our success in dealing with the problem (and its "whiplash") to which Vorenberg refers.

Looking Ahead

Reserved optimism as to the future characterizes the predictions of Don McEvoy, director of community relations and the administration of justice for the National Conference of Christians and Jews ("Observations Through a Murky Crystal Ball"). Admitting the riskiness of such future prospecting, McEvoy nonetheless ventures these thoughts:

> Significant segments of the population will continue to demand higher levels of police professionalism.

> Great changes will occur in the next decade in the educational background of the police, with college training expected.

> Police supervision will be increasingly decentralized, with many experimental programs in community involvement and public accountability —in effect, modified movement toward community control.

> More police departments will move toward establishing different levels of police work, e.g., police agents, community service officers, paraprofessionals, etc.

> The numbers of minority group members recruited for police service will expand dramatically.

> Polarization *within* police departments will increase and will escalate as a matter of community concern.

> There will be less emphasis upon the military model in police agencies.

There will be movement away from specialized community relations units in police organizations, with more stress on the responsibility of every officer to understand and be trained in a community service role.

The criminal code will be drastically re-structured to remove a wide range of victimless crimes from police jurisdiction.

Police structure will be opened to permit more rapid advancement to leadership roles of the qualified.

McEvoy concludes on the note that all of these progressive steps will be opposed, condemned, fought, torpedoed, and sabotaged at every juncture by the established line organizations within police departments. We are not so sure of this. As McEvoy says, two strategies could make a difference:

1. Intensification of work with police line organizations "so they can be exposed to the prospects for change in a non-threatening manner."
2. Continued work with police administrators in management training to help in developing the insights and skills of "democratizing" the police structure.

To this we would add one more dimension: more emphasis upon community relations and community involvement in the criminal justice system across the board, not solely with the police.

Commencement

The end of such a text as this is ideally more in the nature of a beginning—a commencement. It should bring things to a climax point-edly and be done with it. The *motif* should be "on with the work to be done."

Police and community teamwork in dealing with problems, a by-product of which is better relationships, is basically an exercise in par-ticipative democracy. Its chances of success, measured by effective problem-solving, are about as good as our commitment in action is to what we say we believe in theory. It is a mistake either to overestimate or to underestimate the possibilities. Few of us, in the course of a life-time, succeed in living up to our capacity for good.

Participative democracy is a splendid, utopian horizon, with boun-tiful rewards for those who have what it takes to reach for it and grasp even a small part of it. But it is also a mirage to some extent, for many people, seemingly, couldn't care less. It amounts to this:

We can no longer afford to be complacent about our failure to deal effectively with crime, urban disorders, mental illness, addiction, edu-cational failure, and all the problems which accompany poverty and social alienation. The blame—if any can be found—must be very broadly placed. Human problems elicit emotional and subjective, not scientific responses. Social institutions and formal organizations become rigid and resist change. Few individuals are completely open to new ideas or to changes in daily routine. Inertia and habit are basic facts of human existence. It requires determination and a strong sense of purpose to work toward a long-range goal of rational action through the building of knowledge.[18]

Irving Louis Horowitz, writing about Attica, caps it nicely:

Perhaps it is simply time to recognize the universal truth: that freedom is not confined to those outside of prison, nor is slavery a necessary consequence of being inside. The prisoners have already articulated a sense of doing for themselves what must be done. Perhaps it is time for the rest of the American population to redefine its own goals in such a way as to recognize that freedom or slavery is less a consequence of being inside or outside prison walls than it is of one's place in the social order. ["Alias 'Mad Bomber Sam' "]

How to begin? Each of us tends to look for a grand plan to bring about universal regeneration in order to inspire personal action. We forget a simple truth: reaching out to help another person in need is the epitome of individual responsibility at its best. When asked to name the essential ingredient of the ideal community, Solon—the progenitor of Socrates—responded: "... when those who have not been injured become as indignant as those who have."

Notes to Chapter Twenty-four

1. A brief summary of the alternatives is given by William C. Berleman in "Police and Minority Goups: The Improvement of Community Relations."

2. Trojanowics builds his theory on the base developed by Christopher Sower et al., in *Community Involvement*. Sower calls it the *Normative Sponsorship Theory*.

3. See Richard H. Blum, "Drugs, Behavior, and Crime," and by Richard H. Blum et al., *Horatio Alger's Children*, a report prepared for the U.S. Department of Justice, 1972. See also "The Use of Juveniles as informers in Drug-Abuse Matters," a policy statement of the Board of Trustees, National Council on Crime and Delinquency.

4. See such references as Albert D. Biderman, "Surveys of Population Samples for Estimating Crime Incidence"; Jennie McIntyre, "Public Attitudes Toward Crime and Law Enforcement"; John A. Gardiner, "Public Attitudes Toward Gambling and Corruption." Also Gibbons, Jones, and Garbedian, "Gauging Public Opinion About the Crime Problem."

5. Editorial, *The Police Chief* 39, no. 1 (January 1972): 8.

6. Carter, McEachern, and Sigurdson, "The Uncertain Future of Criminal Justice." See also Robert C. Trojanowicz, "Factors That Affect the Functioning of Delinquency Prevention Programs"; and by the same author, "A Comparison of the Behavioral Styles of Policemen and Social Workers," unpublished doctoral dissertation, College of Social Science, Michigan State University, 1969. Also see Robert D. Finney, "A Police View of Social Workers."

7. Address: 165 East 56th St., New York, N.Y. 10022; Director, Harry Fleischman.

8. See Lee P. Brown, "Evaluation of Police-Community Relations Programs."

9. Robert M. Carter, "The Evaluation of Police Programs."

10. These points regarding program evaluation rely considerably on an unpublished monograph by Roger O. Steggerda, "Principles and Guidelines in Evaluative Research," School of Criminal Justice, Michigan State University, March 1972. See also such references on the same subject as R. E. Tyler, ed., *Educational Evaluation: New Roles, New Means;* Elizabeth Herzog, *Some Guidelines for Evaluative Research;* C. H. Weiss, "The Politicization of Evaluation Research."

11. American Institutes for Research, *Project PACE: Police and Community Enterprises* (A Program for Change in Police-Community Behaviors), Final Report, November 1971 (Terry Eisenberg, Robert H. Fosen, Albert S. Glickman), prepared under a grant from the Ford Foundation. See also *Learning to Cope With the C.O.P.S.,* a pamphlet based on the PACE Report, National Conference of Christians and Jews.

12. For an excellent analysis of this matter, see Douglas M. Walters, "Civil Liability for Improper Police Training."

13. See Mark Berger, "The New Haven Misdemeanor Citation Program."

14. Joseph Grange, "Dissent and Society," and William H. Cape, "Policemen ... Dissenters ... and Law-Abiding Citizens."

15. See Reasons and Kuyendall, eds., *Race, Crime, and Justice.* Also The Federal Civil Rights Enforcement Effort *Summary,* U.S. Commission on Civil Rights.

16. As quoted in *The Hot Line* 4, no. 4 (January 1972).

17. See also "A Plan to Cut Crime," *Life,* June 30, 1972, p. 51 ff.

18. Quoted from Twain, Harlow, and Merwin, *Research and Human Services,* p. 93.

Summary
of Part Five

In Part Five, we have discussed programs aimed at bringing about improvement in the relations between police and the community. A great many such programs have come into being in recent years, with considerable variation in style and format: training programs for the police, institutes and metropolitan organization, police-school liaison projects, public relations and public information activities, and miscellaneous other programs. *One of these programs is the*

Human relations or social-psychological training for the police was the earliest type of program in what is today called police-community relations. The development of such special training has been *however* marked by difficulties as to objectives (to change attitudes or behavior or both?), by difficulties *such* ~~to~~ as to top-level administrative commitment, ~~by~~ *and* difficulties in the attitudes of police personnel toward such training, and by difficulties represented by the failure of various facets of police organizations to mesh their functional patterns with what this kind of training stressed. There have also been methodological liabilities, caused by a tendency to adhere tenaciously to instructional techniques known to be relatively ineffective in dealing with such subject matter.

Recently, there have been signs of change. Experimentation with alternative methods and testing of results is being more frequently re-

654

ported in the journals, and some police organizations are demonstrating a certain amount of initiative and courage in opening the door to significant community concern. But the opposition is fierce, as much or more from within police ranks as from outside sources. The basic argument revolves around differing ideas of the role of the police: containing crime versus preventing crime, "real police work" versus "social work." Until this argument is settled, police training in the social psychology of their field will continue to encounter opposition. The reconciliation of the two schools of thought, with particular regard to the obvious importance of cultivating dynamic community concern and action, would not seem on the surface to be very difficult. But as James Q. Wilson has observed, the parties are talking at and past one another, and power seems at the moment to be more the prize than societal welfare.

Institutes on police and community relations date back to 1955, when the first national conference of this kind was conducted at Michigan State University. There have been many since then, in all parts of the country—national, regional, statewide, and local in scope, no two exactly alike, yet all sharing similar general purposes. We summarized the strengths and weaknesses of these institutes, emphasizing the importance of their educational function, the need for reaching those who do not attend such meetings or do not belong to organized groups, the need for setting institute objectives in manageable and measurable terms, and the art of making an institute truly a programmatic forum governed by the participants.

Rather elaborate metropolitan police and community organizations have emerged from the institutes and become well established, in numerous cities, beginning with St. Louis in 1956. Again, the patterns vary from place to place, with police and community relations units in some departments lately giving way to conflict-management divisions featuring team policing, crisis intervention squads, and various other innovations. A controversial issue has been raised in some big cities by the tactics of crime-busting units, by one name or another, the community relations implications of which appear to be questionable. Again, we summarized the strengths and weaknesses of presently existing metropolitan programs.

Relations between youth and the police have been the special focus of many programs, so-called police-school liaison plans among them. Assigning a police officer to the staff of a school sounds like a beneficial arrangement, and it apparently is, in some ways. But it is also an arrangement that can easily deteriorate into role ambiguity and confusion, to the benefit of no one. Such programs have their proponents and opponents, and we noted the arguments on each side. We also listed the recommendations produced by a national conference on the subject held in late 1971. Some other types of police-school cooperative projects were mentioned.

It is probably safe to say that there is generally much more attention being given in police agencies today to public relations and public information than there was only a few years ago. "Getting the word to the public" has come to be recognized as a priority administrative responsibility, and the function is being carried out in myriad ways and with much or little sophistication. For perhaps too many police departments, public relations and community relations mean the same thing, and they never go beyond activities designed and controlled completely by the department, to make the department look good. They have not discovered that there is a significant difference between *looking* good and *being* good. without a doubt

The best public relations for a police organization is the quality of the services it renders to the community. Apprehending those who commit crime is one of these services. Preventing crime is another. Both of these services are utterly dependent on community trust and assistance. And crime, just as civil disorder, is much better prevented than it is dealt with after the fact. Crime prevention and police-community relations are, to a large extent, complementary causes. They can be reversible ends-and-means, and the potential in this vein has hardly been touched.

We briefly described a representative sample of miscellaneous police-community programs, with varying goals, strategies, and levels of sophistication. A wide variety of approaches in this field is both inevitable and wholesome, and the programs are as multistyled as the communities, police organizations, cultures, and people they serve.

The two concluding chapters of Part Five presented the police side and the community side of police and community relations. In summary, we may say: In democratic societies, the existence, the mission, and the authority of the police rest within the community. Like all social institutions, the police are a community creation, ordained to meet basic social needs. Parent and offspring have tended to drift apart in an increasingly complex society in which isolation, alienation, and polarization are among the signs of institutional and systemic dysfunctionality. These very terms are symptomatic of the perplexities of communication in our time and grate on those who insist on simple language to express fundamental ideas. Police and the community: not merely a relationship, but an organic union, for the common good.

Abbreviations

ABA	American Bar Association
ACIR	Advisory Commission on Intergovernmental Relations
ACLU	American Civil Liberties Union
AFL	American Federation of Labor
AFP	American Federation of Police
AFSCME	American Federation of State, County and Municipal Employees
AIR	American Institutes of Research
ANPA	American Newspaper Publishers Association
ASNE	American Society of Newspaper Editors
CIO	Congress of Industrial Organizations
CORE	Congress of Racial Equality
CRC	Civil Rights Commission
CROP	Community Relations Orientation for Police
CSU	Community Services Unit
DPOA	Detroit Police Officers Association
FCIU	Family Crisis Intervention Unit
FOP	Fraternal Order of Police
HEW	(U.S. Department of) Health, Education and Welfare
HUD	(U.S. Department of) Housing and Urban Development
IACP	International Association of Chiefs of Police
IBPO	International Brotherhood of Police Officers
ICPA	International Conference of Police Associations

KKK	Ku Klux Klan
LEAA	Law Enforcement Assistance Administration
LEG	Law Enforcement Group (in N.Y.C.'s PBA)
LTIP	Landlord-Tenant Intervention Program
MDTA	Manpower Development Training Act
NAACP	National Association for the Advancement of Colored People
NAHRW	National Association of Human Rights Workers
NAIRO	National Association for Intergroup Relations Officers (Now NAHRW)
NAPCRO	National Associations for Police and Community Relations Officers
NCC	North City Congress (in North Philadelphia)
NCCD	National Conference on Crime and Delinquency
NCCJ	National Conference of Christians and Jews
NICOVIC	National Information Center on Volunteers in Courts
NFOP	National Fraternal Order of Police
NUL	National Urban League
PACE	Police and Community Enterprise
PAL	Police Athletic League
PAY	Positive Action for Youth
PBA	Police Benevolent Association
PCR	Police and Community Relations
PEP	Prevention Enforcement Patrol
POST	Peace Officers Standards and Training
RAAS	Racial Adjustment Action Society (in Britain)
RAM	Revolutionary Action Movement
SAS	Status Assignment System
SCLC	Southern Christian Leadership Conference
SMS	Self-esteem Maintenance System
SMSA	Standard Metropolitan Statistical Area
SNCC	Student Nonviolent Coordinating Committee
VIPI	Volunteers in Probation Incorporated
WASP	White Anglo-Saxon Protestant

Glossary

For reader convenience in distinguishing between closely associated terms, references are frequently made to one or more of seven special groupings of words under: *Behavior, Cultural, Family, Legal Terms, Police, Role,* and *Social.* The use of the glossary can be an aid in partially reviewing a course.

ACCEPTANCE See SOCIAL. Also CULTURAL (*processes*).

ACCESSORY See *Legal Terms.*

ACCOMMODATION See CULTURAL (*processes*).

ACCOMPLICE See *Legal Terms.*

ACCULTURATION See CULTURAL (*processes*).

ACHIEVED See ROLE.

ACQUIRED See BEHAVIOR.

ADAPTATION See CULTURAL (*responses*).

ADJUSTMENT See SOCIAL Control (*responses to*). Also CULTURAL (*responses*).

ADVERSARY RELATIONSHIP That part of police work which is repressive or punitive and which tends to engender negative relationships with the policed.

AFFECTIVE See LEARNING.

AGENCIES See SOCIAL.

AGGRAVATED ASSAULT See *Legal Terms*.

AGGREGATE See ROLE.

AGGREGATION A collection of individuals or groups, as while awaiting an event; no collective sense of cause. See CROWD, MOB.

AGGRESSION See SOCIAL Control (*responses to*).

ALIENATION See SOCIAL.

ALTERNATION See CULTURAL (*responses*).

ALTERNATIVES See CULTURAL (*concepts*).

AMALGAMATION See CULTURAL (*processes*).

ANOMIE See SOCIAL.

ANONYMITY See CULTURAL (*concepts*).

ARBITRATION See SOCIAL Control (*means of*).

ARRAIGNMENT See *Legal Terms*.

ARREST See *Legal Terms*.

ARSON See *Legal Terms*.

ASCRIBED See ROLE.

ASSAULT See *Legal Terms*.

ASSIMILATION See CULTURAL (*processes*).

ATTACK See SOCIAL Control (*responses to*).

ATTITUDE See ROLE.

ATTORNEY See *Legal Terms*.

ATTRIBUTE See ROLE.

AUDIENCE Listeners and/or observers responding to a single stimulus but not necessarily interacting with each other. See COMMUNITY, PUBLIC.

AUTHORITY The right to act, as stated by law or job description; as distinct from POWER, the personal ability to exercise that right. Thus authority is vested in the office; power in the person. CONTROL may be based on authority or on power, but if based solely on the latter it may be amoral.

AUXILIARIES See POLICE.

AVERAGE The figure resulting from adding all items in a distribution and dividing the sum by their total number. Cf. MEDIAN—the midpoint in a distribution, and MODE—the most frequent statistic in a distribution.

AVOIDANCE See SOCIAL Control (*responses to*).

BACKLASH   A reaction to actions, attitudes or policies, as to discrimination. Or a counter reaction.

BAIL   See *Legal Terms.*

BATTERY   See *Legal Terms.*

BEHAVIOR   Way in which an individual or group does act. The word carries no sense of moral or other values.

Acquired.   Adapted from observed patterns of behavior in others.

Collective.   May involve excesses beyond the sum of the behavioral norms of the individuals involved, as in rioting mobs.

Conditioned.   As modified by environmental factors, etc.

Criminal.   As defined by laws.

Defensive.   Reacting to outside forces.

Deviant.   Not normal. But not necessarily bad (Jesus), although most used for violations of mores, laws, etc.

Normative.   Approaching the standard for the group or culture.

Occupational.   As modified by one's vocation.

Symbolic.   Token actions, gestures, conforming to norms but not necessarily sincere.

Unstructured.   Not based on social norms; unpredictable.

Behaviorism (theories of).   Biologic non-conscious Response to Stimuli $(S>R)$.

Cultural determinism.   Behavior is determined by cultural factors only.

Symbolic interactionism.   Individual Interprets Stimuli in order to Respond $(S+I>R)$.

Phenomenologism.   Bio-social man responds to perceived phenomena.

Psychoanalism.   Behavior results from conflicts between the *id* (biologic desires), the *ego* (perceived realities) and the *super ego* (irrational desires).

BEHAVIORAL

Correlations.   Measurable relations between behavior patterns.

Laws.   The accepted norms, principles, customs re. behavior.

Motivations.   Influences of goals, even if unconsciously.

Norms.   Conforming to accepted standards, expectations.

Patterns.   Observable modes of individual or group action.

Probabilities.   As according to the evidence available.

BENEVOLENT ASSOCIATIONS   See POLICE.

BIAS   See CULTURAL (*concepts*) Prejudice.

BIFURCATION   See CULTURAL (*responses*).

BIGOTRY   See CULTURAL (*concepts*) Prejudice.

BORSTAL   A juvenile detention facility in England (1908–   ) for boys, modeled after the Elmira, N.Y., reformatory, offering vocational education, counseling, etc., in addition to confinement.

BOY   A derogatory (intentional or not) form of addressing a minority group member.

BRUTALITY   See POLICE.

BURGLARY   See *Legal Terms*.

CASTE   See SOCIAL.

CHANGE   See SOCIAL (*processes*). Also CULTURAL (*concepts*).

CIVIL DISOBEDIENCE   Refusal to obey laws, as a matter of principle; passively, and with implied willingness to accept punishment.

CIVIL LIBERTIES   The freedoms guaranteed under the Constitution, particularly the first 10 Amendments (speech, worship, trial by jury, etc.)

CIVIL RIGHTS   The rights and privileges of U.S. citizens, especially under the 13th and 14th Amendments (re. Negroes).

CIVILIAN REVIEW BOARD   See POLICE Review Boards.

CLASS   See SOCIAL.

CLIENT   See ROLE.

CLIQUE   See SOCIAL.

COERCION   See CULTURAL (*processes*).

COGNITIVE   See LEARNING.

COLLECTIVE   See BEHAVIOR.

COMMUNITY   Residents of a limited area having social relationships as in a village or town. A larger city would be a community of communities, or NEIGHBORHOODS—areas whose residents, because of their economic, ethnic, or racial character, may seek local control of their schools, police, etc. The community constitutes the AUDIENCE that reacts to official actions or statements of policy.

COMMUNITY LEADERS   May be either well known office holders or, more realistically, the less visible persons to whom neighborhoods turn for effective leadership.

COMMUNITY RELATIONS   See RELATIONS.

COMPENSATION   See SOCIAL Control (*responses to*).

COMPETITION   See SOCIAL (*processes*).

COMPLAINT   1. A form for filing a grievance of a citizen v. police. 2. A form filing a PETITION in a court. See *Legal Terms*.

COMPROMISE   See CULTURAL (*responses*).

COMPULSORY ARBITRATION   See SOCIAL Control (*means of*).

CONSENSUAL By common agreement.

CONCEPT See ROLE.

CONCILIATION See SOCIAL Control (*means of*).

CONDITIONED See BEHAVIOR.

CONFINEMENT See *Legal Terms*.

CONFLICT See SOCIAL (*processes*), CULTURAL (*concepts*). Also ROLE.

CONFORMITY See SOCIAL Control (*responses to*).

CONSTRUCTION Interpretation, as of the Constitution: *strict*, according to the literal wording, or *loose*, as implied.

CONSTRUCTS See SOCIAL. Also CULTURAL (*concepts*).

CONTINUITIES See CULTURAL (*concepts*).

CONTRA-CULTURAL CONFLICTS See CULTURAL (*concepts*).

CONTROL See SOCIAL Control. Also AUTHORITY.

CONVERSION See CULTURAL (*processes*).

COOPERATION See SOCIAL (*processes*).

CORRECTIONS See *Legal Terms*.

CORRELATIONS See BEHAVIORAL.

CRIME PREVENTION See POLICE (functions).

CRIMES See *Legal Terms*.

CRIMINAL See BEHAVIOR.

CRIMINALISTICS See *Legal Terms*.

CRIMINAL JUSTICE See *Legal Terms*.

CRIMINALIZATION See *Legal Terms*.

CRIMINOLOGY See *Legal Terms*.

CROWD(S) A gathering of people who may be *casual*—looking in a store window and easily broken up; *conventional*—as at a ball game, for a purpose; *aggressive* (mob)—bent on damage, possibly with leadership; or *expressive*, as while dancing in the street. See AGGREGATION, MOB.

CULTURAL Concerning group traits, beliefs, traditions, behavior.

(*concepts*)

Alternatives. A choice of cultural patterns (armed v. unarmed police).

Anonymity. Lacking identity in a group.

Change. Shift from previously accepted beliefs, patterns.

Conflicts. Friction within or between cultures.

Constructs. Established patterns of doing, believing.

Continuities. Persistent customs, patterns, ideas as v. DISCONTINU-ITIES: disruptive changes in these.

Contra-cultural conflicts. Challenging patterns within or between groups.

Differences. Variances from normally accepted patterns, or contrasts in characteristics of groups.

Diffusion. Spread of culture traits from one group to another.

Distance. Degree of difference between culture groups.

Ethnocentrism. Belief that one's own group's ways are best.

Interaction. Implemented communication between groups.

Integration. Fusion of groups or of groups' norms.

Insularity. Isolation of a group from other groups.

Invention. Innovative ability of a group: technical, artistic, philosophical.

Lag. Differential rates of change within or between cultures.

Loss. Disappearance of traits as a result of contacts with other groups.

Marginality. Conflicting allegiances to two or more groups: a black working in a white society. *Double* marginality: black policeman on a white force in a black neighborhood (suspect by both groups).

Minority group. Ethnic or racial group with limited rights and priv-ileges, regardless of its size.

Myths. Traditions, beliefs, which a people cherishes. See MYTH, SO-CIETY and CULTURE.

Pluralism. Idea of a culture comprised of multiple recognized elements (ethnic, racial, economic, political).

Prejudice. Ill-founded, generally negative attitude toward groups, con-cepts, etc. as v.

    Bias. Tendency to favor or oppose without sound reasons, and

    Bigotry. Obstinate devotion to one's own ideas, causes.

Separatism. Belief that certain groups should remain apart.

Shock. Trauma resulting from confronting a new culture.

Specialties. Particular tasks in a larger process: dishwasher in a cafe, wheelmounter on an assembly line.

Stereotype. Baseless but persistent image of persons, groups.

Universal. A way of behaving common to all cultures, or to all persons within a culture.

Universe. All those in a given category: e.g., bachelors.

Values. Conceptions of desirable states of affairs in a social system or culture group.

Visibility. Degree to which ethnic or racial traits are apparent.

(*processes*)

Acceptance.   Receiving a group without compromising its traits.

Accommodation.   Adjustment of groups to each other's ways.

Acculturation.   Acquisition of traits of one group by another.

Alternation.   Vacillating in loyalties to groups' ways.

Amalgamation.   Biological merging of groups.

Assimilation.   Absorption of one group by another.

Bifurcation.   Acceptance of one aspect but not another of a culture (as in business but not socially).

Coercion.   Domination of one group by another.

Compromise.   Making concessions for the sake of achieving a greater goal.

Conflict resolution.   Adjustment of differences between persons, groups.

Conversion.   Acceptance of another individual or group's ideas, ways.

Exploitation.   Use of one group by another.

Extermination.   Eradication of a group. Genocide (Cf. Dachau).

Scapegoating.   Casting upon someone or something else the blame for our own difficulties.

Suppression.   As of a culture group's traits, ideals.

(*responses*)

Adaptation.   Acquiring (modified) traits of another group.

Adjustment.   Conforming to some expectations of another group.

CULTURAL DETERMINISM   See BEHAVIOR (*theories of*).

CUSTODY   See *Legal Terms.*

CUSTOMS   See SOCIAL Control (*means of*).

CYBERNETICS   Comparative study of the automatic control system and brain, and mechanical-electrical communication systems (Webster).

DECENTRALIZATION   See POLICE. Also: outward movement of population from urban centers.

DE FACTO SEGREGATION   Actually existing as by residence distribution, as v. DE JURE—in conformity with legal factors.

DEFENSIVE   See BEHAVIOR.

DE JURE SEGREGATION   See DE FACTO.

DELINQUENT   See *Legal Terms.*

DEMOGRAPHY   Study of population data, with special regard to environmental factors.

DEMONSTRATION   May be peaceful or violent mobilization of people to protest for a cause. Hence legal (if peaceful) or illegal (if violent), depending largely on leaders' cooperation with the police in planning. (March on Washington of Martin Luther King v. riots at the Chicago 1968 Democratic convention). See CIVIL DISOBEDIENCE.

DEVIANCE. See SOCIAL.

DEVIANT (n.) One who behaves atypically.

DEVIANT (adj.). See BEHAVIOR.

DIFFERENCES. See CULTURAL.

DIFFERENTIAL TREATMENT Applying different degrees or types of enforcement at different times and places, or upon the same people at different times, as in SELECTIVE ENFORCEMENT—on every 5th violator, or on youth only, or on certain days. Or in DISCRETIONARY USE OF POLICE POWER by command, or invested in the officer himself, or in "saturation patrols" in crime areas.

DIFFUSION See CULTURAL (concepts).

DISCIPLINARY PROCEDURES Can be INTERNAL (within the department) or EXTERNAL, as by a civilian review board, or can result from an inquiry by an ombudsman.

DISCONTINUITIES See CULTURAL.

DISCRETIONARY USE OF POLICE POWER See DIFFERENTIAL TREATMENT.

DISCRIMINATION See SOCIAL.

DISINTEGRATION See SOCIAL (*processes*).

DISORGANIZATION See SOCIAL.

DISPLACEMENT See SOCIAL Control (*responses to*).

DISTANCE See SOCIAL. Also CULTURAL (*concepts*).

DUE PROCESS See *Legal Terms*.

ECOLOGY Study of organisms and their environment.

ELITE See SOCIAL.

EMBEZZLEMENT See *Legal Terms*.

EQUITATION The art of riding horses through intricate paces and patterns. Figuratively; over-regimentation; resistance to change; decision-making on the basis of precedent and tradition.

ETHNIC As used herein, a grouping of people by cultural characteristics, as v. RACIAL—grouping by physical traits.

ETHNIC JOKES "Ja hear the one about the Wop who . . .". A sudden increase in the number of ethnic or racial jokes can be a clue to coming shortages of jobs, housing, etc., in areas where such groups live in competition.

ETHNOCENTRISM See CULTURAL (*concepts*).

ETIOLOGY Study of the causes of given conditions or situations.

EVALUATION See ROLE.

EXCLUSIONARY RULE   Holds that evidence introduced in court must have been obtained by legal means.

EXPECTATIONS   See ROLE.

EXPLOITATION   See CULTURAL (*processes*).

EXTERMINATION   See CULTURAL (*processes*).

EXTERNALIZATION   See SOCIALIZATION.

FAMILY   Kinship group for reproduction and rearing of children.

FAMILY

(*types of*)
Nuclear.   (From "nucleus"), or *conjugal* family, consists of the immediate parents and their children.

Consanguine.   Family includes persons related by blood plus their nuclear families.

Extended.   At most, a clan, with its dependent septs (branches).

Broken.   Conjugal unit in which parents have been separated by fact, decree, divorce or death.

Census.   U.S. Census definition: a minimum of one parent or guardian and one dependent child.

(*by customs*)
Polygamy.   Family having plural wives or husbands, as v.

Polyandry.   Having plural husbands, as v.

Polygyny.   Having plural wives.

(*by organization*)
Patriarchy.   (Patristic)   Authority and inheritance vested in males.

Matriarchy.   (Matristic)   Authority and inheritance vested in females.

Democratic.   Authority divided between all members of nuclear unit; inheritance by personal decision.

FAMILY   When used in connection with organized crime, means a relatively small number of persons loyal to a leader recognized as dominating a territory for criminal purposes.

FAMILY: CHANGING FUNCTIONS OF   Idea that the "modern" family's functions are changing to surrender training of children to outside agencies (school, church, peer groups, state)—a trend characteristic of some "civilized" and even "primitive" societies throughout history.

FELONIES   See *Legal Terms.*

FIFTH AMENDMENT   "No person shall be held to answer for a capital or otherwise infamous crime, unless on a presentment of indictment by a grand jury . . . nor shall any person be subject for the same offense to be twice put in jeopardy of life or limb; nor shall be compelled in any criminal case to be a witness against himself, nor be denied of life, liberty or property without due process of law; nor shall private property be taken for public use, without just compensation."

FISH   (Not an acronym)   An early symbol of Christianity.

FOLKWAYS   See SOCIAL Control (*means of*).

FORCE FIELD ANALYSIS   Process of identifying forces causing problems and matching them with conditions that counteract them. Drastic example: "If apt to smoke after meals and one wishes to stop smoking, don't eat!"

FORENSICS   See *Legal Terms*.

FORGERY   See *Legal Terms*.

FORMAL v. INFORMAL   See SOCIAL Control (*types of*).

FRATERNAL ORGANIZATIONS   See POLICE Benevolent associations.

FUNCTION   See SOCIAL.   Also POLICE.

GANG   See SOCIAL

GEMEINSCHAFT   See SOCIAL Control (*types of*).

GENERALIZED OTHER   See SOCIALIZATION.

GESELLSCHAFT   See SOCIAL Control (*types of*).

GESTALT   A biological or physiological configuration functioning as a unit. Basis of Gestalt psychology.

GHETTO   Part of a city in which minority people are forced to live for ethnic, racial or economic reasons.

GOSSIP   See SOCIAL Control (*means of*).

GRAND JURY   See *Legal Terms*.

GROUP   See SOCIAL.

HALFWAY HOUSE   See SOCIETY.

HETEROGENOUS   See SOCIETY.

HEURISTIC   Guiding or revealing but not capable of proof.

HIERARCHY   See SOCIAL.

HOMICIDE   See *Legal Terms*.

HOMOGENEOUS   See SOCIETY.

HOUSE OF CORRECTION   See *Legal Terms*.

HUMAN RELATIONS   See RELATIONS.

IDENTIFICATION   See SOCIALIZATION.

IMAGE   See SOCIAL.

IMPLICATIONS   See ROLE.

IMPLY   Means to suggest v. INFER—to deduce ("I infer from what you imply,") as in *implication* and *inference*

INCUMBENT   See ROLE.

INDICTMENT   See *Legal Terms.*

INERTIA   See SOCIAL.

INFERENCE   See IMPLY.

INFRACTIONS   See *Legal Terms.*

INSTITUTIONS   See SOCIAL Control (*means of*).

INSULARITY   See CULTURAL (*concepts*).

INTEGRATION   See SOCIAL (*processes*). Also CULTURAL (*concepts*).

INTERACTION   See SOCIAL (*processes*). Also CULTURAL (*concepts*).

INTERGROUP RELATIONS   See RELATIONS.

INTERNALIZATION   See SOCIALIZATION.

INTERPERSONAL RELATIONS   See RELATIONS.

INTERVENTION   See SOCIAL (*processes*).

INVENTION   See CULTURAL (*concepts*).

ISOMORPHISM   See ROLE.

JAIL   See *Legal Terms*

JUDGE   See *Legal Terms.*

JURY   See *Legal Terms.*

JUVENILE DELINQUENT   Term properly refers to minors, as distinct from "wayward youth," "young or youthful offenders," now coming into use for persons 18–21, or slightly older.

KIDNAPPING   See *Legal Terms.*

LABILE   Changeable, adaptable.

LAG   See CULTURAL (*concepts*).

LARCENY   See *Legal Terms.*

LAW   See *Legal Terms.*

LAW AND ORDER   See *Legal Terms.*

LAW ENFORCEMENT   See POLICE (*functions*).

LAWS   See SOCIAL Control (*means of*). Also BEHAVIORAL and *Legal Terms.*

LEARNING   May be COGNITIVE—essentially an intellectual process based on knowledge or judgment. Or it may be AFFECTIVE—facilitated or impeded by emotions such as desire, joy, fear, prejudice.

LEGAL MORALISM   Idea of making laws to control morals (as re. drugs, alcohol, homosexuality). See CRIMINALIZATION.

LEGAL TERMS

ACCESSORY   Before the fact: aided, though not present. After the fact: knowingly helped in criminal's escape, etc.

LEGAL TERMS (*Continued*)

ACCOMPLICE   Participated in commission of an offense.

ARRAIGNMENT   Hearing at which accused pleads guilty as charged, guilty to a lesser offense (plea bargaining), not guilty, etc.

ARREST   Taking a person into custody.

   v. CONFINEMENT   As while awaiting trial, serving sentence, etc.

   v. CUSTODY   Legal confinement in jail, prison, or other facility.

   v. PROTECTIVE CUSTODY   Holding without a criminal charge.

   v. SEIZURE   Taking, under writ, a person, property, evidence.

ATTORNEY   A trained, licensed member of legal profession.

   v. PROSECUTING ATTORNEY   Official prosecutor for district, county, state, etc.

BAIL   Money, bond, etc., to assure appearance at court for trial.

CORRECTIONS   Post-conviction process including confinement, probation, parole, treatment; and aftercare in juvenile cases.

CRIMES   (general).   Acts or omissions against society or individuals by competent persons in violation of extant laws.

   Felonies.   Acts punishable by death or detention in state or federal prisons (murder, rape, larceny, etc.)

   Misdemeanors.   Less serious offenses (battery, some traffic violations). No jury trial unless classed as "high" or "serious." Punishable by fine and or detention in local or county jail.

   Infractions.   Class of lesser offenses coming into criminal code.

   Torts.   Civil wrongs against individual or property; susceptible to damage suits.

   Violations.   Public wrongs in re. sanitation, fire hazards, etc., punishable by fines, revocation of license, etc.

CRIMES

(*against the person*)

Homicide.   Includes (1) *criminal* (murder, manslaughter); (2) *negligent* (as in auto accident); (3) *innocent* or *excusable* (accidental, or killing dangerous intruder in one's home); (4) *justifiable* (as in performance of duty).

Murder.   *1st degree:* with malice and premeditation, or done while committing a felony (arson, rape); *2nd degree:* with malice, but with no intent until just before the killing (as in a rage).

Manslaughter.   *Voluntary:* without malice, as in self-defense. *Involuntary:* without malice, and done while committing a misdemeanor

Assault.   Threat to do bodily harm.

Aggravated assault.   With intent to do bodily harm.

Battery.   Doing bodily harm.

Rape.   Sexual possession of a woman by force or deception.

LEGAL TERMS *(Continued)*

Statutory rape. Intercourse with a girl below age of consent.

Mayhem. Malicious maiming of a person.

Kidnapping. Abduction and detention of a person against his will.

(against real property)
Arson. Malicious burning of property.

Burglary. (Depending on state law) breaking and entering (in the night?) to commit a felony (theft).

Embezzlement. Taking or misuse of personal property by one to whom it has been entrusted.

Forgery. Making a false document with intent to defraud.

Larceny. Taking another's property with intent to steal. "Grand" or "petty" according to value of goods.

Robbery. Taking property from a person by force. "Armed" involves use of a weapon.

Theft. Felonious taking or removing of personal property.

Uttering and publishing. Passing a false document to defraud.

Vandalism. Willful destruction of property. Punishment (as per extent of damage) by fine and/or imprisonment.

CRIMINALISTICS Field of detection employing physical, social, and medical sciences.

CRIMINALIZATION Classifying and assessing crimes. "Overcriminalization" means to include offenses not thought by some to be crimes (drug addiction, drunkenness, homosexuality). "Decriminalization"

CRIMINAL JUSTICE Whole system, including police, prosecutors, courts, corrections, probation and parole, etc. (some include auxiliary community agencies).

CRIMINOLOGY Study of crime and criminals including classification, causes and prevention.

DELINQUENT One who commits offenses or fails to obey laws.
Juvenile delinquent. Minor who commits acts which if committed by an adult would be a crime, or acts which would not be so considered (truancy, smoking).

DUE PROCESS Principles that limit governmental power to deprive a person of life, liberty, or property.

FORENSICS Science using medical and legal data to determine cause of death, etc.

HALFWAY HOUSE A residence for probationers and parolees in which supervision is provided for their transitional participation in the community.

INDICTMENT Official document of accusation issued by grand jury.

JUDGE Presiding official authorized to decide cases.

MAGISTRATE Judicial official with limited jurisdiction.

LEGAL TERMS (*Continued*)

JURY   Body of persons sworn to inquire into and give verdict upon legally submitted evidence.

  GRAND JURY   Body of persons empowered to investigate and indict upon evidence submitted by a magistrate or upon its own initiative. Advised by prosecuting attorney. Hears legal evidence only. Suspects not represented by counsel and must waive immunity *in re* evidence submitted about other offenses.

  PETIT JURY   (Pronounced "petty"). A trial jury.

LAW

  (*types of*)
  Common.   Based on custom, precedent.

  Statute.   Enacted by legislatures, plus ordinances, etc.

  Constitutional.   The basic law of the land, as interpreted by courts.

  (*fields of*)
  Procedural: regulating processes, especially of courts;
  Substantive: concerning rights and duties. Plus special areas of law such as criminal, administrative, marine, probate, corporate.

LAW AND ORDER   Phrase suggesting hard line enforcement with little regard for human factors.

OFFENSES   Vary by state laws. See CRIMES above.

PAROLE   Conditional release of offenders while serving indeterminate or unexpired sentences.

PETITION   Any formal request to a court for relief.

PLEA BARGAINING   Persuading the defendant to plead guilty to a lesser charge than the one on which he is booked.

PRISON   State or federal place of detention for persons convicted of serious crimes, v.

  JAIL   Local or county facility for persons in lawful custody for minor offenses, or awaiting trial.

PROBATION   Suspension of sentence on stipulated terms.

SUBPOENA   Writ commanding appearance in court (on penalty of failure) to give testimony.

SUMMONS   Writ ordering appearance in court to answer a complaint.

(end of LEGAL TERMS)

LEITMOTIV   A recurring theme.

LIBERTY   Freedom to do, speak, etc., as v. LICENSE—excessive use of liberty.

LOCAL CONTROL   The idea that schools, police, etc., should be organized to maximize neighborhood control of policy but without bearing the appropriate share of financial costs. Cf. DECENTRALIZATION—another term for the same, stressing delegation of functional power to neighborhoods. See POLICE. Also METROPLEXITY.

LOGISTICS   See STRATEGY.

LOSS   See CULTURAL (*concepts*)

MAGINOT LINE Massive French fortifications against invasion which Germans easily by-passed in WWII.

MAGISTRATE See *Legal Terms*.

MANSLAUGHTER See *Legal Terms*.

MARGINALITY See SOCIAL. Also CULTURAL (*concepts*).

MAYHEM See *Legal Terms*.

MEDIAN See AVERAGE.

MEDIATION See SOCIAL Control (*means of*).

METROPLEXITY The aggregate of problems resulting from URBANIZA-TION—the trend of U.S. people to gravitate to cities and suburbs: STAN-DARD METROPOLITAN STATISTICAL AREAS (SMSA). In roughly 80 years, the population has shifted from 80% rural to 80% urban. The problems include providing for, financing and controlling utilities, sanitary, fire and police services: whether by DECENTRALIZATION—operating from local jurisdictions, or under the METROPOLITAN AP-PROACH, pooling *some* police and other services while maintaining separate central city and suburban autonomies, or by politically merging government units to provide a broad financial and administrative base to avoid duplication of services. See LOCAL CONTROL. Also COM-MUNITY.

METROPOLITAN APPROACH See METROPLEXITY.

MINISTERIAL DUTIES See POLICE (*functions*).

MINORITY GROUP See CULTURAL (*concepts*).

MISDEMEANORS See *Legal Terms*.

MOB A potentially or actually disorderly group reacting to a common stimulus. See AGGREGATION, CROWD.

MOBILITY See SOCIAL.

MODE See AVERAGE.

MODEL See SOCIAL. Also ROLE.

MORES See SOCIAL Control (*means of*).

MOTIVATIONS See BEHAVIORAL.

MURDER See *Legal Terms*.

MUTATIS MUTANDIS The necessary changes having been made.

MYTH See CULTURAL (*concepts*). Also MYTH, SOCIETY and CUL-TURE.

MYTH, SOCIETY and CULTURE The concepts can be conceived as meshed gear wheels. Myths are the central *beliefs* around which society *organizes* the culture—the total characteristics of a people. If the myths change (direction) gradually, society may adjust, thus changing the cul-ture. But if the myths change (direction) abruptly or totally, the gears of society are stripped and the culture becomes dysfunctional.

NEIGHBORHOOD See COMMUNITY.

NEIGHBORHOOD CONTROL See LOCAL CONTROL. Also COMMUNITY.

NORMATIVE See BEHAVIOR.

NORMS See BEHAVIORAL.

OCCUPATIONAL See BEHAVIOR.

OFFENSES See *Legal Terms.*

OFFICER FRIENDLY An educational program sponsored by Sears, Roebuck Foundation for elementary schools, using police officers and materials to help children see police as friendly protectors.

OMBUDSMAN An official (first created in Sweden) to receive citizen complaints about and make recommendation to one or more agencies of government, to none of which is he directly responsible.

OPEN CLASS SYSTEM A society in which maximum vertical mobility is assured.

ORDER MAINTENANCE See POLICE (*functions*).

ORWELLIAN Reference to George Orwell's novel *1984* portraying the government as keeping an all-seeing and dominating eye on a thoroughly regimented citizenry. (Big-Brother is watching).

OSTRACISM See SOCIAL.

PAL *P*olice *A*thletic *L*eague, for police-sponsored youth groups.

PANZERS The armored divisions of Adolph Hitler in WWII, largely responsible for his initial successes.

PAROLE See *Legal Terms.*

PATTERNS See BEHAVIORAL.

PECKING ORDER In a poultry yard, each hen picks at the next smaller below it in their "social" order without fear of retaliation. Hence, a social hierarchy of ranks.

PEER GROUPS See SOCIAL Control (*means of*).

PERCEPTION See ROLE. Also see Study 4 (Part II), *The Police and the Community: Studies,* Radelet and Reed

PERFORMANCE See ROLE.

PERSONALITY The syndrome of habits, attitudes and other characteristics of an individual.

PERSONALITY SYSTEM An ordered arrangement of self identities that is characteristic of a particular individual.

PETIT JURY See *Legal Terms.*

PETITION See *Legal Terms.*

PHENOMENOLOGISM See BEHAVIOR (*theories*).

PLEA BARGAINING See *Legal Terms.*

PLURALISM   See CULTURAL (*concepts*).

POLICE (n.)   Agency authorized to enforce law and keep order.

Private.   Licensed property or personal protection service.

Public.   Federal, state, county (sheriff), city, or local.

Special.   Public or private security forces for parks, harbors, transit systems, building, personages, etc.

POLICE (adj.)

Auxiliaries.   Volunteer or paid citizen groups who help with traffic, parades, PCR programs, etc.

Benevolent associations.   Police personnel organizations by rank, specialty, ethnic, racial nature. Often serve as bargaining units.

Brutality.   Physical, verbal or attitudinal discriminatory treatment.

Decentralization.   Theory that control of police should be on a neighborhood basis. See METROPLEXITY.

Professionalism.   Elevating police philosophy, purposes and procedures to level of medicine, law, etc., through training, education, research, and association discipline.

Review boards.   Internal or external (civilian) bodies to exert discipline and/or process complaints.

Role.   See ROLE.

State.   A nation under control of a central police system.

(*functions*)
Crime prevention.   As by use of detection, task forces, PCR programs.

Law enforcement.   By technology, deployment, containment, arrest.

Ministerial duties.   Routinized; not requiring more than technical skills (as in much of traffic enforcement).

Order maintenance.   As through licensing, inspection, traffic control, crowd management, crisis intervention, etc.

Public service.   Public education, emergency service, crisis intervention, family crisis intervention, PCR programs, etc.

POLICE-COMMUNITY RELATIONS   See RELATIONS.

POLICE FUNCTIONS   See POLICE.

POLICE REVIEW BOARDS   See POLICE.

POLICE ROLE   See ROLE.

POLICE STATE   See POLICE.

POLICE UNIONS   See POLICE benevolent associations.

POPULATION MOBILITY   Areal movement of people: geographical, rural-urban, etc. Cf. SOCIAL MOBILITY.

POSITION   See SOCIAL.

POSSE COMITATUS The people a sheriff calls to help him in emergencies.

POWER See AUTHORITY. Also SOCIAL Control.

PRACTICUM That part of a course of study involving practical field experience.

PREJUDICE See CULTURAL (*concepts*).

PRESCRIBED See ROLE.

PRESS RELATIONS See RELATIONS.

PRIMARY v. SECONDARY GROUPS See SOCIAL Control (*types of*).

PRISON See *Legal Terms*.

PRIVATE POLICE See POLICE.

PRIVATE SCHOOL Not supported by public funds. Parochial (church supported) or preparatory (supported by tuition and/or endowment). Term currently being used also for those schools created to avoid integration.

PROBABILITIES See BEHAVIORAL.

PROBATION See *Legal Terms*.

PROBLEM See SOCIAL.

PROFESSIONALISM See POLICE.

PROJECTION See SOCIALIZATION.

PROLETARIAT The masses, hoi polloi (the people).

PROSECUTING ATTORNEY See *Legal Terms*.

PROTECTIVE CUSTODY See *Legal Terms*.

PSYCHIATRY See SOCIOLOGY.

PSYCHOANALISM See BEHAVIOR (*theories of*).

PSYCHOLOGY See SOCIOLOGY.

PUBLIC(S) All of the people, or specific interest groups with possibly different reactions to a common stimulus, as to a policy statement. See AUDIENCE, COMMUNITY, also POLICE.

PUBLIC RELATIONS See RELATIONS.

PUBLIC SERVICE See POLICE (*functions*).

PUNISHMENT See SOCIAL Control (*means of*).

QUASI-CASTE SYSTEM A society in which cultural traditions make vertical mobility extremely difficult for certain people.

RACIAL (As distinct from ETHNIC, which see). There is but one human race. It includes the Caucasian (mostly white); Negroid (mostly black), and the Mongoloid (mostly yellow), color being but one variable group trait, others being lips, hair (type and distribution on body), stature, etc. The Hairy Ainu of Japan, the Maoris of New Zealand and the Melanesians of the South Pacific are, as yet, unclassified, for example. Hence "racial" is a safer term than "race" in descriptions.

RACIAL SUPERIORITY   Idea that one racial group is biologically (hence perhaps intellectually) superior to any other. As in Hitler's claim that the Germans were pure white Aryans (actually the term for the original Indo-Europeans from whom modern racial groups purportedly descend, according to the mono-genetic theory). Popularly called *racism*.

RAPE   See *Legal Terms*.

RATIONALIZATION   See SOCIAL Control (*responses to*).

RECIPROCAL   See ROLE.

REFERENCE   See ROLE.

REGRESSION   See SOCIAL Control (*responses to*).

RELATIONS   "The state of being mutually or reciprocally interested, as in social matters."—Webster. COMMUNITY R. concern the degree of effective communication between the elements of a community in terms of mutual service. POLICE-COMMUNITY R. involve the police in such service as an element of the community. HUMAN R. broadly concern the personal desires, needs and expectations of individuals (INTER-PERSONAL R.) and of sets of people (INTERGROUP R.) PRESS R. concern the procedures by which information is released to or protected by the media. PUBLIC R. concern the image of a client as created through the media.

REPRESSION   See SOCIAL Control (*responses to*).

RESISTANCE   See SOCIAL Control (*responses to*).

REVIEW BOARDS   See POLICE.

REWARD   See SOCIAL Control (*means of*).

ROBBERY   See *Legal Terms*.

ROLE (n.)   Behavior expected of incumbent of a certain position.

   Achieved.   As attained and played by the incumbent. See POLICE.

   Ascribed.   Role to which an incumbent has been assigned.

   Prescribed.   A role as it is expected to be played.

ROLE (adj.)

   Aggregate.   Behavior of a group in a certain situation.

   Attribute.   A characteristic behavior required in a role.

   Attitude.   A positive or negative reaction to a role.

   Client.   A recipient of role behavior.

   Concept.   Set of expectations held by a role incumbent regarding the behavior and attributes of his role, and the behavior and attitudes of a role reciprocal.

   Conflict.   Exposure to and awareness of conflicting expectations in connection with either single or multiple role incumbencies.

   Evaluation.   Observations and judgments made by an actor about the adequacy of personal satisfaction derived from his own role performances.

Expectations. Beliefs and demands about what ought or ought not to be done by a role incumbent.

Implications. Possible results of playing a role in given ways.

Incumbent. Person occupying a given role.

Isomorphism. A condition in which the content of role expectation, self-identity and a cultural value is identical.

Model. Ideal example of performance in a role.

Perception. How incumbent or others see role should be played.

Playing. Performing own role, or acting others' for study.

Performance. Behavior characteristic of an incumbent of one position toward the incumbent of another position.

Reciprocal. Person in a counter role with whom one interacts.

Reference group. A group by whom an actor sees his role performance observed and evaluated, and to whose expectations and evaluations he attends.

Senders. Groups that communicate their expectations as to how roles should be played and performed.

Taking. Assuming the role of another functionally, or experimentally, as in training, therapy, analysis.

ROLE v. STATUS *Role* involves function. *Status* concerns one's place in a social hierarchy of prestige.

RUMOR CLINIC Center to which citizens can turn for clarification of stories of threatened labor shortages, riots, etc., which if not dispelled, can produce violence. Centers have been established by the Urban League, prosecutors' offices, police headquarters, etc. as preventive measures. Also a term coined by Harvard psychologist, Gordon W. Allport, in the 1940s, as applied to an instructional demonstration on the subject of rumor.

SABOTAGE (From the French *sabot*, wooden shoe). Deliberate destruction of property for a purpose (as in political, labor causes) as distinct from VANDALISM (irresponsible destruction).

SANCTION (n./v.). See SOCIAL.

SCAPEGOATING See CULTURAL (processes).

SCOOTER PATROL Special scooter-mounted police assigned to neighborhoods, having back-up emergency support. Introduced by Detroit police as a means of restoring man-on-the-beat relationships.

SCYLLA AND CHARYBDIS (Pronounced Silla, as in silly, and ka-rib'-dis). In the *Iliad*, two demi-gods (actually rocks in the Mediterranean) so vicious and close together as to imperil ships that must sail between them.

SELF-ESTEEM MAINTENANCE SYSTEM (SMS). The hierarchial ordering of cultural values and role concepts within a personality system. Those on top are the most important to the self-esteem; those on the bottom, the least. It is a process of maintaining favorable images of self.

SEIZURE   See *Legal Terms.*

SELECTIVE ENFORCEMENT   See DIFFERENTIAL TREATMENT.

SELF CONCEPT   See SOCIALIZATION.

SENDERS   See ROLE.

SEPARATISM   See CULTURAL (*concepts*).

SHOCK   See CULTURAL (*concepts*).

SIGNIFICANT OTHERS   See SOCIALIZATION.

SINE QUA NON   Something one cannot do without.

SOCIAL   Concerning ways of behaving in, or organizing a group.

Acceptance.   Group approval of behavior.

Agencies.   Political or social organizations.

Alienation.   Estrangement of a person from a group.

Anomie.   Feeling of disorientation or social normlessness.

Caste.   An arbitrary social stratification system, v. CLASS—social ranking based on family, wealth, power, etc.

Clique.   (pronounced "cleek"). Small group of social intimates.

Constructs.   Observable patterns of consistent behavior.

SOCIAL Control.   Process of maintaining social, organizational patterns.

(*means of*)
Arbitration.   The hearing and determination of a dispute by a person chosen by the parties (MEDIATION), or by a person appointed under a statutory authority (COMPULSORY). As v. CONCILIATION—the reconciling of differences in general.

Customs.   Traditional ways of behaving, believing.

Folkways.   Ways of behaving considered pleasant (throwing rice at a wedding).

Mores.   Ways of behaving having moral significance (getting married in a church).

Institutions.   Organized ways of behaving: family, school and church (getting married).

Gossip.   Questionable truths repeated with or without malice.

Laws.   Enacted statutes, ordinances, with sanctions. See *Legal Terms.*

Peer Groups.   Persons of equal rank, class, caste.

Punishment.   Sanctions for unacceptable behavior.

Reward.   Inducements to behaving in approved ways.

(*types of*)
Formal.   By institutional means (laws, sanctions, etc.)

v. Informal.   As by social rejection, ostracism by—

Primary groups.   Gemeinschaft (intimate) relations (family, peers)

v. Secondary groups.   Gesellschaft (impersonal) relations (officials).

(*responses to*)
Adjustment.   Making concessions to achieve greater goals.

Aggression.   Overt hostility in word or action. In *displaced* aggression, A attacks C when he can't attack B.

Attack.   Assault on object of one's frustration.

Avoidance.   Keeping away from need to face realities.

Compensation.   Indulging in B when indulging in A is impossible.

Conformity.   "Going along" when it is expedient to do so.

Displacement.   Shifting viewpoint to rationalize behavior.

(*responses to*)
Rationalization.   Finding excuses for substitute behavior.

Regression.   Unconsciously reverting to earlier behavior.

Repression.   Suppression of one's real feelings.

Resistance.   Reluctance to modifying behavior. Fighting back.

Sublimation.   Unconscious substitution of goals to achieve social acceptance.

Submission.   Capitulation to social pressures.

SOCIAL

Deviance.   Behavior at variance with group norms.

Discrimination.   (1) To distinguish between; (2) Unequal treatment.

Disorganization.   Breakdown of normal patterns of behavior.

Distance.   Degree of dissimilarity between groups.

Elite.   Recognized superior group, by power, birth, etc.

Function.   What an aspect of society is supposed to do.

Gang.   Group of like persons. Connotes crudity.

Group.   (1) Any aggregate of people. (2) Control (normal) v. experimental group.

Hierarchy.   Vertical social arrangement of classes, individuals.

Image.   Impression an individual or group makes on self or others

Inertia.   State of social or cultural arrest.

Marginality.   Sense of identification with two or more groups. (in Econ.) Occupying the most precarious position.

Mobility.   Movement up, down or across social or geographical lines.

Model. Standard or norm. Possibly theoretical.

Ostracism. Rejection or isolation by or from a group.

Position. One's recognized place in the social hierarchy.

Problem. Tension resulting from change in relationships.

Role. See ROLE.

Sanction (v.) To approve certain conduct, programs, etc.

Sanctions (n.) Legal, moral or social pressures imposed to achieve conformity to group expectations.

Status. See SOCIAL Position.

   achieved. Position earned by an incumbent.

   ascribed. Position according to group consensus, or wishes.

Structure. Organization of the elements of a society.

System. Ordered arrangement of interrelated roles about which there is some degree of consensus.

Tolerance. Indulgence of ideas, people, different from one's own.

Values. The accepted beliefs of a group.

Value judgment. Emotional attachment to a norm, idea, belief.

(*processes*)
Change. Shift in existing relationships, status, beliefs, etc.

Competition. Vying of groups or interests for new positions.

Conflict. Frictions resulting from changed relationships.

Cooperation. Joining forces to achieve common goals.

Integration. Fusing of groups to extent of mutual interests, v. Disintegration. Breakdown of former relationships.

Intervention. Introduction of new ideas, procedures, traits, etc.

Stratification. Materialization of a social hierarchy.

SOCIALIZATION Formal or informal learning processes by which individuals become committed to and accept the behavioral norms of a group. The process involves—

Self-concept. How we see ourselves as a result of forming a—

Generalized other. Our evaluation of how others see us, especially—

Significant others. People whose esteem we most treasure. Done by—

Externalization. Expressing ourselves to others, and by—

Internalization. Interpreting others' responses to us. Also by—

Identification. Imagining ourselves in others' roles, or by—

Projection. Expecting others to act or feel as we do.

SOCIETY. The organizational aspects of a culture group. See MYTH, SOCIETY and CULTURE.

   Heterogeneous. Social group comprised of multiple ethnic and/or racial elements.

   Homogeneous. Social group of essentially similar traits.

SOCIOLOGY The study of people in their various social relationships. Cf. PSYCHOLOGY—the study of normal behavior of individuals and/or groups. Cf. PSYCHIATRY—the study and/or treatment of atypical human behavior. Psychiatrists must therefore have medical training to be licensed to practice.

SPECIAL See POLICE.

SPECIALTIES See CULTURAL (*concepts*).

STANDARD METROPOLITAN STATISTICAL AREA (SMSA) Used by U.S. Census Bureau for greater metropolitan areas. See METRO-PLEXITY.

STATUS See SOCIAL. Also ROLE.

STATUS ASSIGNMENT SYSTEM The process of status ordering and giving within a social system. The hierarchy of cultural values and role concepts by the participants of a social system. Those on top possess the most status (prestige); those on bottom, least.

STATUTORY RAPE See *Legal Terms*.

STATE See POLICE.

STEREOTYPE See CULTURAL (*concepts*).

STORE FRONT A rented facility used by police departments to promote PCR. Used variously as a social service, complaint, or social center for citizens. Idea is to humanize police service in an unofficial setting.

STRATEGY Design to strike at the heart of a problem. Cf. LOGISTICS —mobilizing resources to attack a problem.

STRATIFICATION See SOCIAL (*processes*).

STRUCTURE See SOCIAL.

SUB-CULTURE Cultural sub-group having distinct traits, values, etc.

SUBLIMATION See SOCIAL Control (*responses to*).

SUBMISSION See SOCIAL Control (*responses to*).

SUBPOENA See *Legal Terms*.

SUMMONS See *Legal Terms*.

SUPPRESSION See CULTURAL (*processes*).

SYMBOLIC See BEHAVIOR.

SYMBOLIC INTERACTIONISM See BEHAVIOR (*theories*).

SYSTEM See SOCIAL.

SYSTEMATIC   In an organized way. Cf. SYSTEMIC—relating to the whole body, plan, etc.

SYSTEMIC   See SYSTEMATIC.

TACTICS   See STRATEGY.

TAKING   See ROLE.

THEFT   See *Legal Terms*.

TOLERANCE   See SOCIAL.

TORTS   See *Legal Terms*.

TOTALITARIANISM   A regime totally regulated by the state, especially by a single personality (Cf. Hitler).

TYPOLOGY   The study of classifications.

UNIVERSAL   See CULTURAL (*concepts*).

UNIVERSE   See CULTURAL (*concepts*).

UNSTRUCTURED   See BEHAVIOR.

URBANIZATION   See METROPLEXITY.

UTTERING AND PUBLISHING   See *Legal Terms*.

VALUE   See SOCIAL. Also CULTURAL (*concepts*).

VALUE JUDGMENT   See SOCIAL.

VANDALISM   See *Legal Terms*, CRIMES (*against property*).

WHITE PANTHERS   A group of white protestors against drug laws, etc. that surfaced briefly in Michigan in the late 1960s.

Works Cited

Adorno, T. W., Else Frenkel-Brunswik, D. J. Levinson, and R. N. Sanford. *The Authoritarian Personality.* New York: Harper & Brothers, 1950.

Alex, Nicholas. *Black in Blue: A Study of the Negro Policeman.* New York: Appleton-Century-Crofts, 1969.

Allport, Gordon W. *The Nature of Prejudice.* New York: Addison-Wesley, 1954 and 1958. Reprinted as a Doubleday Anchor Book. Garden City, N.Y.: Doubleday & Co., n.d.

————. *The ABC's of Scapegoating.* New York: Association Press, n.d.

————. *The Resolution of Intergroup Tensions.* An Intergroup Education pamphlet. New York: The National Conference of Christians and Jews, n.d.

Allport, Gordon W., and L. Postman. *The Psychology of Rumor.* New York: Henry Holt & Co., 1947.

American Friends Service Committee. *The Struggle for Justice: A Report on Crime and Punishment in America.* New York: Hill & Wang, 1971.

Amos, Robert T., and Reginald M. Washington. "Comparison of Pupil and Teacher Perceptions of Pupil Problems." *Journal of Educational Psychology* 51, no. 5 (1960): 255–258.

Anderson, Stanley V. *Ombudsman for American Government?* Englewood Cliffs, N.J.: Prentice-Hall Spectrum Books, 1968.

Anderton, Jean, and Fred Ferguson. "Police-Community Relations Coffee Klatch Programs." *Police* 13, no. 5 (May–June, 1969): 19–22.

Angell, John E. "Responsiveness—An Obligation and a Technique of the Police Administrator." *The Police Chief,* March 1969.

Arnold, Mark R. "The News Media—Besieged by Critics." *The National Observer,* July 6, 1970, p. A–1.

Ashmore, Harry S. "Government by Public Relations." *The Center Magazine,* 4, no. 5 (September–October 1971): 21–28.

Atshuler, Alan A. *Community Control.* New York: Western Publishing Co., 1970.

Auten, James H. "Determining Training Needs." *Police* 15, no. 1 (September–October 1970): 25–28.

Baehr, Melanie E., John E. Furcon, and Ernest C. Froemel. *Psychological Assessment of Patrolman's Qualification in Relation to Field Performance.* Report submitted by the Industrial Relations Center, University of Chicago, to the Office of Law Enforcement Assistance, U.S. Department of Justice. Washington, D.C.: U.S. Government Printing Office, November 1968.

Bailey, Harry A., Jr., ed. *Negro Politics in America.* Columbus, Ohio: Charles E. Merrill Books, 1967.

Bakal, Carl. "The Failure of Federal Gun Control." *Saturday Review,* July 3, 1971, p. 12.

Baldwin, James. *Nobody Knows My Name.* New York: Dell Publishing Co., 1962.

Ballard, Allen B. "Police Working in the Neighborhood." In *Police and Community Relations: A Sourcebook,* A. F. Brandstatter and Louis A. Radelet, eds., pp. 355–361. Beverly Hills, Calif. Glencoe Press, 1968.

Bannon, James D. "Foot Patrol: The Litany of Law Enforcement." *The Police Chief* 39, no. 4 (April 1972): 44–45.

Banton, Michael. "Social Integration and Police." *The Police Chief,* April 1963.

———. *The Policeman in the Community.* London: Tavistock Publications. New York: Basic Books, 1964.

———. "Social Order and the Police." Preprint from *The Advancement of Science* (British Association) 27 (1970–71): 48–56.

Bard, Morton. "Alternatives to Traditional Law Enforcement." *Police* 15, no. 2 (November–December 1970): 20–23.

Bard, Morton, and Bernard Berkowitz. "Training Police as Specialists in Family Crisis Intervention. A community Psychology Action Program." *Community Mental Health Journal* 3 (1967): 315–317.

Barnard, Chester I. *The Functions of the Executive.* Cambridge. Harvard University Press, 1960.

Barrett, Edward J. "Police Practices and the Law—From Arrest to Release or Charge." *California Law Review* 50, no. 1 (1962): 11–55.

Bayley, David H., and Harold Mendelsohn. *Minorities and the Police: Confrontation in America.* New York: Free Press, 1969.

Bendix, Reinhard. *Max Weber: An Intellectual Portrait.* Garden City, N.Y.: Doubleday & Co., 1962.

Benedict, Ruth. *Patterns of Culture.* New York: Houghton Mifflin, 1954.

Bennis, Warren G., and Philip E. Slater. *The Temporary Society.* New York: Harper & Row, 1968.

Berger, Mark. "The New Haven Misdemeanor Citation Program." *The Police Chief* 39, no. 1 (January 1972): 46–49.

Berkley, George E. *The Democratic Policeman.* Boston: Beacon Press, 1969.

———. "The European Police: Challenge and Change." *Public Administration Review* 28, no. 5 (September–October 1968): 424–430.

Berleman, William C. "Police and Minority Groups: The Improvement of Community Relations." *Crime and Delinquency* 18, no. 2 (April 1972): 160–167.

Berrien, Frederick M., and Wendell H. Bash. *Human Relations: Comments and Cases.* New York: Harper, 1957.

Biderman, Albert D. "Surveys of Population Samples for Estimating Crime Incidence." *The Annals* 374 (November 1967).

Bimstein, Donald. "Improving Departmental Training Programs." *Police* 15 no. 5 (May–June 1971): 22–25.

Birnbaum, Max. "Whose Values Should Be Taught?" *Saturday Review*, June 20, 1964, pp. 60–62.

———. "Sense About Sensitivity Training." *Saturday Review,* November 15, 1969, p. 82.

Bittner, Egon. "The Police on Skid-Row: A Study of Peace-Keeping." *The American Sociological Review* 32 (October 1967): 699–715.

Black, Algernon D. *The People and the Police.* New York: McGraw-Hill, 1968.

Blackwood, George D. "Civil Rights and Direct Action in the Urban North" (paper presented at the 1964 annual meeting of the American Political Science Association in Chicago). *Estratto dolla Rivista Internazionale de Scienze Economiche e Commerciali,* Anno XV, no. 11 (1968).

Blagg, Clifford D. "Improved Community Relations Via Attitude Quantification." *Police* 15, no. 3 (January–February 1971): 47–49.

Block, Herbert, and Arthur Niederhoffer. *The Gang: A Study in Adolescent Behavior.* New York: Philosophical Library, 1958.

Blum, Richard H. "Drugs, Behavior, and Crime." *The Annals* 374 (November 1967): 135–146.

Blum, Richard H., et al. *Horatio Alger's Children.* A report prepared for the U.S. Dept. of Justice. Washington, D.C.: U.S. Government Printing Office, 1972.

Blum, Sam. "The Police." *Redbook Magazine,* February 1967.

Blumer, Herbert. "Collective Behavior." In *New Outline of the Principles of Sociology,* Alfred McClung Lee, ed., pt. 4, pp. 203–211. New York: Barnes & Noble, 1946.

Blumstein, Alfred. "Systems Analysis and the Criminal Justice System." *The Annals* 374 (November 1967): 92–100.

Bordua, David J. "Delinquent Subcultures: Sociological Interpretations of Gang Delinquency." *The Annals,* November 1961, pp. 119–136.

———. "Comments on Police-Community Relations." Paper prepared for the National Advisory Commission on Civil Disorders, 1968. Published in *Law Enforcement Science and Technology II.* Chicago: Illinois Institute of Technology Research Center, 1968. Also in *Connecticut Law Review* 1, no. 1.

Bork, Robert H. "We Suddenly Feel That the Law Is Vulnerable." *Fortune,* December 1971, p. 115 ff.

Borow, Henry, ed. *Man in a World at Work.* Boston: Houghton Mifflin, 1964.

Bouma, Donald H. *Kids and Cops: A Study in Mutual Hostility.* Grand Rapids, Michigan: William B. Erdmans Publishing Co., 1969.

Brannon, Bernard C. "Professional Development of Law Enforcement Personnel." In *Police and Community Relations: A Sourcebook,* A. F. Brandstatter and Louis A. Radelet, eds., pp. 302–316. Beverly Hills, Calif. Glencoe Press, 1968.

Breitman, George. *The Last Year of Malcolm X: The Evolution of a Revolutionary* New York: 1968 (paperback). (Originally published by Merit Publishers, 1967.)

Brennan, James J. "Youth and Police." In *Police and Community Relations: A Sourcebook,* A. B. Brandstatter and Louis A. Radelet, eds., pp. 403–408. Beverly Hills, Calif. Glencoe Press, 1968.

Bronfenbrenner, Urie. "The Split-Level American Family." *Saturday Review,* October 7, 1967, pp. 60–66.

Brown, Lee P. "Police Review Boards: An Historical and Critical Analysis." *Police* 10, no. 6 (July–August, 1966).

———. "Handling Complaints Against the Police." *Police* 12, no. 5 (May–June 1968).

———. "Evaluation of Police-Community Relations Programs." *Police* 14, no. 2 (November–December 1969): 27–31.

————. "Typology: Orientation of Police-Community Relations Programs." *The Police Chief* 38, no. 3 (March 1971): 16–21.

————. *Police-Community Relations Evaluation Project.* Final Report to the National Institute on Law Enforcement and Criminal Justice, Law Enforcement Assistance Administration, U.S. Department of Justice, Grant NI–075. Washington, D.C.: U.S. Government Printing Office, circa 1971.

Brown, William P. "The Police and Community Conflict." In *Police and Community Relations: A Sourcebook,* A. F. Brandstatter and Louis A. Radelet, eds., pp. 322–334. Beverly Hills, Calif. Glencoe Press, 1968.

————. "Mirrors of Prejudice." *The Nation* 208, no. 16 (April 1969): 498–500.

Brunton, Robert L. "Supervision—A Major Problem for Police Departments." *Police,* September–October 1960, p. 14 ff.

Buchanan, Scott. "On Martin Buber." In *Civil Disobedience.* Santa Barbara, California: Center for the Study of Democratic Institutions, April 1966.

Burdman, Milton. "The Conflict Between Freedom and Order." *Crime and Delinquency* 15, no. 3 (July 1969): 371–376.

Bureau of Social Science Research, Inc. *Report on a Pilot Study in the District of Columbia on Victimization and Attitudes Toward Law Enforcement; Field Surveys I.* Report submitted to the President's Commission on Law Enforcement and Administration of Justice. Washington, D.C.: U.S. Government Printing Office, 1967.

Burns, James MacGregor. "Consensus Politics? Not on Your Life." *The New York Times,* February 21, 1972.

Cable, Kenneth M. "The Chief and the Community." *The Police Chief* 38, no. 3 (March 1971): 24–27.

Canlis, Michael N. "Tomorrow Is Too Late." *California Youth Authority Quarterly* 21, no. 1 (1968): 9–16.

Cape, William H. "Policemen . . . Dissenters . . . and Law-Abiding Citizens." *The Police Chief* 38, no. 11 (November 1971): 45–50.

Carmack, William R. "Practical Communication Tools for Group Involvement in Police-Community Programs." *The Police Chief* 32, no. 3 (March 1965): 34–36.

Carmichael, Stokely, and Charles V. Hamilton. *Black Power: The Politics of Liberation in America.* New York: Vintage Books, 1967.

Carpenter, Rod. "Psychology and Its Ever-Changing Ways." *The Police Chief* 38, no. 4 (April 1971): 48–53.

Carter, Robert M. "The Evaluation of Police Programs." *The Police Chief* 38, no. 11 (November 1971): 57–60.

Carter, Robert M., A. W. McEachern, and Herbert R. Sigurdson. "The Uncertain Future of Criminal Justice." *The Police Chief* 38, no. 5 (May 1971): 56–60.

Castelli, Jim. "The Year of the Prisons." *Commonweal* 94, no. 21 (September 1971): 494–497.

Center Magazine 3, no. 3 (May–June 1971). The entire issue is devoted to "Crime and Punishment in America." (Published by the Center for the Study of Democratic Institutions, Santa Barbara, Calif.)

Chackerian, Richard, and Richard F. Barrett. "Police Professionalism and Citizen Evaluation." *Governmental Research Bulletin* 9, no. 1 (January 1972). Institute for Social Research, Florida State University.

Chevigny, Paul. *Police Power: Police Abuses in New York City.* New York: Pantheon Books, 1969.

Civil Disobedience, April 1966. A publication of the Center for the Study of Democratic Institutions, Santa Barbara, Calif.

Cizanckas, Victor L. "Police Patrol for Black Americans." *The Police Chief* 37, no. 2 (February 1970): 26–29.

————. "Experiment in Police Uniforms: An Interim Report." *The Police Chief* 37, no. 4 (April 1970): 28–29.

Clark, John P., and Eugene P. Wenninger. "The Attitude of Juveniles Toward the Legal Institutions." *Journal of Criminal Law, Criminology, and Police Science* 55, no. 4 (1964): 482–489.

Clark, Kenneth B. *Dark Ghetto: Dilemmas of Social Power.* New York: Harper & Row, 1965.

Clark, Ramsey. *Crime in America: Observations on Its Nature, Causes, Prevention and Control.* New York: Simon & Schuster, 1970.

Cleaver, Eldridge, *Soul on Ice,* New York: McGraw-Hill, 1968.

Cloward, Richard A. and Lloyd E. Ohlin. *Delinquency and Opportunity: A Theory of Delinquent Gangs.* Glencoe, Ill.: Free Press, 1960.

Coates, Joseph F. "Wit and Humor: A Neglected Aid in Crowd and Mob Control." *Crime and Delinquency* 18, no. 2 (April 1972): 184–191.

Cohen, Albert K. *Delinquent Boys: The Culture of the Gang.* Glencoe, Ill.: Free Press, 1955.

Cohen, Fred. *The Legal Challenge to Corrections: Implications for Manpower and Training.* Prepared for the Joint Commission on Correctional Manpower and Training. Washington, D.C.: U.S. Government Printing Office, 1969.

Cohen, Jerry, and William S. Murphy. *Burn, Baby, Burn.* New York: E. P. Dutton & Co., 1966.

Cohen, Jozef. *Sensation and Perception.* Eyewitness Series in Psychology. Chicago: Rand McNally, 1969.

Cohen, Mitchell, and Dennis Hale. *The New Student Left.* Boston: Beacon Press, 1967.

Coleman, James S. *The Adolescent Society: The Social Life of the Teenager and Its Impact on Education.* New York: Free Press of Glencoe, 1961.

Coles, Robert, M.D. "A Fashionable Kind of Slander." *Atlantic Monthly* 226, no. 5 (November 1970): 53–55.

Cornelius, A. L. *Cross Examination.* Indianapolis: Bobbs-Merrill, 1929.

Cousins, Norman. "Explanations and Excesses." *Saturday Review,* October 10, 1970, p. 20.

Crawford, James H. "Combined-Selective Patrol." *The Police Chief* 38, no. 8 (August 1971): 32–34.

Cray, Ed. *The Big Blue Line—Police Power vs. Human Rights.* New York: Coward-McCann, 1967.

————. "The Politics of Blue Power. *The Nation* 208, no. 16 (April 1969): 493–496.

Cromwell, Paul F., Jr. "Training-Education-Community Understanding." *The Police Chief* 39, no. 3 (March 1972): 54–56.

Crosby, Muriel E. *An Adventure in Human Relations.* Chicago: Follett, 1965.

Daley, Eliot A. "Is TV Brutalizing Your Child?" *Look,* December 2, 1969, pp. 99–100.

Dalton, Michael D. *The Country Justice.* 6th ed., 1643. London: Assignees of John More, 1635.

Daly, Charles U., ed. *The Media and the Cities.* University of Chicago Center for Policy Study. Chicago: University of Chicago Press, 1968.

Davis, Allison, and Robert J. Havighurst. *Father of the Man.* Boston: Houghton Mifflin, 1947.

Davis, Edgar. "A Method of Approach to the Tasks of a Human Relations Officer." *Police* 15, no. 3 (January–February 1971): 61–64.

Davis, Kenneth C. "Ombudsman in America." *University of Pennsylvania Law Review* 109 (June 1961): 1057.

Davis, Keith. *Human Relations in Business.* New York: McGraw-Hill, 1957.

Dean, John P., and Alex Rosen. *A Manual of Intergroup Relations.* Chicago: University of Chicago Press, 1955.

Dempsey, Robert R. "Police Disciplinary Systems." *The Police Chief* 39, no. 5 (May 1972): 52–56.

Derbyshire, Robert L. "Children's Perceptions of the Police: A Comparative Study of Attitudes and Attitude Change." *Journal of Criminal Law, Criminology, and Police Science* 59 (June 1968): 183–190.

Deutsch, Morton. *Conflict and Its Resolution.* Technical Report No. 1, National Science Foundation Grant G5–302 and Office of Naval Research Contract NONR–4294, October 1, 1965. (Also paper presented at a meeting of the American Psychological Association, September 5, 1965.)

Devlin, Patrick Arthur. "The Police in a Changing Society." *Journal of Criminal Law, Criminology, and Police Science* 57 (July 1966): 124 ff.

Dienstein, William. "Conflict of Beliefs About Cause of Delinquency." *Crime and Delinquency* 6, no. 3 (1960): 287–293.

Dodson, Dan W. "Police and Community Relations as a Political Issue." In *Police and Community Relations: A Sourcebook,* A. F. Brandstatter and Louis A. Radelet, eds., pp. 259–266. Beverly Hills, Calif.: Glencoe Press, 1968.

Doig, Jameson W. "Police Problems, Proposals, and Strategies for Change." *Public Administration Review* 28, no. 5, (September–October 1968): 393–406.

Dollard, John. *Caste and Class in a Southern Town.* New Haven: Yale University Press, 1937.

Donald, J. Ross, and Louis Cobarruviaz. "Eliminating the Language Barrier." *The Police Chief* 38, no. 6 (June 1971): 8.

Dougherty, Richard. "Requiem for the Centre Street Mafia." *Atlantic Monthly* 223, no. 3 (March 1969): 109–114.

————. "The New York Police." *Atlantic Monthly* 229, no. 2 (February 1972): 6–18.

Douglas, Jack D., ed. *Crime and Justice in American Society.* New York: Bobbs-Merrill, 1971.

Downie, Leonard, Jr. *Justice Denied: The Case for Reform of the Courts.* New York: Praeger, 1971.

Doyle, Edward, and George D. Olivet. "An Invitation to Understanding: Workshop in Law Enforcement Integrity." *The Police Chief* 39, no. 5 (May 1972): 34–44.

DuBois, Rachel Davis, and Mew-Soong Li. *Reducing Social Tension and Conflict Through the Group Conversation Method.* New York: Association Press, 1971.

Duffy, John J., Jr. "Stop and Frisk: A Perspective." *Cornell Law Review* 53, no. 5 (1968): 899–915.

Dye, Thomas R., and Brett W. Hawkins, eds. *Politics in the Metropolis: A Reader in Conflict and Cooperation.* Columbus, Ohio: Charles E. Merrill Books, 1967.

Earle, Howard H. "Police Community Relations: The Role of the First-Line Peace Officer." *Police* 14, no. 1 (September–October 1969): 23–28.

————. *Police Community Relations: Crisis in Our Time.* 2nd ed. Springfield, Illinois: Charles C. Thomas, 1969.

Easton, David, and Jack Dennis. *The Development of Basic Attitudes and Values Toward Government and Citizenship During the Elementary School Years.* Final Report CRP 1078. U.S. Department of Health, Education, and Welfare, Office of Education, Bureau of Research. Washington, D.C.: U.S. Government Printing Office, 1968.

Easton, David, and Robert Hess. "The Child's Political World." *Midwest Journal of Political Science* 6 (1962): 229–246.

Echols, Alvin E., Jr. "Deadline, Vengeance, and Tribute: A Prescription for Black Juvenile Delinquency." *Crime and Delinquency* 16, no. 4 (October 1970): 357–362.

Eisenberg, Terry, Robert H. Fosen, and Albert S. Glickman. *Project PACE: Police and Community Enterprise—A Program for Change in Police-Community Behaviors,* Final Report. Prepared under a grant from the Ford Foundation. American Institutes for Research, Silver Springs, Md., November 1971.

Eisenberg, Terry, Albert S. Glickman, and Robert H. Fosen. "Action for Change in Police-Community Behaviors." *Crime and Delinquency* 15, no. 3 (July 1969): 393–406.

Elliott, J. F. "The Crime Control Team." *Police* 13, no. 5 (May–June 1969): 35–41.

Ellison, Ralph. *The Invisible Man.* New York: Random House, 1947. Reprinted by Signet Books, The New American Library.

Epstein, Charlotte. *Intergroup Relations for Police Officers.* Baltimore, Md.: Williams and Wilkins Co., 1962.

Farley, Martha P. and Andrew N. "An American Ombudsman: Due Process in the Administrative State." *Pennsylvania Bar Association Quarterly* 36 (October 1964): 23.

Festinger, Leon. *A Theory of Cognitive Dissonance.* Palo Alto, California: Stanford University Press, 1957.

Fineberg, S. A. *Punishment Without Crime.* New York: Doubleday & Co., 1949.

Finney, Robert D. "A Police View of Social Workers." *Police* 16, no. 6 (February 1972): 59–63.

Fitzgerald, E. T. "The Rumor Process and Its Effect on Civil Disorders." *The Police Chief* 38, no. 4 (April 1971): 16.

Fortas, Abe. *Concerning Dissent and Civil Disobedience.* New York: New American Library, 1968.

Fortier, Kenneth N. "The Police Culture—Its Effect on Sound Police-Community Relations." *The Police Chief* 39, no. 2 (February 1972): 33–35.

Fosdick, Raymond. *American Police Systems.* New York: Century Co., 1920.

Fox, Harry G. "Demonstrations Demand Specialists." *Police* 12, no. 4 (March–April 1968): 33–35.

————. "Community Relations Orientation for Police in Philadelphia, Pennsylvania (CROP)." *The Police Chief* 35, no. 6 (1968): 22.

————. "Preparing for Police Leadership in Community Relations." In *Police and Community Relations: A Sourcebook,* A. F. Brandstatter and Louis A. Radelet, eds. Beverly Hills, California: Glencoe Press, 1968.

————. "Nineteen." *The Police Chief* 38, no. 2 (February 1971): 30–32.

Fox, Harry G., and Clorinda Margolis. "Rap and Rapport: Police and Mental Health Pros." *The Police Chief* 38, no. 12 (December 1971): 46–48.

Freeman, Harrop A. et al. *Civil Disobedience,* April 1966. A Publication of the Center for the Study of Democratic Institutions, Santa Barbara, Calif.

Freiberg, Peter. "Situation Ethnics." *Commonweal* 94, no. 4 (April 1971): 81–83.

Friedenberg, Edgar E. "Hooked on Law Enforcement." *The Nation,* October 16, 1967.

Galliher, John. "Training in Social Manipulation as a Rehabilitative Technique." *Crime and Delinquency* 17, no. 4 (October 1971): 431–436.

Galvin, Raymond T. "Law Enforcement: A Comparative View." *The Police Chief* 38, no. 8 (August 1971): 64–71.

Gardiner, John A. "Public Attitudes Toward Gambling and Corruption." *The Annals* 374 (November 1967).

Geis, Gilbert: "Statistics Concerning Race and Crime." *Crime and Delinquency* 11, no. 2 (1965): 143.

Gellhorn, Walter. "Administrative Procedure Reform: Hardy Perennial." *American Bar Association Journal* 48 (1962): 243–251.

———. "Protecting Citizens Against Administrators in Poland." *Columbia Law Review* 65, no. 4 (1965): 1133–1166.

———. The Swedish Justitie—Ombudsman." *Yale Law Journal* 75, no. 1 (1965): 1–56.

———. "The Norwegian Ombudsman." *Stanford Law Review* 18, no. 2 (1966): 293–321.

———. *Ombudsmen and Others: Citizens' Protectors in Nine Countries.* Cambridge: Harvard University Press, 1966.

———. *When Americans Complain: Governmental Grievance Procedures.* Cambridge: Harvard University Press, 1966.

———. "Police Review Boards: Hoax or Hope?" *Columbia University Forum* Summer, 1966.

Germann, A. C. "The Hip Scene: A New Community." *Police* 12, no. 2 (November–December 1967): 43–45.

———. "The Police: A Mission and Role." *The Police Chief* 37, no. 1 (January 1970).

Gibbons, Don C., Joseph F. Jones, and Peter G. Garbedian. "Gauging Public Opinion About the Crime Problem." *Crime and Delinquency* 18, no. 2 (April 1972): 134–146.

Gibson, James J. *The Senses Considered as Perceptual Systems.* Boston: Houghton Mifflin, 1966.

Gifford, James P. "Dissent in Municipal Employee Organizations." In *Unionization of Municipal Employees,* Robert H. Connery and William V. Farr, eds., pp. 159–172. *Proceedings of the Academy of Political Science.* vol. 30, no. 2. New York: Columbia University, 1970.

Gilbert, G. M. *The Psychology of Dictatorship.* New York: Ronald Press, 1950.

———. *Nuremberg Diary.* New York: Farrar, Straus, 1950. Paperback, Signet Books, 1961.

———. "Stereotype Persistence and Change Among College Students." *Journal of Abnormal and Social Psychology* 46 (1951): 245–254.

———. "What Makes Us Behave as People?" In *Police and Community Relations: A Sourcebook,* A. F. Brandstatter and Louis A. Radelet, eds., pp. 46–53. Beverly Hills, Calif.: Glencoe Press, 1968.

Gillers, Stephen. *Getting Justice: The Rights of People.* New York: Basic Books, 1971.

Gitchoff, C. Thomas, and Richard D. Shope. "Kids vs. Cops: The Police-Youth Discussion Group." *Police* 16, no. 2 (October 1971): 9–13.

Glaser, Daniel. *The Effectiveness of a Prison and Parole System.* Indianapolis, Ind.: Bobbs-Merrill, 1964.

Glazer, Nathan. *Remembering the Answers: Essays on the American Student Revolt.* New York: Basic Books, 1970.

Goldberg, Arthur J. "On the Supreme Court." *The New York Times,* April 12-13, 1971.

———. "The Supreme Court: End of an Era." *Time,* June 21, 1971.

Golden, L. L. L. "Alerting Management." *Saturday Review,* September 11, 1971, p. 70.

Goldner, Norman S., and Ronald Koenig. "White Middle-Class Attitudes Toward an Urban Policemen's Union: A Survey of a Problem in Community-Police Relations." *Crime and Delinquency* 18, no. 2 (April 1972): 168–175.

Goldstein, Herman. "Full Enforcement vs. Police Discretion Not to Invoke Criminal Process." *Public Administration Review* 23, no. 3 (September 1963). Also in *Police and Community Relations: A Sourcebook,* A. F. Brandstatter and Louis A. Radelet, eds., pp. 381–392. Beverly Hills, Calif.: Glencoe Press, 1968.

———. "Administrative Problems in Controlling the Exercise of Police Authority." *Journal of Criminal Law, Criminology, and Police Science* 58, no. 2 (1967): 160–172.

———. "Police Response to Urban Crises." *Public Administration Review* 28, no. 5 (September–October 1968).

Goldstein, Joseph. "Police Discretion Not to Invoke the Criminal Process: Low-Visibility Decisions in the Administration of Justice." *Yale Law Journal* 69 (1960): 543–594.

Goldstein, Leo S. "Characteristics of Police Applicants." *The Police Chief* 39, no. 5 (May 1972): 58–60.

Goode, William J. *Vocabulary for Sociology.* Flushing, N.Y.: Data-Guide, 1959.

Gorer, Geoffrey. "Modification of National Character: The Role of the Police in England." *Journal of Social Issues* 11, no. 2 (1955).

Gosnell, Harold E., and Robert E. Martin. "The Negro as Voter and Officeholder." *Journal of Negro Education* 22 (Fall 1963): 415–425.

Gourley, Dudley D. "A Final Solution to the Problem of Organized Crime." *The Police Chief* 39, no. 2 (February 1972): 18.

Gourley, G. Douglas. *Public Relations and the Police.* Springfield, Ill.: Charles C. Thomas, 1953.

———. "Workshop on Law Enforcement, Public Schools Reveals New Student Attitudes." *Journal of California Law Enforcement* 2, no. 4 (April 1968): 198–200.

Grange, Joseph. "Dissent and Society." *The Police Chief* 38, no. 11 (November 1971): 38–44.

Grauman, Walter. "Lights! Camera! Action! The Role of Television in Law Enforcement." *Police* 12, no. 6 (July–August 1968): 81–83.

Greenstein, Fred I. *Children and Politics.* New Haven: Yale University Press, 1965.

Grinker, R. R., and S. P. Speigel. *Men Under Stress.* Philadelphia: University of Pennsylvania Press, 1945.

Guinier, Ewart. "Impact of Unionization on Blacks." In *Unionization of Municipal Employees,* Robert H. Connery and William V. Farr, eds., pp. 173–181. *Proceedings of the Academy of Political Science,* vol. 30, no. 2 New York: Columbia University, 1970.

Hall, Jerome. *Theft, Law and Society.* 2nd. ed. Indianapolis: Bobbs-Merrill, 1952.

———. "Security and Civil Liberty." *Indiana Law Journal* 28, no. 2 (Winter 1953).

———. "Police and Law in a Democratic Society." *Indiana Law Journal* 28, no. 2 (Winter 1953): 133.

Halverson, Guy. "You and Your Police," a series of 5 articles. *The Christian Science Monitor,* August 10, 11, 12, 13, 14, 1971.

Hamann, Albert D., and Rebecca Becker. "The Police and Partisan Politics in Middle-Sized Communities." *Police* 14, no. 6 (July–August 1970): 18–23.

Hamilton, Lander C. "Collected Essays on the Police Function." *Police* 12, no. 6 (July–August 1968): 18.

Hamm, Carl W. "Pluralistic Planning Within the Criminal Justice System." *Crime and Delinquency* 16, no. 4 (October 1970): 393–402.

Handlin, Oscar. "Community Organization as a Solution to Police-Community Problems." *The Police Chief* 32, no. 3 (March 1965): 18–19.

Hardesty, Thomas J. "Ads for a New Image." *The Police Chief* 38, no. 2 (February 1971): 14.

Hardin, Norman M. "Crime Prevention Through Community Involvement." *Police* 14, no. 2 (November–December 1969): 62–64.

Harlow, Eleanor. "Problems in Police-Community Relations: A Review of the

Literature." *Information Review on Crime and Delinquency* 1, no. 5 (February 1969): 4.

Harris, Sydney J. "Police Power Not the Answer." Lansing *State Journal*, November 25, 1970.

———. "Police Power Waning." Lansing *State Journal*, May 3, 1972.

Hartley, Eugene L. *Problems in Prejudice*. New York: King's Crown Press, 1946.

Havemann, Ernest. "The Paradox of the Prisons." *Life*, September 30, 1957, p. 85.

———. "Prisons in Turmoil." *Newsweek*, September 14, 1970, p. 36.

———. "U.S. Prisons: Schools for Crime." *Time*, January 18, 1971, p. 45.

Hayden, Tom. *Rebellion in Newark: Official Violence and Ghetto Response*. New York: Vintage Books, 1967.

Hentoff, Nat. "A Deepening Chill." *Commonweal* 95, no. 21 (February 1972): 486–488.

Herskovits, M. J. *The Myth of the Negro Past*. New York: Harper & Bros., 1941.

Herzog, Elizabeth. *Some Guidelines for Evaluative Research*. Children's Bureau, U.S. Department of Health, Education, and Welfare. Washington, D.C.: U.S. Government Printing Office, 1959.

———. *About the Poor: Some Facts and Some Fiction*. Children's Bureau Publication No. 451–1967, U.S. Department of Health, Education, and Welfare. Washintgon, D.C.: U.S. Government Printing Office, 1967 and 1968.

Hess, Robert, and Judith V. Torney. *The Development of Basic Attitudes and Values Toward Government and Citizenship During the Elementary School Years*. Bureau of Research CRP 1078, U.S. Department of Health, Education, and Welfare. Washington, D.C.: U.S. Government Printing Office, 1965.

———. *The Development of Political Attitudes in Children*. Chicago: Aldine Publishing Co., 1967.

Hewitt, William H. "New York City's Civilian Complaint Review Board Struggle: Its History, Analysis and Some Notes," 3 pts. *Police*, May–June, July–August, and September–October 1967.

———. "Police Personnel Administration: Lateral Entry." *Police* 15, nos. 3, 4 (January–February, March–April 1971).

Higgins. Lois L. "Historical Background of Policewomen's Service." *Journal of Criminal Law, Criminology, and Police Science* 42 (March–April 1951): 822–833.

Hirsh, Selma. *The Fears Men Live By*. New York: Harper, 1955.

Hohenberg, John. *The Best Cause: Free Press–Free People*. New York: Columbia University Press, 1970.

———. "The Free Press Is on Trial." *Saturday Review*, March 14, 1970, p. 109.

Holcomb, Richard L. *The Police and the Public*. Springfield, Ill.: Charles C. Thomas, 1957.

Hook, Sidney. "Social Protest and Civil Disobedience." *Humanist*, Fall, 1967.

———. *Academic Freedom and Academic Anarchy*. New York: Cowles Books, 1970.

Hopkins, Ernest Jerome. *Our Lawless Police*. New York: Viking Press, 1931.

Horowitz, Irving Louis: "Alias 'Mad Bomber Sam'." *Commonweal* 45, no. 14 (June 1972): 327–331.

Howard, John P. "Integrating Public Relations Training for Police Officers." *Police* 7, no. 1 (September–October): 57–58.

Howlett, Frederick W., and Hunter Hurst. "A Systems Approach to Comprehensive Criminal Justice Planning." *Crime and Delinquency* 17, no. 4 (October 1971): 345–354.

Hovland, Carl, and Muzafer Sherif. "Judgmental Phenomena and Scales of Attitude Measurement: Item Displacement in Thurstone Scales." *Journal of Abnormal and Social Psychology* 47 (1952): 822–833; and 48 (1953): 135–141.

Hughes, Everett C. *Men and Their Work.* Glencoe, Ill.: Free Press, 1958.

Hughes, John J. "Training Police Recruits for Service in the Urban Ghetto." *Crime and Delinquency* 18, no. 2 (April 1972): 176–183.

Hunter, Floyd. *Community Power Structure.* Chapel Hill, N.C.: University of North Carolina Press, 1933.

Hyndman, Don. "The Rule of Law in the Republic." In *Police and Community Relations: A Sourcebook,* A. F. Brandstatter and Louis A. Radelet, eds., pp. 1–7. Beverly Hills, Calif.: Glencoe Press, 1968.

Igleburger, Robert M., and John E. Angell. "Dealing With Police Unions." *The Police Chief* 38, no. 5 (May 1971): 50–55.

Inbau, Fred E. "Public Safety v. Individual Liberties." *The Police Chief* 29, no. 1 (January 1962): 29–33.

———. "More About Public Safety v. Individual Civil Liberties." *Journal of Criminal Law, Criminology, and Police Science* 53, no. 3 (September 1962): 329–332.

———. "Lawlessness Galore." *Vital Speeches* 32 (November 1965): 95–97.

Industrial Relations Center, University of Chicago. *Psychological Assessment of Patrolman's Qualification in Relation to Field Performance.* Report prepared by Melanie E. Baehr, John E. Furcon, and Ernest C. Froemel for the Office of Law Enforcement Assistance, U.S. Department of Justice. Washington, D.C.: U.S. Government Printing Office, November 1968.

International Association of Chiefs of Police. "I.A.C.P. Position Statement on Police Review Boards." *The Police Chief* 32, no. 6 (June 1965): 8–9.

Iyer, Raghavan N. "On Ghandi." In *Civil Disobedience,* April 1966. A publication of the Center for the Study of Democratic Institutions, Santa Barbara, Calif.

Jackson, George. *Soledad Brother: The Prison Letters of George Jackson.* New York: Coward-McCann-Geoghegan and Bantam Books, 1970.

Jacobs, Jane. *The Death and Life of Great American Cities.* New York: Random House, 1961.

Jacobs, Paul. *Prelude to Riot: A View of Urban America From the Bottom.* New York: Random House, 1968.

Jaffee, Carolyn. "The Press and the Oppressed—A Study of Prejudicial News Reporting in Criminal Cases," pts. 1 and 2. *Journal of Criminal Law, Criminology, and Police Science* 56 (1965): 1–17 and 158–173.

James, Howard. "Children In Trouble: A National Scandal." *The Christian Science Monitor,* 1969.

Janowitz, Morris. *The Professional Soldier: A Social and Political Portrait.* Glencoe, Ill.: Free Press, 1964.

———. *Social Control of Escalated Riots.* Chicago: University of Chicago Press, 1968.

Johnson, C. S. *Patterns of Negro Segregation.* New York: Harper & Brothers, 1943.

Johnson, Deborah, and Robert J. Gregory. "Police-Community Relations in the United States: A Review of Recent Literature and Projects." *Journal of Criminal Law, Criminology, and Police Science* 62, no. 1 (March 1971): 94–103.

Johnson, Elmer H. "Interrelatedness of Law Enforcement Programs: A Fundamental Dimension." *Journal of Criminal Law, Criminology, and Police Science* 60, no. 4 (1969): 509–516.

———. *Crime, Corrections and Society.* Rev. ed. Homewood, Ill.: Dorsey Press, 1968.

———. "Report of an Innovation—State Work-Release Programs." *Crime and Delinquency* 16, no. 4 (October 1970): 417-426.

Johnson, Knowlton W. *Examining Behavior and Perceptions of Law Enforcement, Probation and Social Agency Personnel: An Evaluation of an In-Service Train-*

ing Program, Muskegon, Michigan. Center on Police and Community Relations, Michigan State University, May 31, 1971.

Jones, Marshall E. "Police Leadership and Human Relations." *Police* 10, no. 5 (May–June 1966): 42–53.

Jones, Maxwell, et al. *The Therapeutic Community: A New Treatment Method of Psychiatry.* New York: Basic Books, 1953.

Kadish, Sanford H. "Legal Norm and Discretion in the Police and Sentencing Processes." *Harvard Law Review* 75 (1962): 904–931.

———. "The Crisis of Overcriminalization." *The Annals* 374 (November 1967): 157–170.

Kahn, Roger. *The Battle for Morningside Heights: Why Students Rebel.* New York: William Morrow, 1970.

Kalven, Harry, Jr. "On Thoreau." In *Civil Disobedience.* A Publication of the Center for the Study of Democratic Institutions, Santa Barbara, Calif., April 1966.

Kamisar, Yale. "On the Tactics of Police-Prosecution Oriented Critics of the Courts." *Cornell Law Quarterly* 49 (1964): 456–477.

Kane, John J. "Personal and Social Disorganization." In *Police and Community Relations: A Sourcebook,* A. F. Brandstatter and Louis A. Radelet, eds., pp. 61–66. Beverly Hills, Calif.: Glencoe Press, 1968.

Kelly, James P. "Schools v. Cops." *The Police Chief* 38, no. 4 (April 1971): 40–41.

Kelly, Rita Mae, et al. *The Pilot Police Project: A Description and Assessment of a Police-Community Relations Experiment in Washington, D.C.* American Institutes for Research, January 1972.

Keniston, Kenneth. *The Uncommitted: Alienated Youth in American Society.* New York: Harcourt, Brace & World, 1965.

———. *Young Radicals.* New York: Harcourt, Brace & World, 1968.

Keniston, Kenneth, and Michael Lerner. "The Unholy Alliance Against the Campus." *New York Times Magazine,* November 8, 1970, pp. 28–86.

Kent, Deborah Ann, and Terry Eisenberg. "The Selection and Promotion of Police Officers: A Selected Review of Recent Literature." *The Police Chief* 39, no. 2 (February 1972): 20–29.

Kephart, William M. *Racial Factors and Urban Law Enforcement.* Philadelphia: University of Pennsylvania Press, 1957.

Key, Charles R., and Miles R. Warren. "Kansas City: Long Range Planning Program." *The Police Chief* 39, no. 5 (May 1972): 72–75.

Killian, Lewis M. *The Impossible Revolution: Black Power and the American Dream.* New York: Random House, 1968.

Kimble, Joseph Paul. "Night Thoughts of a Police Chief." *The Nation,* April 27, 1970, pp. 490–492.

King, Glen D. "Storefront Centers." *The Police Chief* 38, no. 3 (March 1971): 30–32.

King, Martin Luther, Jr. *Why We Can't Wait.* New York: Harper & Row, 1963–64.

Kirk, Grayson "Limits of Academic Tolerance." *The New York Times,* January 2, 1971, p. 17.

Klein, Herbert T. *The Police: Damned If They Do—Damned If They Don't.* New York: Crown Publishers, 1968.

Klein, Malcolm W., Solomon Kobrin, A. S. McEachern, and Herbert R. Sigurdson. "System Rates: An Approach to Comprehensive Criminal Justice Planning." *Crime and Delinquency* 17, no. 4 (October 1971): 355–372.

Knebel, Fletcher. "Police in Crisis." *Look,* February 6, 1968, p. 14.

———. "A Cop Named Joe." *Look,* July 27, 1971, p. 15; *Newsweek,* September 6, 1971, p. 36.

Kohlberg, Laurence. "Moral Development and Identification in Child Psychology." *Yearbook of the National Society for Studies in Education* 57 (1963).

———. "The Child As Moral Philosopher." *Psychology Today* 11 (September 1968): 12–15.

Kotler, Milton. *Neighborhood Government*. New York: Bobbs-Merrill, 1969.

Krebs, David G. "Perceptual Defense in the Delinquent Child." *Dissertation Abstracts* 25, no. 9 (1964): 53–84.

Kuchel, G. L., and A. P. Pattavina. "Juveniles Look at Their Police." *Police* 13, no. 4 (March–April 1969): 13–17.

Kuykendall, Jack L. "Police and Minority Groups: Toward a Theory of Negative Contacts." *Police* 15, no. 1 (September–October 1970): 47–55.

Kuykendall, Jack L. and James V. Gould. "Cooperative Police Services: A Study Design." *Police* 16, no. 9 (May 1972): 40–47.

Lakin, M. "Some Ethical Issues in Sensitivity Training." *American Psychologist* 24, no. 10 (October 1969): 923–928.

Lane, Robert E. *Political Life*. Glencoe, Ill.: Free Press, 1959.

Lane, Roger. *Policing the City: Boston, 1822–1855*. Cambridge: Harvard University Press, 1967.

LaFave, Wayne R. *Arrest: The Decision to Take a Suspect Into Custody*. Boston: Little, Brown & Co., 1965.

Lasch, Christopher. "The Decline of Dissent." *Katellagete* (Winter 1966–67), p. 17.

Leary, Mary Ellen. "The Trouble With Troubleshooting." *Atlantic Monthly* 223, no. 3 (March 1969): 94–99.

Lee, Alfred McClung, and Norman D. Humphrey. *Race Riot*. (A Study of the 1943 Detroit Riot.) New York: Dryden Press, 1943.

Lee, Edward L., II. "Back To Bikes for Baltimore." *The Police Chief* 39, no. 5 (May 1972): 22.

Lee, W. L. Melville. *A History of Police in England*. London: Methuen & Co., 1901.

LeGrande, J. L. "Nonviolent Civil Disobedience and Police Enforcement Policy." *Journal of Criminal Law, Criminology, and Police Science*, September 1967.

———. "Commentary on Police Supervision." *Police* 13, no. 4 (March–April 1969): 50–57.

Leibman, Morris I. "Civil Disobedience: A Threat to Our Law Society." *American Bar Association Journal* 51 (July 1965): 645–647.

Leonard, V. A. *Police Organization and Management*. Brooklyn: Foundation Press, 1951.

———. *Police Organization and Management*. Brooklyn: Foundation Press, 1964.

———. *The Police, The Judiciary and the Criminal*. Springfield, Ill.: Charles C. Thomas, 1969.

Lett, Harold A. "A Look at Others: Minority Groups and Police-Community Relations." In *Police and Community Relations: A Sourcebook*, A. F. Brandstatter and Louis A. Radelet, eds., pp. 121–128. Beverly Hills, Calif.: Glencoe Press, 1968.

Levy, Burton. "Cops in the Ghetto: A Problem of the Police System." *American Behavioral Scientist* 2, no. 4 (March–April 1968): 31–34.

Levy, Howard, M.D., and David Miller. *Going to Jail: The Political Prisoner*. New York: Grove Press, 1971.

Levy, Ruth J. "Predicting Police Failures." *Journal of Criminal Law, Criminology, and Police Science* 58, no. 2 (1967): 275.

Lewin, Kurt. *Resolving Social Conflicts: Selected Papers on Group Dynamics*. New York: Harper & Bros., 1948.

Liberman, Robert. "Police as a Community Mental Health Resource." *Community Mental Health Journal* 5, no. 2 (April 1969): 111.

Lichtman, Richard, et al. *Civil Disobedience*, April 1966. A publication of the Center for the Study of Democratic Institutions, Santa Barbara, Calif.

Likert, Rensis. *New Patterns of Management*. New York: McGraw-Hill, 1961.

Lincoln, C. Eric. "Patterns of Protest." *Christian Century* 81 (June 1964): 735.

Lippmann, Walter. *Public Opinion*. New York: Harcourt, Brace & Co., 1922.

Lipset, Seymour Martin. "Why Cops Hate Liberals—and Vice Versa." *Atlantic Monthly* 223 (March 1969): 76–83.

Lipsitt, Paul D., and Maureen Steinbruner. "An Experiment in Police-Community Relations: A Small Group Approach." *Community Mental Health Journal* 5, no. 2 (April 1969): 72–80.

Locke, Hubert G. *The Detroit Riot of 1967*. Detroit: Wayne State University Press, 1969.

Lohman, Joseph D. *The Police and Minority Groups*. Chicago: The Chicago Park District, 1947.

————. *Principles of Police Work With Minority Groups*. Louisville, Ky.: Division of Police, 1950.

Lund, Donald A. "Confrontation Management." *Police* 16, no. 7 (March 1972): 56–62.

Lynden, Patricia. "Why I'm a Cop: Interviews From a Reporter's Notebook." *Atlantic Monthly* 223, no. 3 (March 1969): 104–108.

MacIver, R. M., ed. *Discrimination and National Welfare*. Institute for Religious and Social Studies. Distributed by Harper & Bros., New York, 1949.

MacLeish, Archibald. "Trustee of the Culture." *Saturday Review,* December 19, 1970, pp. 18–19.

Maher, Brendan, and Ellen Stein. "The Delinquent's Perception of the Law and Community." In *Controlling Delinquents,* Stanton Wheeler, ed. New York: John Wiley & Sons, 1968.

Mailick, Sidney, and Edward H. Van Ness, eds. *Concepts and Issues in Administrative Behavior*. Englewood Cliffs, N.J.: Prentice-Hall, 1962.

Malcolm X, with the assistance of Alex Haley. *Autobiography of Malcolm X*. 1st paperback ed. New York: Grove Press, 1966.

Malinowski, Bronislaw. *Crime and Custom in Savage Society*. Cambridge, England: Routledge and Kegan Paul, 1966. (Originally published in 1924 by K. Paul, Trench, Trubner and Co., London; Harcourt, Brace & Co., 1926.)

Manella, Frank L. "Humanism in Police Training." *The Police Chief* 38, no. 2 (February 1971): 26–28.

Margolis, Richard J. *Who Will Wear the Badge?* A Study of Minority Recruitment Efforts in Protective Services. U.S. Commission on Civil Rights, Clearinghouse Publication No. 25. Washington, D.C.: U.S. Government Printing Office, 1971.

Martin, John M. *Toward a Political Definition of Juvenile Delinquency*. U.S. Department of Health, Education, and Welfare, Social and Rehabilitation Service, Youth Development and Delinquency Prevention Administration. Washington, D.C.: U.S. Government Printing Office, 1970.

Martin, John M., Joseph P. Fitzpatrick, and Robert E. Gould, M.D. *The Analysis of Delinquent Behavior: A Structural Approach*. New York: Random House, 1970.

Marx, Gary. *Protest and Prejudice: A Study of Belief in the Black Community*. New York: Harper & Row, 1967.

Marx, Jerry. *Officer, Tell Your Story: A Guide to Police Public Relations*. Springfield, Ill.: Charles C. Thomas, 1962.

Masotti, Louis, ed. *Riots, Violence and Disorder: Civil Turbulence in Urban Communities*. Beverly Hills, Calif.: Sage Publications, 1968.

Mathias, William J. "Perceptions of Police Relationships With Ghetto Citizens." Series of 3 articles. *The Police Chief* 38, nos. 3–5 (March–April–May 1971).

Matza, David. *Delinquency and Drift*. New York: John Wiley & Sons, 1964.

McEntire, Davis, and Robert B. Powers. *Guide to Race Relations for Peace Officers*. Office of the Attorney General, State of California, 1946. (Reissued in 1952.)

Republished in 1958 under the same auspices, with the title *Guide to Community Relations for Peace Officers.*

McEvoy, Donald W. "Observations Through a Murky Crystal Ball, Autumn, 1971." *The Hot Line* 4, no. 6 (March 1972). National Conference of Christians and Jews, New York.

McGee, Richard A. "The Administration of Justice: The Correctional Process." In *Police and Community Relations: A Sourcebook,* A. F. Brandstatter and Louis A. Radelet, eds., pp. 414–435. Beverly Hills, Calif.: Glencoe Press, 1968.

McGregor, Douglas. "The Human Side of Enterprise." *The Management Review* 46, (1957): 22–28, 88–92.

McIntyre, Jennie. "Public Attitudes Toward Crime and Law Enforcement." *The Annals* 374 (November 1967).

McLean, L. Deckle. "Psychotherapy for Houston Police." *Ebony* 23, no. 12 (October 1968): 76–82.

McNamara, John H. "Uncertainties in Police Work: The Relevance of Police Recruits' Background and Training." In *The Police: Six Sociological Essays,* David J. Bordua, ed. New York: John Wiley & Sons, 1967.

McNamara, Joseph D. "Profile: Harvard Law School's Center for the Advancement of Criminal Justice." *The Police Chief* 39, no. 1 (January 1972): 24–26.

Meek, Victor. *Cops and Robbers.* London: Gerald Duckworth & Co., 1962.

Melnick, Norman. "The Gain Mutiny." *Newsweek,* December 27, 1971, p. 35.

———. "Uncommon Cop." *New Republic,* January 22, 1972, pp. 15–16.

Meltsner, Michael. "The Future of Correction: A Defense Attorney's View." *Crime and Delinquency* 17, no. 3 (July 1971): 266–270.

Menninger, Karl. *The Crime of Punishment.* New York: Viking Press, 1968.

Meyer, John C., Jr. "Both Sides Now: Police Opinions of the National Police Union." *The Police Chief* 39, no. 4 (April 1972): 68–75.

Meyer, Schuyler M., III, and Charles S. Topham. "Sensitivity Training/Rap Sessions for Police and Pupils." *The Police Chief* 38, no. 9 (September 1971): 63–65.

Michael, Geraldine. "Social Science Education for Police Officers." *The Police Chief* 38, no. 6 (June 1971): 56–61.

Michigan State University, National Center on Police and Community Relations, School of Police Administration and Public Safety. *A National Survey of Police and Community Relations; Field Surveys V.* Report submitted to the President's Commission on Law Enforcement and Administration of Justice. Washington, D.C.: U.S. Government Printing Office, January 1967.

Milander, Henry M. "Communication Patterns: Police and Schools." *Police* 13, no. 6 (July–August 1969): 26–28.

Miller, Herbert F. "Reversing the Crime Trend." *The Police Chief* 38, no. 7 (July 1971): 48–50.

Mills, C. Wright. *The Power Elite.* New York: Oxford University Press, 1956.

Minton, Robert J., ed. *Inside: Prison American Style.* New York: Random House, 1971.

Momboisse, Raymond M. "Demonstrations and Civil Disobedience." *Police* 12, no. 2 (November–December 1967): 76–82.

Morche, J., and J. Colling. "Detroit's New Community Oriented Patrol." *Police* 13, no. 2 (November–December 1968): 93–94.

More, Harry W., Jr., and John T. Nesbit. "Programmed Instruction for Law Enforcement." *Police* 14, no. 2 (November–December 1969): 16–23.

Morgan, James P., Jr. "Responsibilities of Universities to the Criminal Justice System." *Police* 15, no. 2 (November–December 1970): 50–54.

Morris, Albert. "What Is the Role of the Community in the Development of Police Systems?" *Correctional Research Bulletin No. 19.* Boston: Massachusetts Correctional Association, November 1969.

Morris, Earle F. "American Society and the Rebirth of Civil Obedience." *American Bar Association Journal* 54 (1968): 653–657.

Morris, Norval. "Reform: It Must Come." *Life,* September 24, 1971, p. 36.

Morris, Norval, and Gordon Hawkins. *The Honest Politician's Guide to Crime Control.* Chicago: University of Chicago Press, 1970.

Morrison, June. "The Controversial Police-School Liaison Programs." *Police* 13, no. 2 (November–December 1968): 60–64.

Morsell, John A. "A Rationale for Racial Demonstrations. In *Police and Community Relations: A Sourcebook,* A. F. Brandstatter and Louis A. Radelet, eds., pp. 144–151. Beverly Hills, Calif.: Glencoe Press, 1968.

Moynihan, Daniel P. "The Presidency and the Press." *Commentary Magazine,* March 1971.

Mundy, Paul J. "The Implications of Population Trends for Urban Communities." In *Police and Community Relations: A Sourcebook,* A. F. Brandstatter and Louis A. Radelet, eds., pp. 66–72. Beverly Hills, Calif.: Glencoe Press, 1968.

Murphy, Patrick V. "Social Change and the Police." *Police* 16, no. 7 (March 1972): 63–66.

Myrdal, Gunnar. *An American Dilemma: The Negro Problem and Modern Democracy.* New York: Harper & Bros., 1944.

Myren, Richard A. "A Context for Crime." *Police* 13, no. 1 (September–October, 1966): 4.

———. *The Role of the Police.* Prepared for the President's Commission on Law Enforcement and Administration of Justice. Washington, D.C.: U.S. Government Printing Office, 1967.

National Center on Police and Community Relations, Michigan State University, School of Police Administration and Public Safety. *A National Survey of Police and Community Relations; Field Surveys V.* Report submitted to the President's Commission on Law Enforcement and Administration of Justice. Washington, D.C.: U.S. Government Printing Office, January 1967.

National Council on Crime and Delinquency. *Model Rules of Court on Police Action From Arrest to Arraignment.* Council of Judges, National Council on Crime and Delinquency, 1969.

———. "Preventive Detention: A Policy Statement." *Crime and Delinquency* 17, no. 1 (January 1971): 1–8.

———. "A Model Act to Provide for Minimum Standards for the Protection of Rights of Prisoners." *Crime and Delinquency* 18, no. 1 (January 1972): 4–14.

———. "The Use of Juveniles as Informers in Drug-Abuse Matters." *Crime and Delinquency* 18, no. 2 (April 1972): 129–131.

National Opinion Research Center, University of Chicago. *Criminal Victimization in the United States: A Report of a National Survey; Field Surveys II.* Report submitted to the President's Commission on Law Enforcement and Administration of Justice. Washington, D.C.: U.S. Government Printing Office, May 1967.

Nelson, Elmer K., Jr. "Community-Based Correctional Treatment: Rationale and Problems." *The Annals* 374 (November 1967): 82–91.

"New Jersey's Mobile Police Training Centers." *Police* 12, no. 6 (July–August 1968): 95–96.

Newman, Charles L. "Police and Families: Factors Affecting Police Intervention." *The Police Chief* 39, no. 3 (March 1972): 24–30.

Niederhoffer, Arthur. *Behind the Shield.* Garden City, N.Y.: Anchor Books, Doubleday & Co., 1969.

Niederhoffer, Arthur, and Abraham S. Blumberg, eds. *The Ambivalent Force: Perspectives on the Police.* Waltham, Mass.: Ginn & Co., 1970.

Novak, Michael. "The Politics of Resentment." *Commonweal* 92, no. 20 (September 1970): 481–483.

O'Gorman, Ned. "Storefront." *Columbia Forum* 13, no. 3 (Fall 1970): 5–11.

Olson, Bruce T. "Ombudsman on the West Coast: An Analysis and Evaluation of the Watchdog Function of the California Grand Jury." *Police* 12, no. 2 (November–December 1967): 12–20.

———. "Conflicts in Values in Criminal Justice: A Proposed System Analysis." *Police* 14, no. 2 (November–December 1969): 44–48.

———. "The City Policeman: Inner- or Other-Directed" *Public Personnel Review,* April 1970, pp. 102–107.

———. "Police Opinions of Work: An Exploratory Study." *The Police Chief* 38, no. 7 (July 1971): 28–38.

———. "Some Social-Psychological Sources of Tensions on Police Basic Training." *Journal of Law Enforcement Education and Training* 1, no. 1 (September 1971).

O'Neill, Hugh. "The Growth of Municipal Employee Unions." In *Unionization of Municipal Employees, Proceedings of the Academy of Political Science* 30, no. 2; Robert H. Connery and William V. Farr, eds. New York: Columbia University, 1970.

O'Neill, Michael E., and Carlton J. Bloom. "The Field Officer: Is He Really Fighting Crime?" *The Police Chief* 39, no. 2 (February 1972): 30–32.

Packer, Herbert L. "Who Can Police the Police?" *New York Review,* September 8, 1966.

———. *The Limits of the Criminal Sanction.* Palo Alto, Calif.: Stanford University Press, 1968.

Parker, L. Craig, Jr. "Self-Disclosing Behavior in Police Work." *The Police Chief* 38, no. 7 (July 1971): 44–46.

Parker, L. Craig, Jr., Sandra C. Reese, and James Murray. "Authoritarianism in Police College Students and the Effectiveness of Interpersonal Training in Reducing Dogmatism." *Journal of Law Enforcement Education and Training* 1, no. 1 (September 1971).

Parsons, Talcott, and Kenneth B. Clark, eds. *The Negro American.* Boston: Beacon Press, 1967.

Parsons, Talcott, and Edward Shils, eds. *Toward a General Theory of Action.* New York: Harper & Row, 1962.

Parsonson, R. T. "The Regional Trend in Law Enforcement." *The Police Chief* 38, no. 8 (August 1971): 26–28.

Patterson, Franklin K. *The Adolescent Citizen.* Glencoe, Ill.: Free Press, 1960.

Paulsen, Monrad G. "Police Conduct and the Public." In *Police and Community Relations: A Sourcebook,* A. F. Brandstatter and Louis A. Radelet, eds., pp. 266–272. Beverly Hills, Calif.: Glencoe Press, 1968.

Pearman, Robert. "Black Crime, Black Victims." *The Nation* 208, no. 16 (April 1969): 500–503.

Pearson, Gerald H. J. *Adolescence and Conflict of Generations.* New York: W W. Norton, 1958.

Peart, Leo E. "Management by Objectives." *The Police Chief* 38, no. 4 (April 1971): 54–56.

Pepinsky, Harold E. "A Theory of Police Reaction to Mirando v. Arizona." *Crime and Delinquency* 16, no. 4 (October 1970): 379–392.

Perlstein, Gary R. "Policewomen and Policemen: A Comparative Look." *The Police Chief* 39, no. 3 (March 1972): 72–74, and 83; and Time, May 1, 1972, p. 60.

Peters, Mildred. "A Look at Ourselves: Elements of Misunderstanding." In *Police and Community Relations: A Sourcebook,* A. F. Brandstatter and Louis A. Radelet, eds., p. 53 ff. Beverly Hills, Calif.: Glencoe Press, 1968.

Pfautz, Harold W. "The American Dilemma: Perspectives and Proposals for White Americans." In *Urban Violence,* University of Chicago Center for Policy Study, Charles W. Daly, ed. Chicago University of Chicago, 1969.

Pfiffner, John M. *The Supervision of Personnel*. 2nd ed. Englewood Cliffs, N.J.: Prentice-Hall, 1958.

———. "The Community Dimension." In *Occasional Papers: Center for Training and Career Development*. School of Public Administration, University of Southern California, April 1967.

———. "The Function of the Police in a Democratic Society." In *Occasional Papers: Center for Training and Career Development*. School of Public Administration, University of Southern California, April 1967.

———. "Needed: A Geopolitical Approach to Law Observance." In *Occasional Papers: Center for Training and Career Development*. School of Public Administration, University of Southern California, April 1967.

Pfiffner, John M., and Frank P. Sherwood. *Administrative Organization*. Englewood Cliffs, N.J.: Prentice-Hall, 1960.

Phelps, Lourn G., Jeffrey A. Schwartz, and Donald A. Liebman. "Training an Entire Patrol Division in Domestic Crisis Intervention Techniques." *The Police Chief* 38, no. 7 (July 1971): 18–19.

Pierce, Chester M., M.D. "Psychiatric Aspects of Police-Community Relations." *Mental Hygiene* 46, no. 1 (January 1962): 107–115.

Pierce, Lawrence W. "The New York City Formula: VLE (Vigorous Law Enforcement) ECP (Effective Crime Prevention) Coupled with ICI (Increased Community Involvement) Add Up to EDC (Effective Delinquency Control)." In *Police and the Changing Community: Selected Readings*, edited by Nelson A. Watson. Washington, D.C.: International Association of Chiefs of Police, 1965.

Pitchess, Peter J. "Citizen and the Law," *Journal of California Law Enforcement* (date not available), pp. 23–25.

———. "Career Development for Professional Law Enforcement." *Police* 15, no. 1 (September–October 1970): 5–10.

"Playboy Panel: Crisis in Law Enforcement." *Playboy*, March 1966, p. 47.

Poinsett, Alex. "The Dilemma of the Black Policeman." *Ebony* 24, no. 7 (May 1971): 122–131.

The Police and the Children. Liverpool, England: Office of the Chief Constable, 1962.

Police-Community Relations. California State Peace Officers' Training Series No. 79. Bureau of Vocational-Technical Education, The California Community Colleges, Sacramento, August 1968.

Pomeroy, Wesley A. "New Trends in Police Planning." *The Police Chief* 38, no. 2 (February 1971): 16–21.

Portune, Robert G. *Changing Adolescent Attitudes Toward Police*. Cincinnati, Ohio: W. H. Anderson Co., 1971.

Powledge, Fred. *Black Power, White Resistance: Notes on the New Civil War*. Cleveland: World Publishing Co., 1967.

Preiss, Jack J., and Howard J. Ehrlich. *An Examination of Role Theory: The Case of the State Police*. Lincoln, Neb.: University of Nebraska Press, 1966.

The Problem of Discipline/Control and Security in Our Schools. Position Paper No. 1. Education Advisory Committee of the National Urban League, 1971.

Pursley, Robert D. "Traditional Police Organization: A Portent of Failure?" *Police* 16, no. 2 (October 1971): 29–30.

Quinney, Richard, ed. *Crime and Justice in Society*. Boston: Little-Brown, 1969.

Radelet, Louis A. "Implications of Professionalism in Law Enforcement for Police-Community Relations." *Police*, July–August 1966.

———. "The Idea of Community." In *Police and Community Relations: A Sourcebook*, A. F. Brandstatter and Louis A. Radelet, eds., pp. 80–84. Beverly Hills, Calif.: Glencoe Press, 1968.

———. "Who's in Charge of 'Law and Order'?" *Christian Science Monitor*, December 9, 1968.

————. "Public Information and Community Relations." In *Municipal Police Administration*. International City Management Association, 1969.

————. "Attitudes Involved in Relating Community and Police." In *Proceedings of the Institute on Police-Community Relations, University of Southern California, June 1969*.

Radelet, Louis A., and Hoyt Coe Reed. *The Police and the Community: Studies.* Beverly Hills, Calif.: Glencoe Press, 1973.

Rainwater, Lee. "The Revolt of the Dirty-Workers." *Transaction,* November 1967.

Rankin, Theodore L. "PCR—Fact or Farce?" *The Police Chief* 38, no. 3 (March 1971): 62–64.

Reasons, Charles E., and Jack L. Kuykendall, eds. *Race, Crime, and Justice.* Pacific Palisades, Calif.: Goodyear Publishing Co., 1971.

Reddin, Thomas. "Operation Grass Roots." *The Police Chief* 35, no. 6 (1968): 34.

Reich, Charles A. The *Greening of America: How the Youth Revolution Is Trying to Make America Livable.* New York: Random House, 1970.

Reiser, Martin. "Psychological Research in an Urban Police Department." *Police* 16, no. 3 (November 1971): 15–18.

Reiss, Albert J., Jr. "Professionalization of the Police." In *Police and Community Relations: A Sourcebook,* A. F. Brandstatter and Louis A. Radelet, eds., pp. 215–230. Beverly Hills, Calif.: Glencoe Press, 1968.

————. *The Police and the Public.* New Haven: Yale University Press, 1971.

Reiss, Albert J., Jr., and David J. Bordua. "Environment and Organization: A Perspective on the Police." In *The Police: Six Sociological Essays,* David J. Bordua, ed., p. 33. New York: John Wiley & Sons, 1967.

Reiss, Albert J., Jr., and associates, University of Michigan. *Studies in Crime and Law Enforcement in Major Metropolitan Areas; Field Surveys III.* 2 vols. Report submitted to the President's Commission on Law Enforcement and Administration of Justice. Washington, D.C.: U.S. Government Printing Office, 1967.

Reissman, Frank. *The Culturally Deprived Child.* New York: Harper & Row, 1962.

Reith, Charles. *British Police and the Democratic Ideal.* London: Oxford University Press. 1943.

Remington, Frank J. "Social Change, the Law and the Common Good." In *Police and Community Relations: A Sourcebook,* A. F. Brandstatter and Louis A. Radelet, eds., pp. 235–241. Beverly Hills, Calif.: Glencoe Press, 1968.

Reston, James. "Student Involvement or Detachment?" *The New York Times,* November 25, 1970, p. 37.

Rohrer, John H., and Munro S. Edmonson. *Eighth Generation.* New York: Harper, 1960.

Rokeach, Milton. *The Open and Closed Mind: Investigations Into the Nature of Belief Systems and Personality Systems.* New York: Basic Books, 1960.

————. "Police and Community—As Viewed by a Psychologist." In *Police and Community Relations: A Sourcebook,* A. F. Brandstatter and Louis A. Radelet, eds., pp. 50–53. Beverly Hills, Calif.: Glencoe Press, 1968.

Rokeach, Milton, Martin G. Miller, and John A. Snyder. "The Value Gap Between Police and Policed." *Journal of Social Issues,* Winter, 1971.

Roper, Elmo. "Beyond the Riots." *Saturday Review,* October 7, 1967, pp. 24–25.

Rosenthal, Albert H. "The Ombudsman—Swedish Grievance Man." *Public Administration Review* 24, no. 4 (December 1964): 226.

Rosenfeld, Alvin A. "The Friendly Fuzz." *The Nation* 208, no. 16 (April 1969): 503–507.

Rosett, Arthur. "The Negotiated Guilty Plea." *The Annals* 374 (November 1967): 70–81.

Ross, Murray G. *Community Organization: Theory and Principle,* rev. ed. New York: Harper & Bros., 1955.

Rosten, Leo, "Who Speaks for the Young? Some Startling Facts and Fictions." *Look,* May 19, 1970, pp. 16–18.

Rothenberg, David. "Prison Is a Real Education." *The New York Times,* December 3, 1971.

Rowan, Carl T. "How Far From Slavery?" *Minneapolis Star and Tribune,* 1951.

Rowat, Donald C. "Ombudsman for North America." *Public Administration Review* 24, no. 4 (December 1964): 230.

Rowat, Donald C., ed. *The Ombudsman: Citizen's Defender.* Toronto: University of Toronto Press, 1965.

Royal Commission on the Police. Final Report. London: Her Majesty's Stationery Office, 1962.

Roye, Wendell J. *Law and Order in Classroom and Corridor.* Tipsheet No. 6, The National Center for Research and Information on Equal Educational Opportunity. Teachers College, Columbia University, November 1971.

Rubin, Jerry. *Do It!* New York: Simon & Schuster, 1970.

Rubin, Sol. "Needed—New Legislation in Correction." *Crime and Delinquency* 17, no. 4 (October 1971): 392–405.

Rustin, Bayard, et al. *Civil Disobedience,* April 1966. A publication of the Center for the Study of Democratic Institutions, Santa Barbara, Calif.

Sagarin, Edward, and Donal E. J. MacNamara. "The Problem of Entrapment." *Crime and Delinquency* 16, no. 4 (October 1970): 363–378.

Savord, George H. "Selling Law Enforcement to Your Public." *Police* 13, no. 6 (July–August 1969): 6–11.

Sax, Joseph L. "Civil Disobedience: The Law Is Never Blind." *Saturday Review,* September 26, 1968.

Schanche, Don A. *The Panther Paradox: A Liberal's Dilemma.* New York: David McKay, 1970.

Schrag, Clarence. *Crime and Justice: American Style.* Monograph series, Public Health Service Publication, National Institute of Mental Health. Washington, D.C.: U.S. Government Printing Office, 1971.

Schrag, Peter. "The Law-and-Order Issue." *Saturday Review,* November 21, 1970, p. 26.

Schur, Edwin N. *Crimes Without Victims.* Englewood Cliffs, N.J.: Prentice-Hall, 1965.

Scott, Robert H. "Problems in Communication and Cooperation in the Administration of Criminal Justice." In *Police and Community Relations: A Sourcebook,* A. F. Brandstatter and Louis A. Radelet, eds., pp. 430–435. Beverly Hills, Calif.: Glencoe Press, 1968.

Security Planning Corporation. Non-Lethal Weapons for Law Enforcement: Research Needs and Priorities. Report, March 1972, prepared for the National Science Foundation. Washington, D.C.: U.S. Government Printing Office, 1972.

Seeman, Melvin. "On the Meaning of Alienation." *American Sociological Review* 14, (December 1959): 783–791.

Senn, Milton, *A Study of Police Training Programs in Minority Relations.* Law Enforcement Committee of the Los Angeles County Conference on Community Relations, 1952.

Senior, Clarence. *Strangers Then Neighbors: From Pilgrims to Puerto Ricans.* New York: Freedom Books, Anti-Defamation League of B'nai B'rith, 1961.

Sennett, Richard. "The Cities: Fear and Hope." *The New York Times,* October 20, 1970, p. 43.

Serrin, William. "God Help Our City." *Atlantic Monthly* 223, no. 3 (March 1969): 115–121.

Shaftel, George A. and Fannie R. *Role Playing the Problem Story.* New York: National Conference of Christians and Jews, 1952.

Shannon, William V. "A New Look at the Police." *The New York Times,* September 6, 1970.

Shaw, Clifford R., Henry D. McKay, et al. *Delinquency Areas: A Study of the Distribution of School Truants, Juvenile Delinquents, and Adult Offenders in Chicago.* Chicago: University of Chicago Press, 1929.

Shellow, Robert. "The Training of Police Officers to Control Civil Rights Demonstrations." In *Minority Problems,* Arnold M. and Caroline B. Rose, eds., pp. 425–4350. New York: Harper & Row, 1965.

Sherif, Muzafer. *An Outline of Social Psychology.* New York: Harper & Row, 1948.

Sherif, Muzafer and Carolyn. *An Outline of Social Psychology,* rev. ed. New York: Harper & Row, 1948.

Shev, Edward E., and James Wright. "The Uses of Psychiatric Techniques in Selecting and Training Police Officers as Part of Their Regular Training." *Police* 15, no. 5 (May–June 1971): 13–16.

Short, James F., and Fred L. Strodtbeck. *Group Process and Gang Delinquency.* Chicago: University of Chicago Press 1965.

Siebert, Fred S., and George A. Hough, III. *Free Press and Fair Trial.* Athens, Ga.: University of Georgia Press, 1971.

Siegel, Arthur I., Philip Federman, and Douglas Schultz. *Professional Police Human Relations Training.* Springfield, Ill.: Chares C. Thomas, 1963.

Sikes, Melvin P., and Sidney E. Cleveland. "Human Relations Training for Police and Community." *American Psychologist* 23, no. 10 (October 1968): 766–769.

Silberman, Charles E. *Crisis in Black and White.* New York: Random House, 1964.

Silver, Allan. "The Demand for Order in Civil Society: A Review of Some Themes in the History of Urban Crime, Police and Riot." In *The Police: Six Sociological Essays,* David J. Bordua, ed. New York: John Wiley & Sons, 1967.

Silverman, Harold. "Police Attitudes Towards Community Relations Training." *The Police Chief* 35, no. 6 (1968): 57–59.

Simmons, Robert L. "An Answer to Trail Delay." In *Center Report,* February 1972. Center for the Study of Democratic Institutions, Santa Barbara, Calif.

Simon, Herbert A. *Administrative Service.* 2nd ed. New York: Macmillan, 1961.

Skolnick, Jerome H. *Justice Without Trial: Law Enforcement in Democratic Society.* New York: John Wiley & Sons, 1966.

———. *Professional Police in a Free Society.* New York: National Conference of Christians and Jews, 1967.

———. "The Police and the Urban Ghetto." *Research Contributions* of the American Bar Foundation, no. 3 (1968): 11.

———. *The Politics of Protest.* A Staff Report submitted to the National Commission on the Causes and Prevention of Violence. New York: Simon & Schuster, 1969.

Skolnick, Jerome H., and J. Richard Woodworth. "Bureaucracy, Information, and Social Control: A Study of a Morals Detail." In *The Police: Six Sociological Essays.* New York: John Wiley & Sons, 1967.

Skousen, W. Cleon. "Sensitivity Training—A Word of Caution." *Law and Order* 15, no. 11 (1967): 10.

Slavin, James M. "How Can Policing Become a Profession?" *Proceedings of the Fifth National Institute on Police and Community Relations,* May 25, 1959. Michigan State University.

Slingsby, Stephen. "Militants vs. Traditionalists: The New Power Struggle for the Uncommitted." *Detroit Magazine, Detroit Free Press,* September 3, 1967.

Smith, Alexander B., and Harriet Pollack. "Crimes Without Victims." *Saturday Review,* December 4, 1971, pp. 27–29.

_____. *Crime and Justice in a Mass Society*. Waltham, Mass.: Xerox College Publishing, 1972.

Smith, Leroy A. "Lateral Entry: An Inside Job." *The Police Chief* 38, no. 8 (August 1971): 52–55.

Smith, Lillian. *Killers of the Dream*. New York: W. W. Norton & Co., 1949.

Snibbe, Richard H. "A Concept for Police in Crime Prevention." *Police* 13, no. 6 (July–August 1969): 29–32.

Sower, Christopher, et al. *Community Involvement*. Glencoe, Ill.: Free Press, 1957.

Spencer, Gilmore, and Robert Nichols. "A Study of Chicago Police Recruits: Validation of Selection Procedures." *The Police Chief* 38, no. 6 (June 1971): 50–55.

Spergel, Irving. *Racketville, Slumtown, Haulberg: An Exploratory Study of Delinquent Subcultures*. Chicago: University of Chicago Press, 1964.

Spreen, Johannes F. "Police Responsibility for a Community in Turmoil." *Police* 14, no. 4 (March–April 1970).

Steele, John L. "The People's Right to Know: How Much or How Little?" *Time*, January 11, 1971. pp. 16–17.

Stein, Maurice. *The Eclipse of Community: An Interpretation of American Studies*. Princeton, N.J.: Princeton University Press, 1960.

Sterling, James W. *Changes in Role Concepts of Police Officers During Recruit Training*. Washington, D.C.: International Association of Chiefs of Police, June 1969.

Stinchcombe, Arthur L. "Institutions of Privacy in the Determination of Police Administrative Practice." *American Journal of Sociology* 69, no. 2 (September 1963): 150–161.

_____. *Rebellion in a High School*. Chicago: Quadrangle Books, 1969.

Stouffer, S. A. "An Analysis of Conflicting Social Norms." *American Sociological Review* 14 (1949): 707–717.

Stouffer, S. A., et al. *The American Soldier: Combat and Its Aftermath*. Princeton, N.J.: Princeton University Press, 1949.

Strecher, Victor G. "When Subcultures Meet: Police-Negro Relations." In *Science and Technology in Law Enforcement*, Sheldon Yefsky, ed. Chicago: Thompson Co., 1967.

_____. *The Environment of Law Enforcement: A Community Relations Guide*. Englewood Cliffs, N.J.: Prentice-Hall, 1971.

Sutherland, Edwin H., and Donald R. Cressey. *Principles of Criminology*. 7th ed. Philadelphia: J. B. Lippincott, 1966.

Sutton, Horace. "Drugs: Ten Years to Doomsday?" *Saturday Review*, November 14, 1970, p. 18.

Sykes, Gresham. *The Society of Captives: A Study of a Maximum Security Prison*. Princeton, N.J.: Princeton University Press, 1958.

Taba, Hilda, Elizabeth H. Brady, and John T. Robinson. *Intergroup Education in Public Schools*. Washington, D.C.: American Council on Education, 1952.

Tamm, Quinn. "Police Professionalism and Civil Rights." *The Police Chief* 21, no. 9 (September 1964): 30.

_____. "Objective-Performance Management Training." *The Police Chief* 39, no. 2 (February 1972): 12–13.

Taylor, Charles R., and John R. Kleberg. "A Decade of Police Training in Illinois: A Basic Police Training Course Evaluation." *Police* 13, no. 4 (March–April 1969): 28–34.

Tebbel, John. "The Stories the Newspapers *Do* Cover." *Saturday Review*, April 11, 1970, p. 66.

_____. "Press Power Revisited." *Saturday Review*, June 13, 1970, p. 53.

Terris, Bruce J. "The Role of the Police." *The Annals* 374 (November 1967).

Thomas, Paul A. "New Pressures in Corrections: A Case Study." *Police* 16, no. 1 (September 1971): 25–28.

Thompson, James R. "Supreme Court and the Police: 1968." *Journal of Criminal Law, Criminology, and Police Science* 57, no. 4 (December 1966): 425.

Thrasher, Frederick. *The Gang: A Study of 1,313 Gangs in Chicago.* Chicago: University of Chicago Press, 1927.

Tobin, Richard L. "Reporters, Subpoenas, Immunity, and the Court." *Saturday Review*, December 11, 1971, pp. 63–64.

Toch, Hans. "A Note on Police 'experience'." *Police* 11, no. 4 (March–April 1967): 87–89.

————. "Last Word on the Hippies." *The Nation* 205 (December 1967): 582–588.

————. "Cops and Blacks: Warring Minorities." *The Nation* 208, no. 16 (April 1969): 491.

————. *Violent Men: An Inquiry Into the Psychology of Violence.* Chicago: Aldine Publishing Co., 1969.

————. "Quality Control in Police Work." *Police* 16, no. 1 (September 1971): 42–44.

Toffler, Alvin. *Future Shock.* New York: Bantam Books, 1971.

Tompkins, Dorothy Campbell. *Bibliography on Juvenile Gangs in the United States Since World War II.* Berkeley: University of California, 1965.

Trager, Helen G., and Marian Badke Yarrow. *They Learn What They Live: Prejudice in Young Children.* New York: Harper & Bros., 1952.

Turner, William W. *The Police Establishment.* New York: G. P. Putnam's Sons, 1968.

Twain, David, Eleanor Harlow, and Donald Merwin. *Research and Human Services: A Guide to Collaboration for Program Development.* New York: Jewish Board of Guardians, September 1970.

Tyler, R. E. ed. *Educational Evaluation: New Roles, New Means.* Chicago: University of Chicago Press, 1969.

University of California, School of Criminology. *The Police and the Community; Field Surveys IV.* A Report to the President's Commission on Law Enforcement and Administration of Justice. Washington, D.C.: U.S. Government Printing Office, October 1966.

University of Chicago, Industrial Relations Center. *Psychological Assessment of Patrolman's Qualification in Relation to Field Performance.* Report prepared by Melanie E. Baehr, John E. Furcon, and Ernest C. Froemel for the Office of Law Enforcement Assistance, U.S. Department of Justice. Washington, D.C.: U.S. Government Printing Office, November 1968.

University of Chicago National Opinion Research Center. *Criminal Victimization in the United States: A Report of a National Survey; Field Surveys II.* A report submitted to the President's Commission on Law Enforcement and Administration of Justice. Washington, D.C.: U.S. Government Printing Office, May 1967.

University of Michigan. *Studies in Crime and Law Enforcement in Major Metropolitan Areas; Field Surveys III.* 2 vols. Report prepared by Albert J. Reiss, Jr., and associates for the President's Commission on Law Enforcement and Administration of Justice. Washington, D.C.: U.S. Government Printing Office, 1967.

U.S., Commission on Civil Rights. Reports listed are available from U.S. Government Printing Office, Washington, D.C.

The Federal Civil Rights Enforcement Effort Summary, Clearinghouse Publication no. 31, 1971.

Mexican Americans and the Administration of Justice in the Southwest, 1970. Report of the United States Commission on Civil Rights, 1959.

Who Will Wear the Badge? A Study of Minority Recuitment Efforts in Protect Services, prepared by Richard J. Margolis. Clearinghouse Publication no. 25, 1971.

U.S., Congress, House. Select Committee on Crime. Third Report, *Juvenile Justice and Corrections,* 91st Cong., 2nd sess., January 2, 1971. Washington, D.C.: U.S. Government Printing Office, 1971.

U.S., Congress, Senate. Committee on Labor and Public Welfare. *Indian Education: A National Tragedy—A National Challenge.* Washington, D.C.: U.S. Government Printing Office, 1969.

U.S., Department of Health, Education, and Welfare. Reports listed are available from U.S. Government Printing Office, Washington, D.C.

About the Poor: Some Facts and Some Fictions. Publication no. 451–1967. Prepared by Elizabeth Herzog for the Children's Bureau, 1967 and 1968.

Community-Based Correctional Programs: Models and Practices. Monograph Series, Public Health Service Publication no. 2130. National Institute of Mental Health, 1971.

Crime and Justice: American Style. Monograph Series, Public Health Service Publication. Prepared by Clarence Schrag for the National Institute of Mental Health, 1971.

Delinquency Today: A Guide for Community Action, rev. Youth Development and Delinquency Prevention Administration, 1971.

The Development of Basic Attitudes and Values Toward Government and Citizenship During the Elementary School Years. CRP 1078. Prepared by Robert Hess and Judith V. Torney for the Office of Education, Bureau of Research, 1965.

The Development of Basic Attitudes and Values Toward Government and Citizenship During the Elementary School Years. Final Report CRP 1078. Prepared by David Easton and Jack Dennis for the Office of Education, Bureau of Research, 1968.

Some Guidelines for Evaluative Research. Prepared by Elizabeth Herzog for the Children's Bureau, 1959.

Toward a Political Definition of Juvenile Delinquency. Prepared by John M. Martin for the Youth Development and Delinquency Prevention Administration, 1970.

U.S., Department of Justice. Reports listed are available from U.S. Government Printing Office, Washington, D.C.

Criminal Justice Agencies in the United States. LEAA Publication no. SD-D-1. Law Enforcement Assistance Administration, 1970.

Horatio Alger's Children. A report prepared by Richard H. Blum, et al., for the U.S. Department of Justice, 1972.

National Jail Census, 1970. Series SC-no. 1. National Criminal Justice Information and Statistics Service, Law Enforcement Assistance Administration, February 1971.

Police-Community Relations Evaluation Project. Final Report. Prepared by Lee P. Brown for the National Institute on Law Enforcement and Criminal Justice, Law Enforcement Assistance Administration, Grant NI–075, circa 1971.

Police Training and Performance Study. PR 70–4. National Institute of Law Enforcement and Criminal Justice, Law Enforcement Administration, September 1971.

Psychological Assessment of Patrolman's Qualifications in Relation to Field Performance. Report prepared by the Industrial Relations Center, University of Chicago (Melanie E. Baehr, John E. Furcon, and Ernest C. Froemel) for the Office of Law Enforcement Assistance, November 1968.

Training Police as Specialists in Family Crisis Intervention. Law Enforcement Assistance Administration, n.d.

U.S., National Advisory Commission on Civil Disorders. *Report of the National Advisory Commission on Civil Disorders.* (Kerner Report.) Washington, D.C.: U.S. Government Printing Office, 1968.

U.S., National Commission on the Causes and Prevention of Violence. Reports listed are available from U.S. Government Printing Office, Washington, D.C.

To Establish Justice, To Insure Domestic Tranquility, Commission Report, 1969.

The Politics of Protest. Staff Report of the Task Force on Violent Aspects of Protest and Confrontation, prepared by Jerome H. Skolnick, 1969.

The Commission's Task Force Reports include:

Assassination and Political Violence, 1969.

Crimes of Violence, 1969.

Firearms and Violence in American Life, 1969.

Law and Order Reconsidered, 1969.

Violence in America: Historical and Comparative Perspectives, 1969.

Violence and the Media, 1969.

U.S., National Science Foundation. *Non-Lethal Weapons for Law Enforcement: Research Needs and Priorities.* Report, March 1972, prepared by the Security Planning Corporation. Washington, D.C.: U.S. Government Printing Office, 1972.

U.S., President's Commission on Campus Unrest. *Report: Campus Unrest.* Washington, D.C.: U.S. Government Printing Office, 1970.

U.S., President's Commission on Crime in the District of Columbia. *Report of the President's Commission on Crime in the District of Columbia.* Washington, D.C.: U.S. Government Printing Office. 1966.

U.S., President's Commission on Law Enforcement and Administration of Justice. Reports listed are available from U.S. Government Printing Office, Washington, D.C.

The Challenge of Crime in a Free Society, Commission Report, 1967.

The Role of the Police. Prepared for the Commission by Richard A. Myren, 1967.

Crimes of Violence. Prepared for the Commission by Marvin E. Wolfgang, 1967.

Field Surveys I. Report on a Pilot Study in the District of Columbia on Victimization and Attitudes Toward Law Enforcement. Prepared for the Commission by the Bureau of Social Science Research, In., 1967.

Field Surveys II. Criminal Victimization in the United States: A Report of a National Survey. Prepared for the Commission by the National Opinion Research Center, University of Chicago, May 1967.

Field Surveys III. Studies in Crime and Law Enforcement in Major Metropolitan Areas. 2 vols. Prepared for the Commission by the University of Michigan, Albert J. Reiss, Jr., and associates.

Field Surveys IV. The Police and the Community. Prepared for the Commission by the University of California, School of Criminology, October 1966.

Field Surveys V. A National Survey of Police and Community Relations. Prepared for the Commission by the National Center on Police and Community Relations, Michigan State University, School of Police Administration and Public Safety, January 1967.

Task Force Report: Corrections, 1967.

Task Force Report: The Courts, 1967.

Task Force Report: The Police, 1967.

U.S., President's Committee on Civil Rights. *To Secure These Rights: The Report of the President's Committee on Civil Rights.* Washington, D.C.: U.S. Government Printing Office, 1947.

U.S., President's Task Force on Prisoner Rehabilitation. *The Criminal Offender—What Should Be Done?* Washington, D.C.: U.S. Government Printing Office, April 1970.

Vanagunas, Stanley. "Police Entry Testing and Minority Employment: Implications of a Supreme Court Decision." *The Police Chief* 39, no. 4 (April 1972): 62–64.

Van Den Haag, Ernest. "America's No. 1 Dilemma: The Breakdown of Authority." In *Reader's Digest Almanac and Yearbook*, 1970, pp. 33–42.

Vanderwicken, Peter. "The Angry Young Lawyers." *Fortune*, September 1971, p. 74.

Vickery, William E. "Educating Citizens for Democratic Intergroup Relations, 1960–1980." Chap. 9 in the *30th Yearbook of the National Council for the Social Studies,* 1960.

Wald, Patricia M. *Law and Poverty: 1965,* edited by Abram Chayes and Robert L. Wald. Working paper for the National Conference on Law and Poverty, under cosponsorship of the Attorney-General of the United States and the Director of the Office of Economic Opportunity, Washington, D.C., June 23–25, 1965. Washington, D.C.: U.S. Government Printing Office, 1965.

Walters, Douglas M. "Civil Liability for Improper Police Training." *The Police Chief* 38, no. 11 (November 1971): 28–36.

Wambaugh, Joseph. *The New Centurions.* Boston: Little, Brown & Co., 1970.

———. *The Blue Knight.* Boston: Little, Brown & Co., 1972.

Wand, Hal. "Extra Eyes and Ears for a Police Department." *Police* 13, no. 4 (March–April 1969): 96–98.

Waskow, Arthur I. "Community Control of the Police." *Transaction,* December 1969, pp. 4–7.

Wasserstein, Bruce, and Mark J. Green, eds. *With Justice for Some.* Boston: Beacon Press, 1971.

Wasserstrom, Richard, et al. *Civil Disobedience,* April 1966. A publication of the Center for the Study of Democratic Institutions, Santa Barbara, Calif.

Watson, Nelson A. *IACP Training Guides: Attitudes—A Factor in Performance; Human Relations Training for Police—A Syllabus; Improving the Officer–Citizen Contact;* and *Issues in Human Relations—Threats and Challenges.* Washington, D.C.: International Association of Chiefs of Police, n.d.

———. "Developing Guidelines for Police Practices. *The Police Chief* 31, no. 9 (September 1964): 32–39.

———. *Police-Community Relations.* Washington, D.C.: International Association of Chiefs of Police, 1966.

———. "Group Behavior and Civil Disobedience." In *Police and Community Relations: A Sourcebook,* A. F. Brandstatter and Louis A. Radelet, eds., pp. 103–113. Beverly Hills, Calif.: Glencoe Press, 1968.

Watson, Nelson, ed. *Police and the Changing Community: Selected Readings.* Washington, D.C.: International Association of Chiefs of Police, 1965.

Watson, Nelson A., and James W. Sterling. *Police and Their Opinions.* Washington, D.C.: International Association of Chiefs of Police, 1969.

Wattenberg, William W., and Noel Bufé. "The Effectiveness of Police Youth Bureau Officers." *Journal of Criminal Law, Criminology, and Police Science* 54, no. 4 (1963): 470–475.

Webb, Donald G. "Police Administrators and the Personnel Incentive Policy." *The Police Chief* 38, no. 4 (April 1971): 66–70.

Weber, Max. *Essays in Sociology.* Trans. and ed. by Hans Gerth and C. Wright Mills: New York: Oxford University Press, 1958.

Weckler, J. E., and T. E. Hall. *The Police and Minority Groups.* Chicago: The International City Managers' Association, 1944.

Weiss, C. H. "The Politicization of Evaluation Research." *Journal of Social Issues* 26 (1970): 57–68.

Wenninger, Eugene P., and John P. Clark. "A Theoretical Orientation for Police Studies." In *Juvenile Gangs in Context,* Malcolm W. Klein, ed., pp. 161–172. Englewood Cliffs, N.J.: Prentice-Hall, 1967.

Werthman, Carl, and Irving Piliavin. "Gang Members and the Police." In *The Police: Six Sociological Essays,* David J. Bordua, ed., p. 75. New York: John Wiley & Sons, 1967.

Westley, William A. "Violence and the Police." *American Journal of Sociology* 59 (July 1953): 34–41.

———. "The Escalation of Violence Through Legitimation." *The Annals* 364 (March 1966): 126.

Whisenand, Paul M. "Municipal Police Services in a Disaster Preparedness Program: A Role Analysis." *Police* 13, no. 3 (January–February 1969): 65–73.

Whisenand, Paul M., and George Felkenes. "An Ombudsman for Police: An Overview and Critical Appraisal." *The Police Chief* 34, no. 11 (1967).

Whyte, William Foote. *Street Corner Society*. Chicago: University of Chicago Press, 1943.

Wiehofen, Henry. *The Urge to Punish: New Approaches to the Problems of Mental Responsibility for Crime*. New York: Farrar, Straus, & Cudahy, 1956.

Wildstrom, Stephen H. "Mugged by the Sheriffs: An Anecdote." *The Nation* 208, no. 16 (April 1969): 496–497.

Wilensky, Harold L. "The Professionalization of Everyone." *American Journal of Sociology* 70, no. 2 (September 1964): 137–158.

Williams, Edward Bennett. *One Man's Freedom*. New York: Atheneum, 1962.

———. "What's Needed to Speed Up Justice?" *U.S. News & World Report,* September 21, 1970, pp. 94–98.

Williams, R. M., Jr. *The Reduction of Intergroup Tensions*. Social Science Research Council, 1947.

Wilson, James Q. *Negro Politics*. Glencoe, Ill.: Free Press, 1960.

———. "The Police and Their Problems: A Theory." In *Public Policy* (Yearbook of the Harvard University Graduate School of Public Administration), 1963.

———. "Police Morale, Reform and Citizen Respect: The Chicago Case." In *The Police: Six Sociological Essays,* David J. Bordua, ed., p. 158. New York: John Wiley & Sons, 1967.

———. *City Politics and Public Policy*. New York: John Wiley & Sons, 1968.

———. "Controlling the Police." *Harvard Today,* Autumn 1968.

———. "Dilemmas of Police Administration." *Public Administration Review* 28, no. 5 (September–October 1968): 407.

———. "The Patrolman's Dilemma." *New York,* September 1968, pp. 19–20.

———. *Varieties of Police Behavior: The Management of Law and Order in Eight Communities*. Cambridge: Harvard University Press, 1968.

———. "What Makes a Better Policeman?" *Atlantic Monthly* 223, no. 3 (March 1969): 131.

Wirths, Claudine Gibson. "The Development of Attitudes Toward Law Enforcement." *Police* 3, no. 2 (November–December 1958): 50–52.

Wolff, Paul, ed. *The Rule of Law*. New York: Simon & Schuster, 1971.

Wolfgang, Marvin E. *Crimes of Violence*. A report to the President's Commission on Law Enforcement and Administration of Justice. Washington, D.C.: U.S. Government Printing Office, 1967.

———. "Making the Criminal Justice System Accountable." *Crime and Delinquency* 18, no. 1 (January 1972): 15–22.

Wolfgang, Marvin E., and Bernard Cohen. *Crime and Race: Conceptions and Misconceptions*. New York: Institute of Human Relations Press, Paperback Series, 1970.

Wolfgang, Marvin E., and Franco Ferracuti. *The Subculture of Violence: Toward an Integrated Theory of Criminology.* London: Tavistock Publications, Social Science Paperback, 1967.

Wolfgang, Marvin, ed. "Patterns of Violence." *The Annals* 364 (1966): 1–248.

Yablonsky, Lewis. *The Violent Gang.* New York: Macmillan, 1962.

———. "Hippies: Their Past and Their Future." *Transaction 5,* no. 2 (December 1967).

———. *The Hippie Trip.* New York: Pegasus (Western Publishing Co.). 1968.

Young, Whitney M. *Beyond Racism.* New York: McGraw-Hill, 1969.

Zinn, Howard. *The Politics of History.* Boston: Beacon Press: 1970.

Bibliography

Items listed are primarily recent titles (since 1967) but also include a few classic works.

Adams, Thomas F. *Law Enforcement: An Introduction to the Police Role in the Community.* Englewood Cliffs, N.J.: Prentice-Hall, 1968.

Abrahamsen, David, M.D. *Our Violent Society.* New York: Funk & Wagnalls, 1970.

Ahern, James F. *Police in Trouble: Our Frightening Crisis in Law Enforcement.* New York: Hawthorne Books, 1972.

Aichorn, August. *Wayward Youth.* New York: Viking Press, 1969.

Alex, Nicholas. *Black in Blue: A Study of the Negro Policeman.* New York: Appleton-Century-Crafts, 1969.

Alexander, Rae Pace. *Young and Black in America.* New York: Random House, 1970.

Altshuler, Alan. *Community Control: The Black Demand for Participation in Large American Cities.* New York: Pegasus, 1970.

American Bar Association. *Drug Addiction: Crime or Disease?* Bloomington, Ind.: Indiana University Press. 1970.

American Civil Liberties Union. *Fifty Years of Civil Liberties: The Annual Report of the American Civil Liberties Union.* New York: Arno Press, 1970.

American Friends Service Committee. *Struggle for Justice: A Report on Crime and Punishment in America.* New York: Hill & Wang, Inc. 1971.

Anderson, Stanley V. *Ombudsmen for American Government?* Englewood Cliffs, N.J.: Prentice-Hall Spectrum Books, 1968.

712

Answers to Your Questions About American Indians. Washington, D.C.: U.S. Government Printing Office, 1969.

Anthony, Earl. *Picking up the Gun: A Report on the Black Panthers.* New York: Dial Press, 1970.

Anti-Defamation League, et al. *Negro History and Literature: A Selected Annotated Bibliography.* New York: Anti-Defamation League, 1969.

Aptheker, Herbert, ed. *Documentary History of the Negro People in the U.S. From Colonial Times to the Founding of the NAACP in 1910.* New York: Citadel Press, 1969.

Arens, Richard. *Make Mad the Guilty: The Insanity Defense in the District of Columbia.* Springfield, Ill.: Charles C. Thomas, 1969.

Arnold, William R. *Juveniles on Parole: A Sociological Perspective.* New York: Random House. 1970.

Asch, Sidney H. *Police Authority and the Rights of the Individual.* New York: Arco, 1968.

Ashley, T. Ludlow, et al. *The Quality of Inequality: Urban and Suburban Public Schools.* Chicago: Center for Police Study, University of Chicago, 1969.

Asinof, Eliot. *People vs. Blutcher.* New York: Viking Press, 1970.

Astor, Gerald. *The New York Cops.* New York: Scriber's, 1971.

Baehr, Melanie E., John E. Furcon, and Ernest C. Froemel. *Psychological Assessment of Patrolman Qualifications in Relations to Field Performance.* Washington, D.C.: Office of Law Enforcement Assistance, U.S. Department of Justice, 1968.

Bagdikian, Ben H. et al. *The Media and the Cities.* Chicago: Center for Policy Study, University of Chicago, 1969.

Baltimore Committee on the Administration of Justice Under Emergency Conditions. *Report,* Baltimore, May 31, 1968.

Banfield, Edward C. *The Unheavenly City: The Nature and Future of Our Urban Crisis.* Boston: Little, Brown, 1970.

Banton, Michael. *Race Relations.* New York: Basic Books, 1968.
———. *The Policeman in the Community.* New York: Basic Books, 1964.

Barbour, Floyd B. (ed.). *The Black Power Revolt.* Boston: Porter Sargent, 1968.
———. *The Black Seventies.* Boston: Porter Sargent, 1970.

Bassiouni, M. Cherif. *Criminal Law and Its Processes: The Law of Public Order.* Springfield, Ill.: Charles C. Thomas, 1969.
———. *The Law of Dissent and Riots.* Springfield, Ill.: Charles C. Thomas, 1971.

Bayley, David H., and Harold Mendelsohn. *Minorities and the Police: Confrontation in America.* New York: Free Press, 1969.

Becker, Harold K. *Issues in Police Administration.* Metuchen, N.J.: Scarecrow Press, 1970.

Becker, Howard S., ed. *Campus Power Struggle.* Chicago: Aldine, 1970.

Bedau, Hugo Adam. *Civil Disobedience Theory and Practice.* New York: Pegasus, 1969.

Bell, Daniel, and Irving Kristol. *Confrontation: The Student Rebellion and the Universities.* New York: Basic Books, 1969.

Bellush, Jewell and Stephen David. *Race and Politics in New York City: Six Case Studies in Policy Making.* New York: Praeger, 1970.

Berger, Peter L. and Richard J. Neuhaus. *Movement and Revolution.* Garden City, N.Y.: Doubleday, 1970.

Bergman, Peter N. *Chronological History of the Negro in America.* New York: Harper & Row, 1970.

Berkley, George E. *The Democratic Policeman.* Boston: Beacon Press, 1969.

Bersani, Carl A. *Crime and Delinquency: A Reader.* New York: Macmillan, 1970.

Berube, Maurice R., and Marilyn Gittell. *Confrontation at Ocean Hill-Brownsville: The New York School Strikes of 1968*. New York: Praeger, 1969.

Bibliography on the Urban Crisis. Washington, D.C.: U.S. Government Printing Office, 1969.

Bichel, Alexander M. *The Supreme Court and the Idea of Progress*. New York: Harper & Row, 1970.

Bierstedt, Robert. *The Social Order* 3d ed. New York: McGraw-Hill, 1970.

Birmingham, John. *Our Time Is Now*. New York: Praeger, 1970.

Bittner, Egon. *The Functions of Police in Modern Society*. Chevy Chase, Md.: National Institutes of Mental Health, 1970.

Black, Charles L. *Structure and Relationship in Constitutional Law*. Baton Rouge, La.: Louisiana State University Press, 1969.

Block, Herbert A., and Gilbert Geis. *Man, Crime, and Society*. New York: Random House, 1970.

Bloom, Leonard. *The Social Psychology of Race Relations*. Morristown, N.J.: General Learning Press, 1972.

Blumberg, Abraham S., ed. *Law and Order: The Scales of Justice*. Chicago: Aldine, 1970.

Bonger, Willem (Abridged by Turk, Austin T.) *Criminality and Economic Conditions*. Bloomington, Ind.: Indiana University Press, 1970.

Booth, Alan, and John Edwards. *Social Participation in Urban Society*. Cambridge, Mass.: Schenkman, 1970.

Bopp, William J. *The Police Rebellion*. Springfield, Ill.: Charles C. Thomas, 1971.

Bordua, David J., ed. *The Police: Six Sociological Essays*. New York: John Wiley & Sons, 1967.

Boskin, Joseph. *Urban Violence in the Twentieth Century*. Beverly Hills, Calif.: Glencoe Press. 1969.

Bosmajian, Haig, ed. *The Principles and Practices of Freedom of Speech*. Boston: Houghton Mifflin, 1970.

Bottomley, A. Keith. *Prison Before Trial*. London: G. Bell, 1970.

Bouma, Donald. *Kids and Cops*. Grand Rapids, Mich.: William B. Erdmans, 1969.

Bouma, Donald and James Hoffman. *The Dynamics of School Integration: Problems and Approaches in a Northern City*. Grand Rapids, Mich.: William B. Erdmans, 1969.

Bracey, John H., Jr. *Black Nationalism in America*. New York: Bobbs-Merrill, 1970.

Bracey, John H., Jr., August Meier, and Elliott Rudwick, eds. *Black Nationalism in America*. New York: Bobbs-Merrill, 1970.

Braden, William. *The Age of Aquarius: Technology and the Cultural Revolution*. Chicago: Quadrangle Books, 1970.

Bragdon, Henry, and John C. Pittenger. *The Pursuit of Justice*. New York: Macmillan, 1969.

Braly, Malcolm. *On the Yard*. New York: Fawcett World Library, 1969.

Brandstatter, A. F., and Allen A. Hyman. *Fundamentals of Law Enforcement*. Beverly Hills, Calif.: Glencoe Press, 1971.

Brandstatter, A. F., and Louis A. Radelet. *Police and Community Relations: A Sourcebook*. Beverly Hills, Calif.: Glencoe Press. 1968.

Brazier, Arthur, et al. *Black Self Determination: The Story of the Woodlawn Organization*. Grand Rapids, Mich.: William B. Erdmans, 1969.

Brennan, James, and Donald W. Olmstead. *Police Work With Delinquents: Analysis of a Training Program*. East Lansing: Social Sciences Research Bureau, Michigan State University, 1965.

Bromley, David G. and Charles F. Longino, *White Racism and Black America*. Morristown, N.J.: General Learning Press, 1972.

Brown, Michael. *The Politics and Anti-Politics of the Young*. Beverly Hills. Calif.: Glencoe Press, 1969.

Buckman, Peter. *The Limits of Protest*. New York: Bobbs-Merrill, 1970.

Bullock, Henry Allen. *A History of Negro Education in the South From 1619 to the Present*. Cambridge, Mass.: Harvard University Press, 1969.

Bundy, McGeorge. *Reconnection for Learning: A Community School System for New York City*. New York: Praeger, 1969.

Burby's Law Refresher Series. *Criminal Law and Procedure*, 4th ed. St. Paul, Minn.: West Publishing Co., 1969.

Burma, John H., ed. *Mexican-Americans in the U.S.: A Reader*. Cambridge, Mass.: Schenkman, 1970.

Burris, Donald S. *The Right to Treatment*. New York: Springer, 1969.

Burpo, John H. *The Police Labor Movement: Problems and Perspectives*. Springfield, Ill.: Charles C. Thomas, 1971.

Caffi, Andrea. *A Critique of Violence*. New York: Bobbs-Merrill, 1970.

Cahn, Edgar S., ed. *Our Brother's Keeper: The Indian in White America*. New York: World Publishing Co., 1969.

Califans, Joseph A., Jr. *The Student Revolution: A Global Confrontation*. New York: W. W. Norton, 1970.

Canton, Norman F. *The Age of Protest: Dissent and Rebellion in the Twentieth Century*. New York: Hawthorne Books, 1970.

Capaldi, Nicholas, ed. *Clear and Present Danger*. New York: Pegasus, 1970.

Carmichael, Stokely, and Charles V. Hamilton. *Black Power: The Politics of Liberation in America*. New York: Vintage Books. 1967.

Carney, Frank J., Hans W. Mattick, and John A. Callaway. *Action on the Streets: A Handbook for Inner City Youth Work*. New York: Association Press, 1969.

Carter, Robert, and Leslie T. Wilkins. *Probation and Parole: Selected Reading*. New York: John Wiley & Sons, 1970.

Center for the Study of Democratic Institutions. *The Establishment and All That*. Santa Barbara, Calif.: The Center for the Study of Democratic Institutions, 1970.

Cerrantes, Lucius F. *The Dropout: Causes and Cures*. Ann Arbor, Mich.: University of Michigan Press, 1969.

Chace, William, and Peter Collier. *Justice Denied: The Black Man in White America*. Chicago: Harcourt, Brace & World, 1970.

Challenge of Crime in a Free Society. President's Commission on Law Enforcement and Administration of Justice. Washington, D.C.: U.S. Government Printing Office, 1967.

Chambliss, William J. *Crime and the Legal Process*. New York: McGraw-Hill, 1968.

Chametzky, Jules, and Sidney Kaplan. *Black and White in American Culture*. Amherst, Mass.: University of Massachusetts Press, 1970.

Chevigny, Paul. *Police Power*. New York: Pantheon, 1969.

Chitty, Elizabeth N., and Ben Arthur. *Ely: Too Black, Too White*. Amherst, Mass.: University of Massachusetts Press, 1970.

Cicourel, Aaron V. *The Social Organization of Juvenile Justice*. New York: John Wiley & Sons, 1968.

Civil Disorders After Action Reports. Washington, D.C.: International Association of Chiefs of Police, Professional Standards Division, 1968.

Clark, N. Terry. *Community Structure, Power, and Decision-Making: Comparative Analyses*. San Francisco: Chandler, 1968.

Clark, Ramsey. *Crime in America*. New York: Simon & Schuster, 1970.

Clark, Thomas D. *The Emerging South*. 2d ed. New York: Oxford University Press, 1969.

Clarke, John Henrik. *Malcolm X: The Man and His Time.* New York: Macmillan, 1969.

Clavir, Judy, and John Spitzer, eds. *The Conspiracy Trial.* New York: Bobbs-Merrill, 1970.

Cleaver, Eldridge. *Soul on Ice.* New York: McGraw-Hill, 1968.

Coffey, Alan, Edward Eldefonso, and Walter Hartinger. *Human Relations: Law Enforcement in a Changing Community.* Englewood Cliffs, N.J.: Prentice-Hall, 1971.

————. *Police-Community Relations.* Englewood Cliffs, N.J.: Prentice-Hall, 1971.

Cohen, Bruce J., ed. *Crime in America.* Itasca, Ill.: Peacock, 1970.

Cohen, Nathan, ed. *The Los Angeles Riots: A Socio-Psychological Study.* New York: Praeger, 1970.

Cohen, Stanley A. *A Law Enforcement Guide to United States Supreme Court Decisions.* Springfield, Ill.: Charles C. Thomas, 1971.

Cole, Jonathan O. and J. R. Wittenborn. *Drug Abuse: Social and Psychopharmacological Effects.* Springfield, Ill.: Charles C. Thomas, 1969.

College Volunteers, A Guide to Action: Helping Students Help Others. Washington, D.C.: U.S. Government Printing Office, 1969.

Comer, James P., M.D. *Beyond Black and White.* New York: New York *Times* Co., 1972.

Commission on Community Interrelations. *Survey on Preparations for Urban Violence and Appendix: Special Study on Preparations for Urban Violence.* New York: American Jewish Congress, 1968.

Commission on Human Rights. *To Continue Action for Human Rights: Federal Report.* Washington, D.C.: U.S. Government Printing Office, 1969.

Committee for Economic Development. *Training and Jobs for the Urban Poor.* New York: Committee for Economic Development, 477 Madison Avenue, New York: 10022, 1970.

Conant, Ralph W. *The Prospects for Revolution.* New York: Harper & Row, 1971.

Conant, Ralph W., and Molly Apple Levin, eds. *Problems in Research on Community Violence.* New York: Praeger, 1969.

Connery, Robert H. and Caraley Demetrios, eds. *Governing the City: Challenges and Options for New York.* New York: Praeger, 1969.

Conrad, Earl. *The Invention of the Negro.* New York: Paul S. Erickson, 1969.

Correctional Institutions, vol. 2. Washington, D.C.: U.S. Government Printing Office, 1969.

Corson, William R. *Promise or Peril: The Black College Student in America.* New York: W. W. Norton, 1970.

Cousens, Frances Reissman. *Public Civil Rights Agencies and Fair Employment: Promise and Performance.* New York: Praeger, 1969.

Cray, Ed. *The Enemy in the Streets: Police Malpractice in America.* New York: Doubleday Anchor Books, 1972.

Cressey, Donald R., and David A. Ward. *Delinquency, Crime, and Social Process.* New York: Harper & Row, 1969.

Crime Commission of Philadelphia. *Attack on Crime: Design of a Regional Approach to Law Enforcement in the Delaware Valley.* Philadelphia: Crime Commission of Philadelphia (mimeo), 1969.

Crime Commission of Philadelphia. *Violence Today: A Judicial Concern (Proceedings of the 4th Judicial Sentencing Institute, Redford, Pa., 1968).* Philadelphia: Crime Commission of Philadelphia, 1969.

Critchley, T. A. *The Conquest of Violence: Order and Liberty in Britain.* New York: Schocken Books, 1970.

Cruickshank, William M., James L. Paul, and John B. Junkala. *Misfits in the Public Schools.* Syracuse, N.Y.: Syracuse University Press, 1969.

Cumming, Elaine. *Systems of Social Regulation.* New York: Atherton Press, 1968.

Dawson, Robert O. *Sentencing.* (From American Bar Association Administration of Criminal Justice Series). Boston: Little, Brown, 1969.

Deloria, Vine, Jr. *We Talk, You Listen: New Tribes, New Turf.* New York: Macmillan, 1970.

Dentler, Robert A. *American Community Problems.* New York: McGraw-Hill, 1968.

DeTocqueville, Alexis. *Democracy in America.* 2 vols. New York: Schocken Books, 1970.

Detroit Urban League. *A Survey of Attitudes of Detroit Negroes After the Riot of 1967.* Detroit: The Detroit Urban League, 208 Mack Avenue, Detroit, Michigan, 1967.

Dinitz, Simon, Russell R. Dynes, and Alfred C. Clarke, eds. *Deviance: Studies in the Process of Stigmatization and Societal Reaction.* New York: Oxford University Press. 1969.

Dinitz, Simon and Walter Reckless. *Critical Issues in the Study of Crime.* New York: Little, Brown, 1968.

Downs, Anthony. *Who Are the Urban Poor?* New York: Committee for Economic Development, 1970.

Draper, Theodore. *The Rediscovery of Black Nationalism.* New York: Viking Press, 1970.

Dressler, David. *Practice and Theory of Probation and Parole.* New York: Columbia University Press, 1970.

Drucker, Peter F. *The Age of Discontinuity: Guidelines to Our Changing Society.* New York: Harper & Row, 1970.

Drug Dependence—Youth in Rebellion. Washington, D.C.: U.S. Government Printing Office, 1969.

DuBois, W.E.B. *Dusk of Dawn: An Essay Toward an Autobiography of a Race Concept.* New York': Schocken Books, 1969.

Durham, Lewis E., Jack R. Gibbs, and Eric S. Knowles. *A Bibliography of Research —Explorations in Human Relations Training and Research.* Washington, D.C.: National Institute for Applied Behavioral Science, 1967.

Dymally, Mervyn M. *The Black Man in American Politics.* New York: Praeger, 1970.

Earle, Howard H. *Police-Community Relations: Crisis in Our Time,* 2d ed. Springfield, Ill.: Charles C. Thomas, 1970.

————. *Student-Instructor Guide on Police-Community Relations.* Springfield, Ill.: Charles C. Thomas, 1970.

Edwards, George. *The Police on the Urban Frontier: A Guide to Community Understanding.* New York: Institute of Human Relations Press, The American Jewish Committee, 1968.

Eisner, Victor. *The Delinquency Label: The Epidemiology of Juvenile Delinquency.* New York: Random House, 1968.

Eldefonso, Edward. *Youth Problems and Law Enforcement.* Englewood Cliffs, N.J.: Prentice-Hall, 1972.

Eldefonso, Edward, Alan Coffey, and Richard C. Grace. *Principles of Law Enforcement.* New York: John Wiley & Sons, 1968.

Elliott, J. F. and Thomas J. Sardino. *Crime Control Team: An Experiment in Municipal Police Department Management and Operations.* Springfield, Ill.: Charles C. Thomas, 1971.

Ellis, William W. *White Ethics and Black Power: The Emergence of the West Side Organization.* Chicago: Aldine, 1969.

Emerson, Robert E. *Judging Delinquents: Context and Process in Juvenile Court.* Chicago: Aldine, 1969.

Empey, LaMar T. *The Silverlake Experiment: Testing Delinquency Theory and Community Intervention.* Chicago: Aldine, 1971.

Empey, LaMar T. and Steven G. Lubeck. *Delinquency Prevention Strategies.* Washington, D.C.: U.S. Government Printing Office, 1970.

Endleman, Shalom. *Violence in the Streets.* Chicago: Quadrangle Books, 1970.

Epstein, Charlotte. *Intergroup Relations for Police Officers.* Baltimore, Md.: Williams and Wilkins, 1962.

Epstein, Jason. *The Great Conspiracy Trial.* New York: Random House, 1970.

Equal Opportunity: A Bibliography of Research on Equal Opportunity in Housing. Washington, D.C.: U.S. Government Printing Office, 1969.

Erber, Ernest, ed. *Urban Planning in Transition.* New York: Viking Press, 1969.

Etzkowitz, Henry, and Gerald M. Schaflander. *Ghetto Crisis: Riots or Reconciliation?* Boston: Little, Brown, 1969.

Evard, Franklin H. *Successful Parole.* Springfield, Ill.: Charles C. Thomas, 1971.

Eyman, Joy S. *Prisons for Women: A Practical Guide for Administrative Problems.* Springfield, Ill.: Charles C. Thomas, 1971.

Fager, Charles E. *White Reflections on Black Power.* Grand Rapids, Mich.: William B. Eerdmans, 1968.

Fantini, Mario, Marilyn Gittell, and Richard Magat. *Community Control and the Urban School.* New York: Praeger, 1970.

Finn, James, ed. *A Conflict of Loyalties: The Case for Selective Conscientious Objection.* New York: Pegasus, 1969.

Flammang, C. J. *The Police and the Underprotected Child.* Springfield, Ill.: Charles C. Thomas, 1970.

Foley, James A., and Robert K. Foley. *The College Scene: Students Tell It Like It Is.* New York: Cowles Book, 1970.

Forer, Lois G. *No One Will Listen: An Indictment of the Juvenile Court System.* New York: John Day, 1970.

Fort, Joel. *The Pleasure Seekers: The Drug Crisis, Youth and Society.* Indianapolis, Ind.: Bobbs-Merrill, 1970.

Fortas, Abe. *Concerning Dissent and Civil Disobedience—We Have an Alternative to Violence.* New York: Signet Books, New American Library, 1968.

Fox, Vernon B. *Guidelines for Corrections Programs in Community and Junior Colleges.* Washington, D.C.: American Association of Junior Colleges, 1969.

Frazier, Thomas R. *Afro-American History.* Chicago: Harcourt, Brace & World, 1970.

Freeman, Howard, and Norman R. Kurtz, eds. *America's Troubles: A Casebook in Social Conflict.* Englewood Cliffs, N.J.: Prentice-Hall, 1969.

Freeman, Linton C., and Morris H. Sunshine. *Patterns of Residential Segregation.* Cambridge, Mass.: Schenkman, 1969.

Friendly, Alfred, and Ronald Goldfarb. *Crime and Publicity: The Impact of News on the Administration of Justice.* New York: Twentieth Century Fund, 1967.

Galarza, Gallegos, and Samora. *Mexican Americans of the Southwest.* New York: Anti-Defamation League, 1969.

Ganz, Alan S., Hans W. Mattick, Kenneth J. Northcott, and Jerome H. Skolnick. *The Cities and the Police.* Chicago: The University of Chicago Round Table, 1968.

Garabedian, Peter G., and Don C. Gibbons, eds. *Becoming Delinquent: Correctional Process and Delinquent Careers.* Chicago: Aldine, 1970.

Gardiner, John A. *Traffic and the Police: Variations in the Law Enforcement Policy.* Cambridge, Mass.: Harvard University Press, 1969.

Gardner, Erle Stanley. *Cops on Campus and Crime in the Streets.* New York: William Morrow, 1970.

Garn, Stanley M. *Human Races.* 2d ed. Springfield, Ill.: Chares C. Thomas, 1969.

Gawthrop, Louis C., ed. *The Administrative Process and Democratic Theory.* Boston: Houghton Mifflin, 1970.

Gayle, Addison, J. *The Black Situation.* New York: Horizon Press, 1970.

Gaylin, Willard, M.D. *In the Service of Their Country (War Resistors in Prison).* New York: Viking Press, 1970.

Gellhorn, Walter. *When Americans Complain: Governmental Grievance Procedures.* Cambridge, Mass.: Harvard University Press, 1966.

George, B. J., Jr. *Gault and the Juvenile Court.* Ann Arbor, Mich.: Institute of Continuing Legal Education, 1967.

Germann, A. C., Frank D. Day, and Robert G. Gallati. *Introduction to Law Enforcement.* rev. ed. Springfield, Ill.: Charles C. Thomas, 1969.

Gibbons, Don C. *Delinquent Behavior.* Englewood Cliffs, N.J.: Prentice-Hall, 1970.

———. *Society, Crime, and Criminal Careers: An Introduction to Criminology.* Englewood Cliffs, N.J.: Prentice-Hall, 1968.

Gibson, William M. *Lessons in Conflict: Legal Education Materials for Secondary Schools.* Boston: Boston School of Law, 1970.

Gilbert, Ben W. and The Staff of the Washington Post. *Ten Blocks From the White House: Anatomy of the Washington Riots of 1968.* New York: Frederick A. Praeger, 1968.

Gittell, Marilyn and Alan G. Hevesi. *The Politics of Urban Education.* New York: Frederick A. Praeger, 1969.

Glaser, Daniel, ed. *Crime in the City.* New York: Harper & Row, 1970.

Gold, Martin. *Delinquent Behaviors in an American City.* Belmont, Calif.: Brooks-Cole, 1970.

Goldberg, W. A. *Guide to Corrections.* East Lansing, Mich.: (mimeo) Available Gibson's Book Store, 128 W. Grand River, 1969.

Goldman, Nathan. *The Differential Selection of Juvenile Offenders for Court Appearance.* Paramus, N.J.: National Council on Crime and Delinquency, 1968.

Goldman, Peter. *Report from Black America.* New York: Simon & Schuster, 1970.

Goldstein, Joseph E., ed. *Crime, Law and Society: A Collection of Essays on Insanity as a Legal Defense.* Detroit: Detroit Free Press, Oct. 1970.

Gossett, Thomas F. *Race, The History of an Idea in America.* New York: Schocken Books. 1969.

Gourley, G. Douglas, *Effective Municipal Police Organization.* Beverly Hills, Calif.: Glencoe Press, 1971.

———. *Public Relations and the Police.* Springfield, Ill.: Charles C. Thomas, 1953.

Grad, Frank P. *Alcoholism and the Law.* Dobbs Ferry, N.Y.: Oceana Publications, 1970.

Graham, Hugh Davis and Ted Robert Gurr, eds. *The History of Violence in America—Historical and Comparative Perspectives.* New York: Frederick A. Praeger, 1969.

Green, Robert L., ed. *Racial Crisis in American Education.* Chicago: Follett, 1970.

Greenberg, Harold. *Social Environment and Behavior.* Cambridge, Mass.: Schenkman, 1970.

Grier, William H., and Price M. Cobbs, *Black Rage.* New York: Basic Books, 1968.

Griffin, John Howard. *The Church and the Black Man.* Dayton, Ohio: Pflaum, 1970.

Grimshaw, Allen D., ed. *Racial Violence in the United States.* Chicago: Aldine–Atherton, 1971.

Grosman, Brian A. *The Prosecutor.* Toronto: University of Toronto Press, 1970.

Grupp, Stanley E. *Theories of Punishment.* Bloomington, Ill.: Indiana University Press, 1972.

Hacker, Andrew. *The End of the American Era.* New York: Atheneum, 1970.

Hadden, Jeffrey K., Louis H. Masotti, Kenneth Seminatore, and Jerome Corsi. *A Time to Burn? An Evaluation of the Present Crisis in Race Relations.* Chicago: Rand McNally, 1969.

Hannerz, Ulf. *Soulside: Inquiries Into Ghetto Culture and Community.* New York: Columbia University Press, 1970.

Hansen, David A., and Thomas R. Culley. *The Police Leader.* Springfield, Ill.: Charles C. Thomas, 1971.

Hapgood, Hutchins. *The Spirit of the Ghetto: Studies of the Jewish Quarter of New York.* New York: Schocken Books, 1970.

Hare, Nathan. *The Black Anglo-Saxons.* New York: Macmillan, 1970.

Harris, M. A. (Spike). *A Negro History Tour of Manhattan.* Westport, Conn.: Greenwood, 1969.

Harris, M. A. and Morriss Levitt. *Teachers Guide to a Negro History Tour of Manhattan.* Westport, Conn.: Greenwood, 1970.

Harris, Richard. *Justice: The Crisis of Law, Order and Freedom in America.* New York: E. P. Dutton, 1970.

————. *The Fear of Crime.* New York: Frederick A. Praeger, 1969.

Haskins, James. *Diary of a Harlem Schoolteacher.* New York: Grove Press, 1970.

Hazard, Geoffrey C. *Law in a Changing America.* Englewood Cliffs, N.J.: Prentice-Hall, 1969.

Heidt, Sarajane and Amitai Etzioni, eds. *Societal Guidance: A New Approach to Social Problems.* New York: Thomas Y. Crowell, 1969.

Helfer, Ray E., M.D. and Henry Kempe, M.D. *The Battered Child.* Chicago: University of Chicago Press, 1968.

Henderson, David: *De Mayor of Harlem.* New York: E. P. Dutton, 1970.

Hendin, Herbert. *Black Suicide.* New York: Basic Books, 1969.

Hentoff, Nat, ed. *Black Anti-Semitism and Jewish Racism.* Woodbury, N.Y.: Barron's Educational Series, 1970.

Hernandez, Luis F. *The Forgotten American.* New York: Anti-Defamation League, 1969.

Hersey, John. *The Algiers Motel Incident.* New York: Alfred A. Knopf, 1968.

Hewitt, William H., and Charles L. Newman. *Police-Community Relations: An Anthology and a Bibliography.* Mineola, N.Y.: Foundation Press, 1970.

Heyer, Monte. *Am I a Racist?* New York: Association Press, 1970.

Hill, Albert Fay. *The North Avenue Irregulars.* New York: Cowles, 1968.

Hirschi, Travis. *Causes of Delinquency.* Berkeley: University of California Press, 1969.

Hofstadter, Richard, and Michael Wallace, eds. *American Violence: A Documentary History.* New York: Alfred A. Knopf, 1970.

Holcomb, Richard L. *The Police and the Public.* Springfield, Ill.: Charles C. Thomas, 1969.

Hook, Sidney. *Academic Freedom and Academic Anarchy.* New York: Cowles Book, 1969.

Hoover, J. Edgar. *Communism—History and Evaluation in the U.S.* New York: Random House, 1969.

Hormachea, C. R., and M. Hormachea. *Confrontation: Violence and the Police.* Boston: Holbrook Press, (Allyn & Bacon), 1971.

Horwitz, John J. *Team Practice and the Specialist: An Introduction to Interdisciplinary Teamwork.* Springfield, Ill.: Charles C. Thomas, 1970.

Howard, John R., ed. *The Awakening Minorities: American Indians, Mexican-Americans, and Puerto Ricans.* Chicago. Aldine Publishing Co., 1970.

Iannone, Nathan F. *Supervision of Police Personnel.* Englewood Cliffs, N.J.: Prentice-Hall, 1970.

Inbau, Fred E., and James R. Thompson. *Administration of Criminal Justice*. Mineola, New York: Foundation Press, 1970.

Indian Education: *A National Tragedy—A National Challenge*. Washington, D.C.: U.S. Government Printing Office, 1969.

Institute for the Study of Crime and Delinquency. *The Non-Prison*: *A New Approach to Treating Youthful Offenders*. St. Paul, Minn.: Bruce Publishing Co., 1970.

Institute for Training in Municipal Administration. *Municipal Police Administration* (*A Manual*), 6th ed. Washington, D.C.: International City Management Association, 1969.

Institute of Criminal Law and Procedure. *Rehabilitation Planning Services for the Criminal Defense*. Washington, D.C.: U.S. Government Printing Office, 1970.

Institute of Social, Economic and Government Research. *Survey Manual for Comprehensive Urban Planning*: *The Use of Opinion Surveys and Sampling Techniques in Planning Process*. Fairbanks, Alaska: University of Alaska Press, 1969.

Jackson, Percival E. *Dissent in the Supreme Court*. Norman, Okla.: University of Oklahoma Press, 1969.

Jacobs, Paul. *Prelude to Riot*: *A View of Urban America From the Bottom*. New York: Random House, 1968.

James, Howard. *Children in Trouble*. New York: David McKay, 1970.

————. *Crisis in the Courts*. New York: David McKay, 1968.

Janowitz, Morris. *Social Control of Escalated Riots*. Chicago: The University of Chicago Center for Policy Study, 1968.

Jemilo, Robert F. *A Ten Point Program on Police-Community Relations*: *Planned Aggressive Prevention*. Chicago: The Young Men's Christian Association of Metropolitan Chicago, 1966.

Johnson, Elmer Hubert. *Crime, Correction and Society*. rev. ed. Homewood, Ill.: Dorsey Press, 1969.

Johnston, Norman, Leonard Savitz, and Marvin E. Wolfgang, eds. *The Sociology of Punishment & Corrections*. New York: John Wiley & Sons, 1970.

Jordan, Philip D. *Frontier Law and Order*. Lincoln, Neb.: University of Nebraska Press, 1970.

July, Robert W. *A History of the African People*. New York: Charles Scribner's Sons, 1970.

Justice, Blair. *Assessing Potentials for Racial Violence*. Houston: Rice University, 1968.

Kahn, Roger. *The Battle for Morningside Heights*: *Why Students Rebel*. New York: William Morrow, 1970.

Kain, John F. *Race and Poverty*: *The Economics of Discrimination*. Englewood Cliffs, N.J.: Prentice-Hall, 1969.

Kavolis, Vytautas. *Comparative Perspectives on Social Problems*. Boston: Little, Brown, 1969.

Kay, Barbara A., and Clyde B. Vedder. *Probation and Parole*. Springfield, Ill.: Charles C. Thomas, 1969.

Keating, Edward M. *Free Huey! The Murder Trial of Black Panther Leader Huey Newton*. New York: E. P. Dutton, 1970.

Keller, Oliver J. Jr., and Benedict S. Alper. *Halfway Houses*: *Community-Centered Correction and Treatment*. Lexington, Mass.: D.C. Heath, 1970.

Kelman, Steven. *Push Comes to Shove*: *The Escalation of Student Protest*. Boston: Houghton Mifflin, 1970.

Kenney, John P. *Police Administration*. Springfield, Ill.: Charles C. Thomas, 1972.

Kenney, John P., and Dan G. Pursuit. *Police Work With Juveniles*. Springfield, Ill.: Charles C. Thomas, 1969.

Klein, Herbert T. *The Police: Damned If They Do—Damned If They Don't.* New York: Brown Publishers, 1969.

Klein, Malcolm W., and Barbara G. Myerhoff, eds. *Juvenile Gangs in Context: Theory Research and Action.* Englewood Cliffs, N.J.: Prentice-Hall, 1967.

Klotter, John C. *Constitutional Law for Police.* Cincinnati: W. H. Anderson, 1970.

Knight, Etheridge. *Black Voices From Prison.* New York: Pathfinder Press, 1970.

Knopf, Terry Ann. *Youth Patrols: An Experiment in Community Participation.* Waltham, Mass.: Brandeis University, the Lemberg Center for the Study of Violence, 1969.

Knowles, Louis, and Kenneth Prewitt. *Institutional Racism in America.* Englewood Cliffs, N.J.: Prentice-Hall, 1969.

Knudten, Richard D. and Stephen Schafer. *Juvenile Delinquency: A Reader.* New York: Random House, 1970.

Kobetz, Robert W. *The Police Role and Juvenile Delinquency.* Gaithersberg, Md.: International Association of Chiefs of Police, 1971.

Kruger, Daniel H., and Charles T. Schmidt, Jr. *Collective Bargaining in Public Service.* New York: Random House, 1969.

Kurland, Philip. *The Supreme Court Review 1969* (Decisions of the year with analyses). Chicago: University of Chicago Press, 1970.

Lambert, John R. *Crime, Police and Race Relations.* New York: Oxford University Press, 1970.

Lansberry, J. Robert. *Introduction to Criminal Justice.* Santa Cruz, Calif.: Davis Publishing Co., 1968.

Lasch, Christopher. *The Agony of the American Left—Protest Without A Problem.* New York: Random House, 1969.

Laurence, John. *History of Capital Punishment.* New York: Citadel Press, 1932/1969.

Law Enforcement Assistance Administration, U.S. Department of Justice. *A Look at Criminal Justice Research* (technological). Washington, D.C.: U.S. Government Printing Office, 1971.

Law-Medicine Institute, Boston University. *Police-Community Relations Project: Pilot Project.* Boston: Boston University, Law-Medicine Institute, Training Center in Youth Development, 1966.

Lawler, Irvin D. *Training Program in Human Relations for Cadet and In-Service Officers.* Detroit: Detroit Police Department, 1952.

Lecky, Robert S., and H. Elliott Wright. *Black Manifesto: Religion, Racism and Reparation.* New York: Sheed & Ward, 1970.

Lee, Alfred McClung, and Norman D. Humphrey. *Race Riot: Detroit, 1943.* New York: Octagon, 1968.

LeMelle, Tilden J., and Wilbert J. LeMelle. *The Black College: A Strategy for Relevancy.* New York: Praeger, 1969.

Leonard, V. A. *The Police Communications System.* Springfield, Ill.: Charles C. Thomas, 1970.

———. *Police Crime Prevention.* Springfield, Ill.: Charles C. Thomas, 1971.

———. *The Police Enterprise: Its Organization and Management.* Springfield, Ill.: Charles C. Thomas, 1969.

———. *The Police, the Judiciary, and the Criminal.* Springfield, Ill.: Charles C. Thomas, 1969.

Lerman, Paul, ed. *Delinquency and Social Policy.* New York: Praeger, 1970.

Liebow, Elliot. *Tally's Corner: A Study of Negro Streetcorner Men.* Boston: Little, Brown, 1968.

Lincoln, C. Eric, ed. *Martin Luther King, Jr.* New York: Hill & Wang, 1970.

Lincoln, James. *Anatomy of a Riot.* New York: McGraw-Hill, 1968.

Lindesmith, Alfred R. *The Addict and the Law*. Bloomington, Ind.: Indiana University Press, 1970.

Lipset, Seymour Martin. *Rebellion in the University*. Boston: Little, Brown, 1972.

Lipset, Seymour Martin, and P. G. Altbach, eds. *Students in Revolt*. Boston: Houghton Mifflin, 1970.

Lipsky, Michael, ed. *Law and Order: Police Encounters*. Chicago: Aldine, 1970.

Locke, Hubert G. *The Detroit Riot of 1967*. Detroit: Wayne State University Press, 1969.

Lofland, John. *Deviance and Identity*. Englewood Cliffs, N.J.: Prentice-Hall, 1969.

Lohman, Joseph D. *The Police and Minority Groups*. Chicago: Chicago Park Police, 1947.

Lohman, Joseph D., and Gordon E. Misner. *The Police and the Community: The Dynamics of Their Relationship in a Changing Society; Field Surveys IV*. Vols. 1, 2. Washington, D.C.: U.S. Government Printing Office, 1967.

Lohman, Joseph D., James T. Carey, Joel Goldfarb, and Michael J. Rowe. *The Handling of Juveniles From Offense to Disposition*. 7 vols. Berkeley, Calif.: University of California School of Criminology, 1965.

London *Times* News Team. *The Black Man In Search of Power*. Camden, N.J.: Thomas Nelson, 1969.

Ludwig, Frederick J. *Supreme Court Decisions and Law Enforcement*. Dobbs Ferry, N.Y.: Oceana Publications, 1969.

Lystad, Mary H. *The College Scene and Changing Social Values*. Morristown, N.J.: General Learning Press, 1972.

Mack, Raymond W. *Prejudice and Race Relations*. Chicago: Quadrangle Books, 1970.

MacNamara, Donal E. *Perspectives on Correction*. New York: Thomas Y. Crowell, 1971.

Mapp, Edward C. *Blacks in American Films: Today and Yesterday*. Metuchen, N.J.: Scarecrow Press, 1972.

Martin, John M., Joseph P. Fitzpatrick and Robert E. Gould. *The Analysis of Delinquent Behavior: A Structural Approach*. New York: Random House, 1970.

Masotti, Louis H. and Don R. Bowen. *Riots and Rebellion: Civil Violence in the Urban Community*. Beverly Hills, Calif.: Sage Publications, 1968.

Masotti, Louis H. and Jerome Corsi. *Shoot-Out in Cleveland: Black Militants and the Police, July 23, 1968*. New York: Praeger, 1969.

Matthiessen, Peter. *Sal Si Puedes: Cesar Chavez and the New American Revolution*. New York: Random House, 1970.

————. *The New American Revolution*. New York: Random House, 1970.

Matza, David. *Becoming Deviant*. Englewood Cliffs, N.J.: Prentice-Hall, 1969.

Maxwell, James A. *Financing State and Local Governments*. Washington, D.C.: Brookings Institution, 1969.

Meier, August, ed. *Black Experience 2: The Transformation of Activism*. Chicago: Aldine, 1970.

Messner, Gerald. *Another View: To Be Black in America*. Chicago: Harcourt, Brace & World, 1970.

Methvin, Eugene H. *The Riot Makers*. New Rochelle, N.Y.: Arlington House, 1970.

Meyerson, Martin, ed. *The Conscience of the City*. New York: George Braziller, 1970.

Middleton, John. *Black Africa: Its People and Cultures Today*. New York: Macmillan, 1970.

Milio, Nancy. *9226 Kercheval: The Storefront That Did Not Burn*. Ann Arbor, Mich.: University of Michigan Press, 1970.

Miller, Derek. *Growth to Freedom: The Psychological Treatment of Delinquent Youth*. Bloomington, Ind.: Indiana University Press, 1970.

Miller, Kelly. *Radicals and Conservatives and Others on the Negro in America.* New York: Schocken Books, 1970.

Milner, Neal A. *The Court and Law Enforcement: The Impact of Miranda.* Beverly Hills, Calif.: Sage Publications, 1971.

Minton, Robert J. *Inside: Prison American Style.* New York: Random House, 1971.

Mitchell, J. Paul. *Race Riots in Black and White.* Englewood Cliffs, N.J.: Prentice-Hall, 1970.

Momboisse, Raymond M. *Blueprint of Revolution: The Rebel, The Party, the Techniques of Revolt.* Springfield, Ill.: Charles C. Thomas, 1970.

————. *Community Relations and Riot Prevention.* Springfield, Ill.: Charles C. Thomas, 1970.

————. *Riots, Revolts and Insurrections.* Springfield, Ill.: Charles C. Thomas, 1970.

Moore, Chuck (As told to). *I Was a Black Panther.* New York: Doubleday & Co., 1970.

Morgan, John S. *The Negro Breakthrough.* New York: Macmillan, 1970.

Morison, Samuel Eliot, Frederick Merk, and Frank Freidel. *Dissent in Three American Wars.* Cambridge, Mass.: Harvard University Press, 1970.

Morris, Joe Alex. *First Offender: A Volunteer Program for Youth in Trouble With the Law.* New York: Funk & Wagnalls, 1970.

Morris, Norval, and Gordon Hawkins. *The Honest Politician's Guide to Crime Control.* Chicago: University of Chicago Press, 1970.

Moynihan, Daniel Patrick. *Maximum Feasible Misunderstanding: Community Action in the War on Poverty.* New York: Free Press, 1969.

————. *Toward a National Urban Policy.* New York: Basic Books, 1970.

————. *Violent Crime: The Challenge to Our Cities. The Report of the National Commission on the Causes and Prevention of Violence.* New York: George Braziller, 1970.

Murphy, Thomas P., and F. Gerald Brown. *Emerging Patterns in Urban Administration.* Lexington, Mass.: Heath Lexington Books, D. C. Heath Co., 1970.

Murray, Albert. *The Omni-Americans: New Perspectives on Black Experience and American Culture.* New York: E. P. Dutton, 1970.

Murton, Thomas, and Joseph Hyams. *Accomplices to the Crime: The Arkansas Prison Scandal.* New York: Grove Press, 1969.

Muse, Benjamin. *The American Negro Revolution: From Non-Violence to Black Power 1963–1967.* Bloomington, Ind.: Indiana University Press, 1970.

Mushkin, Selma J., and John F. Cotton. *Sharing Federal Funds for State and Local Needs: Grants-in-Aid and PPB Systems.* New York: Praeger, 1970.

McCord, William, et al. *Life Styles in the Black Ghetto.* New York: W. W. Norton, 1969.

McLennan, Barbara N. *Crime in Urban Society.* New York: Dunellen, 1970.

McPherson, James Alan. *Hue and Cry.* New York: Fawcett World Library, 1970.

National Advisory Commission on Civil Disorders. *Report* (A Bantam Book: QZ4273). New York: New York *Times* Company, 1968.

National Advisory Council on Economic Opportunity. *Continuity and Changes in Anti-Poverty Programs.* Washington, D.C.: U.S. Government Printing Office, 1969.

National Center on Police and Community Relations of the School of Police Administration and Public Safety, Michigan State University. *A National Survey of Police and Community Relations—Field Surveys V.* Washington, D.C.: U.S. Government Printing Office, 1967.

National Commission on Causes and Prevention of Violence. See under U.S. listings.

National Commission on Reform of Federal Criminal Laws. *Final Report: A Proposed New Federal Criminal Code* (Title 18, United States Code). Washington, D.C.: U.S. Government Printing Office, 1971.

National Council on Crime and Delinquency. *Juvenile Justice Confounded: Pretentions and Realities of Treatment Services.* Paramus, N.J.: National Council on Crime and Delinquency, 1972.

National Criminal Justice Reference Service. *LEAA Reference List of Publications* (free) Washington, D.C.: U.S. Department of Justice, 633 Indiana Avenue, Washington, D.C. 20530, 1971.

National Institute of Mental Health. See under U.S., Department of Health, Education, and Welfare.

National Institute of Law Enforcement and Criminal Justice, U.S. Department of Justice, LEAA. *Police Training and Performance Study.* Washington, D.C.: U.S. Government Printing Office, 1970.

National School of Public Relations Association. *Black Studies in Schools,* no. 2. Washington, D.C.: National Education Association, 1970.

Nearing, Scott. *Black America.* New York: Schocken Books, 1970.

Negro and the City: Adapted From a Special Issue of Fortune On: "Business and the Urban Crisis." New York: Time–Life Books, 1968.

Neighborhood Youth Corps. Washington, D.C.: U.S. Government Printing Office, 1969.

New Jersey. *Governor's Select Commission on Civil Disorder: Report for Action.* Trenton, N.J., 1968.

Newman, Charles L. *Personnel Practices in Adult Parole Systems.* Springfield, Ill.: Charles C. Thomas, 1971.

Niederhoffer, Arthur, and Abraham S. Blumberg. *The Ambivalent Force: Perspectives on the Police.* Waltham, Mass.: Ginn & Co., 1970

Nielsen, Swven C. *General Organizational and Administrative Concepts for University Police.* Springfield, Ill.: Charles C. Thomas, 1971.

Ng, Larry, ed. *Alternatives to Violence: A Stimulus to Dialogue.* New York: Time–Life Books, 1968.

Norrgard, David L. *Regional Law Enforcement.* Chicago: Public Administration Service, 1969.

O'Connor, George W., and Nelson A. Watson. *Juvenile Delinquency and Youth Crime, the Police Role. An Analysis of: Philosophy, Policy, Opinion.* Gaithersberg, Md: International Association of Chiefs of Police, 1965.

Olson, Bruce. *Regional Law Enforcement Training.* Detroit: Metropolitan Fund, 1968.

O'Neill, William L., ed. *American Society Since 1945.* Chicago: Quadrangle Books, 1970.

Operation Open City, New York Urban League. *Enforcing Open Housing.* New York: Friends of Operation Open City, 1970.

Oppenheimer, Martin. *The Urban Guerilla.* Chicago: Quadrangle Books, 1970.

Oppenheimer, Martin, and George Lakey. *A Manual for Direct Action.* Chicago: Quadrangle Books, 1969.

Ornati, Oscar A. *Transportation Needs of the Poor—A Case Study of New York City.* New York: Praeger, 1970.

Ovington, Mary White. *Half A Man: The Status of a Negro in New York.* New York: Schocken Books, 1970.

Packer, Herbert S. *The Limits of the Criminal Sanction,* Stanford, Calif.: Stanford University Press, 1968.

Patrick, Clarence H. *The Police, Crime and Society.* Springfield, Ill.: Charles C. Thomas, 1971.

Paynton, Clifford E. and Robert Blackey. *Why Revolution?* Morristown, N.J.: General Learning Press, 1971.

People of Watts. *The Aftermath.* New York: Grove Press, 1969.

Perkins, Rollin M. *Criminal Law*. 2d ed. Mineola, New York: Foundation Press, 1969.

Perlman, Harvey S., and Thomas Allington. *The Tasks of Penology: A Symposium on Prisons and Correctional Law*. Lincoln, Nebraska: University of Nebraska Press, 1969.

Perucci, Robert. *The Triple Revolution: Social Problems in Depth*. Boston: Little, Brown, 1969.

Petroni, Frank A., Ernest A. Hirsch, and Lillian Petroni. *Two, Four, Six, Eight, When You Gonna Integrate?* New York: Behavioral Publications, 1971.

Pickett, Robert S. *House of Refuge*. Syracuse, N.Y.: Syracuse University Press, 1969.

Pilisuk, Marc, ed. *Poor Americans: How the Poor White Live*. Chicago: Aldine, 1970.

Police and the Civil Rights Acts. Gaithersberg, Md.: International Association of Chiefs of Police, 1965.

Police, the Community, and You. Washington, D.C.: Women's International League for Peace and Freedom, 120 Maryland Avenue, N.E., 20002, 1968.

Poston, Richard W. *The Gang and the Establishment*. New York: Harper & Row, 1971.

President's Commission on Law Enforcement and Administration of Justice; Prepared by The Institute for Defense Analyses. *Task Force Report: Science and Technology*. Washington D.C.: U.S. Government Printing Office, 1967.

President's Commission on Law Enforcement and Administration of Justice. *Task Force Report: The Police*. Washington, D.C.: U.S. Government Printing Office, 1967.

President's Council on Youth Opportunity. *Manual for Youth Coordinators*. Washington, D.C.: U.S. Government Printing Office, 1969.

President's Task Force on Prisoner Rehabilitation. *The Criminal Offender—What Should Be Done?* Washington, D.C.: U.S. Government Printing Office, 1970.

Probation/Parole, vol. 1. Washington, D.C.: U.S. Government Printing Office, 1969.

Puzo, Mario. *The Godfather*. New York: Fawcett World Library, 1970.

Quinney, Richard. *Crime and Justice in Society*. Boston: Little, Brown, 1969.

———. *The Social Reality of Crime*. Boston: Little, Brown, 1970.

Radano, Gene. *Walking the Beat*. Cleveland: World Publishing Co., 1968.

Radzinowicz, Sir Leon and Marvin E. Wolfgang, eds. *Crime and Justice*. 3 vols. New York: Basic Books, 1972.

Rainwater, Lee. *Behind Ghetto Walls: Black Family Life in a Federal Slum*. Chicago: Aldine, 1970.

Rainwater, Lee, ed. *Black Experience I: Soul*. Chicago: Aldine, 1970.

Rapoport, Roger, and Laurence J. Kirshbaum. *Is the Library Burning?* New York: Random House, 1970.

Rathbone, Josephine L., and Carol Lucas. *Recreation in Total Rehabilitation*. Springfield, Ill.: Charles C. Thomas, 1970.

Reasons, Charles E. and Jack L. Kuykendall, eds. *Race, Crime and Justice*. Pacific Palisades, Calif.: Goodyear, 1972.

Reid, Tim, and Julyan Reid, eds. *Student Power and the Canadian Campus*. Toronto: Peter Martin Associates, 1970.

Reich, Charles A. *The Greening of America*. New York: Random House, 1970.

Reiss, Albert J., Jr. *The Police and the Public*. New Haven: Yale University Press, 1971.

———. *Studies in Crime and Law Enforcement in Major Metropolitan Areas*. vols. 1 and 2, *Field Surveys III*. Washington, D.C.: U.S. Government Printing Office, 1967.

Report (and Appendix) of the President's Commission on Crime in the District of Columbia. Washington, D.C.: U.S. Government Printing Office, 1966.
Report of the Advisory Panel Against Armed Violence. Washington, D.C.: U.S. Government Printing Office, 1969.
Report of the National Advisory Commission on Civil Disorders. Washington, D.C.: U.S. Government Printing Office, 1968.
Richette, Lisa A. *The Throwaway Children.* Philadelphia: J. R. Lippincott, 1968.
Roberts, Albert R. *Sourcebook on Prison Education: Past, Present and Future.* Springfield, Ill.: Charles C. Thomas, 1971.
Robinson, Armstead L., Craig C. Foster, and Donald H. Ogilvie. *Black Studies in the University: A symposium.* New Haven: Yale University Press, 1970.
Rogan, Donald L. *Campus Apocalypse: The Student Search Today.* New York: Seabury Press, 1970.
Rolph, C. H. *Law and the Common Man.* Springfield, Ill.: Charles C. Thomas, 1968.
Rose, Thomas. *Violence in America.* New York: Random House, 1969.
Rosenquist, Carl M. and Edwin I. Megargee. *Delinquency in Three Cultures.* Austin, Texas: University of Texas Press, 1969.
Ross, H. Lawrence. *Settled Out of Court.* Chicago: Aldine, 1970.
Risso, Peter H., ed. *Ghetto Revolts.* Chicago: Aldine, 1970.
Rubin, Jerry, *Do It!* New York: Simon & Schuster, 1970.
Rubin, Sol. *Crime and Juvenile Delinquency.* 3d ed. Dobbs Ferry, N.Y.: Oceana Publications, 1970.
Rubin, Ted. *Law as an Agent of Delinquency Prevention.* Washington, D.C.: U.S. Government Printing Office, 1971.
Rubington, Earl and Martin S. Weinberg. *Deviance: The Interactionist Perspective.* New York: Macmillan, 1968.
Saint Louis Council on Police-Community Relations. *Police Community Relations 1966–1967 Program.* Saint Louis: Saint Louis Metropolitan Police Department, 1967.
Sanders, Marion K. *The Professional Radical: Conversations With Saul Alinsky.* New York: Harper & Row, 1970.
Saunders, Charles B., Jr. *Police Education and Training: Key to Better Law Enforcement.* Washington, D.C.: Brookings Institution, 1970.
Saunders, Charles B. *Upgrading the American Police.* Washington, D.C.: Brookings Institution, 1970.
Sauter, Van Gordon and Burleigh Hines. *Nightmare in Detroit: A Rebellion and Its Victims.* Chicago: Henry Regnery, 1968.
Sayler, Richard H., Barry B. Bayer, and Robert E. Gooding, Jr., eds. *The Warren Court.* New York: Chelsea House, 1969.
Scammon, Richard M., and Ben J. Wattenberg. *The Real Majority.* New York: Coward-McCann, 1970.
Schafer, Stephen. *Compensation and Restitution to Victims of Crime.* rev. Montclair, N.J.: Patterson Smith, 1970.
———. *Juvenile Delinquency: An Introduction.* New York: Random House, 1970.
Schanche, Don A. *The Panther Paradox: A Liberal's Dilemma.* New York: David McKay, 1970.
Schlesinger, Arthur M., Jr. *The Crisis in Confidence: Ideas, Power and Violence in America.* Boston: Houghton Mifflin, 1969.
Schreiber, Flora Rheta. *A Job With a Future in Law Enforcement and Related Fields.* New York: Grosset & Dunlap, 1970.
Schuchter, Arnold. *Reparations: The Black Manifesto and Its Challenge to White America.* Philadelphia: Lippincott, 1970.
Schultz, John. *No One Was Killed: Documentation and Meditation: Convention Week, Chicago—August 1968.* Chicago: Big Table Publishers, 1969.

Schur, Edwin M. *Narcotic Addiction in Britain and America*. Bloomington, Ind.: Indiana University Press, 1970.

————. *Our Criminal Society: The Social and Legal Sources of Crime in America*. Englewood Cliffs, N.J.: Prentice-Hall, 1969.

Schwab, Joseph J. *College Curriculum and Student Protest*. Chicago: University of Chicago Press, 1970.

Schwartz, Louis B., and S. R. Goldstein. *Law Enforcement Handbook for Police*. Saint Paul, Minn.: West Publishing Co., 1970.

Schwartz, Richard D. and Jerome H. Skolnik. *Society and the Legal Order*. New York: Basic Books, 1970.

Scott, Benjamin. *The Coming of the Black Man: Manifesto on Black Power*. Boston: Beacon Press, 1969.

Sears, David O. *The Politics of Violence: The New Urban Black Man and the Watts Riot*. Boston: Houghton Mifflin, 1970.

Select Committee on Crime, U.S. House of Representatives. *Juvenile Justice and Corrections*. Washington, D.C.: U.S. Government Printing Office, 1971.

Seligman, Ben B. *Permanent Poverty*. Chicago: Quadrangle Books, 1970.

Selznick, Gertrude J., and Stephen Steinberg. *The Tenacity of Prejudice: Anti-Semitism in Contemporary America*. New York: Harper & Row, 1969.

Servin, Manuel. *The Mexican-Americans: An Awakening Minority*. New York: Macmillan, 1970.

Shaw, Clifford, and Henry D. McKay. *Juvenile Delinquency and Urban Areas: A Study of Rates of Delinquency In Relation to Differential Characteristics of Local Communities and American Cities*. rev. Chicago: University of Chicago Press, 1969.

Shapiro, Martin M., ed. *The Supreme Court and Public Policy*. Glenview, Ill.: Scott, Foresman, 1969.

Sheldon, Charles. *The Supreme Court: Politicians in Robes*. New York: Macmillan, 1970.

Shepard, Harold L., ed. *Poverty and Wealth In America*. Chicago: Quadrangle Books, 1970.

Shepardson, Mary, and Blodwen Hammond. *The Navajo Mountain Community*. Berkeley, Calif.: University of California Press, 1970.

Sherwood, Norman. *The Youth Service Bureau: A Key to Delinquency Prevention*. Paramus, N.J.: National Council on Crime and Delinquency, 1972.

Shiloh, Ailon. *Studies in Human Sexual Behavior: The American Scene*. Springfield, Ill.: Charles C. Thomas, 1970.

Short, James F., Jr., ed. *Modern Criminals*. Chicago: Aldine, 1970.

Sinclair, Ian. *Hostels for Probationers*. London: Her Majesty's Stationery Office, 1971.

Skolnick, Jerome H. *Justice Without Trial: Law Enforcement in Democratic Society*. New York: John Wiley & Sons, 1966.

————. *Professional Police in a Free Society*. New York: National Conference of Christians and Jews, 1968.

Skolnick, Jerome and Elliott Currie. *Crisis in American Institutions*. Boston: Little, Brown, 1970.

Slough, M. C. *Privacy, Freedom and Responsibility*. Springfield, Ill.: Charles C. Thomas, 1969.

Smith, Alexander B. and Harriet Pollack. *Crime and Justice in a Mass Society*. Waltham, Mass.: Xerox College Publishing Corp., 1972.

Smith, R. Dean, and Richard Kobetz. *Guidelines for Civil Disorder and Mobilization Planning: Prepared for the President's Advisory Commission on Civil Disorders*. Gaithersberg, Md.: International Association of Chiefs of Police, Research, Development, and Planning Division, 1968.

Solomon, Arthur, Perry Steven, and Robert Devine. *Interpersonal Communication: Cross Disciplinary Approach.* Springfield, Ill.: Charles C. Thomas, 1970.

Spender, Stephen. *Year of the Young Rebels.* New York: Random House, 1969.

Spiegel, John P. *The Tradition of Violence in Our Society.* Waltham, Mass.: Lemberg Center for the Study of Violence, Brandeis University, 1968.

Stavis, Barrie. *John Brown: The Sword and the Word.* Cranbury, N.J.: A. S. Barnes & Co., 1970.

Stein, David Lewis. *Living the Revolution: The Yippies in Chicago.* Indianapolis, Ind.: Bobbs-Merrill, 1969.

Steiner, Stan. *La Raza: The Mexican Americans.* New York: Harper & Row, 1970.

———. *The New Indians.* New York: Dell, 1969.

Steinfield, Melvin. *Cracks in the Melting Pot: Readings in Racism and Discrimination in American History.* New York: Macmillan, 1970.

Sterling, James W. *Changes in Role Concept of Police Officers.* Gaithersberg, Md.: International Association of Chiefs of Police, Research, Development and Planning Division, 1968.

Stone, Chuck. *Black Political Power in America.* New York: Bobbs-Merrill, 1969.

Stratton, John R., and Robert M. Terry. *Prevention of Delinquency: Problems and Programs.* New York: Macmillan, 1968.

Strecher, Victor G. *The Environment of Law Enforcement: A Community Relations Guide.* Englewood Cliffs, N.J.: Prentice-Hall, 1971.

Supplemental Studies for the National Advisory Commission on Civil Disorders. Washington, D.C.: U.S. Government Printing Office, 1968.

Susman, Jackwell, ed. *Crime and Justice 1970–1971.* New York: 56 E. 13th St., New York 10003: AMS Press, 1972.

Sutherland, Edwin H., and Donald R. Cressey. *Principles of Criminology.* 8th ed. Philadelphia: Lippincott, 1970.

Suttles, Gerald D. *The Social Order of the Slum: Ethnicity and Territory in the Inner City.* Chicago: University of Chicago Press, 1968.

Sykes, Gresham M. and Thomas E. Drabek. *Law and the Lawless: A Reader in Criminology.* New York: Random House, 1969.

Szurek, S. A., and I. N. Berlin, eds. *The Antisocial Child: His Family and His Community.* Palo Alto, Calif.: Science and Behavior Books, 1970.

Taylor, Karl K., and Fred W. Soady, Jr., eds. *Violence: An Element of American Life.* Boston: Holbrook Press, 1972.

Terry, Robert W. *For Whites Only.* Grand Rapids, Mich.: William E. Eerdmans, 1970.

Thurow, Lester C. *Poverty and Discrimination.* Washington, D.C.: Brookings Institution, 1969.

Toch, Hans H. *Violent Men: An Inquiry Into the Psychology of Violence.* Chicago: Aldine, 1969.

Towler, Juby E. *The Police Role in Racial Conflicts.* 2d ed. Springfield, Ill.: Charles C. Thomas, 1969.

Treanor, Gerald F. Jr. *Riots and Municipalities.* Report no. 152. Washington, D.C.: National Institute of Municipal Law Officers, 1968.

Tresolini, Roco J., and Martin Shapiro. *American Constitutional Law.* rev. New York: Macmillan, 1970.

Trubowitz, Julius. *Changing the Racial Attitudes of Children—The Effects of an Activity Group Program in New York City Schools.* New York: Praeger, 1969.

Tucker, Sterling. *Beyond the Burning: Life and Death of the Ghetto.* New York: Association Press, 1970.

———. *Black Reflections on White Power.* Grand Rapids, Mich.: William B. Eerdmans, 1969.

Tumin, Melvin M. *Comparative Perspectives on Race Relations.* Boston: Little, Brown, 1969.

———. *Research Annual on Intergroup Relations—1970.* Chicago: Quadrangle Books, 1970.

Turk, Austin. *Criminality: A Sociological Perspective.* Chicago: Rand McNally, 1969.

Turner, Kenneth A. *Juvenile Justice: Juvenile Court Problems, Procedures and Practices in Tennessee.* Charlottesville, Va.: Michie, 1969.

Turner, William W. *The Police Establishment.* New York: G. P. Putnam'. Sons, 1968.

Tussman, Joseph. *Experiment at Berkeley.* New York: Oxford University Press, 1969.

Ulmer, S. Sidney. *Military Justice and the Right to Counsel.* Lexington, Ky.: University of Kentucky Press, 1970.

Urban Outlook, Bibliography of Films, Filmstrips, Etc. Washington, D.C.: U.S. Government Printing Office, 1969.

U.S., Advisory Panel Against Armed Violence. *Report of the Advisory Panel Against Armed Violence.* Washington, D.C.: U.S. Government Printing Office, 1969.

U.S., Commission on Civil Rights. Reports listed are available from the U.S. Government Printing Office, Washington, D.C.
  Racism in America and How to Combat It, 1970.
  The Unfinished Education: Outcomes for Minorities in Five Southwestern States. Mexican-American Education Series Report 2, 1971.

U.S., Commission on Human Rights. *To Continue Action for Human Rights: Federal Report.* Washington, D.C.: U.S. Government Printing Office, 1969.

U.S., Congress. House. Select Committee on Crime. *Juvenile Justice and Corrections.* Washington, D.C.: U.S. Government Printing Office, 1971.

U.S., Congress, Senate. Committee on Labor and Public Welfare. *Indian Education: A National Tragedy—A National Challenge.* Washington, D.C.: U.S. Government Printing Office, 1969.

U.S., Department of Health, Education, and Welfare. National Institute of Mental Health. Reports listed are available from U.S. Government Printing Office, Washington, D.C.
  Civil Commitment of Special Categories of Offenders. Public Health Service Publication no. 2131, 1971.
  Community-Based Correctional Programs: Models and Practices. Public Health Service Publication no. 2130, 1971.
  Diversion From the Criminal Justice System. Public Health Service Publication no. 2129, 1971.
  Graduated Release. Public Health Service Publication no. 2128, 1971.
  The Juvenile Court: A Status Report. Public Health Service Publication no. 2132, 1971.

U.S., Department of Housing and Urban Development. *The Model Cities Program: A History and Analysis of the Planning Process in Three Cities: Atlanta, Ga.; Seattle, Wash.; Dayton, Ohio.* Washington, D.C.: U.S. Government Printing Office, 1969.

U.S., Department of Justice. Reports listed are available from U.S. Government Printing Office, Washington, D.C.
  Psychological Assessment of Patrolman's Qualifications in Relation to Field Performance. Report Prepared by Melanie E. Baehr, John E. Furcon, and Ernest C. Froemel, Industrial Relations Center, University of Chicago, for the Office of Law Enforcement Assistance, November 1968.
  Correctional Institutions, vol. 2, 1969.

A Look at Criminal Justice Research (Technological). Law Enforcement Assistance Administration, 1971.

Police Training and Performance Study, PR 70-4. National Institute of Law Enforcement and Criminal Justice, Law Enforcement Administration, 1971.

U.S., National Advisory Commission on Civil Disorders. Reports listed are available from U.S. Government Printing Office, Washington, D.C.

Report of the National Advisory Commission on Civil Disorders, 1968. (Kerner Report.)

Supplemental Studies for the National Advisory Commission on Civil Disorders, 1968.

U.S., National Advisory Council on Economic Opportunity. *Continuity and Changes in Anti-Poverty Programs*. Washington, D.C.: U.S. Government Printing Office, 1969.

U.S., National Commission on Causes and Prevention of Violence. Reports listed are available from U.S. Government Printing Office, Washington, D.C.

Assassination and Political Violence, 1969.

Criminal Justice, 1969.

Mass Media and Violence, 1969.

Miami Report, 1969.

Political Assassination, 1969.

The Politics of Protest: Violent Aspects of Protest and Confrontation, 1969.

Progress Report of the National Commission on the Causes and Prevention of Violence, 1969.

Rights in Concord: The Response to the Counter-Inaugural Protest Activities in Washington, D.C., 1969.

Shoot-out in Cleveland, 1969.

Shut It Down! A College Crisis (San Francisco State College, October 1968–April 1969), 1969.

To Establish Justice, To Insure Domestic Tranquillity, 1969.

Violence in America: Historical and Comparative Perspectives, vols. 1 and 2, 1969.

U.S., National Commission on Reform of Federal Criminal Laws. *Final Report: A Proposed New Federal Criminal Code* (Title 18, United States Code). Washington, D.C.: U.S. Government Printing Office, 1971.

U.S., President's Commission on Crime in the District of Columbia. *Report of the President's Commission on Crime in the District of Columbia*. Washington, D.C.: U.S. Government Printing Office, 1966.

U.S., President's Commission on Law Enforcement and Administration of Justice. Reports listed are available from U.S. Government Printing Office, Washington, D.C.

Challenge of Crime in a Free Society, 1967.

Field Surveys IV. The Police and the Community: The Dynamics of their Relationship in a Changing Society, 1967.

Field Surveys V. A National Survey of Police and Community Relations, 1967.

Task Force Report: The Police, 1967.

Task Force Report: Science and Technology, 1967.

U.S., President's Council on Youth Opportunity. *Manual for Youth Coordinators*. Washington, D.C.: U.S. Government Printing Office, 1969.

U.S., President's Task Force on Prisoner Rehabilitation. *The Criminal Offender—What Should Be Done?* Washington, D.C.: U.S. Government Printing Office, 1970.

U.S. News and World Reports. *Communism and the New Left*. Washington, D.C.: Books by U.S. News and World Reports, Inc., 1969.

Vedder, Clyde B. *Juvenile Offenders*. Springfield, Ill.: Charles C. Thomas, 1969.

Vedder, Clyde B., and Barbara A. Kay. *Penology*. Springfield, Ill.: Charles C. Thomas, 1969.

Vedder, Clyde B., and Dora B. Somerville. *The Delinquent Girl*. Springfield, Ill.: Charles C. Thomas, 1970.

Vietroisz, Thomas, and Bennett Harrison. *The Economic Development of Harlem*. New York: Praeger, 1970.

Von Hoffman, Nicholas. *We Are The People Our Parents Warned Us Against*. New York: Fawcett World Library, 1969.

Voss, Harwin L. *Reader in Juvenile Delinquency*. Boston: Little, Brown, 1970.

Wade, Richard C., et al. *Urban Violence*. Chicago: Center for Policy Study, University of Chicago, 1969.

Wagstaff, Thomas. *Black Power: The Radical Response to White America*. Beverly Hills, Calif.: Glencoe Press, 1969.

Walker, Daniel. *Rights in Conflict: The Violent Confrontation of Demonstrators and Police in the Parks and Streets of Chicago During the Week of the Democratic National Convention of 1968*. New York: Bantam Books, 1968.

Wambaugh, Joseph. *The New Centurions:* A novel about police work as an intimate social function. Boston: Little, Brown, 1970.

————. *The Blue Knight*. Boston: Little, Brown, 1972.

Wasserman, Miriam. *The School Fix, N.Y.C., U.S.A.* New York: E. P. Dutton, 1970.

Watson, Nelson A. *Attitudes—A Factor in Performance*. Gaithersberg, Md.: International Association of Chiefs of Police, Research, Development and Planning Division, 1968.

————. *Human Relations Training for Police: A Syllabus*. Gaithersberg, Md.: International Association of Chiefs of Police, Research and Development Division, 1968.

————. *Improving the Officer-Citizen Contact*. Gaithersberg, Md.: International Association of Chiefs of Police, Research, Development and Planning Division, 1968.

————. *Issues in Human Relations: Threats and Challenges*. Gaithersberg, Md.: International Association of Chiefs of Police, Research, Development and Planning Division, 1969.

————. *Police-Community Relations*. Gaithersberg, Md.: International Association of Chiefs of Police, Research, Development and Planning Division, 1966.

————. *Police Procedures in the Handling of Juveniles*. Address before the American Bar Association, Family Law Annual Meeting, 1966.

————. ed. *Police and the Changing Community: Selected Readings*. Gaithersberg, Md.: International Association of Chiefs of Police, Research, Development and Planning Division, 1965.

Watson, Nelson A., and Robert N. Walker, eds. *Juvenile Delinquency in Police Education: Proceedings of Workshop for Police Professors, Michigan State University, 1966*. Gaithersberg, Md.: International Association of Chiefs of Police, 1966.

We the Black People of the United States. Washington, D.C.: U.S. Government Printing Office, 1969.

Weaver, James, and Gary Weaver, eds. *The University and Revolution*. Englewood Cliffs, N.J.: Prentice-Hall, 1969.

Weinreb, Lloyd L. *Criminal Law: Cases, Comments, Questions*. Mineola, N.Y.: Foundation Press, 1969.

Weinstein, Allen, and Frank Orro Gatell. *The Segregation Era: 1863–1954*. New York: Oxford University Press, 1970.

Weinstein, James, and David W. Eakins. *For a New America*. New York: Random House, 1970.

Wells, Ida B. *Crusade for Justice.* Chicago: University of Chicago Press, 1970.

Westley, William A. *Violence and the Police.* Cambridge, Mass.: M.I.T. Press, 1970.

Wheeler, Stanton, ed. *Controlling Delinquents.* New York: John Wiley & Sons, 1968.

Whisenand, Paul M. *Police Supervision: Theory and Practice.* Englewood Cliffs, N.J.: Prentice-Hall, 1971.

Whitehead, Donn. *Attack on Terror: The FBI Against the Ku Klux Klan in Mississippi.* New York: Funk & Wagnalls, 1970.

Whittemore, L. H. *Cop.* New York: Fawcett World Library, 1970.

Who Will Listen If You Have a Civil Rights Complaint? Washington, D.C.: U.S. Government Printing Office, 1969.

Wilkins, Leslie T. *Evaluation of Penal Measures.* New York: Random House, 1969.

Wilson, James Q. *City Politics and Public Policy.* New York: John Wiley & Sons, 1968.

————. *Varieties of Police Behavior: The Management of Law and Order in Eight Communities.* Cambridge, Mass.: Harvard University Press, 1968.

————. ed. *The Metropolitan Enigma.* Garden City, N.Y.: Doubleday & Co., 1970.

Wittenborn, J. R., Henry Brill, and Sarah A. Wittenborn. *Drugs and Youth: Proceedings of the Rutgers Symposium on Drug Abuse.* Springfield, Ill.: Charles C. Thomas, 1969.

Wolf, Kurt. *Patterns of Self Destruction: Depression and Suicide.* Springfield, Ill.: Charles C. Thomas, 1970.

Wolfgang, Marvin E. *The Culture of Youth.* Washington, D.C.: U.S. Government Printing Office, 1968.

Wolfgang, Marvin E., and Bernard Cohen. *Crime and Race.* Rev. New York: Institute of Human Relations Press, The American Jewish Committee, 165 E. 56th St., 1970.

Wood, Forrest G. *Black Scare: The White Racist Response to Emancipation and Reconstruction.* Berkeley, Calif.: University of California Press, 1970.

Wright, R. Gene, and John A. Marlo. *The Police Officer and Criminal Justice.* New York: McGraw-Hill, 1970.

Yablonsky, Lewis. *The Hippie Trip.* New York: Pegasus Publishing Co., 1969.

Young, Whitney. *Beyond Racism: Building an Open Society.* New York: McGraw-Hill, 1970.

Yuan, D. Y. *The Chinese-American Population: A Study of Voluntary Segregation.* Morristown, N.J.: General Learning Press, 1972.

Zarr, Melvyn. *The Bill of Rights and the Police.* Dobbs Ferry, N.Y.: Oceana Publications, 1970.

Zimmerman, Joseph F. *Subnational Politics: Reading in State and Local Government.* 2d. ed. New York: Holt, Rinehart & Winston, 1970.

Zinn, Howard. *The Politics of History.* Boston: Beacon Press, 1970.

Zuk, Gerald H. *Family Therapy.* New York: Behavioral Publications, 1972.

Index

Subject Index